OCR Gateway
GCSE Chemistry
Teacher Handbook

Author:
Adelene Cogill • Sam Holyman

Series Editor:
Philippa Gardom Hulme

Contents

Introduction ... iv
Assessment and progress ... vi
Differentiation and skills ... viii
Kerboodle ... x

Working Scientifically ... 2

- WS1 The power of science ... 2
- WS2 Methods, models, and communication ... 4
- WS3 Asking scientific questions ... 6
- WS4 Planning an investigation ... 8
- WS5 Obtaining high-quality data ... 10
- WS6 Presenting data ... 12
- WS7 Interpreting data ... 14
- WS8 Errors and uncertainties ... 16

C1 Particles ... 18

- C1.1 **The particle model**
- C1.1.1 Introducing particles ... 18
- C1.1.2 Chemical and physical changes ... 20
- C1.1.3 Limitations of the particle model ... 22
- C1.1 Checkpoint ... 24
- C1.2 **Atomic structure**
- C1.2.1 Atomic structure ... 26
- C1.2.2 Isotopes ... 28
- C1.2.3 Developing the atomic model ... 30
- C1.2 Checkpoint ... 32
- C1 Topic summary ... 34

C2 Elements, compounds, and mixtures ... 36

- C2.1 **Purity and separating mixtures**
- C2.1.1 Relative formula mass ... 36
- C2.1.2 Empirical formula ... 38
- C2.1.3 Pure and impure substances ... 40
- C2.1.4 Filtration and crystallisation ... 42
- C2.1.5 Distillation ... 44
- C2.1.6 Chromatography ... 46
- C2.1.7 Purification and checking purity ... 48
- C2.1 Checkpoint ... 50
- C2.2 **Bonding**
- C2.2.1 Metals and non-metals ... 52
- C2.2.2 Electronic structures ... 54
- C2.2.3 Forming ions ... 56
- C2.2.4 Ionic compounds ... 58
- C2.2.5 Simple molecules ... 60
- C2.2.6 Giant covalent structures ... 62
- C2.2.7 Polymer molecules ... 64
- C2.2.8 Structure of metals ... 66
- C2.2.9 Developing the Periodic Table ... 68
- C2.2.10 Atomic structure and the Periodic Table ... 70
- C2.2 Checkpoint ... 72
- C2.3 **Properties of materials**
- C2.3.1 Carbon ... 74
- C2.3.2 Changing state ... 76
- C2.3.3 Bulk properties of materials ... 78
- C2.3.4 Nanoparticles ... 80
- C2.3 Checkpoint ... 82
- C2 Topic summary ... 84

C3 Chemical reactions ... 86

- C3.1 **Introducing chemical reactions**
- C3.1.1 Formulae of elements and molecules ... 86
- C3.1.2 Formulae of ionic compounds ... 88
- C3.1.3 Conservation of mass ... 90
- C3.1.4 Chemical equations ... 92
- C3.1.5 Half equations and ionic equations ... 94
- C3.1.6 The mole ... 96
- C3.1.7 Mole calculations ... 98
- C3.1 Checkpoint ... 100
- C3.2 **Energetics**
- C3.2.1 Exothermic and endothermic reactions ... 102
- C3.2.2 Reaction profiles ... 104
- C3.2.3 Calculating energy changes ... 106
- C3.2 Checkpoint ... 108
- C3.3 **Types of chemical reaction**
- C3.3.1 Redox reactions ... 110
- C3.3.2 The pH scale ... 112
- C3.3.3 Neutralisation ... 114
- C3.3.4 Reactions of acids ... 116
- C3.3.5 Hydrogen ions and pH ... 118
- C3.3 Checkpoint ... 120
- C3.4 **Electrolysis**
- C3.4.1 Electrolysis of molten salts ... 122
- C3.4.2 Electrolysis of solutions ... 124
- C3.4.3 Electroplating ... 126
- C3.4 Checkpoint ... 128
- C3 Topic summary ... 130

C4 Predicting and identifying reactions and products ... 132

- C4.1 **Predicting chemical reactions**
- C4.1.1 Group 1 – the alkali metals ... 132

C4.1.2	Group 7 – the halogens	134
C4.1.3	Halogen displacement reactions	136
C4.1.4	Group 0 – the noble gases	138
C4.1.5	The transition metals	140
C4.1.6	Reactivity of elements	142
C4.1	Checkpoint	144
C4.2	**Identifying the products of chemical reactions**	
C4.2.1	Detecting gases	146
C4.2.2	Detecting cations	148
C4.2.3	Detecting anions	150
C4.2.4	Instrumental methods of analysis	152
C4.2	Checkpoint	154
C4	Topic summary	156

C5 Monitoring and controlling chemical reactions — 158

C5.1	**Monitoring chemical reactions**	
C5.1.1	Theoretical yield	158
C5.1.2	Percentage yield and atom economy	160
C5.1.3	Choosing a reaction pathway	162
C5.1.4	Concentration of solution	164
C5.1.5	Titrations	166
C5.1.6	Titration calculations	168
C5.1.7	Gas calculations	170
C5.1	Checkpoint	172
C5.2	**Controlling reactions**	
C5.2.1	Rate of reaction	174
C5.2.2	Temperature and reaction rate	176
C5.2.3	Concentration, pressure, and reaction rate	178
C5.2.4	Particle size and reaction rate	180
C5.2.5	Catalysts and reaction rate	182
C5.2	Checkpoint	184
C5.3	**Equilibria**	
C5.3.1	Reversible reactions	186
C5.3.2	Equilibrium position	188
C5.3.3	Choosing reaction conditions	190
C5.3	Checkpoint	192
C5	Topic summary	194

C6 Global Challenges — 196

C6.1	**Improving processes and products**	
C6.1.1	Fertilisers	196
C6.1.2	Making fertilisers	198
C6.1.3	The Haber process	200
C6.1.4	The Contact process	202
C6.1.5	Making ethanol	204
C6.1.6	Extracting metals	206
C6.1.7	Extracting iron	208
C6.1.8	Extracting aluminium	210
C6.1.9	Biological metal extraction	212
C6.1.10	Alloys	214
C6.1.11	Corrosion	216
C6.1.12	Reducing corrosion	218
C6.1.13	Different materials	220
C6.1.14	Composite materials	222
C6.1.15	Choosing materials	224
C6.1.16	Recycling materials	226
C6.1	Checkpoint	228
C6.2	**Organic chemistry**	
C6.2.1	Alkanes	230
C6.2.2	Alkenes	232
C6.2.3	Alcohols	234
C6.2.4	Carboxylic acids	236
C6.2.5	Alkanes from crude oil	238
C6.2.6	Cracking oil fractions	240
C6.2.7	Addition polymers	242
C6.2.8	Biological polymers	244
C6.2.9	Condensation polymers	246
C6.2.10	Producing electricity using chemistry	248
C6.2	Checkpoint	250
C6.3	**Interpreting and interacting with Earth Systems**	
C6.3.1	Forming the atmosphere	252
C6.3.2	Pollution and the atmosphere	254
C6.3.3	Climate change	256
C6.3.4	Water for drinking	258
C6.3	Checkpoint	260
C6	Topic summary	262

C7 Practical skills — 264

C1	Reactivity trend	264
C2	Electrolysis	266
C3	Separation techniques	268
C4	Distillation	270
C5	Identification of species	272
C6	Titration	274
C7	Production of salts	276
C8	Measuring rates of reaction	278

Answers for all questions — 280

Introduction

About the series

This series has been specifically designed to support the new OCR Gateway GCSE Science suite of resources. The student books have been endorsed by OCR, and our author teams and experts have been working closely with OCR to develop a blended suite of resources to support the new specifications.

All resources in this series have been carefully designed to support students of all abilities on their journey through GCSE Science. The demands of the new specifications are fully supported, with maths, practicals, and synoptic skills developed throughout, and all new subject content fully covered.

The series is designed to be flexible, enabling you to co-teach Foundation and Higher tiers, and Combined and Separate Sciences. Content is clearly flagged throughout the resources, helping you to identify the relevant content for your students.

Assessment is an important feature of the series, and is supported by our unique assessment framework, helping students to track and make progress. Users of *Activate* will recognise features of this assessment framework, and this series has been developed to segue perfectly from *Activate* into GCSE.

The series is edited by Philippa Gardom Hulme. Philippa Gardom Hulme brings a wealth of teaching and authoring experience to her role as Series Editor of OUP's *OCR Gateway GCSE Science* series. She builds on her authoring success with GCSE revision guides, the *Activate Chemistry* Student Book, and numerous Kerboodle resources. A former teacher in a variety of comprehensive schools and more recently an Oxford University PGCE tutor, she understands the demands of modern education and draws on her experience to deliver this new and innovative course that builds upon *Activate* and the legacy of previous *OCR Gateway GCSE Science* editions.

Your Teacher Handbook

This Teacher Handbook aims to save you time and effort by offering lesson plans, differentiation suggestions, and assessment guidance on a page-by-page basis that is a direct match to the Student Book.

With learning outcomes differentiated you can tailor the lessons and activities to suit your students and provide progression opportunities for students of all abilities.

Lesson plans are written for 55-minute lessons but are flexible and fully adaptable so you can choose the activities that suit your class best.

Separate Science-only content is contained within whole topics and clearly flagged from the Combined Sciences content, enabling you co-teach using one Teacher Handbook.

Lesson

Specification links

This indicates the area of the OCR Gateway GCSE (9–1) Chemistry specification this lesson covers. Relevant Working Scientifically and Mathematical requirements links are also provided.

Differentiated outcomes

This table summarises the possible lesson outcomes. They are ramped and divided into three ability bands. The three ability bands are explained in the Assessment and progress section. Each ability band has two to three outcomes defined, designed to cover the specification content for different ability levels.

An index of questions and activities is given for each learning outcome, helping you to assess your students informally as you progress through each lesson.

Suggested lesson plan

A suggested route through the lesson is provided, including ideas for support, extension, and homework. The right-hand column indicated where Kerboodle resources are available.

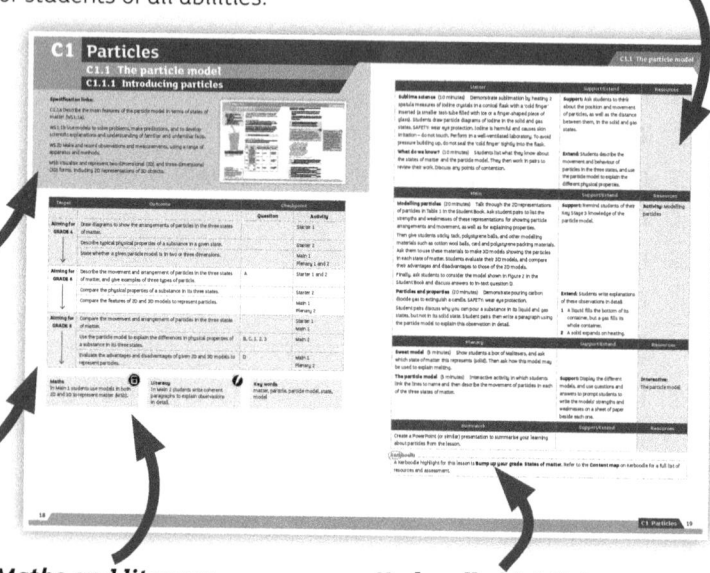

Maths and literacy

These boxes provide suggestions of how Maths and Literacy skills can be developed in the lesson. Where relevant, the Maths skills are linked to the Mathematical requirements of the specification.

Kerboodle highlights

A resource from the Kerboodle course for the lesson is suggested here. The Content Map on Kerboodle provides a full list of resources and assessment.

iv

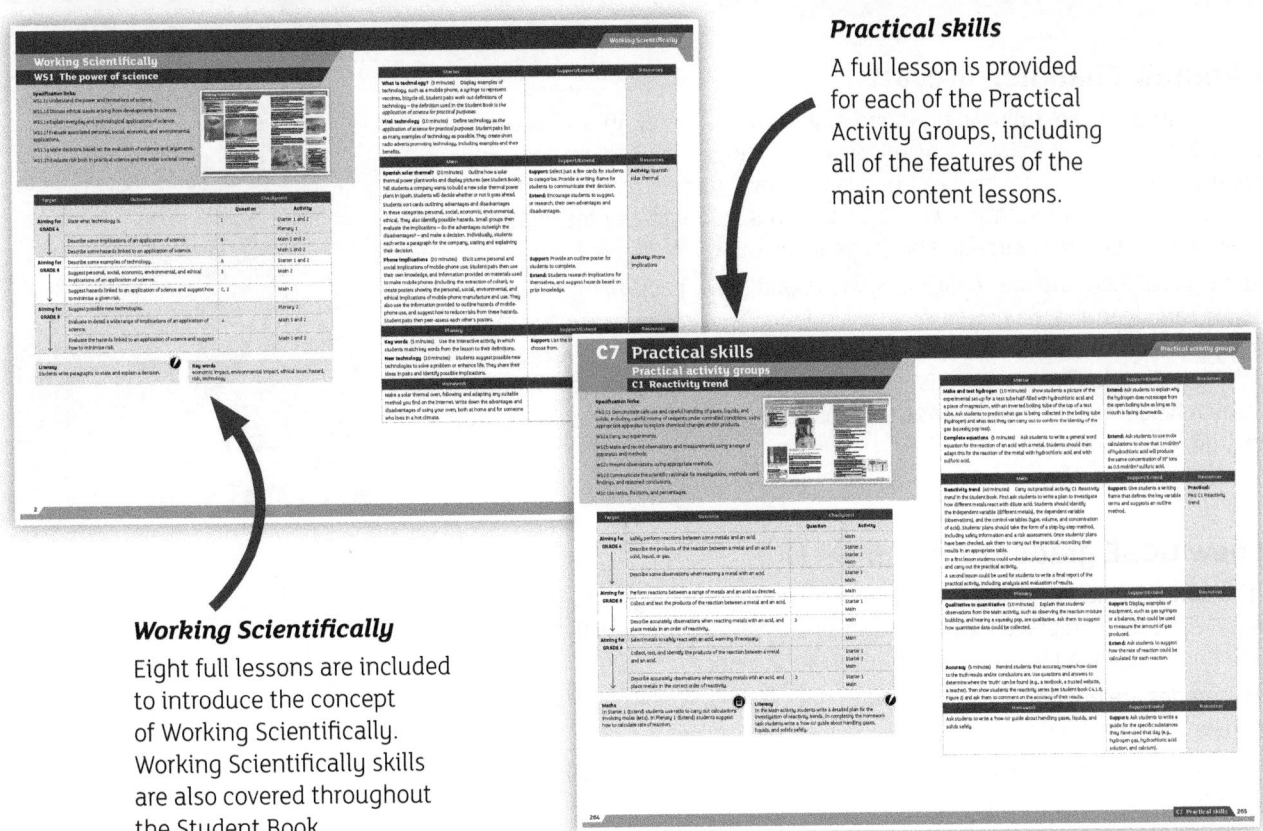

Practical skills

A full lesson is provided for each of the Practical Activity Groups, including all of the features of the main content lessons.

Working Scientifically

Eight full lessons are included to introduce the concept of Working Scientifically. Working Scientifically skills are also covered throughout the Student Book.

Checkpoint lesson

Overview

The Checkpoint lesson is a suggested follow-up lesson after students have completed the automarked Checkpoint Assessment on Kerboodle. There are three routes through the lesson, with the route for each student being determined by their mark in the assessment. Each route aims to support students with progressing up an assessment band.

Chapter overview

This text provides a brief overview of the chapter, including the key concepts students should be confident with.

Checkpoint lesson plan

This table provides a differentiated lesson plan for the Checkpoint follow-up lesson. This includes learning outcomes, starters and plenaries, supporting information for the follow-up worksheets (including any descriptions of relevant practicals), and progression suggestions to support students with progressing up a band.

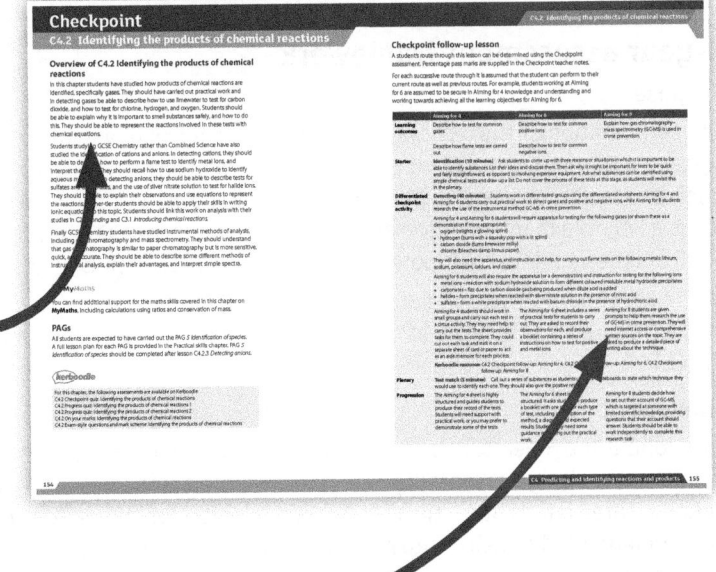

Assessment and progress

Dr Andrew Chandler-Grevatt

To ensure students are fully supported to make progress through the new linear exams, OCR Gateway GCSE (9–1) Sciences was developed in consultation with assessment consultant, Dr Andrew Chandler-Grevatt. Andrew worked with the team to develop an assessment framework that supports students and teachers in tracking and promoting progress through Key Stage 3 and GCSE.

Andrew has a doctorate in school assessment, and a real passion for science teaching and learning. Having worked as a science teacher for ten years, of which five were spent as an AST, Andrew has a real understanding of the pressures and joys of teaching in the classroom. His most recent projects include *Activate for KS3 Science*, for which he developed a unique assessment framework to support schools in the transition away from levels.

The new GCSE grading system (9–1)

With the new specifications and criteria comes a new grading system. The old system of grades A*–G, is being replaced with a numerical system with grades 9–1. Grade 9 is the highest, and is designed to award exceptional performance.

The new grades are not directly equivalent to the old A*–C system, although some comparisons can be drawn:

- Approximately the same proportion of students will achieve a grade 4 or above as currently achieve a grade C or above.
- Approximately the same proportion of students will achieve a grade 7 or above as currently achieve an A or above.
- The bottom of grade 1 will be aligned with the bottom of grade G.

A 'good pass' is considered to be a grade 5 or above.

Throughout the course, resources and assessments have been designed to help students working at different grades to make progress.

5-year assessment framework

Purpose

The combination of the removal of levels, new performance measures, new grading system, and more demanding GCSEs makes it more important than ever to be able to track and facilitate progress from Year 7 and all the way through secondary. Assessment plays a key role in intervention and extension, and these are both vital in helping students of all abilities achieve their potential, and add value to their projected GCSE grade.

In the absence of levels, and as we learn more about the new GCSE grades, it is important that a framework is in place in order to inform learning, teaching, and assessment from Y7-Y11.

Framework

Throughout the 5 years, it is useful to define three ability bands, which can be used to inform the design of learning outcomes, learning resources, and assessments. By defining three bands, realistic and valuable intervention and extension can be designed and implemented to help students of all abilities make progress, and improve their grade projection.

At KS3, the model is designed with the aim of encouraging every student to gain a 'secure' grasp of each concept and topic, so that they are ready to progress. These students will be on track to secure a 'good pass' (grade 5 or above) at GCSE.

In the KS3 course Activate three bands have been defined:

- **Developing**, in which students are able to know and understand a concept, and demonstrate their knowledge in simple and familiar situations.

- **Secure**, in which students are able to apply their knowledge and skills to familiar and some unfamiliar situations, undertake analysis, and understand more complex concepts.
- **Extending**, in which students are able to evaluate and create, apply their knowledge to complex and unfamiliar situations, and demonstrate advanced use of skills.

Using the framework throughout KS3 helps you to identify which students are ready to progress, and approximately what GCSE grades they should be aiming for.

At GCSE, students can then be differentiated into three bands, aiming for different grades.

- **Aiming for 4** is for students working at the lower grades 1–3, who would have been Developing at KS3, and aspiring to a Grade 4 at GCSE. Resources and assessments for these students are supportive, and focus on developing understanding of core concepts.
- **Aiming for 6** is for students working at grades 4–6, who would have been Secure at KS3. Resources and assessments for these students help to embed core concepts, by encouraging application and analysis, and beginning to explore more complex ideas and situations.
- **Aiming for 8** provides extension for students working at grades 7–9, who are able to grasp complex concepts, and demonstrate higher order skills, such as evaluation and creation in complex and unfamiliar situations.

The framework is summarised in the table below.

Key stage 3	Band	Developing		Secure		Extending	
	Level	3	4	5	6	7	8
GCSE	Band	Aiming for 4			Aiming for 6		Aiming for 8	
	Grades	1	2	3	4	5	6	7	8	9
	Demand	Low			Standard			High		

Informing learning outcomes

The assessment framework has informed the design of the learning outcomes throughout the course. Learning outcomes are differentiated, and there is a set of learning outcomes for every lesson for each ability band.

The checkpoint assessment system

This series includes a checkpoint assessment system for intervention and extension, designed to help students of all abilities make continuous progress through the course. The system also helps you and your students to monitor achievement, and ensure all students are on-track and monitored through the new linear assessments.

Checkpoint assessments are provided in Kerboodle. These are automarked objective tests with diagnostic feedback. Once students have completed their assessment, depending on their results, they will complete one of three follow-up activities, designed for intervention and extension. Students are supported with activity sheets, and lesson plans and overviews are provided for the teacher. The three follow-up routes are:

1. **Aiming for 4** is for students who achieved a low score. These resources support students by helping to develop and embed core concepts.
2. **Aiming for 6** is for students who achieved a medium score. These resources encourage students to embed and extend core concepts, and begin to apply their knowledge in more complex or unfamiliar situations.
3. **Aiming for 8** is for students who have achieved a high score. These resources encourage extensive use of more complex skills, in more complex and unfamiliar situations, helping them to reach for the top grades.

Differentiation and skills

Maths skills 🔢 and 🔵 MyMaths

With the introduction of the new GCSE competence in maths, the support and development of maths skills in a scientific context will be vital for success.

The Student Books contain a maths skills reference section that covers all the maths required for the specification, explained in a scientific context and with a worked example for reference. Where maths skills are embedded within the scientific content, the maths is demonstrated in a Using Maths feature providing a worked example and an opportunity for students to have a go themselves.

In Kerboodle you will find maths skills interactives that are automarked and provide formative feedback. Calculation sheets provide opportunities for practice of the maths skills and links to MyMaths are shown in the Lesson Player and Teacher Handbook where additional resources exist that can be used to reinforce the maths skill. These include practice sheets and Invisi-pen worked examples.

Literacy skills

Literacy skills enable students to effectively communicate their ideas about science and access the information they need. Though the marks allocated for QWC are no longer present in the new specifications, a good degree of literacy is required to read and answer longer, structured exam questions, to access the more difficult concepts introduced in the new GCSE Programme of Study, and to be able to effectively interpret and answer questions.

The Student Books flag opportunities to develop and practise literacy skills through the use of the pen icon. Key words are identified in the text and a glossary helps students get to grips with new scientific terms.

In Kerboodle, you will find Literacy Skills Interactives that help assess literacy skills, including the spelling of key words. Additional Literacy worksheets are available to reinforce skills learnt and provide practice opportunities.

The Teacher Handbook flags literacy suggestions and opportunities relating to the lesson. All of these features will help to develop well-rounded scientists able to access information and communicate their ideas effectively.

Working Scientifically

Working Scientifically is new to the 2016 GCSE criteria. It is divided up into four areas and is integrated into the teaching and learning of Biology, Chemistry, and Physics. The four areas are:

1. Development of scientific thinking in which students need to be able to demonstrate understanding of scientific methods and the scientific process, how these may develop over time, and their associated limitations.

2. Experimental skills and strategies in which students ask scientific questions based on observations, make predictions using scientific knowledge and understanding, carry out investigations to test predictions, make and record measurements, and evaluate methods.

3. Analysis and evaluation in which students apply mathematical concepts and calculate results, present and interpret data using tables and graphs, draw conclusions and evaluate data, and are able to distinguish accuracy, precision, repeatability, and reproducibility.

4. Scientific vocabulary, quantities, units, symbols, and nomenclature in which students calculate results and manipulate data using scientific formulae using basic analysis, SI units, and IUPAC chemical nomenclature where appropriate.

Working Scientifically is integrated throughout the Student Book with flagged Practical boxes, flagged Required Practical boxes, and questions. A dedicated Working Scientifically reference chapter is also provided at the back of the Student Book to refer to during investigations, when answering Working Scientifically questions, and to enable investigative skills to be developed.

In Kerboodle there are Practicals and Activities resources with their own Working Scientifically objectives and additional targeted Working Scientifically skills sheets, as well as other resources such as simulations and Webquests to target specific skills areas. Questions are ramped in difficulty and opportunities to build up to and practise the practical-based questions for the exam are provided.

For the Practical Activity Groups, the guidance provided to students acknowledges the differing degrees of support and independence required, with targeted support sheets to the key grade descriptors of Grade 4, 6, and 8, with a view to move the students over that Grade point onwards.

In the Teacher Handbook lessons will often have a Working Scientifically focus in mind for the activities in that lesson. Working Scientifically Learning Outcomes, where specified, are differentiated to show the expectations for the differing ability levels. Each Student Book and Teacher Handbook starts with a Working Scientifically chapter, to help introduce key skills before commencing the course.

For the purpose of the practical-based questions in the examination, practicals are flagged and practice opportunities are provided throughout the Student Book in the summary questions and exam-style questions.

Differentiation

Building upon the principles of *Activate* at Key Stage 3.

Differentiation using the checkpoint system

The end-of-chapter Checkpoint lessons will help you to progress students of every ability, targeting the key Grade boundaries of 4, 6, and 8 to enable students to review, consolidate, and extend their understanding at each of the grade lesson points.

The tasks focused at students to become secure at Grades 4 and 6 are designed to help them become more secure in their understanding and consolidate the chapter. Teacher input will help them grasp important concepts from the chapter with the opportunity for some extension for Grade 6 students.

The tasks focused at students to become secure and extend at Grade 8 are designed to develop and challenge. Students will work more independently on these tasks to free up the teacher to be able to focus on those that found the chapter more challenging.

Teacher Handbook

Lesson outcomes are differentiated and suggestions for activities throughout the lesson plans are accompanied by support and extension opportunities.

Student Book

Summary questions per lesson are ramped with a darker shading indicating a more challenging question. In the end-of-chapter summary questions and exam-style questions, ramping occurs within the question (as would be seen in a typical exam question).

Practicals and Activities

All Practicals and Activities are differentiated. Where more complex areas are covered, additional support sheets may be provided to allow lower attaining students to access the activity.

For all Practical Activity Groups that may be assessed in an exam, specific support sheets are provided targeting the progression of students across the key Grades 4, 6, and 8.

Additional skills sheets may be used in conjunction with practicals to provide additional support in generic competencies such as constructing a graph etc.

Interactive assessments

All interactive assessments are ramped in difficulty and support is provided in the feedback directing students where they can improve. In chapters with both levels of content, Higher and Foundation versions of assessment are available.

Written assessments

End-of-section tests and end-of-year tests have Foundation and Higher versions.

Kerboodle

OCR Gateway GCSE Sciences Kerboodle is packed full of guided support and ideas for running and creating effective GCSE Science lessons, and for assessing and facilitating students' progress. It is intuitive to use and customisable.

Kerboodle is online, allowing you and your students to access the course anytime, anywhere.

OCR Gateway GCSE Sciences Kerboodle consists of:
- lessons, resources, and assessment
- access to *OCR Gateway GCSE Science* Student Books for both teachers and students.

Lessons, Resources, and Assessment

OCR Gateway GCSE Sciences Kerboodle offers new, engaging lesson resources, as well as a fully comprehensive assessment package, written to match the *OCR Gateway GCSE (9–1) Science* specifications.

Kerboodle offers comprehensive and flexible support for the *OCR Gateway GCSE (9–1) Science* specifications, enabling you to follow our suggested lessons and schemes of work or to create your own lessons and schemes and share them with other members of your department.

You can **adapt** many of the resources to suit your students' needs, with all non-interactive activities available as editable Word documents. You can also **upload** your own resources so that everything is accessed from one location.

Set homework and assessments through the Assessment system and **track** progress using the Markbook.

Lessons

Click on the **Lessons tab** to access the *OCR Gateway GCSE Sciences* lesson presentations and notes.

Ready-to-play lesson presentations complement every spread in the Teacher Handbook and Student Book. Each lesson presentation is easy to launch and features lesson objectives, starters, activity guidance, key diagrams, plenaries, and homework suggestions. The lesson presentations and accompanying note sections are 100% customisable. You can personalise the lessons by adding your own resources and notes, or build your own lesson plans using our resources.

Your lessons and notes can be accessed by your whole department and they are ideal for use in cover lessons.

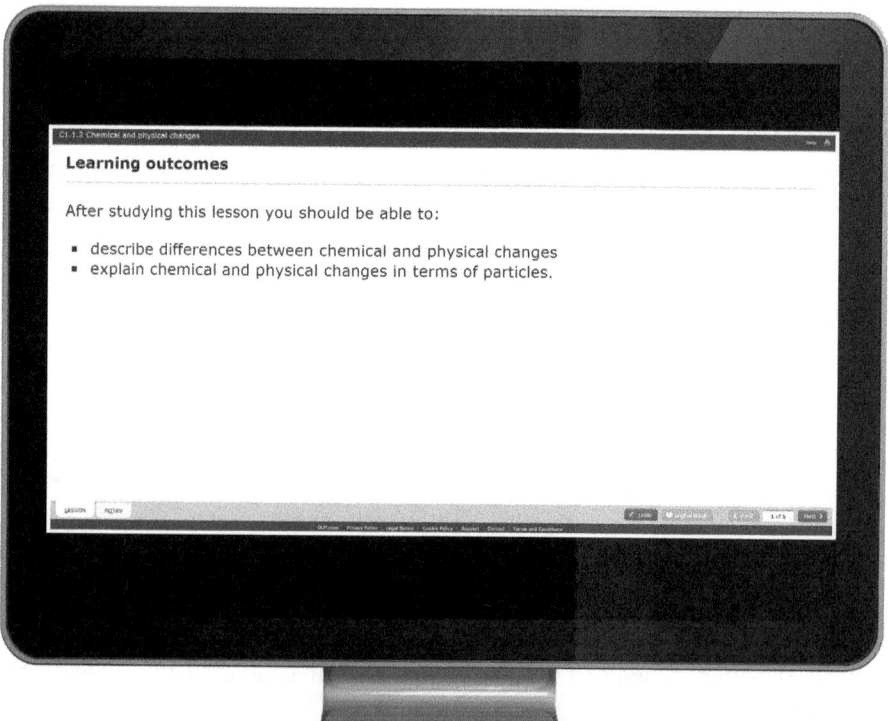

Resources

Click on the Resources tab to access the full list of OCR Gateway GCSE Sciences resources. Use the navigation panel on the left hand side to find resources for any lesson, chapter, or topic.

Fully customisable content to cater to all your classes. Resources can be created using the create button.

Existing resources can be uploaded on to the platform using the upload button.

Navigation panel and search bar allow for easy navigation between resources by course and chapter.

Page navigator shows resources matching to particular pages in the Student Book.

Resources matching every lesson in the *AQA GCSE Chemistry* series are shown here.

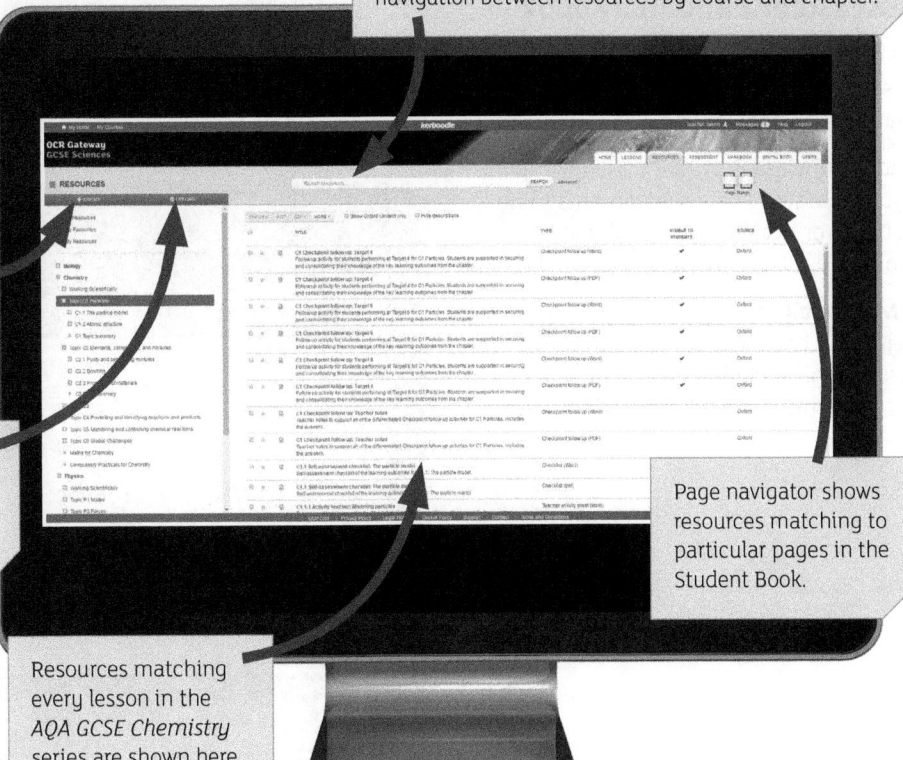

 Practicals and Activities Fully editable resources provided for every lesson to guide students through a practical or activity with fully integrated Working Scientifically skills. Teacher and Technician notes are provided for all practicals and activities to give further ideas on differentiation, answers, example data where appropriate, and a list of resources required by technicians.

 Interactive starters or plenaries Accompany each lesson, and can be used front-of-class to maximise student participation.

 Skills sheets Editable worksheets that target Maths, Literacy, and Working Scientifically skills. They provide guidance and examples to help students whenever they need to use a particular skill.

 Skills interactives Automarked interactive activities with formative feedback that focus on key maths and literacy skills. You can use these activities in your class to help consolidate core skills relevant to the lesson, or they can be assigned as homework by accessing them through the Assessment tab.

 Animations and videos Help students to visualise difficult concepts or to learn about real-life contexts, with engaging visuals and narration. They are structured to clearly address a set of learning objectives and are followed by interactive question screens to help consolidate key points and to provide formative feedback.

 Simulations Allow students to control variables and look at outcomes for experiments that are difficult to carry out in the classroom or focus on tricky concepts.

 Podcasts Available for every chapter to help review and consolidate key points. The podcast presents an audio summary with transcript, followed by a series of ramped questions and answers to assist students in their revision.

 Targeted support sheets Available for the full ability range and are provided to help students progress as they complete their GCSE. **Bump up your Grades** target common misconceptions and difficult topics to securely move students over the key boundaries of Grades 4, 6, and 8. Extension activities provide opportunities for higher-ability students to apply their knowledge and understanding to new contexts, whilst **Go Further** worksheets aim to inspire students to consider the subject at A Level and beyond.

 WebQuests Research-based activities set in a real-life context. WebQuests are fun and engaging activities that can be carried out individually or within a group and are ideal for peer-review.

 Checklists and chapter maps Self-assessment checklists for students of the key learning points from each chapter to aid consolidation and revision. For teachers there is an additional chapter-map resource that provides an overview of the chapter, specific opportunities to support and extend, and information on tackling common misconceptions.

Assessment and markbook

All of the assessment material in Kerboodle has been quality assured by our expert Assessment Advisor. Click on the **Assessment tab** to find the wide range of assessment materials to help you deliver a varied, motivating, and effective assessment programme.

Once your classes are set up in Kerboodle, you can assign them assessments to do at home or in class individually or as a group.

A **Markbook** with reporting function helps you to keep track of your students' results. This includes both automarked assessments and work marked by you.

Practice or test?

Many of the automarked assessments in the OCR Gateway GCSE Sciences Kerboodle are available in formative or summative versions.

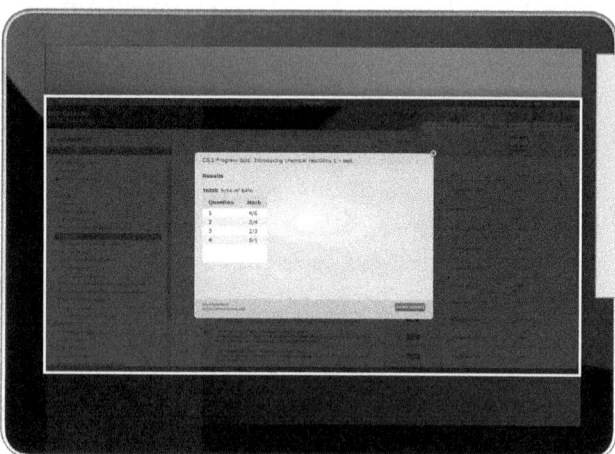

Test versions of the assessment provide feedback on performance at the end of the test. Students are only given one attempt at each screen but can review them and see which answers they get wrong after completing the activity. Marks are reported to the Markbook.

Practice versions of the assessment provide screen-by-screen feedback, focusing on misconceptions, and provide hints for the students to help them revise their answer. Students are given the opportunity to try again. Marks are reported to the Markbook.

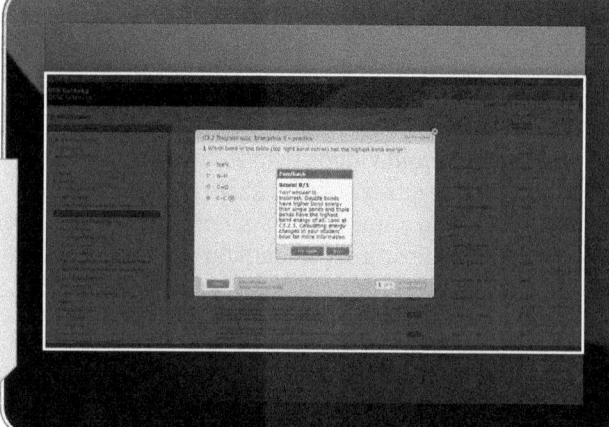

Assessment per chapter

Through each chapter there are many opportunities for assessment and determining/monitoring progress.

- **Progress quizzes** Automarked assessments that focus on the content of the chapters. They are quick, engaging quizzes designed to be taken throughout the course to monitor progress and to focus revision.
- **Checkpoint assessments** Automarked assessments designed to determine whether students have a secure grasp of concepts from the chapter. These assessments are ramped in difficulty and can be followed up by the differentiated Checkpoint lesson activities.
- **On Your Marks** Improve students' exam skills by analysing questions, looking at other students' responses, interpreting mark schemes, and answering exam-style questions.
- **Homework activities** Automarked quizzes with ramped questions targeting the key Grades 4, 6, and 8 boundaries designed to help students apply and embed their knowledge and understanding from the classroom.

Formal testing

- **End-of-chapter tests** Provide students with the opportunity to practise answering exam-style questions in a written format. There are differentiated Foundation and Higher versions, with separate options for the combined sciences and the separate sciences. Accompanied by a fully comprehensive mark scheme, data can be entered manually into the Markbook.
- **Mid-point and end-of-course written tests** Provide students with the opportunity to practise answering exam-style questions in a full-length paper. There are differentiated Foundation and Higher versions, with separate options for the combined sciences and the separate sciences. Accompanied by a fully comprehensive mark scheme, data can be entered manually into the Markbook.

Kerboodle Book

The *OCR Gateway GCSE Sciences* Kerboodle Books are digital versions of the Student Books for you to use at the front of the classroom.

Access to the Kerboodle Book is automatically available as part of the Lessons, Resources, and Assessment package for both you and your students.

A set of tools is available with the Kerboodle Book so that you can personalise your book and make notes. Like all resources offered on Kerboodle, the Kerboodle Book can also be accessed using a range of devices.

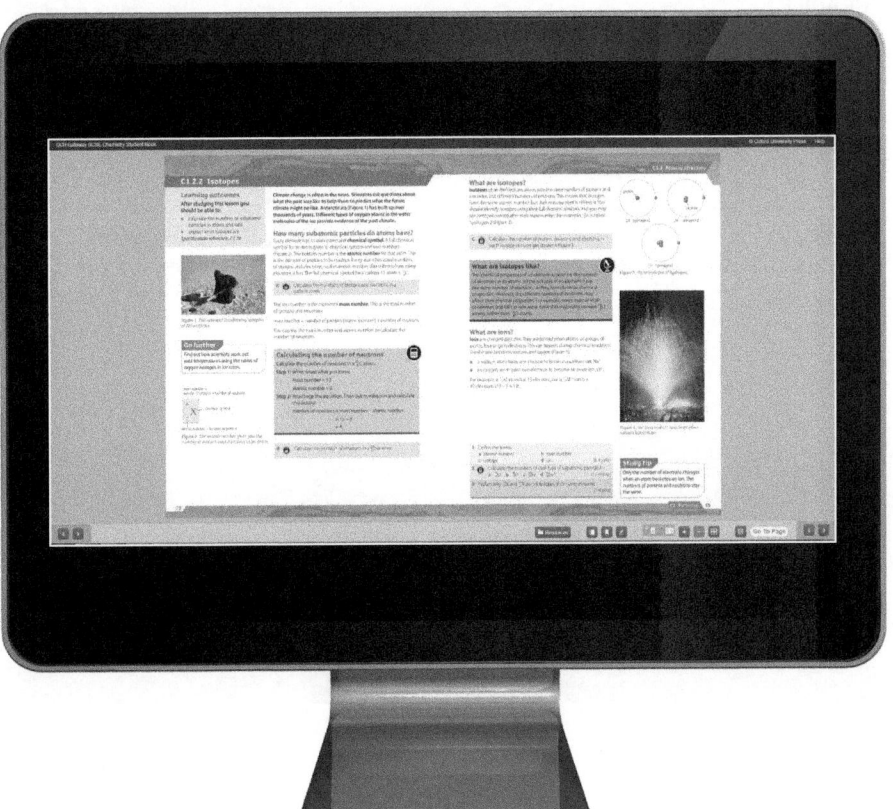

xiii

Working Scientifically

WS1 The power of science

Specification links:

WS1.1c Understand the power and limitations of science.

WS1.1d Discuss ethical issues arising from developments in science.

WS1.1e Explain everyday and technological applications of science.

WS1.1f Evaluate associated personal, social, economic, and environmental applications.

WS1.1g Make decisions based on the evaluation of evidence and arguments.

WS1.1h Evaluate risk both in practical science and the wider societal context.

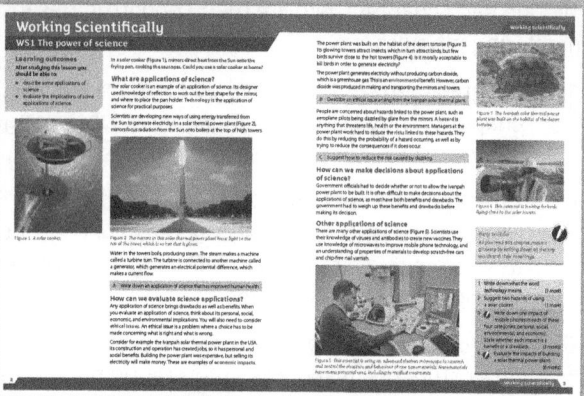

Target	Outcome	Checkpoint	
		Question	Activity
Aiming for GRADE 4	State what technology is.	1	Starter 1 and 2 Plenary 1
	Describe some implications of an application of science.	B	Main 1 and 2
	Describe some hazards linked to an application of science.		Main 1 and 2
Aiming for GRADE 6	Describe some examples of technology.	A	Starter 1 and 2
	Suggest personal, social, economic, environmental, and ethical implications of an application of science.	3	Main 2
	Suggest hazards linked to an application of science and suggest how to minimise a given risk.	C, 2	Main 2
Aiming for GRADE 8	Suggest possible new technologies.		Plenary 2
	Evaluate in detail a wide range of implications of an application of science.	4	Main 1 and 2
	Evaluate the hazards linked to an application of science and suggest how to minimise risk.		Main 1 and 2

Literacy
Students write paragraphs to state and explain a decision.

Key words
economic impact, environmental impact, ethical issue, hazard, risk, technology

Working Scientifically

Starter	Support/Extend	Resources
What is technology? (5 minutes) Display examples of technology, such as a mobile phone, a syringe to represent vaccines, bicycle oil. Student pairs work out definitions of technology – the definition used in the Student Book is *the application of science for practical purposes*. **Vital technology** (10 minutes) Define technology as *the application of science for practical purposes*. Student pairs list as many examples of technology as possible. They create short radio adverts promoting technology, including examples and their benefits.		

Main	Support/Extend	Resources
Spanish solar thermal? (20 minutes) Outline how a solar thermal power plant works and display pictures (see Student Book). Tell students a company wants to build a new solar thermal power plant in Spain. Students will decide whether or not it goes ahead. Students sort cards outlining advantages and disadvantages in these categories: personal, social, economic, environmental, ethical. They also identify possible hazards. Small groups then evaluate the implications – do the advantages outweigh the disadvantages? – and make a decision. Individually, students each write a paragraph for the company, stating and explaining their decision.	**Support:** Select just a few cards for students to categorise. Provide a writing frame for students to communicate their decision. **Extend:** Encourage students to suggest, or research, their own advantages and disadvantages.	**Activity:** Spanish solar thermal
Phone implications (20 minutes) Elicit some personal and social implications of mobile-phone use. Student pairs then use their own knowledge, and information provided on materials used to make mobile phones (including the extraction of coltan), to create posters showing the personal, social, environmental, and ethical implications of mobile-phone manufacture and use. They also use the information provided to outline hazards of mobile-phone use, and suggest how to reduce risks from these hazards. Student pairs then peer-assess each other's posters.	**Support:** Provide an outline poster for students to complete. **Extend:** Students research implications for themselves, and suggest hazards based on prior knowledge.	**Activity:** Phone implications

Plenary	Support/Extend	Resources
Key words (5 minutes) Use the interactive activity in which students match key words from the lesson to their definitions. **New technology** (10 minutes) Students suggest possible new technologies to solve a problem or enhance life. They share their ideas in pairs and identify possible implications.	**Support:** List the key words for students to choose from.	**Interactive:** Key words

Homework		
Make a solar thermal oven, following and adapting any suitable method you find on the Internet. Write down the advantages and disadvantages of using your oven, both at home and for someone who lives in a hot climate.		

WS2 Methods, models, and communication

Specification links:

WS 1.1a Understand how scientific methods and theories develop over time, to include new technology allowing new evidence to be collected and changing explanations as new evidence is found.

WS1.1b Use models to solve problems, make predictions, and to develop scientific explanations and understanding of familiar and unfamiliar facts, to include representational, spatial, descriptive, computational, and mathematical models.

WS1.1i Recognise the importance of peer review of results and of communicating results to a range of audiences.

WS1.4a Use scientific vocabulary, terminology, and definitions.

M5b Visualise and represent 2D and 3D forms including 2D representations of 3D objects.

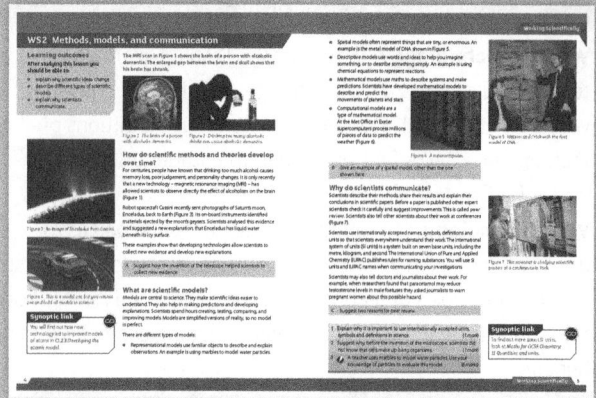

Target	Outcome	Checkpoint	
		Question	Activity
Aiming for GRADE 4	State one way in which new technology has allowed new evidence to be collected.	A	Starter 1 and 2
	Describe different types of scientific model.	B	Main 1
	State the meaning of peer review.		Main 2
Aiming for GRADE 6	Explain how new evidence might lead scientists to develop a new explanation.	2	Starter 1 and 2
	Compare different types of scientific model.		Main 1
	Explain the purposes of peer review, and why scientists use internationally accepted units, symbols, and definitions.	C, 1	Main 2
Aiming for GRADE 8	Evaluate the contribution of a particular technology to the development of scientific explanations.		Starter 2
	Evaluate a scientific model.	3	Main 1
	Suggest possible criteria for peer review.		Plenary 2

Maths
Students evaluate 2D and 3D representations of objects.

Literacy
Students read and critique a scientific article.

Key words
model, peer review

4

Working Scientifically

Starter	Support/Extend	Resources
New technology, new science (5 minutes) Display an MRI scan showing alcoholic dementia. Tell students that MRI is a relatively new technology. Students discuss what scientists might have learnt about alcoholic dementia from brain scans that they could not have learnt by direct observation. There are many examples of new technology that allow scientists to collect new evidence. **Learning from microscopes** (10 minutes) Students observe cork cells through a microscope, as Robert Hooke did in the 1660s. Students list what we have learnt from microscopes (a new technology 400 years ago).	**Extend:** Students research examples to illustrate how new technology allows scientists to collect new evidence.	

Main	Support/Extend	Resources
Models, models, models (20 minutes) New technologies help scientists to collect new evidence and develop explanations. Scientists may also use models to help develop new explanations. Students read about models in the Student Book. They then evaluate models set up as a circus. For each model, they consider how it is like and unlike the real situation, and judge its usefulness. Suggestions for models: • Marbles to represent water molecules • Plastic models showing a red sphere joined to two white spheres to represent water molecules • A physical model of the Solar System • A word equation and a balanced symbol equation to model the burning reaction of methane, placed next to a lighted Bunsen burner • A weather forecast animation set up on a computer (suggested search term: *forecast model animations*).	**Support:** Provide a writing frame for students to record and organise their model evaluations. **Extend:** Students suggest how computer models compare to physical models.	**Activity:** Models, models, models
Peer review (20 minutes) Scientists publish new explanations in scientific journals. Some scientists recently published a paper saying that chocolate lowers the risk of stroke and heart disease. Is this true? Student pairs list questions they would like to ask the scientists about their work. Introduce peer review, in which other scientists review papers. Students read a simplified version of the paper, and look for answers to their questions. They then apply peer-review criteria to decide whether they think the paper should have been published.	**Support:** Provide straightforward questions for students to answer about the chocolate research. **Extend:** Students suggest how the scientists could extend the study to support their claim.	**Activity:** Peer review

Plenary	Support/Extend	Resources
What have I learnt? (5 minutes) Students write down three things they have learnt in the lesson, as well as one thing they would like to learn more about. **Peer-review criteria** (10 minutes) Use the interactive activity in which students select appropriate criteria for peer review from a list of possible criteria.		**Interactive:** Peer review criteria

Homework		
Research how computer models are used to make predictions. Alternatively, find the answers to the questions posed in Plenary 1.		

WS3 Asking scientific questions

Specification links:
WS1.2a Use scientific theories and explanations to develop hypotheses.

WS1.2b Plan experiments or devise procedures to make observations, produce or characterise a substance, test hypotheses, check data, or explore phenomena.

M4c Plot two variables from experimental or other data.

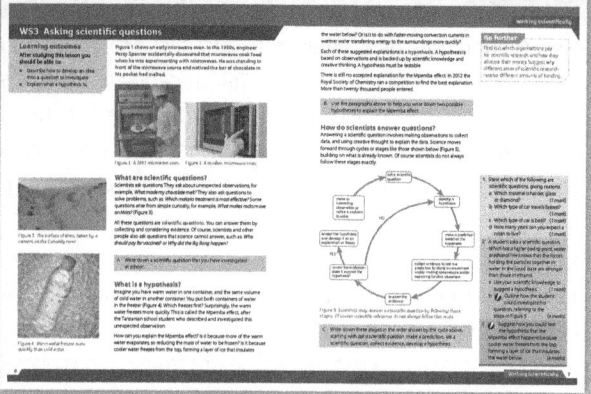

Target	Outcome	Checkpoint	
		Question	Activity
Aiming for GRADE 4 ↓	State what a scientific question is.		Starter 1 and 2, Plenary 1
	State what a hypothesis is.		Plenary 1
	Describe some steps in answering a scientific question.		Main 1
Aiming for GRADE 6 ↓	Recognise scientific questions and questions that are not scientific.	A, 1	Starter 1
	Identify statements that are hypotheses.	B	
	Explain a series of steps to answer a scientific question.	2	Main 1 and 2
Aiming for GRADE 8 ↓	Suggest a scientific question to investigate.		Starter 2
	Suggest a hypothesis to explain an observation.	2	Main 1
	Suggest how to test a given hypothesis to answer a scientific question.	3	Main 1, Plenary 2

Maths
Students plot variables from experimental data (M4c).

Literacy
Students write a paragraph to explain whether the evidence they collect in an investigation supports the hypothesis.

Key words
hypothesis, scientific question

6

Working Scientifically

Starter	Support/Extend	Resources
Scientific or not? (5 minutes) Tell students what a scientific question is. Then use the interactivity in which students identify questions that are scientific and those that are not. Suggested questions: How big is Pluto? How can we prevent meningitis? Who should pay for vaccines? What is made when petrol burns? **Questions, questions** (10 minutes) Tell students what a scientific question is. Demonstrate, but do not explain, the reaction of aluminium with iodine. Student pairs list scientific questions that they would like to answer about what they have seen.	**Support:** Begin by giving scientific questions that they have previously investigated. **Extend:** Students suggest their own scientific and non-scientific questions.	**Interactive:** Scientific or not?

Main	Support/Extend	Resources
A question of volume (35 minutes) Pose a scientific question: What will happen to sea levels as a result of global warming? Gather initial responses – students will probably say that melting ice will make sea levels rise. Then remind students that many substances expand on heating; might this be the same for water? Tell students that they will follow the steps shown in Figure 5 in the Student Book to answer the scientific question. Students use the Practical sheet to guide them in developing a hypothesis (e.g., on heating, particles in liquid water move faster and slightly apart from each other, resulting in an increase in volume) and making a prediction (e.g., heating a water sample will result in an increase in its volume). They test their prediction by placing coloured water in a flask fitted with a bung with two holes. In one hole is a thermometer. In the other hole is a glass tube. Students heat the water and record in a table the height of the water column in the glass tube at different temperatures. Students analyse the evidence by drawing a line graph. They then decide whether the evidence supports the hypothesis and write a paragraph to explain their decision. **One step at a time** (5 minutes) Students study Figure 5, and match what they did in the investigation to the steps shown.	**Support:** Provide a results table and graph axes. Provide a writing frame to help students record their decision. **Extend:** Students suggest alternative methods for investigating this hypothesis.	**Practical:** A question of volume

Plenary	Support/Extend	Resources
Key words (5 minutes) Students write definitions for the two key words of the lesson, and peer-assess one another's definitions. **Matching steps** (10 minutes) Return to one of the scientific questions posed in the starter. Students suggest what they would do for each step shown in Figure 5 to answer the question.		

Homework		
Choose a scientific question from the starter activity, or from the Student Book. Describe and explain what you would do for each step shown in Figure 5 to answer the question.	**Support:** Provide a simple question and writing frame to guide students in this task.	

WS4 Planning an investigation

Specification links:

WS1.1h Evaluate risks both in practical science and the wider societal context.

WS1.2b Plan experiments or devise procedures to make observations, produce or characterise a substance, test hypotheses, check data, or explore phenomena.

WS1.2c Apply a range of techniques, instruments, apparatus, and materials to select those appropriate to the experiment.

M4c Plot two variables from experimental or other data.

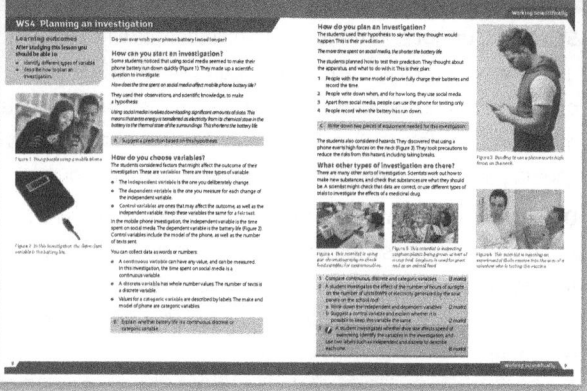

Target	Outcome	Checkpoint	
		Question	Activity
Aiming for GRADE 4 ↓	State what a variable is, and state the meanings of these terms: independent variable, dependent variable, control variable.		Starter 1, Plenary 1
	State examples of continuous, discrete, and categoric variables.		Main 2
	Describe the steps in a plan for an investigation to make observations, including making a prediction.	A, C	Main 1
Aiming for GRADE 6 ↓	Explain whether given variables in an investigation are independent, dependent, or control variables.		Main 1
	Compare continuous, discrete, and categoric variables.	1	
	Describe and explain the steps in a plan for an investigation to make observations.		Main 1
Aiming for GRADE 8 ↓	Determine the variables to change, measure, and control when planning an investigation.	2, 3	Starter 2, Plenary 2
	Determine whether given variables in an investigation are continuous, discrete, or categoric.	B, 3	Main 2, Plenary 2
	Justify decisions made in a plan for an investigation to make observations.		Main 1

Maths
Students plot bar charts from their investigation data (M4c).

Literacy
Students define key words.

Key words
categoric variable, continuous variable, control variable, dependent variable, discrete variable, fair test, independent variable, prediction

Working Scientifically

Starter	Support/Extend	Resources
Defining variables (5 minutes) Students use Key Stage 3 knowledge to match key words (variable, independent variable, dependent variable, control variable) to their definitions. **Phone variables** (10 minutes) Display the scientific question *How does the time spent on social media affect mobile-phone battery life?* Students use Key Stage 3 knowledge to suggest the following variables for an investigation to answer this question: one independent variable, one dependent variable, two control variables.	**Support:** List variables for students to choose from. **Extend:** Students write their own definitions of the key words.	**Interactive:** Defining variables

Main	Support/Extend	Resources
Temperature and dissolving (30 minutes) Students plan and carry out an investigation to compare the temperature changes on dissolving different substances in water (e.g., ammonium chloride, ammonium nitrate, potassium nitrate, copper sulfate, potassium chloride, calcium chloride, sodium carbonate). Students start by identifying variables (independent – substance; dependent – temperature change; control – starting temperature of water, amount of substance). They then consider the hazards, and how to minimise risks from these hazards (see CLEAPSS Student Safety Sheets). Next, students decide what to do, and draw a results table, with the independent variable in the column on the left. Students then carry out the investigation and collect data. **Dissolving variables** (10 minutes) Explain the differences between continuous, discrete, and categoric variables, including examples. Students categorise the variables in their investigation (substance – categoric; temperature change – continuous). Since one variable is categoric, they draw bar charts to display their results.	**Support:** Provide a writing frame to help students plan their investigation. **Extend:** When planning their investigations, students justify each decision they make. They also explain how they know which type of variable is which. **Support:** If time is short, focus on the variable categories only – do not ask students to draw bar charts.	**Practical:** Temperature and dissolving

Plenary	Support/Extend	Resources
Variable quiz (10 minutes) Students make up a five-question quiz on variables. They swap quizzes and answer the questions. **Swimming and shoe size** (5 minutes) Students answer question 3 in the Student Book, and peer-assess each other's answers. In the peer assessment, they point out things that have been done well, and suggest any improvements or corrections.		

Homework		
Devise an investigation to answer the question *How does coffee drinking affect reaction time?* You may need to use the Internet for suggestions on how to measure reaction time.		

WS5 Obtaining high-quality data

Specification links:

WS1.3c Carry out and represent mathematical and statistical analysis.

WS1.3g Evaluate data in terms of accuracy, precision, repeatability, and reproducibility.

WS1.4f Use an appropriate number of significant figures in calculation.

M2b Find arithmetic means.

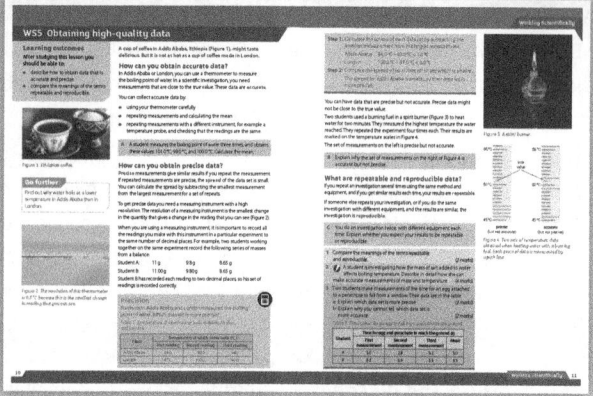

Target	Outcome	Checkpoint	
		Question	Activity
Aiming for GRADE 4	State what is meant by accurate data and precise data.		Starter 1, Main 1, Plenary 1
	State the meanings of repeatable and reproducible.	C	Main 2, Plenary 1
Aiming for GRADE 6	Compare the meanings of accurate and precise when applied to data.	B, 3	Main 1
	Compare the meanings of repeatable and reproducible.	1	Main 2
Aiming for GRADE 8	Suggest how to maximise the accuracy and precision of data collected in an investigation.	A, 2	Starter 2, Plenary 2
	Suggest how to devise an investigation that is repeatable and reproducible.		Plenary 2

Maths
Students calculate mean values for data sets (M2b), and give answers to a suitable number of significant figures (M2a).

Literacy
Students write paragraphs about the difference between accuracy and precision.

Key words
accurate, precise, repeatable, reproducible, resolution, spread

Working Scientifically

Starter	Support/Extend	Resources
How accurate? (10 minutes) Demonstrate the volume change when salt dissolves in water by placing 300–400 g of salt in a 1 dm³ volumetric flask. Add enough water to cover the salt, swirl to wet it, and let air bubbles float to the top. Then add water to fill the flask to the mark. Shake to speed up dissolving. When no more salt dissolves, mark the new – lower – level of the solution. Ask student pairs to discuss how to get accurate data for the decrease in height. Answers: use the ruler carefully; repeat the procedure and calculate a mean; measure the height with a different instrument and check that the value is the same as for the ruler. **Heart beat** (5 minutes) Students suggest how to get an accurate value for their resting pulse rate. Answers: place fingers on the pulse and count carefully; repeat and calculate a mean; use a pulse-rate monitor and check that the value is the same as for placing fingers on the pulse.		

Main	Support/Extend	Resources
Hand-span precision (25 minutes) Elicit that accurate data is data that is close to the true value. State that precise has a different meaning – if data is precise, it has similar values. In pairs, students measure each other's hand spans by marking the positions of the thumb and little finger on a piece of paper, and using a ruler to measure the distance between them. Each student repeats the procedure three times, records the measurements, and calculates the spread. In pairs, students compare their results: whose measurements are more precise? Students write a paragraph to explain the difference between accuracy and precision. **Thumb width** (15 minutes) In pairs, students measure each other's thumb widths three times using a technique as for hand span. They swap partners and repeat. Finally, students return to their original partner and devise a different method for measuring thumb width, using callipers, for example. Students record all measurements. Use the investigation to explain the difference between repeatability and reproducibility (see Student Book). Students complete a passage to explain the difference between the two terms.	**Support:** Supply results tables for students to complete. Supply a passage for students to complete to explain the difference between accuracy and precision. **Extend:** Students write their own paragraphs to explain the difference between repeatability and reproducibility.	**Practical:** Hand-span precision

Plenary	Support/Extend	Resources
Reproducibility and repeatability (5 minutes) Students complete a paragraph to consolidate their understanding of reproducibility and repeatability. **Accurate advice** (10 minutes) Students write instructions to a younger student to explain how to collect accurate and precise data.	**Extend:** Students write corrected versions of the false sentences.	**Interactive:** Reproducibility and repeatability

Homework		
Make a small parachute from a handkerchief or similar item. Suspend a weight from it. Collect data on its time to fall to the ground from a given height. Explain what you did to collect precise and accurate data. Describe how you could find out if the data is repeatable and reproducible.		

WS6 Presenting data

Specification links:

WS1.3a Present observations and other data using appropriate methods.

WS1.3b Translate data from one form to another.

M4c Plot two variables from experimental or other data.

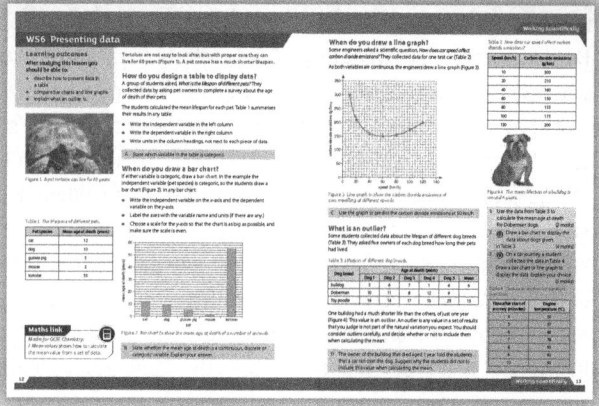

Target	Outcome	Checkpoint	
		Question	Activity
Aiming for GRADE 4 ↓	Draw a bar chart or line graph to present data, given fully labelled axes.		Main 2 and 3
	Identify the value of the dependent variable, given the value of the independent variable, from a bar chart.		Main 2
	State what an outlier is.		Main 1
Aiming for GRADE 6 ↓	Draw a bar chart or line graph to present data, including choosing which type of chart/graph to draw, labelling axes, and choosing suitable scales.	B, 2	Starter 1 Main 2 and 3
	Identify the value of the dependent variable, given a value of the independent variable, from a bar chart or line graph.	C	Plenary 1 and 2
	Calculate the mean from a set of data.	1	Main 1
Aiming for GRADE 8 ↓	Draw a bar chart or line graph to present data and justify the choice of bar chart or line graph. Decide which variables to place on which axes.	A, 3	Starter 2 Main 2
	Predict values for the dependent variable, given values for the independent variable, from a bar chart or line graph.		Main 2 Plenary 2
	Justify a decision to include or not to include an outlier when calculating the mean from a set of data.	D	Main 1

Maths
Students plot bar charts and line graphs (M4c).

Literacy
Students compose questions about their graphs.

Key words
bar chart, line graph

12

Working Scientifically

Starter	Support/Extend	Resources
Displaying dogs (5 minutes) Display pictures of different dog breeds. Give values for the mean adult mass of dogs of each breed (Great Dane – 54 kg; Pekingese – 5 kg; Rottweiler – 39 kg). Ask whether this data is better displayed as a bar chart or line graph, and why. (Answer – bar chart, since one variable is categoric.)	**Support:** Point out that one of the variables (dog breed) is categoric.	
Line graph or bar chart? (10 minutes) Display tables showing different data sets. For each, students decide and justify whether the data should be presented as a bar chart or line graph.	**Extend:** Students suggest data sets for which bar charts or line graphs should be drawn.	**Interactive:** Line graph or bar chart?

Main	Support/Extend	Resources
Means and outliers (10 minutes) Give students the adult masses of six adult dogs of the same breed, including one outlier. Students calculate mean values. Point out the outlier. Discuss whether or not to include the outlier in calculating the mean. Tell students the outlier dog was ill, and could not eat enough. Have they changed their minds about whether to include this value in calculating the mean? (Suitable Great Dane values: 50, 54, 58, 56, 38, 50)		
Line graphs (15 minutes) On the same axes, students use supplied data to plot growth curves for different puppy breeds (mass versus age). They peer-evaluate each other's graphs, checking that variables have been plotted on the correct axes, that the axes are labelled, that the scales are suitable, and that the curves for each dog breed are clearly labelled. Students then make up questions about their graph and swap with a partner, who answers the questions.	**Support:** Provide labelled axes. Ask students to plot data for one dog breed only. **Extend:** Students justify drawing a line graph for this data.	**Activity:** Line graphs and bar charts
Bar charts (15 minutes) Pass around equal-sized cuboids made from materials of different densities. Tell students that they will find out whether there is a link between the position of an element in the Periodic Table, and its density. Give data for six elements, as well as their relative positions in the Periodic Table. Students plot the data for the two groups on one bar chart. They then note any patterns in the data. Below is some suitable data for elements in adjacent groups of the periodic table:	**Support:** Supply labelled axes and ask students to plot data for one group only. **Extend:** Students find the density for elements in other adjacent groups of the Periodic Table, and add this to their bar charts.	

Element	Density (g/cm^3)	Element	Density (g/cm^3)
cobalt	8.9	nickel	8.9
rhodium	12.4	palladium	12.0
iridium	22.5	platinum	21.4

Plenary	Support/Extend	Resources
Emissions and car speed (5 minutes) Students study the line graph in the Student Book. In pairs, they take turns to describe what it shows. They then answer in-text question C.		
Questions, questions (10 minutes) Students make up questions about their bar charts and swap with a partner, who answers the questions.		

Homework
Use the data provided to plot a bar chart or line graph. Justify your choice of graph type.

WS7 Interpreting data

Specification links:

WS1.3e Interpreting observations and other data.

WS1.3f Presenting reasoned explanations.

WS1.3g Evaluating data in terms of accuracy, precision, repeatability, and reproducibility.

M2g Use a scatter diagram to identify a relationship between two variables.

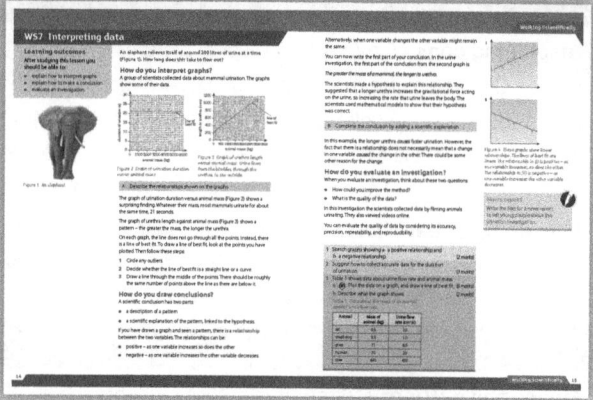

Target	Outcome	Checkpoint	
		Question	Activity
Aiming for GRADE 4	Draw a line of best fit on a simple graph.		Main 2
	Describe the relationship shown by a graph using non-specialist terms.	A	
	Describe one way of evaluating an investigation.		Starter 1
Aiming for GRADE 6	Draw a line of best fit on a graph that does not include outliers.		Main 2
	Describe the relationship shown by a graph using terms such as positive relationship.	A, 1, 3	Starter 2
	Explain at least two ways of evaluating investigations, including the quality of data.	2	Main 3
Aiming for GRADE 8	Draw the line of best fit on a graph that includes outliers.		Main 2
	Describe in detail the relationship shown by a graph using technical terms. If appropriate, suggest and justify whether any relationship shown could be causal.	C, 3	
	Suggest how to evaluate both the method and quality of data for a given investigation.		Main 3

Maths
Students interpret scatter graphs.

Literacy
Students write conclusions for investigations.

Key words
line of best fit, relationship

14

Working Scientifically

Starter	Support/Extend	Resources
Urination duration (10 minutes) Show a video of an animal such as an elephant urinating. Individually, students outline how they could collect high-quality data to compare the duration of urination for different mammal species. Each student shares their ideas with a partner, who evaluates their method, suggesting improvements that would enable them to collect more accurate data. Answers might include: make a video and then measure urination duration several times; find the mean of repeated readings.	**Support:** Suggest methods for students to evaluate.	
What do graphs show? (5 minutes) Use the interactive activity in which students have to identify, from graph sketches, whether a graph shows a positive relationship, a negative relationship, or no relationship.		**Interactive:** What do graphs show?

Main	Support/Extend	Resources
Urination duration – any relation? (15 minutes) For several mammal species, provide data of urination duration and mean adult mass. Students plot the data as a scatter graph. Elicit that there is no relationship between the data – the data shows that, whatever the mass, urination duration is around 21 seconds. Students write conclusions for the investigation.	**Support:** Provide a writing frame for the conclusion.	**Activity:** Urination duration – any relation?
Mass, urethra length, and lines of best fit (15 minutes) For several species, provide data of mean adult mass and urethra length. Students plot the data as a scatter graph. Elicit that the data shows a positive relationship. Students write conclusions for the investigation. Provide further scatter graphs (some including outliers) so that students can practise drawing lines of best fit, as well as identifying whether each shows a positive relationship, a negative relationship, or no relationship.	**Support:** Provide a writing frame for the conclusion. **Extend:** Provide data so that students can sketch extra scatter diagrams of their own.	
Evaluating an investigation (10 minutes) If students did the activity in Starter 1, remind them how they evaluated the method. Now give further data for the urination experiment, and ask students to evaluate the data in terms of its precision. They can do this by calculating the spread of each data set. For which animal is the data most precise?	**Support:** Provide a series of questions to support students in evaluating the precision of the data.	

Plenary	Support/Extend	Resources
Relationships (5 minutes) Ask students to sketch graphs showing each of these relationships in turn – positive, negative, none.		
Evaluation (10 minutes) Read out statements about evaluation, some true and some false. Students use mini-whiteboards to indicate which are true and which are false.		

Homework
Make a poster to display your learning from the lesson.

WS8 Errors and uncertainties

Specification links:
WS1.3d Representing distribution of results and making estimations of uncertainty.

WS1.3h Identifying potential sources of random and systematic error.

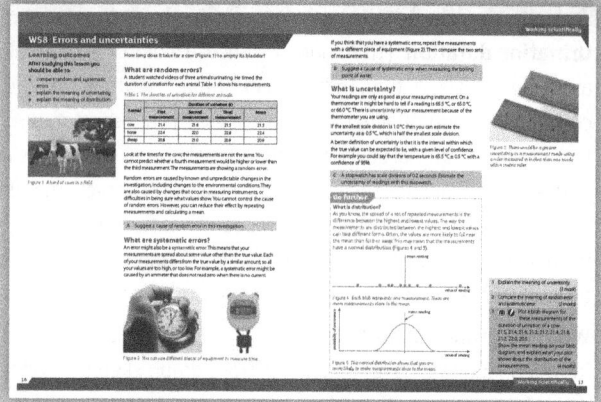

Target	Outcome	Checkpoint	
		Question	Activity
Aiming for GRADE 4	State the meanings of random error and systematic error.		Main 1 / Plenary 2
	State the scientific meaning of uncertainty.	1	Main 2 / Plenary 2
	State the meaning of the spread of a set of data.		Main 3 / Plenary 2
Aiming for GRADE 6	Compare random and systematic error and suggest causes of these types of error.	A, B, 2	Starter 1 and 2 / Main 1 / Plenary 1
	Estimate the uncertainty of a given measuring instrument using scale divisions.	C	Main 2
	Recognise and sketch a plot showing normal distribution.		Main 3
Aiming for GRADE 8	State whether a given error is random or systematic, and justify this choice.		Main 1
	Compare the uncertainties of two given measuring instruments using scale divisions.		Main 2
	Plot a blob diagram and explain what it shows about the distribution of measurements.	3	

Maths
Students identify plots of normal distribution and explain what they mean.

Literacy
Students describe the difference between random and systematic errors.

Key words
normal distribution, random error, systematic error, uncertainty

16

Working Scientifically

Starter	Support/Extend	Resources
Timing errors I (10 minutes) Show a video clip of a 200m sprint. Students use stopwatches or other timing devices to measure the winning time. They then write down their results. Repeat the exercise twice more, so that each student has a set of three results. Ask students to compare their three results. Are they all the same? In pairs, students suggest reasons for any differences. **Timing errors II** (5 minutes) Ask students to think back to measuring urination duration. Imagine they watched a video of an animal urinating three times. Would they get the same measurements each time? If not, why not?	**Support:** Provide a table for recording results. **Extend:** Tell students they will consider two types of error – random error and systematic error. Can they suggest any differences in their meanings?	

Main	Support/Extend	Resources
Boiling salty water (20 minutes) Students add 4 spatula measures of salt to approximately 100 cm^3 of water. They heat the solution in a beaker and measure and record its boiling temperature. They repeat this twice more, thus collecting a set of three results. Students consider their results. Why might they be different? Introduce the idea of random errors, and state that these cannot be controlled, but that their effects can be reduced by repeating measurements and calculating a mean. Then explain systematic errors. Gather mean values for the boiling temperature of salty water from all groups. Does it appear that one or more groups might have a systematic error? (Any group whose values are consistently lower or higher than those of other groups might have a systematic error.) Ask students to suggest what they might do about these errors. (Repeat with a different thermometer.) **Uncertainty circus** (10 minutes) Introduce the scientific meaning of uncertainty, and compare to the everyday meaning. Explain how to estimate the uncertainty of a measuring instrument as half of its smallest scale division. Set up a circus of measuring instruments. Students examine each and estimate the uncertainty in readings taken with the instrument. **Distribution** (10 minutes) Ask students to calculate the spread of their measurements for the boiling-water practical. Then take the results from the group with the biggest spread and draw a blob plot on the board. Explain that, for a given set of measurements, the measurements are likely to be distributed with more nearer the mean than further away. Students answer question 3 in the Student Book.	**Support:** Provide results tables and gap fill exercises for students to summarise their learning. **Extend:** Students read about a second way of estimating uncertainty, as described in the Student Book. They also compare the uncertainties of two instruments for measuring the same quantity, such as time. **Extend:** Point out the special case of a normal, or Gaussian, distribution, as shown in the Student Book.	**Practical:** Looking at errors

Plenary	Support/Extend	Resources
Random versus systematic (10 minutes) Students write down the difference between random and systematic errors, and peer-assess. **Key words** (5 minutes) Read definitions of the key words, without saying which is which. Students write down the key words.	**Support:** Give key words for students to choose from.	**Interactive:** Key words

Homework		
Answer all of the questions in the Student Book that you have not already answered.		

C1 Particles

C1.1 The particle model
C1.1.1 Introducing particles

Specification links:

C1.1a Describe the main features of the particle model in terms of states of matter (WS1.1a).

WS1.1b Use models to solve problems, make predictions, and to develop scientific explanations and understanding of familiar and unfamiliar facts.

WS2b Make and record observations and measurements, using a range of apparatus and methods.

M5b Visualise and represent two-dimensional (2D) and three-dimensional (3D) forms, including 2D representations of 3D objects.

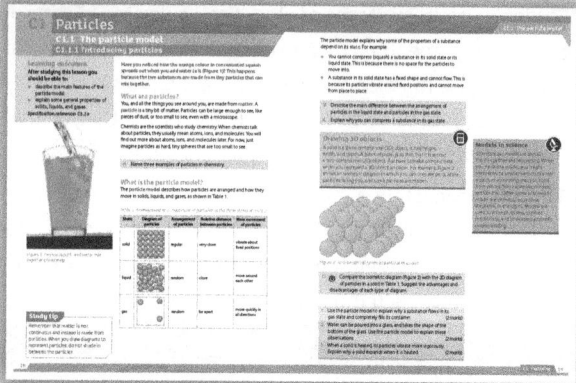

Target	Outcome	Checkpoint Question	Checkpoint Activity
Aiming for GRADE 4 ↓	Draw diagrams to show the arrangements of particles in the three states of matter.		Starter 1
	Describe typical physical properties of a substance in a given state.		Starter 2
	State whether a given particle model is in two or three dimensions.		Main 1, Plenary 1 and 2
Aiming for GRADE 6 ↓	Describe the movement and arrangement of particles in the three states of matter, and give examples of three types of particle.	A	Starter 1 and 2
	Compare the physical properties of a substance in its three states.		Starter 2
	Compare the features of 2D and 3D models to represent particles.		Main 1, Plenary 2
Aiming for GRADE 8 ↓	Compare the movement and arrangement of particles in the three states of matter.		Starter 1, Main 1
	Use the particle model to explain the differences in physical properties of a substance in its three states.	B, C, 1, 2, 3	Main 2
	Evaluate the advantages and disadvantages of given 2D and 3D models to represent particles.	D	Main 1, Plenary 2

Maths
In Main 1 students use models in both 2D and 3D to represent matter (M5b).

Literacy
In Main 2 students write coherent paragraphs to explain observations in detail.

Key words
matter, particle, particle model, state, model

C1.1 The particle model

Starter	Support/Extend	Resources
Sublime science (10 minutes) Demonstrate sublimation by heating 2 spatula measures of iodine crystals in a conical flask with a 'cold finger' inserted (a smaller test-tube filled with ice or a finger-shaped piece of glass). Students draw particle diagrams of iodine in the solid and gas states. SAFETY: wear eye protection. Iodine is harmful and causes skin irritation – do not touch. Perform in a well-ventilated laboratory. To avoid pressure building up, do not seal the 'cold finger' tightly into the flask. **What do we know?** (10 minutes) Students list what they know about the states of matter and the particle model. They then work in pairs to review their work. Discuss any points of contention.	**Support:** Ask students to think about the position and movement of particles, as well as the distance between them, in the solid and gas states. **Extend:** Students describe the movement and behaviour of particles in the three states, and use the particle model to explain the different physical properties.	

Main	Support/Extend	Resources
Modelling particles (20 minutes) Talk through the 2D representations of particles in Table 1 in the Student Book. Ask student pairs to list the strengths and weaknesses of these representations for showing particle arrangements and movement, as well as for explaining properties. Then give students sticky tack, polystyrene balls, and other modelling materials such as cotton wool balls, card and polystyrene packing materials. Ask them to use these materials to make 3D models showing the particles in each state of matter. Students evaluate their 3D models, and compare their advantages and disadvantages to those of the 2D models. Finally, ask students to consider the model shown in Figure 2 in the Student Book and discuss answers to in-text question D. **Particles and properties** (20 minutes) Demonstrate pouring carbon dioxide gas to extinguish a candle. SAFETY: wear eye protection. Student pairs discuss why you can pour a substance in its liquid and gas states, but not in its solid state. Student pairs then write a paragraph using the particle model to explain this observation in detail.	**Support:** Remind students of their Key Stage 3 knowledge of the particle model. **Extend:** Students write explanations of these observations in detail: 1 A liquid fills the bottom of its container, but a gas fills its whole container. 2 A solid expands on heating.	**Activity:** Modelling particles

Plenary	Support/Extend	Resources
Sweet model (5 minutes) Show students a box of Maltesers, and ask which state of matter this represents (solid). Then ask how this model may be used to explain melting. **The particle model** (5 minutes) Interactive activity in which students link the lines to name and then describe the movement of particles in each of the three states of matter.	**Support:** Display the different models, and use questions and answers to prompt students to write the models' strengths and weaknesses on a sheet of paper beside each one.	**Interactive:** The particle model

Homework	Support/Extend	Resources
Create a PowerPoint (or similar) presentation to summarise your learning about particles from the lesson.		

kerboodle

A Kerboodle highlight for this lesson is **Bump up your grade: States of matter.** Refer to the **Content map** on Kerboodle for a full list of resources and assessment.

C1 Particles

C1.1.2 Chemical and physical changes

Specification links:

C1.1b Explain, in terms of the particle model, the distinction between physical changes and chemical changes.

WS1.1b Use models to solve problems, make predictions, and develop scientific explanations and understanding of familiar and unfamiliar facts.

WS2b Make and record observations and measurements, using a range of apparatus and methods.

M5b Visualise and represent two-dimensional (2D) and three-dimensional (3D) forms, including 2D representations of 3D objects.

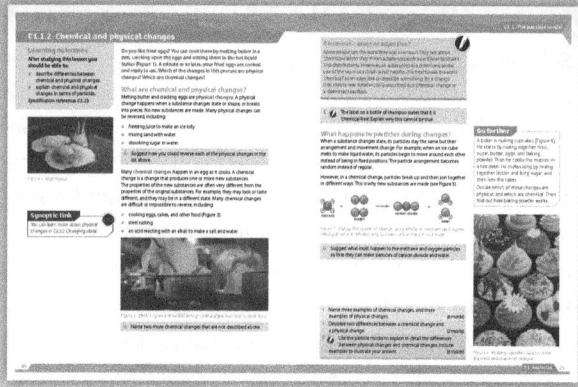

Target	Outcome	Checkpoint	
		Question	Activity
Aiming for GRADE 4 ↓	Make observations, and give examples of physical and chemical changes.	A, B, 1	Starter 1, Main 1
	State the definitions of physical and chemical changes.		Main 1
	Compare reactants and products in a chemical reaction using particle diagrams or physical models.		Main 2
Aiming for GRADE 6 ↓	State whether an observed change is physical or chemical.		Main 1, Plenary 1
	Compare the features of physical and chemical changes.	2	Main 1, Plenary 1 and 2
	Deduce whether a given change is physical or chemical by interpreting particle diagrams of reactants and products.	D	Starter 2, Plenary 1
Aiming for GRADE 8 ↓	Justify classifying a given observed change as physical or chemical.		Main 1
	Explain the differences between physical and chemical changes using the particle model.	3	Main 2
	Draw particle diagrams of reactants and products to model a chemical reaction.		Main 2

Maths
In Main 2 students use 2D diagrams to represent 3D objects (M5b).

Literacy
In Plenary 1 students write formative assessment comments for peers.

Key words
physical change, chemical change, chemical reaction

C1.1 The particle model

Starter	Support/Extend	Resources
Exploding balloons (10 minutes) Fill a balloon with 300 cm^3 of hydrogen and anchor it with a 1 kg mass. Place it 5 m away from all observers. Ignite the balloon by touching it with a lit taper joined to a metre rule. Repeat with a stoichiometric mixture of oxygen and hydrogen in a second balloon (do not use more than 300 cm^3 of the mixture). Elicit that a chemical change has occurred. SAFETY: wear eye protection. Students use the particle model to draw diagrams of the hydrogen molecules in the first balloon and the mixture of hydrogen and oxygen molecules in the second balloon. **States of matter** (5 minutes) Draw a chlorine molecule as two green spheres connected with a black line. Ask students to draw several chlorine molecules to model the element in the solid, liquid, and gas states. Elicit that changing the state of a sample of chlorine is a physical change.	**Support:** Remind students of the particle model studied last lesson. **Extend:** Ask students to draw diagrams to represent particles of the reactants (hydrogen and oxygen, as molecules) and product (water, as a molecule) in the demonstration.	

Main	Support/Extend	Resources
Chemical and physical changes (20 minutes) Set up five stations around the room. Students visit each station in pairs or groups of three, and outline each activity in a sentence and note their observations. They then classify each change as physical or chemical, and use the particle model to justify their decisions. 1 Place 2 cm^3 of dilute hydrochloric acid into a test tube. Add a 1 cm length of magnesium ribbon. 2 Place 2 cm^3 of water into a test tube and add 1 spatula of sodium chloride, then stir. 3 Place 2 cm^3 of dilute sulfuric acid into a test tube and add 1 spatula of copper carbonate, then stir. 4 Place an ice cube in a beaker and observe over time. 5 Place 2 cm^3 of copper sulfate solution in a test tube. Then add 2 cm^3 of sodium hydroxide solution one drop at a time. **Molecular models** (20 minutes) Student pairs use molecular model kits to make the following: two hydrogen molecules (connect two white balls), one oxygen molecule (connect two red balls), and two molecules of water (connect two white balls to one red ball). They use these 3D models to draw 2D diagrams of the particles in a mixture of hydrogen and oxygen (as in the second balloon in Starter 1) and in the water that is made. Students compare the particles before and after the reaction, using the particle model to explain why making a mixture is a physical change, but synthesising water from its elements is a chemical change.	**Support:** You might need to remind students of the definitions of physical and chemical changes. Complete each experiment as a class and discuss the observations and conclusions before proceeding to the next task. **Extend:** Ask students to design a table to record classifications and justifications, and fill it in as they go around the circus.	**Practical:** Chemical and physical changes

Plenary	Support/Extend	Resources
Text message (10 minutes) Students summarise their learning in the lesson as a text message or series of three tweets, one linked to each learning outcome strand. Students peer assess each other's work. **Chemical and physical changes** (5 minutes) Students write sentences to describe, explain and give examples of chemical and physical changes. Alternatively, students could complete the Interactive activity.	**Extend:** Students make a key to classify physical changes from practical observations.	**Interactive:** Chemical and physical changes

Homework	Support/Extend	Resources
Choose one physical change and one chemical change, and illustrate both with labelled 2D particle models. Or complete the interactive activity on chemical and physical changes.		

kerboodle
A Kerboodle highlight for this lesson is **Literacy sheet: Chemical and physical changes.** Refer to the **Content map** on Kerboodle for a full list of resources and assessment.

HIGHER TIER
C1.1.3 Limitations of the particle model

Specification links:

C1.1a Describe the main features of the particle model in terms of states of matter and change of state (WS1.1a).

C1.1c Explain the limitations of the particle model in relation to changes of state when particles are represented by inelastic spheres (e.g. like bowling balls) (WS1.1c).

WS1.1b Use models to solve problems, make predictions, and develop scientific explanations and understandings of familiar and unfamiliar facts.

M1c Use ratios, fractions, and percentages.

M5b Visualise and represent two-dimensional (2D) and three-dimensional (3D) forms, including 2D representations of 3D objects.

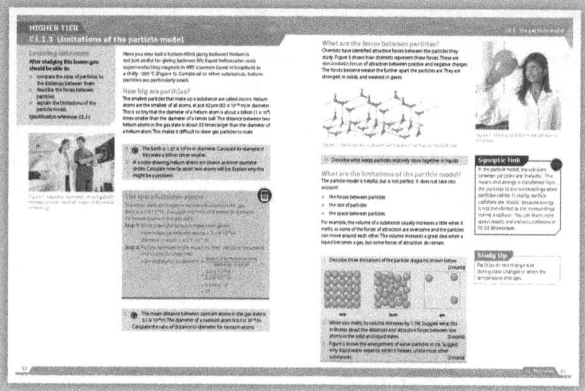

Target	Outcome	Checkpoint	
		Question	**Activity**
Aiming for GRADE 4 ↓	Name the type of force that acts between particles.	D	Starter 2 Plenary 1
	Compare the relative distances between particles in the three states of matter.		Main 1
	Describe one way in which the particle model is unlike the situation it represents.		Starter 1
Aiming for GRADE 6 ↓	Describe how the strength of the forces between particles changes with distance.		Starter 2 Plenary 2
	State typical distances between particles in the gas state.		Main 1 Plenary 2
	Describe three limitations of the particle model.	1	Main 2 Plenary 2
Aiming for GRADE 8 ↓	Explain why the strength of the forces between particles affects the properties of a substance.	2, 3	
	Calculate the ratio of particle diameter to distance between particles for a substance in the gas state, and use ratios to calculate the sizes of objects in scale models.	A, B, C	Main 1
	Use mathematical ideas to explain some limitations of the particle model.		Main 2

Maths
In Starter 1 students use 2D and 3D models to represent particles (M5b), and in Main 1 students use ratios (M1c).

Literacy
In Plenary 1, given definitions, students identify key words.

Key words
atom, electrostatic force

kerboodle

A Kerboodle highlight for this lesson is **Maths skills: Size of atoms.** Refer to the **Content map** on Kerboodle for a full list of resources and assessment.

22

C1.1 The particle model

Starter	Support/Extend	Resources
Burst balloon (5 minutes) Show students a 2D picture of the particles in a gas. Then show two demonstrations – activating an air freshener at the front of the room, and blowing up a balloon until it bursts. In groups of three or four, students use their observations to suggest limitations of this representation of the particle model. (Because the model does not show the particles moving, it cannot explain diffusion or gas pressure.) **Make sentences** (10 minutes) Explain that there are electrostatic forces of attraction between particles. Student pairs then select one or more correct endings for each sentence starter below. The correct endings are italicised. 1 The volume of a substance usually increases a little on melting because... the particles expand; *some forces of attraction between the particles are overcome; the particles can move around each other*. 2 When a liquid becomes a gas...*most forces of attraction between particles are overcome; some forces of attraction remain*; no forces of attraction remain. 3 In the air, distances between particles are... similar to the diameters of the particles; *much greater than the diameters of the particles*; much smaller than the diameters of the particles. 4 As the distance between particles increases, the strength of the force of attraction between them...*decreases*; increases.	**Extend:** Ask students to suggest which observations can be explained using the 2D representations of the particle model. **Support:** Ask students to relate their observations to the model (e.g. can this representation of the model explain gas diffusion?)	

Main	Support/Extend	Resources
Size and scale (15 minutes) In this activity students look at the relative sizes of various tiny objects, using numbers in standard form. **Scrap the particle model? Limitations of the particle model** (25 minutes) Students make simple posters to describe the particle model. They describe its limitations, including the fact that it does not take into account the forces between particles, the size of particles, nor the space between particles. Then divide the class into two groups, one for and the other against the motion *The particle model should be scrapped*. Allow time for students to prepare their points for a debate. Carry out the debate and take a vote.	**Support:** Students colour in one square of graph paper to represent a helium atom. Then count 55 squares away and colour another square, and repeat. This shows the space needed to represent gases using the particle model. **Extend:** Students do further calculations on atomic radius. **Support:** Use questions and answers to generate a list of pros and cons for the particle model before the debate. **Extend:** Students use standard form to compare the sizes of common small objects.	**Activity:** Limitations of the particle model

Plenary	Support/Extend	Resources
Define (5 minutes) Students give the key word or phrase for these definitions: Smallest particle that can exist on its own (atom); force between molecules (electrostatic force of attraction); simplified version of what happens which helps us understand observations and make predictions (model). **Limitations of the particle model** (5 minutes) Interactive activity in which students are introduced to a selection of very small objects whose dimensions are given in standard form and are then asked to arrange them into size order. Students then practise converting between different units before looking at some of the limitations of the particle model.	**Support:** Ask students to match key words to definitions. **Support:** Allow students to work in small groups to generate the key points.	**Interactive:** Limitations of the particle model

Homework	Support/Extend	Resources
Write down the diameter of a helium atom and the distance between two helium atoms in metres, without using standard form.		

Checkpoint
C1.1 The particle model

Overview of C1.1 The particle model

In this chapter students have studied the particle model. Building on concepts studied at Key Stage 3, they should understand what is meant by a particle and be familiar with the types of particle in matter. They should be able to describe how the particles are arranged in the three states of matter, and typical physical properties of a substance in a given state. It can be effective to fill a syringe with air and show how easy it is to compress, and compare this with the same syringe full of water. Students should be able to compare and evaluate different representations of the particle model. They should be able to discuss the advantages and disadvantages of representing the particles in two or three dimensions.

In studying physical and chemical changes, students should be able to define these changes and distinguish between them. They should have use models to represent and interpret reactants and products in a chemical reaction. This use of models leads to chemical equations, and can be used to illustrate the conservation of matter, and show bonds between the particles. Chemical change is a fundamental concept in chemistry and students should have used molecular models with colour-coded atoms and easily quantified numbers of bonds for each atom to demonstrate that not only are atoms conserved but also the total number of bonds between them.

Students should be able to describe the forces between particles and how these affect the properties of a substance. They should be aware of the relative distances between particles in the different states of matter. The ability of gases to fill their container can be shown using bromine or nitrogen dioxide (prepared in fume cupboard by reacting copper with concentrated nitric acid).

Higher-tier students should understand the limitations of the particle model, that it does not truly represent the sizes of the particles and the distances and forces between them. They should also be aware that the particle model represents particles as inelastic spheres.

You can find additional support for the maths skills covered in this chapter on **MyMaths**, including using models in both 2D and 3D to represent matter, and using ratios.

For this chapter, the following assessments are available on Kerboodle:
C1.1 Checkpoint quiz: The particle model
C1.1 Progress quiz: The particle model 1
C1.1 Progress quiz: The particle model 2
C1.1 On your marks: The particle model
C1.1 Exam-style questions and mark scheme: The particle model

C1.1 The particle model

Checkpoint follow-up lesson

A student's route through this lesson can be determined using the Checkpoint assessment. Percentage pass marks are supplied in the Checkpoint teacher notes.

For each successive route through it is assumed that the student can perform to their current route as well as previous routes. For example, students working at Aiming for 6 are assumed to be secure in Aiming for 4 knowledge and understanding and working towards achieving all the learning objectives for Aiming for 6.

	Aiming for 4	Aiming for 6	Aiming for 8
Learning outcomes	Classify diagrams of particles to represent solids, liquids, and gases.	Draw particle diagrams to represent solids, liquids, gases, compounds, elements, and mixtures.	Evaluate the particle model.
	Describe the changes of state.	Draw particle models to represent changes of state.	
	Recall a definition, with an example, of chemical and physical change.	Use the particle model to explain the difference between a physical change and a chemical change.	
Starter	**Match (5 minutes)** Each small group of students will need a selection of particle diagrams with examples of elements in different states, compounds in different states, and mixtures in different states. Ask them to classify the diagrams, then invite each group to explain their classification (either state of matter or element, compound, or mixture).		
	Chemical or physical? (10 minutes) Ask students to classify the following demonstrations as chemical or physical changes. Demonstrate the gas test for hydrogen by exploding a hydrogen-filled balloon (chemical change). Explain that water is a product of this demonstration. Then put some water on the outside of the bottom of a 100 cm beaker and place it on a small piece of cardboard. In a fume cupboard, put 5 cm^3 of volatile ether into the beaker and swirl to encourage evaporation. As the ether evaporates (physical change), the water on the outside of the beaker freezes (physical change) and so the beaker can be picked up and the cardboard will follow.		
Differentiated checkpoint activity	**The particle model (40 minutes)** Explain that students will be using the particle model to describe changes and revise the content of C1.1 *The particle model*. Students answer each question on the differentiated worksheets.		
	Aiming for 4 students will need red and blue pens. The sheet provides structured tasks including matching exercises to support students with revising and summarising the particle model.	Aiming for 6 students may benefit from using molecular model kits. The sheet provides questions to guide students in drawing different particle models, prompting them to explain the difference between chemical and physical changes.	Aiming for 8 students will need beakers, spatulas, and cornflour suspension. The sheet asks them to evaluate the use of the particle model to explaining observations of mixtures.
	Kerboodle resource: C1.1 Checkpoint follow-up: Aiming for 4, C1.1 Checkpoint follow-up: Aiming for 6, C1.1 Checkpoint follow-up: Aiming for 8		
Plenary	**Describe the image (5 minutes)** Each student will need a mini-whiteboard, pen, and eraser. Display the particle model images from the Match starter, one at a time. Students should describe the image in terms of (a) state and (b) element, compound, or mixture.		
	Pictionary (5 minutes) You will need a bag of cards each stating some information about a substance, including element, compound, or mixture, and its state. You could also include descriptions of changes of state or simple chemical reactions. Students work in small teams around a bench or table. Ask one student from each team to come to the front and choose a card from the bag. In their teams, students draw a particle model to describe the substance. Points can be awarded and you could reward the winning team.		
Progression	Aiming for 4 students should be able to identify particle model diagrams for the three states of matter and recall the names for the state changes. Encourage them to describe the properties of each state of matter using the particle model.	Aiming for 6 students should be able to draw particle diagrams of elements, compounds, and mixtures in the three states of matter. Encourage them to represent a simple chemical reaction in terms of particles, and draw the particle diagrams for the state changes.	Encourage Aiming for 8 students to critically consider the use of the particle model to describe the behaviour of matter.

C1.2 Atomic structure

C1.2.1 Atomic structure

Specification links:

C1.2b Describe the atom as a positively charged nucleus surrounded by negatively charged electrons, with the nuclear radius much smaller than that of the atom, and with most of the mass in the nucleus.

C1.2c Recall the typical size (order of magnitude) of atoms and small molecules.

C1.2d Recall relative charges and approximate relative masses of protons, neutrons, and electrons.

WS1.1c Understand the power and limitations of science.

WS1.4a Use scientific vocabulary, terminology, and definitions.

WS1.4b Recognise the importance of scientific quantities and understand how they are determined.

WS1.4c Use SI units and IUPAC chemical nomenclature unless inappropriate.

WS1.4d Use prefixes and powers of ten for orders of magnitude.

WS1.4e Interconvert units.

WS1.4f Use an appropriate number of significant figures in calculations.

M1b Recognise expressions in standard form.

M1c Use ratios, fractions, and percentages.

M4a Translate information between graphical and numeric form.

CM1.2i Relate size and scale of atoms to objects in the physical world.

CM1.2ii Estimate size and scale of atoms and nanoparticles.

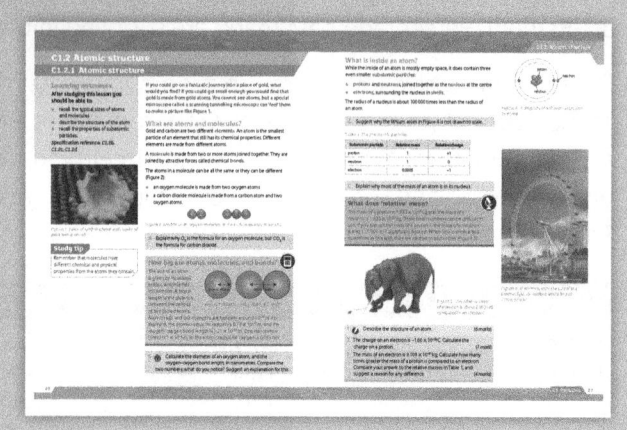

Target	Outcome	Checkpoint	
		Question	Activity
Aiming for GRADE 4	List the subatomic particles in an atom.	1	Main 1 Plenary 1
	Qualitatively describe: the relative sizes of an atom, chemical bonds, and simple molecules.		Main 1 and 2
	State the size of a typical atom.	B, 3	Main 1 and 2
Aiming for GRADE 6	Describe the subatomic particles in an atom.	1	Starter 1 Main 1 and 2 Plenary 1 and 2
	Use standard form to describe the sizes of atoms, chemical bonds, and molecules.		Main 2 Homework
	Use data to calculate the sizes, masses, and charges of subatomic particles.	2	Main 2 Homework
Aiming for GRADE 8	Outline evidence for the structure of the atom.	D	Plenary 2
	Explain why a relative scale is used to compare subatomic particles.	C	Main 2 Homework
	Use data to calculate the relative sizes, masses, and charges of subatomic particles.	3	

C1.2 Atomic structure

Maths
In Main 2 students make relative comparisons (CM1.2i). Students work with standard form in completing the Homework task (M1b).

Literacy
In Plenary 2 students explain observations from an experiment.

Key words
elements, atom, molecule, bonds, atomic radius, bond length, subatomic particles, protons, neutrons, nucleus, electrons, shells

Starter	Support/Extend	Resources
Bending water (5 minutes) Give students a piece of polythene and a duster. They rub the plastic with the duster (to create a static charge), before holding it near to a stream of running water (e.g., a slow-flowing tap or a burette of water). Students should observe the water bending as the charge on the plastic interacts with the electrons in the water molecules. Ask students to suggest what is occurring.	**Support:** Explain that a charge is created by rubbing the plastic. What does this tell us about water?	
Chemical samples (10 minutes) Give students some samples of elements and compounds in sealed containers labelled with their names and symbols. Students sort them into: elements and compounds; substances made up of molecules and those not made up of molecules; pure and impure substances. After each sorting, discuss the criteria for each category and check that students understand what is meant by the terms element, compound, and molecule.	**Extend:** Ask students to draw particle diagrams to represent each category.	

Main	Support/Extend	Resources
Model of an atom (20 minutes) Give students a selection of materials such as polystyrene balls (of different sizes), wire, string, and card. Ask them to make a model of a helium atom. They then use sticky notes to add information about the structure of their model atom, e.g. the charges and masses of the subatomic particles. Students also write down the radius of a helium atom, which is 0.031 nm (3.1×10^{-11} m).	**Support:** Guide students by drawing their attention to Figure 4 and Table 1 of the Student Book.	**Activity:** Model of an atom
Relative size (20 minutes) Give students two test-tube racks and a set of test-tubes. Students measure out 1 g of sand in a test-tube and label this as a neutron: it has a mass of 1 and no charge. Ask students to make a relative model of an electron and a proton using sand and test-tubes. Students then use these model subatomic particles to make a large model of a form (isotope) of hydrogen that has one proton and one neutron in the nucleus and one electron (deuterium). Students should think about the distance between the particles in the nucleus and the diameter of the nucleus, as well as the distance between the nucleus and the electrons. You may need to use the school field to allow enough space.		

Plenary	Support/Extend	Resources
Atom anatomy (5 minutes) Interactive activity where students drag labels to a diagram and complete the sentences.		**Interactive:** The model of the atom
Rutherford (10 minutes) Explain that Rutherford fired helium nuclei at very thin gold foil. He found that most of the nuclei passed through the foil, while some bounced straight back. Ask students to think about the structure of the atom and explain these observations.		

Homework	Support/Extend	Resources
Change the following numbers from standard form to numbers showing all the digits: 0.73×10^{-10}; 1.21×10^{-10}, 1×10^{-9}, 0.073 nm, 1.673×10^{-27}, 1.675×10^{-27}.	**Extend:** Students use the Student Book to determine the significance of these numbers.	

kerboodle
A Kerboodle highlight for this lesson is **Literacy skills: More about atoms**. Refer to the **Content map** on Kerboodle for a full list of resources and assessment.

C1.2.2 Isotopes

Specification links:

C1.2e Calculate the numbers of protons, neutrons, and electrons in atoms and ions, given the atomic number and mass number of isotopes, to include definitions of an ion, atomic number, mass number, and an isotope, also the standard notation to represent these.

WS1.3c Carrying out and representing mathematical and statistical analysis, to include arithmetic means, mode, and median.

WS1.4b Recognise the importance of scientific quantities and understand how they are determined.

M3b Change the subject of an equation.

M3d Solve simple algebraic equations.

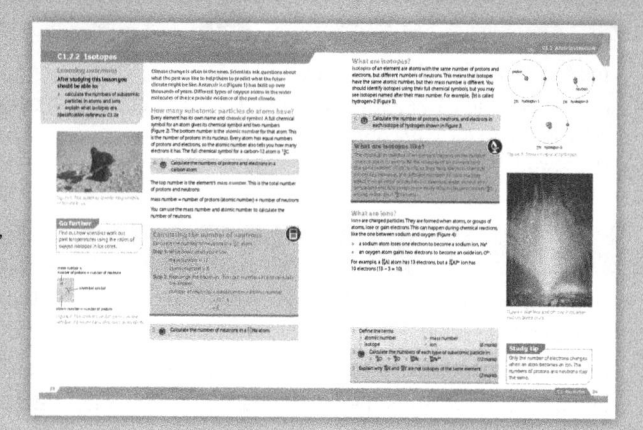

Target	Outcome	Checkpoint	
		Question	Activity
Aiming for GRADE 4	State definitions of the terms ion, atomic number, mass number, and isotope.	1	Starter 1 and 2 Main 1 and 2
	Describe how an atom becomes an ion.		Starter 2
	State the number of protons, neutrons, and electrons from given values of atomic number and mass number.	2	Main 1 and 2 Plenary 1
Aiming for GRADE 6	Use an example to describe the similarities and differences between isotopes in terms of subatomic particles.		Plenary 2 Homework
	Use standard notation to represent an ion.		Starter 2 Main 2 Homework
	State the numbers of protons, neutrons, and electrons in an atom when a Periodic Table is supplied.	A, B, C, 2	Main 1 and 2 Plenary 1
Aiming for GRADE 8	Explain why isotopes of the same element may have different physical properties but identical chemical properties.	3	Plenary 2
	Use and interpret standard notation to represent atoms, ions, and isotopes.	2	Main 1 and 2 Homework
	State the number of protons, neutrons, and electrons for an ion when a Periodic Table is supplied.	2	Main 2 Homework

Maths
In Main 2 students calculate the number of subatomic particles from atomic number and mass number of an atom or isotope (M3b, M3d).

Literacy
In Main 1 students explain how to calculate the number of subatomic particles.

Key words
chemical symbol, atomic number, mass number, isotopes, ions

C1.2 Atomic structure

Starter	Support/Extend	Resources
Atom anatomy recap (5 minutes) Ask students to fill in gaps to complete a paragraph about atom anatomy. Students can then link key terminology with definitions, and complete a 'true and false' activity about atomic structure. **Introduction to ions** (10 minutes) Ask students to draw a diagram of a hydrogen atom, showing all the subatomic particles. Explain that it can either gain an electron or lose an electron. Ask a volunteer to draw two diagrams showing this. Ask students to suggest which would have a positive charge and which would have a negative charge, and to explain why.	**Extend:** Explain that atoms achieve greater stability with a full outer shell of electrons, and that this is why ions form.	

Main	Support/Extend	Resources
Elemental (25 minutes) Split the class into groups of about six students and give samples of the first 20 elements in sealed containers to each group. Alternatively, display one sample of each of these elements in the classroom, and give each group a set of 20 cards showing photographs of the first twenty elements. SAFETY: Colourless gases can just be air. Fluorine can be simulated by washing out the sample jar with pale yellow paint and allowing it to dry. Green paint can be used for chlorine. Group 1 metals should be small pieces stored under oil in sealed vessels. All substances should have the appropriate safety labels. Ask students to use the Periodic Table to order the elements, then to write the atomic number and mass number for each element onto a sticky note, which should be placed in front of the sample or on the card. Students use this information to calculate the number of each type of subatomic particle, adding this to the sticky notes too. Encourage students to find a pattern in the data. **Ideas about ions** (15 minutes) Explain how ions are formed, and outline how to calculate the number of subatomic particles in an ion. Then ask students to complete tasks and questions about the numbers of protons, neutrons, and electrons in ions.	**Extend:** Provide formulae for the common ions of these elements, and ask students to determine the number of subatomic particles in these examples.	**Activity:** Ideas about ions

Plenary	Support/Extend	Resources
Isotopes (5 minutes) Interactive activity in which students complete sentences by choosing the correct words and then link isotopes of carbon with the correct number of protons, neutrons, and electrons. **Hydrogen** (10 minutes) Show students atomic structures of the three isotopes of hydrogen as in Figure 3. Ask them to note the similarities (number of electrons, number of protons, atomic number, and chemical properties) and differences (number of neutrons, mass number, electronic structure and physical properties).	**Support:** Focus students on hydrogen and helium and ask questions only about these two elements. **Extend:** Show students the standard notation for carbon isotopes, and ask them to determine the number of subatomic particles in each isotope. Students could complete the Interactive.	**Interactive:** Isotopes

Homework	Support/Extend	Resources
Write down the number of each type of subatomic particle for the two main chlorine isotopes. List the atomic number and mass number for each isotope, showing how they are used to calculate the subatomic particles.	**Support:** Give students the standard notation for each isotope. **Extend:** Students also write the number of subatomic particles for chloride ions of both isotopes, and write their symbols.	

kerboodle
A Kerboodle highlight for this lesson is **Homework: The particle model**. Refer to the **Content map** on Kerboodle for a full list of resources and assessment.

C1.2.3 Developing the atomic model

Specification links:

C1.2a Describe how and why the atomic model has changed over time, to include the models of Dalton, Thomson, Rutherford, Bohr, and Geiger and Marsden (WS1.2b).

WS 1.1a Understand how scientific methods and theories develop over time, to include new technology allowing new evidence to be collected and changing explanations as new evidence is found.

WS1.1i Recognise the importance of peer review of results and of communicating results to a range of audiences.

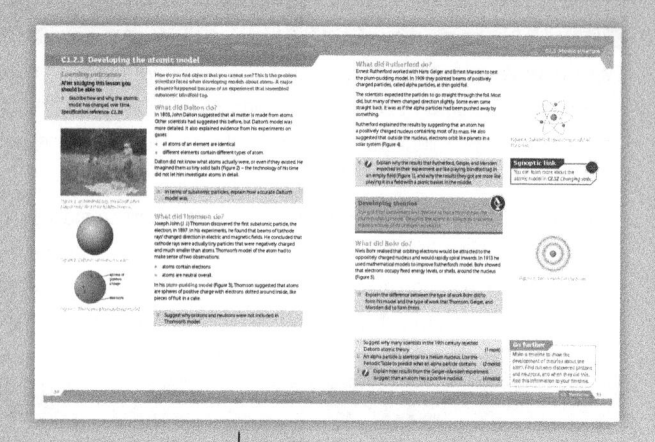

Target	Outcome	Checkpoint	
		Question	Activity
Aiming for GRADE 4	Recall the main features of the plum-pudding model and the Bohr model.	B, D	Starter 2, Main 1 and 2
↓	Describe the contributions Dalton, Thomson, Rutherford, Bohr, Geiger, and Marsden made to the atomic model.		Main 1 and 2, Plenary 1
↓	State what an atom is.		Starter 1
Aiming for GRADE 6	Describe the development of the atomic model.	D, 1	Main 1 and 2, Plenary 1
↓	Explain the contributions of Dalton, Thomson, Rutherford, Bohr, Geiger, and Marsden to the development of the atomic model.	D, 3	Main 1 and 2
Aiming for GRADE 8	Explain why the atomic model has changed over time.	A, 1, 3	Main 1 and 2, Plenary 2
↓	Justify amendments to the model of the atom.	B, C, 1	Main 1 and 2, Plenary 2

Literacy
In Main 2 students summarise the findings of key scientists in the development of the atomic model.

Key words
plum-pudding model

C1.2 Atomic structure

Starter	Support/Extend	Resources
What is an atom? (5 minutes) Ask students to answer the question. Then pick three students to read out their ideas. Discuss the answers as a class, drawing out a more scientific description. Then show *The Fuse School's* presentation *What is an Atom?* **Interpret models** (10 minutes) Give small groups of students a polystyrene ball, a ball of modelling clay studded with beads, and a Bohr model of a hydrogen atom. Students suggest how each model could represent an atom, which is likely to be the oldest representation of an atom, and which is likely to be the present-day representation.	**Support:** Ask students to find the definition of an atom in the Student Book glossary. **Extend:** Ask students to think about the structure and properties of an atom. **Extend:** Ask students to evaluate each model.	

Main	Support/Extend	Resources
Timeline: Developing the atomic model (20 minutes) Students draw an arrow in landscape on an A3 piece of paper. They then write down ideas to create a timeline, focussing on the contributions of Dalton, Thomson, Rutherford, Bohr, and Geiger and Marsden. Their timelines should include key dates, observations, and models. In tackling this task, students could draw on a number of resources including the Student Book. **Scientists' summary** (20 minutes) Give students six index cards, one for each of the scientists. They write the name of the scientist, their birth and death dates, what experiments they did (if any) and how they refined the atomic model.	**Support:** Encourage students to represent Figures 2, 3, 4, and 5 in the Student Book on their timeline. **Extend:** Students research how the atomic model is still being refined, such as using particle accelerators to discover quarks. **Extend:** You may wish to add Democritus, Schrödinger, and Heisenberg.	**Activity:** Developing the atomic model

Plenary	Support/Extend	Resources
Discovery (5 minutes) Students to match the scientist with their discovery. (Dalton – all matter is made of atoms and different elements are made of different atoms; Thomson – atoms are neutral but contain electrons; Rutherford – positive nucleus; Bohr – electrons are in shells [energy levels]) **Development of a model** (10 minutes) Students to discuss how ideas are shared in science, and why it is easier now for new ideas to be taken on board than in the past.	**Extend:** Ask students to think about how technology has helped and hindered the development of scientific ideas.	**Interactive:** Developing the atomic model

Homework	Support/Extend	Resources
List the advantages and disadvantages of the atomic models developed by Dalton, Thomson, Rutherford, and Bohr.	**Extend:** Explain the limits of each model and why it needed to be modified.	

kerboodle
A Kerboodle highlight for this lesson is **Podcast: The particle model**. Refer to the **Content map** on Kerboodle for a full list of resources and assessment.

Checkpoint
C1.2 Atomic structure

Overview of C1.2 Atomic structure

In this chapter students have studied the structure of the atom. They should have an understanding of the relative sizes of atoms, chemical bonds, and simple molecules, and be able to state the size of a typical atom. They should be able to describe the different subatomic particles and use the terms atomic number and mass number. They should describe the atom as a positively charged nucleus surrounded by negatively charged electrons, with the nuclear radius much smaller than that of the atom and with most of the mass in the nucleus. They should be able to use a Periodic Table to state the numbers of protons, neutrons, and electrons in an atom, and be able to calculate the sizes, masses, and charges of subatomic particles. The link between electron arrangements and the position of the element in the Periodic Table is highlighted in C2.2.2 *Electronic structures* and C2.2.10 *Atomic structure and the Periodic Table*.

Students should understand ionisation and be able to represent ions. They should be able to define an isotope and know how isotopes of an element differ and how they are the same.

Students should be aware of evidence for the structure of the atom and its development from the plum-pudding model to the Bohr model, and be able to interpret this evidence. They should be aware of the contributions of Dalton, Thomson, Rutherford, Bohr, Geiger, and Marsden to the development of the atomic model. They should link this work with C2.2.9 *Developing the Periodic Table* which also highlights the ways in which scientific theories and models evolve as more evidence becomes more available.

MyMaths

You can find additional support for the maths skills covered in this chapter on **MyMaths**, including using models in both 2D and 3D to represent matter, and using ratios.

kerboodle

For this chapter, the following assessments are available on Kerboodle:
C1.2 Checkpoint quiz: Atomic structure
C1.2 Progress quiz: Atomic structure 1
C1.2 Progress quiz: Atomic structure 2
C1.2 On your marks: Atomic structure
C1.2 Exam-style questions and mark scheme: Atomic structure

C1.2 Atomic structure

Checkpoint follow-up lesson

A student's route through this lesson can be determined using the Checkpoint assessment. Percentage pass marks are supplied in the Checkpoint teacher notes.

For each successive route through it is assumed that the student can perform to their current route as well as previous routes. For example, students working at Aiming for 6 are assumed to be secure in Aiming for 4 knowledge and understanding and working towards achieving all the learning objectives for Aiming for 6.

	Aiming for 4	Aiming for 6	Aiming for 8
Learning outcomes	Describe the structure of an atom and the key properties of protons, neutrons, and electrons.	Describe in detail the structure of an atom and the key properties of protons, neutrons, and electrons.	Explain how the atomic model has changed over time, drawing on the work of Dalton, Thompson, Rutherford, and Bohr.
	Describe what an isotope is and calculate the different numbers of neutrons in isotopes.	Describe in detail what an isotope is and how to calculate the different numbers of neutrons in isotopes.	
	Describe the three states of matter.	Compare and contrast physical and chemical changes.	
Starter	**Periodic Table quiz (5 minutes)** Hold a quickfire quiz on the Periodic Table. Provide students with a Periodic Table. Questions should include asking for symbols for named elements, element names from symbols, and numbers of electrons, protons, or neutrons.		
	Chemical change (5 minutes) Demonstrate the reaction between magnesium and oxygen by burning a small piece of magnesium ribbon in a Bunsen burner flame (appropriate safety precautions should be taken, including reminding students not to look directly at the flame). Ask – is this a chemical or physical change? How do you know? Reinforce that it is a chemical change because new products are formed. Use a word and formula equation to show how the original atoms have been rearranged to make new products.		
Differentiated checkpoint activity	**Poster (45 minutes)** Explain that students will be producing a poster to revise their work on particles. Students answer each question on the differentiated worksheets. They will need A3 paper and coloured pencils. Students would benefit from access to the Student book as well as the Internet or detailed printed resources on atomic models (Aiming for 4 and Aiming for 6 – the current atomic model; Aiming for 8 – changing atomic models over time).		
	The Aiming for 4 sheet contains structured tasks to support students in producing a poster about the structure of the atom, isotopes, and states of matter.	The Aiming for 6 sheet contains information and questions to answer to guide students as they produce a poster to describe the structure of the atom, isotopes, and comparing physical and chemical changes.	Aiming for 8 students produce a poster to show how and why the atomic model has changed over time, drawing on the work of Dalton, Thompson, Rutherford, and Bohr.
	Kerboodle resource: C1.2 Checkpoint follow-up: Aiming for 4, C1.2 Checkpoint follow-up: Aiming for 6, C1.2 Checkpoint follow-up: Aiming for 8		
Plenary	**Review (5 minutes)** Ask students to lay out their posters on benches around the room. Students choose another person's poster to review. They should read the poster and decide on two strong points about the poster and one point that could be improved on.		
	Learning points (5 minutes) Ask student pairs decide on three key learning points from the chapter. Review these as a class. Address any misconceptions should they arise.		
Progression	The Aiming for 4 sheet contains structured tasks including a linking exercise and multiple choice. Students may need prompting to move on to the next task at the appropriate time.	The Aiming for 6 sheet is fairly structured with information and questions to answer before students produce the poster.	The Aiming for 8 sheet contains prompts and questions for students to consider when designing their poster. A possible extension would be to find out about the work of other scientists in the field.

C1 Particles: Topic summary

C1.1 The particle model
C1.2 Atomic structure
C2.1 Purity and separating mixtures

Spec ref	Statement	Book spreads
C1.1a	Describe the main features of the particle model in terms of states of matter and change of state	C1.1.1, C1.1.3
C1.1b	Explain in terms of the particle model the distinction between physical changes and chemical changes	C1.1.2
C1.1c	Explain the limitations of the particle model in relation to changes of state when particles are represented by inelastic spheres (e.g. like bowling balls)	C1.1.3
C1.2a	Describe how and why the atomic model has changed over time	C1.2.3
C1.2b	Describe the atom as a positively charged nucleus surrounded by negatively charged electrons, with the nuclear radius much smaller than that of the atom and with most of the mass in the nucleus	C1.2.1
C1.2c	Recall the typical size (order of magnitude) of atoms and small molecules	C1.2.1
C1.2d	Recall relative charges and approximate relative masses of protons, neutrons, and electrons	C1.2.1
C1.2e	Calculate numbers of protons, neutrons, and electrons in atoms and ions, given atomic number and mass number of isotopes	C1.2.2

Maths

Specification		Book spread	
Spec ref	Statement	Main content	Maths chapter
CM1.1i	Represent three-dimensional shapes in two dimensions and vice versa when looking at chemical structures, e.g. allotropes of carbon		16
CM1.2i	Relate size and scale of atoms to objects in the physical	C1.2.1	11
CM1.2ii	Estimate size and scale of atoms and nanoparticles	C1.2.1	2, 8, 11

Working scientifically

Specification		Book spread	
Spec ref	Statement	Main content	WS chapter
WS1.1a	Understand how scientific methods and theories develop over time, to include new technology allowing new evidence to be collected and changing explanations as new evidence is found.	C1.2.3	WS2
WS1.1b	Use models to solve problems, make predictions, and to develop scientific explanations and understanding of familiar and unfamiliar facts.	C1.1.1, C1.1.2, C1.1.3	WS2
WS1.1c	Understand the power and limitations of science.	C1.2.1	WS1
WS1.1i	Recognise the importance of peer review of results and of communicating results to a range of audiences.	C1.2.3	WS2
WS1.3c	Carrying out and representing mathematical and statistical analysis, to include arithmetic means, mode, and median.	C1.2.2	WS5
WS1.4a	Use scientific vocabulary, terminology, and definitions.	C1.2.1	WS2
WS1.4b	Recognise the importance of scientific quantities and understand how they are determined.	C1.2.1, C1.2.2	
WS1.4c	Use SI units and IUPAC chemical nomenclature unless inappropriate.	C1.2.1	
WS1.4d	Use prefixes and powers of ten for orders of magnitude.	C1.2.1	
WS1.4e	Interconvert units.	C1.2.1	
WS1.4f	Use an appropriate number of significant figures in calculations.	C1.2.1	WS5
WS2b	Make and record observations and measurements, using a range of apparatus and methods.	C1.1.1, C1.1.2	

C2 Elements, compounds, and mixtures
C2.1 Purity and separating mixtures
C2.1.1 Relative formula mass

Specification links:

C2.1c Calculate relative formula masses of species separately and in a balanced chemical equation, to include the definition of relative atomic mass, relative molecular mass, and relative formula mass.

WS1.3c Carry out and represent mathematical and statistical analysis.

WS1.4c Use SI units and IUPAC chemical nomenclature unless inappropriate.

CM2.1i Understand that arithmetic computation, ratio, percentage, and multistep calculations permeate quantitative chemistry (M1a, M1c, M1d).

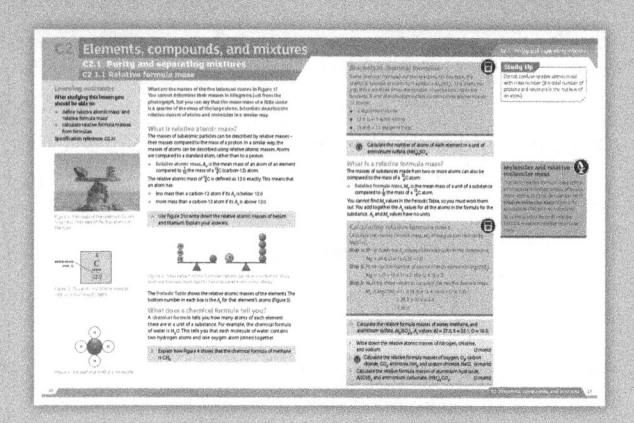

Target	Outcome	Checkpoint Question	Checkpoint Activity
Aiming for GRADE 4	State definitions of relative atomic mass, relative molecular mass, and relative formula mass.		Main 2, Plenary 1
	Use the Periodic Table to find the chemical symbol for an element.		Main 1
	Use the Periodic Table to give the relative atomic mass of an element.	1	Main 1
Aiming for GRADE 6	Use data from the Periodic Table to compare the relative atomic masses of different elements.	A	Main 2
	Interpret simple formulae to list the number of each type of atom present.	C	Main 1
	Calculate the relative formula mass or relative molecular mass of a simple substance when the relative atomic mass and formula are given.		Main 2, Plenary 2, Homework
Aiming for GRADE 8	Explain why relative formula mass is a useful measurement.		Main 2
	Interpret diagrams of molecular compounds to write chemical formulae.	B	Plenary 2
	Calculate the relative formula mass or relative molecular mass of substances from diagrams or formulae (including those with brackets).	D, 2, 3	Main 2, Plenary 2

Maths
In Main 2 students calculate the relative molecular mass or relative formula mass.

Literacy
In Main 2 students explain how to calculate the relative molecular or relative formula mass of a substance.

Key words
relative atomic mass, Periodic Table, chemical formula, relative formula mass

C2.1 Purity and separating mixtures

Starter	Support/Extend	Resources
Make models (5 minutes) Give students molecular model kits. Explain what represents bonds in the model. Ask students to make models of water, hydrogen, oxygen, and methane molecules, including all the bonds for each atom.	**Support:** Draw students' attention to Figure 4 in the Student Book and ask them to note the colours used to represent hydrogen and carbon atoms.	
Atoms and their masses (10 minutes) Ask students to briefly revise the structure of the atom from their notes on C1.2 Atomic structure. Students write down a definition of relative molecular mass and devise a worked example showing how to calculate the relative molecular mass of a simple molecule.	**Extend:** Ask students to make a model of a carbon dioxide molecule.	

Main	Support/Extend	Resources
Chemical calculations (20 minutes) Explain to students the meaning of chemical formula. Then ask students to interpret the chemical formulae of HCl, and CH_3Cl. Ask students to define the term relative atomic mass, and find the values on the Periodic Table for Cl, H, and C. Students then use this information to calculate the relative molecular masses for the examples above. Students then calculate the relative formula masses of other substances by completing the task and questions on the Kerboodle resource. **Calculate molecular mass** (20 minutes) Go through a worked example to show how to calculate the relative formula mass of magnesium hydroxide. Students then tackle the tasks on the Kerboodle calculation sheet.	**Support:** Provide the steps to calculate the relative formula mass: 1 Identify the different types of atom in the formula, and the number of each type of atom that is present. 2 Use the Periodic Table to find the atomic mass of each element in the formula. 3 Multiply the number of each atom in the formula by its atomic mass. 4 Add the masses together. **Extend:** Ask students to explain the difference between relative molecular mass and relative formula mass. **Extend:** Ask students to complete Question 3 in the Student Book.	**Activity:** Chemical calculations

Plenary	Support/Extend	Resources
Terminology (5 minutes) Ask students to explain the difference between Ar (chemical symbol for argon) and A_r (symbol for relative atomic mass). **Target mass** (10 minutes) Challenge students to use the molecular model kit to make as many molecules as possible with a relative formula mass of 84 and to write down their formulae. Alternatively, ask students to complete the Interactive activity: Relative formula mass.	**Extend:** Ask students to write down the chemical formulae.	**Interactive:** Relative formula mass

Homework	Support/Extend	Resources
Choose a substance from the Student Book spread, write its name and formula, and then calculate the relative formula mass or relative molecular mass of the compound. If you choose an element, it should be a non-metal in a molecule (e.g., sulfur, eight atoms of sulfur in a puckered ring). You should not choose a metal such as magnesium, as this is reported by its empirical formula.		

kerboodle

A Kerboodle highlight for this lesson is **Calculation sheet: Chemical calculations**. Refer to the **Content map** on Kerboodle for a full list of resources and assessment.

C2 Elements, compounds, and mixtures

C2.1.2 Empirical formula

Specification links:

C2.1c Calculate relative formula masses of species separately and in a balanced chemical equation, to include the definition of relative atomic mass, relative molecular mass, and relative formula mass.

C2.1d Deduce the empirical formula of a compound from the relative numbers of atoms present, or from a model or diagram, and vice versa.

WS1.3c Carry out and represent mathematical and statistical analysis.

WS1.4c Use SI units and IUPAC chemical nomenclature unless inappropriate.

WS2b Make and record observations and measurements using a range of apparatus and methods.

M1c Use ratios, fractions, and percentages.

CM2.1iv Use arithmetic computation and ratios when determining empirical formulae and balancing equations (M3b, M3c).

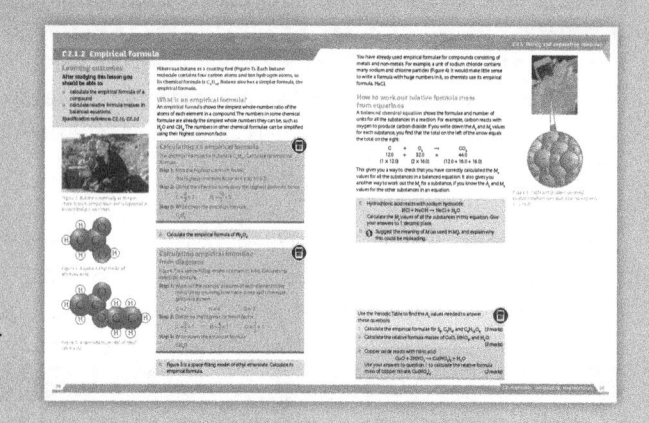

Target	Outcome	Checkpoint	
		Question	Activity
Aiming for GRADE 4	State a definition of empirical formula.		Main 1
	Calculate the empirical formula for a simple covalent compound when the molecular formula is given.	A, 1	Main 2 Plenary 1 and 2
	Use a balanced symbol equation to calculate the relative formula mass or relative molecular mass of any substance shown in the equation.	C, 2, 3	Starter 1 and 2 Main 2
Aiming for GRADE 6	Use an example to explain how a molecular formula and an empirical formula can be the same.		Plenary 1
	Calculate the empirical formula for a compound from a diagram.	B	Plenary 2
	Explain when the term relative molecular mass can be used.		Homework
Aiming for GRADE 8	Explain why ionic compounds are always referred to by their empirical formulae.		Homework
	Calculate an empirical formula from a molecular formula that contains brackets.		Main 2
	Explain how the sum of the M_r values of the reactants must equal the sum of the M_r values of the products in a balanced symbol equation.		Main 2

Maths
In Main 2 students calculate the relative formula mass of a compound and the empirical formula of a compound (M1c).

Key words
empirical formula, balanced chemical equation, relative molecular mass

C2.1 Purity and separating mixtures

Starter	Support/Extend	Resources
Burning carbon (5 minutes) Set up a Bunsen burner on a flame-proof mat. Then, wearing eye protection, sprinkle half a spatula of powdered carbon into the flame. For a more impressive reaction, heat carbon powder on a deflagrating spoon until it is glowing orange, then put it into a gas jar of oxygen. Ask students to write a balanced symbol equation for the reaction and to calculate the relative formula mass of each substance in the equation. **Fire hands** (10 minutes) Half-fill a washing-up bowl with detergent and water. Take off any jewellery and wet your hands and arms. Using a long rubber hose connected to the gas tap, blow methane-filled bubbles. Catch them on your hands, then move over to a Bunsen burner set to the safety flame and ignite the bubbles. Explain that methane has reacted with oxygen to make carbon dioxide and water. Write up the balanced symbol equation. Ask students to calculate the relative formula mass of each substance in the equation.	**Support:** Draw students' attention to the symbol equation in the Student Book section *How to work out relative formula mass from equations* and ask them to use this to write a word equation. **Support:** Ask students to write a word equation for the reaction.	

Main	Support/Extend	Resources
Determine an empirical formula (20 minutes) Pairs of students design a results table to record their data. Using a balance, students weigh a crucible and lid. Students then clean a 10 cm piece of magnesium ribbon with emery paper before loosely coiling it and placing it in the crucible. Students should record the mass of the crucible, lid, and magnesium. Students then strongly heat the magnesium in the crucible supported on a pipe-clay triangle over a blue Bunsen burner flame, leaving the crucible lid slightly ajar to allow air to enter. Students should occasionally lift up the lid slightly to allow more air in, whilst preventing any magnesium oxide from escaping. Ask students to heat the crucible until all the magnesium has turned to a whitish-grey powder, then allow it to cool before reweighing the crucible, lid, and contents. Ask students to use the data gathered to calculate the mass of magnesium and oxygen used. Explain the meaning of the term empirical formula, and ask students to determine the empirical formula of magnesium oxide. **Ethyl ethanoate** (20 minutes) Give small groups of students cotton buds dipped in nail polish remover (one cotton bud per group). Allow them to smell it, and explain that one of its ingredients is ethyl ethanoate, shown in Figure 3 in the Student Book. Students write the molecular formula and then use this to calculate the empirical formula. They then tackle the task and follow-up questions on the Activity sheet, where they deduce the empirical formulae of a large number of compounds.	**Support:** Give students the steps to use to calculate the empirical formula. **Extend:** Ask students to comment on the accuracy of their conclusion. You may wish to give more examples of these calculations for students to complete. **Support:** Give students the formulae of the substances and the relative atomic masses for hydrogen, carbon, and oxygen.	**Activity:** Empirical formula

Plenary	Support/Extend	Resources
Match (5 minutes) Students match molecular formulae with empirical formulae, for example, C_6H_6 matches with CH. **Butane** (10 minutes) Ask students to look at Figure 1 in the Student Book. Students use the information in the section *Calculating an empirical formula* to draw a space-filling model of butane. They then use the method in the section *Calculating empirical formulae from diagrams* to demonstrate how the empirical formula is the same no matter which method is used to generate it.	**Extend:** Provide more than one molecular formula for each empirical formula. **Support:** Use molecular models. **Extend:** Students write a balanced symbol equation for the combustion of butane, and calculate the M_r of each species.	**Interactive:** Empirical formula

Homework	Support/Extend	Resources
Explain why relative formula mass is a more useful term than relative molecular mass. Refer to ionic compounds.		

C2.1.3 Pure and impure substances

Specification links:

C2.1a Explain what is meant by the purity of a substance, distinguishing between the scientific and everyday use of the term pure.

C2.1b Use melting point data to distinguish pure from impure substances.

C2.1e Explain that many useful materials are formulations of mixtures, to include alloys.

WS1.4a Use scientific vocabulary, terminology, and definitions.

WS2b Make and record observations and measurements, using a range of apparatus and methods.

M4c Plot two variables from experimental or other data.

CM2.1i Understand that arithmetic computation, ratio, percentage, and multistep calculations permeate quantitative chemistry (M1a, M1c, M1d).

CM2.1ii Provide answers to an appropriate number of significant figures (M2a).

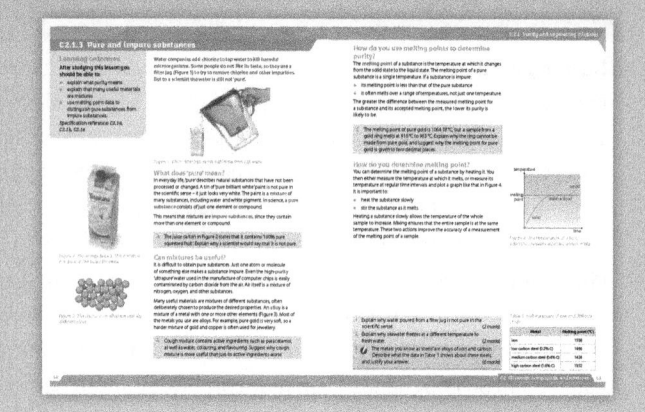

Target	Outcome	Checkpoint Question	Checkpoint Activity
Aiming for GRADE 4 ↓	State definitions of the terms pure and mixture.		Starter 1 Main Plenary 1 and 2
	Give an example of a pure substance and a mixture.		Starter 1 and 2
	Safely determine the melting point of a substance.		Main
Aiming for GRADE 6 ↓	Explain the different meanings of pure in everyday and scientific language.	A, 1	Starter 1
	Identify a substance as either pure or a mixture.		Plenary 2
	Identify a substance from melting point data.		Plenary 2
Aiming for GRADE 8 ↓	Suggest why a mixture is often more useful than a pure substance.	B	Starter 2
	Explain the effect on melting point of adding different substances to a pure substance.	2, 3	Starter 2 Plenary 2 Homework
	Evaluate the purity of a sample from its melting point data.	C	Plenary 2

Maths
In Main 1 students plot a line graph, draw a line of best fit, and read values off the graph (M4c).

Literacy
In Plenary 1 students use bullet points to summarise.

Key words
mixture, pure substance, impure substances, purity, alloy, melting point

C2.1 Purity and separating mixtures

Starter	Support/Extend	Resources
Purity (5 minutes) Give small groups of students labelled samples of distilled water in a sealed container, de-ionised water in an open container, and 'pure' mineral water in a sealed bottle. Ask the groups to order them in terms of purity and explain their reasoning. **Salt and water** (10 minutes) Before the lesson, make ice cubes from distilled water. Demonstrate crushing the ice cubes. Explain to students that this is pure water and invite a volunteer to draw a particle model of ice (the particle model of a solid). Then ask a volunteer to pour a spatula of sodium chloride onto the ice and observe. Ask students to explain what they have observed, and what this shows about the melting point of brine compared with water.	**Support:** Encourage students to read the Student Book section *What does 'pure' mean?*, so that they are clear about what scientifically pure means. **Extend:** Ask students to think of a real-world application for this phenomenon.	

Main	Support/Extend	Resources
Measurement of melting point (35 minutes) Supply each student pair with a boiling tube half-filled with Salol. Students place the boiling tube in a water bath (warm water in a 250 cm³ beaker) and record the temperature every 20 seconds until well after the mixture has completely melted, stirring throughout. Students design results tables to record their data and then plot a graph with a line of best fit in order to read off the melting point of the substance. You could follow this activity with the graph activity on the Working Scientifically sheet: *The melting point of stearic acid*.	**Support:** Use questions and answers to establish how to draw the graph, demonstrating using an interactive white board with a graph paper background. **Extend:** The accepted melting point of stearic acid is 70 °C. Ask students to comment on the accuracy of their result. **Extend:** Ask students to use Figure 3 in the Student Book to draw diagrams showing particles in each metal and alloy in Table 1. Challenge students to explain why the addition of carbon lowers the melting point (the addition of extra carbon atoms disrupts the forces of attraction within the material).	**Practical:** Measurement of melting point

Plenary	Support/Extend	Resources
Pure versus impure (5 minutes) Ask students to look at the data in Table 1 in the Student Book and explain why they cannot plot these data on a line graph (the data are discrete, not continuous). Challenge students to describe the pattern shown by the data (as the percentage of carbon in the alloy increases, melting point decreases). The interactive activity *Pure and impure substances* can be used to reinforce this activity. **Sort** (10 minutes) Display five different melting-point graphs similar to the one created in Main 1, and a data table giving the melting points of the substances shown in the graphs. Ask students to classify each substance as pure or impure, and identify each substance.	**Support:** Use questioning to ensure that students can correctly determine the melting point from each graph.	**Interactive:** Pure and impure substances

Homework	Support/Extend	Resources
Copy the sketch graph in Figure 4 in the Student Book and add particle model diagrams to illustrate the solid, melting, and liquid parts of the graph. Explain how the graph shows that the ice is pure. Then predict how the shape of the graph would change if a small amount of salt was mixed with the ice. Explain your prediction.	**Extend:** Explain why the temperature does not change as a substance changes state.	

kerboodle

A Kerboodle highlight for this lesson is **Working Scientifically: The melting point of stearic acid**. Refer to the **Content map** on Kerboodle for a full list of resources and assessment.

C2.1.4 Filtration and crystallisation

Specification links:

C2.1f Describe, explain, and exemplify the processes of filtration and crystallisation, to include knowledge of the techniques of filtration and crystallisation.

WS1.2b Plan experiments or devise procedures to make observations, produce or characterise a substance, test hypotheses, check data, or explore phenomena.

WS1.2c Apply knowledge of a range of techniques, instruments, apparatus, and materials to select those appropriate to the experiment.

WS2a Carry out experiments.

WS2b Make and record observations and measurements, using a range of apparatus and methods.

WS2c Present observations using appropriate methods.

M1c Use ratios, fractions, and percentages.

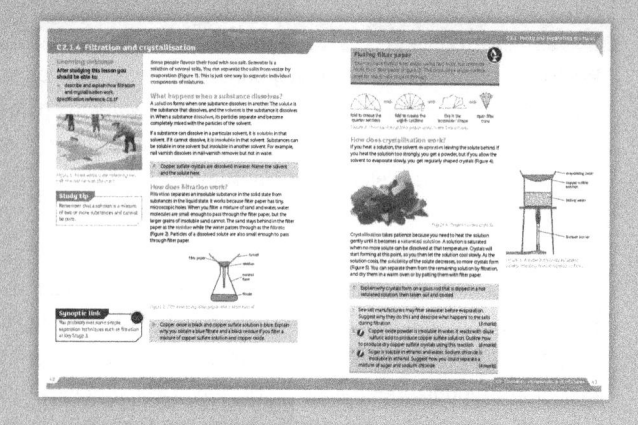

Target	Outcome	Checkpoint	
		Question	Activity
Aiming for GRADE 4 ↓	Safely separate a mixture to collect an insoluble substance from a liquid or solution.		Main Homework
	Safely separate a solution to collect the solute.		Main
	Identify the solute, solvent, residue, and filtrate in named solutions or suspensions that have been separated.	A	Main
Aiming for GRADE 6 ↓	Describe the process of filtering.	1	Plenary 1 Main
	Describe the process of crystallisation.	2	Plenary 1 Main
	Suggest and describe a suitable technique to separate a named solution or suspension.	3	Starter 1 Main
Aiming for GRADE 8 ↓	Explain how filtration separates an insoluble solid from a liquid or solution.	B	Main Plenary 2
	Explain how crystallisation separates the components of a solution.	C	Main
	Evaluate different techniques for folding filter paper.		Starter 2

Maths
In the Main activity (Extend) students calculate the percentage mass of a substance in a mixture (M1c).

Literacy
In the Main activity (extend) students use ideas about particles to explain how filtration and crystallisation work.

Key words
solution, solute, solvent, dissolves, soluble, insoluble, filtration, residue, filtrate, evaporates, crystallisation, saturated solution, solubility

C2.1 Purity and separating mixtures

Starter	Support/Extend	Resources
Deduction (5 minutes) Provide small groups of students with sealed samples of copper sulfate crystals, carbon powder, and a mixture of copper sulfate and carbon powder. Include labels and hazard symbols. Ask the student groups to list what they know about the properties of copper sulfate and carbon powder. Students can then use their lists to suggest how to separate the mixture of copper sulfate and carbon powder.	**Support:** Have test-tubes available containing the substances, to which water may be added to show solubility.	
Fold that filter paper (10 minutes) Give students a piece of filter paper each and ask them to fold it for use in a funnel. Examples may include fluting, forming a cone, and ripping the paper to make it fit. Use questions and answers to evaluate the different techniques.	**Support:** Have examples of the three different folding methods already made up so that students can refer to these.	

Main	Support/Extend	Resources
Making a salt (40 minutes) Ask small groups of students to work together to produce a sample of copper(II) sulfate salt from copper(II) carbonate powder and 0.5 mol/dm³ sulfuric acid, through the techniques of filtration and crystallisation. SAFTEY: Wear eye protection. Take care not to get burnt/scalded by hot equipment. Take care when using the sulfuric acid and with the copper sulfate solution that is produced.	**Support:** Provide students with the relevant steps to put into the correct sequence. **Extend:** Measure the mass of the mixture and the mass of the pure carbon and copper sulfate. Ask students to compare the masses and work out the percentage by mass of each substance in the mixture. **Extend:** Challenge students to use ideas about particles to explain how filtration and crystallisation work.	**Practical:** Making a salt

Plenary	Support/Extend	Resources
Apparatus for filtration and crystallisation (5 minutes) Display unlabelled diagrams of the apparatus for filtration and crystallisation (see Student Book Figures 2 and 5). Ask students to label the key parts.		**Interactive:** Filtration and crystallisation
Filtration model (10 minutes) Provide small groups of students with a sieve, flour, and dried kidney beans. Student groups use this equipment to model filtration and then explain their model.	**Extend:** Ask students to explain how filtration is an improvement on decanting.	

Homework	Support/Extend	Resources
Suggest how various mixtures could be separated.		

kerboodle
A Kerboodle highlight for this lesson is **Working Scientifically: Separating mixtures**. Refer to the **Content map** on Kerboodle for a full list of resources and assessment.

C2.1.5 Distillation

Specification links:

C2.1f Describe, explain, and exemplify the processes of simple distillation and fractional distillation, to include knowledge of the techniques of simple distillation and fractional distillation.

WS1.2b Plan experiments or devise procedures to make observations, produce or characterise a substance, test hypotheses, check data, or explore phenomena.

WS1.2c Apply knowledge of a range of techniques, instruments, apparatus, and materials to select those appropriate to the experiment.

WS1.4a Use scientific vocabulary, terminology, and definitions.

WS2a Carry out experiments.

WS2b Make and record observations and measurements, using a range of apparatus and methods.

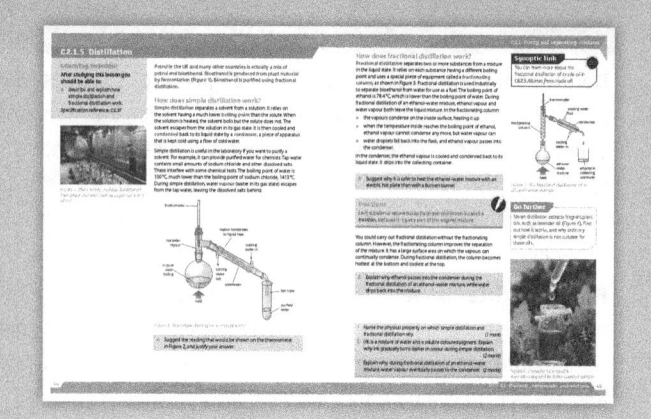

Target	Outcome	Checkpoint	
		Question	Activity
Aiming for GRADE 4	List and recognise the key equipment used in a simple distillation.		Starter 2, Main 1, Plenary 1 and 2
	Safely use distillation to separate two miscible liquids.		Main 1
	State the types of mixtures that can be separated by distillation.		Main 2
Aiming for GRADE 6	Describe the process of simple distillation.		Main 1, Homework
	Describe the process of fractional distillation.		Main 2
	Suggest and describe a suitable technique to separate a named solution or mixture of miscible liquids.	B	Main 1 and 2
Aiming for GRADE 8	Explain how simple distillation separates a solution.	1, 2	Main 1
	Explain how fractional distillation separates a mixture of liquids.	C, 1, 3	Main 2
	Predict and justify the value shown on a thermometer in a distillation, given the mixture and relevant data.	A	Main 1 and 2

Literacy
In completing the Homework task students write a step-by-step method.

Key words
simple distillation, boiling point, condensed, condenser, vapour, fractional distillation, fractionating column, fraction

C2.1 Purity and separating mixtures

Starter	Support/Extend	Resources
Deceptive demo (5 minutes) Measure 50 cm³ of water into one measuring cylinder and 50 cm³ of ethanol into a second measuring cylinder. Ask students to suggest what the total volume will be when both liquids are mixed. Mix the liquids together in a 100 cm³ measuring cylinder. The volume will be less than 100 cm³. Challenge students to use their knowledge of mixtures and solutions to explain this observation.	**Support:** Give students only the correct apparatus, and draw their attention to Figure 2 in the Student Book.	
Simple distillation apparatus (10 minutes) Give small groups of students a selection of apparatus, including the apparatus needed for distillation, filtration, and crystallisation. Ask the groups to set up the apparatus for simple distillation. Then tour the groups, pointing out the good points (e.g., boss being used correctly) and negative points (e.g., stand used backwards). Students may need to complete their annotated diagrams as part of their homework.		

Main	Support/Extend	Resources
Simple distillation (25 minutes) Ask pairs of students to pour diluted ink solution into a boiling tube to a depth of about 2 cm and add a few anti-bumping granules. Students then connect this tube to a test-tube via an L-shaped delivery tube with a bung and complete a simple distillation. Ask students to predict the colour of the mixture and the temperature on the thermometer as the distillation proceeds. Point out that simple distillation is used to separate a solvent from a solution, and ask students to discuss further examples, including how the technique can be used to obtain pure water from seawater.	**Extend:** Challenge students to use ideas about particles to explain how simple distillation works.	**Practical:** Simple distillation
Fractional distillation (15 minutes) Use Quickfit apparatus to demonstrate the separation of ethanol from a mixture with water using fractional distillation. Use questions and answers to ensure that students understand the process and point out that the technique has been used to separate two miscible liquids. Then ask students to copy Figure 3 from the Student Book and add labels to fully explain how fractional distillation works.	**Support:** Give students key words to include in their labels. **Extend:** Ask students to apply what they have learnt to the fractional distillation of air. You may wish to show a video clip.	

Plenary	Support/Extend	Resources
Distillation: which apparatus? (5 minutes) Interactive activity in which students label a distillation diagram and then link together key terms with their definitions.		**Interactive:** Distillation
Compare and contrast (10 minutes) Show students the Quickfit apparatus for a simple distillation. Ask student pairs to compare this apparatus with that used in the experiment carried out in Main 1.	**Extend:** How could the experiment in Main 1 be improved (e.g., cold cloths around the delivery tube)?	

Homework	Support/Extend	Resources
Write a step-by-step method to complete a simple distillation of brine to collect pure water.		

kerboodle

A Kerboodle highlight for this lesson is **Extension: An important use of fractional distillation**. Refer to the **Content map** on Kerboodle for a full list of resources and assessment.

The Practical Skills lesson for PAG 4 *Distillation* could follow this lesson.

C2 Elements, compounds, and mixtures

C2.1.6 Chromatography

Specification links:

C2.1g Describe the techniques of paper and thin-layer chromatography.

C2.1h Recall that chromatography involves a stationary and a mobile phase, and that separation depends on the distribution between the phases, to include identification of the mobile and stationary phases.

C2.1i Interpret chromatograms, including measuring R_f values, to include the recall and the use of the formula.

WS1.2b Plan experiments or devise procedures to make observations, produce or characterise a substance, test hypotheses, check data, or explore phenomena.

WS1.2c Apply knowledge of a range of techniques, instruments, apparatus, and materials to select those appropriate to the experiment.

WS1.3c Carry out and represent mathematic and statistical analysis.

WS1.4a Use scientific vocabulary, terminology, and definitions.

WS2a Carry out experiments.

WS2b Make and record observations and measurements, using a range of apparatus and methods.

M2a Use an appropriate number of significant figures.

M3c Substitute numerical values into algebraic equations using appropriate units for physical quantities.

CM2.1i Understand that arithmetic computation, ratio, percentage, and multistep calculations permeate quantitative chemistry (M1a, M1c, M1d).

CM2.1ii Provide answers to an appropriate number of significant figures (M2a).

Target	Outcome	Checkpoint	
		Question	Activity
Aiming for GRADE 4	State definitions for the stationary and mobile phases in chromatography.		Plenary 2
	Safely complete a paper chromatogram.		Main 2
	Recall the formula for the R_f value.		Starter, Main 1 and 2, Plenary 1
Aiming for GRADE 6	Describe how to complete paper chromatography.		Main 2
	Describe how to complete thin-layer chromatography.		Main 1
	Calculate R_f values given a chromatogram.	B, 1	Main 1 and 2, Plenary 1
Aiming for GRADE 8	Explain how separation occurs in a chromatography experiment.	A, 3	Homework
	Explain how chromatograms for the same substances can be different when phases are changed.	2	Main 1 and 2
	Interpret a chromatogram.	1	Main 1 and 2, Plenary 1

Maths
In Main 1 and Main 2 students calculate R_f values (M2a, M3c).

Literacy
For homework students explain how to interpret chromatograms.

Key words
chromatography, phases, stationary phase, mobile phase, paper chromatography, thin-layer chromatography, chromatogram, R_f values, gas chromatography, carrier gas

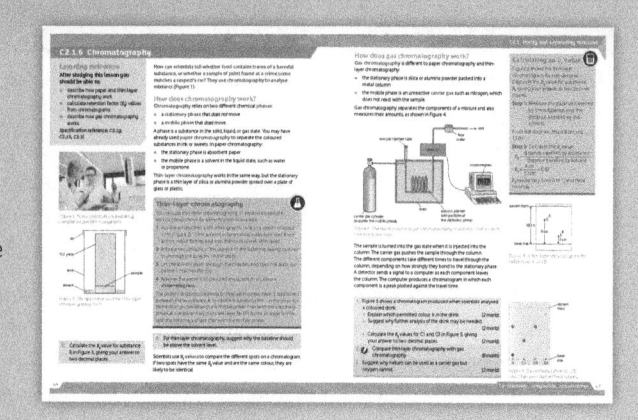

C2.1 Purity and separating mixtures

Starter	Support/Extend	Resources
Equation steps (5 minutes) Ask students to read the Student Book section *Calculating an R_f value* and create a step-by-step flow chart to describe how to calculate the R_f value of a substance from its chromatogram.	**Support:** You may need to provide the equation triangle and demonstrate how to use it. **Extend:** Encourage students to calculate the R_f values for the substances shown in Figure 3.	

Main	Support/Extend	Resources
Chromatography detectives (20 minutes) Students work in small groups to try to match up the ink left on a ransom note with ink from five different pens, which belong to five different suspects. Ideally, students tackle this task using thin-layer chromatography, but paper chromatography is a suitable alternative. Students should calculate the R_f value for each of the ink samples and compare them with the ink from the ransom note to work out which person's pen matches the one used to write the note.	**Extend:** Ask students to use the internet to research thin-layer chromatography.	
Paper chromatography (20 minutes) Ask students to draw a horizontal pencil line 1 cm from the bottom edge of a rectangular piece of chromatography paper. Students then put pencil crosses on the line, 1 cm apart, and label them for different food colourings. Using a capillary tube, students spot three drops of food colouring on each labelled cross. Students then roll the chromatography paper into a cylinder, with the pencil line at the bottom, and secure it with a paper clip. Students insert the cylinder into about 0.5 cm depth of water in a beaker so that the bottom edge of the cylinder is in the water, but the pencil line is above the water level. Students then leave the chromatogram to develop so that the solvent line is above the last coloured dot. Finally students remove the paper, uncoil it, and allow it to dry. Students then tackle the questions on the Kerboodle calculation sheet on R_f values.	**Support:** Ask students to describe how a chromatogram can tell you whether a substance is soluble in the solvent used, how pure the substance is, and what the substance is.	**Practical:** Paper chromatography

Plenary	Support/Extend	Resources
Chromatogram quiz (5 minutes) Show students a selection of chromatograms and ask them to interpret them in order to answer questions.		
Chromatography (5 minutes) Interactive activity in which students link key phrases to their definitions and then calculate R_f values.	**Support:** Explain that the word search includes all the key words from the Student Book.	**Interactive:** Chromatography

Homework	Support/Extend	Resources
Explain how chromatography separates a mixture.	**Extend:** Research gas chromatography, and consider how separation methods are chosen.	

kerboodle
A Kerboodle highlight for this lesson is **Calculation sheet: R_f values**. Refer to the **Content map** on Kerboodle for a full list of resources and assessment.

The Practical Skills lesson for PAG *3 Separation techniques* could follow this lesson.

C2.1.7 Purification and checking purity

Specification links:

C2.1j Suggest suitable purification techniques given information about the substances involved.

C2.1k Suggest chromatographic methods for distinguishing pure from impure substances, to include paper, thin-layer (TLC), and gas chromatography.

WS1.4a Use scientific vocabulary, terminology, and definitions.

M3c Substitute numerical values into algebraic equations using appropriate units for physical quantities.

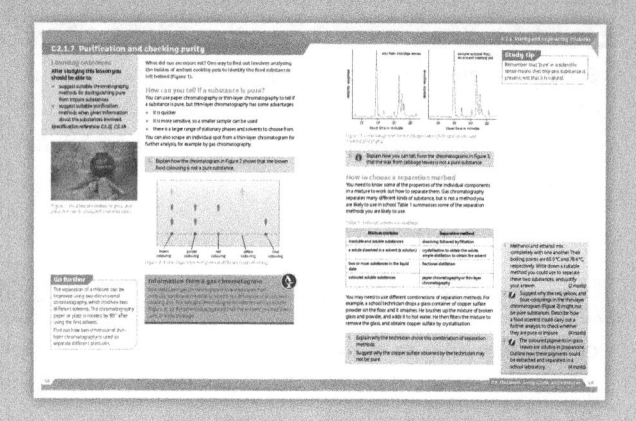

Target	Outcome	Checkpoint Question	Checkpoint Activity
Aiming for GRADE 4	Describe one purification technique to separate a simple mixture.	1	Plenary 1, Main 2
	Describe the processes of paper, thin-layer, and gas chromatography.		Starter 2, Main 2
	Use a chromatogram to classify a substance as pure or a mixture.		Starter 1
Aiming for GRADE 6	Suggest a multi-step separation technique for a mixture.	3	Homework
	Explain the processes of paper, thin-layer, and gas chromatography.		Starter 2, Main 1
	Explain how a chromatogram can be used to identify a pure substance or a mixture.	A, B	Starter 1, Main 2
Aiming for GRADE 8	Explain how a multi-step method can be used to separate a given mixture.	C	Homework
	Evaluate the different types of chromatography.	C, 2	Starter 2, Main 1
	Justify the use of different purification techniques in different circumstances.		Main 1

Maths
In Starter 1 (Extend) students calculate R_f values (M3c).

Literacy
In Main 1 students write an article about chromatography.

C2.1 Purity and separating mixtures

Starter	Support/Extend	Resources
Interpret (5 minutes) Ask students to look at Figure 2 in the Student Book and draw as many conclusions as they can from the chromatogram. Then use questions and answers to help students build up a list of all the information that the chromatogram can give. **Chromatography comparison** (10 minutes) Ask students to design a table with the following column headings: stationary phase; mobile phase; advantages; disadvantages. Students complete the table to compare and contrast paper, thin-layer, and gas chromatography.	**Extend:** Ask students to calculate the R_f values for the food colourings in Figure 2. **Support:** Provide students with a partially completed table, with only one missing entry in each row.	

Main	Support/Extend	Resources
Mind map (20 minutes) Ask students to design a mind map that summarises all the separation techniques they have studied. Students should include a labelled diagram of each technique, and state examples of what each technique is used to separate. **Purity** (20 minutes) Students consolidate their learning about purity and purification by analysing some gas chromatograms and exploring when and why different separation techniques can be used.	**Extend:** Encourage students to digitise their work using free mind-mapping software.	**Activity:** Purity and purification

Plenary	Support/Extend	Resources
Which technique? (5 minutes) Ask students to match the separation technique to the mixture: 1 Solution, collecting the solvent (simple distillation) 2 Solution, collecting the solute (crystallisation) 3 Insoluble compound from a liquid (filtration) 4 Suspension (filtration) **Exam question** (10 minutes) Provide small groups of students with a 5-mark exam question about this topic. Ask students to produce a mark scheme rather than answer the question. The mark scheme should include points for which marks are awarded (indicating the most desirable points), other acceptable answers, and common misconceptions that would not be awarded credit. Then show students the actual mark scheme and ask them to compare the two.	**Support:** Use a question from a Foundation exam paper.	**Interactive:** Separating mixtures

Homework	Support/Extend	Resources
Outline a series of separation techniques to separate out each part of seawater to leave a sample of water that is safe to drink. Summarise your method and results in a table with the following column headings: mixture; separation technique; outcome. (Filter seawater to remove any insoluble material such as sand and plant matter, collect the filtrate solution, distil, collect the distillate that boils at 100°C as this will be pure water.)	**Extend:** Explain how you could show that your method produced pure water.	

Checkpoint
C2.1 Purity and separating mixtures

Overview of C2.1 Purity and separating mixtures

In this chapter students have studied elements, compounds, and mixtures, how to describe them, and how to separate different mixtures. They should know the terms relative atomic mass, relative molecular mass, and relative formula mass, understanding that the relative atomic mass is a weighted mean of the different isotopes present. They should have used the Periodic Table to find the chemical symbol and relative atomic mass of an element.

In studying compounds, students should be able to use and interpret formulae, including those involving brackets, and calculate the relative formula mass or relative molecular mass. They should understand what is meant by an empirical formula and be able to find this from the molecular formula or from a model. Students should be able to apply conservation of mass to chemical reactions, and find the relative molecular mass of a product using the relative formula or molecular masses of the other reactants and products.

Students should be able to define the terms pure and impure, and give examples. They should be able to use melting point to identify a substance and understand how this can indicate purity.

Students should have used filtration to separate an insoluble substance from a liquid, and crystallisation to separate a solute from a solution. They should understand the terms solute, solvent, residue, and filtrate, and be able to suggest a suitable technique to separate a named solution or suspension.

In studying distillation students should be able to describe the processes of simple and fractional distillation, safely use distillation to separate two miscible liquids, and suggest a suitable distillation technique to separate a named solution.

Students should understand the techniques of paper chromatography and thin-layer chromatography. They should be able to define the terms mobile and stationary phase, and use the R_f value to identify an unknown substance.

Students should be able to suggest a suitable purification technique for a given mixture and explain how a substance can be identified as pure or a mixture.

MyMaths

You can find additional support for the maths skills covered in this chapter on **MyMaths**, including calculations using ratios and percentages and working with graphs.

PAGs

All students are expected to have carried out the PAG *3 Separation techniques* and the PAG *4 Distillation*. A full lesson plan for each PAG is provided in the Practical skills chapter. PAG *3 Separation techniques* should be completed after lesson C2.1.6 *Chromatography*. PAG *4 Distillation* should be completed after lesson C2.1.5 *Distillation*.

C2.1 Purity and separating mixtures

kerboodle

For this chapter, the following assessments are available on Kerboodle:
C2.1 Checkpoint quiz: Purity and separating mixtures
C2.1 Progress quiz: Purity and separating mixtures 1
C2.1 Progress quiz: Purity and separating mixtures 2
C2.1 On your marks: Purity and separating mixtures
C2.1 Exam-style questions and mark scheme: Purity and separating mixtures

Checkpoint follow-up lesson

A student's route through this lesson can be determined using the Checkpoint assessment. Percentage pass marks are supplied in the Checkpoint teacher notes.

For each successive route through it is assumed that the student can perform to their current route as well as previous routes. For example, students working at Aiming for 6 are assumed to be secure in Aiming for 4 knowledge and understanding and working towards achieving all the learning objectives for Aiming for 6.

	Aiming for 4	Aiming for 6	Aiming for 8
Learning outcomes	Use melting point data to identify pure substances and mixtures.	Explain the difference between the scientific and everyday use of the term pure.	Justify a separation process for a given mixture.
	Describe the processes of filtration, crystallisation, simple distillation, and fractional distillation.	Calculate the relative formula mass of compounds.	Calculate the relative formula mass of species including in balanced chemical equations.
	Outline a simple method for paper chromatography.	Interpret chromatograms including calculating R_f values.	Explain how chromatography separates different components of a mixture.
Starter	**Water (5 minutes)** Show students a bottle of mineral water, a glass of tap water, and water collected from a simple distillation set-up. Ask students to list the similarities (they all contain mainly water) and differences (tap water and bottled water are solutions and contain other substances as well as water, but distilled water is scientifically pure and contains only water particles).			
	What a state! (5 minutes) Provide some melting point and boiling point data for pure substances such as water, bromine, and sodium as well as similar data for mixtures such as wax, petrol, and salt water. Ask students to consider the state of each chemical at room temperature and then sort them into pure and impure substances. Then ask students to explain how from the melting point data they can determine if a substance is scientifically pure (it has a sharp melting point, whereas mixtures melt over a range).			
Differentiated checkpoint activity	**Poster (45 minutes)** Explain that students will be producing a set of revision cards. Students answer each question on the differentiated worksheets. Each student will need three index cards and a selection of coloured pens or pencils and highlighters.			
	The Aiming for 4 sheet contains structured tasks to support students as they produce cards revising and summarising purity and separation techniques. Students will require scissors and glue sticks.	The Aiming for 6 sheet contains questions to guide students as they produce revision cards about purity, relative formula mass, and chromatography. Students will require scissors and glue sticks.	Aiming for 8 students produce cards that summarise separation techniques and justify when they are used, as well as defining relative atomic mass is, relative formula mass, and relative molecular mass and how they are related.
	Kerboodle resource: C2.1 Checkpoint follow-up: Aiming for 4, C2.1 Checkpoint follow-up: Aiming for 6, C2.1 Checkpoint follow-up: Aiming for 8			
Plenary	**Revision card review (5 minutes)** Ask students to lay out their revision cards on benches around the room. Students choose another person's cards to review. They should read the cards and decide on two strong points about the cards and one point that could be improved on.			
	Think, pair, share (5 minutes) Ask students to think about one fact they have revised and one fact they have learnt in the lesson. They should then discuss with a partner and together decide on the best revised fact and the best new fact. Then finally compare as a group for each bench or table and agree on the best two facts. Ask each group to share their ideas with the class.			
Progression	Aiming for 4 students should be able to outline filtration, crystallisation, simple distillation, fractional distillation, and chromatography.	Aiming for 6 students should be able to explain the difference between the everyday use and scientific use of the term pure. They should also be able to interpret a chromatogram and calculate the relative formula mass of a given compound.	Aiming for 8 students should be able to justify which separation technique should be used for a given mixture and explain how chromatography separates different parts of a mixture. They should also be able to calculate the relative formula mass of chemical species.

C2 Elements, compounds, and mixtures

C2.2 Bonding
C2.2.1 Metals and non-metals

Specification links:

C2.2a Describe metals and non-metals and explain the differences between them on the basis of their characteristic physical and chemical properties.

WS1.3f Present reasoned explanations.

WS1.4a Use scientific vocabulary, terminology, and definitions.

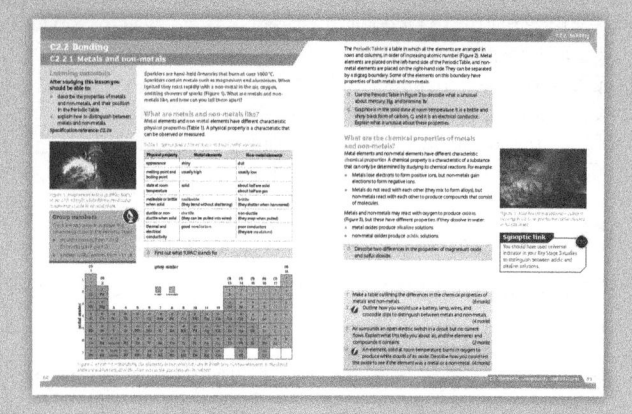

Target	Outcome	Checkpoint	
		Question	Activity
Aiming for GRADE 4	List the physical properties of metals and non-metals.	2	Starter 1 and 2 Main 1 Plenary 2
	State where metals and non-metals are found in the Periodic Table.		Starter 2 Plenary 1
	Use the Periodic Table to classify an element as a metal or a non-metal.		Starter 2 Plenary 1
Aiming for GRADE 6	Describe the differences between the chemical properties of metals and non-metals.	1, 4	Plenary 2
	Describe an experiment to determine whether an element is a metal or a non-metal.	2, 4	Main 1 and 2
	Identify patterns in the Periodic Table for the physical properties of elements.		Plenary 1
Aiming for GRADE 8	Predict the physical and chemical properties of an element based on its position in the Periodic Table.	B	Plenary 1
	Evaluate an experiment designed to classify an element as a metal or a non-metal.	2, 4	Main 1 and 2 Homework
	Identify elements in the Periodic Table with anomalous properties.	B, C	Homework

Key words
metal, non-metal, physical properties, malleable, brittle, ductile, conductors, insulators, Periodic Table, chemical properties, oxides, alkaline, acidic

52

C2.2 Bonding

Starter	Support/Extend	Resources
Splat! (5 minutes) Ask student pairs to write the key words on an A3 piece of paper in large text, spread out across the page. Then ask questions that are answered by the key words. Students put their hand as quickly as possible on the appropriate key word to show the answer. The first person in each pair to put their hand on the correct word gets a point.	**Support:** Prepare the A3 sheets in advance.	
Classify (10 minutes) Give groups of students pictures of different elements. Ask students to sort the samples into metals and non-metals using the Periodic Table. Use questions and answers to encourage students to list the observations they are making in order to carry out their classification. These observations can form the beginning of a list of the physical properties of metals and non-metals.	**Extend:** Introduce the idea of a metalloid.	

Main	Support/Extend	Resources
Investigate properties (25 minutes) Ask pairs of students to test materials for flexibility and conductivity. Students should design a results table to record their observations and then draw conclusions consistent with the results. 1 To test flexibility: Clamp the material to be tested to the end of the desk, with the end of the material extending beyond the edge. Clamp a ruler to the end of the desk vertically, with the top of the ruler (0 cm) level with the free end of the material. Hang a 200 g mass on the free end of the material and measure the deflection of the free end after 30 seconds. 2 To test electrical conductivity: Make a simple series circuit with the material to be tested, three wires, two crocodile clips, a lamp, a multimeter or ammeter, and a low-voltage power supply. Use this circuit to observe whether the material conducts electricity. 3 To test thermal conductivity: Use petroleum jelly to hold a drawing pin onto a rod of the material to be tested. Place the other end of the rod into just-boiled water and time how long it takes for the drawing pin to fall off.	**Support:** Give students the results table to complete. **Extend:** Allow students to use a secondary source to research the melting points and boiling points of the materials tested.	**Practical:** Metals and non-metals
Oxides (15 minutes) Demonstrate that metals produce alkaline oxides and non-metals produce acidic oxides. Have a gas jar of oxygen containing about 1 cm depth of water mixed with a few drops of universal indicator. On a deflagrating spoon, place a 3 cm length of magnesium ribbon, twisted into a spiral. Ignite the metal over a blue Bunsen burner flame and put it into the gas jar of oxygen. The universal indicator colour change shows that the oxide formed is alkaline. Repeat the demonstration with a new gas jar of oxygen and about a quarter of a spatula of sulfur flowers. The universal indicator colour change shows that the oxide formed is acidic. Ask students to record their observations and conclusions. Use a well-ventilated room or fume cupboard and do not look directly at the magnesium flame.	**Extend:** Link combustion of sulfur to acid rain.	

Plenary	Support/Extend	Resources
Predict the properties (5 minutes) Give groups of students an element and ask them to use its appearance to classify it as a metal or non-metal. Then ask students to predict further chemical and physical properties of the element, based on its position in the Periodic Table.	**Support:** Draw students' attention to Table 1 in the Student Book.	
Metals and non-metals (5 minutes) Students use the interactive to sort properties according to whether describe metals or non-metals.		**Interactive:** Metals and non-metals

Homework
Explain why it is not possible to classify a material as a metal or a non-metal by testing for electrical conductivity alone.

C2.2.2 Electronic structures

Specification links:

C2.2b Explain how the atomic structure of metals and non-metals relates to their position in the Periodic Table.

C2.2c Explain how the position of an element in the Periodic Table is related to the arrangement of electrons in its atoms and hence to its atomic number.

WS1.1b Use models to solve problems, make predictions, and develop scientific explanations and understanding of familiar and unfamiliar facts.

WS1.4a Use scientific vocabulary, terminology, and definitions.

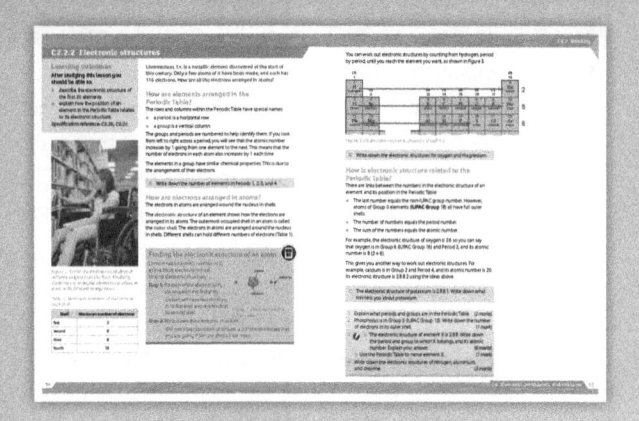

Target	Outcome	Checkpoint Question	Checkpoint Activity
Aiming for GRADE 4	State definitions of a group and a period in the Periodic Table.	1	
	State the maximum number of electrons in each of the first three shells.		Main 1 and 2 Homework
↓	Draw the electronic structure of the first 20 elements given the number of electrons.		Main 1 and 2 Plenary 2 Homework
Aiming for GRADE 6	Identify an element given the group and period number, and vice versa.	A	Starter 1
	Use simplified electronic structure notation to draw the electronic structure of the first 20 elements in the Periodic Table.		Main 1 and 2 Homework
↓	Draw the electronic structure of the first 20 elements using the Periodic Table to determine their number of electrons.	B	Main 1 and 2 Homework
Aiming for GRADE 8	Determine the electronic structure of each of the first 20 elements given group number and period number.	2	Main 1 and 2 Homework
	Interpret simplified electronic notation for the first 20 elements to determine group number, period number, and element.	C, 4	Main 1 and 2 Plenary 1 Homework
↓	Justify the study of the electronic structures of only the first 20 elements at GCSE level.		Main 2

Maths
In Main 1 students determine the number of electrons in each shell.

Literacy
For homework students summarise how electrons are arranged in atoms.

Key words
period, group, electronic structure, outer shell

C2.2 Bonding

Starter	Support/Extend	Resources
Guess the element (5 minutes) Give students group and period numbers in the Periodic Table and ask them to write the symbol of the element on mini-whiteboards. For example, Group 0, Period 1 (He). **Label** (10 minutes) Show students a helium-filled balloon. Ask them to name the element contained in the balloon. Then ask for a volunteer to draw the subatomic particles in a helium atom. Invite more volunteers to label the subatomic particles and to explain how they knew the number of each type of subatomic particle in the helium atom.	**Support:** Define group and period using a worked example. **Support:** Show students a diagram of a helium atom and ask them to label each subatomic particle.	

Main	Support/Extend	Resources
Electronic structures (20 minutes) Demonstrate how to build up the electronic structure of an argon atom. Then ask students to draw the electronic structures of lithium, carbon, neon, magnesium, fluorine, and chlorine. Students should complete the atomic structure worksheet, which gives practice at extracting information about atoms from the Periodic Table. **First 20 elements** (20 minutes) Explain that the GCSE electronic structure model works for the first 20 elements in the Periodic Table only. Encourage students to draw an outline of the Periodic Table for the first 20 elements, and to include each element's electronic structure in its symbol tile. Challenge students to identify a pattern in the electronic structures and group numbers, and then to identify a second relationship between the period numbers and numbers of electron shells.	**Support:** Give students diagrams showing the electronic structures of the elements listed in the main activity, without the names of the elements and in a different order. Students write the name of the element represented in each diagram. **Support:** The patterns may be easier to see if students draw the electronic structures in a blank Periodic Table outline with group and period numbers detailed. See Student Book spread C2.2.10, Figure 3. **Extend:** Introduce the idea of sub-shells and how this concept relates to the Periodic Table.	**Activity:** Electronic structures

Plenary	Support/Extend	Resources
Name that element (5 minutes) Give students electronic structures and ask them to write the element they represent on mini-whiteboards: 1 2 (He) 2 2.1 (Li) 3 2.8.8 (Ar) 4 2.2 (Be) 5 2.4 (C) **Electronic structures** (5 minutes) Interactive activity in which students match the element to its group in the Periodic Table and then type in the number of electrons in each shell.		**Interactive:** Electronic structures

Homework
Summarise how electrons are arranged in atoms. Practise writing the electronic structure of the first 20 elements in the Periodic Table.

kerboodle

A Kerboodle highlight for this lesson is **Maths skills: The arrangement of electrons in atoms**. Refer to the **Content map** on Kerboodle for a full list of resources and assessment.

C2.2.3 Forming ions

Specification links:

C2.2f Construct dot-and-cross diagrams for [simple covalent and] binary ionic substances.

C2.2h Explain how the reactions of elements are related to the arrangement of electrons in their atoms and hence to their atomic number.

WS1.1b Use models to solve problems, make predictions, and develop scientific explanations and understanding of familiar and unfamiliar facts.

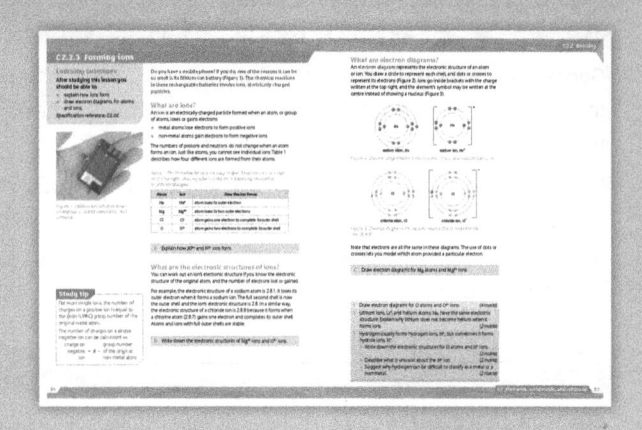

Target	Outcome	Checkpoint Question	Checkpoint Activity
Aiming for GRADE 4	State the definition of the term ion.		Starter 1, Main 2
↓	Recognise an ion from its symbol.		Starter 2
↓	Draw or state the electronic structure of an ion given its charge and the electronic structure of the neutral atom.	B	Starter 2, Main 1 and 2
Aiming for GRADE 6	Use electron diagrams to explain how ions are formed.		Starter 2, Main 1 and 2
↓	Explain whether a given electron diagram represents an atom or an ion.	C, 1	Main 2
↓	Draw the electronic structure of an ion given its charge and the number of electrons in the neutral atom.		Main 2
Aiming for GRADE 8	Explain the charge on a given ion in terms of subatomic particles and electron transfer.	A	Starter 1 and 2, Main 2
↓	Explain how atoms and ions of different elements can have the same electronic structure.	2	Plenary 1
↓	Predict the electronic structure of an ion given its position in the Periodic Table.	3	Main 2, Homework

Maths
In Main 2, students translate information from numeric to graphical form.

Literacy
In Main 2, students construct a flow chart.

Key words
ion, electron diagram

C2.2 Bonding

Starter	Support/Extend	Resources
Charges (5 minutes) Ask students to list the different subatomic particles and state the number of each in a sodium atom. Explain that a sodium ion is a sodium atom whose outer electron has been removed. Then ask students to list the different subatomic particles and state the number of each in a sodium ion, to justify the charge on a sodium ion being +1. **Sodium chloride** (10 minutes) Ask students to draw the electronic structures of sodium and chlorine. Explain how the electron in the outer shell of a sodium atom is given to a chlorine atom when the two elements react, and that this is how ions are formed. Students modify their work to show the symbols and electronic structures of the ions. Demonstrate the reaction by heating a small piece of sodium on a deflagrating spoon until it starts to combust. In a fume cupboard, quickly remove the lid of a gas jar of chlorine, and put the burning metal into the gas.	**Extend:** Ask students to consider a transition metal that has more than one stable ion. **Extend:** Ask students to write an equation for this reaction.	

Main	Support/Extend	Resources
Making sense of ions (20 minutes) Remind students that electrons exist is shells around the nucleus of an atom and remind students of the total number of electrons in each shell for the first 20 elements: • first shell: 2 electrons • second shell: 8 electrons • third shell: 8 electrons • fourth shell: 2 electrons Then introduce students to ions, explaining that they are an electrically charged particle formed when an atom or group of atoms gains or loses electrons. Students then work through the activity sheet to draw the electron diagram of lithium, before practicing drawing electron diagrams of other ions. **Ideas about ions** (20 minutes) Ask students to make a flow chart to explain how you can use atomic number and mass number to determine the numbers of subatomic particles in an ion. Then ask students to swap flow charts with one another and use the charts to determine the numbers of subatomic particles in a variety of ionic compounds.	**Extend:** Develop the flow chart by adding additional branches to explain how to determine the subatomic particles in a negative ion, a positive ion, and an isotope.	**Activity:** Making sense of ions

Plenary	Support/Extend	Resources
Which ions? (5 minutes) Ask students to write the electronic structures of all the atoms or ions that have the following structures: 1 2 (He, H$^-$, Li$^+$, Be^{2+}) 2 2.8 (N^{3-}, O^{2-}, F$^-$, Ne, Na$^+$, Mg^{2+}, Al^{3+}) **Turning atoms into ions** (5 minutes) Interactive activity in which students match terms and definitions and then decide whether symbols represent atoms or ions.		**Interactive:** Turning atoms into ions

Homework		
Explain which ion aluminium forms. Answers should include electron diagrams.		

C2 Elements, compounds, and mixtures 57

C2.2.4 Ionic compounds

Specification links:

C2.2d Describe and compare the nature and arrangement of chemical bonds in: **i** ionic compounds [**ii** simple molecules **iii** giant covalent structures **iv** polymers **v** metals].

C2.2e Explain chemical bonding in terms of electrostatic forces and the transfer [or sharing] of electrons.

C2.2f Construct dot-and-cross diagrams for [simple covalent and] binary ionic substances.

C2.2g Describe the limitations of particular representations and models to include dot-and-cross diagrams, ball-and-stick models, and 2D and 3D representations.

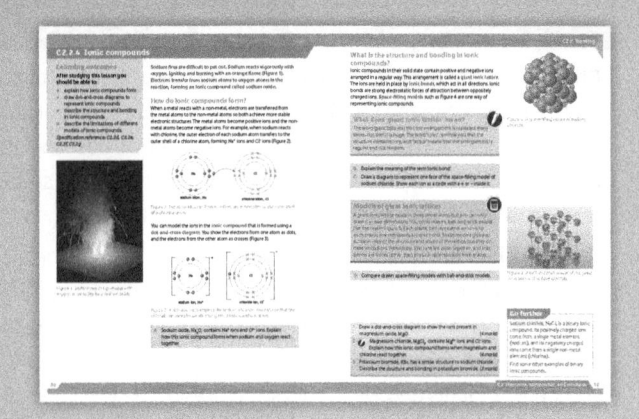

WS1.1b Use models to solve problems, make predictions, and develop scientific explanations and understanding of familiar and unfamiliar facts.

M1c Use ratios, [fractions, and percentages].

M5b Visualise and represent 2D and 3D forms including two dimensional representations of 3D objects.

CM2.2ii Represent 3D shapes in 2D and vice versa when looking at chemical structures, (e.g., allotropes of carbon) (M5b).

CM2.2iii Translate information between diagrammatic and numerical forms (M4a).

Target	Outcome	Checkpoint Question	Checkpoint Activity
Aiming for GRADE 4	State that ionic compounds tend to form between a metal and a non-metal.		Starter 2, Main 1 and 2, Plenary 2
	Draw dot-and-cross diagrams to represent simple binary ionic compounds in which one electron per atom is transferred.	B	Main 1 and 2
	Describe the structure and bonding in an ionic compound.	3, C	Main 1, Homework
Aiming for GRADE 6	Explain the formation of ionic bonds in terms of electron transfer.	A, 2	Main 1
	Draw dot-and-cross diagrams to represent ionic compounds in which more than one electron per atom is transferred.	1	Homework
	Explain how a given model represents an ionically bonded compound.		Main 2, Homework
Aiming for GRADE 8	Justify the formation of ionic bonds in terms of the stability of the atoms and ions involved.		Main 1, Plenary 2
	Justify how a space-filling model for a given compound arises from its dot-and-cross diagram.		Main 2
	Evaluate different models to represent ionic compounds.		Main 2, Homework

Maths
In Starter 2, students calculate the charges on ions and the ratio of ions required to make a stable ionic compound (M1c). Represent 3D shapes in two dimensions (M5b).

Literacy
In Main 2 students write evaluations of models.

Key words
ionic compound, dot-and-cross diagram, giant ionic lattice, ionic bonds, space-filling model, ball-and-stick model

C2.2 Bonding

Starter	Support/Extend	Resources
3D to 2D (5 minutes) Show students a 3D ball-and-stick model of sodium chloride (see Figure 5). Ask them to draw this as a 3D space-filling diagram (see Figure 4) and then as a 2D representation (see Figure 2). **Examine ionic compounds** (10 minutes) Give students a series of binary ionic compounds (e.g., sodium chloride, magnesium oxide, lithium chloride, magnesium sulfide) and the formula of the compound. Students work in pairs to suggest the formula of each ion in the compound. If ball-and-stick or space-filling models of these ionic compounds are available, ask students to match these with the samples.	**Extend:** Ask students to suggest what represents the chloride ions, the sodium ions, and the bonds between the particles. **Support:** Include the formulae of the ionic compounds on the labels. **Extend:** Ask students to draw the dot-and-cross diagrams of the ions.	

Main	Support/Extend	Resources
Ionic compounds (40 minutes) Explain that sodium chloride has the same properties no matter how it is made. Ask pairs of students to measure out 10 cm³ of dilute hydrochloric acid into a beaker and a few drops of universal indicator. Students then add dilute sodium hydroxide from a dropping pipette until the indicator shows the solution is neutral. Students then add activated charcoal to remove the indicator, filter the mixture, and collect the colourless filtrate. After allowing crystallisation to occur, students observe the sodium chloride crystals. Students then use dot-and-cross diagrams to explain why sodium ions are attracted to chloride ions. Students then look at a dot-and-cross diagram, space-filling model, and ball-and-stick model of sodium chloride to evaluate the advantages and disadvantages of each model.	**Support:** Refer students to Figures 2 and 3. **Extend:** Ask students to write an outline flow chart to explain the stages of the experiment to make and collect sodium chloride crystals. **Support:** Prompt students to compare the models using questions (e.g., 'Does the model show that ions have a charge?' and 'Does the model show that ions are in a fixed arrangement when the compound is in the solid state?').	**Activity:** Ionic compounds

Plenary	Support/Extend	Resources
Ionic structures (5 minutes) Interactive activity where students select the correct words to complete a paragraph and then select true or false for a series of statements. **Iron sparklers** (10 minutes) Ask students to dip the end of a splint into water and then into iron filings. Wearing eye protection, students then hold the metal in the top of the inner cone of a blue Bunsen burner flame. Students should notice a sparkler effect. Ask students to suggest the product formed (iron oxide), write an equation to summarise the reaction, and identify and justify the bonding present in the product (ionic).	**Extend:** Explain that ionic compounds can conduct electricity when the ions are free to move. Ask students to suggest which model best represents this. **Extend:** Explain that in this case iron(III) oxide is formed, in which the iron has a 3+ charge. Ask students to draw a dot-and-cross diagram of this ionic compound.	**Interactive:** Ionic structures

Homework		
Draw a dot-and-cross diagram of potassium fluoride and use it to explain the bonding present. Then draw dot-and-cross diagrams for magnesium oxide and magnesium sulfide. Finally, draw a space-filling diagram for potassium fluoride and use it to explain the structure of this compound.	**Support:** The outer shell electronic structure of potassium is the same as that of sodium, and the outer shell electronic structure of fluoride is the same as that of chloride.	

C2.2.5 Simple molecules

Specification links:

C2.2d Describe and compare the nature and arrangement of chemical bonds in: [**i** ionic compounds] **ii** simple molecules [**iii** giant covalent structures **iv** polymers **v** metals].

C2.2e Explain chemical bonding in terms of electrostatic forces and the [transfer or] sharing of electrons.

C2.2f Construct dot-and-cross diagrams for simple covalent [and binary ionic] substances.

C2.2g Describe the limitations of particular representations and models to include dot-and-cross diagrams, ball-and-stick models, and 2D and 3D representations.

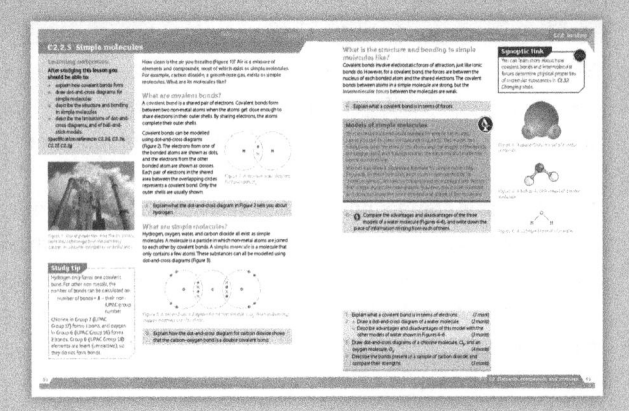

C2.2h Explain how the reactions of elements are related to the arrangement of electrons in their atoms and hence to their atomic number.

WS1.1b Use models to solve problems, make predictions, and develop scientific explanations and understanding of familiar and unfamiliar facts.

WS1.1c Understand the power and limitations of science.

WS1.3f Present reasoned explanations.

WS1.4a Use scientific vocabulary, terminology, and definitions.

M1c Use ratios, [fractions, and percentages].

CM2.2ii Represent 3D shapes in 2D and vice versa when looking at chemical structures (e.g., allotropes of carbon) (M5b).

CM2.2iii Translate information between diagrammatic and numerical forms (M4a).

Target	Outcome	Checkpoint	
		Question	Activity
Aiming for GRADE 4	State that covalent compounds form between non-metal atoms.		Starter 1 and 2 Main 1 and 2
	Recognise covalent bonding and identify substances as covalently bonded.		Main 1 and 2
↓	Draw dot-and-cross diagrams of simple covalent substances, limited to the first 20 elements and single bonds.	2, 3	Starter 1 Main 1 and 2 Plenary 1
Aiming for GRADE 6	Describe the formation of covalent bonds in terms of electron sharing.		Main 1
	Describe structure and bonding in simple molecular substances.	4	Main 1
↓	Draw displayed formulae or dot-and-cross diagrams of covalent compounds, limited to the first 20 elements with single and/or double bonds.	3	Starter 1 Main 1 and 2 Plenary 1
Aiming for GRADE 8	Explain how covalent bonds form between non-metal atoms.	A, B, C, 1	Main 1
	Evaluate different models to represent covalent compounds.	D, 2	Plenary 1
↓	Suggest the displayed formula, space-filling, or dot-and-cross diagrams for covalent compounds, including those with multiple bonds.		Starter 1 Main 2 Homework

Maths
In Main 1 students calculate the number of bonds in a covalent molecule (M1c).

Literacy
In Main 1 students write prose to explain how covalent bonds form.

Key words
covalent bond, simple molecule, intermolecular force, ball-and-stick models, displayed formula

C2.2 Bonding

Starter	Support/Extend	Resources
Match (5 minutes) Display the dot-and-cross diagrams, space-filling models, and molecular formulae of hydrogen, oxygen, chlorine, hydrogen chloride, methane, carbon dioxide, ammonia, and water. Ask students to group the diagrams and models by substance, matching all the different representations. Point out that in all these substances, which are made up of atoms of non-metal elements only, the atoms are held together by shared pairs of electrons – covalent bonds. **Create water** (10 minutes) Ask students to model hydrogen molecules, oxygen molecules, and water using molecular model kits. Point out that in water, which is made up of atoms of non-metal elements only, the atoms are held together by shared pairs of electrons – covalent bonds.	**Support:** Use only hydrogen, carbon dioxide, and water (since these are featured in the Student Book). **Extend:** Include displayed formulae of the substances. **Support:** Give students the formulae and explain which parts of the modelling kit represent the bonds and the hydrogen and oxygen atoms. **Extend:** Ask students to write an equation for the reaction demonstrated.	

Main	Support/Extend	Resources
Water models (25 minutes) Remind students that water is made up of atoms of two non-metal elements, hydrogen and oxygen. Each hydrogen atom shares a pair of electrons with the oxygen atom, forming a covalent bond. Ask students to use molecular model kits to make molecules of water. Then ask them to draw a dot-and-cross diagram and displayed formula of the water molecule. Students should label the covalent bonds and add prose to explain how the bonds are formed. Then ask students to join water molecule models together using sticky tack so that the oxygen atom of one molecule is facing a hydrogen atom of another, to model water as ice. Explain that there is an attraction between the molecules and that this is why ice has a crystal structure. Ask students to draw a space-filling diagram of ice and label this to explain how the structure is held together by intermolecular forces. Point out that the covalent bonds within molecules are much stronger than the forces of attraction between molecules. **Covalent bonding** (15 minutes) Students work through the activity sheet to describe the covalent bonding in chlorine, oxygen, methane, and other simple molecules. Students then create an infomercial to advertise covalent bonds. Their advert should be no more than 30 seconds.	**Support:** Refer students to Figures 4 and 6 in the Student Book. **Extend:** Introduce the idea that the oxygen in a water molecule has a slight negative charge, and the hydrogen has a slight positive charge. **Support:** Give students the formula of each chemical in the reaction and a blank table to help them complete the equations.	**Activity:** Covalent bonding

Plenary	Support/Extend	Resources
Justify your model (5 minutes) Ask small groups of students to consider space-filling models, ball-and-stick models, displayed formulae, and dot-and-cross diagrams representing simple covalent molecules. The groups should suggest which is the best model and justify their choice. **Simple molecules** (5 minutes) Interactive activity in which students match molecules to the correct diagram and then select the correct words to complete a passage about covalent bonding.	**Support:** Use the water molecule as an example, focusing on Figures 4, 5, and 6 from the Student Book. **Extend:** Ask students to use their models to suggest why simple molecules have low melting points.	**Interactive:** Simple molecules

Homework		
Draw the dot-and-cross diagrams and displayed formulae of methane and ammonia.	**Extend:** Draw the dot-and-cross diagram of nitrogen.	

kerboodle
A Kerboodle highlight for this lesson is **Activity: Covalent bonding**. Refer to the **Content map** on Kerboodle for a full list of resources and assessment.

C2.2.6 Giant covalent structures

Specification links:

C2.2d Describe and compare the nature and arrangement of chemical bonds in: [**i** ionic compounds **ii** simple molecules] **iii** giant covalent structures [**iv** polymers **v** metals].

C2.2e Explain chemical bonding in terms of electrostatic forces and the [transfer or] sharing of electrons.

C2.2f Construct dot-and-cross diagrams for simple covalent [and binary ionic] substances.

C2.2g Describe the limitations of particular representations and models to include dot-and-cross diagrams, ball-and-stick models, and 2D and 3D representations.

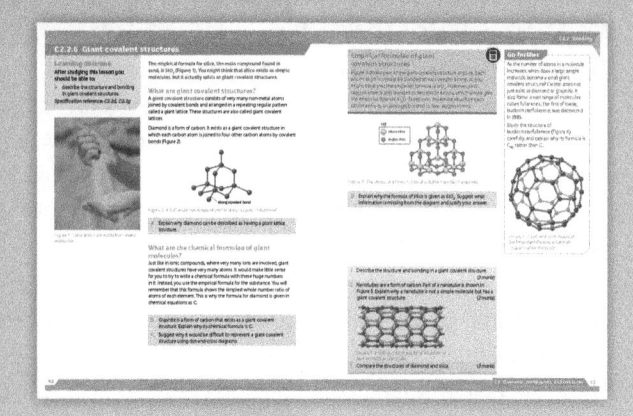

C2.2h Explain how the reactions of elements are related to the arrangement of electrons in their atoms and hence to their atomic number.

WS1.1b Use models to solve problems, make predictions, and develop scientific explanations and understanding of familiar and unfamiliar facts.

WS1.1c Understand the power and limitations of science.

WS1.3f Present reasoned explanations.

WS1.4a Use scientific vocabulary, terminology, and definitions.

M1c Use ratios, [fractions, and percentages].

CM2.2ii Represent 3D shapes in 2D and vice versa when looking at chemical structures (e.g., allotropes of carbon) (M5b).

CM2.2iii Translate information between diagrammatic and numerical forms (M4a).

Target	Outcome	Checkpoint Question	Checkpoint Activity
Aiming for GRADE 4	State that covalent compounds form between non-metal atoms.		Starter 1 and 2 Main 1 Plenary 1 and 2
↓	State examples of substances with giant covalent structures.		Starter 1 and 2 Main 1 and 2 Plenary 1 and 2
↓	Draw a 3D representation of a giant covalent structure.		Main 2
Aiming for GRADE 6	Describe the formation of covalent bonds in terms of electron sharing.		Main 1 and 2
	Describe the structure and bonding in giant covalent structures.	1	Starter 1 and 2 Main 1 and 2 Plenary 1
↓	Determine the empirical formula of a substance with a giant covalent structure.		Plenary 2
Aiming for GRADE 8	Use examples to explain how covalent bonds hold together a giant covalent structure.	A, 2, 3	Starter 1 and 2 Main 1 and 2 Plenary 1
	Evaluate different models to represent covalent compounds.	C, D	
↓	Justify the use of empirical formulae to describe substances that have giant covalent structures.	B, D	Plenary 2

Maths
In Plenary 2 students generate empirical formulae (M1c).

Literacy
In Main 1 students create questions and answers.

Key words
giant covalent structure

62

C2.2 Bonding

Starter	Support/Extend	Resources
Silicon dioxide (5 minutes) Ask students to draw a dot-and-cross diagram of silicon dioxide. It is likely that many students will draw a structure similar to that of carbon dioxide. Explain that silicon dioxide forms a giant covalent molecule and refer students to Figure 3 in the Student Book. **Carbon model** (10 minutes) Give students a molecular model kit and ask them to use only single bonds to make a model of carbon. Encourage students to show their models to the class and compare the different structures. Ask students to look at Figures 2, 4, and 5 and show them a model of graphite. Explain that these are all examples of giant covalent structures.	**Support:** Remind students that the outer shells of silicon and carbon have the same number of electrons. Students could look at their work on carbon dioxide in lesson C2.2.5 to help them. **Extend:** Explain that these are examples of allotropes. Sulfur and phosphorus also form allotropes with simple molecules. Students could generate models of these elements.	

Main	Support/Extend	Resources
Carbon dioxide versus silicon dioxide (30 minutes) Introduce carbon dioxide and silicon dioxide to students, explaining how the bonding is the same (covalent bonds) but the structures are different (carbon dioxide is a simple covalent molecule whereas silicon dioxide has a giant covalent structure). Ask students to create a comparison table featuring a diagram of each substance. Students should label the diagrams fully to explain the bonding and the differences between the structures. **Carbon structure and bonding** (10 minutes) Give each student an A4 sheet of paper and ask them to fold it in half (portrait) to form a narrow column. Ask students to write questions about covalent bonds and giant covalent structures in the left-hand column, using the Student Book to help them. Students then swap their questions with a partner, who writes the answers in the right-hand column. The paper is then returned to the first student, who should consider the answers and modify their questions as required.	**Support:** Give students a set of questions and a set of answers. Students should match up questions and answers to create the question/answer sheet.	**Activity:** Carbon dioxide versus silicon dioxide

Plenary	Support/Extend	Resources
Giant covalent structures (5 minutes) Students use the interactive to complete a paragraph summarising the key points from the lesson. **Generate empirical formulae** (10 minutes) Show students a ball-and-stick model of diamond and silicon dioxide. Ask students to write the chemical formulae of the two substances. Then ask students to suggest why an empirical formulae would be more useful. Ask students to write the empirical formulae of the two substances.	**Extend:** Ask students to suggest why graphene is highly conducting (there is one freely moving electron from each carbon atom). **Extend:** Ask students to justify their answers.	**Interactive:** Giant covalent structures

Homework		
Draw the dot-and-cross diagram for a section of diamond.	**Extend:** Suggest what might be on the ends of the diamond structure (oxygen).	

kerboodle

A Kerboodle highlight for this lesson is **Literacy sheet: Giant covalent compounds**. Refer to the **Content map** on Kerboodle for a full list of resources and assessment.

C2.2.7 Polymer molecules

Specification links:

C2.2d Describe and compare the nature and arrangement of chemical bonds in: [**i** ionic compounds **ii** simple molecules **iii** giant covalent structures] **iv** polymers [**v** metals].

C2.2e Explain chemical bonding in terms of electrostatic forces and the [transfer or] sharing of electrons.

C2.2g Describe the limitations of particular representations and models to include dot-and-cross diagrams, ball-and-stick models, and 2D and 3D representations.

C2.2h Explain how the reactions of elements are related to the arrangement of electrons in their atoms and hence to their atomic number.

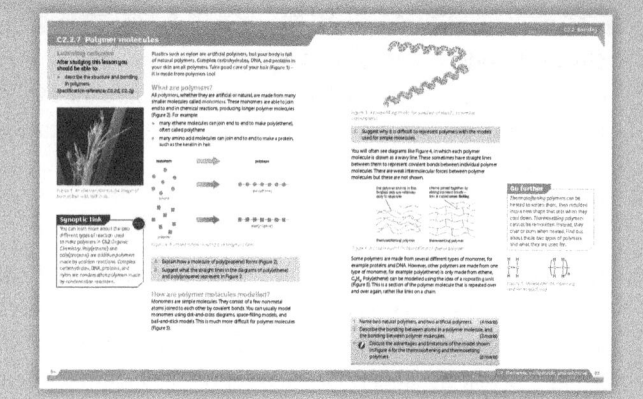

WS1.1b Use models to solve problems, make predictions, and develop scientific explanations and understanding of familiar and unfamiliar facts.

WS1.1c Understand the power and limitations of science.

WS1.3f Present reasoned explanations.

WS1.4a Use scientific vocabulary, terminology, and definitions.

CM2.2ii Represent 3D shapes in two dimensions and vice versa when looking at chemical structures [(e.g. allotropes of carbon)] (M5b).

CM2.2iii Translate information between diagrammatic and numerical forms (M4a).

Target	Outcome	Checkpoint Question	Checkpoint Activity
Aiming for GRADE 4	State definitions of the terms monomer and polymer and give examples of each.		Main 1, Homework
	Describe the difference between the properties of thermosoftening and thermosetting polymers.		Main 2
	Identify a monomer and polymer in a model.		Main 1, Plenary 2
Aiming for GRADE 6	Describe the formation of a polymer.	A	Main 1
	Describe an experiment to classify a polymer as thermosoftening or thermosetting.		Main 2
	Explain a model to represent a polymer.	B, C, 2	Main 1, Plenary 2
Aiming for GRADE 8	Explain how monomers join together to form an addition polymer.	A	Main 1, Plenary 2, Homework
	Explain how the structures of thermosoftening and thermosetting polymers affect their properties.		Starter 2, Main 2
	Evaluate different models to represent polymers.	C, 3	Plenary 2

Maths
In Main 1 students make 3D models to represent polymers and polymerisation, which involves translating from the 2D images in the Student Book.

Literacy
The Homework activity requires students to explain how monomers join together to form polymers.

Key words
polymers, monomers, repeating unit

C2.2 Bonding

Starter	Support/Extend	Resources
Plastic everywhere (5 minutes) Give students 1 minute to note down as many plastic things as they can think of that they have used today. Then choose a student to read their list out. Ask the rest of the class to raise their hand if they have noted the same use. Then ask volunteers if there are any unusual uses of plastics they could add (e.g., plastic coating on a medical capsule).	**Support:** Give students a 'feely box' containing different plastic items.	
Slime (10 minutes) Before the lesson, make some slime by mixing 40 cm³ of PVA solution, 5 cm³ of borax solution, and 2 cm³ of food colouring in a plastic cup. Stir vigorously for 2 minutes to allow cross links to form. Allow students to feel both the slime and some PVA solution, and ask them to compare the properties of PVA solution with those of the slime. Explain that the PVA solution is like the first diagram in Figure 4, but when borax is added, cross links form as in the second diagram in Figure 4, which make the material more rigid.	**Extend:** This could be developed into a main activity in which students investigate the time taken for a coin to descend in a measured depth of different slime samples made by adding different amounts of borax solution.	

Main	Support/Extend	Resources
Polymerisation models (20 minutes) Use Figure 2 to explain to students how monomers join to form polymers. Split the class into three groups. Give one group a molecular model kit, another group cooked spaghetti and sticky tack, and the third group beads, string, and a necklace. Ask each group to use their materials to model polymers and polymerisation.	**Support:** Draw students' attention to Figures 2 and 5 to help them model the formation of poly(ethene). **Extend:** Ask students to model the difference between thermosoftening and thermosetting polymers.	
Classifying plastics (20 minutes) Demonstrate the differences between the properties of thermosoftening and thermosetting plastics when heated. In a fume cupboard, set up a Bunsen burner, tripod, and gauze on a flame-proof mat. Place a 1 cm² sample of each plastic on the tin lid, and place the tin lid on the gauze. Heat strongly over a blue flame and observe. Use an unlit splint to demonstrate the consistency of the materials. The thermosoftening plastic will be soft and sticky when touched, but the thermosetting plastic will remain hard. Ask students to design a results table to record their observations.	**Extend:** Ask students to use Figure 4 to explain their observations.	**Practical:** Classifying plastics

Plenary	Support/Extend	Resources
Poly(tetrafluoroethene) (5 minutes) Show students a section of a model of poly(tetrafluoroethene) made of at least three monomers. Students identify the structure of the monomer, the repeating unit of the polymer, and state the type of polymerisation used. Then show students but-2-ene and ask them to identify the polymer.		**Interactive:** Poly(tetrafluoroethene)
Model presentation (10 minutes) Ask student groups to present their model from Main 1, highlighting the features that represent the monomers, the bonds, and the polymer.	**Extend:** Ask students to vote for the best model and to justify their choice.	

Homework		
Model propene and poly(propene) using displayed formulae and repeating unit notation. Use these models to explain in terms of electrons how monomers join to become polymers.	**Support:** Use Figure 5 in the Student Book to help you.	

kerboodle
A Kerboodle highlight for this lesson is **Working Scientifically: Using models – polymers**. Refer to the **Content map** on Kerboodle for a full list of resources and assessment.

C2.2.8 Structure of metals

Specification links:

C2.2d Describe and compare the nature and arrangement of chemical bonds in: [**i** ionic compounds **ii** simple molecules **iii** giant covalent structures **iv** polymers] **v** metals.

C2.2e Explain chemical bonding in terms of electrostatic forces [and the transfer or sharing of electrons].

C2.2g Describe the limitations of particular representations and models to include dot-and-cross diagrams, ball-and-stick models, and 2D and 3D representations.

C2.2h Explain how the reactions of elements are related to the arrangement of electrons in their atoms and hence to their atomic number.

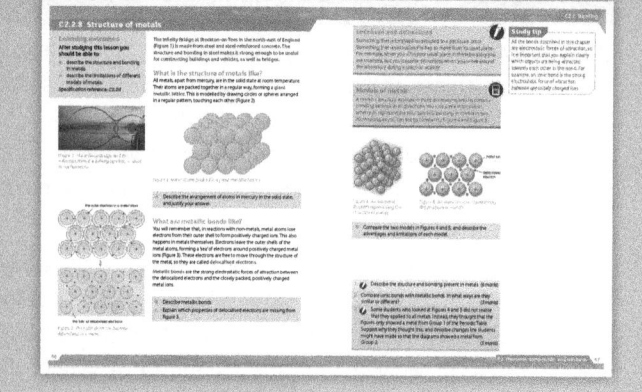

WS1.1b Use models to solve problems, make predictions, and develop scientific explanations and understanding of familiar and unfamiliar facts.

WS1.1c Understand the power and limitations of science.

WS1.4a Use scientific vocabulary, terminology, and definitions.

WS1.3f Present reasoned explanations.

CM2.2i Estimate the size and scale of atoms and nanoparticles (M1c).

CM2.2ii Represent 3D shapes in 2D and vice versa when looking at chemical structures [(e.g., allotropes of carbon)] (M5b).

CM2.2iii Translate information between diagrammatic and numerical forms (M4a).

Target	Outcome	Checkpoint Question	Checkpoint Activity
Aiming for GRADE 4	List examples of substances with metallic bonds.		Starter 1, Plenary 1
	Describe the lattice structure of a metallic crystal.	1	Starter 1 and 2, Main 1 and 2, Plenary 2
	Recognise a model of a metallic lattice.		Starter 2, Main 1
Aiming for GRADE 6	Describe the formation of metallic bonds.	B	Main 2, Plenary 2
	Use a model to explain the lattice structure of a metallic crystal.		Main 1
	Compare metallic bonds with covalent and ionic bonds.	2	Main 2, Plenary 2, Homework
Aiming for GRADE 8	Explain in detail how metallic bonds form.		Main 2
	Evaluate different models to represent metallic bonds and metallic crystals.	C, D 3	Main 1
	Justify the use of a specific model to explain an observation or make a prediction.	A	Main 1

Maths
In Starter 2 students represent metallic structures with 3D models (M5b).

Literacy
In Starter 2 students annotate diagrams to explain metallic bonding and the structure of a metal crystal.

Key words
giant metallic lattice, delocalised electrons, metallic bonds

C2.2 Bonding

Starter	Support/Extend	Resources
Examine metal crystals (5 minutes) Explain that metals are made up of grains, which can be seen using a microscope. Suitable images can be found by using the search term 'photomicrograph of metals' in an image search engine. Show students photomicrograph images showing grains and grain boundaries. If possible, show examples of metal crystals and explain that these are formed when the grains order themselves to form a regular pattern.		
Bonding in metals (5 minutes) Students label a diagram of metallic bonding to show the key features. They then complete a matching exercise to briefly summarise the key features of the three types of bonding they have studied — ionic, covalent, and metallic.	**Support:** Draw students' attention to Table 1 in Student Book spread C1.1.1.	**Interactive:** Bonding in metals

Main	Support/Extend	Resources
Metal crystal models (20 minutes) Show the students any available pre-made metallic models. Students then use soap bubbles to represent metal atoms in a metallic crystal. Half-fill a Petri dish with dilute soap solution. Students blow similar-sized bubbles into the Petri dish using a pipette, to create a raft of bubbles. Ask students to consider how the bubble raft models a metal crystal. Students should sketch the model and annotate the diagram to explain how it models a metal crystal. Then ask students to consider the advantages and disadvantages of this model over those created in Starter 2 and those shown in Figures 2, 3, 4, and 5.	**Extend:** Allow students to model an alloy by blowing different-sized bubbles using a normal dropping pipette and observing the result. The regular pattern of bubbles will be disrupted.	
Growing silver crystals (20 minutes) Wearing eye protection, students half-fill a boiling tube with 0.4 mol/dm³ silver nitrate solution and place it in a boiling tube rack. Ask students to coil copper wire into a spring shape and lower it into the solution. Students observe as the displacement reaction forms silver crystals on the copper wire. Better crystals result if the reaction is left for a few days. Ask students to note their observations and then describe the structure and bonding in the silver metal crystal using labelled diagrams. Then lead a discussion to elicit from students the differences and similarities between metallic bonds, covalent bonds, and ionic bonds.	**Extend:** Ask students to explain in detail how metallic bonds form.	**Practical:** Growing silver crystals

Plenary	Support/Extend	Resources
5, 4, 3, 2, 1 (5 minutes) Ask students to write a list of: five metal symbols; four metal properties; three magnetic elements; two metals used in jewellery; one metal that is a liquid at room temperature. Students could show their answers on mini-whiteboards for instant feedback and praise. Discuss how the structure and bonding of metals gives rise to these properties and uses.	**Support:** Use questions and answers to build up a class list on the board. Display a Periodic Table that has a colour-coded key showing metals and non-metals and the state of each element at room temperature.	
Metals versus carbon nanotubes (10 minutes) Work with students to analyse examination questions comparing metals with carbon nanotubes by looking at sample student answers along with examiner's comments.		

Homework
List the similarities and differences between metallic crystals and ionic crystals.

kerboodle

A Kerboodle highlight for this lesson is **Podcast: Bonding.** Refer to the **Content map** on Kerboodle for a full list of resources and assessment.

C2.2.9 Developing the Periodic Table

Specification links:

C2.2i Explain in terms of atomic number how Mendeleev's arrangement was refined into the modern Periodic Table.

WS1.1a Understand how scientific methods and theories develop over time.

WS1.4a Use scientific vocabulary, terminology, and definitions.

M4a Translate information between graphical and numeric form.

CM2.2iii Translate information between diagrammatic and numerical forms (M4a).

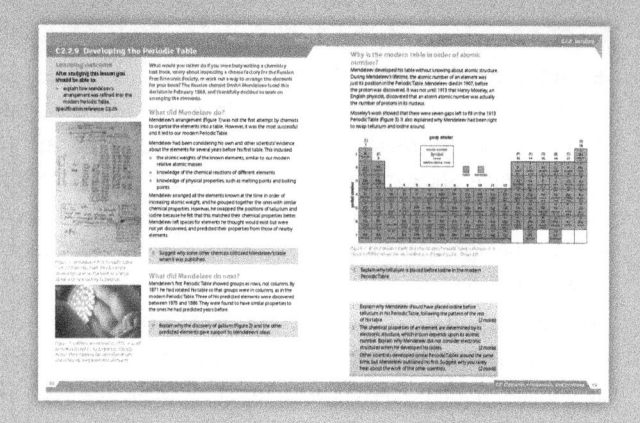

Target	Outcome	Checkpoint	
		Question	Activity
Aiming for GRADE 4 ↓	Describe how the elements are listed in the Periodic Table.		Starter 1 and 2, Main 1 and 2, Plenary 1 and 2
	Use the Periodic Table to determine the symbol, atomic number, and relative atomic mass of an element.		Main 1
Aiming for GRADE 6 ↓	Explain how Mendeleev organised the elements in the Periodic Table.	C, 1	Main 2
	Explain why Mendeleev's Periodic Table was not adopted straight away.	A	Main 2, Plenary 1
Aiming for GRADE 8 ↓	Explain why the modern Periodic Table is not the same as Mendeleev's Periodic Table.	B	Plenary 1, Homework
	Evaluate the Periodic Table as a method of displaying information about the elements.	2, 3	Main 1

Maths
In Main 1 students find patterns in the Periodic Table (M4a).

Literacy
In Main 2 students could write a letter from the point of view of Mendeleev.

68

C2.2 Bonding

Starter	Support/Extend	Resources
Geography of the Periodic Table (5 minutes) Ask students to draw an outline of the Periodic Table and label metals, non-metals, alkali metals, halogens, transition metals, noble gases, group numbers, and period numbers.	**Support:** Show the outline Periodic Table on the board and use questions and answers to build up the labelled diagram as a class. **Extend:** Ask students to highlight the metalloids.	
What do you know? (10 minutes) Ask students to draw a table with the following column headings: what I know; what I want to know; what I know now. Ask students to complete the first column with bullet points about what they already know about the Periodic Table, and the second column with questions that they would like to have answered during the lesson.	**Support:** Allow students to work in small groups, with a higher ability student in each to help support the group.	

Main	Support/Extend	Resources
Arrange the elements (20 minutes) Give small groups of students an activity sheet with part-completed information cards on a selection of elements (e.g., sodium, argon, gold, chlorine, potassium, neon, lithium, fluorine, hydrogen, carbon, oxygen, or bromine), and a large Periodic Table printed on A3. Ask students to complete the information cards and classify the elements in different ways. Then give students a selection of samples of elements (including those listed above) in sealed, labelled containers. Ask students to look at the elements and to place them on the large Periodic Table. Encourage students to notice any patterns in the elements in terms of their bonding, structure, atomic number, and mass number.	**Support:** Give students completed information cards for each element.	**Activity:** Arranging the elements
The development of the Periodic Table (20 minutes) Students use secondary resources including the Student Book and the internet to make a timeline to show how the elements were ordered in different ways. The timeline should include dates, the scientist who proposed the idea, and an outline of the idea (including an image if available).		**Activity:** The development of the Periodic Table

Plenary	Support/Extend	Resources
The history of the Periodic Table (10 minutes) Interactive where students summarise their learning from the lesson by completing sentences on the work of chemists to arrange the elements.	**Support:** Ask students to fill in missing words in prose explaining how Mendeleev ordered the elements in the Periodic Table.	**Interactive:** The history of the Periodic Table
What do you know now? (10 minutes) Ask students to look back at the tables created in Starter 2. Using a different colour, students should make any necessary corrections in the first column, answer the questions in the second column, and list any other information they have found out in the last column.	**Extension:** Invite students to put any unanswered questions to you or to other students.	

Homework		
List the similarities and differences between Mendeleev's Periodic Table (Figure 1) and the modern Periodic Table (Figure 3).		

kerboodle
A Kerboodle highlight for this lesson is **Webquest: The early Periodic Table**. Refer to the **Content map** on Kerboodle for a full list of resources and assessment.

C2.2.10 Atomic structure and the Periodic Table

Specification links:

C2.2h Explain how the reactions of elements are related to the arrangement of electrons in their atoms and hence to their atomic number.

WS1.1a Understand how scientific methods and theories develop over time.

WS1.4a Use scientific vocabulary, terminology, and definitions.

M4a Translate information between graphical and numeric form.

CM2.2iii Translate information between diagrammatic and numerical forms (M4a).

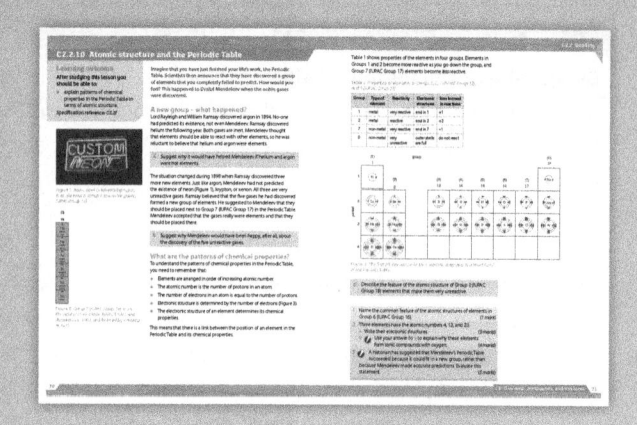

Target	Outcome	Checkpoint	
		Question	Activity
Aiming for GRADE 4 ↓	State the number of electrons in the outer electron shells for the elements in Groups 1 and 8 (IUPAC 18).		Main 1
	Describe the trend in the reactions of the Group 1 elements.		Starter 2
	Describe the trend in the reactions of the Group 7 elements.		Starter 2
Aiming for GRADE 6 ↓	Use the Periodic Table to suggest the electronic structure for the first 20 elements.	2	Main 1
	Predict and explain the trend in reactivity of elements in Groups 2 and 6.		Plenary 2
	Use the Periodic Table to make predictions about the chemical reactions of elements with oxygen.	2	Plenary 2
Aiming for GRADE 8 ↓	Use the Periodic Table to suggest the number of outer-shell electrons and the number of electron shells for an element.		Starter 2 Main 1 and 2 Plenary 2
	Explain, in terms of electronic structure, why noble gases are described as inert.	A, B, C	Starter 1 Main 1
	Evaluate the versatility of the Periodic Table as new elements are discovered.	3	

Maths
In Main 1 and Main 2 students find patterns in the Periodic Table (M4a).

Literacy
In Starter 2 students explain a trend in the reactions of the Group 1 elements with water.

C2.2 Bonding

Starter	Support/Extend	Resources
Noble gases (5 minutes) Show students a helium-filled balloon. Carefully insert a glass straw through the mylar valve and push gently on the balloon to release the gas. Aim the gas jet over a lit candle or the yellow flame of a Bunsen burner. Ask students to explain why the flame goes out. **Reactivity trends** (10 minutes) Introduce the trend in reactivity down Group 1. Explain to students what causes this change in reactivity. Then introduce the trend in reactivity down Group 7. Explain why this trend is different to Group 1. If possible, these reactivity trends could be demonstrated.	**Extend:** Ask students to draw the electronic structure of helium and explain why the element is inert.	

Main	Support/Extend	Resources
Electron structures and the Periodic Table (40 minutes) Give students a simplified version of the OCR Periodic Table photocopied onto an A3 sheet of paper, with plenty of space around the Periodic Table. Ask students to annotate the table to explain how electronic structure relates to position in the Periodic Table, how predictions of electronic structure can be made, why the noble gases are unreactive, the difference in electronic structures of simple ions of the first 20 elements, and the trend in boiling point of the noble gases. Their annotations should be illustrated with real examples, for example, Group 1 elements all have one electron in their outer shell (e.g., Li 2,1 and Na 2,8,1).	**Support:** Give students diagrams of the electronic structures of the first 20 elements, without their names and in a random order. Students cut and stick these diagrams in the correct places in their outline Periodic Table. **Extension:** Introduce students to the idea of sub-shells and how this concept relates to the Periodic Table.	**Activity:** Electron structures and the Periodic Table

Plenary	Support/Extend	Resources
Element symbols (5 minutes) Ask students to give the symbol of an element with a given number of electrons in the outer shell and a given number of electron shells. Students will need access to a periodic table for this activity. **Predict trends** (10 minutes) Ask students to consider the trends in reactivity of Groups 1 and 7. Students should use this information to predict the trends in reactivity of Groups 2 and 6.		**Interactive:** Element symbols

Homework		
Copy Table 1 and extend it to include all the groups of the Periodic Table. Point out that some groups include both metals and non-metals.		

kerboodle
A Kerboodle highlight for this lesson is **Extension: Putting the periodicity into the Periodic Table**. Refer to the **Content map** on Kerboodle for a full list of resources and assessment.

Checkpoint

C2.2 Bonding

Overview of C2.2 Bonding

In this chapter students have studied bonding and electronic structure. They have compared the physical and chemical properties of metals and non-metals, and should know the position of these in the Periodic Table. They should be able to define a group and a period, relate the arrangement of electrons in an element to its position in the Periodic Table, and draw the electronic structure of the first 20 elements.

Continuing their study of ions and electron transfer, students should be able to use electron diagrams to explain how ions are formed and give the electronic structure of an ion. They should understand that ionic compounds tend to form between a metal and a non-metal, and use dot-and-cross diagrams to represent simple binary ionic compounds. They should understand that atoms and ions with full outer shells are stable, and use this as the basis for working out which ions are formed.

In studying covalent compounds, students should know that these form between non-metal elements, be able to recognise covalently bonded substances, and draw dot-and-cross diagrams to represent them. They should understand that a covalent bond is the attraction of the nuclei of two atoms for the electrons, forming a strong bond within the molecule, even though simple molecular substances have low melting points and weak intermolecular forces. Students have gone on to study to giant covalent structures, giving examples and modelling these substances.

Students should be able to describe how a polymer is formed from monomers, and describe the differences between thermosoftening and thermosetting polymers.

Their study of modelling different types of bonding has concluded with metallic bonding, describing the lattice structure of a metallic crystal, giving examples, and comparing metallic bonds with covalent and ionic bonds.

Finally students have studied Mendeleev's work and its refinement to form the modern Periodic Table. They have related the reactions of elements to their electron arrangement and hence to their position in the Periodic Table, and studied trends in reactivity in the elements of Groups 2 and 6.

MyMaths

You can find additional support for the maths skills covered in this chapter on **MyMaths**, including calculations using ratios, translating information from numeric to graphical form, working with 2D and 3D models, and finding patterns.

kerboodle

For this chapter, the following assessments are available on Kerboodle:
C2.2 Checkpoint quiz: Bonding
C2.2 Progress quiz: Bonding 1
C2.2 Progress quiz: Bonding 2
C2.2 On your marks: Bonding
C2.2 Exam-style questions and mark scheme: Bonding

C2.2 Bonding

Checkpoint follow-up lesson

A student's route through this lesson can be determined using the Checkpoint assessment. Percentage pass marks are supplied in the Checkpoint teacher notes.

For each successive route through it is assumed that the student can perform to their current route as well as previous routes. For example, students working at Aiming for 6 are assumed to be secure in Aiming for 4 knowledge and understanding and working towards achieving all the learning objectives for Aiming for 6.

	Aiming for 4	Aiming for 6	Aiming for 8
Learning outcomes	Describe and classify substances as metals or non-metals based on their properties and position in the Periodic Table.	Explain how the position of the element in the Periodic Table is related to the electronic structure of the element.	Explain how reactions of elements are related to their electronic structure and therefore their atomic number.
	Recall a definition of covalent bonds and ionic bonds.	Draw dot-and-cross diagrams to show simple covalent and binary ionic compounds.	Describe the structure of simple covalent substances, giant covalent substances, ionic compounds, metals, and polymers.
	Give examples of substances that have simple covalent structures, giant covalent structures, ionic compounds, metals, and polymers.	Describe the structure of simple covalent substances, giant covalent substances, ionic compounds, metals, and polymers.	Evaluate different models for representing structure and bonding.
Starter	**Electronic relationships (5 minutes)** Provide each student with symbol tiles of a Periodic Table. Show the electronic structures of the first 20 elements and ask students to note them in their symbol tiles. Ask them to conclude the relationship between electronic structure and position (the number of electron shells is the same as the period number, and the number of outer-shell electrons is the same as the group number).			
	5, 4, 3, 2, 1 (5 minutes) Ask students to write the symbols of five metals, the symbols of four non-metals, the formulae of three simple covalent compounds, the formulae of two ionic compounds, and the formula of one giant covalent substance.			
Differentiated checkpoint activity	**Bonding summary (45 minutes)** Students work in differentiated groups to produce a large visual summary of the topic bonding. Groups answer each question on the differentiated worksheets. Each group will need a large (A1) sheet of paper, a selection of coloured pens or pencils, and Post-it notes.			
	The Aiming for 4 sheet provides sentences from which students identify key words for the visual summary. It guides students as they build up their summary.	The Aiming for 6 sheet provides students with the key words to use on their summary, and encourages them to draw ideas from other groups. Students include dot-and-cross diagrams to exemplify covalent and ionic bonding.	The Aiming for 8 sheet provides fewer prompt questions and covers more advanced content. It guides students to design and produce a visual summary with illustrations. They are encouraged to critically review other groups' summaries. Students will require access to the Student Book.
	Kerboodle resource: C2.2 Checkpoint follow-up: Aiming for 4, C2.2 Checkpoint follow-up: Aiming for 6, C2.2 Checkpoint follow-up: Aiming for 8			
Plenary	**Highlight (5 minutes)** Each student needs a highlighter pen. Ask students to review their group's visual summary and highlight three branches which they did not know until they generated their summary.			
	Tweet (5 minutes) Ask students to summarise the learning outcomes in 140 characters.			
Progression	Aiming for 4 students should be able to classify a substance as a metal or non-metal and define, with examples, covalent and ionic bonding. They should also be able to recall the different structures and give examples of them.	Aiming for 6 students should be able to explain ionic and covalent bonding using dot-and-cross diagrams. They should understand that the position of an element in the Periodic Table gives information about the electronic structure.	Aiming for 8 students should be able to explain structure and bonding in a variety of substances and evaluate the different models for bonding.

C2 Elements, compounds, and mixtures

C2.3 Properties of materials
C2.3.1 Carbon

Specification links:

C2.3a Recall that carbon can form four covalent bonds.

C2.3b Explain that the vast array of natural and synthetic organic compounds occurs due to the ability of carbon to form families of similar compounds, chains, and rings.

C2.3c Explain the properties of diamond, graphite, fullerenes, and graphene in terms of their structures and bonding.

WS1.4a Use scientific vocabulary, terminology, and definitions.

M5b Visualise and represent two dimensional (2D) and three-dimensional (3D) forms, including 2D representations of 3D objects.

CM2.3i Represent three-dimensional shapes in two dimensions and vice versa when looking at chemical structures (e.g., allotropes of carbon).

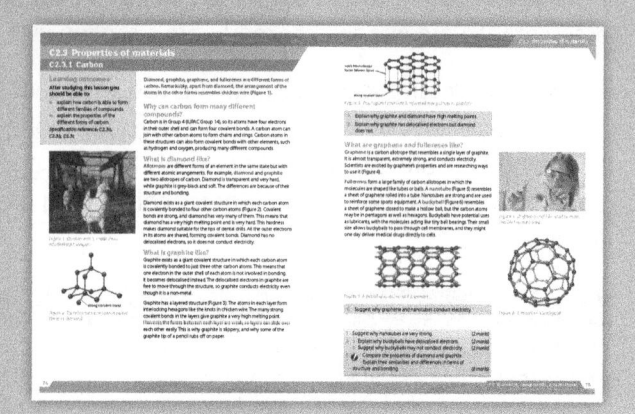

Target	Outcome	Checkpoint Question	Checkpoint Activity
Aiming for GRADE 4	Describe the structure and bonding in graphite and diamond.		Main 2
	List the properties of graphite and diamond.		Starter 1, Main 2, Plenary 1
	Name examples of carbon allotropes.		Starter 1, Main 2
Aiming for GRADE 6	Explain how carbon can form different families of compounds.		Main 1
	Explain the properties of graphite and diamond in terms of structure and bonding.	A, B, 3	Main 2, Plenary 1, Homework
	Explain the term allotrope using carbon to illustrate.		Starter 2, Main 1 and 2
Aiming for GRADE 8	Explain the uses of graphite and diamond in terms of their properties.		Starter 1, Main 2, Plenary 1
	Predict the properties of carbon allotropes, given information about their structure and bonding.	C, 1, 2	Main 2
	Predict the properties or structure of Group 4 elements.		Plenary 2

Maths
In Main 1, students create 2D representations of carbon structures (M5b), calculate the subatomic particles in carbon atoms, and generate their electronic structures.

Literacy
In Homework, students explain the melting points of allotropes of carbon.

Key words
allotropes, diamond, graphite, graphene, fullerenes, nanotube, buckyball

C2.3 Properties of materials

Starter	Support/Extend	Resources
Uses of carbon (5 minutes) Students explore a 'feely' tray featuring a diamond drill bit, a pencil, carbon lubricant powder, activated charcoal, coal, and (if possible) a piece of diamond jewellery (or costume jewellery). Ask students what the samples have in common.	**Extend:** Ask students to identify the property of each material that makes it suitable for its purpose.	
Allotrope chocolate (10 minutes) Ahead of the lesson, buy two large bars of milk chocolate and allow one to melt slightly before cooling it quickly in a fridge. Students take a chunk of each chocolate as they enter, snap them, and compare how easily they break. They then suck the two samples of chocolate and compare them. The cocoa butter in the melted and cooled chocolate takes a different physical form than that in the original bar, changing the properties of the chocolate to give it a smoother taste, greater malleability, and a fuller flavour. Use this model to help in defining allotropes.		

Main	Support/Extend	Resources
Spotlight on carbon (10 minutes) Ask students to draw the electronic structure for carbon. Student pairs use this structure to suggest why carbon forms so many different elemental structures and organic compounds. Elicit the answer, that since carbon has four electrons in its outer shell it can form four covalent bonds.		
Carbon blogging (30 minutes) Introduce students to carbon, the bonding, properties, and uses of graphite, and the bonding, properties, and uses of diamond.	**Extend:** Students should explain the properties in terms of structure and bonding.	**Activity:** Carbon blogging
Students then create a comparison table that includes the structure, describes the properties, and explains them in terms of structure and bonding.		
Students then use their comparison table to summarise the key points about carbon in the form of graphite and diamond as a blog article.		
Students should include a labelled diagram and links to at least one other interesting web page.		

Plenary	Support/Extend	Resources
Giant covalent structures (5 minutes) Students use the interactive to label diagrams of diamond and graphite. They then sort statements according to whether they describe diamond or graphite.	**Extension:** Add statements about bonding.	**Interactive:** Giant covalent structures
Silicon (10 minutes) Ask students to draw a predicted structure of silicon, which is hard, crystalline, and has a high melting point. Students should add labels to explain the structure and the bonding they have drawn.	**Support:** Encourage students to consider which allotrope of carbon has the properties described, and use this to determine the structure for silicon.	
	Extend: Ask students to look back at the structure of silica in C2.2.6 and predict its properties based on its structure and bonding.	

Homework	Support/Extend	Resources
Explain why buckyballs have low melting and boiling points, but graphite has a high melting point.		

kerboodle

A Kerboodle highlight for this lesson is **Activity: News articles**. Refer to the **Content map** on Kerboodle for a full list of resources and assessment.

C2.3.2 Changing state

Specification links:

C2.3d Use ideas about energy transfers and the relative strength of chemical bonds and intermolecular forces to explain the different temperatures at which changes of state occur.

C2.3e Use data to predict states of substances under given conditions.

WS1.2a Use scientific theories and explanations to develop hypotheses.

WS1.3f Present reasoned explanations.

WS1.4a Use scientific vocabulary, terminology, and definitions.

WS1.4c Use SI units and IUPAC chemical nomenclature unless inappropriate.

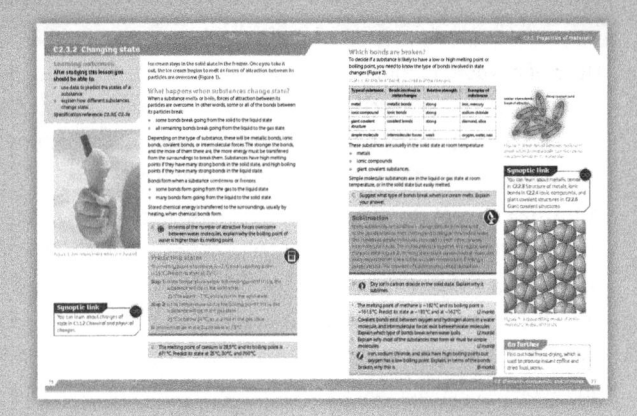

Target	Outcome	Checkpoint	
		Question	Activity
Aiming for GRADE 4 ↓	Describe changes of state in terms of bonds and forces of attraction.		Main 1
	State what is meant by melting point and boiling point.		Starter 1, Main 1
	Explain why the boiling point of a substance is always higher than its melting point.	A	Starter 1
Aiming for GRADE 6 ↓	Explain changes of state in terms of bonds and interactions between particles.	2	Main 1
	Use melting and boiling point data to determine the state of a substance at a given temperature.	B, 1	Starter 1
	Use melting and boiling point data to interpret the relative strengths of forces of attraction.		Plenary 2
Aiming for GRADE 8 ↓	Use an example to explain sublimation.	D	Plenary 1
	Use melting and boiling point data to suggest the type of substance and/or type of bonds present in a sample.	C, 3	Main 2, Homework
	Explain how to use melting and boiling point data to interpret the relative strengths of forces of attraction.	4	Plenary 2

Maths
Interpreting melting and boiling point data.

Literacy
In Plenary 2 students explain how melting point and boiling point data can be used to compare the strength of bonds.

Key words
melts, boils, condenses, freezes, sublime

76

C2.3 Properties of materials

Starter	Support/Extend	Resources
Water (5 minutes) Ask students to sketch a thermometer and label the melting point of water and the boiling point of water. They then label regions where water is a solid, liquid, and gas. Give students some temperatures and ask them to predict the state of water at these temperatures. **Solids, liquids, and gases** (10 minutes) Students use the interactive to identify if well-known substances are in the solid, liquid, or gas state at room temperature. They then match the change of state key word to its description.	**Extend:** Ask students to suggest what would happen to the melting and boiling point if the atmospheric pressure was reduced, e.g., up a mountain.	**Interactive:** Solids, liquids, and gases

Main	Support/Extend	Resources
Cartoon strip (10 minutes) Remind students of the particle model for states of matter in C1.1.1. They draw a cartoon strip to explain in terms of bonding and structure what happens when an ice cube is placed in a pan of boiling water. **Cooling curves** (35 minutes) Students complete the practical to get temperature data from stearic acid as it cools. Boil the kettle and half-fill the beaker with water to make a warm water bath. Half-fill a boiling tube with stearic acid and put in the water bath until the solid has melted. Insert the bulb of the thermometer into the stearic acid. Remove the boiling tube and put in a boiling-tube rack. Measure the temperature of the stearic acid every 30 seconds for 10 minutes or until the substance has been solid for two minutes. Students then plot a cooling curve (temperature against time). Ask students to annotate the graph with the sections where the stearic acid is liquid, freezing, and solid. Encourage students to use state symbol notation and draw annotated particle diagrams to show how the particles are moving and arranged in each section of the graph. SAFETY: Wear eye protection. Be aware that the kettle and hot water bath will be hot enough to burn skin.	**Support:** Allow students to work in small groups to support their learning. **Extend:** Allow students to use an online data book to research the actual melting points of these substances.	**Practical:** Cooling curves

Plenary	Support/Extend	Resources
Sublimation (10 minutes) Add two pellets of solid carbon dioxide to a party balloon and tie up the top. Hold the tied end and run hot water from the tap over the balloon and observe. Ask students to explain what is happening. SAFETY: wear hand and eye protection. Use tweezers. **Strengths of bonds** (10 minutes) Provide students with melting and boiling point data for different substances, and ask students to list the substances in order of the strength of their attractive forces. Students justify this conclusion.	**Support:** You may wish to demonstrate adding the pellets to a conical flask of warm water. **Extend:** Use a pin to make a small hole in the rubber of the balloon after the pellets have sublimed. As carbon dioxide is denser than air, it can be poured into a test-tube half full of limewater to test for the gas.	

Homework	Support/Extend	Resources
Explain why it is not possible to distinguish between metallic crystal, ionic bonding, or giant molecular structures by melting point alone.		

kerboodle

A Kerboodle highlight for this lesson is **Working Scientifically: Planning an experiment (investigating states of matter)**. Refer to the **Content map** on Kerboodle for a full list of resources and assessment.

C2 Elements, compounds, and mixtures 77

C2.3.3 Bulk properties of materials

Specification links:

C2.3f Explain how the bulk properties of materials (ionic compounds; simple molecules; giant covalent structures; polymers and metals) are related to the different types of bonds they contain, their bond strengths in relation to intermolecular forces, and the ways in which their bonds are arranged.

WS1.1b Use models to solve problems, make predictions, and develop scientific explanations and understanding of familiar and unfamiliar facts.

WS1.4a Use scientific vocabulary, terminology, and definitions.

CM2.3i Represent three-dimensional (3D) shapes in two dimensions and vice versa when looking at chemical structures (e.g., allotropes of carbon).

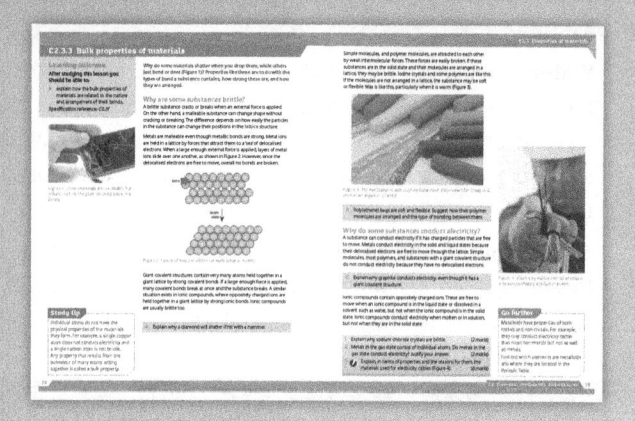

Target	Outcome	Checkpoint	
		Question	Activity
Aiming for GRADE 4	State a definition of the term bulk properties.		Main
	List the main bulk properties of ionic compounds, simple molecules, giant covalent structures, polymers, and metals.		Main, Plenary 1 and 2
	Recognise models of ionic compounds, simple molecules, giant covalent structures, polymers, and metals.		Starter 1
Aiming for GRADE 6	Explain that individual atoms do not exhibit the bulk properties of a material.		Main
	Explain how structure and bonding cause the bulk properties of a material.	A, B, C 1	Main, Plenary 2
	Use models of ionic compounds, simple molecules, giant covalent structures, polymers, and metals to explain bulk properties.		Main, Starter 2
Aiming for GRADE 8	Justify the choice of a material for a function based on its bulk properties.	3	Plenary 1
	Predict the bulk properties of a material given information about its structure and bonding.	2	Main, Plenary 2
	Evaluate models of ionic compounds, simple molecules, giant covalent structures, polymers, and metals used to explain bulk properties.		Main, Starter 2

Maths
In Starter 1 and Starter 2 students explore 3D models.

Literacy
In Main 1 students use analogy to explain how the bulk properties of a material are not the same as the properties of small particles of the material.

Key words
lattice

C2.3 Properties of materials

Starter	Support/Extend	Resources
Models (5 minutes) Split the class into two teams. Show students models of metal crystal lattices, ionic lattices, graphite, diamond, and simple molecules. Put these in a bag and ask for a volunteer from each team to come to the front. The volunteers turn with their backs to the class and take out a model each. Each volunteer describes their model to their team and the first team to name the bonding and structure described gets a point. Repeat for some of the other models.		
Explaining bulk properties (10 minutes) In preparation for the lesson, students complete the interactive activity to remind themselves of the properties of ionic compounds, simple covalent molecules, and the structure and bonding of metals.		**Interactive:** Explaining bulk properties

Main	Support/Extend	Resources
Investigating bulk properties (40 minutes) Give groups of students samples of materials with these structures: polymer (acrylic strip), metallic (copper rod), giant covalent (graphite rod), simple covalent (wax candle), and ionic lattice (sodium chloride crystals). Students draw a table with the following headings: substance; bonding; structure; Is the substance malleable or brittle?; Does the substance conduct electricity?. Students try to bend each material and classify it as malleable or brittle. Using a simple series circuit made of a low voltage power supply, connecting wires, crocodile clips and an ammeter or multimeter, students can test whether the materials are electrical conductors or insulators. Students then draw conclusions consistent with their results about how structure and bonding affect the properties of a substance.	**Extend:** You may wish to provide beakers and allow students to investigate the solubility of the materials, and then whether or not any resulting solution conducts electricity.	**Practical:** Investigating bulk properties

Plenary	Support/Extend	Resources
Name the structure (5 minutes) Hand out the materials investigated in the Main. Call out statements about the bulk properties of a material. Students hold up the material being described and suggest a use for the material.	**Extend:** Ask students to suggest a suitable use for this material based on its bulk properties.	
Explain (10 minutes) Pair students up and split the five types of materials between the students (one student will have three types of materials and the other student will have two types of materials).		
Students write a brief explanation of the bulk properties of their materials. They then swap their explanations with their partners. They then review the explanations, highlight and correct any misconceptions, and add in any extra detail.		

Homework	Support/Extend	Resources
Explain why it is not possible to distinguish between metallic crystal, ionic bonding, or giant molecular structures by conductivity alone.		

GCSE CHEMISTRY ONLY
C2.3.4 Nanoparticles

Specification links:

C2.3g Compare nano dimensions to typical dimensions of atoms and molecules.

C2.3h Describe the surface-area-to-volume relationship for different-sized particles and describe how this affects properties.

C2.3i Describe how the properties of nanoparticulate materials are related to their uses.

C2.3j Explain the possible risks associated with some nanoparticulate materials.

WS1.1c Understand the power and limitations of science.

WS1.1d Discuss ethical issues arising from developments in science.

WS1.1e Explain everyday and technological applications of science.

WS1.1f Evaluate associated personal, social, economic, and environmental implications.

WS1.1h Evaluate risks both in practical science and in the wider societal context.

WS1.1i Recognise the importance of peer review of results and of communicating results to a range of audiences.

WS1.3c Carry out and represent mathematical and statistical analysis.

M1b Recognise expressions in standard form.

M1c Use ratios, fractions, and percentages.

M1d Make estimates of the results of simple calculations, without using a calculator.

M4a Translate information between graphical and numeric forms.

M5c Calculate area of triangles and rectangles, surface area and volume of cubes.

CM2.3ii Relate size and scale of atoms to objects in the physical world.

CM2.3iii Estimate size and scale of atoms and nanoparticles.

CM2.3iv Interpret, order, and calculate with numbers written in standard form when dealing with nanoparticles.

CM2.3v Use ratios when considering relative sizes and surface-area-to-volume comparisons.

CM2.3vi Calculate surface areas and volumes of cubes.

Target	Outcome	Checkpoint Question	Checkpoint Activity
Aiming for GRADE 4	State the relative size of nanoparticles and use this to classify substances.	A	Starter 2
	Calculate the surface area of a cube given the formula.		Main 1
	List some examples of the use of nanotechnology.		Starter 1, Plenary 1 and 2, Homework
Aiming for GRADE 6	Describe how the properties of nanoparticles relate to their uses.	2	Starter 1, Plenary 2, Homework
	Describe and explain how the surface-area-to-volume ratio affects properties.	1	Main 1
	List the advantages and disadvantages of nanotechnology.	2	Main 2, Plenary 1
Aiming for GRADE 8	Use standard form where appropriate, to describe the size of nanoparticles.	B, C	Starter 2
	Calculate the surface-area-to-volume ratio of a cube.	D	Main 1
	Evaluate the uses of nanotechnology.	3	Plenary 1, Homework

C2.3 Properties of materials

Maths
In Main 1 students calculate surface area and volume of cubes (M5c) and determine surface-area-to-volume ratio (M1c).

Literacy
In Main 2 students create a presentation about nanotechnology.

Key words
nanoparticle, nanoparticulate

Starter	Support/Extend	Resources
Guess the lesson (5 minutes) Provide small groups of students with samples of everyday items containing nanotechnology (e.g., deodorants or fabric conditioners containing microencapsulated fragrances for long-lasting scent; sun cream; plasters and cosmetics containing silver). Task students with finding the link between the products. **Manipulate maths** (5 minutes) Ask students to covert the diameters in Table 1 in the Student Book into metres and then into standard form.	**Extend:** Ask students to convert the diameters into other metric units, such as micrometres, or into imperial units.	

Main	Support/Extend	Resources
Nanoscience (40 minutes) Draw students' attention to the worked example in Student Book section *Calculating surface-area-to-volume ratio*. Ask students to work in small groups. Give them 64 1 cm³ cubes that stick together (often found in mathematics departments). Ask students to make a cube 4×4×4 and record the volume and the surface area. Repeat for cubes 2×2×2 and 1×1×1. Students should record their results in an appropriate table. Ask students to add a column of surface area:volume ratio. Explain that each side length of the cube is half the side length of the cube before and ask them to draw conclusions consistent with the results. **What is nanotechnology?** (20 minutes) Working in small groups, students imagine that they are nanotechnology researchers seeking to secure further funding to continue with their research. Using trusted websites, students prepare a presentation to explain the uses of nanotechnologies: how they work; and why they are profitable; as well as an evaluation of the safety of the use of nanotechnology.	**Support:** Students may need help to reinforce how to carry out the calculations. **Extend:** Link with biology: how surface-area-to-volume ratio affects biological systems.	**Practical:** Nanoscience

Plenary	Support/Extend	Resources
Should we develop nanotechnology? (10 minutes) Outline different viewpoints about the development and use of nanotechnology before asking students to state and justify their own opinions. **Uses of nanoparticles** (5 minutes) Interactive activity in which students type in answers to complete sentences about nanoparticles and then answer a question about using nanoparticles in suncream.	**Extend:** Ask students their opinion, then share different viewpoints and invite students to explain whether or not their opinion has changed, and why.	**Interactive:** Uses of nanoparticles

Homework	Support/Extend	Resources
Working in small groups, students imagine that they are nanotechnology researchers seeking to secure further funding to continue with their research. Using trusted websites, students prepare a presentation to explain the uses of nanotechnologies: how they work; and why they are profi table; as well as an evaluation of the safety of the use of nanotechnology.		

kerboodle
A Kerboodle highlight for this lesson is **Extension: Applications of nanoscience**. Refer to the **Content map** on Kerboodle for a full list of resources and assessment.

Checkpoint

C2.3 Properties of materials

Overview of C2.3 Properties of materials

In this chapter students have studied the properties of materials, starting with carbon. They should be familiar with allotropes of carbon, and be able to describe the structure, bonding, and properties of graphite, diamond, graphene, and fullerenes. They should understand that carbon atoms can form four covalent bonds and that this enables carbon to form many different families of compounds.

Students should be able to describe changes of state in terms of bonds and forces of attraction. They should be able determine the state of a substance at a given temperature from melting and boiling point data, and use these data to interpret the relative strengths of forces of attraction and therefore suggest the type bonding present in of substance. They should be able to explain that substances with strong bonds between the particles require more energy to separate the particles than those with weak bonds between the particles. Students should be familiar with sublimation and give an example.

In studying the bulk properties of materials, students should understand that materials are chosen for particular functions based on their bulk properties, be able to relate a substance's properties to its structure and bonding, and use models to explain these properties.

Students studying GCSE chemistry rather than Combined Science have studied nanoparticles and should have an understanding of the size and properties of nanoparticles, along with examples of their uses and risks associated with these uses. They should be able to calculate the surface-area-to-volume ratio and explain how this affects the properties of a material – because nanoparticles have a very high surface-area-to-volume ratio they have very different properties from those of the same materials in bulk.

MyMaths

You can find additional support for the maths skills covered in this chapter on **MyMaths**, including using models in both 2D and 3D to represent matter, and calculations using ratios.

kerboodle

For this chapter, the following assessments are available on Kerboodle:
C2.3 Checkpoint quiz: Properties of materials
C2.3 Progress quiz: Properties of materials 1
C2.3 Progress quiz: Properties of materials 2
C2.3 On your marks: Properties of materials
C2.3 Exam-style questions and mark scheme: Properties of materials

C2.3 Properties of materials

Checkpoint follow-up lesson

A student's route through this lesson can be determined using the Checkpoint assessment. Percentage pass marks are supplied in the Checkpoint teacher notes.

For each successive route through it is assumed that the student can perform to their current route as well as previous routes. For example, students working at Aiming for 6 are assumed to be secure in Aiming for 4 knowledge and understanding and working towards achieving all the learning objectives for Aiming for 6.

	Aiming for 4	**Aiming for 6**	**Aiming for 8**
Learning outcomes	Recognise and describe the three main types of bonding (covalent, ionic, and metallic).	Describe the main types of bonding and related structures (simple covalent, giant covalent, giant ionic lattice, and metallic).	Use experimental results to identify bonding types present.
		Explain what occurs when each type of substance is melted or boiled.	
Starter	**Covalent and ionic models (5 minutes)** Show molecular models of simple covalent structures (e.g., a molecule of oxygen), giant covalent structures (e.g., diamond), and ionic substances (e.g., sodium chloride). An animation of the delocalised electrons within metallic bonding could also be shown. Discuss how electrons are shared or transferred within each type of bonding, and the properties of each type of substance.		
	Dot and cross (5 minutes) Model the use of dot-and-cross diagrams to represent the bonding in substances, for example, for sodium chloride and methane. Highlight that dots and crosses represent electrons, and that the number of electrons in the outer shell of each element corresponds to the group number. Describe how electrons are shared in covalent molecules and how diagrams for these show overlapping shells, while in ionic substances electrons are transferred and each ion is shown in square brackets with a charge. Emphasise that dots and crosses can show which atom electrons have come from.		
Differentiated checkpoint activity	**Activity 1 Fact sheet (40 minutes)** Explain that students will be producing a fact sheet about different types of bonding using the differentiated worksheets.		
	Aiming for 4 students complete their sheet to produce a fact sheet on the three main types of bonding.	The Aiming for 6 sheet includes a series of tasks and questions for students to complete to produce a fact sheet about the main types of bonding.	Aiming for 8 students use the results shown on their sheet to decide on the bonding types present in the substances investigated. They are then asked to write detailed explanations of how the results have led to their decisions.
	Kerboodle resource: C2.3 Checkpoint follow-up: Aiming for 4, C2.3 Checkpoint follow-up: Aiming for 6, C2.3 Checkpoint follow-up: Aiming for 8		
Plenary	**Three facts (10 minutes)** Draw four columns on an interactive whiteboard or flip chart, with the headings simple covalent, giant covalent, ionic, and metallic bonding. Ask pairs or small groups to think of three facts for each type of bonding. Then ask them to compare with neighbouring groups before discussing the facts as a class. Address any misconceptions that have arisen. Then ask students to describe, or draw using a simple cartoon-style drawing, what happens when each type of substance melts or boils.		
Progression	Aiming for 4 students should recognise and describe the three main types of bonding (covalent, ionic, and metallic). The sheet contains structured tasks including a linking exercise and true or false exercise.	Aiming for 6 students should be able to describe the main types of bonding and structures (simple covalent, giant covalent, giant ionic lattice, and metallic) and to explain what occurs when substances with each type of bonding melt or boil. The sheet is fairly structured but also asks students to write a mini-story about bonding in changes of state.	Aiming for 8 students should be able to analyse and explain experimental results to decide what bonding and structure is present in unknown substances. They should understand why some substances behave in an anomalous way. As an extension, students could be given a selection of substances to experiment on to determine their bonding, by testing conduction, solubility, and by researching their melting and boiling points.

C2 Elements, compounds, and mixtures

C2 Elements, compounds, and mixtures: Topic summary

C2.1 Purity and separating mixtures
C2.2 Bonding
C2.3 Properties of materials

Spec ref	Statement	Book spreads
C2.1a	Explain what is meant by the purity of a substance, distinguishing between the scientific and everyday use of the term 'pure'	C2.1.3
C2.1b	Use melting point data to distinguish pure from impure substances	C2.1.3
C2.1c	Calculate relative formula masses of species separately and in a balanced chemical equation	C2.1.1, C2.1.2
C2.1d	Deduce the empirical formula of a compound from the relative numbers of atoms present or from a model or diagram and vice versa	C2.1.2
C2.1e	Explain that many useful materials are formulations of mixtures	C2.1.3
C2.1f	Describe, explain, and exemplify the processes of filtration, crystallisation, simple distillation, and fractional distillation	C2.1.4, C2.1.5
C2.1g	Describe the techniques of paper and thin-layer chromatography	C2.1.6
C2.1h	Recall that chromatography involves a stationary and a mobile phase and that separation depends on the distribution between the phases	C2.1.6
C2.1i	Interpret chromatograms, including measuring R_f values	C2.1.6
C2.1j	Suggest suitable purification techniques given information about the substances involved	C2.1.7
C2.1k	Suggest chromatographic methods for distinguishing pure from impure substances	C2.1.7
C2.2a	Describe metals and non-metals and explain the differences between them on the basis of their characteristic physical and chemical properties	C2.2.1
C2.2b	Explain how the atomic structure of metals and non-metals relates to their position in the periodic table	C2.2.2, C2.2.5
C2.2c	Explain how the position of an element in the periodic table is related to the arrangement of electrons in its atoms and hence to its atomic number	C2.2.2, C2.2.5
C2.2d	Describe and compare the nature and arrangement of chemical bonds in: i. ionic compounds ii. simple molecules iii. giant covalent structures iv. polymers v. metals	C2.2.4, C2.2.6–8
C2.2e	Explain chemical bonding in terms of electrostatic forces and the transfer or sharing of electrons	C2.2.4, C2.2.6–8
C2.2f	Construct dot-and-cross diagrams for simple covalent and binary ionic substances	C2.2.3, C2.2.3–6
C2.2g	Describe the limitations of particular representations and models to include dot-and-cross diagrams, ball-and-stick models, and two- and three-dimensional representations	C2.2.4–8, C2.2.10
C2.2h	Explain how the reactions of elements are related to the arrangement of electrons in their atoms and hence to their atomic number	C2.2.3, C2.2.5–8
C2.2i	Explain in terms of atomic number how Mendeleev's arrangement was refined into the modern periodic table	C2.2.9
C2.3a	Recall that carbon can form four covalent bonds	C2.3.1
C2.3b	Explain that the vast array of natural and synthetic organic compounds occur due to the ability of carbon to form families of similar compounds, chains, and rings	C2.3.1
C2.3c	Explain the properties of diamond, graphite, fullerenes, and graphene in terms of their structures and bonding	C2.3.1
C2.3d	Use ideas about energy transfers and the relative strength of chemical bonds and intermolecular forces to explain the different temperatures at which changes of state occur	C2.3.2
C2.3e	Use data to predict states of substances under given conditions	C2.3.2
C2.3f	Explain how the bulk properties of materials (ionic compounds; simple molecules; giant covalent structures; polymers; and metals) are related to the different types of bonds they contain, their bond strengths in relation to intermolecular forces and the ways in which their bonds are arranged	C2.3.3
C2.3g	Compare 'nano' dimensions to typical dimensions of atoms and molecules	C2.3.4
C2.3h	Describe the surface-area-to-volume relationship for different sized particles and describe how this affects properties	C2.3.4
C2.3i	Describe how the properties of nanoparticulate materials are related to their uses	
C2.3j	Explain the possible risks associated with some nanoparticulate materials	C2.3.4

Maths

Specification		Book spread	
Spec ref	Statement	Main content	Maths chapter
CM2.1i	Arithmetic computation, ratio, percentage and multistep calculations permeates quantitative chemistry	C2.1.1, C2.1.3, C2.1.6	3
CM2.1ii	Provide answers to an appropriate number of significant figures	C2.1.3, C2.1.6	5
CM2.1iii	Change the subject of a mathematical equation		10
CM2.1iv	Arithmetic computation and ratio when determining empirical formulae, balancing equations	C2.1.2	3
CM2.2i	Estimate size and scale of atoms and nanoparticles	C2.2.8	8
CM2.2ii	Represent three-dimensional shapes in two dimensions and vice versa when looking at chemical structures, e.g. allotropes of carbon	C2.2.4–8	16
CM2.2iii	Translate information between diagrammatic and numerical forms	C2.2.4–10	14
CM2.3i	Represent three-dimensional shapes in two dimensions and vice versa when looking at chemical structures, e.g. allotropes of carbon	C2.3.1, C2.3.3	16
CM2.3ii	Relate size and scale of atoms to objects in the physical world	C2.3.4	8
CM2.3iii	Estimate size and scale of atoms and nanoparticles	C2.3.4	8
CM2.3iv	Interpret, order and calculate with numbers written in standard form when dealing with nanoparticles	C2.3.4	2
CM2.3v	Use ratios when considering relative sizes and surface area to volume comparisons	C2.3.4	3
CM2.3vi	Calculate surface areas and volumes of cubes	C2.3.4	15

Working scientifically

Specification		Book spread	
Spec ref	Statement	Main content	WS chapter
WS1.1a	Understand how scientific methods and theories develop over time, to include new technology allowing new evidence to be collected and changing explanations as new evidence is found.	C2.2.9, C2.2.10	WS2
WS1.1b	Use models to solve problems, make predictions and to develop scientific explanations and understanding of familiar and unfamiliar facts.	C2.2.2–8, C2.3.3	WS2
WS1.1c	Understand the power and limitations of science.	C2.2.5–8, C2.3.4	WS1
WS1.1d	Discuss ethical issues arising from developments in science.	C2.3.4	WS1
WS1.1e	Explain everyday and technological applications of science.	C2.3.4	WS1
WS1.1f	Evaluate associated personal, social, economic, and environmental implications.	C2.3.4	WS1
WS1.1h	Evaluate risks both in practical science and in the wider societal context.	C2.3.4	WS1, WS4
WS1.1i	Recognise the importance of peer review of results and of communicating results to a range of audiences.	C2.3.4	WS2
WS1.2a	Use scientific theories and explanations to develop hypotheses.	C2.3.2	WS3
WS1.2b	Plan experiments or devise procedures to make observations, produce or characterise a substance, test hypotheses, check data, or explore phenomena.	C2.1.4–6	WS3, WS4
WS1.2c	Apply knowledge of a range of techniques, instruments, apparatus, and materials to select those appropriate to the experiment.	C2.1.4–6	WS4
WS1.3c	Carrying out and representing mathematical and statistical analysis, to include arithmetic means, mode, and median.	C2.1.1, C2.1.2, C2.1.6, C2.3.4	WS5
WS1.3f	Present reasoned explanations.	C2.2.1, C2.2.5–8, C2.3.2	WS7
WS1.4a	Use scientific vocabulary, terminology, and definitions.	C2.1.3, C2.1.5–7, C2.2.1, C2.2.2, C2.2.5–10, C2.3.1–3	WS2
WS1.4c	Use SI units and IUPAC chemical nomenclature unless inappropriate.	C2.1.1, C2.1.2, C2.3.2	
WS2a	Carry out experiments.	C2.1.4–6	
WS2b	Make and record observations and measurements, using a range of apparatus and methods.	C2.1.2–6	
WS2c	Present observations using appropriate methods.	C2.1.4	

C2 Elements, compounds, and mixtures

C3 Chemical reactions

C3.1 Introducing chemical reactions
C3.1.1 Formulae of elements and molecules

Specification links:

3.1a Use chemical symbols to write the formulae of elements and simple covalent [and ionic] compounds.

WS1.4a Use scientific vocabulary, terminology, and definitions.

M1c Use ratios, fractions, and percentages.

CM3.1i Use arithmetic computation and ratio when [determining empirical formulae and] balancing equations (M1a, M1c).

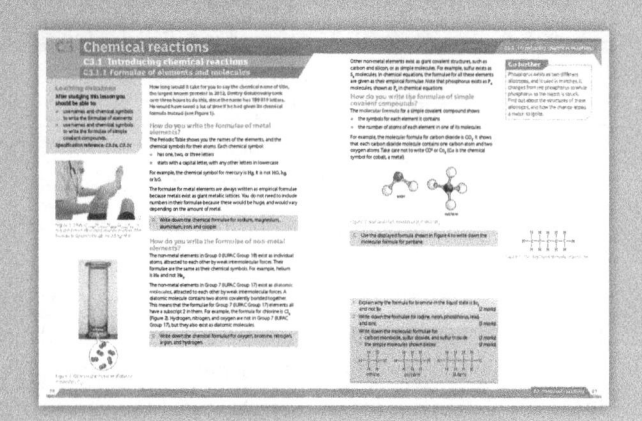

Target	Outcome	Checkpoint	
		Question	Activity
Aiming for GRADE 4 ↓	Name the elements in a familiar simple covalent substance, given the formula.		Starter 2
	Use the Periodic Table to find symbols for elements.	A	Starter 1
Aiming for GRADE 6 ↓	State the number of atoms of each element in an unfamiliar simple covalent substance, given the formula.	1	Starter 2, Main 2
	Write the molecular formula of a compound that exists as simple covalent molecules, given the name or the number of atoms of each element present.	B, 2, 3a	Main 1, Plenary 1
Aiming for GRADE 8 ↓	Explain why metal elements and noble gases are described using only the symbol of the element.	A, 2	Plenary 2
	Write the molecular formula for a simple covalent compound, given the structural formula.	C, 3b	Plenary 1

Maths
In Main 2 and Plenary 1 students generate formulae for simple covalent molecules (M1c).

Literacy
In Main 1 students learn to spell the names of compounds correctly.

Key words
diatomic molecules, molecular formula

C3.1 Introducing chemical reactions

Starter	Support/Extend	Resources
Symbol bingo (5 minutes) Give students bingo cards showing a selection of element symbols. Read out the names of the elements. Students cross off the corresponding symbol if it appears on their card. The first student to cross off all the elements on their card shouts 'Bingo!'. **Structure challenge** (10 minutes) Ask pairs of students to use molecular model kits to make as many structure as they can with the formula C_6H_{10}, and to name the elements in the compound.	**Support:** Give the formula of water and of methane. Ask students to use molecular model kits to model the structures of these simple compounds. **Extend:** Ask students to draw the displayed formula for each example.	

Main	Support/Extend	Resources
Formulae of elements and compounds (20 minutes) Ask students to define the terms molecular and empirical formulae, using the Student Book for information. Students also complete a table to show the structure and molecular formula of some covalent compounds. **Titin** (20 minutes) Draw students' attention to Figure 1. Ask students to rationalise the formula to find the ratio of the different types of atom present in titin. Students then calculate the relative formula mass of this compound. Finally, ask students how many molecules there would be in 0.5 kg of titin (and therefore approximately how many molecules of titin there would be in the human body).	**Support:** Show students a sample of glucose, and write its chemical formula on the board: $C_6H_{12}O_6$. Ask students to give the number of each type of atom in one molecule of the substance, and to find the ratio of different types of atom present in titin. Students then calculate the relative formula mass of this compound. **Extend:** Encourage students to use an image search engine to find pictures of models of the titin molecule online.	**Activity:** Formulae of elements and compounds

Plenary	Support/Extend	Resources
Match the compound (5 minutes) Ask students to match the names of simple covalent compounds to ball-and-stick diagrams. Then ask students to write the formulae of the compounds. **Chemical symbols** (10 minutes) Display on the board the chemical symbol of hydrogen (H_2), argon (Ar), and iron (Fe). Ask students to suggest why the chemical symbol of argon and iron does not have any subscript numbers.	**Support:** Use only water, methane, and pentane (since these are featured in the Student Book).	**Interactive:** Match the compound

Homework	Support/Extend	Resources
Create a table giving the names and formulae of 10 compounds that have not been mentioned in the lesson.		

C3 Chemical reactions

C3.1.2 Formulae of ionic compounds

Specification links:

3.1a Use chemical symbols to write the formulae of elements and simple covalent and ionic compounds.

3.1d Use the formulae of common ions to deduce the formula of a compound.

WS1.4a Use scientific vocabulary, terminology, and definitions.

WS1.4c Use SI units and IUPAC chemical nomenclature unless inappropriate.

M1c Use ratios, fractions, and percentages.

CM3.1i Use arithmetic computation and ratio when [determining empirical formulae and] balancing equations (M1a, M1c).

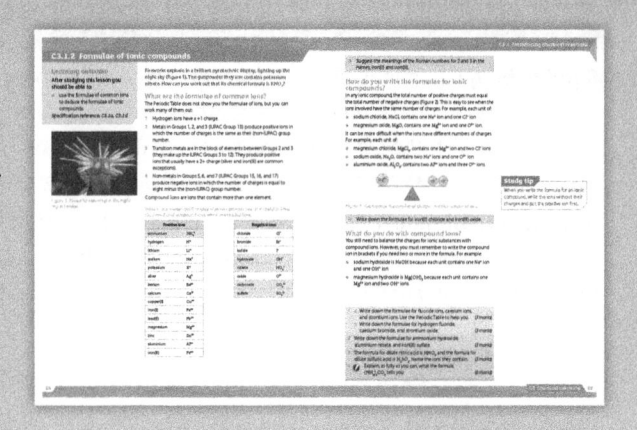

Target	Outcome	Checkpoint	
		Question	Activity
Aiming for GRADE 4	State the charges on ions in Groups 1, 2, 6 (IUPAC 16), and 7 (IUPAC 17).	1a	Starter 1 and 2
			Main 1 and 2
			Plenary 2
	State the ions in familiar ionic substances, given the formulae.	3	Main 2
	State that transition metals can make more than one type of ion.		Main 2
			Homework
Aiming for GRADE 6	Determine the number and type of elements in unfamiliar ionic substances, given the formulae.		Plenary 1
	Write the formula of ionic compounds containing one metal and one non-metal, given the name.	1b	Main 1
	Write the formula of a named ion, including using the Roman numeral convention.	A	Starter 1
			Homework
Aiming for GRADE 8	Explain how a compound can contain both covalent and ionic bonds.	4	
	Write the formulae of ionic compounds that include compound ions.	C, 2, 3	Main 1 and 2
			Plenary 1 and 2
	Name ionic compounds that contain transition metals using the Roman numeral convention.	B, 2	Homework

Maths
In Main 1 and Main 2 students generate ionic formulae using ratios (M1c).

Key words
compound ions

C3.1 Introducing chemical reactions

Starter	Support/Extend	Resources
Ions and group numbers (5 minutes) Interactive in which students match monatomic ions to their group in the Periodic Table. **Draw that ion** (10 minutes) Ask students to draw the electronic structures of atoms or ions – one at a time – on mini-whiteboards, limited to the first 20 elements in the Periodic Table. Encourage students to write the shorthand notation for each electronic structure as well as the diagram.	**Support:** Ask students which type of elements make positive ions (metals) and which make negative ions (non-metals). Elicit the connection between group number and charge (Groups 1–3 have a positive charge equal to their group number).	**Interactive:** Ions and group numbers

Main	Support/Extend	Resources
Formulae of ions (20 minutes) Explain how to work out the formulae of ionic compounds, including those that include compound ions. The key point to note is that the total number of positive charges must be equal to the total number of negative charges. Give students some examples of ionic compounds and ask them to generate their ionic formulae. **Formulae of ionic compounds** (20 minutes) Ask students to draw a grid with positive metal ions across the top (including those from Groups 1 and 2) and negative ions down the side (including those from Groups 6 and 7). Then ask students to complete the grid to show the formulae for all the compounds that could theoretically be made from each pair of ions. Point out that some of these compounds do not actually exist. Then give students the formulae of five compounds, such as copper(II) sulfate and iron(III) oxide, and ask them to state the ions they are made up of.	**Extend:** Encourage students to use an image search engine to find pictures of models of molecular ions online, and to use these to write formulae for the ions. **Extend:** Ask students to include transition metal ions (such as Fe^{2+} and Fe^{3+}) and compound ions in their grid. **Extend:** Ask students to show the name of each compound as well as its formula.	**Activity:** Formulae of ionic compounds

Plenary	Support/Extend	Resources
Choose the formula (5 minutes) Give students a compound name and three different formulae. Ask students to select the correct formula from the list. The correct formulae are italicised. 1 Sodium chloride: NaCl, *NaCl*, SCl 2 Aluminium oxide: *Al_2O_3*, AlO, Al_3O_2 3 Lithium oxide: *Li_2O*, LiO_2, LiO 4 Magnesium hydroxide: *$Mg(OH)_2$*, MgOH, $MgOH_2$ 5 Ammonium sulfate: $NH_4(SO_4)_2$, NH_4SO_4, *$(NH_4)_2SO_4$* **Name that formula** (10 minutes) Ask students to generate the names of five ionic compounds. They should start with those containing one metal and one non-metal element, and then move on to compounds that include ions made up of more than one atom. Ask students to swap their lists with a partner and write the formulae for the compounds, then swap back and check each other's formulae, awarding a score out of 5. Students may wish to discuss their marking. Provide clarification where needed.	**Support:** For each compound, give only the correct formula and one of the incorrect ones for students to choose from. **Extend:** Ask student pairs to make up similar questions for one another, and to peer assess the answers.	

Homework	Support/Extend	Resources
Choose three ionic compounds made from transition metals and write their formulae.	**Extend:** Explain how Roman numerals can be used to indicate the charge on the metal ion. Name the compounds using the Roman numeral convention (e.g., iron(II) sulfate).	

kerboodle

A Kerboodle highlight for this lesson is **Calculation sheet: Ionic formulae**. Refer to the **Content map** on Kerboodle for a full list of resources and assessment.

C3.1.3 Conservation of mass

Specification links:

3.1i Recall and use the law of conservation of mass.

3.1j Explain any observed changes in mass in non-enclosed systems during a chemical reaction and explain them using the particle model.

M1a Recognise and use expressions in decimal form.

M1c Use ratios, fractions, and percentages.

CM3.1i Use arithmetic computation and ratio when determining empirical formulae and balancing equations (M1a, M1c).

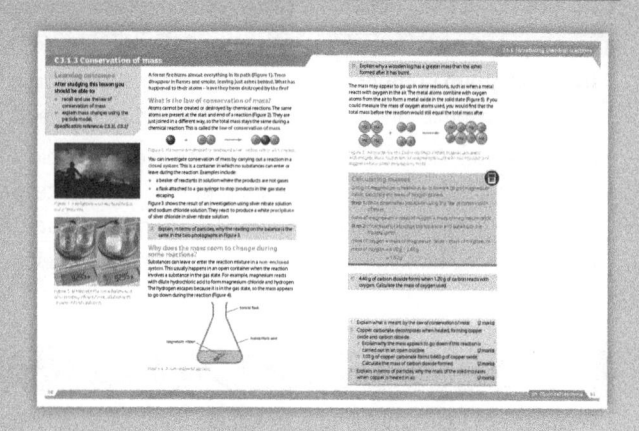

Target	Outcome	Checkpoint	
		Question	Activity
Aiming for GRADE 4 ↓	State the law of conservation of mass.		Starter 2 / Main 1
	Predict the total mass of the products or reactants in a closed chemical system, given the total mass of the reactants or products.		Plenary 2
Aiming for GRADE 6 ↓	Use the particle model to explain the law of conservation of mass.	A, 1	
	Predict the total mass of the products or reactants in a non-enclosed chemical system, given the total mass of the reactants or products.		Main 2 / Plenary 2 / Homework
Aiming for GRADE 8 ↓	Explain why, in some chemical reactions performed in the laboratory, there appears to be a change in total mass.	B, 2a, 3	Starter 1 / Plenary 1 / Main 2
	Calculate the mass of one substance from a balanced symbol equation, given the masses of the other substances.	C, 2b	Main 2 / Plenary 2

Maths
In Main 1 and Main 2 students calculate masses of reacting substances using the law of conservation of mass (M1a, M1c).

Literacy
In Plenary 2, students explain the conservation of mass principle.

Key words
law of conservation of mass, closed system, precipitate, non-enclosed system

C3.1 Introducing chemical reactions

Starter	Support/Extend	Resources
Compare systems (5 minutes) Show students a nail rusting in a little water in an open test-tube, and a nail rusting in a similar test-tube sealed with a bung. Ask students to determine which system is closed and which is non-enclosed, and explain the difference between them. **Mass and equations** (10 minutes) Ask students to use molecular model kits to make hydrogen, chlorine, and hydrogen chloride molecules. Students should place the elements on the left and the compound on the right. Ask students to make additional molecules until they have balanced the number and type of atoms on each side. Then ask students to use the Periodic Table to calculate the total mass of the reactants and of the products, and explain why they are the same.	**Extend:** Introduce the idea of closed, non-enclosed, and isolated systems, with a focus on chemical and energy transfer. **Support:** Allow students to work in small groups.	

Main	Support/Extend	Resources
Investigating mass changes during reactions (25 minutes) Working in small groups, students investigate the conservation of mass in different precipitation reactions. Students measure 10 cm³ of potassium iodide solution into a measuring cylinder and use a balance to record the mass. They then measure 10 cm³ of lead nitrate solution into a second measuring cylinder and again record the mass. They record the total mass of the reactants. They then mix the potassium iodide and lead nitrate solutions, and record their observations and the final mass. Repeat with clean measuring cylinders using barium chloride and sodium sulfate. Ask students to design their own results table and draw conclusions consistent with their results. **Mass in thermal decomposition** (15 minutes) Student pairs thermally decompose copper(II) carbonate in a boiling tube. Ask students to write an equation for the process. Then ask students to calculate the relative formula masses of copper carbonate, carbon dioxide, and copper oxide using the Periodic Table. Finally, ask students to predict the mass of the reactant if 44 g, 22 g, and 11 g of carbon dioxide were made.	**Extend:** Encourage students to write equations for the reactions investigated. Links can be made to ionic equations, making insoluble salts, and testing for sulfate ions. **Support:** Show students a simulation of the thermal decomposition.	**Practical:** Investigating mass changes during reactions

Plenary	Support/Extend	Resources
Mass change (5 minutes) Students use the interactive to sort chemical systems according to whether they would show a loss of mass, whether there would be no change in mass, or whether there would be an increase in mass. **Calculate masses** (10 minutes) Focus on the thermal decomposition of 100 g of calcium carbonate. Ask students to predict the mass of the products if it were completed in: 1 a closed system 2 a non-enclosed system. Then ask students to explain the difference in these values.		**Interactive:** Mass change

Homework	Support/Extend	Resources
Write an equation to illustrate a chemical system of your choice. Predict the observed mass change of the reaction in both a closed system and a non-enclosed system.	**Extend:** Justify your predictions.	

kerboodle
A Kerboodle highlight for this lesson is **Literacy interactive: Conservation of mass**. Refer to the **Content map** on Kerboodle for a full list of resources and assessment.

C3.1.4 Chemical equations

Specification links:

3.1b Use the names and symbols of common elements and compounds and the principle of conservation of mass to write formulae and balanced chemical equations [and half equations].

3.1c Use the names and symbols of common elements from a supplied Periodic Table to write formulae and balanced chemical equations where appropriate.

3.1f Describe the physical states of products and reactants using state symbols (s, l, g, and aq).

WS1.4c Use SI units and IUPAC chemical nomenclature unless inappropriate.

M1c Use ratios, fractions, and percentages.

CM3.1i Use arithmetic computation and ratio when [determining empirical formulae and] balancing equations (M1a, M1c).

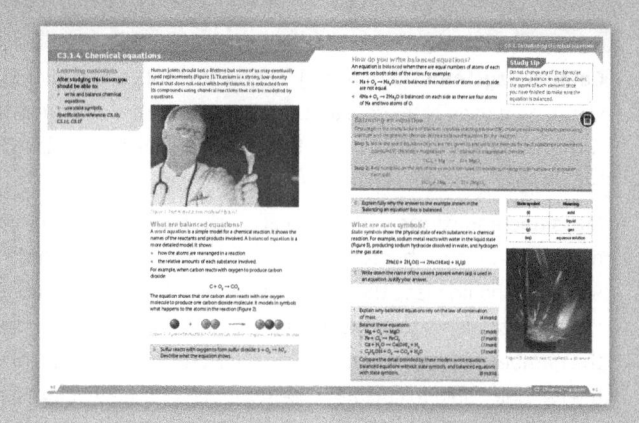

Target	Outcome	Checkpoint Question	Checkpoint Activity
Aiming for GRADE 4	Write a word equation, given a statement naming the reactants and products.		Main 1
	Identify the reactants and products in a word or symbol equation.	A	Starter, Main 1
	Recognise state symbols for solids, liquids, and gases.		Plenary 1, Main 1 and 2
Aiming for GRADE 6	Explain why a symbol equation must be balanced.	B, 1	Main 2, Plenary 2
	Balance symbol equations with formulae that do not contain brackets.	2a,b,d	Main 1 and 2, Plenary 2, Homework
	Add state symbols to balanced symbol equations and explain what they mean.	C	Plenary 1, Main 1 and 2
Aiming for GRADE 8	Write a balanced symbol equation, given a statement describing a familiar chemical reaction.		Starter, Main 1 and 2, Plenary 2
	Balance symbol equations with formulae that include brackets.	2c	Main 2
	Evaluate the use of the terms equations, balanced symbol equations, and state symbols to describe a chemical system.	3	Main 2

Maths
Throughout this lesson students balance equations (M1c).

Literacy
In Main 2 students create a flow chart to explain how to balance equations.

Key words
word equation, balanced equation, state symbols

92

HIGHER TIER
C3.1.5 Half equations and ionic equations

Specification links:

3.1b Use the names and symbols of common elements and compounds and the principle of conservation of mass to write formulae and balanced chemical equations and half equations.

3.1d Use the formulae of common ions to deduce the formula of a compound.

3.1e Construct balanced ionic equations.

WS1.4c Use SI units and IUPAC chemical nomenclature unless inappropriate.

M1c Use ratios, fractions, and percentages.

CM3.1i Use arithmetic computation and ratio when [determining empirical formulae and] balancing equations (M1a, M1c).

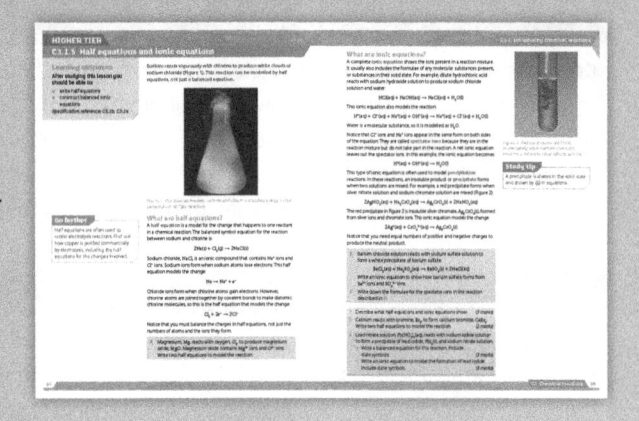

Target	Outcome	Checkpoint	
		Question	Activity
Aiming for GRADE 6 ↓	Determine the ions in a compound, including those containing compound ions.		Starter 1
			Plenary 2
	Balance an ionic equation or half equation and explain what the equation shows.	1	Starter 2
			Main 1 and 2
			Plenary 1 and 2
	Explain why precipitation reactions can be described by ionic equations.		Main 1
Aiming for GRADE 8 ↓	Write an ionic equation or half equations, given a description of a chemical reaction.	A, B, 2, 3	Starter 2
			Main 1 and 2
			Plenary 2
	Explain what spectator ions are, and determine them in a given example.	C	Main 1

Maths
In Main 1, Main 2, Plenary 1, and Plenary 2 students balance equations (M1c).

Key words
half equation, ionic equation, spectator ion, precipitation, precipitate

94

C3.1 Introducing chemical reactions

Starter	Support/Extend	Resources
State the ions (5 minutes) Show students some examples of ionic compounds and ask them to determine the ions that they contain. **Copper oxide and zinc sausages** (15 minutes) Mix 2 g of copper(II) oxide and 1.6 g of zinc powder and put the mixture into sample bottles for pairs of students. Ask each student pair to pour the mixture into a 'sausage' shape about 5 cm long on a flame-proof mat or clean tin lid. Students use a blue Bunsen burner flame to heat one end of the 'sausage' until it begins to glow, and then take away the flame. Students should allow the reaction to complete and pour the cool residue into a 100 cm³ beaker. They should then add a little dilute hydrochloric acid to dissolve the zinc oxide and leave red-brown copper. Rinse the copper with water so that students can handle it. Ask students to explain what happens to the copper ions and the zinc atoms in the reaction, and write half equations for the reaction.	**Extend:** Encourage students to include state symbols in their equations.	

Main	Support/Extend	Resources
Half equations and ionic equations (25 minutes) Ask students to use a dimple dish to test solutions of copper(II) chloride, iron(II) chloride, and iron(III) chloride with dilute sodium hydroxide solution, to see whether a coloured precipitate of the metal hydroxide forms. Students should place 2 drops of the solution to be tested into a dimple and add 2 drops of sodium hydroxide solution. Ask students to design a suitable results table to note the colour of any precipitate formed. Point out that the precipitation reactions can be described by ionic equations, and explain why. Then ask students to write a balanced symbol equation and an ionic equation for each reaction. **Thermite** (15 minutes) Demonstrate the thermite reaction. Ask students to write word and balanced symbol equations for this reaction, and then draw dot-and-cross diagrams of the atoms and ions. Ask students to draw a coloured arrow from the aluminium in the reactant to the aluminium oxide product. Show students that the aluminium atoms each lose three electrons to become aluminium ions. Then generate the half equation for this reaction. Repeat, now focusing on the iron ion forming the iron atom.	**Support:** Explain how to complete the ionic equation for copper(II) ions and encourage students to use this to write an equation for iron(II) ions. **Extend:** Ask students to identify spectator ions and justify their choice. **Extend:** Encourage students to include state symbols in their reactions.	**Practical:** Half equations and ionic equations

Plenary	Support/Extend	Resources
Classify equations (5 minutes) Show students examples of unbalanced symbol equations, half equations, and ionic equations. Ask students to classify and balance them. **Generate equations** (10 minutes) Give students some examples of word equations for familiar reactions. Ask students to generate balanced symbol equations as well as half equations or ionic equations for the reactions.		**Interactive:** Classify equations

Homework	Support/Extend	Resources
When acidified barium chloride solution is added to sodium sulfate solution, a white precipitate of barium sulfate and a solution of sodium chloride are formed. Write a word equation, symbol equation, and ionic equation to represent this reaction.		

kerboodle

A Kerboodle highlight for this lesson is **Maths skills: Writing half equations**. Refer to the **Content map** on Kerboodle for a full list of resources and assessment.

HIGHER TIER
C3.1.6 The mole

Specification links:

3.1g Recall and use the definitions of the Avogadro constant (in standard form) and of the mole.

3.1h Explain how the mass of a given substance is related to the amount of that substance in moles and vice versa.

WS1.4b Recognise the importance of scientific quantities and understand how they are determined.

WS1.4c Use SI units and IUPAC chemical nomenclature unless inappropriate.

WS1.4d Use prefixes and powers of ten for orders of magnitude.

WS1.4f Use an appropriate number of significant figures in calculation.

M1a Recognise and use expressions in decimal form.

M1b Recognise expressions in standard form.

M1c Use ratios, fractions, and percentages.

M2a Use an appropriate number of significant figures.

CM3.1i Use arithmetic computation and ratio when determining empirical formulae and balancing equations (M1a, M1c).

CM3.1ii Carry out calculations with numbers written in standard form when using the Avogadro constant (M1b).

CM3.1iii Provide answers to an appropriate number of significant figures (M2a).

CM3.1iv Convert units where appropriate, particularly from mass to moles (M1c).

Target	Outcome	Checkpoint Question	Checkpoint Activity
Aiming for GRADE 6	Calculate the number of particles in a sample of a substance, given the amount in moles.	B, 2	Main, Homework
	State the formula that links the amount in moles, mass, and molar mass and use the Periodic Table to determine the molar mass of elements and compounds.		Starter, Main, Plenary 2
	Use the Periodic Table to determine the molar mass of monatomic and polyatomic elements and compounds.	A, 2a, 2b, 2c	Main, Plenary 2, Homework
Aiming for GRADE 8	Explain the relationship between the mole and the Avogadro constant.	C	Starter, Main, Homework
	Calculate the mass or amount in moles of a given sample of a substance.	3	Main, Plenary 2, Homework
	Use standard form in calculations involving amounts of substance.	2	Main, Plenary 2, Homework

Maths
Throughout this lesson students calculate mass, moles, molar mass, and number of particles (M1a, M1c). They express numbers in standard form (M1b), use an appropriate number of significant figures (M2a), and interconvert units from mass to moles (M1c).

Key words
mole, Avogadro constant, molar mass

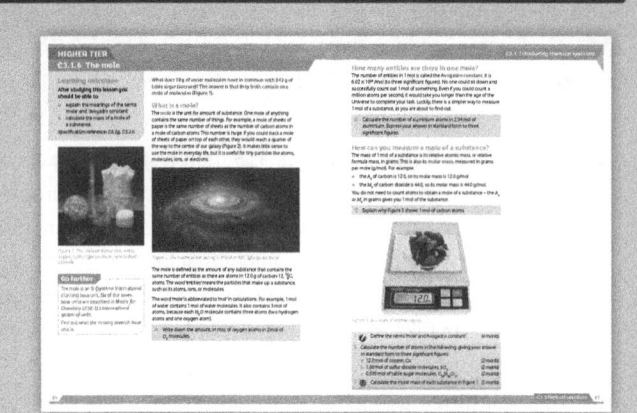

C3.1 Introducing chemical reactions

Starter	Support/Extend	Resources
Mole equations (5 minutes) Interactive activity where students match the quantity with the correct equation. They then select the correct words to complete a passage. **Equation subjects** (10 minutes) Display the equation showing how the mass of a substance is related to its molar mass and the amount: Mass (g) = molar mass (g/mol) × amount (mol) Ask students to rearrange the equation to generate two further equations, one in which molar mass is the subject, and a second in which amount is the subject. Students should then write the units of each term in a different colour.	**Extend:** Ask students to write an expression to link the Avogadro constant, amount, and molar mass. Students should express this in terms of molar mass and then substitute it into the main equation.	**Interactive:** Mole equations

Main	Support/Extend	Resources
Moles (40 minutes) Provide pairs of students with samples of 1 mol of different elements in sealed boiling tubes, each labelled with the element and the mass. Ask students to design a suitable results table and record (for each element) the symbol of the element, the mass of 1 mol of that element, and its relative atomic mass. Then ask students to predict what the mass of 1 mol of water would be, and reveal the answer (18 g). Explain that a mole is a measurement based on the number of particles in a sample. Show samples of 1 mol of different compounds and ask students to predict the masses. Use a top-pan balance to check their predictions. Next, tell students that 1 mol of any substance has the same number of particles (6.02×10^{23}). Ask students to give the number of water molecules in 18 g of water, as well as the number of hydrogen atoms (12.04×10^{23}), and the number of oxygen atoms (6.02×10^{23}). Students should also answer questions that ask them to calculate masses, molar masses, and amounts in moles.	**Support:** Remind students to use the Periodic Table to find relative atomic masses.	**Activity:** The mole

Plenary	Support/Extend	Resources
Mole jokes (5 minutes) Share some mole jokes with the class. For example: - What do you call a sauce made from 6×10^{23} pieces of avocado? A guacamole! - How many guacs are in a bowl of guacamole? Avocado's number! - How much does Avogadro exaggerate? He makes mountains out of mole hills. **The mass of a mole** (10 minutes) Ask students to calculate the mass of 1 mol of the following: 1 oxygen atoms (16 g) 2 oxygen molecules (32 g) 3 water molecules (18 g). Encourage students to show their working.		

Homework	Support/Extend	Resources
Calculate the molar mass of oxygen as separate atoms, and of oxygen as O_2 molecules. State the number of oxygen atoms in a sample of oxygen atoms and a sample of O_2 molecules with a mass equal to the molar mass.		

HIGHER TIER
C3.1.7 Mole calculations

Specification links:

3.1k Deduce the stoichiometry of an equation from the masses of reactants and products and explain the effect of a limiting quantity of a reactant.

3.1l Use a balanced equation to calculate masses of reactants or products.

WS1.3c Carry out and represent mathematical and statistical analysis.

WS1.4c Use SI units and IUPAC chemical nomenclature unless inappropriate.

M1a Recognise and use expressions in decimal form.

M1b Recognise expressions in standard form.

M1c Use ratios, fractions, and percentages.

CM3.1i Use arithmetic computation and ratio when determining empirical formulae and balancing equations (M1a, M1c).

CM3.1ii Carry out calculations with numbers written in standard form when using the Avogadro constant (M1b, WS1.4d).

CM3.1iii Provide answers to an appropriate number of significant figures (M2a, WS1.4f).

CM3.1iv Convert units where appropriate, particularly from mass to moles (M1c).

Target	Outcome	Checkpoint	
		Question	Activity
Aiming for GRADE 6	Define a limiting reactant.		Main 2 Plenary 1 and 2
	Identify a limiting reactant, given the mole values for a reaction.	3b	
	Calculate the number of moles of a substance used or produced in a chemical reaction, given the amounts of all of the other substances.	A, 3	Starter 1 and 2 Main 1 Homework
Aiming for GRADE 8	Explain the effect of a limiting amount of a reactant.		Homework
	Use mass data to determine the stoichiometry and generate a balanced symbol equation for a reaction.	C, 2	Main 1
	Calculate the mass of a substance used or produced in a chemical reaction, given the mass of the limiting reactant.	B, 1, 3	Main 1

Maths
In Starter 2, Main 1, Main 3, and the Homework task students calculate masses and numbers of moles of reacting substances (M1a, M1b, M1c).

Literacy
In Main 2 students justify the classification of a reactant as limiting or in excess, and in Plenary 1 students write three key facts to summarise the lesson.

Key words
excess, limiting, stoichiometry

C3.1 Introducing chemical reactions

Starter	Support/Extend	Resources
Calculate moles (5 minutes) Ask students to calculate the number of moles in: 1 12 g of carbon 2 9.0 g of water 3 34 g of ammonia 4 1.6 g of methane	**Support:** Encourage students to use an equation triangle to help them.	
Thermal decomposition of copper carbonate (10 minutes) Allow pairs or small groups of students to thermally decompose a large spatula measure of copper carbonate in a boiling tube over a blue Bunsen burner flame. Ask students to write the balanced symbol equation for this reaction and calculate the molar mass of each substance in the equation.	**Extend:** Encourage students to include state symbols in their equation.	

Main	Support/Extend	Resources
Reduction of copper oxide with hydrogen (25 minutes) Demonstrate the reduction of copper oxide with hydrogen. Assemble the apparatus shown in Figure 2 with 3 g of copper(II) oxide. Connect the hydrogen cylinder and turn on so that a gentle stream of gas from the hole in the tube can be felt on the cheek. Leave for about 30 s to flush out the air, then ignite the gas. Using a Bunsen burner, heat the copper oxide until the powder has changed colour from black to red. Turn off the gas and allow the product to cool before weighing it. Ask students to use the worked example in Student Book section *Calculating stoichiometry* to calculate the number of moles of reactants used and product made. Then ask students to write a balanced symbol equation.	**Extend:** Ask students to state and justify the limiting and excess reactant and write half equations for this reaction.	**Practical:** Mole calculations
Bunsen burner flames (15 minutes) Ask pairs or small groups of students to set up a Bunsen burner. Explain that when the air hole is open, the methane fully reacts with oxygen to make just carbon dioxide and water. But when the air hole is closed, the amount of oxygen is restricted and a mixture of products is formed, including carbon dioxide, carbon monoxide, carbon, and water. Ask students to write balanced symbol equations for each type of flame, then to annotate these in a different colour to indicate the limiting reactant and the reactant that is present in excess. Ask students to justify their classification.		

Plenary	Support/Extend	Resources
Mole calculation summary (5 minutes) Students use the interactive to match up mass, molar mass, and amount in moles with the the correct expression to calculate them. They then use mole calculations to deduce the correct stoichiometry of a chemical equation.	**Support:** Ask students to focus on the learning outcomes and use these as a basis for each point.	**Interactive:** Mole calculation summary
Thought experiment (10 minutes) Show students an image of iron rusting. Ask them to suggest what is needed for rusting to occur (iron, oxygen, and water). Ask students to imagine a nail placed in an airtight container half-filled with water. Which reactant is limiting, and which is in excess?	**Extend:** Ask students to suggest how different rust-prevention techniques work in terms of limiting air and water.	

Homework		
Choose a chemical reaction and imagine that 100 g of one of the reactants is used. Determine the maximum mass of the products in your chosen reaction.		

kerboodle

A Kerboodle highlight for this lesson is **Working Scientifically: Mole calculations**. Refer to the **Content map** on Kerboodle for a full list of resources and assessment.

Checkpoint
C3.1 Introducing chemical reactions

Overview of C3.1 Introducing chemical reactions

In this chapter, building on work in C2 *Elements, compounds, and mixtures*, students should be able use and interpret formulae for simple covalent compounds. They should know why substances with giant ionic and giant covalent structures are described using empirical formula, and noble gases using just the element symbol.

In studying ionic compounds, students should be able to state the charges on ions in Groups 1, 2, 6 (IUPAC 16), and 7 (IUPAC 17) and know that transition metals can form ions of different charges. They should be able to use formulae for ionic compounds, including using the Roman numeral convention.

Students should be able to apply the law of conservation of mass to chemical reactions and understand that this underpins the need to balance equations. They should be able to find the mass of one substance from an equation given the masses of the other substances, and explain any observed changes in mass in non-enclosed systems during a chemical reaction, explaining them using the particle model. They have described reactions using word and symbol equations, including balancing and the inclusion of state symbols.

The use of equations is extended in the higher-tier topics of half equations and ionic equations, using these to describe precipitation reactions. Building on earlier work in the chapter, higher-tier students should be able to deduce the stoichiometry of an equation from the masses of reactants and products, and identify a limiting reagent in a reaction. They should be able to define the Avogadro constant (in standard form) and have carried out mole calculations to find the number of moles or mass of a substance used or produced in a chemical reaction, given the amount of the limiting reactant.

MyMaths

You can find additional support for the maths skills covered in this chapter on **MyMaths**, including calculations using ratios and the law of conservation of mass, expressing numbers in standard form, using an appropriate number of significant figures, and interconverting units from mass to moles.

kerboodle

For this chapter, the following assessments are available on Kerboodle:
C3.1 Checkpoint quiz: Introducing chemical reactions
C3.1 Progress quiz: Introducing chemical reactions 1
C3.1 Progress quiz: Introducing chemical reactions 2
C3.1 On your marks: Introducing chemical reactions
C3.1 Exam-style questions and mark scheme: Introducing chemical reactions

C3.1 Introducing chemical reactions

Checkpoint follow-up lesson

A student's route through this lesson can be determined using the Checkpoint assessment. Percentage pass marks are supplied in the Checkpoint teacher notes.

For each successive route through it is assumed that the student can perform to their current route as well as previous routes. For example, students working at Aiming for 6 are assumed to be secure in Aiming for 4 knowledge and understanding and working towards achieving all the learning objectives for Aiming for 6.

	Aiming for 4	**Aiming for 6**	**Aiming for 8**
Learning outcomes	Generate the formula of simple covalent compounds.	Generate balanced chemical equations.	Generate balanced ionic equations.
	Use the formula of common ions to generate the formula of ionic compounds and compound ions.	Add state symbols to a balanced ionic equation.	Recall and use the concepts of Avogadro's number and the mole.
	Add state symbols to a balanced chemical equation.	Use the particle model to explain observed mass changes in an open system.	Explain the effect of a limiting reactant on a chemical system.
	Recall the law of conservation of mass.		
Starter	**Name that ion! (5 minutes)** Show students the electronic structures 2.2.8 and 2.8.8, then ask them to write the formulae of all the ions that have each of these electronic structures (that are isoelectronic).		
	Formulae (5 minutes) Students will need a Periodic Table and a list of common ions. Show labelled samples of substances such as an ice cube, sulfur, bromine. Ask them to use the Periodic Table and the list of common ions to write the formula, including state symbols, for each chemical. Then use questions and answers to list the correct formulae on the board so that students can check their work.		
Differentiated checkpoint activity	**Activity 1 Poster (45 minutes)** Explain that students will be producing a poster to summarise the topic *Introducing chemical reactions*. Students answer each question on the differentiated worksheets. They will need A3 or A4 paper, a ruler, pencil, and coloured pens.		
	The Aiming for 4 sheet provides structured activities which should be completed and could be included on posters. Students may require scissors and glue sticks.	The Aiming for 6 sheet provides questions to help stimulate students' ideas as they produce their posters.	The Aiming for 8 sheet provides fewer prompt questions which cover more advanced content.
	Kerboodle resource: C3.1 Checkpoint follow-up: Aiming for 4, C3.1 Checkpoint follow-up: Aiming for 6, C3.1 Checkpoint follow-up: Aiming for 8		
Plenary	**Poster review (5 minutes)** Ask students to lay out their posters on benches around the room. Students choose another person's poster to review. They should read the poster and decide on two strong points about the poster and one point that could be improved on.		
	Review (5 minutes) Ask students to look back at the learning objectives. They should draw an emoticon to describe how they feel about each objective, and then write themselves a SMART target to help move their consolidation forward.		
Progression	Aiming for 4 students should identify the key points being covered in each task. Encourage them to write the key point as a question which they then answer on their poster.	Provide Aiming for 6 students with a more challenging reaction to balance, such as the complete combustion of decane, and also consider mass gain such as the rusting of an iron nail.	Encourage Aiming for 8 students to generate and balance more complicated symbol equations, such reactions studied in chemical identification, for example the test for sulfate in C4.2.3 *Detecting anions*.

C3.2 Energetics
C3.2.1 Exothermic and endothermic reactions

Specification links:

3.2a Distinguish between endothermic and exothermic reactions on the basis of the temperature change of the surroundings.

WS1.3a Present observations and other data using appropriate methods.

WS1.3e Interpreting observations and other data.

WS1.3f Present reasoned explanations.

WS2a Carry out experiments.

WS2b Make and record observations and measurements, using a range of apparatus and methods.

M4a Translate information between graphical and numeric form.

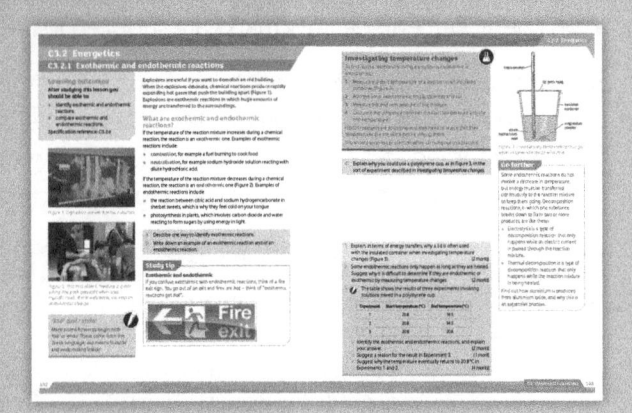

Target	Outcome	Checkpoint	
		Question	Activity
Aiming for GRADE 4	State definitions of the terms exothermic and endothermic.		Plenary 2
	Identify a reaction as exothermic or endothermic when the temperature change is given.	3	Starter 2 Main Plenary 1
	State an example of an exothermic and an endothermic reaction.	B	Starter 1 and 2 Main Plenary 1 and 2
Aiming for GRADE 6	Describe the observations that indicate whether a reaction is exothermic or endothermic.	A	Starter 1 and 2 Main Plenary 2
	Describe an experiment to determine if a reaction is exothermic or endothermic.		Main Homework
	Explain the use of endothermic and exothermic reactions for a stated function.		Starter 1 Plenary 2
Aiming for GRADE 8	Draw a line graph to calculate the maximum temperature change during a reaction, determine when the reaction stopped, and predict the temperature at different times during the reaction.	3	Main
	Evaluate an experiment to classify a reaction as exothermic or endothermic.	C, 1, 2, 3	Main
	Compare endothermic and exothermic reactions.		Starter 1 Plenary 2

Maths
In Main 1 students draw a line graph, read from a line graph, and calculate temperature changes (M4a).

Literacy
In Plenary 2 students make posters to define and exemplify exothermic and endothermic changes. In completing the Homework task students write a method for an experiment to classify a reaction as exothermic or endothermic.

Key words
exothermic, combustion, neutralisation, endothermic

102

C3.2 Energetics

Starter	Support/Extend	Resources
Exothermic and endothermic (5 minutes) Draw a table on the board with the headings Definition, Effect on surrounding temperature, and Example. Use this table to introduce the key terms endothermic and exothermic, talking through each column. Students should copy down the table once it is complete. **Ice and water** (10 minutes) Give student pairs a half-filled cup of icy water and a thermometer. Ask them to record the temperature of the icy water and then to add several large spatula measures of sodium chloride, mix, and observe the temperature of the mixture. Ask students whether the change is chemical or physical (physical), and whether the change is exothermic or endothermic (endothermic). Then set up a demonstration of a similar experiment using a data logger with a temperature probe. Ask students to predict the shape of the graph. Allow the experiment to run throughout the lesson, encouraging students to look at the results throughout.		

Main	Support/Extend	Resources
Investigating temperature changes (40 minutes) Students investigate the temperature change when sodium hydroxide solution and hydrochloric acid react in a sealed polystyrene cup. They can follow the method given in the Student Book. Ask students to design their own results table and record their results in order to draw a graph. Remind them that the scales do not have to start at zero (the y-axis will probably start at about 15 °C). Consider concentrating on evaluating methodology in terms of the reproducibility and repeatability of the evidence generated. Following the practical, point out that one of its purposes was to find out whether the reaction is exothermic or endothermic. State that the fact that the temperature increased initially shows that the reaction is exothermic. **Classify reactions** (15 minutes) Ask pairs of students to use temperature probes, data loggers, or thermometers to monitor the temperature change in and classify a variety of exothermic or endothermic changes. Suitable changes include dissolving ammonium nitrate, citric acid, and sodium hydrogencarbonate; and adding ammonium nitrate to barium hydroxide. Ask students to design their own results and conclusions table to note their observations and classifications.	**Support:** Students may struggle to draw the line of best fit for this reaction, in which case this could be demonstrated on the board. **Extend:** Ask students to write half equations for this reaction.	**Practical:** Investigating temperature changes

Plenary	Support/Extend	Resources
Ice and water results (5 minutes) Review the data-logging results from Starter 2 and ask students to explain why the temperature fell initially, and then rose. **Compare reactions** (10 minutes) Students complete the interactive where they sort statements according to whether they describe endothermic reactions or exothermic reactions. They then review descriptions of reactions and associated temperature changes to decide whether the reaction is endothermic or exothermic.	**Support:** Give students information to cut up and stick on to the correct poster.	**Interactive:** Compare reactions

Homework	Support/Extend	Resources
Write a method for an experiment that will enable you to classify the reaction between dilute hydrochloric acid and magnesium as exothermic or endothermic.		

kerboodle

A Kerboodle highlight for this lesson is **Animation: Exothermic and endothermic reactions**. Refer to the **Content map** on Kerboodle for a full list of resources and assessment.

C3.2.2 Reaction profiles

Specification links:

3.2b Draw and label a reaction profile for an exothermic and an endothermic reaction.

3.2c Explain activation energy as the energy needed for a reaction to occur.

WS1.3b Translate data from one form to another.

WS1.3c Carry out and represent mathematical and statistical analysis.

WS1.3d Represent distributions of results and make estimations of uncertainty.

WS1.3e Interpret observations and other data.

M4a Translate information between graphical and numeric form.

CM3.2i Interpret charts and graphs when dealing with reaction profiles (M4a).

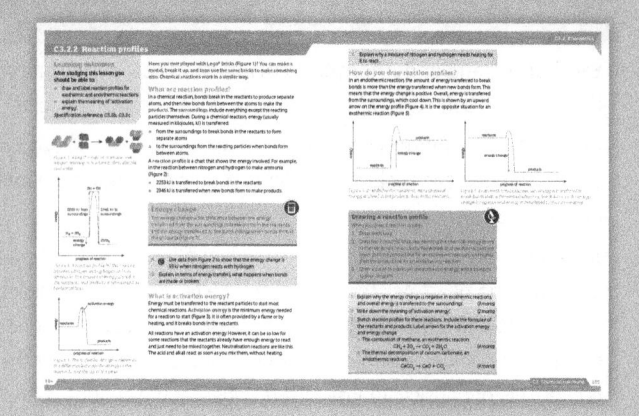

Target	Outcome	Checkpoint	
		Question	Activity
Aiming for GRADE 4 ↓	State a definition of activation energy.	2	Plenary 1
	Identify a reaction as exothermic or endothermic from the reaction profile.		Main 1 and 2 Plenary 1 and 2
	Identify bond breaking as endothermic and bond making as exothermic.	A	Main 1
Aiming for GRADE 6 ↓	Describe activation energy using a reaction profile.		Plenary 2 Homework
	Sketch a general reaction profile for an exothermic and an endothermic reaction.		Main 1 and 2 Homework
	Explain why bond breaking is endothermic and bond making is exothermic.	B	Main 1
Aiming for GRADE 8 ↓	Explain, in terms of bonds, the need for activation energy.	C	Main 1
	Sketch a specific reaction profile for a given reaction.	3	Main 1 and 2 Homework
	Use the particle model to model a chemical reaction in terms of bond breaking and bond making.	1	Main 1

Maths
In Main 1 and Main 2 students draw and interpret a reaction profile (M4a).

Key words
products, surroundings, reaction profile, energy change, activation energy

C3.2 Energetics

Starter	Support/Extend	Resources
Sherbet (5 minutes) Give each student a sample of sherbet to eat on the way into the classroom. Ask students to classify the reaction as exothermic or endothermic, and to justify their classification. **Ethanol spray** (10 minutes) Demonstrate spraying ethanol into a blue Bunsen burner flame to create a fireball. You can add different metal salts to change the colour of the flame. Ask students to classify the reaction as exothermic or endothermic, and to suggest how they know. Ask students to write a balanced symbol equation for the reaction.	**Extend:** Encourage students to include state symbols in their equation.	

Main	Support/Extend	Resources
Reaction profiles (burning hydrogen) (20 minutes) Demonstrate a hydrogen explosion as detailed. Then allow students to test the gas on a small scale themselves. Prepare a boiling tube of hydrogen with a bung in the top. Students should wear chemical splash-proof eye protection and put a lighted splint into the open mouth of the boiling tube. They should observe a pop. This demonstration must be carefully monitored by a teacher or technician. Ask students to write equations for the reaction and then illustrate the reaction in a reaction profile diagram. They should annotate the activation energy and describe this as the energy provided by the flame, and add the actual chemicals which are the reactants and the products.	**Support:** You may wish to use question and answer to complete the task on the board before students copy the information into their notes. **Extend:** Ensure students write balanced symbol equations with state symbols.	**Practical:** Reaction profiles
Reaction profiles (burning methane) (20 minutes) Light a Bunsen burner and turn it to the blue flame. Ask students to write an equation to illustrate this reaction. Then give students a molecular modelling kit. Encourage students to work in small groups to illustrate the combustion of methane by making the models of the reactants and then forming the products. Ask students to explain why energy is needed to break the bonds and then why energy is released when bonds are made. Students should then sketch the reaction profile for this reaction.	**Support:** Supply the balanced symbol equation. Ask students to make the reactants and then rearrange the atoms to make the products. **Extend:** Give each group of students a different chemical reaction to model.	

Plenary	Support/Extend	Resources
Energy changes (5 minutes) Interactive in which students complete a paragraph on the energy changes involved in the making and breaking of bonds. They then label two reaction profile diagrams as endothermic or exothermic, identifying the reactants, products, and activation energy.		**Interactive:** Energy changes
Interpret (10 minutes) Ask students to focus on Figure 2 in the Student Book and determine all the information that they can from the diagram.	**Support:** Prompt students using questions (e.g., 'What are the reactants and the products?', 'What is the word and symbol equation for this reaction?', and 'Is this reaction exothermic or endothermic?'). **Extend:** Ask students to calculate the energy transferred to the surroundings in the reaction, and the activation energy of the reaction.	

Homework	Support/Extend	Resources
Choose a chemical reaction and draw a fully labelled reaction profile for the reaction.		

kerboodle

A Kerboodle highlight for this lesson is **Calculation sheet: Reaction profiles**. Refer to the **Content map** on Kerboodle for a full list of resources and assessment.

HIGHER TIER
C3.2.3 Calculating energy changes

Specification links:

3.2d Calculate energy changes in a chemical reaction by considering bond making and bond breaking energies.

WS1.1b Use models to solve problems, make predictions, and develop scientific explanations and understanding of familiar and unfamiliar facts.

WS1.3b Translate data from one form to another.

WS1.3c Carry out and represent mathematical and statistical analysis.

WS1.4c Use SI units and IUPAC chemical nomenclature unless inappropriate.

M1a Recognise and use expressions in decimal form.

M4a Translate information between graphical and numeric form.

CM3.2ii Use arithmetic computation when calculating energy changes (M1a).

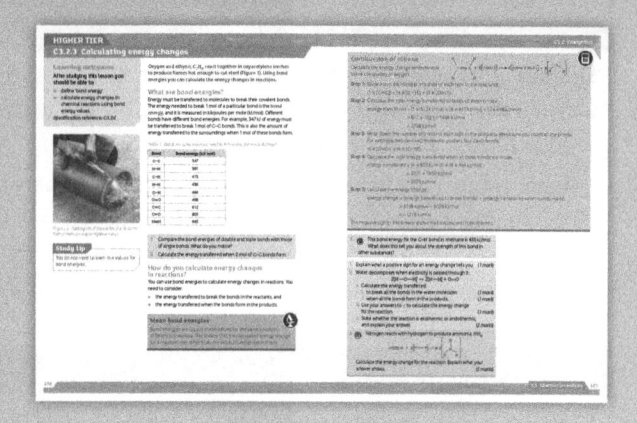

Target	Outcome	Checkpoint	
		Question	Activity
Aiming for GRADE 6	Define the term bond energy.		Starter 1
	Calculate the number and type of bonds in a molecule, given the displayed formula.	2	Main
		3	Plenary 1 and 2
	Use bond energy data to calculate the energy change in a given reaction.	B	Main
		2	Plenary 2
		3	Homework
Aiming for GRADE 8	Compare bond energies for different bonds, and suggest reasons for differences.	A, C, 1	Plenary 2
	Draw displayed formulae of familiar covalent molecules.		Main
			Plenary 2
			Homework
	Explain why the calculated energy change may not be the same as the actual value.		Plenary 1

Maths
In Main students carry out bond energy calculations (M1a). In Starter 2 students draw and interpret a reaction profile (M4a).

Literacy
In Plenary 1 students explain why the calculated energy change for the combustion of ethene is different from the observed value.

Key words
bond energy

C3.2 Energetics

Starter	Support/Extend	Resources
Explain bond energy (5 minutes) Ask students to define bond energy, and then to explain why bond energies always have positive values. **Combustion of ethene** (10 minutes) Ask students to use Student Book section *Combustion of ethene* to draw a labelled reaction profile for the reaction.	**Support:** Remind students of the generic exothermic reaction profile sketched in Plenary 1, C3.2.2.	

Main	Support/Extend	Resources
Calculating bond energies (40 minutes) Go through the worked example in the Student Book of calculating the energy change for the combustion of ethene. Students use the worked example to summarise the steps in performing this calculation: • Draw displayed formulae for the balanced symbol equation. • Total each type of bond on the reactants side. • Total each type of bond on the product side. • Calculate the energy required to break the reactant bonds. • Calculate the energy transferred to the surroundings when the product bonds are made. • *Energy change = energy required to break reactant bonds – energy transferred to the surroundings when products are made.* Students then use their summary to answer further questions.		**Activity:** Calculating bond energies

Plenary	Support/Extend	Resources
Explain the difference (5 minutes) Ask students to suggest why the value calculated from bond energies for the combustion of ethene is different from the value that would be observed from measurements made in the laboratory. **Energy calculations** (10 minutes) Students label a reaction profile, identify true and false statements about breaking and making bonds, and calculate the energy change for some reactions when the balanced symbol equation and mean bond energies are given.	**Extend:** Encourage students to consider experimental error as well as calculation error. **Extend:** You may wish to allow students to complete this review individually, or you could invite teams to compete and give a prize to the winning team.	**Interactive:** Energy calculations

Homework	Support/Extend	Resources
Complete more bond energy calculations.		

kerboodle
A Kerboodle highlight for this lesson is **Maths skills: Bond energies**. Refer to the **Content map** on Kerboodle for a full list of resources and assessment.

Checkpoint
C3.2 Energetics

Overview of C3.2 Energetics

In this chapter students have studied exothermic and endothermic reactions. They should be able to identify a reaction as exothermic or endothermic based on observations, and state examples of each. They should be able to describe an experiment to determine if a reaction is exothermic or endothermic, and explain uses of endothermic and exothermic reactions.

Students should be able to apply the conservation of energy, and understand that an exothermic reaction has lost energy to its surroundings, measured as a temperature rise of the surroundings by a thermometer. Using a reaction profile, students should be able to identify a reaction as exothermic – losing energy to the surroundings, or endothermic – gaining energy from the surroundings. They should also be able to correctly mark the activation energy on a reaction profile, and describe the activation energy for a reaction as the minimum energy the reactant particles must possess before reaction can take place. They should be able to explain why bond breaking is endothermic and bond making is exothermic and relate this to the particle model. Students should link this work with other topics, for example C3.3 *Types of chemical reaction*, C3.4 *Electrolysis*, and C5.3 *Equilibria*.

In studying the higher-tier topic of calculating energy changes, higher-tier students should have studied bond energy, and compared bond energies for different bonds. In using bond energy data to calculate the energy change in a given reaction, they should be able to deduce which bonds are involved and how many.

MyMaths

You can find additional support for the maths skills covered in this chapter on **MyMaths**, including calculations and working with graphs.

kerboodle

For this chapter, the following assessments are available on Kerboodle:
C3.2 Checkpoint quiz: Energetics
C3.2 Progress quiz: Energetics 1
C3.2 Progress quiz: Energetics 2
C3.2 On your marks: Energetics
C3.2 Exam-style questions and mark scheme: Energetics

C3.2 Energetics

Checkpoint follow-up lesson

A student's route through this lesson can be determined using the Checkpoint assessment. Percentage pass marks are supplied in the Checkpoint teacher notes.

For each successive route through it is assumed that the student can perform to their current route as well as previous routes. For example, students working at Aiming for 6 are assumed to be secure in Aiming for 4 knowledge and understanding and working towards achieving all the learning objectives for Aiming for 6.

	Aiming for 4	Aiming for 6	Aiming for 8
Learning outcomes	Classify reactions as exothermic or endothermic based on temperature data.	Draw a labelled reaction profile for endothermic and exothermic reactions.	Justify a classification of a chemical reaction as endothermic or exothermic.
	Describe a chemical reaction as bonds breaking in the reactants and bonds being made in the products.	Explain the need for activation energy in a chemical reaction.	Calculate the energy change in a reaction using bond energy information.
Starter	**Label (5 minutes)** Sketch the reaction profile for an exothermic reaction and for an endothermic reaction on the board. Ask individual students to label the reactants, the products, energy change, activation energy, exothermic reaction, and endothermic reaction.		
	Formulae (10 minutes) Provide small groups of students with a re-useable hand warmer and a single-use sports cool pack. Students should discuss their observations as they use these devices, classify each change as an exothermic or endothermic change, and justify their classifications.		
Differentiated checkpoint activity	**Activity 1 MP3 revision file (40 minutes)** Students will need access to sound-recording equipment such as tablet PCs, mobile phones, or a computer with a microphone and speakers or headphones. Explain that students will be working in differentiated groups to produce a script for a spoken MP3 sound file to revise and summarise the topic of energetics. Students answer each question on the differentiated worksheets. They could record their work on their own device and email it to the teacher. The best files could be uploaded to the VLE for other students to share.		
	The Aiming for 4 sheet provides structured activities to support students with revising and summarising the information about energetics.	The Aiming for 6 sheet provides questions to guide the content students include in their monologue.	The Aiming for 8 sheet provides fewer prompt questions which cover more advanced content.
	Kerboodle resource: C3.2 Checkpoint follow-up: Aiming for 4, C3.2 Checkpoint follow-up: Aiming for 6, C3.2 Checkpoint follow-up: Aiming for 8		
Plenary	**MP3 review (10 minutes)** Review the lesson by making a composite MP3 file. Ask one group of students to read their introduction, a second group to read their main section, a third group to read their questions and answers, and a final group to read their summary section.		
	Blurb (5 minutes) Ask students to summarise their MP3 file in a catchy blurb which could be used on a website to encourage students to click and download the file.		
Progression	Aiming for 4 students should be able to define exothermic and endothermic reactions and describe a model for a chemical reaction. Students may like to begin to use energy profile diagrams for familiar reactions such as the combustion of hydrogen to form water.	Aiming for 6 students should be able to explain the difference between endothermic and exothermic reactions, using labelled reaction profiles with little prompting. Students should be able to articulate the need for activation energy in a chemical reaction and relate this to a reaction profile.	Aiming for 8 students should be able to justify the classification of a given reaction as exothermic or endothermic, and be comfortable constructing and explaining reaction profiles for both kinds of reaction. Students should be able to calculate the energy change for a reaction using bond energy data.

C3.3 Types of chemical reaction
C3.3.1 Redox reactions

Specification links:

3.3a Explain reduction and oxidation in terms of loss or gain of oxygen, identifying which species are oxidised and which are reduced.

3.3b Explain reduction and oxidation in terms of gain or loss of electrons, identifying which species are oxidised and which are reduced. **H**

WS1.4a Use scientific vocabulary, terminology, and definitions.

M1c Use ratios, fractions, and percentages.

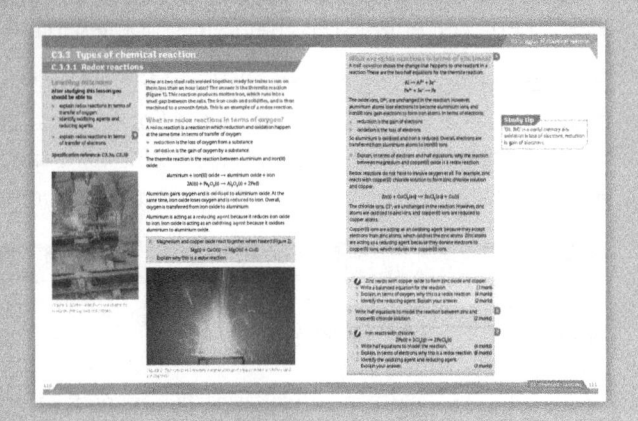

Target	Outcome	Checkpoint	
		Question	Activity
Aiming for GRADE 4	State definitions of reduction, oxidation, and redox.		Main 1
			Plenary 1 and 2
	State an example of a redox reaction.		Starter 1 and 2
			Main 1 and 2
			Plenary 1 and 2
	Describe an oxidising agent and a reducing agent.	1	Starter 1
			Main 1 and 2
			Plenary 1
Aiming for GRADE 6	Explain reduction, oxidation, and redox in terms of electrons.	A, B, 3	Main 1 and 2
			Plenary 1 and 2
			Homework
	Balance half equations.		Main 1 and 2
			Plenary 2
	Identify substances as oxidising agents or reducing agents, given the balanced symbol equation.	1, 3	Starter 1
			Main 1
			Plenary 1 and 2
Aiming for GRADE 8	Write balanced half equations to illustrate reduction and oxidation.	B, 2, 3	Main 1 and 2
			Plenary 2
			Homework
	Explain why oxidation or reduction does not happen in isolation.		Main 1
	Construct balanced symbol equations by combining half equations and adding spectator ions.		Main 1 and 2 **H**

Maths
Throughout this lesson students balance half equations (M1c).

Literacy
In Plenary 2 students justify which substance is being oxidised and which is being reduced in a reaction, and explain why it is a redox reaction.

Key words
redox, reduction, oxidation, oxidised, reduced, reducing agent, oxidising agent, half equation

C3.3 Types of chemical reaction

Starter	Support/Extend	Resources
Screaming jelly baby (5 minutes) Demonstrate the screaming jelly baby experiment. Explain that molten potassium chlorate is an oxidising agent that rapidly oxidises the sugar in jelly babies. **Microscale displacement** (10 minutes) Give students a laminated sheet of paper. Ask students to use a dropping pipette to drop three drops of iron(III) sulfate onto the paper, and then add one or two magnesium turnings. Prompt students to note the colour change. Invite students to use a magnet to move the metal piece around in the reaction mixture. Ask students to write an equation to summarise this reaction.	**Extend:** Ask students to write the combustion reaction for a simple sugar with an oxidising agent simplified to [O].	

Main	Support/Extend	Resources
Best thermite reaction (15 minutes) Remind students of the thermite reaction demonstrated in C3.1.5. Demonstrate two or three different methods for the thermite reaction and ask students to justify which is the best. Point out that the reaction is a redox reaction, and write a balanced equation on the board. Ask students to identify the oxidising and reducing agents in the reaction, and to explain why oxidation and reduction cannot happen in isolation. **Reduction of copper(II) oxide** (25 minutes) Allow pairs or small groups of students to use carbon powder to reduce copper(II) oxide. Ask students to mix 1 spatula measure of powdered copper(II) oxide with 2 spatula measures of powdered charcoal (carbon) in a crucible, then cover the surface of the mixture with a 0.5 cm layer of powdered charcoal. Students then place the crucible in a pipe-clay triangle over a blue Bunsen burner flame and heat strongly for 10 minutes. Ask students to allow the crucible and contents to cool, then, using tongs, add the contents to a half-full beaker of cold water and swirl the beaker. The copper will sink to the bottom and the carbon will make a suspension. Students should add more water and keep on pouring and swirling so that only the denser material is left at the bottom of the beaker. Students should decant the water and observe the copper at the bottom of the beaker. Ask students to write a balanced symbol equation to model the reaction. Students should also identify the reducing agent.	**Extend:** Ask students to use ideas about electron transfer to justify why the thermite reaction can be classified as a redox reaction, and to write and balance half equations to show the oxidation and reduction that occur in this reaction. Then ask students to use their balanced half equations to explain why oxidation or reduction cannot happen in isolation. [H] **Extend:** Ask students to write half equations for these reactions, and to use ideas about electron transfer to explain what happens to the copper when copper(II) oxide is reduced. [H]	**Practical:** Reduction of copper(II) oxide

Plenary	Support/Extend	Resources
Sorting redox reactions (5 minutes) Show students a series of statements and have them sort them according to whether they describe reduction, oxidation, or redox. **Displacement demo** (10 minutes) Demonstrate a displacement reaction by adding a coil of magnesium ribbon to a test-tube half-filled with iron(III) sulfate. Ask students to state and justify which substance is being oxidised and which is being reduced, and to explain why this is a redox reaction.	**Support:** Do not use statements that contain electrons or half equations. **Extend:** Explain in terms of electrons why this is a redox reaction, and write half equations. [H]	**Interactive:** Redox reactions

Homework	Support/Extend	Resources
Write an equation to illustrate: 1 oxidation in terms of gain of oxygen 2 oxidation in terms of loss of hydrogen 3 reduction in terms of loss of oxygen 4 reduction in terms of gain of hydrogen 5 a redox reaction.	**Extend:** Write half equations to illustrate: [H] 1 oxidation in terms of loss of electrons 2 reduction in terms of gain of electrons.	

C3.3.2 The pH scale

Specification links:

3.3c Recall that acids form hydrogen ions when they dissolve in water, and solutions of alkalis contain hydroxide ions.

3.3h Recall that relative acidity and alkalinity are measured by pH.

3.3k Describe techniques and apparatus used to measure pH.

WS1.4a Use scientific vocabulary, terminology, and definitions.

M2c Construct and interpret frequency tables and diagrams, bar charts, and histograms.

CM3.3i Understand that arithmetic computation, ratio, percentage, and multistep calculations permeate quantitative chemistry (M1a, M1c, M1d).

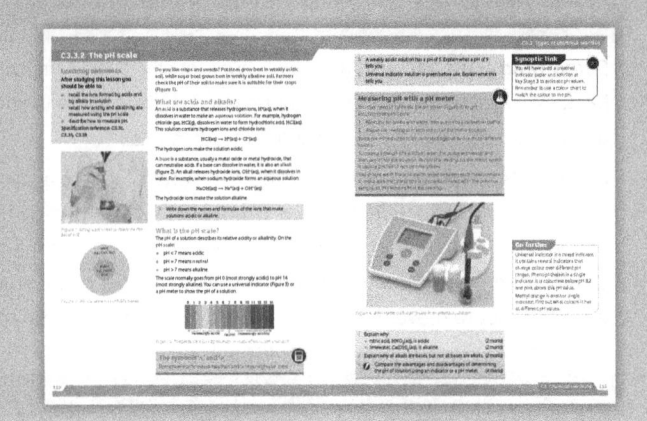

Target	Outcome	Checkpoint	
		Question	Activity
Aiming for GRADE 4 ↓	State definitions of an acid and an alkali and give examples.		Starter 1 / Main / Plenary 2
	Identify a solution as acidic or alkaline given its pH.	B, C	Main / Plenary 1 and 2
	Safely use an indicator to classify a substance as an acid or an alkali.		Starter 2 / Main
Aiming for GRADE 6 ↓	Explain the terms acid and alkali in terms of ions.	A, 1	Main / Plenary 1
	Describe a method to use universal indicator or a pH probe to determine the pH of a solution.		Main / Homework
	Explain the pH scale in terms of acidity and alkalinity.	B, C	Main
Aiming for GRADE 8 ↓	Use ionic equations to explain how acids produce hydrogen ions and alkalis produce hydroxide ions in solution.		Main / Plenary 1
	Evaluate the use of indicators or pH probes and data loggers to determine the pH of a solution.	3	Starter 2 / Main / Homework
	Explain the difference between an alkali and a base.	2	Plenary 2

Maths
In Plenary 2 students complete a Venn diagram (M2c).

Literacy
In completing the Homework task, students write a method for finding the pH of a substance.

Key words
acid, aqueous solution, base, alkali, pH, pH scale, neutral, calibrate, buffer

C3.3 Types of chemical reaction

Starter	Support/Extend	Resources
5, 4, 3, 2, 1 (5 minutes) Ask students to use their general knowledge and information from KS3 to write a list of: five everyday acids, four bases used in a laboratory, three properties of acids, two properties of alkalis, and one example of a neutral substance. Students could show you their answers on mini-whiteboards for instant feedback and praise. **Home-made anthocyanin indicator** (10 minutes) Give students three cubes of fresh beetroot. Wearing eye protection, students should place one cube in dilute hydrochloric acid, one in dilute sodium hydroxide solution, and one into a neutral buffer. Ask students to make observations and then to swap the beetroot chunks into different solutions to illustrate that the colour changes reversibly. Ask students to suggest what the beetroot is behaving as (an acid/base indicator).	**Support:** Use questions and answers to build up a class list on the board. **Extend:** Encourage students to use correct chemical formulae for their answers where possible.	

Main	Support/Extend	Resources
Investigating pH scale (30 minutes) Students can appreciate the dilution of the pH scale by investigating the colours of universal indicator in solutions of different concentrations. Ask pairs or small groups of students to label 13 test-tubes with numbers from 1 to 13 and carry out the following steps: 1 Put 10 cm³ of 0.1 mol/dm³ hydrochloric acid into the first test-tube. 2 Take 1 cm³ of the solution from test-tube 1 and add it to test-tube 2 with 9 cm³ of de-ionised water. 3 Take 1 cm³ of the solution from test-tube 2 and add it to test-tube 3 with 9 cm³ of de-ionised water. 4 Repeat this for the first 6 test-tubes. 5 Put deionised water into test-tube 7. 6 Put 0.1 mol/dm³ of sodium hydroxide solution into test-tube 13 and successively dilute as before to fill the remaining test-tubes 12–8. 7 Add a few drops of universal indicator to each tube. Students should see the full spectrum of colours of the indicator. Students then work in pairs or small groups to test the pH of a range of solutions. Students should place a few drops of each solution to be tested in a well of a dimple dish. Then ask students to add a few drops of universal indicator solution or dip in strips of universal indicator paper. Students should compare the resultant colour with Figure 3 to determine the pH and classify the solution as acidic, alkaline, or neutral. Ask students to design a results table in which to record their work. Finally, explain the terms acid and alkali in terms of ions – an acid forms hydrogen ions when it dissolves in water, and solutions of alkalis contain hydroxide ions. Use ionic equations to explain how these ions are produced in solution.	**Extend:** Ask students to draw particle models of the different concentrations of acids and alkali solutions. **Extend:** Ask students to write ionic equations to explain: 1 how hydrogen chloride produces hydrogen ions when it dissolves in water to form hydrochloric acid 2 how sodium hydroxide forms hydroxide ions when it dissolves in water. **Support:** Use household substances rather than laboratory substances. **Extend:** Ask students to half-fill test-tubes with the solutions to be tested and use a pH probe.	**Practical:** Investigating the pH scale

Plenary	Support/Extend	Resources
Classify substances (5 minutes) Give each student a red, a blue, and a green card. Read out statements, or the names of substances, or chemical formulae, and ask students to hold up a red card for acid, a blue card for base or alkali, and a green card for neutral substances. **The pH scale** (10 minutes) Provide students with pH values, colours of universal indicator, and other statements that describe acids and alkalis. Students have to classify whether each statement or value is describing an acid or an alkali.	**Extend:** Include ions and ionic equations.	**Interactive:** The pH scale

Homework	Support/Extend	Resources
Write a method for an experiment to determine the pH of a substance.	**Extend:** Justify your method.	

kerboodle

A Kerboodle highlight for this lesson is **Maths skills: Plotting a pH curve**. Refer to the **Content map** on Kerboodle for a full list of resources and assessment.

C3 Chemical reactions 113

C3.3.3 Neutralisation

Specification links:

3.3d Describe neutralisation as an acid reacting with an alkali or a base to form a salt plus water.

3.3e Recognise that aqueous neutralisation reactions can be generalised to hydrogen ions reacting with hydroxide ions to form water.

WS1.4a Use scientific vocabulary, terminology, and definitions.

M1c Use ratios, fractions, and percentages.

CM3.3i Understand that arithmetic computation, ratio, percentage, and multistep calculations permeate quantitative chemistry (M1a, M1c, M1d).

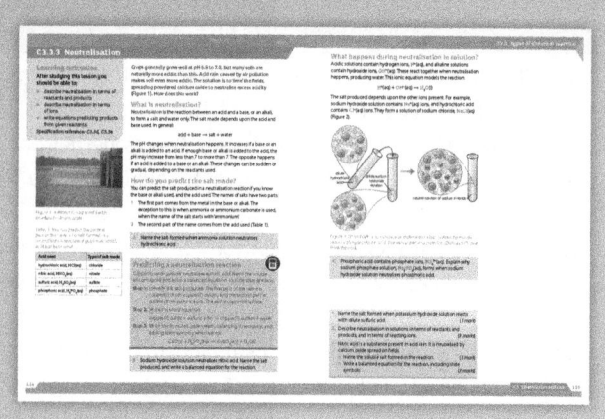

Target	Outcome	Checkpoint	
		Question	Activity
Aiming for GRADE 4 ↓	State a definition of neutralisation.		Starter 2, Main
	Describe some uses of neutralisation.		Main, Plenary 2
	Predict the name of a salt made from a named alkali and common strong acids.	A, B, 1, 3	Starter 1, Main
Aiming for GRADE 6 ↓	Describe neutralisation in terms of reactants, products, and reacting ions.	2	Main
	Write a balanced symbol equation to describe a neutralisation reaction.	B	Starter 2, Main
	State the formula of the salt made from a given alkali and strong acid.		Starter 1 and 2, Main
Aiming for GRADE 8 ↓	Write an ionic equation for the neutralisation of an alkali by an acid.		Plenary 1, Main
	Write balanced symbol equations with state symbols for unfamiliar neutralisation reactions.	3	Starter 1, Main
	Use the particle model to explain how the products of neutralisation form.	C	Main, Plenary 1

Maths
In Main 1 students use ratios to compare the volumes of reacting solutions in neutralisation reactions (M1c).

Literacy
In Plenary 2 students write an outline method to prepare a sample of potassium nitrate.

Key words
neutralisation, salt

C3.3 Types of chemical reaction

Starter

Acid table (5 minutes)   Ask students to complete a table of acids, their formulae, the type of salt they make, and an example of a salt made from each acid.

Acid	Formula	Type of salt	Example
hydrochloric	HCl	chloride	sodium chloride
nitric	HNO_3	nitrate	sodium nitrate
sulfuric	H_2SO_4	sulfate	sodium sulfate
phosphoric	H_3PO_4	phosphate	sodium phosphate

Support/Extend

Extend: Ask students to include the formulae of the salts.

Egg race (10 minutes)   Ask pairs of students, wearing eye protection, to put 10 cm³ of dilute hydrochloric acid and a few drops of universal indicator solution into a 100 cm³ beaker. Pairs of students then race to make a neutral solution by adding dilute sodium hydroxide solution to the beaker. If they overshoot, students can add more acid.

Extend: Ask students to write the balanced symbol equation for the reaction, with state symbols.

Main

Investigating neutralisation (40 minutes)   Ask pairs or small groups of students to use a measuring cylinder to transfer 15 cm³ of sodium hydroxide solution and a few drops of universal indicator into a conical flask. Students then slowly add hydrochloric acid from a burette until a neutral solution is achieved. They will need to record the start and end volume on the burette to calculate the volume of solution added. Students then mix activated charcoal with the solution to remove the universal indicator, filter the solution, and then crystallise the salt. Ask students to explain the reaction in terms of particles, and to write a balanced symbol equation, with state symbols, to describe the reaction. Students should also name the salt they have made.

Support/Extend

Support: Monitor the change in pH using a pH meter or datalogger with pH probe.

Resources

Practical: Investigating neutralisation

Plenary

Explain (5 minutes)   Ask students to justify the fact that the ionic equation for the neutralisation reaction between an acid and an alkali is always the same.

Neutralisation (10 minutes)   Provide students with a list of acid and metal oxide reactions. Students identify the name and formula of the salt that will be formed.

Support/Extend

Support: Ask students to state some uses of neutralisation reactions.

Resources

Interactive: Neutralisation

Homework

Explain the steps in the method to make copper(II) sulfate from copper(II) oxide and sulfuric acid, as introduced in Student Book section *Predicting a neutralisation reaction*.

---

kerboodle

A Kerboodle highlight for this lesson is **Literacy sheet: Making salts**. Refer to the **Content map** on Kerboodle for a full list of resources and assessment.

C3.3.4 Reactions of acids

Specification links:

3.3f Recall that carbonates and some metals react with acids, and write balanced equations predicting products from given reactants.

WS1.4a Use scientific vocabulary, terminology, and definitions.

M1c Use ratios, fractions, and percentages.

M2c Construct and interpret frequency tables and diagrams, bar charts, and histograms.

CM3.3i Understand that arithmetic computation, ratio, percentage, and multistep calculations permeate quantitative chemistry (M1a, M1c, M1d).

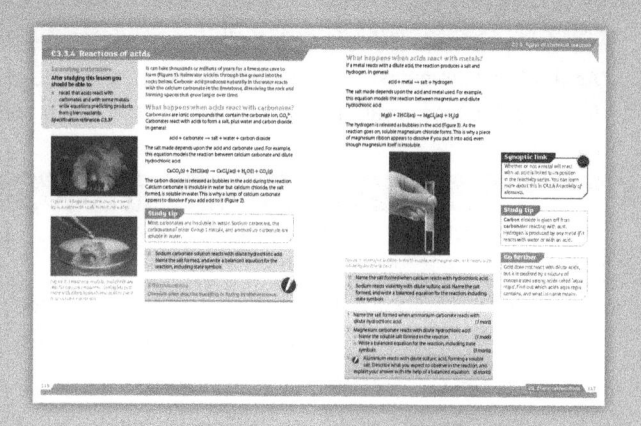

Target	Outcome	Checkpoint	
		Question	Activity
Aiming for GRADE 4	Predict the names of the products of a reaction between a metal or a metal carbonate and an acid.	B, C, 1, 2	Main 1 and 2
	Write a word equation to model a reaction between a metal or a metal carbonate and an acid.		Main 1 and 2, Plenary 1, Homework
	Describe how to test and identify a gas made when a metal or a metal carbonate reacts with an acid.		Starter 2
Aiming for GRADE 6	Predict the observations that might be made during a reaction between a metal or a metal carbonate and an acid.	3	Main 1 and 2, Homework
	Write a balanced symbol equation to model a reaction between a metal or a metal carbonate and an acid.	3	Main 1 and 2, Homework
	Describe how to make and collect a dry sample of a named salt from a reaction between a metal or a metal carbonate and an acid.		Main 1
Aiming for GRADE 8	Explain why the reaction between a metal or a metal carbonate and an acid is classified as a neutralisation reaction.		Main 1 and 2, Plenary 1
	Write a balanced symbol equation, including state symbols, to model a reaction between a metal or a metal carbonate and an acid.	A, C, 2	Main 1 and 2, Homework
	Explain how the reactions of metals and metal carbonates with acids can be used to determine the reactivity of the metal.		Main 1 and 2

Maths
In Starter 2 (Extend), Main 1 and Main 2 Students generate balanced symbol equations (M1c). In Plenary 2 students complete a Venn diagram (M2c).

Literacy
In Starter 1 students describe observations using their senses.

Key words
carbonates, effervescence

C3.3 Types of chemical reaction

Starter	Support/Extend	Resources
Make observations (5 minutes) Ask students, wearing eye protection, to half-fill a test-tube with hydrochloric acid and to add one small piece of calcium metal. Students make observations, ensuring that they note any temperature change, effervescence, movement of the piece of metal, and how it seems to disappear. **Determine the gas** (10 minutes) Give students two boiling tubes of carbon dioxide labelled A, and two boiling tubes of hydrogen labelled B. Ask students to add about 1 cm³ of limewater to one A tube and one B tube, and observe. Then ask students to introduce a lighted splint into each of the second A and B tubes, and observe again. Ask students to identify the gases formed, and justify their answers.	**Support:** Ensure that students note observations made using their senses, rather than conclusions about the products that have been formed. **Extend:** Write the balanced symbol equations for the reaction between limewater and carbon dioxide, and between hydrogen and oxygen.	

Main	Support/Extend	Resources
Reactions of metal carbonates with hydrochloric acid (25 minutes) Ask pairs of students to prepare one chloride salt by reacting 25 cm³ of 0.50 mol/dm³ hydrochloric acid with about 1 spatula measure of one of the following metal carbonates: copper(II) carbonate, zinc carbonate, calcium carbonate, or sodium carbonate. The gas produced can be bubbled through limewater to show that it is carbon dioxide. When the reaction is complete, ask students to filter the mixture into a second conical flask, pour the solution into an evaporating basin, and heat it until the solution has halved in volume. Leave the solution in a warm place for crystallisation to occur. Point out that, in each reaction, the carbonate has neutralised the acid. Ask students to write a balanced symbol equation, with state symbols, for the reaction they have carried out, as well as for the reactions of other pairs. When crystals have formed (next lesson), allow students time to look at each other's crystals. **Microscale reactivity** (15 minutes) Ask students to put a piece each of copper, zinc, magnesium, and calcium into separate dimples in a dimple dish. Then, ask students to add a few drops of a dilute acid (e.g., hydrochloric acid, nitric acid, or sulfuric acid) using a dropping pipette, and observe. Ask students to write a balanced symbol equation with state symbols to model each reaction, and then list the metals in order of reactivity.	**Extend:** Discuss the reactivity of the metal carbonates. **Support:** Ask students to write only word equations for these reactions.	**Practical:** Reactions of metal carbonates with hydrochloric acid

Plenary	Support/Extend	Resources
Reactions of acids (10 minutes) Interactive where students complete the general word equation for the reaction of an acid and a metal to form a salt and hydrogen. They then order sentences to explain how salts are made. **Venn diagram** (10 minutes) Ask students to draw a Venn diagram with a large circle labelled 'bases' and a smaller circle inside this labelled 'alkalis', as seen in C3.3.2, Plenary 2. Then ask students to write the metal carbonates used during the lesson, and those mentioned in the Student Book, in the correct part of the diagram.	**Support:** Recap the definitions of the terms base and alkali.	**Interactive:** Reactions of acids

Homework	Support/Extend	Resources
Predict the observations that might be made during the reaction between magnesium and phosphoric acid, and write an equation for the reaction.		

kerboodle
A Kerboodle highlight for this lesson is **Bump up your grade: Reactions of acids.** Refer to the **Content map** on Kerboodle for a full list of resources and assessment.

The Practical Skills lesson for PAG *7 Production of salts* could follow this lesson.

HIGHER TIER
C3.3.5 Hydrogen ions and pH

Specification links:

3.3i Describe neutrality and relative acidity and alkalinity in terms of the effect of the concentration of hydrogen ions on the numerical value of pH (whole numbers only).

3.3j Recall that as hydrogen ion concentration increases by a factor of ten, the pH value of a solution decreases by a factor of one.

WS1.1b Use models to solve problems, make predictions, and to develop scientific observations and understanding of familiar and unfamiliar facts.

WS1.4a Use scientific vocabulary, terminology, and definitions.

M4a Translate information between graphical and numeric form.

M4c Plot two variables from experimental or other data.

CM3.3i Understand that arithmetic computation, ratio, percentage, and multistep calculations permeate quantitative chemistry (M1a, M1c, M1d).

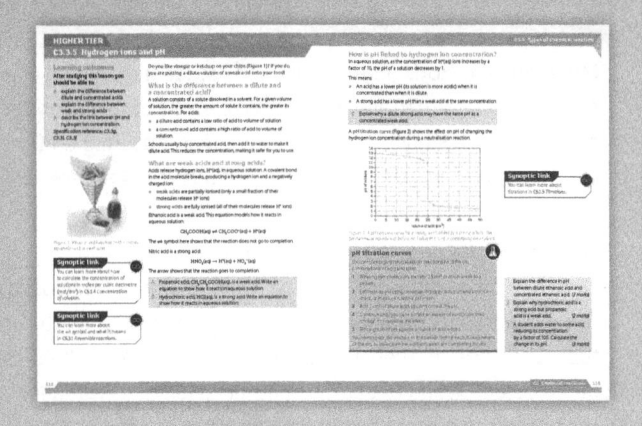

Target	Outcome	Checkpoint	
		Question	Activity
Aiming for GRADE 6 ↓	Describe what is meant by a strong acid and a weak acid.	A, B	Plenary 1
	Describe how an acid can be dilute or concentrated.		Plenary 2
	Collect data to plot a pH curve.		Main
Aiming for GRADE 8 ↓	Explain the difference between a strong acid and a weak acid.	C, 2	Starter 2
			Plenary 1
	Explain the difference between a concentrated acid or alkali and a dilute acid or alkali.	1	Plenary 2
	Interpret pH curves to determine the titre and the strength of reactants.	3	Starter 1
			Main

Maths
In Main 2 students plot a pH curve and draw a line of best fit (M4a, M4c).

Key words
concentration, dilute, concentrated, weak acids, strong acids, pH titration curve

118

C3.3 Types of chemical reaction

Starter	Support/Extend	Resources
Interpret a pH graph (5 minutes) Ask students to look at Figure 2 and interpret the graph. Students should state the dependent and independent variables and their units, and describe the shape of the graph. **Particle diagrams** (10 minutes) Ask students to draw particle diagrams to model a strong acid and a weak acid, using a red circle for a H$^+$ ion, a green circle for the negative ion (A$^-$), a yellow circle for the undissociated acid (HA), and a blue circle for a water molecule.	**Extend:** Ask students to draw particle diagrams of dilute and concentrated strong acids and dilute and concentrated weak acids.	

Main	Support/Extend	Resources
Obtaining a pH curve (40 minutes) Explain that students are going to add hydrochloric acid to sodium hydroxide solution. Ask students to predict how the pH will change as 1 cm^3 increments are added of acid. Then allow pairs of students to carry out the practical as described below: 1 Fill a burette with hydrochloric acid to the 0 cm^3 mark. Using a burette clamp, support the burette over a beaker. 2 Measure 20 cm^3 of sodium hydroxide solution and place this in the beaker. Use the pH probe to measure the pH. 3 Add 1 cm^3 of hydrochloric acid from the burette. Swirl the mixture and record the pH. 4 Repeat, adding 1 cm^3 measures of hydrochloric acid until 25 cm^3 of acid have been added. Ask students to draw a line graph with a line of best fit to display their results.	**Support:** Allow students to use a data logger to record the data. This could also be used to plot the graph. **Extend:** Ask students to annotate areas of their graph to explain why the pH changes in terms of which ion is in excess.	**Practical:** Obtaining a pH curve

Plenary	Support/Extend	Resources
Strong and weak acids (5 minutes) Interactive in which students complete the paragraph to describe the difference between strong and weak acids, and how the pH of an acid is affected by acid strength and concentration. Then give students a list of acids to classify as strong or weak acids. For example: • Hydrochloric acid (strong) • Citric acid (weak) • Ethanoic acid (weak) • Sulfuric acid (strong) • Nitric acid (strong) **Concentrated versus dilute** (10 minutes) Wearing eye protection, demonstrate placing 10 cm^3 of 0.1 mol/dm^3 hydrochloric acid in a 250 cm^3 beaker. Add water to dilute the acid, using a pH probe to monitor the pH. Ask students to explain what is observed. Students should recognise that the added water decreases the concentration of H$^+$ ions, increasing the pH.	**Extend:** Give students the formula for each example and ask them to write a balanced symbol equation to illustrate the ionisation that occurs when the acid is in solution. **Extend:** Encourage students to use numbers to explain the dilution observed, and to describe the relationship between concentration and pH.	**Interactive:** Strong and weak acids

Homework	Support/Extend	Resources
Predict the shape of the pH curve for the addition of potassium hydroxide solution to nitric acid, and write an equation.		

kerboodle

A Kerboodle highlight for this lesson is **Calculation sheet: pH and H$^+$ concentration**. Refer to the **Content map** on Kerboodle for a full list of resources and assessment.

Checkpoint
C3.3 Types of chemical reaction

Overview of C3.3 Types of chemical reaction

In this chapter students have studied both redox and neutralisation reactions, and the pH scale. They should be able to define reduction, oxidation, and redox reactions, and give examples of redox reactions and oxidising and reducing agents. Students consider redox reactions in terms of loss or gain of oxygen, and higher-tier students go on to explain the process as gain and loss of electrons. These students should be able to write balanced half equations for reduction and oxidation, combine them, and add spectator ions to represent redox reactions.

In studying the pH scale, students should be able to define an acid and an alkali and give examples of these. They should recognise a solution as acidic or alkaline given its pH, and be able to use an indicator or pH probe safely to determine the pH of a solution. They should associate an increase in acidity with a decrease in pH number.

Students should be able to define neutralisation as an acid reacting with an alkali or a base to form a salt plus water, and describe some uses of neutralisation. They should be able to predict the salt produced from the neutralisation reaction between a given alkali and strong acid, and use equations to describe such reactions. They should recognise that aqueous neutralisation reactions can be generalised to hydrogen ions reacting with hydroxide ions to form water.

Students have studied the reactions of acids with metals and with metal carbonates, and should be able to use equations to model these reactions. They should have tested and identified the gas produced. Students have made and collected a dry sample of a named salt from such a reaction.

A higher-tier topic covers strong and weak acids and alkalis, and dilute and concentrated acids alkalis. Students should be able to explain the difference between these, and also to interpret pH curves to determine the titre and strength of reactants in a neutralisation reaction.

MyMaths

You can find additional support for the maths skills covered in this chapter on **MyMaths**, including calculations using ratios, using a Venn diagram, and working with graphs.

PAGs

All students are expected to have carried out the PAG 7 *Production of salts*. A full lesson plan for each PAG is provided in the Practical skills chapter. PAG 7 *Production of salts* should be completed after lesson C3.3.4 *Reactions of acids*.

kerboodle

For this chapter, the following assessments are available on Kerboodle:
C3.3 Checkpoint quiz: Types of chemical reaction
C3.3 Progress quiz: Types of chemical reaction 1
C3.3 Progress quiz: Types of chemical reaction 2
C3.3 On your marks: Types of chemical reaction
C3.3 Exam-style questions and mark scheme: Types of chemical reaction

C3.3 Types of chemical reaction

Checkpoint follow-up lesson

A student's route through this lesson can be determined using the Checkpoint assessment. Percentage pass marks are supplied in the Checkpoint teacher notes.

For each successive route through it is assumed that the student can perform to their current route as well as previous routes. For example, students working at Aiming for 6 are assumed to be secure in Aiming for 4 knowledge and understanding and working towards achieving all the learning objectives for Aiming for 6.

	Aiming for 4	Aiming for 6	Aiming for 8
Learning outcomes	Describe oxidation and reduction in terms of gain and loss of oxygen.	Explain a classification of a reaction that is oxidation and reduction.	Explain reduction and oxidation in terms of electrons and using half equations.
	Describe an acid and an alkali.	Describe and explain neutralisation reactions using prose and equations.	Explain the difference between strength and concentration.
	Recall that pH measures relative alkalinity and acidity.	Outline how to measure the pH of a chemical.	Explain how the concentration of hydrogen ions changes as you move through the pH scale from 0 to 14.
Starter	**Colour code (5 minutes)** Give each student a red, green, and blue card to represent acid, neutral, and alkali, respectively. Then provide examples of chemicals (either images or actual bottles of chemicals) and ask students to hold up a card to show the classification of the chemical.		
	Define (5 minutes) Read out statements and examples of oxidation and reduction. Students should shout out a classification for each statement. Encourage a scribe to note the statements into a table and allow students to copy this table into their notes.		
Differentiated checkpoint activity	**Activity 1 Poster (45 minutes)** Explain that students will be producing a puzzle to summarise the topic *Types of chemical reaction*. Students answer each question on the differentiated worksheets.		
	Aiming for 4 students produce a word search. The sheet provides structured tasks to support them in producing their word search.	Aiming for 6 students write a crossword. The sheet provides clues and an outline of the crossword grid to help them.	Aiming for 8 students make a puzzle. The sheet provides prompts for the students to consider when designing their puzzle. Students may need squared paper.
	Kerboodle resource: C3.3 Checkpoint follow-up: Aiming for 4, C3.3 Checkpoint follow-up: Aiming for 6, C3.3 Checkpoint follow-up: Aiming for 8		
Plenary	**Puzzle review (5 minutes)** Ask students to work in small groups to contrast and compare their puzzles. Each group should choose the best puzzle and justify their choice. The best puzzles can be photocopied and used as revision homework.		
	Annotate (5 minutes) Give students an image, such as a person taking a heartburn remedy, a camp fire, or someone removing rust from a rusty bike. Ask students to annotate these to show if they depict oxidation, reduction, or neutralisation reactions.		
Progression	Aiming for 4 students should be able to define oxidation and reduction reactions and give examples of each. Students could begin to refine their definitions of oxidation and reduction by considering electrons, and define neutralisation.	Aiming for 6 students should be able to describe neutralisation reactions and refine their definition of oxidation and reduction reactions. Students could be extended by using equations to illustrate different chemical reactions.	Aiming for 8 students should be able to explain the difference between strength and concentration. Students could begin to use the particle model to illustrate these concepts.

C3.4 Electrolysis
C3.4.1 Electrolysis of molten salts

Specification links:

3.4b Predict the products of electrolysis of binary ionic compounds in the molten state.

3.4d Describe electrolysis in terms of the ions present and reactions at the electrodes.

WS1.2a Use scientific theories and explanations to develop hypotheses.

WS1.2b Plan experiments or devise procedures to make observations, produce or characterise a substance, test hypotheses, check data, or explore phenomena.

WS1.2c Apply knowledge of a range of techniques, instruments, apparatus, and materials to select those appropriate to the experiment.

WS1.4a Use scientific vocabulary, terminology, and definitions.

M1c Use ratios, fractions, and percentages.

CM3.4i Use arithmetic computation and ratio when determining empirical formulae and balancing equations (M1a, M1c).

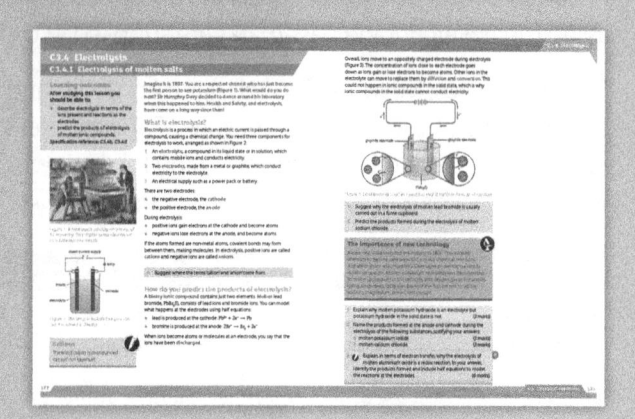

Target	Outcome	Checkpoint	
		Question	Activity
Aiming for GRADE 4	Explain why solid compounds of a metal with a non-metal do not conduct electricity.	1	Main
			Plenary 2
	State that electrolysis breaks ionic compounds down into their component elements.		Starter 1
			Main
	Predict the products of electrolysis.	B, C	Main
			Plenary 1
			Homework
Aiming for GRADE 6	Describe the components of an electrolysis circuit, and how to mobilise the ions in the electrolyte.	1	Main
	Describe the process of electrolysis.		Main
	Predict the products at the anode and the cathode during the electrolysis of molten ionic compounds.	C, 2	Main
			Plenary 1
			Homework
Aiming for GRADE 8	Explain why electrolysis provides evidence for the existence of ions.		Main
			Plenary 2
	Explain the process of electrolysis in detail.		Main
	Write half equations for the reactions that occur at the anode and the cathode, and explain in terms of electron transfer why these are redox reactions.	3	Main
			Plenary 1
			Homework

Maths
Throughout this lesson students write balanced symbol and half equations (M1c).

Literacy
In Plenary 2 students explain why ionic compounds conduct electricity in the liquid state, but not in the solid state.

Key words
electrolysis, electrolyte, electrodes, cathode, anode, cations, anions, binary ionic compound, molten, discharged, diffusion, convection

C3.4 Electrolysis

Starter	Support/Extend	Resources
Key words (5 minutes) Provide students with a list of key terms from the lesson and their definitions. Students match each key term to its definition. **Ionic compound models** (10 minutes) Ask small groups of students to make a model of an ionic compound such as sodium chloride using molecular modelling kits. Ask students to use their model to explain what happens to the particles in an ionic compound when it is heated above its melting point.		

Main	Support/Extend	Resources
Electrolysis of zinc chloride (40 minutes) Show students samples of zinc, zinc chloride, and chlorine. Encourage students to note the difference in appearance of the chemicals. Explain the process of electrolysis and encourage students to predict the products at each electrode. Demonstrate the electrolysis of zinc chloride as outlined below. Use question and answer to ensure students make all the relevant observations. Students draw a labelled diagram and then add information to explain how the ions move to each electrode and how they become the elements. Half-fill a crucible with zinc chloride and balance it in a pipe-clay triangle on a tripod. Submerge the ends of carbon electrodes electrodes in the powder, making sure they do not touch. Connect the electrodes into a series circuit with an ammeter and a low voltage power supply. Put the Bunsen burner under the crucible and heat moderately until the zinc chloride melts. At the anode, bubbles of chlorine vapour can be seen. Run the electrolysis for up to 15 minutes. Once finished, let the crucible cool. Using tongs, put the cooled crucible into a beaker of water and let any leftover zinc chloride dissolve. Filter the water to get the metallic zinc. SAFETY: Zinc chloride is corrosive and chlorine is toxic. Carry out in a fume cupboard. Take care with any students who have breathing problems. Wear chemical splash-proof eye protection throughout and wash hands after demonstration.	**Support:** Allow students to use prose to explain what is happening to the ions at each electrode. **Extend:** Ensure students write half equations and classify the reaction as oxidation or reduction. [H] **Extend:** Discuss how this process could be used to coat metal items with copper.	**Practical:** Electrolysis of zinc chloride

Plenary	Support/Extend	Resources
Predict the products (5 minutes) Ask students to write balanced symbol equations to show the products of the electrolysis of molten zinc chloride and of molten aluminium oxide. **Electrolysis** (5 minutes) Interactive where students complete a paragraph to explain how ionic compounds conduct electricity in solution and when molten. Students then label a diagram of an electrolysis experiment to identify the different species involved, the anode, and the cathode.	**Extend:** Ask students to write half equations and determine which species is oxidised and which is reduced. [H]	**Interactive:** Electrolysis

Homework	Support/Extend	Resources
Write a balanced symbol equation to represent what happens when electricity is passed through molten copper chloride. Determine which species is oxidised and which is reduced. Higher-tier students should also write half equations. [H]		

kerboodle
A Kerboodle highlight for this lesson is **Literacy skills: Electrolysis**. Refer to the **Content map** on Kerboodle for a full list of resources and assessment.

C3.4.2 Electrolysis of solutions

Specification links:

3.4a Recall that metals (or hydrogen) are formed at the cathode and non-metals are formed at the anode in electrolysis using inert electrodes.

3.4c Describe competing reactions in the electrolysis of aqueous solutions of ionic compounds in terms of the different species present.

WS1.4a Use scientific vocabulary, terminology, and definitions.

M1c Use ratios, fractions, and percentages.

CM3.4i Use arithmetic computation and ratio when determining empirical formulae and balancing equations (M1a, M1c).

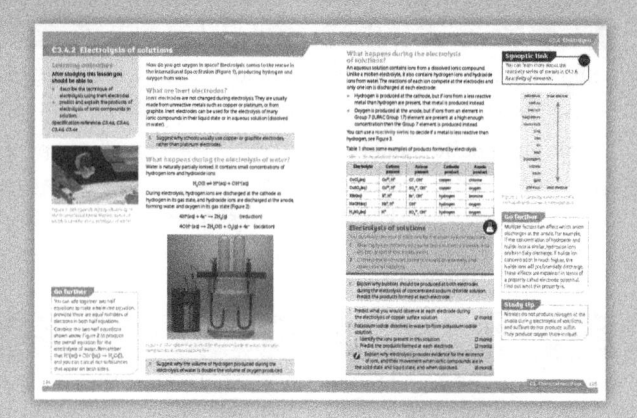

Target	Outcome	Checkpoint	
		Question	Activity
Aiming for GRADE 4 ↓	State that inert electrodes are made from unreactive metals or graphite.	A	Main
	Name some products of the electrolysis of solutions.		Starter 1 and 2 / Main / Plenary 1 and 2
	Set up an electrolysis circuit and collect/observe some products formed by the electrolysis of a solution.		Plenary 1 / Main
Aiming for GRADE 6 ↓	Explain why inert electrodes are used for the electrolysis of water (and aqueous solutions) and state the products of this reaction.		Main / Starter 2
	Predict and describe the products at each electrode during the electrolysis of a solution.	1	Starter 2 / Main / Plenary 1
	Identify products formed by the electrolysis of a solution.		Main
Aiming for GRADE 8 ↓	Write half equations to explain the formation of the products at each electrode during the electrolysis of water.		Main
	Predict and explain the products at each electrode during the electrolysis of a solution.	B, C, 2	Main / Starter 2
	Collect and identify the products at each electrode during the electrolysis of a solution.		Main

Maths
In Main 2 students write half equations and balanced symbol equations (M1c).

Literacy
In Plenary 2 students write a flow chart to determine the products of the electrolysis of a solution.

Key words
inert electrode, reactivity series

The Practical Skills lesson for PAG 2 Electrolysis could follow this lesson.

124

C3.4 Electrolysis

Starter	Support/Extend	Resources
Electrolysis of aqueous solutions (5 minutes) Interactive where students complete a crossword to summarise what they have learnt so far about electrolysis. **Predict the products** (5 minutes) Ask students to predict the products of the electrolysis of silver chloride, copper(II) sulfate, sodium nitrate, and sodium sulfate solutions, using Table 1 to help them.	**Support:** Give students the formulae of the compounds.	**Interactive:** Electrolysis of aqueous solutions

Main	Support/Extend	Resources
Electrolysis of brine (40 minutes) Split the lass into small groups. Introduce the electrolysis of brine and ask students to write an outline plan, including the dependent and control variables and predictions. If the plan is safe allow students to complete their investigation, recording their observations in a table. Encourage students to write a conclusion and evaluation. Bubbles can be seen around the anode. Students could add universal indicator to their solutions and they will see the solution around the anode first turn red and later become colourless. Bubbles also form around the cathode, and the solution turns purple. Ask students to explain their observations. Point out that inert electrodes are used in this practical, and ask students to explain why (Answer – electrodes made from reactive metals might react with the products of electrolysis).	**Support:** To help predict the electrolysis products of a solution, ask students to state the ions present and then consider which ions will move to which electrode. Explain that the least reactive ion will be turned into an atom. **Extend:** Ask students to suggest why inert electrodes are used for the electrolysis of aqueous solutions. **Extend:** Ask students to write half equations and construct a balanced symbol equation from the half equations of their electrolysis. **H** **Extend:** Ask students to determine which species is oxidised and which is reduced.	**Practical:** Electrolysis of brine

Plenary	Support/Extend	Resources
Electrolysis of solutions (10 minutes) Give students a list of salt solutions. Ask students to predict what experimental observations they would make if two carbon electrodes were inserted into the solutions and a low-voltage power supply added. **Flow chart** (10 minutes) Ask students to make a flow chart to help determine the products of the electrolysis of a solution.	**Extend:** Ask students to predict the products of the reaction. **Support:** Prompt students to include the following questions: Does the electrolyte contain a metal above hydrogen in the reactivity series? Does it contain a halide? Does it contain a molecular ion?	

Homework	Support/Extend	Resources
Write a risk assessment for the electrolysis of brine, knowing that chlorine gas, sodium hydroxide, and hydrogen are formed.		

kerboodle
A Kerboodle highlight for this lesson is **WebQuest: Extracting aluminium.** Refer to the **Content map** on Kerboodle for a full list of resources and assessment.

C3.4.3 Electroplating

Specification links:

C3.4e Describe the technique of electrolysis using inert and non-inert electrodes.

M1c Use ratios, fractions, and percentages.

CM3.4i Use arithmetic computation and ratio when determining empirical formulae and balancing equations (M1a, M1c).

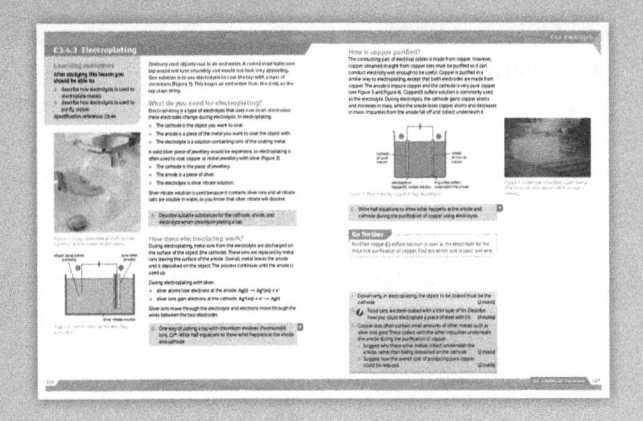

Target	Outcome	Checkpoint	
		Question	Activity
Aiming for GRADE 4	State that electrolysis can be used to electroplate metals.		Starter 1
			Main 1 and 2
	Describe some components of an electroplating circuit.		Main 1 and 2
↓	Explain that copper can be purified by electrolysis.		Main 1
Aiming for GRADE 6	Describe the process of electroplating.	2	Main 1 and 2
			Homework
	Suggest suitable substances for the anode, cathode, and electrolyte when electroplating.	A	Main 1 and 2
↓	Explain how electrolysis is used to purify copper.	3	Main 1
Aiming for GRADE 8	Write half equations to show what happens at the anode and the cathode during electroplating.	B	Starter 2
			Main 1 and 2
			Plenary 1
	Explain in detail the components of an electroplating circuit.	1	Main 1 and 2
↓	Write half equations to explain what happens at the anode and the cathode during the purification of copper using electrolysis.	C	Main 1
			Plenary 2

Maths
In Starter 2 students write balanced equations (M1c).

Literacy
In Plenary 2 students write a story to explain what happens to copper particles in an electroplating process.

Key words
electroplating, non-inert electrodes

kerboodle
A Kerboodle highlight for this lesson is **Literacy sheet: Electroplating**. Refer to the **Content map** on Kerboodle for a full list of resources and assessment.

C3.4 Electrolysis

Starter	Support/Extend	Resources

Have a think (5 minutes)   Give small groups of students an electroplated item on which the coating has begun to wear away, such as a spoon or a piece of jewellery. Ask students to suggest what they are about to study in the lesson.

From words to equations (10 minutes)   Ask students to change the following prose into a set of balanced half equations:
1 If a positive electrode is made from nickel, the nickel atoms can lose two electrons to become nickel ions: $Ni(s) \rightarrow Ni^{2+}(aq) + 2e^-$
2 The electrolyte can be made from a soluble nickel salt: $NiCl_2(s) + (aq) \rightarrow NiCl_2(aq)$
3 If a negative electrode attracts nickel ions from the electrolyte, the nickel ions gain two electrons from the negative electrode and become nickel atoms: $Ni^{2+}(aq) + 2e^- \rightarrow Ni(s)$

Support: Give students the equations and ask them to write the prose.

[H]

Main	Support/Extend	Resources

Electroplating with copper (15 minutes)   Demonstrate plating a small metal object such as a washer using copper(II) sulfate solution. Secure a copper anode to one side of a beaker half-filled with copper(II) sulfate solution, and secure the metal object to be plated to the other side of the beaker. The metal object is the cathode. Then make a simple series circuit with wires and a low-voltage power supply, run the current for about 5 minutes, turn off the power, and observe the metal object. Ensure students understand that the copper deposited at the cathode is pure, and the copper used to make the anode is impure.

Extend: Ask students to use half equations to explain what is happening at each electrode.

Mass and electroplating (25 minutes)   In small groups, students study how the amount of zinc deposited on a copper strip depends on the length of time for which electrolysis is carried out.
1 Thoroughly clean a 10 cm strip of copper with emery paper, then wash it with propanone. Once dry, note its mass to the nearest 0.01 g.
2 Support the copper strip in zinc sulfate solution by hooking it around a small glass rod.
3 Use card or polystyrene to hold the copper electrode a fixed distance apart from a zinc electrode.
4 Set up a simple electrolysis circuit with the copper strip connected directly to the negative terminal and the zinc strip connected through the ammeter to the positive terminal. Use 9 V for 10 minutes and record the current.
5 Turn off the power and remove the copper strip, wash it with propanone and, when completely dry, reweigh it to the nearest 0.01 g.
6 Calculate the increase in mass of the copper.
Students repeat the process for different times or using different voltages, designing their own results table and drawing conclusions from their results.

Extend: Ask students to use half equations to explain what is happening at each electrode.

Practical: Mass and electroplating

Plenary	Support/Extend	Resources

Half equations (5 minutes)   Ask students to write half equations to explain how an object can be plated with silver using a silver anode and silver nitrate solution.

Interactive: Half equations for electroplating

[H]

Story of the copper particle (10 minutes)   Ask students to imagine that they are a copper particle and explain what happens to them as they move from the anode to the cathode (refer to Main 1).

Extend: Ask students to draw a cartoon to illustrate their story.

Homework	Support/Extend	Resources

Compare and contrast electrolysis and electroplating.

C3 Chemical reactions 127

Checkpoint
C3.4 Electrolysis

Overview of C3.4 Electrolysis

In this chapter students have studied electrolysis of molten salts, electrolysis of solutions, and electroplating. They should be able to use the terms electrolysis, electrode, electrolyte, cathode and cations, anode and anions. Students should be able to explain why solid ionic compounds do not conduct electricity but molten ionic compounds do. They should be able to state that electrolysis breaks ionic compounds down into their component elements, describe an electrolysis circuit, and predict the products of electrolysis at the anode and cathode. Higher-tier students should be able to write half equations for the reactions at the anode and cathode, and explain in terms of electron transfer why these are redox reactions. They should link this work with half equations from C3.1 *Introducing chemical reactions* and redox reactions from C3.3 *Types of chemical reaction*.

In studying the electrolysis of solutions using inert electrodes, students should recall that metals (or hydrogen) are formed at the cathode and non-metals are formed at the anode. They should understand why inert electrodes are used for the electrolysis of aqueous solutions and give examples of suitable materials for these electrodes. They should be able to describe competing reactions in the electrolysis of aqueous solutions of ionic compounds in terms of the different species present. They should have carried out electrolysis of a solution and collected and identified the products. Higher-tier students should be able to write half equations for the reactions at each electrode during the electrolysis of water.

Students should know that electrolysis can be used to electroplate metals, and be able to describe the process, including suitable substances for the anode, cathode, and electrolyte.

MyMaths

You can find additional support for the maths skills covered in this chapter on **MyMaths**, including calculations using ratios.

PAGs

All students are expected to have carried out the PAG *2 Electrolysis*. A full lesson plan for each PAG is provided in the Practical skills chapter. PAG *2 Electrolysis* should be completed after lesson C3.4.2 *Electrolysis of solutions*.

kerboodle

For this chapter, the following assessments are available on Kerboodle:
C3.4 Checkpoint quiz: Electrolysis
C3.4 Progress quiz: Electrolysis 1
C3.4 Progress quiz: Electrolysis 2
C3.4 On your marks: Electrolysis
C3.4 Exam-style questions and mark scheme: Electrolysis

C3.4 Electrolysis

Checkpoint follow-up lesson

A student's route through this lesson can be determined using the Checkpoint assessment. Percentage pass marks are supplied in the Checkpoint teacher notes.

For each successive route through it is assumed that the student can perform to their current route as well as previous routes. For example, students working at Aiming for 6 are assumed to be secure in Aiming for 4 knowledge and understanding and working towards achieving all the learning objectives for Aiming for 6.

	Aiming for 4	Aiming for 6	Aiming for 8
Learning outcomes	Describe what happens to an ionic substance when it is electrolysed.	Describe what happens during electrolysis.	Explain, including half equations, what happens when a substance is electrolysed.
	Describe what happens at the positive and negative electrodes to form elements.	Explain what happens at the electrodes using the terms reduction and oxidation.	Predict what will happen at the electrodes during an electrolysis.
Starter	**Electrolysis in action (10 minutes)** Show a video clip of electrolysis in action. Emphasise that electrolysis occurs because when ionic substances are molten or dissolved, their ions become free and are able to move, and that they will be attracted to the oppositely charged electrode. Recap that ions gain or lose electrons at the electrodes to form neutral elements. This could be modelled by students, using counters to represent electrons.		
Differentiated checkpoint activity	**Electrolysis poster (35 minutes)** Explain that students will be producing a poster about electrolysis using the differentiated worksheets. Students will need A3 or A4 paper and coloured pencils.		
	The Aiming for 4 sheet includes a cut and paste task. Students will require scissors and glue sticks.	The Aiming for 6 sheet encourages students to design their own poster, providing prompt questions that it should answer. They are asked to draw diagrams showing what happens to the ions.	The Aiming for 8 sheet encourages students to design their own poster explaining what happens during the electrolysis of potassium chloride. They are prompted to include equations, half equations, and diagrams, and to analyse the change in terms of oxidation and reduction.
	Kerboodle resource: C3.4 Checkpoint follow-up: Aiming for 4, C3.4 Checkpoint follow-up: Aiming for 6, C3.4 Checkpoint follow-up: Aiming for 8		
Plenary	**Poetry (10 minutes)** Ask students to think of an easy poem or song to help them remember what happens during electrolysis, specifically at each electrode. Ask some students to perform their song or poem to the rest of the class.		
Progression	The Aiming for 4 sheet contains structured tasks to guide students through their revision.	The Aiming for 6 sheet provides guidance for students to revise what happens when a substance is electrolysed.	Aiming for 8 students should be able to explain, including half equations, what happens when a substance is electrolysed.

C3 Chemical reactions: Topic summary

C3.1 Introducing chemical reactions
C3.2 Energetics
C3.3 Types of chemical reactions
C3.4 Electrolysis

Spec ref	Statement	Book spreads
C3.1a	Use chemical symbols to write the formulae of elements and simple covalent and ionic compounds	C3.1.1, C3.1.2
C3.1b	Use the names and symbols of common elements and compounds and the principle of conservation of mass to write formulae and balanced chemical equations and half equations	C3.1.4, C3.1.4
C3.1c	Use the names and symbols of common elements from a supplied Periodic Table to write formulae and balanced chemical equations where appropriate	C3.1.4
C3.1d	Use the formula of common ions to deduce the formula of a compound	C3.1.2, C3.1.4
C3.1e	Construct balanced ionic equations	C3.1.4 [H]
C3.1f	Describe the physical states of products and reactants using state symbols (s, l, g, and aq)	C3.1.4
C3.1g	Recall and use the definitions of the Avogadro constant (in standard form) and of the mole	C3.1.6 [H]
C3.1h	Explain how the mass of a given substance is related to the amount of that substance in moles and vice versa	C3.1.6 [H]
C3.1i	Recall and use the law of conservation of mass	C3.1.3
C3.1j	Explain any observed changes in mass in non-enclosed systems during a chemical reaction and explain them using the particle model	C3.1.3
C3.1k	Deduce the stoichiometry of an equation from the masses of reactants and products and explain the effect of a limiting quantity of a reactant	C3.1.7 [H]
C3.1l	Use a balanced equation to calculate masses of reactants or products	C3.1.7 [H]
C3.2a	Distinguish between endothermic and exothermic reactions on the basis of the temperature change of the surroundings	C3.2.1
C3.2b	Draw and label a reaction profile for an exothermic and an endothermic reaction	C3.2.2
C3.2c	Explain activation energy as the energy needed for a reaction to occur	C3.2.2
C3.2d	Calculate energy changes in a chemical reaction by considering bond making and bond breaking energies	C3.2.3 [H]
C3.3a	Explain reduction and oxidation in terms of loss or gain of oxygen, identifying which species are oxidised and which are reduced	C3.3.1
C3.3b	Explain reduction and oxidation in terms of gain or loss of electrons, identifying which species are oxidised and which are reduced	C3.3.1 [H]
C3.3c	Recall that acids form hydrogen ions when they dissolve in water and solutions of alkalis contain hydroxide ions	C3.3.2
C3.3d	Describe neutralisation as acid reacting with alkali or a base to form a salt plus water	C3.3.3
C3.3e	Recognise that aqueous neutralisation reactions can be generalised to hydrogen ions reacting with hydroxide ions to form water	C3.3.3
C3.3f	Recall that carbonates and some metals react with acids and write balanced equations predicting products from given reactants	C3.3.4
C3.3g	Use and explain the terms dilute and concentrated (amount of substance) and weak and strong (degree of ionisation) in relation to acids	[H]
C3.3h	Recall that relative acidity and alkalinity are measured by pH	C3.3.2
C3.3i	Describe neutrality and relative acidity and alkalinity in terms of the effect of the concentration of hydrogen ions on the numerical value of pH (whole numbers only)	C3.3.5 [H]
C3.3j	Recall that as hydrogen ion concentration increases by a factor of ten the pH value of a solution decreases by a factor of one	C3.3.5 [H]
C3.3k	Describe techniques and apparatus used to measure pH	C3.3.2
C3.4a	Recall that metals (or hydrogen) are formed at the cathode and non-metals are formed at the anode in electrolysis using inert electrodes	C3.4.2
C3.4b	Predict the products of electrolysis of binary ionic compounds in the molten state	C3.4.1
C3.4c	Describe competing reactions in the electrolysis of aqueous solutions of ionic compounds in terms of the different species present	C3.4.1
C3.4d	Describe electrolysis in terms of the ions present and reactions at the electrodes	C3.4.1
C3.4e	Describe the technique of electrolysis using inert and non-inert electrodes	C3.4.3

Maths

Specification Spec ref	Statement	Book spread Main content	Maths chapter
CM3.1i	Arithmetic computation and ratio when determining empirical formulae, balancing equations	C3.1.1–7, C3.2.2	3
CM3.1ii	Calculations with numbers written in standard form when using the Avogadro constant	C3.1.6, C3.1.7, C3.2.3	2
CM3.1iii	Provide answers to an appropriate number of significant figures	C3.1.6, C3.1.7	5
CM3.1iv	Convert units where appropriate particularly from mass to moles	C3.1.6, C3.1.7	11, 12
CM3.2i	Interpretation of charts and graphs when dealing with reaction profiles		13, 14
CM3.2ii	Arithmetic computation when calculating energy changes		11
CM3.3i	Arithmetic computation, ratio, percentage, and multistep calculations permeates quantitative chemistry	C3.3.2–5	3
CM3.4i	Arithmetic computation and ratio when determining empirical formulae, balancing equations	C3.4.1–3	3

H

Working scientifically

Specification Spec ref	Statement	Book spread Main content	WS chapter
WS1.1b	Use models to solve problems, make predictions, and to develop scientific explanations and understanding of familiar and unfamiliar facts.	C3.2.3, C3.3.5	WS2
WS1.2a	Use scientific theories and explanations to develop hypotheses.	C3.4.1	WS3
WS1.2b	Plan experiments or devise procedures to make observations, produce or characterise a substance, test hypotheses, check data, or explore phenomena.	C3.4.1	WS3, WS4
WS1.2c	Apply knowledge of a range of techniques, instruments, apparatus, and materials to select those appropriate to the experiment.	C3.4.1	WS4
WS1.3a	Present observations and other data using appropriate methods.	C3.2.1	WS6
WS1.3b	Translate data from one form to another.	C3.2.2, C3.2.3	WS6
WS1.3c	Carrying out and representing mathematical and statistical analysis, to include arithmetic means, mode, and median.	C3.1.7, C3.2.2, C3.2.3	WS5
WS1.3e	Interpreting observations and other data.	C3.2.1, C3.2.2	WS7
WS1.3f	Present reasoned explanations.	C3.2.1	WS7
WS1.4a	Use scientific vocabulary, terminology, and definitions.	C3.1.1, C3.1.2, C3.3.1–5, C3.4.1, C3.4.2	WS2
WS1.4b	Recognise the importance of scientific quantities and understand how they are determined.	C3.1.6	
WS1.4c	Use SI units and IUPAC chemical nomenclature unless inappropriate.	C3.1.2, C3.1.4–7, C3.2.3	
WS1.4d	Use prefixes and powers of ten for orders of magnitude.	C3.1.6	
WS1.4f	Use an appropriate number of significant figures in calculation.	C3.1.6	WS5
WS2b	Make and record observations and measurements, using a range of apparatus and methods.	C3.2.1	
WS2c	Present observations using appropriate methods.	C3.2.1	

C3 Chemical reactions

C4 Predicting and identifying reactions and products
C4.1 Predicting chemical reactions
C4.1.1 Group 1 – the alkali metals

Specification links:

4.1a Recall the simple properties of Group 1, [7, and 0].

4.1b Explain how observed simple properties of Group 1, [7, and 0] depend on the outer shell of electrons of the atoms, and predict properties from given trends down the group.

WS1.2a Use scientific theories and explanations to develop hypotheses.

WS1.4a Use scientific vocabulary, terminology, and definitions.

Ws1.4c Use SI units and IUPAC chemical nomenclature unless inappropriate.

M1c Use ratios, fractions, and percentages.

M4a Translate information between graphical and numeric form.

M4c Plot two variables from experimental or other data.

CM4.1i Use arithmetic computation and ratio when determining empirical formulae and balancing equations (M1a, M1c).

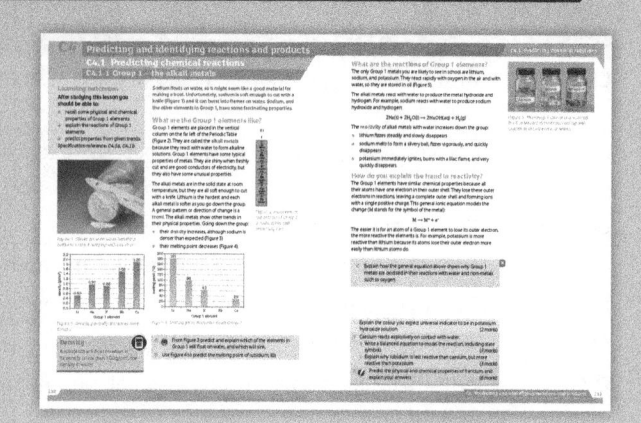

Target	Outcome	Checkpoint Question	Checkpoint Activity
Aiming for GRADE 4	Describe some physical properties of the Group 1 elements.		Starter 2, Main
	Record the observations noted when Group 1 elements react with water.		Main
	State that Group 1 metals react vigorously with water, and name the products formed.	2	Main
Aiming for GRADE 6	Interpret data to describe trends in the physical properties of the Group 1 elements.	A, 2	Plenary 2, Homework
	Explain the observations noted when Group 1 elements react with water.	1	Main
	Write balanced equations for the reactions of the Group 1 elements with water.	2	Main
Aiming for GRADE 8	Predict the physical properties of a Group 1 element, given data about other members of the group.	B, 3	Starter 2, Plenary 1
	Explain in detail the observations noted when Group 1 elements react with water.		Main
	Use knowledge of electronic structures to explain in detail the trend in reactivity of the Group 1 elements.	C, 3	Plenary 2

Literacy
In Plenary 2 students describe trends in Group 1.

Key words
Group 1, alkali metals, trend, density, reactivity

C4.1 Predicting chemical reactions

Starter	Support/Extend	Resources
Group 1 (5 minutes) Interactive where students summarise the electron arrangements and properties of the Group 1 elements. Students then complete a crossword of the key words for the lesson. **Display information** (10 minutes) Students plot a line graph of melting point versus atomic number using Figure 4 and the Periodic Table. Ask students to use their graph to predict the melting point of rubidium.	**Extend:** Ask students to look for patterns in the electronic structures, including the numbers of electronic shells and outer-shell electrons. **Support:** Provide graph paper with the axes and scales already drawn.	**Interactive:** Group 1

Main	Support/Extend	Resources
Reactions of alkali metals with water (40 minutes) Show students the Group 1 metals lithium, sodium, and potassium. Point out that they are stored under oil and encourage students to predict why this is so. Demonstrate cutting the metals and quickly show the metallic lustre of the metal before it tarnishes. Note the trend in reactivity by observing the speed at which the metals tarnish. Then demonstrate the reactions of these metals with water in a glass trough. You may wish to put some universal indicator in the water to show the change in pH. Ask students to design a table to write equations for the reactions between all the Group 1 metals with oxygen and with water, and to record their observations as the reactions occur.	**Support:** Guide students through understanding how and why the reactions of these metals change as you go down the group. **Extend:** Ask students to write an ionic equation for the production of hydroxide ions in solution and use this to explain why the pH increases when alkali metals react with water.	**Practical:** Reactions of alkali metals with water

Plenary	Support/Extend	Resources
Group 1 predictions (5 minutes) Explain that francium is radioactive and very little of it exists on Earth at any one time. Ask students to use the information that they have about Group 1 elements and the trends in their properties to predict what francium would look like, its physical properties, and how it would react with water. **Group 1 trends** (10 minutes) Ask students to look back at what they have learnt about Group 1 and state any trends in properties going down the group. Ask students to list how the electronic structures change from the top to the bottom of the group.	**Extend:** Encourage students to use the electronic structures drawn in Starter 1 to explain why reactivity increases as you go down the group.	

Homework	Support/Extend	Resources
Make a 'Fascinating fact' poster about Group 1 elements, including their physical and chemical properties and their uses.		

kerboodle

A Kerboodle highlight for this lesson is **Literacy sheet: Patterns and trends in Group 1**. Refer to the **Content map** on Kerboodle for a full list of resources and assessment.

C4.1.2 Group 7 – the halogens

Specification links:

4.1a Recall the simple properties of Group [1, 7, and 0].

4.1b Explain how observed simple properties of Group [1, 7, and 0] depend on the outer shell of electrons of the atoms, and predict properties from given trends down the group.

WS1.2a Use scientific theories and explanations to develop hypotheses.

WS1.4a Use scientific vocabulary, terminology, and definitions.

WS1.4c Use SI units and IUPAC chemical nomenclature unless inappropriate.

M4a Translate information between graphical and numeric form.

M4c Plot two variables from experimental or other data.

CM4.1i Use arithmetic computation and ratio when determining empirical formulae and balancing equations (M1a, M1c).

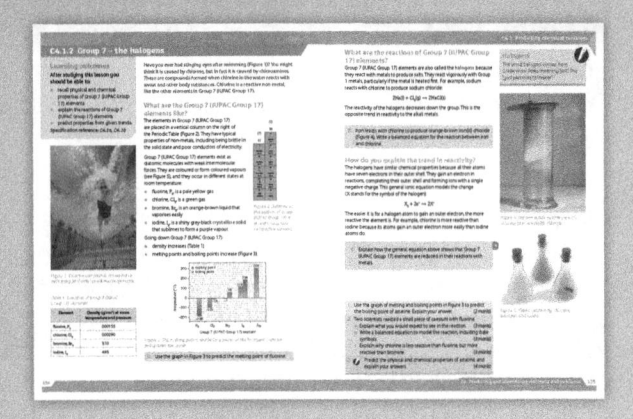

Target	Outcome	Checkpoint Question	Checkpoint Activity
Aiming for GRADE 4	Describe some physical properties of the Group 7 (IUPAC Group 17) elements.		Starter 1 and 2 Plenary 1 Homework
	Name the salt formed when a Group 7 (IUPAC Group 17) element reacts with a metal, and write the word equation for the reaction.		Main 1 and 2
	State that Group 7 (IUPAC Group 17) elements react vigorously with metals.		Main 1 and 2
Aiming for GRADE 6	Interpret data to describe trends in the physical properties of the Group 7 (IUPAC Group 17) elements.		Starter 2 Main 2 Homework
	Write balanced chemical equations for the reactions of Group 7 (IUPAC Group 17) elements with metals, given the formula of the salt formed.		Main 1 and 2 Plenary 2
	Describe the trend in reactivity of the Group 7 (IUPAC Group 17) elements.		Main 1 and 2
Aiming for GRADE 8	Predict the physical properties of a Group 7 (IUPAC Group 17) element, given data about other members of the group.	A, 1, 3	Main 2 Homework
	Write balanced chemical equations for the reactions of Group 7 (IUPAC Group 17) elements with metals.	B, C	Main 1 and 2 Plenary 2
	Use knowledge of electronic structures to explain in detail the trend in reactivity of the Group 7 (IUPAC Group 17) elements.	2	Main 1 and 2

Maths
In completing the Homework task students use ICT to draw a graph and make a prediction from it (M4a, M4c).

Literacy
In Main 2 students write examiner's comments in response to fictitious student answers to exam questions.

Key words
Group 7, crystalline, halogens

C4.1 Predicting chemical reactions

Starter	Support/Extend	Resources
Sublimation of iodine (5 minutes) Prepare a sealed boiling tube containing a few crystals of iodine, a small beaker of just boiled water, and a separate beaker of iced water. Put the boiling tube into each beaker and observe the sublimation of iodine, noting the mauve vapour. **Group 7 (IUPAC Group 17) trends** (10 minutes) Ask students to use the information in the Student Book to state the trends in colour, melting point, and density of the Group 7 (IUPAC Group 17) elements.	**Extend:** Write a balanced symbol equation, including state symbols, for this physical change. **Extend:** Ask students to think about the size of the molecules and how this could be used to explain the trend in melting point.	

Main	Support/Extend	Resources
Reactivity in Group 7 (IUPAC Group 17) (25 minutes) Ask pairs of students to discuss and predict the relative vigour of the reactions of chlorine, bromine, and iodine with iron, and to give reasons for their predictions. Then demonstrate the reactions of these halogens with iron. Ask students to note their observations in a table and decide whether their observations support their predictions. Then ask students to write balanced equations, including state symbols, for the reactions. **Exam focus** (15 minutes) Provide small groups of students with an exam question on halogens, with fictitious candidate responses. Ask the groups to discuss the responses, use the Student Book to consider the marking of the work, and make suggestions as though they were examiners. Then reveal the marking and the examiner's comments, and invite students to discuss any similarities and differences between their thoughts and the examiner's comments.	**Support:** Help students make their predictions by reminding them that chlorine reacts very vigorously with many substances. **Extend:** Encourage students to explain the trend in reactivity using the electronic structures of the atoms. **Support:** Use questions only from the Foundation tier.	**Practical:** Reactivity of Group 7

Plenary	Support/Extend	Resources
Group 7 (IUPAC Group 17) (10 minutes) Interactive activity in which students fill in the gaps of a series of sentences that summarise the properties of Group 7 elements. Students then complete a crossword of key words from the lesson. **Balanced equations** (15 minutes) Ask students to write balanced symbol equations for the reactions of the halogens with iron.	**Extend:** Ask students to write ionic equations for these reactions.	**Interactive:** Group 7

Homework	Support/Extend	Resources
Use ICT to draw a graph of the density data from Table 1, and use this to predict the density of astatine.		

kerboodle

A Kerboodle highlight for this lesson is **Literacy interactive: The halogens**. Refer to the **Content map** on Kerboodle for a full list of resources and assessment.

C4.1.3 Halogen displacement reactions

Specification links:

4.1a Recall the simple properties of Group, [1, 7 and 0].

4.1d Predict possible reactions and probable reactivities of elements from their positions in the Periodic Table.

WS1.2a Use scientific theories and explanations to develop hypotheses.

WS1.4a Use scientific vocabulary, terminology, and definitions.

WS1.4c Use SI units and IUPAC chemical nomenclature unless inappropriate.

M1c Use ratios, fractions, and percentages.

CM4.1i Use arithmetic computation and ratio when determining empirical formulae and balancing equations (M1a, M1c).

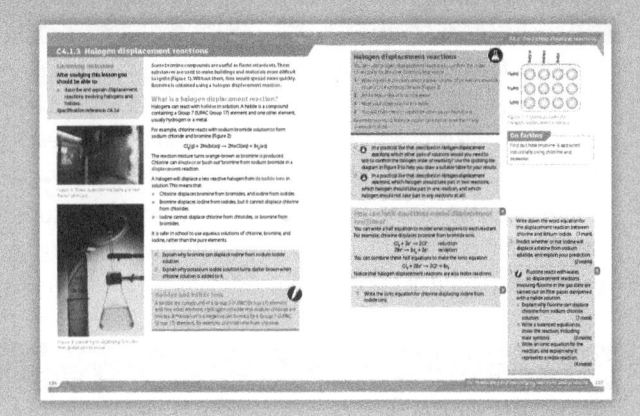

Target	Outcome	Checkpoint	
		Question	Activity
Aiming for GRADE 4 ↓	State that a more reactive halogen can displace a less reactive halogen from its compounds.		Main 2
	Record the observations noted when halogens react with halide ions in solution.		Main 2
	State the products when a halogen reacts with a halide ion.	1	Main 2
Aiming for GRADE 6 ↓	Use the order of reactivity of the halogens to explain the outcome of a displacement reaction.	A	Main 2
	Use observations from halogen displacement reactions to identify the more reactive halogen in the reaction.	B	Main 2
	Write balanced chemical equations for halogen displacement reactions.	3	Main 2 Homework
Aiming for GRADE 8 ↓	Predict possible reactions from the order of reactivity of the halogens, or their positions in the Periodic Table.	2, D	Starter 2 Plenary 1 and 2
	Use observations from halogen displacement reactions to deduce the order of reactivity of the halogens.		Main 2
	Write half equations for each reactant in a halogen displacement reaction, and use them to identify which species have been oxidised and which have been reduced.	C, E, 3	Main 2

Maths
In Starter 2 students write balanced symbol equations (M1c).

Literacy
In Main 2 students draw a cartoon to explain how displacement occurs.

Key words
halides, displace, displacement, halide ions

C4.1 Predicting chemical reactions

Starter	Support/Extend	Resources
What's the difference? (5 minutes) Ask students to explain the difference between halogens and halides, illustrating their answer with fluorine. **Halogens and aluminium** (10 minutes) Demonstrate the reaction of aluminium with chlorine, bromine, and iodine. Ask students to state the order of reactivity of these elements based on their reactions with aluminium and drawing on knowledge gained in C4.1.2. Ask students to write balanced symbol equations to model these reactions.	**Extend:** Students use dot-and-cross diagrams to explain the difference between halogens and halides. **Support:** Ask students to write just word equations for the reactions.	

Main	Support/Extend	Resources
Investigate halogens (15 minutes) Students begin by observing the colours of halogen solutions in water and in an organic solvent. Ask pairs of students to pour about 2 cm³ each of chlorine water, bromine water, and iodine solution into separate test tubes. Then ask them to add 1 cm³ of cyclohexane to each tube, agitate, and note the colour. Students should then allow the two layers to settle. **Displacement reactions** (25 minutes) Students next investigate displacement reactions between halogens in solution and potassium halide salt solutions. Ask pairs of students to pour about 2 cm³ of each of the aqueous halogen solutions into separate test tubes. Then, one tube at a time, ask them to add 2 cm³ of potassium chloride, followed by 1 cm³ of cyclohexane. Students should stopper the tube and, holding a thumb over the bung, shake the mixture by inverting the test-tube a few times. Ask students to observe and record the colour of the cyclohexane layer, then repeat with potassium bromide and potassium iodide. Students should note which pairs of substances react, and explain their observations. Ask students to draw a cartoon that personifies halogens and halides. Students should use their characters to explain how displacement occurs.	**Support:** Complete the displacement reactions on a microscale using dimple dishes and two drops of each solution. This reduces the risk. **Extend:** Ask students to write half equations and balanced ionic equations for the reactions, and determine which species is oxidised and which is reduced. **H** **Support:** You may wish to provide students with the captions to illustrate.	**Practical:** Displacement reactions

Plenary	Support/Extend	Resources
Demonstrate sodium chloride (5 minutes) Ask students to predict the reaction between sodium and chlorine, bromine, and iodine. Link to the reactions of chlorine with iron (as seen in Main 1, C4.1.2) and with aluminium (as seen in Starter 2). **Electronic structures** (10 minutes) Students use the interactive to link the correct electronic structure with the first four halogens. They then complete a paragraph to explain why reactivity increases going down the group.	**Extend:** Students should state whether the formation of the ion is an oxidation or reduction, and justify their classification.	**Interactive:** Electronic structures

Homework	Support/Extend	Resources
Predict the physical properties of astatine, and write equations for the displacement reactions between chlorine, bromine, iodine, and potassium astatide.		

kerboodle

A Kerboodle highlight for this lesson is **Homework: Predicting chemical reactions.** Refer to the **Content map** on Kerboodle for a full list of resources and assessment.

C4.1.4 Group 0 – the noble gases

Specification links:

4.1a Recall the simple properties of Group [1, 7, and] 0.

4.1b Explain how observed simple properties of Group [1, 7, and] 0 depend on the outer shell of electrons of the atoms, and predict properties from given trends down the group.

WS1.2a Use scientific theories and explanations to develop hypotheses.

WS1.4a Use scientific vocabulary, terminology, and definitions.

Ws1.4c Use SI units and IUPAC chemical nomenclature unless inappropriate.

M4a Translate information between graphical and numeric form.

M4c Plot two variables from experimental or other data.

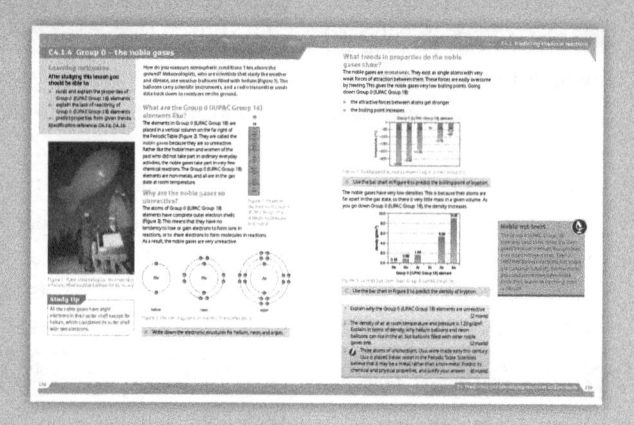

Target	Outcome	Checkpoint Question	Checkpoint Activity
Aiming for GRADE 4	Describe some physical properties of the noble gases.		Starter 1 and 2 Plenary 2 Homework
	State that noble gases are unreactive.		Main 1 Plenary 2
↓	Explain that noble gases exist as separate atoms.		Main 2
Aiming for GRADE 6	Interpret data to describe trends in the physical properties of the noble gases.	2	Starter 2 Plenary 2 Plenary 1
	Relate the lack of reactivity of the noble gases to their outer shell electronic structure.	A, 1	Main 1
↓	Use the monatomic nature of the noble gases to explain their low boiling points and densities.		Main 2
Aiming for GRADE 8	Predict the physical properties of a noble gas element, given data about other members of the group.	B, C	Starter 2 Plenary 1
	Use knowledge of electronic structures to explain in detail the lack of reactivity of the noble gases.	3	Main 1 Plenary 2
↓	Use the relative strengths of the forces between atoms to explain the trend in boiling point of the noble gases.	3	Main 2 Plenary 2

Literacy
In completing the Homework task students write a prediction and justify it.

Key words
Group 0, noble gases, monatomic

C4.1 Predicting chemical reactions

Starter	Support/Extend	Resources
Discharge tubes (5 minutes) Demonstrate discharge tubes filled with noble gases connected to a low-voltage power supply. Encourage students to note the colours that are generated and explain that these tubes are bent into different shapes to make coloured advertising signs. **Scatter graph** (10 minutes) Ask students to draw a scatter graph of boiling point versus proton number for the Group 0 (IUPAC Group 18) elements using data from Figure 4 and the Periodic Table, and to draw a line of best fit. Then ask students to predict the boiling point of krypton.	**Support:** Provide graph paper with the axes and scales already drawn. **Extend:** Ask students to convert the temperatures to kelvin.	

Main	Support/Extend	Resources
Noble gas structure (20 minutes) Ask students to draw the electronic structure of the first three noble gases, and to label the numbers of protons and neutrons in the nucleus. Then ask students to use their diagrams to explain why this group of elements is very unreactive. **Particle model** (20 minutes) Ask pairs of students to design a model to represent the particle model of the noble gases. Students should use the model to demonstrate why noble gases have low densities (not many particles in a given volume) and low melting points (weak attractive forces between particles). Students could take photos of their model and then annotate the different images to explain the physical properties of the noble gases. Students could also explain how their models are like, and unlike, the real situation.	**Extend:** Challenge students to find out the different isotopes of these elements and to draw the structures of these as well. Ask students to explain the difference in properties between the isotopes (they hold the same chemical properties but different physical properties).	**Activity:** Noble gas structure

Plenary	Support/Extend	Resources
Floating gases (5 minutes) Use Figure 5 to help you predict which noble gases would float and which would sink in air. The density of dry air is 1.2 kg/m³. Justify your answers. **Trends in the noble gases** (10 minutes) Ask students to match the trend with an explanation: 1 Melting point increases as you go down the group… because the forces of attraction between the atoms increase as the size of the atom increases. 2 Boiling point increases as you go down the group… because the forces of attraction between the atoms increase as the size of the atom increases. 3 Density increases as you go down the group… because there is more mass per volume as the atoms increase in mass. 4 Reactivity increases as you go down the group… because the atoms get larger, so their outer electrons are less strongly attracted to the nucleus.		**Interactive:** Trends in the noble gases

Homework	Support/Extend	Resources
Give students a list of uses of the noble gases, for example, an incandescent light bulb (argon), a laser pointer (neon or krypton), and a party balloon (helium). Students suggest why each noble gas is used for this purpose.	**Support:** Provide students with a list of the reasons why the noble gases are used in these examples. Students have to match them up.	

GCSE CHEMISTRY ONLY

C4.1.5 The transition metals

Specification links:

4.1c Recall the general properties of transition metals and their compounds and exemplify these by reference to a small number of transition metals.

WS1.4a Use scientific vocabulary, terminology, and definitions.

M2c Construct and interpret frequency tables and diagrams, bar charts, and histograms.

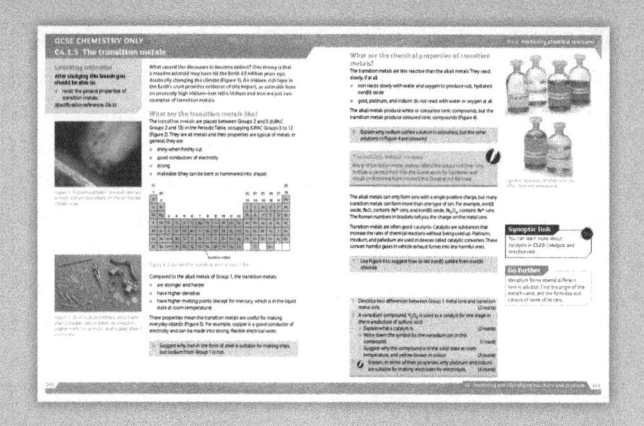

Target	Outcome	Checkpoint	
		Question	Activity
Aiming for GRADE 4	Describe some physical properties of transition metals.		Starter 1 and 2, Plenary 2
	Describe some simple reactions of transition metals.		Main
	State that transition metals can form more than one kind of ion.		Starter 1, Plenary 1
Aiming for GRADE 6	Compare the physical properties of transition metals with those of Group 1 metals.	A, 1	Plenary 2
	Describe how to distinguish transition metal compounds from each other and from Group 1 compounds.	B, C	Plenary 2
	Deduce the charge on a transition metal ion, given the names of compounds that include it.		Plenary 1
Aiming for GRADE 8	Explain in detail how the uses of transition metals depend on their physical properties.	A, 3	Starter 2
	Explain the use of transition metals as catalysts.	2	Main, Homework
	Deduce the charge on a transition metal ion, given the formulae of its compounds.	2	Plenary 1, Homework

Maths
In Plenary 2 students draw a Venn diagram (M2c).

Literacy
In Main 2 students write questions to form a key for the identification of metal samples.

Key words
transition metals, catalysts

140

C4.1 Predicting chemical reactions

Starter	Support/Extend	Resources
Observe transition metal compounds (5 minutes) Give students a selection of labelled transition metal compounds and ask them to draw conclusions consistent with their observations. Students should determine that the samples all contain transition metals and that they are all coloured. **Properties and uses** (10 minutes) Ask students to list the properties of transition metals that are common to all metals. Then ask them to give examples to illustrate how each property makes a named transition metal fit for one of its uses (e.g., copper is used to make electrical wire as it is ductile and a good electrical conductor).	**Extend:** Ask students to write the formula of each metal compound.	

Main	Support/Extend	Resources
Properties of transition elements (40 minutes) Ask students to draw a Venn diagram made of two circles that slightly overlap. Label one circle as Group 1 (alkali metals) and the second as transition metals. Students write the properties of Group 1 in the first circle. They then write the properties of transition metals in the second circle and write the common properties in the overlap. Using different coloured pens, students write examples of symbols and names of elements in the appropriate parts of the Venn diagram. Then ask students to focus on the properties of the transition metals and their uses. Students use the properties of the transition elements to justify why the uses of chromium, manganese, iron, cobalt, nickel, and copper.	**Support:** Give students the outline of the Venn diagram and show them the different properties for them to copy into the correct part of the Venn diagram. **Extend:** Encourage students to use examples outside those listed in the specification and to speculate why the alkali metals and transition elements differ.	**Practical:** Properties of transition elements

Plenary	Support/Extend	Resources
The transition elements (5 minutes) Students complete the interactive where they match the symbol of each transition metal to its name and then select the correct answer to complete sentences about transition metals. **Metal identification key** (10 minutes) Ask students to work in pairs to develop two keys: one couplet, and one branched key. Each should use the properties of two transition elements (zinc and copper) and two Group 1 elements (lithium and sodium) as the basis for the identification of these metals. Then ask students to swap keys with other pairs and use them to identify samples of the metals (do not give out samples of sodium).		**Interactive:** The transition elements

Homework	Support/Extend	Resources
Use the Student Book and the internet to research the transition metal catalysts used for the following: 1 the Contact process 2 the Haber process 3 making margarine 4 catalytic converters.	**Extend:** From formulae of several transition metal compounds, deduce the charge on the transition metal ion in each case.	

kerboodle

A Kerboodle highlight for this lesson is **Support: Transition metals are marvellous**. Refer to the **Content map** on Kerboodle for a full list of resources and assessment.

C4.1.6 Reactivity of elements

Specification links:

4.1e Explain how the reactivity of metals with water or dilute acids is related to the tendency of the metal to form its positive ion.

4.1f Deduce an order of reactivity of metals based on experimental results.

WS1.1b Use models to solve problems, make predictions, and develop scientific explanations and understanding of familiar and unfamiliar facts.

WS1.2a Use scientific theories and explanations to develop hypotheses.

WS1.4a Use scientific vocabulary, terminology, and definitions.

WS1.3e Interpreting observations and other data.

WS2a Carry out experiments.

M1a Recognise and use expressions in decimal form.

M1c Use [fractions,] ratios, [and percentages].

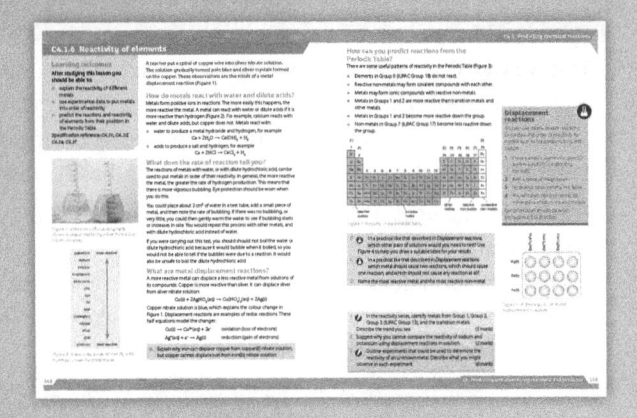

Target	Outcome	Checkpoint Question	Checkpoint Activity
Aiming for GRADE 4 ↓	Record observations noted when metals react with water and dilute acids.		Main 1
	Describe the products of a metal displacement reaction.		Starter 2, Main 2
Aiming for GRADE 6 ↓	Use observations from metal reactions to place them in an order of reactivity.	B, C, D	Main 1, Plenary 2, Homework
	Write balanced equations for metal displacement reactions.		Main 2
	Use the order of reactivity of metals to predict reactions.	1	Main 2
Aiming for GRADE 8 ↓	Explain why some metals are more reactive than others.	A, 2	Main 2
	Write half equations for metal displacement reactions and distinguish those that model oxidation and those that model reduction.		Main 2
	Use the order of reactivity of metals to predict reactions, and justify these predictions.	1, 3	Plenary 1

Maths
In Main 1 and Main 2 students write balanced symbol equations. In Main 2 (Extend) students write ionic equations (M1c). In Main 1 (Extend) students plot a graph of volume of gas produced against time (M4c).

Literacy
In Plenary 1 students write a prediction about a reaction, and justify their prediction.

142

C4.1 Predicting chemical reactions

Starter	Support/Extend	Resources
The reactivity series (5 minutes) Remind students of the reactivity series they first met in C3.4.2. Show the reactivity series and have students create mnemonic to remember the order. **Microscale displacement** (10 minutes) Demonstrate the microscale displacement of iron from iron chloride by magnesium. Put three drops of iron(III) chloride solution on a piece of plastic and add one magnesium turning. Students should note that the solution is decolourised as magnesium chloride is produced. Then hold a magnet near the droplet. The iron that is displaced will be attracted to the magnet. Ask students to describe and explain their observations.	**Extend:** Ask students to suggest which species is oxidised and which is reduced.	

Main	Support/Extend	Resources
Rate of bubbling (25 minutes) Ask pairs or small groups of students to investigate calcium, zinc, and copper reacting with cold water, warm water, and dilute hydrochloric acid. Students should pour about 2 cm depth of the liquid or solution into a test tube, and then add a small piece of the metal. Ask students to design a results table to record their observations. Then ask students to write balanced symbol equations to model each reaction that occurs, and use their data to list the metals in order of reactivity. **Metal displacement reactions** (15 minutes) Give students a series of word equations for reactions between a a metal and metal solution. Students use the reactivity series to identify which reactions will occur, justifying their decisions. For each reaction that will occur, students should write a balanced symbol equation.	**Extend:** Ask students to use a gas syringe to measure the gas produced every 30 seconds for 5 minutes. Then ask students to plot a graph of the results. **Extend:** Ask students to write half equations for the reaction that occur, and to distinguish those that model oxidation from those that model reduction.	**Practical:** Rate of bubbling

Plenary	Support/Extend	Resources
Predict reactions (5 minutes) Ask students to predict the reaction between magnesium and cold water, based on their observations from Main 1. Ask students to justify their prediction. **Group 1 metals and water** (10 minutes) Interactive where students sort metals according to whether they react with water. They then put the metals of the reactivity series in order.	**Support:** Work as a class to come up with a mnemonic to remember the order of the reactivity series.	**Interactive:** The reactivity series

Homework	Support/Extend	Resources
Write an outline method to explain how you could use displacement reactions to determine a reactivity series.		

kerboodle
A Kerboodle highlight for this lesson is **Go further: Mobile devices**. Refer to the **Content map** on Kerboodle for a full list of resources and assessment.

The Practical Skills lesson for PAG *1 Reactivity trend* could follow this lesson.

Checkpoint
C4.1 Predicting chemical reactions

Overview of C4.1 Predicting chemical reactions

In this chapter students have looked at patterns in the reactions of Groups 1, 7, 0, and the transition metals. In studying the reactions of the Group 1 elements, they should have observed reactions between halogens and halide ions, and be able to state the products and use the order of reactivity of the halogens to explain the outcome of these displacement reactions. They should be able to represent halogen displacement reactions as chemical equations and predict possible reactions based on the position of halogens in the Periodic Table.

In studying Group 0, students should be able to describe physical properties of the noble gases and relate their lack of reactivity to their outer shell electronic structure. They should be able to use the monatomic nature of the noble gases to explain their low boiling points and densities. Students should be able to predict the physical properties of a noble gas element from data about other members of the group.

Students studying GCSE Chemistry rather than Combined Science should be able to recall the physical properties and reactions of transition metals and their compounds, and give examples. They should have compared the physical properties of transition metals with those of Group 1 metals, and be able to describe how to distinguish transition metal compounds from each other and from Group 1 compounds. They should be able to deduce the charge on a transition metal ion given the names of its compounds. Students should be aware of the uses of transition metals including as catalysts.

Building on work in C3.3 *Types of chemical reaction*, all students should be able to explain how the reactivity of a metal with water or dilute acids is related to its tendency to form its positive ion, and should have used the order of reactivity of metals to predict reactions.

MyMaths

You can find additional support for the maths skills covered in this chapter on **MyMaths**, including calculations using ratios and the law of conservation of mass, using graphs, and drawing Venn diagrams.

PAGs

All students are expected to have carried out the PAG *1 Reactivity trend*. A full lesson plan for each PAG is provided in the Practical skills chapter. PAG *1 Reactivity trend* should be completed after lesson C4.1.6 *Reactivity of elements*.

kerboodle

For this chapter, the following assessments are available on Kerboodle:
C4.1 Checkpoint quiz: Predicting chemical reactions
C4.1 Progress quiz: Predicting chemical reactions 1
C4.1 Progress quiz: Predicting chemical reactions 2
C4.1 On your marks: Predicting chemical reactions
C4.1 Exam-style questions and mark scheme: Predicting chemical reactions

C4.1 Predicting chemical reactions

Checkpoint follow-up lesson

A student's route through this lesson can be determined using the Checkpoint assessment. Percentage pass marks are supplied in the Checkpoint teacher notes.

For each successive route through it is assumed that the student can perform to their current route as well as previous routes. For example, students working at Aiming for 6 are assumed to be secure in Aiming for 4 knowledge and understanding and working towards achieving all the learning objectives for Aiming for 6.

	Aiming for 4	**Aiming for 6**	**Aiming for 8**
Learning outcomes	Recall the simple properties of Groups 1, 7, and 0.	Explain the trend in properties of Groups 1, 7, and 0.	Predict the properties of elements based on the trends for a group.
	Recall the general properties of transition metals.	Give examples to illustrate the properties of transition metals.	Predict possible reactions and probable reactivity of elements from their positions in the Periodic Table.
	Complete word equations for reactions between metals and acids or water.	Explain how the reactivity of metals with water or dilute acids is related to the tendency of the metal to form its positive ion.	Deduce an order of reactivity of metals based on experimental results.
Starter	**General equations (5 minutes)** Ask students to write general equations for the reactions of metals with water, acid, and oxygen.		
	Dot and cross (10 minutes) Ask students to draw the dot-and-cross diagrams for the first three Group 1 metals. Then ask them to list all the similarities (same number of electrons in the outer shell) and all the differences between the diagrams (different number of nucleons, different mass, different number of electron shells).		
Differentiated checkpoint activity	**Poster (40 minutes)** Explain that students will be producing a question and answer sheet to summarise the topic *Predicting chemical reactions*. Students answer each question on the differentiated worksheets.		
	The Aiming for 4 sheet provides structured tasks to support students in making a set of questions and answers that they can use to quiz themselves when revising the topic.	The Aiming for 6 sheet provides questions to guide the content students include as they prepare a revision quiz.	The Aiming for 8 sheet provides fewer prompt questions which cover more advanced content.
	Kerboodle resource: C4.1 Checkpoint follow-up: Aiming for 4, C4.1 Checkpoint follow-up: Aiming for 6, C4.1 Checkpoint follow-up: Aiming for 8		
Plenary	**Question review (5 minutes)** Ask students to swap their question and answer sheet with another student. They should review each other's work and list anything that might need changing because the science is incorrect.		
	Objective check (5 minutes) Rewrite each objective for the lesson as a question and answer. Alternatively, students could highlight questions and the answers on their prepared sheets that represent the objectives.		
Progression	Aiming for 4 students should be able to recall the simple properties of Groups 1, 7, 0 and the transition metals. They can build on this by stating and explaining the trends in these properties. Students should be able to describe chemical reactions in word equations and work towards completing symbol equations.	Aiming for 6 students should be able to describe trends in properties for Groups 1, 7, 0, and the transition metals. They should use symbol equations to describe reactions and begin to add state symbols. Students should be able to explain why a chemical reaction is likely to take place in terms of the ease of making the metal ion. They can start to relate this to the reactivity series.	Aiming for 8 students should be able to predict the properties of elements in Groups 1, 7, 0 and the transition metals based on the trends seen in the Periodic Table. They should begin to apply their knowledge to predict the trends in properties of elements in other groups of the Periodic Table. Students should be able to draw conclusions about reactivity based on results. They should work towards being be able to predict the reactions of an unknown element based on its reaction with various elements and compounds.

C4 Predicting and identifying reactions and products

C4.2 Identifying the products of chemical reactions
C4.2.1 Detecting gases

Specification links:

4.2a Describe tests to identify selected gases.

WS2a Carry out experiments.

WS2b Make and record observations and measurements, using a range of apparatus and methods.

WS2c Present observations using appropriate methods.

M1c Use ratios, [fractions, and percentages].

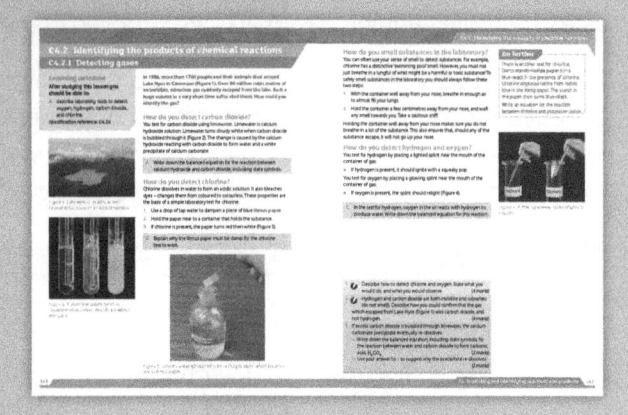

Target	Outcome	Checkpoint	
		Question	Activity
Aiming for GRADE 4	Recognise that limewater turns cloudy when carbon dioxide is bubbled through it.	2	Starter 2 Main 2 Plenary 2 Homework
	Describe the results of positive tests for hydrogen and oxygen.		Main Plenary 1 and 2
↓	Recognise that substances need to be smelt safely.		Starter 1
Aiming for GRADE 6	Describe in detail how to use limewater to test for carbon dioxide.	2	Starter 2 Main Plenary 2 Homework
	Describe in detail how to test for chlorine, hydrogen, and oxygen.	B, 1	Main Plenary 2
↓	Smell substances safely in the laboratory.		Starter 1
Aiming for GRADE 8	Write balanced chemical equations to explain the reactions that occur when carbon dioxide is bubbled through limewater.	A, 3	Starter 2
	Write equations for the reactions that occur in the tests for hydrogen and oxygen.	C	Main
↓	Explain why it is important to smell substances safely.		Starter 1

Maths
In Starter 2 students write balanced symbol and half equations (M1c).

Key words
limewater, litmus paper, starch–iodide paper

C4.2 Identifying the products of chemical reactions

Starter	Support/Extend	Resources
How to smell gases (5 minutes) Demonstrate how to smell substances safely. Allow students to smell chlorine water, dilute ammonia, and oxygen. **Limewater test** (10 minutes) Give each student a straw and a test-tube half-filled with limewater. Wearing eye protection, students gently exhale through the straw into the limewater and note what they observe. Explain that carbon dioxide is an acidic gas and limewater is a solution of the alkali calcium hydroxide. Ask students to write a balanced symbol equation for the reaction.	**Extend:** Explain why it is important to smell substances safely. **Extend:** Ask students to add state symbols to the equation and use this to explain why limewater goes cloudy when carbon dioxide is present.	

Main	Support/Extend	Resources
Circus: gases (40 minutes) Set up three stations around the room. Students visit each station in pairs or groups of three. Ask students to make and test the following: 1 **Carbon dioxide:** Half-fill a test-tube with limewater and place in a test-tube rack. Put the end of a delivery tube into the liquid. Add about 25 cm³ of hydrochloric acid to a conical flask and add a few marble chips. Quickly put a bung on the conical flask and observe the limewater. 2 **Hydrogen:** Fill a water trough and test tube with water. Submerge the test tube in the trough, still full of water. Add about 100 cm³ of hydrochloric acid into a conical flask and add a spatula of zinc granules. Put a bung in the conical flask and put the end of the delivery tube into the water bath. Wait about a minute to ensure the air has been removed from the system. Then collect the gas in a test-tube by delivery over water. Put a bung on the test-tube whilst the lip is still under the water. Test the gas by removing the bung and holding a lighted splint at the neck of the test tube. 3 **Oxygen:** Add about 25 cm³ hydrogen peroxide to a conical flask with 1 spatula of manganese dioxide. Light a splint and gently blow or tap it so that it is only glowing. Hold the glowing splint in the neck of the conical flask and observe. Ask students to draw a labelled diagram of the apparatus for each reaction, to describe in detail how to test for the gas produced, and to note the result of this test.		**Practical:** Making and testing gases

Plenary	Support/Extend	Resources
Testing for gases (10 minutes) Interactive activity in which students match the substance with its chemical test. **Which gas?** (5 minutes) Ask students to imagine they have been given three unlabelled test tubes that contain hydrogen, carbon dioxide, and oxygen. Students write a quick guide for how to identify each gas, including safety considerations.		**Interactive:** Testing for gases

Homework	Support/Extend	Resources
Write an outline method for testing a gas to find out whether it is carbon dioxide.		

kerboodle

A Kerboodle highlight for this lesson is **Literacy interactive: Detecting gases**. Refer to the **Content map** on Kerboodle for a full list of resources and assessment.

GCSE CHEMISTRY ONLY
C4.2.2 Detecting cations

Specification links:

4.2b Describe tests to identify aqueous cations and aqueous anions.

4.2c Describe how to perform a flame test.

4.2d Identify species from test results.

4.2e Interpret flame tests to identify metal ions.

WS1.4a Use scientific vocabulary, terminology, and definitions.

WS1.2b Plan experiments or devise procedures to make observations, produce or characterise a substance, test hypotheses, check data, or explore phenomena.

WS1.2c Apply knowledge of a range of techniques, instruments, apparatus, and materials to select those appropriate to the experiment.

WS2a Carry out experiments.

WS2b Make and record observations and measurements, using a range of apparatus and methods.

M1c Use ratios, fractions, and percentages.

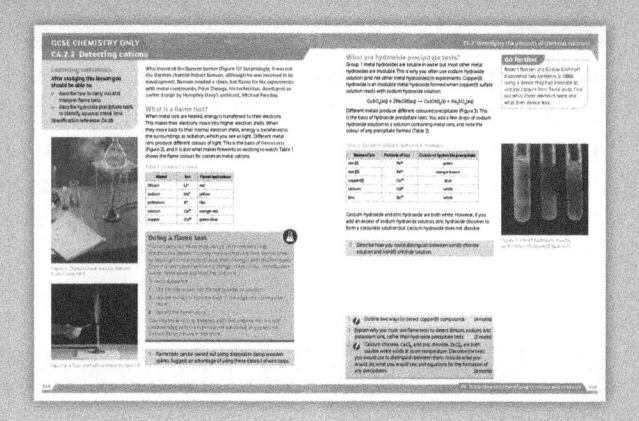

Target	Outcome	Checkpoint	
		Question	Activity
Aiming for GRADE 4 ↓	Describe some steps in performing a flame test to identify metal ions.		Main 2, Plenary 1
	Record observations when metal ions are heated.		Main 2
	Recognise that sodium hydroxide can be used to identify aqueous metal ions.		Main 1
Aiming for GRADE 6 ↓	Describe in detail how to perform a flame test to identify metal ions.		Main 2, Plenary 1
	Interpret flame test results to identify the metal ions present in a substance.	1, 2	Main 2, Plenary 2
	Explain how to use sodium hydroxide to identify aqueous metal ions.	B, 1	Main 1, Plenary 2, Homework
Aiming for GRADE 8 ↓	Explain why each step in the flame test is necessary to obtain a valid result.	A	Main 2
	Explain why different metal ions produce different colours when heated.		Main 2
	Explain in detail, including equations, how aqueous cations can be identified with sodium hydroxide solution.	3	Main 1, Homework

Maths
In Main 1 (Extend) and in completing the Homework task students write balanced symbol and ionic equations (M1c).

Literacy
In Plenary 1 students order statements to write a method to carry out a flame test.

Key words
flame tests

C4.2 Identifying the products of chemical reactions

Starter	Support/Extend	Resources
Fireworks (5 minutes) Explain to students that the colours of fireworks are caused by different metal compounds. Different metals burn in different colours. Ask students to suggest how this could be used by scientists analytically. **Equations** (10 minutes) Show students the word equations for the reactions they will carry out in Main 1. Ask students to write balanced symbol equations with state symbols.		

Main	Support/Extend	Resources
Identifying positive ions (25 minutes) Ask pairs of students to place 2 drops of each solution to be tested (iron(II) chloride, iron(III) chloride, copper(II) sulfate, calcium chloride, zinc nitrate) in a dimple on a spotting tile, followed by 2 drops of sodium hydroxide solution. Students should design a results table in which to note the colour of any precipitate formed. Ask students to conclude which metal ions are present in each solution. **Flame tests** (15 minutes) Ask students to read the method outlined in the Student Book section *Doing a flame test* to carry out flame tests on metal salts. Provide students with a list of metal salts and have them predict what results they would expect from a flame test. Ask students to use information from the Student Book to help them explain why different metal ions produce different colours when heated. Then ask students to evaluate this technique and to consider why it cannot be used to identify solutions with more than one metal ion, or to differentiate easily between lithium and calcium compounds.	**Extend:** Ask students to write balanced symbol equations, with state symbols, to help them to explain in detail how aqueous cations can be identified with sodium hydroxide solution. **Extend:** Include some mixtures of metal salts. Students should identify how it would be difficult to use flame tests to identify the metals in these mixtures. **Extend:** Ask students to explain why each step in the flame test is necessary to obtain a valid result.	**Practical:** Identifying positive ions

Plenary	Support/Extend	Resources
Method sort (5 minutes) Show students the procedure for carrying out a flame test as separate sentences. Ask them to sequence the steps correctly. **Testing for positive ions** (10 minutes) Interactive activity in which students match flame test results to the metal ion present. Students then sort cations according to whether they form a coloured or a white precipitate when sodium hydroxide is added to them.	**Extend:** Ask students to suggest what simple laboratory test could be used to differentiate between copper(II) chloride and barium chloride.	**Interactive:** Testing for positive ions

Homework	Support/Extend	Resources
Write balanced symbol equations for the reaction between sodium hydroxide solution and metal chlorides, limited to the ions listed in Table 2 in the Student Book.	**Extend:** Ask students to write ionic equations for these reactions.	

kerboodle
A Kerboodle highlight for this lesson is **Bump up your grade: Detecting cations**. Refer to the **Content map** on Kerboodle for a full list of resources and assessment.

GCSE CHEMISTRY ONLY
C4.2.3 Detecting anions

Specification links:

4.2b Describe tests to identify aqueous cations and aqueous anions.

WS1.4a Use scientific vocabulary, terminology, and definitions.

WS2a Carry out experiments.

WS2b Make and record observations and measurements, using a range of apparatus and methods.

M1c Use ratios, fractions, and percentages.

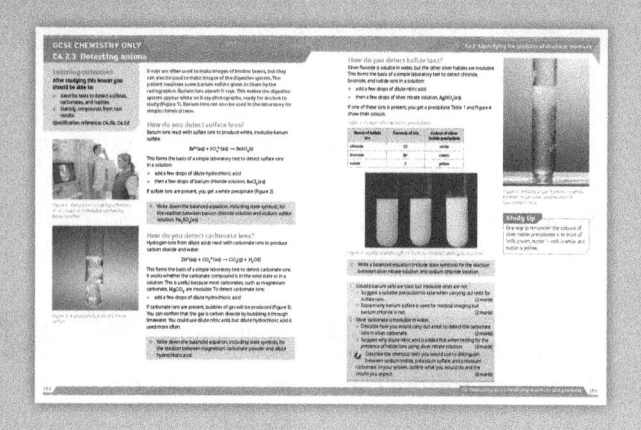

Target	Outcome	Checkpoint Question	Checkpoint Activity
Aiming for GRADE 4 ↓	Describe some steps and expected results for sulfate and carbonate anion tests.		Starter 2, Main
	State that aqueous halide ions form a precipitate with silver nitrate solution and that this can be used to identify them.		Main, Plenary 2, Homework
	Record observations when carrying out tests for anions.		Main
Aiming for GRADE 6 ↓	Describe in detail how to test for sulfate and carbonate anions.	1, 2	Main
	Explain how silver nitrate solution can be used to test for halide ions.	3	Main
	Explain observations noted when testing for anions.		Main
Aiming for GRADE 8 ↓	Describe in detail how to identify sulfate and carbonate anions, and write equations for all reactions that occur.	A, B	Main
	Explain in detail how silver nitrate solution can be used to identify halide ions, and write equations for all reactions that occur.	C	Main
	Explain in detail observations noted when testing for anions, and write equations for all reactions that occur.		Main, Plenary 2, Homework

Maths
In Main 1 (Extend) students write ionic equations (M1c).

Literacy
In Main 2 students write an outline method for testing anions.

C4.2 Identifying the products of chemical reactions

Starter	Support/Extend	Resources
Matching anions (5 minutes) Ask students to match the names of the anions in this section of the Student Book with their formulae. **Metal carbonates and acid** (10 minutes) Put half a spatula measure of calcium carbonate powder into a test-tube. Then add some hydrochloric acid and observe. Ask students to suggest how this could be used to show that the powder is a carbonate.	**Extend:** Ask students to calculate the relative formula mass of the ions.	**Interactive:** Matching anions

Main	Support/Extend	Resources
Circus: anions (40 minutes) Set up three stations around the room. Students visit each station in pairs. Ask students to test for different anions as described below. As they perform each test, students write an outline method describing the test, highlighting the reagents with one colour of highlighter pen, and the expected positive result with another colour. 1 Sulfate test: place 2 drops of the solution to be tested in a dimple. Add 2 drops of hydrochloric acid solution and 2 drops of barium chloride solution. Note the colour of any precipitate formed. 2 Halide test: place 2 drops of the solution to be tested in a dimple. Add 2 drops of nitric acid solution and 2 drops of silver nitrate solution. Note the colour of any precipitate formed. 3 Carbonate test: half-fill a test-tube with limewater and put it in a test-tube rack. Half-fill a second test-tube with the solution to be tested. Mount it at 45° using a stand, boss, and clamp. Add about 2 cm^3 of dilute acid and quickly insert a bung and delivery tube so that any gas produced bubbles through the limewater. Observe whether the limewater goes cloudy. Use microscale testing where possible to reduce the risk and the cost.	**Extend:** Ask students to write the ionic equations for all the tests.	**Practical:** Circus: anions

Plenary	Support/Extend	Resources
True or false? (5 minutes) Ask students to put their thumbs up for true and thumbs down for false. Read out the following statements: 1 Barium sulfate is soluble in water (false). 2 Metal carbonates are bases (true). 3 Silver chloride is a white solid at room temperature (true). 4 The reagents for testing for halide ions are nitric acid and silver nitrate (true). 5 Most metal carbonates are soluble in water (false). **Secret identity** (10 minutes) Ask students to identify mystery substances based on questions, such as 'What substance produces a green flame, a blue precipitate when mixed with sodium hydroxide solution, but a white precipitate when mixed with nitric acid and silver nitrate solution?' (copper(II) chloride).	**Support:** Allow students to work in small teams before giving their answer.	

Homework	Support/Extend	Resources
Explain how simple laboratory techniques may be used to identify lithium chloride and sodium bromide solutions.		

A Kerboodle highlight for this lesson is **WebQuest: Identifying chemicals**. Refer to the **Content map** on Kerboodle for a full list of resources and assessment.

The Practical Skills lesson for PAG 5 *Identification of species* could follow this lesson.

GCSE CHEMISTRY ONLY

C4.2.4 Instrumental methods of analysis

Specification links:

4.2f Describe the advantages of instrumental methods of analysis.

4.2g Interpret an instrumental result, given appropriate data in chart or tabular form, when accompanied by a reference set of data in the same form.

WS1.1e Explain everyday and technological applications of science.

WS1.2c Apply knowledge of a range of techniques, instruments, apparatus, and materials to select those appropriate to the experiment.

WS1.2d Recognise when to apply knowledge of sampling techniques to ensure any samples collected are representative.

WS1.2e Evaluate methods and suggest possible improvements and further investigations.

WS1.3e Interpret observations and other data.

M1c Use ratios, fractions, [and percentages].

CM4.2i Interpret charts, particularly in spectroscopy (M4a).

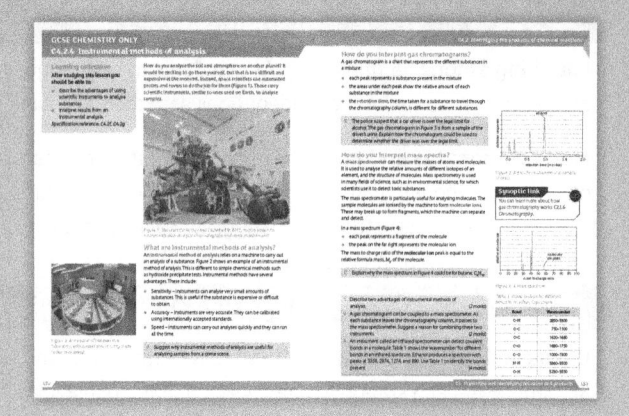

Target	Outcome	Checkpoint	
		Question	Activity
Aiming for GRADE 4	State that scientific instruments can be used to identify substances and recall one use of instrumental analysis.		Starter 1 Plenary 1
	List some methods of instrumental analysis.		Main 1 and 2 Plenary 1
↓	Recognise that the spectrum produced by an instrument is unique for a particular substance.		Main 1 and 2 Plenary 1
Aiming for GRADE 6	Describe some advantages of instrumental analysis.	A, 1	Main 2 Plenary 2 Homework
	Describe some details of the different methods of instrumental analysis available.		Main 1
↓	Interpret simple spectra to suggest the relative formula mass of a substance or the bonds present.	B, 3	Main 1
Aiming for GRADE 8	Justify the use of particular instruments to analyse given substances or mixtures of substances.		Plenary 2 Homework
	Explain why different instrumental techniques are used together.	2	Main 1 and 2
↓	Use data and spectra to suggest functional groups in a sample.	B, 3	Main 1

Maths
In Starter 2 (Extend) students calculate retention factors (M1c).

Literacy
In Main 2 students prepare persuasive arguments.

Key words
instrumental method of analysis, retention time, mass spectrometer, molecular ions, molecular ion peak

C4.2 Identifying the products of chemical reactions

Starter	Support/Extend	Resources
History of the laboratory (5 minutes) Show students images of science laboratories from different stages in history, up to the most high-tech labs available to today's scientists. Ask students to suggest how and why research environments have changed. **Paper chromatography** (10 minutes) Ask students to sketch the experimental setup used to separate dyes in pen ink (paper chromatography, met in C2.1.6). Then ask students to sketch what they would expect the chromatogram to look like if the ink contained three dyes. Finally ask students what is the stationary phase and what is the mobile phase.	**Extend:** Ask students to give the formula to calculate retention factors.	

Main	Support/Extend	Resources
Gas chromatograms (20 minutes) If you have not already done so, remind students of paper chromatography that they studied in C2.1.6. Ask them to suggest what is the stationary phase and what is the mobile phase. Then introduce gas chromatography. Ask them to suggest what are the stationary phase (coil) and the mobile phase (gas) in a gas chromatogram, and how the retention time is calculated. Then ask students to explain why gas chromatography is better than paper chromatography. Explain that gas chromatography is often used with mass spectroscopy, and discuss why these techniques are often used together. Show students a mass spectrum of butane, explaining that the substance is a hydrocarbon. Then ask students to identify the molecular ion peak of this compound, predict its molecular mass, and suggest its molecular formula. **Debating instrumental analysis** (20 minutes) Explain that instrumental analysis allows quantitative data to be collected, which is very important when providing evidence to a court, such as in a pollution control case. Review the advantages and disadvantages of instrumental analysis techniques. Then split the class into two groups, one for and the other against the motion *Instrumental analysis should not be used to analyse substances in samples taken by the Environment Agency*. Ask students to prepare and present persuasive arguments in support of their case.	**Support:** A number of instructional video clips of analytical techniques and instruments can be found by searching on the RSC website.	**Activity:** Debating instrumental analysis

Plenary	Support/Extend	Resources
Match (5 minutes) Ask students to match up the instrumental technique with its uses: 1 Gas chromatography (separating mixtures, identifying substances) 2 Mass spectroscopy (determining molecular mass, providing information about the structure of a substance, identifying substances) 3 Infrared spectroscopy (providing information about the structure of a substance, identifying substances). **Dragon's den** (10 minutes) Ask students to work in small groups to prepare a 1-minute pitch to encourage an analytical laboratory owner to invest in new instrumental techniques.		**Interactive:** Matching instrumental techniques and uses

Homework	Support/Extend	Resources
Make a poster to explain the benefits and drawbacks of instrumental techniques compared with traditional simple laboratory tests.		

kerboodle
A Kerboodle highlight for this lesson is **Literacy sheet: Instrumental analysis**. Refer to the **Content map** on Kerboodle for a full list of resources and assessment.

Checkpoint
C4.2 Identifying the products of chemical reactions

Overview of C4.2 Identifying the products of chemical reactions

In this chapter students have studied how products of chemical reactions are identified, specifically gases. They should have carried out practical work and in detecting gases be able to describe how to use limewater to test for carbon dioxide, and how to test for chlorine, hydrogen, and oxygen. Students should be able to explain why it is important to smell substances safely, and how to do this. They should be able to represent the reactions involved in these tests with chemical equations.

Students studying GCSE Chemistry rather than Combined Science have also studied the identification of cations and anions. In detecting cations, they should be able to describe how to perform a flame test to identify metal ions, and interpret the result. They should recall how to use sodium hydroxide to identify aqueous metal ions. In detecting anions, they should be able to describe tests for sulfates and carbonates, and the use of silver nitrate solution to test for halide ions. They should be able to explain their observations and use equations to represent the reactions. Higher-tier students should be able to apply their skills in writing ionic equations to this topic. Students should link this work on analysis with their studies in C2.2 *Bonding* and C3.1 *Introducing chemical reactions*.

Finally GCSE Chemistry students have studied instrumental methods of analysis, including gas chromatography and mass spectrometry. They should understand that gas chromatography is similar to paper chromatography but is more sensitive, quick, and accurate. They should be able to describe some different methods of instrumental analysis, explain their advantages, and interpret simple spectra.

MyMaths

You can find additional support for the maths skills covered in this chapter on **MyMaths**, including calculations using ratios and conservation of mass.

PAGs

All students are expected to have carried out the PAG *5 Identification of species*. A full lesson plan for each PAG is provided in the Practical skills chapter. PAG *5 Identification of species* should be completed after lesson C4.2.3 *Detecting anions*.

kerboodle

For this chapter, the following assessments are available on Kerboodle:
C4.2 Checkpoint quiz: Identifying the products of chemical reactions
C4.2 Progress quiz: Identifying the products of chemical reactions 1
C4.2 Progress quiz: Identifying the products of chemical reactions 2
C4.2 On your marks: Identifying the products of chemical reactions
C4.2 Exam-style questions and mark scheme: Identifying the products of chemical reactions

C4.2 Identifying the products of chemical reactions

Checkpoint follow-up lesson

A student's route through this lesson can be determined using the Checkpoint assessment. Percentage pass marks are supplied in the Checkpoint teacher notes.

For each successive route through it is assumed that the student can perform to their current route as well as previous routes. For example, students working at Aiming for 6 are assumed to be secure in Aiming for 4 knowledge and understanding and working towards achieving all the learning objectives for Aiming for 6.

	Aiming for 4	**Aiming for 6**	**Aiming for 8**
Learning outcomes	Describe how to test for common gases.	Describe how to test for common positive ions.	Explain how gas chromatography–mass spectrometry (GC-MS) is used in crime prevention.
	Describe how flame tests are carried out.	Describe how to test for common negative ions.	
Starter	**Identification (10 minutes)** Ask students to come up with three reasons or situations in which it is important to be able to identify substances. List their ideas and discuss them. Then ask why it might be important for tests to be quick and fairly straightforward, as opposed to involving expensive equipment. Ask what substances can be identified using simple chemical tests and draw up a list. Do not cover the process of these tests at this stage, as students will revisit this in the plenary.		
Differentiated checkpoint activity	**Detecting (40 minutes)** Students work in differentiated groups using the differentiated worksheets. Aiming for 4 and Aiming for 6 students carry out practical work to detect gases and positive and negative ions, while Aiming for 8 students research the use of the instrumental method GC-MS in crime prevention.		
	Aiming for 4 and Aiming for 6 students will require apparatus for testing for the following gases (or shown these as a demonstration if more appropriate): • oxygen (relights a glowing splint) • hydrogen (burns with a squeaky pop with a lit splint) • carbon dioxide (turns limewater milky) • chlorine (bleaches damp litmus paper).		
	They will also need the apparatus, and instruction and help, for carrying out flame tests on the following metals: lithium, sodium, potassium, calcium, and copper.		
	Aiming for 6 students will also require the apparatus (or a demonstration) and instruction for testing for the following ions: • metal ions – reaction with sodium hydroxide solution to form different coloured insoluble metal hydroxide precipitates • carbonates – fizz due to carbon dioxide gas being produced when dilute acid is added • halides – form precipitates when reacted with silver nitrate solution in the presence of nitric acid • sulfates – form a white precipitate when reacted with barium chloride in the presence of hydrochloric acid.		
	Aiming for 4 students should work in small groups and carry out each test in a circus activity. They may need help to carry out the tests. The sheet provides tasks for them to complete. They could cut out each task and stick it on a separate sheet of card or paper to act as an aide memoire for each process.	The Aiming for 6 sheet includes a series of practical tests for students to carry out. They are asked to record their observations for each, and produce a booklet containing a series of instructions on how to test for positive and metal ions.	Aiming for 8 students are given prompts to help them research the use of GC-MS in crime prevention. They will need internet access or comprehensive written sources on the topic. They are asked to produce a detailed piece of writing about the technique.
	Kerboodle resource: C4.2 Checkpoint follow-up: Aiming for 4, C4.2 Checkpoint follow-up: Aiming for 6, C4.2 Checkpoint follow-up: Aiming for 8		
Plenary	**Test match (5 minutes)** Call out a series of substances as students use mini-whiteboards to state which technique they would use to identify each one. They should also give the positive result.		
Progression	The Aiming for 4 sheet is highly structured and guides students to produce their record of the tests. Students will need support with practical work, or you may prefer to demonstrate some of the tests.	The Aiming for 6 sheet is fairly structured. It asks students to produce a booklet with one page for each type of test, including a description of the method, a diagram, and expected results. Students may need some guidance in carrying out the practical work.	Aiming for 8 students decide how to set out their account of GC-MS, which is targeted at someone with limited scientific knowledge, providing questions that their account should answer. Students should be able to work independently to complete this research task.

C4 Predicting and identifying reactions and products: Topic summary

C4.1 Predicting chemical reactions
C4.2 Identifying the products of chemical reactions

Spec ref	Statement	Book spreads
C4.1a	Recall the simple properties of Groups 1, 7, and 0	C4.1.1, C4.1.2, C4.1.3, C4.1.4
C4.1b	Explain how observed simple properties of Groups 1, 7, and 0 depend on the outer shell of electrons of the atoms and predict properties from given trends down the groups	C4.1.1, C4.1.2, C4.1.4
C4.1c	Recall the general properties of transition metals and their compounds and exemplify these by reference to a small number of transition metals	C4.1.5
C4.1d	Predict possible reactions and probable reactivity of elements from their positions in the periodic table	C4.1.3
C4.1e	Explain how the reactivity of metals with water or dilute acids is related to the tendency of the metal to form its positive ion	C4.1.6, C4.1.6
C4.1f	Deduce an order of reactivity of metals based on experimental results	
C4.2a	Describe tests to identify selected gases	C4.2.1
C4.2b	Describe tests to identify aqueous cations and aqueous anions	C4.2.2, C4.2.3
C4.2c	Describe how to perform a flame test	C4.2.2
C4.2d	Identify species from test results	C4.2.2
C4.2e	Interpret flame tests to identify metal ions	C4.2.2
C4.2f	Describe the advantages of instrumental methods of analysis	C4.2.4
C4.2g	Interpret an instrumental result given appropriate data in chart or tabular form, when accompanied by a reference set of data in the same form	C4.2.4

Maths

Specification		Book spread	
Spec ref	Statement	Main content	Maths chapter
CM4.1i	Arithmetic computation and ratio when determining empirical formulae, balancing equations	C4.1.1, C4.1.2, C4.1.3	3
CM4.2i	Interpret charts, particularly in spectroscopy	C4.2.4	6

Working scientifically

Specification		Book spread	
Spec ref	Statement	Main content	WS chapter
WS1.1b	Use models to solve problems, make predictions, and to develop scientific explanations and understanding of familiar and unfamiliar facts.	C4.1.6	WS2
WS1.1e	Explain everyday and technological applications of science.	C4.2.4	WS1
WS1.2a	Use scientific theories and explanations to develop hypotheses.	C4.1.1, C4.1.2, C4.1.3, C4.1.4, C4.1.6	WS3
WS1.2b	Plan experiments or devise procedures to make observations, produce or characterise a substance, test hypotheses, check data, or explore phenomena.	C4.2.2	WS3, WS4
WS1.2c	Apply knowledge of a range of techniques, instruments, apparatus, and materials to select those appropriate to the experiment.	C4.2.2, C4.2.4	WS4
WS1.2d	Recognise when to apply knowledge of sampling techniques to ensure any samples collected are representative	C4.2.4	
WS1.2e	Evaluate methods and suggest possible improvements and further investigations.	C4.2.4	
WS1.3c	Carrying out and representing mathematical and statistical analysis, to include arithmetic means, mode, and median.		WS5
WS1.3e	Interpreting observations and other data.	C4.1.6, C4.2.4	WS7
WS1.4a	Use scientific vocabulary, terminology, and definitions.	C4.1.1, C4.1.2, C4.1.3, C4.1.4, C4.1.5, C4.1.6, C4.2.2, C4.2.3	WS2
WS1.4c	Use SI units and IUPAC chemical nomenclature unless inappropriate.	C4.1.1, C4.1.2, C4.1.3, C4.1.4	
WS2a	Carry out experiments.	C4.2.1, C4.2.2, C4.2.3	
WS2b	Make and record observations and measurements, using a range of apparatus and methods.	C4.2.1, C4.2.2, C4.2.3	
WS2c	Present observations using appropriate methods.	C4.2.1	

C5 Monitoring and controlling chemical reactions
C5.1 Monitoring chemical reactions
C5.1.1 Theoretical yield — GCSE CHEMISTRY ONLY

Specification links:

5.1g Calculate the theoretical amount of a product from a given amount of reactant.

WS1.3c Carry out and represent mathematical and statistical analysis.

M1a Recognise and use expressions in decimal form.

M1c Use ratios, fractions, and percentages.

CM5.1iv Understand that arithmetic computation, ratio, percentage, and multistep calculations permeate quantitative chemistry (M1a, M1c, M1d).

CM5.1v Use arithmetic computation when calculating yields and atom economy (M1a, M1c).

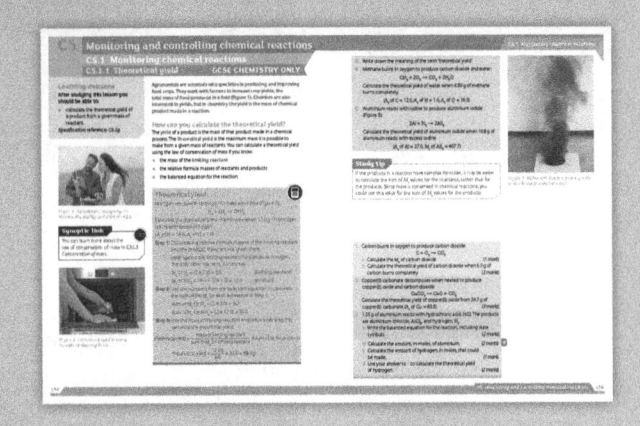

Target	Outcome	Checkpoint Question	Checkpoint Activity
Aiming for GRADE 4	Calculate the relative formula mass of elements and compounds that exist as diatomic molecules.		Main / Homework
	State that the mass of a product obtained in a chemical reaction is the yield.		Main / Plenary 1 and 2
Aiming for GRADE 6	Calculate the relative formula mass of molecules and compounds containing simple ions.	1a	Main
	Define the term theoretical yield.	A	Main / Plenary 1
	Calculate the theoretical yield of a product from a given mass of reactant, given the equation for the reaction.	B, C, 1b, 2	Starter 1 and 2 / Main / Plenary 2 / Homework
Aiming for GRADE 8	Calculate the relative formula mass of compounds containing ions made up of atoms of more than one element.		Plenary 2
	Justify the use of the law of conservation of mass and the identity of the limiting reactant in theoretical yield calculations.		Main / Plenary 1
	Calculate the theoretical yield of a product from a given mass of reactant in a given reaction.	3	Starter 1 and 2 / Main / Plenary 2 / Homework

Maths
Throughout this lesson students calculate relative formula mass and theoretical yield (M1a, M1c).

Literacy
In Main 1 students make a flow chart to explain how to calculate theoretical yield.

Key words
yield, theoretical yield, limiting reactant

C5.1 Monitoring chemical reactions

Starter	Support/Extend	Resources
Ammonia maths (5 minutes) Give students the balanced symbol equation for the reaction of concentrated ammonia and hydrochloric acid and ask them to predict the maximum mass of ammonium chloride produced if the total mass of the reactants was 5.35 g. **Ammonia fountain** (10 minutes) Give students three reactions written out in prose. Ask students to suggest an equation for each reaction and to identify the limiting reactant and the reactant present in excess.	**Extend:** Ask students to write the balanced symbol equation for each reaction, and to predict the maximum mass of produce that would be made if 5 g of the limiting reactant was used.	

Main	Support/Extend	Resources
Calculating theoretical yield (20 minutes) Go through Student Book section *Theoretical yield*, showing how to calculate the theoretical yield of ammonia. Then ask students to make a flow chart to explain how to calculate theoretical yield, and use this to answer Questions 1b and 2. Students then write a balanced symbol equation for the reaction of magnesium with oxygen, identifying the limiting reactant and the reactant in excess. Provide students with a length of magnesium ribbon, around 5 cm long, and have them measure the mass to 0.01 g. They find the relative atomic mass of magnesium and calculate the relative formula mass of oxygen, to calculate the theoretical yield of magnesium oxide. Their length of ribbon should be labelled with the students' name and stored safely for the next lesson, where they will conduct the reaction.	**Support:** Provide students with the relevant steps to put into the correct sequence. **Extend:** Ask students to measure the mass of the product after combustion and suggest why it is not the same as the theoretical yield.	**Activity:** Calculating theoretical yield

Plenary	Support/Extend	Resources
Higher or lower? (5 minutes) Ask students to suggest the effect that each of the following would have on the actual yield of a product compared with the theoretical yield: 1 Product still has solvent in it (higher yield) 2 Not all of the reactants reacted (lower yield) 3 The reaction is reversible (lower yield) 4 Not all of the product was transferred (lower yield) 5 A smaller mass of limiting reactant was used (lower yield) 6 A larger mass of limiting reactant was used (higher yield). **Calculate yield** (10 minutes) Calculate the mass of ammonium sulfate produced when 0.98 g of sulfuric acid reacts with excess ammonium hydroxide.	**Extend:** Ask students what effect adding a larger mass of the reactant in excess would have (no effect). **Support:** Give the balanced symbol equation for the reaction and the following steps: 1 Calculate the relative formula mass of each substance. 2 Which is the limiting reactant? 3 Work out the ratio between the limiting reactant and the desired product. 4 Calculate the mass of the desired product.	**Interactive:** Higher or lower?

Homework	Support/Extend	Resources
Write a balanced symbol equation for making water from its elements. Use this to determine the mass of water made when 2 g of hydrogen reacts with excess oxygen.	**Extend:** Make sure you use moles in your calculations.	

GCSE CHEMISTRY ONLY

C5.1.2 Percentage yield and atom economy

Specification links:

5.1h Calculate the percentage yield of a reaction product from the actual yield of a reaction.

5.1i Define the atom economy of a reaction.

5.1j Calculate the atom economy of a reaction to form a desired product from the balanced equation.

WS1.2a Use scientific theories and explanations to develop hypotheses.

WS1.2b Plan experiments or devise procedures to make observations, produce or characterise a substance, test hypotheses, check data, or explore phenomena.

WS1.2c Apply knowledge of a range of techniques, instruments, apparatus, and materials to select those appropriate to the experiment.

WS1.2d Recognise when to apply knowledge of sampling techniques to ensure any samples collected are representative.

WS1.3c Carry out and represent mathematical and statistical analysis.

WS2a Carry out experiments.

WS2b Make and record observations and measurements using a range of apparatus and methods.

M1a Recognise and use expressions in decimal form. M1c Use ratios, fractions, and percentages.

CM5.1iv Understand that arithmetic computation, ratio, percentage, and multistep calculations permeate quantitative chemistry (M1a, M1c, M1d). CM5.1v Use arithmetic computation when calculating yields and atom economy (M1a, M1c).

Target	Outcome	Checkpoint Question	Checkpoint Activity
Aiming for GRADE 4	State that the actual yield of a reaction may be less than the theoretical yield.		Main
	Calculate the percentage yield of a reaction, given the equation for the process, the actual yield, and the theoretical yield.		Main, Plenary 2
	Calculate the atom economy of a reaction, given the equation for the process, the relative masses of all the products, and the relative mass of the desired product.		Starter 2, Plenary 1
Aiming for GRADE 6	Suggest some reasons why the percentage yield of a reaction may be less than 100%.	B	Plenary 2
	Calculate the percentage yield of a product, given the theoretical yield and the actual yield.	A, 1	Main, Plenary 2
	Define the term atom economy and calculate the atom economy of a reaction, given the balanced chemical equation.	C, 2	Starter 1 and 2
Aiming for GRADE 8	Suggest why percentage yield may be less than 100% for given reactions.	B	Main, Plenary 2
	Calculate the percentage yield of a product, given the mass of the reactants and the actual yield.		Main, Plenary 2
	Evaluate different processes used to make the same substance, in order to compare their atom economies.	3	Plenary 1

Maths
In Main 1, Main 2, Plenary 1, and Plenary 2 students calculate percentage yield and atom economy (M1a, M1c).

Literacy
In completing the Homework task students explain the importance of calculating percentage yield and atom economy for industrial processes.

Key words
actual yield, percentage yield, reversible reaction, atom economy

160

C5.1 Monitoring chemical reactions

Starter	Support/Extend	Resources
Key terms (5 minutes) Students use the interactive to match the key terms from this lesson (theoretical yield, limiting reactant, reactant in excess, actual yield, percentage yield, atom economy) to their definition. **Atom economy** (10 minutes) Explain the meaning of atom economy, and show that it can be expressed as: $$\text{atom economy} = \frac{\text{sum of } M_r \text{ of the desired product}}{\text{sum of } M_r \text{ of all products}} \times 100$$ Ask pairs of students to compare percentage yield and atom economy. (Percentage yield concerns the desired product of a reaction only, and involves comparing the actual mass of product obtained with the theoretical maximum mass. Atom economy considers all the products of a reaction, and works out the percentage of the total amount of products that is the desired product. Percentage yield compares masses, while atom economy compares amounts of substance, in moles.)	**Extend:** Just provide students with the key terms and have them write a definition.	**Interactive:** Yield key terms

Main	Support/Extend	Resources
Finding the percentage yield (40 minutes) Build on the work done in the previous lesson and revisit the oxidation of magnesium in air. Ask student pairs to refer back to the theoretical yield of magnesium oxide calculated in C5.1.1. Remind students that the actual yield of a reaction may be less than the theoretical yield. Then ask students to combust their piece of magnesium ribbon in a crucible, measure the mass of the cooled product, and use this to calculate the percentage yield.	**Extend:** Ask students to suggest why the yield is less than 100%. (Some magnesium oxide might have escaped from the reaction vessel when the lid was opened, and some of the magnesium remains unreacted.)	**Practical:** Finding the percentage yield

Plenary	Support/Extend	Resources
Ethanol (5 minutes) Ask students to write a balanced symbol equation for ethene reacting with water to make ethanol. Then ask students to explain why this process has 100% atom economy. **Calculate atom economy** (10 minutes) Explain that 100 tonnes of calcium carbonate can undergo thermal decomposition to make carbon dioxide and calcium oxide. Calcium oxide is then used to make building materials such as cement. Ask students to calculate the atom economy of this reaction and suggest why the percentage yield would be less than 100%. (Some of the calcium carbonate remains unreacted; the reaction is reversible, so some of the products reform calcium carbonate.)	**Support:** Remind students what atom economy is a measure of. **Extend:** Ask students to compare this process of ethanol production with fermentation. **Extend:** State that 28 tonnes of calcium oxide were made. Ask students to calculate the percentage yield.	

Homework	Support/Extend	Resources
Explain the importance of calculating percentage yield and atom economy for an industrial process.		

kerboodle

A Kerboodle highlight for this lesson is **Calculation sheet: Atom economy calculations**. Refer to the **Content map** on Kerboodle for a full list of resources and assessment.

GCSE CHEMISTRY ONLY — HIGHER TIER
C5.1.3 Choosing a reaction pathway

Specification links:

5.1k Explain why a particular reaction pathway is chosen to produce a specified product given appropriate data.

WS1.3c Carry out and represent mathematical and statistical analysis.

WS1.3f Present reasoned explanations.

M1a Recognise and use expressions in decimal form.

M1c Use ratios, fractions, and percentages.

CM5.1v Use arithmetic computation when calculating yields and atom economy (M1a, M1c).

CM5.1vi Change the subject of a mathematical equation (M3b, M3c).

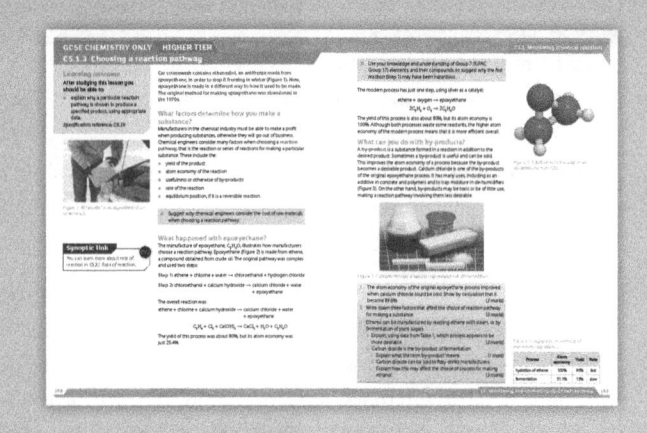

Target	Outcome	Checkpoint Question	Checkpoint Activity
Aiming for GRADE 6	List some of the factors that chemists consider when choosing a reaction pathway.	2	Starter 1, Plenary 1 and 2
	Explain why reaction pathways with high atom economies are desirable.		Starter 1, Plenary 2, Homework
↓	Define the term by-product and explain how selling a by-product can improve the atom economy of a reaction.	3	Plenary 1
Aiming for GRADE 8	Perform practicals to make a substance in two different ways. Use this example to explain in detail the factors that chemists consider when choosing a reaction pathway.	A, B	Main, Plenary 2
	Evaluate the suitability of a process using the atom economies and yields of the reactions involved.	3	Main, Homework
↓	Demonstrate by calculation how selling a by-product can be used to improve the atom economy of a reaction.	1	Plenary 1, Homework

Maths
In Main 1 and Main 2 students calculate atom economy (M1a, M1c).

Literacy
In completing the Homework task students justify their choice of reaction pathway.

Key words
reaction pathway, by-product

C5.1 Monitoring chemical reactions

Starter	Support/Extend	Resources
List (5 minutes) Ask students to list all the ways they can think of to make carbon dioxide in chemical reactions (e.g., combusting carbon, reacting a metal carbonate with an acid, and thermally decomposing calcium carbonate). Ensure students understand that there are many ways to make the same substance and that industrial chemists need to choose the best reaction pathway to produce the desired product in a timely and affordable way. **Producing ethene** (10 minutes) Students use the interactive to complete word and balance symbol equations with state symbols to describe the production of ethene from ethanol and decane.		**Interactive:** Producing ethene

Main	Support/Extend	Resources
Making ethene (40 minutes) Split the class into two groups. One group should produce ethene from ethanol and the other class should produce ethene from decane. Students work in pairs for this practical. 1 Put a piece of mineral wool soaked in ethanol or decane into a boiling tube. 2 Clamp the tube almost horizontally, with the mouth slightly upwards, and place some pumice chips into the tube, about 2 cm above the mineral wool. 3 Connect a bung with a delivery tube to collect the gas under displacement. Ask students to calculate the atom economy of this reaction. Students then swap results to compare the atom economies of the two methods to produce ethene.	**Support:** This experiment is high-risk. You may wish to demonstrate it rather than completing it as a class practical. **Extend:** Use bromine water to test the ethanol and the gas collected, to show that the product and the reactant have different properties.	**Practical:** Making ethene

Plenary	Support/Extend	Resources
By-products (5 minutes) Ask students to justify why it is important to consider the by-products of a reaction when considering which reaction pathway to choose for the industrial production of a product. **Which procedure?** (10 minutes) Explain that ethene is an important feedstock substance in industry, and can be made by fermenting ethanol (as seen in Main 1) or cracking decane (as seen in Main 2). Ethanol can be made from renewable raw materials by fermentation, which is considered to be a carbon-neutral process. Decane is made from the fractional distillation of crude oil, which is a finite resource. Ask students to use this information, together with their knowledge of the two experiments carried out in Main 1 and Main 2, and the atom economy of the reactions, to justify which method they would use to make ethene – fermentation or cracking.	**Support:** Ask students to base their answer on the process described in Student Book section *What happened with epoxyethane?*	

Homework	Support/Extend	Resources
Consider the production of ethanol by fermentation or by the hydration of ethene. Which reaction pathway would you choose and why?		

kerboodle

A Kerboodle highlight for this lesson is **Homework: Monitoring chemical reactions**. Refer to the **Content map** on Kerboodle for a full list of resources and assessment.

HIGHER TIER
C5.1.4 Concentration of solution

Specification links:

5.1a Explain how the concentration of a solution in mol/dm³ is related to the mass of the solute and the volume of the solution.

5.1f Explain how the mass of a solute and the volume of the solution is related to the concentration of the solution.

WS1.3c Carry out and represent mathematical and statistical analysis.

WS1.4a Use scientific vocabulary, terminology, and definitions.

WS1.4c Use SI units and IUPAC chemical nomenclature unless inappropriate.

M1b Recognise expressions in standard form.

M1c Use ratios, fractions, and percentages.

M2a Use an appropriate number of significant figures.

M3b Change the subject of an equation.

CM5.1i Make calculations with numbers written in standard form when using the Avogadro constant (M1b).

CM5.1iii Convert units where appropriate, particularly from mass to moles (M1c).

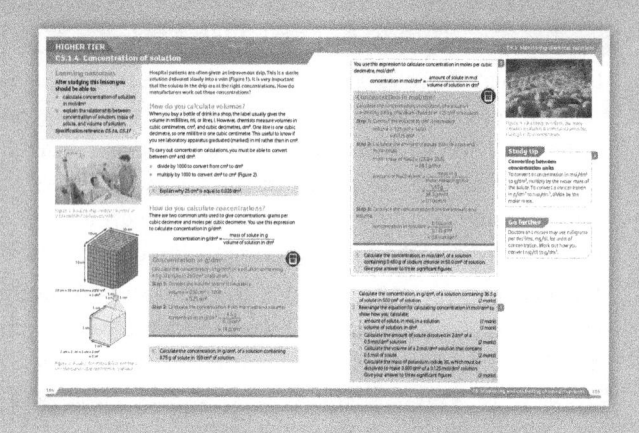

Target	Outcome	Checkpoint	
		Question	Activity
Aiming for GRADE 6	State that 1 ml = 1 cm³ and convert volumes given in cm³ to dm³ by calculation.	A	Starter 1
	Calculate concentrations in g/dm³.	B, 1	Main 2
			Plenary 2
	Calculate concentrations in mol/dm³.		Main 1 and 2
			Plenary 2
Aiming for GRADE 8	Explain why it is useful to convert cm³ to dm³ in calculations.		Plenary 1
	Convert concentrations in g/dm³ to mol/dm³ and vice versa by calculation.	C	Plenary 1
			Homework
	Rearrange the concentration equation to calculate the volume of solution or the amount of solute in mol.	2, 3	Plenary 1

Maths
Throughout this lesson students rearrange algebraic expressions (M3b), substitute numbers including those in standard form (M1b), and calculate terms to an appropriate number of significant figures (M1c, M2a).

Literacy
In Main 2 students make a flow chart to explain how to calculate concentration.

C5.1 Monitoring chemical reactions

Starter	Support/Extend	Resources
Conversions (5 minutes) Ask students to convert the following and to write their answers on mini-whiteboards: 1 $100\,cm^3$ to ml and dm^3 2 $2\,dm^3$ to cm^3 and ml 3 $500\,ml$ to cm^3 and dm^3. **Concentration** (10 minutes) Ask students to draw a particle diagram of a concentrated orange squash solution and a dilute orange squash solution, using orange for the squash particles and blue for the water particles.	**Support:** Provide students with the conversion factors. **Extend:** Tell students that they had $100\,cm^3$ of the concentrated solution. They took $10\,cm^3$ of the concentrated solution and diluted it with $90\,cm^3$ of water. Students draw a particle diagram that represents this dilution (i.e., the particle diagram for the diluted solution should contain 10% of the squash particles from the concentrated solution).	

Main	Support/Extend	Resources
Make a standard solution (30 minutes) Give pairs of students a $250\,cm^3$ volumetric flask and ask them to make a $1\,mol/dm^3$ solution of sodium hydrogensulfate. 1 Calculate the mass of anhydrous sodium hydrogensulfate required and weigh this out. 2 Add a little water to the sodium chloride and transfer it to the volumetric flask, rinsing the weighing boat and transferring the washings. 3 Make the solution up to $100\,cm^3$, ensuring that the bottom of the meniscus is in line with the graduated mark. 4 Stopper the flask and shake it three times. 5 Label the flask with students' names, contents, concentration, and date. SAFETY: Sodium hydrogensulfate is harmful. Wear eye protection and wash hands after making the solution. **Concentration flow chart** (10 minutes) Ask students to make a flow chart to explain how to calculate concentration. Students should then use this to attempt Questions 1, 2, and 3.	**Support:** Lead students through the calculations on the board.	**Practical:** Make a standard solution

Plenary	Support/Extend	Resources
Expressing concentration (5 minutes) Students use the interactive to link the different arrangements of the expression for concentration with the correct subject of the equation. Students link concentration expressions in g/dm^3 and mol/dm^3. **Calculate masses for solutions** (10 minutes) Ask students to calculate the mass of each of the following substances that is needed to make a $1\,mol/dm^3$ solution: 1 Sodium hydroxide 2 Sodium carbonate 3 Hydrochloric acid.	**Support:** Provide students with the formulae of the substances. **Extend:** Ask students to calculate the concentrations of these solutions in g/dm^3.	**Interactive:** Expressing concentration

Homework	Support/Extend	Resources
Use mathematics to show that a saline drip with a concentration of $9\,g/dm^3$ has the same concentration of sodium chloride as saline labelled $0.154\,mol/dm^3$.		

kerboodle
A Kerboodle highlight for this lesson is **Calculation sheet: Concentrations of solutions.** Refer to the **Content map** on Kerboodle for a full list of resources and assessment.

GCSE CHEMISTRY ONLY — HIGHER TIER
C5.1.5 Titrations

Specification links:

5.1b Describe the technique of titration.

WS2a Carry out experiments.

WS2b Make and record observations and measurements using a range of apparatus and methods.

WS2c Present observations using appropriate methods.

M2a Use an appropriate number of significant figures.

M2b Find arithmetic means.

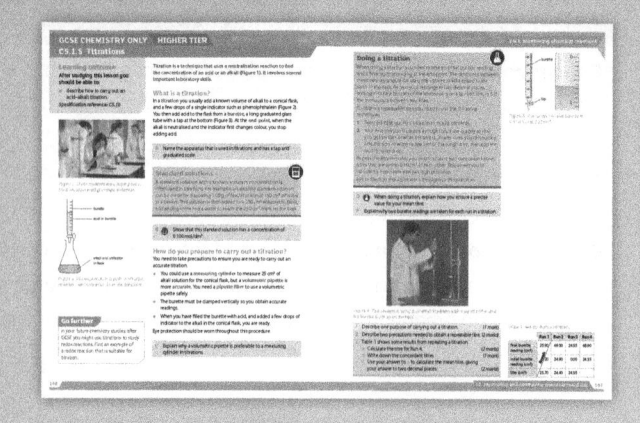

Target	Outcome	Checkpoint Question	Checkpoint Activity
Aiming for GRADE 6 ↓	Name the apparatus used in an acid–alkali titration.	A, 1	Main 1 and 2 / Plenary 1 and 2
	Perform an acid–alkali titration and obtain a titre value.		Main 2
	Record initial and final burette readings to 2 decimal places and select suitable titres to calculate the mean titre.	3	Main 2
Aiming for GRADE 8 ↓	Explain in detail how to carry out an acid–alkali titration safely and with accuracy and precision.	B, D, E, 2	Starter 1 / Main 2 / Plenary 1 and 2
	Perform an acid–alkali titration to obtain concordant titre values.		Main 2
	Justify the use of a volumetric pipette and a burette in titrations.	C	Homework

Maths
In Main 2 students record readings to an appropriate number of decimal places and calculate the mean (M2a, M2b).

Literacy
In Plenary 2 students explain safety precautions, including writing a risk assessment. In completing the Homework task students justify the procedure for reading volumes.

Key words
titration, burette, end-point, standard solution, volumetric flask, measuring cylinder, volumetric pipette, accurate, pipette filler, titre, meniscus, repeatable, concordant titres, precision

C5.1 Monitoring chemical reactions

Starter	Support/Extend	Resources
Safety first (10 minutes) Ask students to justify the following safety precautions for carrying out the titration in Main 2: 1 Do not fill the burette above head height (so that solutions do not get into your eyes). 2 Use a pipette filler (so that chemicals are not drawn into your mouth). 3 Wear eye protection (to protect your eyes, as sodium hydroxide is corrosive and hydrochloric acid is an irritant). 4 Wash hands after the practical (to remove any traces of corrosive or irritating solutions). **Choose your instrument** (10 minutes) Give small groups of students a measuring jug, measuring cylinders of different sizes, a dropping pipette, a bulb pipette, and a burette. Ask students to discuss the resolution, advantages, and disadvantages of each type of measuring instrument.	**Extend:** Ask students to write a full risk assessment for the titration in Main 2. **Support:** Define the terms accuracy (close to the correct value) and reliability (similar results each time).	

Main	Support/Extend	Resources
Pipettes and burettes (10 minutes) Demonstrate the use of a pipette and a burette with water. Ask student pairs to practise using the equipment with water. Ensure students can measure the volume in the pipette correctly and use the filler appropriately. Check that each student can read the burette scale appropriately. **Titration** (30 minutes) Ask students to carry out a titration using 0.1 mol/dm³ sodium hydroxide in a conical flask with phenolphthalein indicator and 0.1 mol/dm³ hydrochloric acid in a burette. Students should repeat the titration until they obtain at least two concordant titres, then calculate the mean titre. Students then record in detail how they carried out their titration, explaining each step.	**Extend:** Encourage students to record burette readings to 2 decimal places.	**Practical:** Titration

Plenary	Support/Extend	Resources
Titration apparatus (5 minutes) Give students an unlabelled diagram of titration apparatus and ask them to add labels. **Titration method** (5 minutes) Give students the steps in a titration method and ask them to order them to describe the method.	**Extend:** Provide the first step, and then go around the class with each student adding the next step.	**Interactive:** Titration apparatus

Homework	Support/Extend	Resources
Justify why volumes should be measured with the eye level with the graduation mark, and looking at the bottom of the meniscus. Then justify the use of a volumetric pipette and burette in titrations, rather than measuring cylinders.		

kerboodle

A Kerboodle highlight for this lesson is **Literacy sheet: Titrations**. Refer to the **Content map** on Kerboodle for a full list of resources and assessment.

The Practical Skills lesson for PAG *6 Titration* could follow this lesson.

GCSE CHEMISTRY ONLY — HIGHER TIER
C5.1.6 Titration calculations

Specification links:

5.1c Explain the relationship between the volume of a solution of known concentration of a substance and the volume or concentration of another substance that react completely together.

WS1.3c Carry out and represent mathematical and statistical analysis.

WS1.4a Use scientific vocabulary, terminology, and definitions.

WS1.4b Recognise the importance of scientific quantities and understand how they are determined.

WS1.4c Use SI units and IUPAC chemical nomenclature unless inappropriate.

M1c Use ratios, fractions, and percentages.

M2a Use an appropriate number of significant figures.

CM5.1ii provide answers to an appropriate number of significant figures (M2a).

CM5.1iii convert units where appropriate, particularly from mass to moles (M1c).

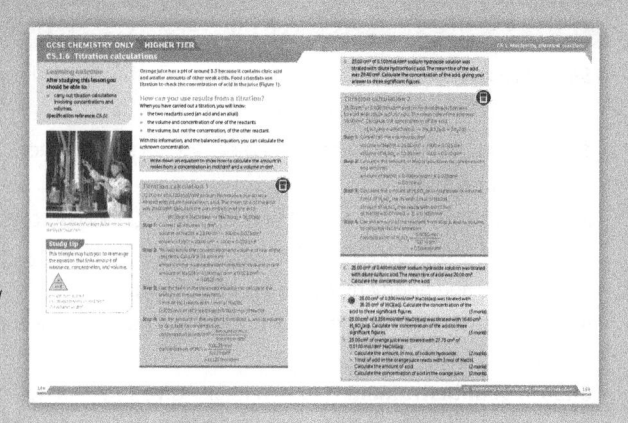

Target	Outcome	Checkpoint Question	Checkpoint Activity
Aiming for GRADE 6	Calculate the number of moles of substance in a standard solution used in a titration, given its volume and concentration.	A, B, C, 1, 2, 3a	Starter 1 and 2 Main 2 Plenary 1 and 2
	Calculate the number of moles of a substance of unknown concentration in a titration, given the equation or ratio of reacting moles.	3b	Main 1 and 2 Plenary 1 and 2
	Calculate the concentration of a solution following a titration, given the number of moles and volume.	B, C, 1, 2, 3c	Starter 1 Main 1 and 2 Plenary 1 and 2 Homework
Aiming for GRADE 8	Use titration results to calculate the number of moles of substance in a standard solution used in a titration.	B, C, 1, 2, 3a	Starter 1 Main 1 and 2 Plenary 1 and 2
	Write a balanced equation for the reaction in a titration and use this to calculate the number of moles of reactant in a solution of unknown concentration.	B, C, 1, 2	Main 1 and 2 Plenary 1 and 2
	Calculate the concentration of a solution following a titration to the appropriate number of significant figures.	B, C, 1, 2, 3c	Starter 1 Main 1 and 2 Plenary 1 and 2

Maths
Throughout this lesson students carry out calculations involving moles using ratios, providing answers to the appropriate number of significant figures (M1c, M2a).

Literacy
In Starter 2 students spot the mistakes and write a corrected version of a passage.

C5.1 Monitoring chemical reactions

Starter	Support/Extend	Resources
Mole equations (5 minutes) Ask students to list all the relationships they can remember that include amount of substance in moles.	**Support:** Provide the equations with one missing term. **Extend:** Ask students to change the subject of the equations, and incorporate common unit conversion factors into the equations.	**Interactive:** Mole equations
Spot the mistake (10 minutes) Ask students to look at the passage below. Students should identify the mistakes and suggest what should be written to correct them: In an acidic solution of sodium hydroxide, a concentration of 0.4 g of solid was used and made into a standard solution of 100 dm^3. (Sodium hydroxide solution is alkaline; 0.4 g is a mass, not a concentration; 100 dm^3 is much too large a volume, use cm^3 as the unit.)	**Extend:** Ask students to calculate the concentration of this solution.	

Main	Support/Extend	Resources
Labelled titration set-up (25 minutes) Ask students to draw a labelled diagram of an acid–base titration. If students labelled a diagram of titration apparatus in C5.1.5, Plenary 1 they can add to (or refer to) this now. Ask students to annotate their new diagram to show that, for example, the burette contains hydrochloric acid of concentration 0.5 mol/dm^3, the average titre was 24.5 cm^3, and in the conical flask there is 25 cm^3 of sodium hydroxide solution of unknown concentration plus a few drops of indicator. Students should add extra annotations to show how they calculate the number of moles of acid that were added, the number of moles of alkali that reacted with the acid, and the concentration of the alkali. **Model calculations** (15 minutes) Work through Student Book sections *Titration calculations 1* and *Titration calculations 2* as a class and ensure that students are aware of the key steps in titration calculations. Then ask students to complete questions 1, 2, and 3.	**Extend:** Ask students to choose a suitable indicator and suggest the visual observations that would be made during the reaction.	**Activity:** Labelled titration set-up

Plenary	Support/Extend	Resources
Look back (5 minutes) Ask students to use their titration results from C5.1.5, Main 2 to calculate the concentration of the alkali in that experiment. **Make your own question** (10 minutes) Ask students to choose an acid, its concentration, and the titre. They should then choose an alkali. Ask students to write a balanced symbol equation for the reaction. On the assumption that they are using 20 cm^3 of the alkali, students should then calculate the concentration of their alkali.	**Extend:** Ask students to evaluate whether the chosen reactants and concentrations are safe and suitable for an acid–base titration.	

Homework	Support/Extend	Resources
Calculate the concentrations of all the reactants in question 1, 2, or 3 in units of g/cm^3.		

kerboodle

A Kerboodle highlight for this lesson is **Maths skills: Titrations**. Refer to the **Content map** on Kerboodle for a full list of resources and assessment.

GCSE CHEMISTRY ONLY — HIGHER TIER
C5.1.7 Gas calculations

Specification links:

5.1d Describe the relationship between molar amounts of gases and their volumes and vice versa.

5.1e Calculate the volumes of gases involved in reactions using the molar gas volume at room temperature and pressure (assumed to be 24 dm³).

WS1.3c Carry out and represent mathematical and statistical analysis.

WS1.4a Use scientific vocabulary, terminology, and definitions.

WS1.4c Use SI units and IUPAC chemical nomenclature unless inappropriate.

WS1.4d Use prefixes and powers of ten for orders of magnitude.

WS1.4f Use an appropriate number of significant figures in calculation.

M3b Change the subject of an equation.

M3c Substitute numerical values into algebraic equations using appropriate units for physical quantities.

M3d Solve simple algebraic equations.

CM5.1i Make calculations with numbers written in standard form when using the Avogadro constant (M1b).

CM5.1iii Convert units where appropriate, particularly from masses to moles.

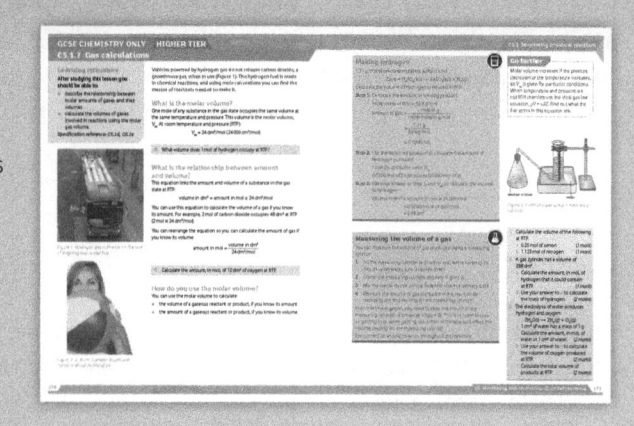

Target	Outcome	Checkpoint Question	Checkpoint Activity
Aiming for GRADE 6 ↓	State that 1 mol of a gas occupies 24 dm³ at RTP and use this to calculate the volumes of gases at room temperature and pressure (RTP).	A, 1	Starter 1 and 2 / Plenary 1 and 2
	Calculate the volume of gas produced in a reaction, given the appropriate equations and/or a stepped calculation.		Main 2
	Perform an experiment to determine the volume of gas produced in a reaction.		Main 1
Aiming for GRADE 8 ↓	Rearrange the gas equation to calculate the moles or volume of any gas at RTP.	B, 2	Starter 2
	Calculate the volume or mass of a gas produced in a reaction.	2, 3	Main 2
	Compare the amount of gas produced by experiment with the calculated theoretical yield and suggest reasons for any discrepancies.		Main 1 / Homework

Maths
Throughout this lesson students convert units (M3d), manipulate equations (M3b), and calculate terms (M3c).

Literacy
In Main 2 students make a flow chart to explain how to calculate the amount of gas in moles.

Key words
molar volume

C5.1 Monitoring chemical reactions

Starter	Support/Extend	Resources
One mole (5 minutes) Ask students what connects 12 g carbon, 16 g of water, and 32 g of sulfur (they are all one mole of the substance). Ask students what a mole is (the amount of a substance that contains 6.02×10^{23} atoms of molecules). Then explain to students that one mole of any gas has the volume 24 dm^3 at room temperature and pressure.	**Extend:** Ask students to express 24 dm^3 as litres and cm^3.	
Mathematical magic (10 minutes) Ask students to manipulate the following equation to show three different subjects: volume in dm^3 = amount in mol × 24 dm^3/mol Then ask students to include an extra term to show the equation if the volume were given in cm^3.	**Extend:** Ask students to substitute into this equation the formula for calculating the amount (in moles) from mass values.	

Main	Support/Extend	Resources
Molar volume of a gas (30 minutes) Ask pairs of students to place around 0.30 g of sodium hydrogencarbonate into a boiling tube and record the exact mass. They should then fill a specimen tube with 2 mol/dm^3 hydrochloric acid. Students should then place the specimen tube inside the boiling tube and stopper it with a bung, through which a delivery tube is connected to a 100 cm^3 gas syringe. When students tip the boiling tube, the acid will react with the sodium hydrogencarbonate. Students should collect the gas produced in the gas syringe, and record the volume when the reaction is compete. Ask students to calculate the number of moles of acid and sodium hydrogencarbonate at the start, and use these values to predict the maximum number of moles of gas that could be produced. Then ask students to measure the volume of gas produced and use this to estimate its amount in moles.	**Support:** Provide students with the balanced symbol equation. **Extend:** Calculate the percentage yield for this reaction.	**Practical:** Molar volume of a gas
Calculate the volume of a gas (10 minutes) Ask students to make a flow chart to explain how to calculate the amount of a gas in moles. Students should then use their flow charts to answer Questions 2 and 3.		

Plenary	Support/Extend	Resources
True or false? (5 minutes) Interactive activity in which students complete a paragraph about mole calculations with gases. In addition, students should answer the following true or false questions. 1 All gases have the same molar volume under STP (true). 2 Changing temperature has no effect on the molar gas volume (false). 3 Molar gas volume is measured in moles (false). 4 The volume of a gas is measured in dm^3/mol (false). 5 One mole of any gas at standard room temperature and pressure is 24 dm^3 (true).	**Support:** Use questions and answers to revise the particle model for a gas, and how a gas produces gas pressure through its particles colliding with the sides of the container.	**Interactive:** Volumes of gases
Predict molar gas volume (10 minutes) Ask students to predict how the molar gas volume of a substance would change if the gas were heated or cooled. Students should use the particle model to explain their answer.		

Homework	Support/Extend	Resources
Calculate the percentage yield of carbon dioxide obtained in the thermal decomposition of 12.35 g of copper(II) carbonate. The volume of carbon dioxide obtained at room temperature and pressure was 2.00 dm^3.	**Support:** Provide students with the balanced symbol equation. **Extend:** Ask students to suggest reasons why the yield was less than 100%.	

kerboodle
A Kerboodle highlight for this lesson is **Calculation sheet: Molar volumes of gases**. Refer to the **Content map** on Kerboodle for a full list of resources and assessment.

Checkpoint

C5.1 Monitoring chemical reactions

Overview of C5.1 Monitoring chemical reactions

This chapter has concentrated mainly on GCSE Chemistry only topics. GCSE Chemistry students have studied how reactions are monitored, including yield and atom economy. They should be able to use relative formula masses to calculate the theoretical yield of a reaction given the amount of reactant. Students should understand that the actual yield of a reaction may be less than the theoretical yield and be able to calculate the percentage yield. They should also be able to define and calculate the atom economy of a reaction, given the balanced equation, and understand how this analysis is used to evaluate different processes to make a product. They should link this work with the law of conservation of mass, balanced equations, and limiting reactants in C3.1 *Introducing chemical reactions*.

The later part of the chapter is for higher-tier GCSE Chemistry students. In studying reaction pathways they should be able to explain why reaction pathways with high atom economies are desirable, including the sale of by-products to improve the atom economy of a process. They should have evaluated the suitability of a process using atom economies and yields.

Higher-tier students, including those taking Combined Science, have studied concentrations of solutions. They should be able to convert concentrations expressed as masses of solute and volumes of solution into mol/dm^3 and vice versa. Higher-tier GCSE Chemistry students should have performed an acid–alkali titration to obtain concordant titre values, and should be able to describe how to carry out an acid–alkali titration with accuracy and precision. In analysing titration results they should be able to calculate the concentration of a solution and hence the number of moles of substance in the solution, working to an appropriate number of significant figures.

Finally higher-tier GCSE Chemistry students have carried out gas calculations and should be able to calculate the volumes of gases involved in reactions using the molar gas volume of $24\ dm^3$ at room temperature and pressure.

MyMaths

You can find additional support for the maths skills covered in this chapter on **MyMaths**, including calculations using ratios and the law of conservation of mass, working with algebraic expressions and numbers in standard form, and calculating terms to an appropriate number of significant figures.

PAGs

All students are expected to have carried out the PAG *6 Titration*. A full lesson plan for each PAG is provided in the Practical skills chapter. PAG *6 Titration* should be completed after lesson C5.1.5 *Titrations*.

kerboodle

For this chapter, the following assessments are available on Kerboodle:
C5.1 Checkpoint quiz: Monitoring chemical reactions
C5.1 Progress quiz: Monitoring chemical reactions 1
C5.1 Progress quiz: Monitoring chemical reactions 2
C5.1 On your marks: Monitoring chemical reactions
C5.1 Exam-style questions and mark scheme: Monitoring chemical reactions

C5.1 Monitoring chemical reactions

Checkpoint follow-up lesson

A student's route through this lesson can be determined using the Checkpoint assessment. Percentage pass marks are supplied in the Checkpoint teacher notes.

For each successive route through it is assumed that the student can perform to their current route as well as previous routes. For example, students working at Aiming for 6 are assumed to be secure in Aiming for 4 knowledge and understanding and working towards achieving all the learning objectives for Aiming for 6.

	Aiming for 4	**Aiming for 6**	**Aiming for 8**
Learning outcomes	Describe titration.	Calculate the theoretical amount of a substance from a balanced symbol equation.	Complete titration calculations.
	Define different types of yield and atom economy.	Calculate theoretical yield, percentage yield, and atom economy.	Evaluate a reaction using data including yield and atom economy.
Starter	**Equation triangles (5 minutes)** Ask students to put the following formulae into equation triangles: moles = mass/relative formula mass; moles = concentration × volume; volume = 24 × moles.		
	Label (5 minutes) Give students a photocopied outline of an unlabelled titration set-up and ask them to label each piece of equipment.		
Differentiated checkpoint activity	**Spider diagram (45 minutes)** Explain that students will be producing a spider diagram to summarise the topic *Monitoring chemical reactions*. Students answer each question on the differentiated worksheets. They will need A4 paper, coloured pencils, and rulers.		
	The Aiming for 4 sheet provides structured activities that can be used to generate the sections of the spider diagram on titrations and on yield and atom economy.	The Aiming for 6 sheet provides key words to be included, and encourages students to use a separate branch of the diagram to summarise yield and atom economy.	The Aiming for 8 sheet provides fewer prompt questions which cover more advanced content. Students are asked to produce an illustrated spider diagram about titrations and evaluating reaction pathways in terms of yield and atom economy.
	Kerboodle resource: C5.1 Checkpoint follow-up: Aiming for 4, C5.1 Checkpoint follow-up: Aiming for 6, C5.1 Checkpoint follow-up: Aiming for 8		
Plenary	**Swap (5 minutes)** Ask students to swap their spider diagram with another student. They should review each other's work using the department marking policy.		
	Reflection (5 minutes) Ask students to write one fact that they revised in the lesson, and one new piece of information that they have learnt.		
Progression	Aiming for 4 students should be able to describe a titration and recall the definitions for different yields and atom economy. They could begin to complete calculations to illustrate these concepts.	Aiming for 6 students should be able to complete yield and atom economy calculations. Students could begin to justify a reaction pathway based on calculations.	Aiming for 8 students should be able to complete titration calculations. Students could begin to convert units.

C5.2 Controlling reactions
C5.2.1 Rate of reaction

Specification links:

5.2a Suggest practical methods for determining the rate of a given reaction.

5.2b Interpret rate-of-reaction graphs.

WS1.2b Plan experiments or devise procedures to make observations, produce or characterise a substance, test hypotheses, check data, or explore phenomena.

WS1.2c Apply knowledge of a range of techniques, instruments, apparatus, and materials to select those appropriate to the experiment.

WS1.2d Recognise when to apply knowledge of sampling techniques to ensure any samples collected are representative.

WS1.3a Present observations and other data using appropriate methods.
WS1.3b Translate data from one form to another.

WS1.3c Carry out and represent mathematical and statistical analysis. WS1.3d Represent distribution of results and make estimations of uncertainty.

WS1.3e Interpret observations and other data. WS1.3f Present reasoned explanations.

WS1.3g Evaluate data in terms of accuracy, precision, repeatability, and reproducibility.

WS1.3h Identify potential sources of random and systematic error.

WS1.3i Communicate the scientific rationale for investigations, methods used, findings, and reasoned conclusions.

WS2a Carry out experiments. WS2b Make and record observations and measurements using a range of apparatus and methods.

M4a Translate information between graphical and numeric form. M4c Plot two variables from experimental or other data.

M4e Draw and use the slope of a tangent to a curve as a measure of rate of change.

CM5.2ii Draw and interpret appropriate graphs from data to determine rate of reaction (M4a, M4b, M4c).

CM5.2iii Determine gradients of graphs as a measure of rate of change to determine rate (M4d, M4e).

Target	Outcome	Checkpoint Question	Checkpoint Activity
Aiming for GRADE 4	State that reactions with a high rate proceed quickly and produce a large amount of product in a short time, and that those with a low rate take longer to produce the same amount of product.	A	Starter 2
	Explain that the volume of gas produced in a reaction can be used as a measure of reaction rate.	B	Main 1
	Use a graph to describe how rate of reaction changes with time.		Main 1 and 2
Aiming for GRADE 6	Define the term rate of reaction.		Starter 1 and 2 / Main 2
	Explain how to use a gas syringe, measuring cylinder, or top-pan balance to monitor the volume of gas produced in a reaction.		Main 1 / Plenary 2
	Calculate rate of reaction from a graph.	C, D, 2	Main 2 / Plenary 1
Aiming for GRADE 8	Explain how equations can be used to calculate rate of reaction.	1	Main 2 / Plenary 1
	Explain how the volume of gas produced in a reaction can be used to calculate rate of reaction.	3	Main 1 and 2 / Plenary 1
	Plot appropriate graphs from experimental data and use them to calculate rate of reaction.		Main 1 and 2 / Plenary 1

174

C5.2 Controlling reactions

Maths
In Main 1 students plot and interpret a graph of volume of gas produced against time (M4a, M4c). In Main 2 students draw tangents and calculate their gradients to determine rate of reaction (M4e).

Literacy
In Plenary 1 students write concise summaries of how to calculate rate of reaction. In completing the Homework task students write an outline method to monitor the rate of a specific reaction.

Key words
rate of reaction, gas syringe

Starter	Support/Extend	Resources
Units (5 minutes) Ask students to use the equations in the Student Book to suggest what the unit of rate of reaction would be. **Order reactions** (10 minutes) Show students an image of a rusty nail, a firework, and a lighted candle. Ask students to discuss which chemical reaction the items represent (oxidation) and to put them in order of rate of reaction, slowest to fastest.	**Support:** Remind students of the units for concentration and time.	**Interactive:** Units of rate

Main	Support/Extend	Resources
Measure the volume of a gas over time (30 minutes) Point out that there are different ways of following the rate of a reaction, such as using a gas syringe to measure the volume of gas produced over time, or measuring the decrease in mass of a reaction mixture as a gas is evolved. Students then write a balanced symbol equation for the reaction between magnesium and hydrochloric acid. Then ask pairs of students to react 25 cm³ of 0.5 mol/dm³ hydrochloric acid with a 5 cm length of magnesium ribbon. This time students should use a gas syringe to measure the total volume of the gas collected every 10 s for 1 minute. (If gas syringes are not available, the gas can be collected by bubbling through a trough of water into a water-filled measuring cylinder.) Ask students to use their results to plot a graph of volume of gas (y-axis) versus time (x-axis) and describe qualitatively how the rate of reaction changed over time.	**Extend:** Ask students to predict the effect on the rate of reaction if the concentration were doubled, and then repeat the experiment with 1 mol/dm³ hydrochloric acid.	**Practical:** Measure the volume of gas over time
Interpret a graph (10 minutes) Ask students to look at a copy of Figure 3 and identify the independent and dependent variables. Then ask students to draw tangents to the curve at 40 s, 120 s, and 180 s. Students should calculate the gradients of these tangents in order to find the instantaneous rate of reaction at these times. Finally, ask students to calculate the mean rate of reaction between 40 s and 120 s.	**Support:** Before starting, ensure that all students understand the meaning of the term 'Rate of reaction'. **Extend:** Encourage students to use particle models to explain why rate of reaction changes over the course of the reaction.	

Plenary	Support/Extend	Resources
Sticky note (5 minutes) Give each student a sticky note and ask them to summarise how to calculate the rate of reaction from a graph. **Methods** (10 minutes) Ask student pairs to discuss reasons for the choice of method used to monitor the rate of reaction in Main 1. Then ask them to suggest another method of monitoring the rate of a reaction that produces a gaseous product. You may wish show a top-pan balance with a conical flask on it.	**Support:** Use questions and answers to elicit that the gas produced could be lost to the atmosphere, producing a measurable mass loss.	

Homework	Support/Extend	Resources
Write an outline method to monitor the rate of reaction of the catalytic decomposition of hydrogen peroxide.	**Support:** You will have the symbol equation.	

kerboodle
A Kerboodle highlight for this lesson is **Calculation sheet: Calculating rates.** Refer to the **Content map** on Kerboodle for a full list of resources and assessment.

C5 Monitoring and controlling chemical reactions 175

C5.2.2 Temperature and reaction rate

Specification links:

5.2b Interpret rate-of-reaction graphs.

5.2c Describe the effect of changes in temperature, [concentration, pressure, and surface area] on rate of reaction.

5.2d Explain the effects on rates of reaction of changes in temperature, [concentration, and pressure] in terms of frequency and energy of collision between particles.

WS1.3a Present observations and other data using appropriate methods.

WS1.3b Translate data from one form to another.

WS1.3c Carry out and represent mathematical and statistical analysis.
WS1.3d Represent distribution of results and make estimations of uncertainty.

WS1.3e Interpret observations and other data. WS1.3f Present reasoned explanations.

WS1.3g Evaluate data in terms of accuracy, precision, repeatability, and reproducibility. WS1.3h Identify potential sources of random and systematic error.

WS1.3i Communicate the scientific rationale for investigations, methods used, findings, and reasoned conclusions.

WS1.4c Use SI units and IUPAC chemical nomenclature unless inappropriate.

WS2b Make and record observations and measurements using a range of apparatus and methods.

M4a Translate information between graphical and numeric form. M4c Plot two variables from experimental or other data.

CM5.2ii Draw and interpret appropriate graphs from data to determine rate of reaction (M4a, M4b, M4c).

CM5.2iii Determine gradients of graphs as a measure of rate of change to determine rate (M4d, M4e).

Target	Outcome	Checkpoint	
		Question	Activity
Aiming for GRADE 4	State that particles must collide in order to react.		Main 2
	State that rate of reaction increases with temperature.		Main 1, Plenary 2
↓	Record some reaction times at different temperatures in rate-of-reaction experiments.		Main 1
Aiming for GRADE 6	Define the term successful collision and explain how the number of successful collisions can be increased.	A	Main 2, Homework
	Use collision theory to explain the effect of temperature on rate of reaction.	2, 3	Starter 1, Main 2, Plenary 1
↓	Use experimental data to calculate rate of reaction at different temperatures.	B, C, 3	Main 1, Plenary 2
Aiming for GRADE 8	Explain collision theory in detail.		Main 2
	Use collision theory to justify a detailed explanation of the effect of temperature on rate of reaction.	3	Homework
↓	Interpret a graph of rate of reaction against temperature and explain its shape.	3	Plenary 1

Maths
In Main 1 students plot and interpret graphs of reaction rate at different temperatures (M4a, M4c).

Literacy
In Main 2 students create a cartoon to explain why increasing the temperature increases the rate of reaction. In Plenary 1 students write a three-point summary.

Key words
collide, successful collision, inversely proportional, reaction time, directly proportional

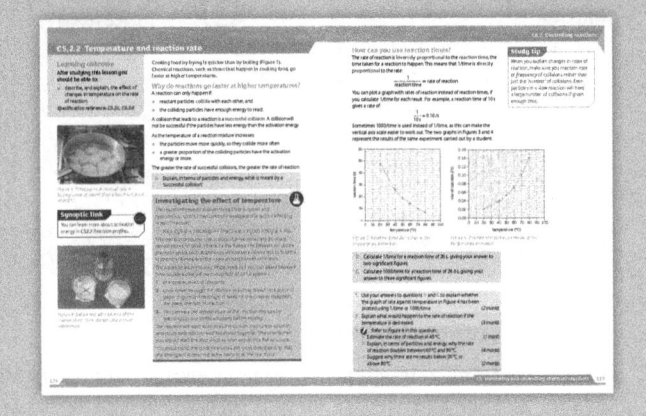

C5.2 Controlling reactions

Starter	Support/Extend	Resources
Temperature and movement (5 minutes) Ask students to consider the particle model and suggest how the kinetic energy of particles changes as temperature increases. **Keeping food cool** (10 minutes) Ask students to suggest why we put food in the fridge to help it last longer.	**Support:** Encourage students to act out the movement of particles. **Support:** Explain that the solid sulfur formed in the reaction stops the light from being transmitted through the liquid. **Extend:** Connect the light meter to a data logger and ask students to predict the shape of the graph of light transmitted against time.	

Main	Support/Extend	Resources
Effect of temperature on rate of reaction (30 minutes) Set up an ice bath, a cold water bath (tap water), a warm water bath (approximately 40 °C), and a hot water bath (approximately 60 °C) on each bench. Students should place a conical flask containing 30 cm³ of distilled water into each of the water/ice baths to acclimatise. Students should then add an indigestion tablet to each conical flask, quickly stopper the flask (using a bung connected to a delivery tube and gas syringe), and use a stopwatch to measure how long it takes to produce a set volume of carbon dioxide. Ask students to plot a graph of time taken for volume of gas to be produced against temperature, and use this to predict the time taken at 80 °C. Finally, ensure that all students are aware that the reaction rate increases with temperature. SAFETY: Complete in a well-ventilated room, wearing eye protection, and wash hands after completing the practical. **Collision** (10 minutes) Ask students to create a cartoon to explain in terms of collision theory why increasing temperature increases rate of reaction.	**Support:** Ask each pair of students to perform the reaction at just one or two temperatures, and then pool results. **Support:** Provide students with statements to illustrate: 1 At low temperatures particles move slowly. 2 At low temperatures, collisions do not happen often and when they do, they are of low energy. 3 At high temperatures particles move fast. 4 At high temperatures there are many high-energy collisions which often lead to a product being made.	**Practical:** Effect of temperature on rate of reaction

Plenary	Support/Extend	Resources
Interpreting graphs (10 minutes) Show students a graph of rate of reaction against temperature. Students use collision theory to explain the shape of the graph. **The effect of temperature** (5 minutes) Students use the interactive to complete a paragraph summarising the key points from the lesson.	**Extend:** Ask students to justify their predictions using collision theory. **Support:** Allow students to work in small groups to generate the key points.	**Interactive:** The effect of temperature

Homework	Support/Extend	Resources
Define a successful collision, then explain how you would change the temperature to increase the number of successful collisions in a given time. Describe how this would affect the rate of reaction.		

kerboodle
A Kerboodle highlight for this lesson is **Working Scientifically: Recording data**. Refer to the **Content map** on Kerboodle for a full list of resources and assessment.

C5.2.3 Concentration, pressure, and reaction rate

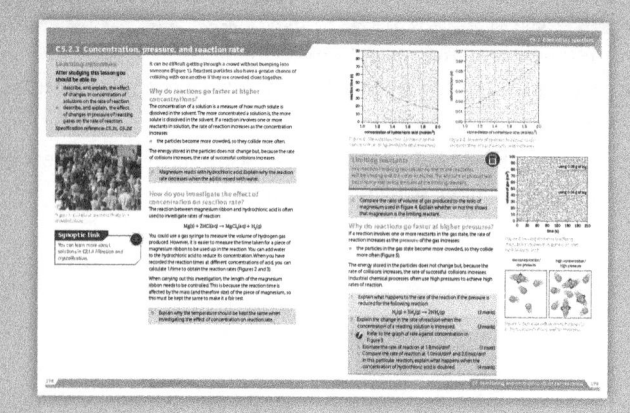

Specification links:

5.2b Interpret rate-of-reaction graphs.

5.2c Describe the effect of changes in [temperature,] concentration, pressure, [and surface area] on rate of reaction.

5.2d Explain the effects on rates of reaction of changes in [temperature,] concentration, and pressure in terms of frequency and energy of collision between particles.

WS1.3a Present observations and other data using appropriate methods.

WS1.3b Translate data from one form to another.

WS1.3c Carry out and represent mathematical and statistical analysis.

WS1.3d Represent distribution of results and make estimations of uncertainty.

WS1.3e Interpret observations and other data. WS1.3f Present reasoned explanations.

WS1.3g Evaluate data in terms of accuracy, precision, repeatability, and reproducibility. WS1.3h Identify potential sources of random and systematic error.

WS1.3i Communicate the scientific rationale for investigations, methods used, findings, and reasoned conclusions.

WS1.4c Use SI units and IUPAC chemical nomenclature unless inappropriate.

WS2b Make and record observations and measurements using a range of apparatus and methods.

M4a Translate information between graphical and numeric form. M4c Plot two variables from experimental or other data.

CM5.2ii Draw and interpret appropriate graphs from data to determine rate of reaction (M4a, M4b, M4c).

CM5.2iii Determine gradients of graphs as a measure of rate of change to determine rate (M4d, M4e).

Target	Outcome	Checkpoint Question	Checkpoint Activity
Aiming for GRADE 4 ↓	State that rate of reaction increases as concentration increases.	A	Main 1 and 2, Plenary 2
	State that rate of reaction increases as pressure increases.		Main 2
	Record some reaction times at different concentrations in rate-of-reaction experiments.		Main 1
Aiming for GRADE 6 ↓	Define the term concentration and use collision theory to explain how concentration affects rate of reaction.	A, 2	Starter 2, Main 1 and 2, Plenary 1 and 2
	Define the term pressure and use collision theory to explain how pressure affects rate of reaction.	1	Starter 1, Main 2
	Use experimental data to calculate rate of reaction at different concentrations.	3	Main 1
Aiming for GRADE 8 ↓	Use detailed collision theory to explain the relationship between concentration and rate of reaction.		Main 1
	Explain why the temperature should be kept constant when investigating the effect of concentration or pressure on rate of reaction.	B	Main 1
	Interpret a graph of rate of reaction against concentration and explain its shape.	3	Plenary 2

Maths
In Main 1 students plot and interpret graphs of reaction rate at different concentrations (M4a, M4c).

Literacy
In Plenary 2 students explain results using collision theory. In the Homework students outline an experiment to investigate how changing the pressure affects the rate of a given reaction.

Key words
pressure

C5.2 Controlling reactions

Starter	Support/Extend	Resources
Marshmallow madness (5 minutes) Demonstrate placing a marshmallow inside an inverted bell jar connected to a vacuum pump, and use grease to seal the jar to a piece of acrylic. Turn on the pump. Ask students what is happening to the amount of air per unit volume (reducing) and what this means in terms of particles (fewer air particles in the jar). Ask students to explain their observations of the marshmallow.		
Concentration models (10 minutes) Give each student a mini-whiteboard. Ask students to draw two particle models, side by side, to represent a solution of dilute hydrochloric acid and a solution of concentrated hydrochloric acid. Students should include a key with their diagrams. Students display their particle diagrams for instant feedback.	**Support:** Use questions and answers to remind students of the particle model of a liquid and a solution. **Extend:** Dilute double-concentrate squash so that it is 50% squash and 50% water. Ask students to draw a particle model for this.	

Main	Support/Extend	Resources
Investigating concentration (20 minutes) Split the class into three groups, and assign each group one of three concentrations of hydrochloric acid. Students react their solution with a 5 cm length of magnesium ribbon and collect the gas produced in a gas syringe. (If gas syringes are not available, the gas can be collected by bubbling through a trough of water into a water-filled measuring cylinder.) Ask students to record the total volume of the gas collected every 10 s for 2 minutes. Students swap their results with students from the other two groups. They use their collated results to plot a graph of volume of gas (y-axis) versus time (x-axis) for each concentration of acid, on the same axes. Ask students to draw tangents to their curves at three different points, and calculate the instantaneous rate of reaction at each of these times. Then ask them to compare the rates of reaction at each time, and suggest how concentration affects rate of reaction.	**Extend:** Ask students to calculate the amount in moles of each reactant and then suggest which is the limiting reactant and which is in excess. **Extend:** Students list the variables they need to control in their investigation. They should identify temperature. Ask them to explain why temperature needs to be controlled, with reference to what they learnt in the previous lesson.	**Practical:** Investigating concentration
Rate-of-reaction models (20 minutes) Demonstrate calcium reacting with 0.1 mol/dm³ hydrochloric acid and 1 mol/dm³ hydrochloric acid. Ask students to draw two labelled particle diagrams to explain the observed difference in the rate of reaction.	**Extend:** Explain that calcium reacts with oxygen in the air. Ask students to draw labelled particle diagrams to show the rate of oxidation of calcium in air and in air pressurised to 200 kPa (2 atmospheres), and explain the difference.	

Plenary	Support/Extend	Resources
Effect of concentration and pressure (5 minutes) Interactive in which students identify whether particle diagrams show high concentration and pressure or low concentration and pressure.	**Support:** Remind students that gas pressure is caused by gas particles colliding with the sides of the container.	**Interactive:** Effect of concentration or pressure
Predicting graph shapes (10 minutes) Ask students to sketch a graph of rate of reaction against concentration. They should use collision theory to explain the shape of the graph they have sketched.		

Homework	Support/Extend	Resources
Outline an experiment to investigate how changing the pressure affects the rate of reaction between Alka-Seltzer and water in an open test-tube and then in a bunged test-tube.		

kerboodle
A Kerboodle highlight for this lesson is **Homework: Controlling reactions.** Refer to the **Content map** on Kerboodle for a full list of resources and assessment.

C5.2.4 Particle size and reaction rate

Specification links:

5.2b Interpret rate-of-reaction graphs.

5.2c Describe the effect of changes in [temperature, concentration, pressure, and] surface area on rate of reaction.

5.2e Explain the effects on rates of reaction of changes in the size of the pieces of a reacting solid in terms of surface-area-to-volume ratio.

WS1.3a Present observations and other data using appropriate methods.

WS1.3b Translate data from one form to another.

WS1.3c Carry out and represent mathematical and statistical analysis.

WS1.3d Represent distribution of results and make estimations of uncertainty.

WS1.3e Interpret observations and other data. WS1.3f Present reasoned explanations.

WS1.3g Evaluate data in terms of accuracy, precision, repeatability, and reproducibility. WS1.3h Identify potential sources of random and systematic error.

WS1.3i Communicate the scientific rationale for investigations, methods used, findings, and reasoned conclusions.

WS1.4c Use SI units and IUPAC chemical nomenclature unless inappropriate.

WS2b Make and record observations and measurements using a range of apparatus and methods.

M1c Use ratios, fractions, and percentages. M4a Translate information between graphical and numeric form.

M4c Plot two variables from experimental or other data. M4e Draw and use the slope of a tangent to a curve as a measure of rate of change.

CM5.2ii Draw and interpret appropriate graphs from data to determine rate of reaction (M4a, M4b, M4c).

CM5.2iii Determine gradients of graphs as a measure of rate of change to determine rate (M4d, M4e).

CM5.2iv Use proportionality when comparing factors affecting rate of reaction (M1c).

Target	Outcome	Checkpoint	
		Question	Activity
Aiming for GRADE 4	State that small pieces of a solid have a larger surface-area-to-volume ratio than larger pieces.		Starter 1
	State that pieces of solid with a large surface area react more quickly than those with a smaller surface area.	A, 2	Main Plenary 1 and 2
	Record data in rate-of-reaction experiments for pieces of solid with different surface areas.		Main
Aiming for GRADE 6	Explain how to conduct a fair test and obtain valid results when investigating the effect of particle size on rate of reaction.	B, C, D	Main
	Use collision theory to explain how surface area affects rate of reaction.	A, 2	Plenary 1
	Use experimental data to demonstrate the effect of surface area on rate of reaction.		Main
Aiming for GRADE 8	Calculate the surface-area-to-volume ratio for different-sized pieces of solid.		Starter 1
	Use detailed collision theory to justify the relationship between surface area and rate of reaction.		Plenary 1
	Use experimental data to calculate mean rates of reaction for different surface areas.	1	Main

Maths
In Starter 1 (Extend) students calculate surface-area-to-volume ratios (M1c). In Main 1 students plot and interpret graphs of reaction rate with different-sized pieces (M4a, M4c, M4e).

Literacy
In completing the Homework task students write a method for a practical experiment.

Key words
rate

C5.2 Controlling reactions

Starter	Support/Extend	Resources
Cubes (5 minutes) Ask students to calculate the volume and surface area of a large cube made up of eight 1 cm³ cubes (8 cm³ and 24 cm²). Then ask students to calculate the total volume and surface area of eight 1 cm³ cubes (8 cm³ and 48 cm²). Ask students to compare the combined surface area of the eight smaller cubes with the surface area of the one big cube at the start (total surface area of smaller cubes is greater).	**Support:** Give students modeling cubes (may be available in the mathematics department) to help them. **Extend:** Ask students to calculate the surface-area-to-volume ratio for the larger cube and for the eight smaller cubes, and compare them.	**Interactive:** Collision theory and surface area
Collision theory and surface area (10 minutes) Interactive in which students are introduced to collision theory and the effect of surface area on the rate of a reaction. Students complete a paragraph that describes collision theory and then put statements in order to describe how increasing the surface area of a solid increases the rate of the reaction.	**Extend:** Ask students to write a balanced symbol equation and explain why this is an example of oxidation.	

Main	Support/Extend	Resources
Investigating the effect of surface area (40 minutes) Demonstrate the effect of surface area on rate of reaction using three grades of marble chips (calcium carbonate). Set up three reactions, one for each size of chip: 1 Weigh out 2.5 g of marble chips. 2 Measure 25 cm³ of 2 mol/dm³ hydrochloric acid into a conical flask and place it on a balance. 3 Add the marble chips, plug the flask loosely with cotton wool, and simultaneously start a timer. Note the mass every 30 s for 5 minutes. Ask which variables were kept constant, and why, as well as the purpose of the cotton-wool plug. Students plot the data from the three different grades on the same axes (total loss of mass on y-axis versus time on x-axis). They then calculate the mean rate of reaction over the first 2 minutes for each of the three grades of marble chips and draw conclusions.	**Support:** Provide graph paper with labelled axes for students to plot the data. **Extend:** Ask students to calculate the moles of each reactant used and suggest the maximum mass loss. **Extend:** Ask students to explain why sulfuric acid cannot be used in this experiment.	**Practical:** Investigating the effect of surface area

Plenary	Support/Extend	Resources
Sugar combustion (10 minutes) Demonstrate the effect of increased surface area on the combustion of sugar. Hold a sugar cube in a blue Bunsen burner flame and observe. Then blow icing sugar into the blue Bunsen burner flame. Ask students for observations and discuss the difference in terms of collision theory.		
Collision theory (5 minutes) Ask students to draw a labelled diagram to explain the difference in reactivity of magnesium ribbon with hydrochloric acid and powdered magnesium with hydrochlorics acid. Their diagrams should include how surface area affects the number of collisions and therefore the rate of reaction in this experiment.		

Homework	Support/Extend	Resources
Write a method to investigate, using a gas syringe, how the surface area of calcium carbonate affects its reaction with acid.		

kerboodle
A Kerboodle highlight for this lesson is **Calculation sheet: Calculating surface areas**. Refer to the **Content map** on Kerboodle for a full list of resources and assessment.

C5.2.5 Catalysts and reaction rate

Specification links:

5.2f Describe the characteristics of catalysts and their effect on rates of reaction.

5.2g Identify catalysts in reactions.

5.2h Explain catalytic action in terms of activation energy.

5.2i Recall that enzymes act as catalysts in biological systems.

WS1.4a Use scientific vocabulary, terminology, and definitions.

M4a Translate information between graphical and numeric form.

M4c Plot two variables from experimental or other data.

CM5.2ii Draw and interpret appropriate graphs from data to determine rate of reaction (M4a, M4b, M4c).

CM5.2iii Determine gradients of graphs as a measure of rate of change to determine rate (M4d, M4e).

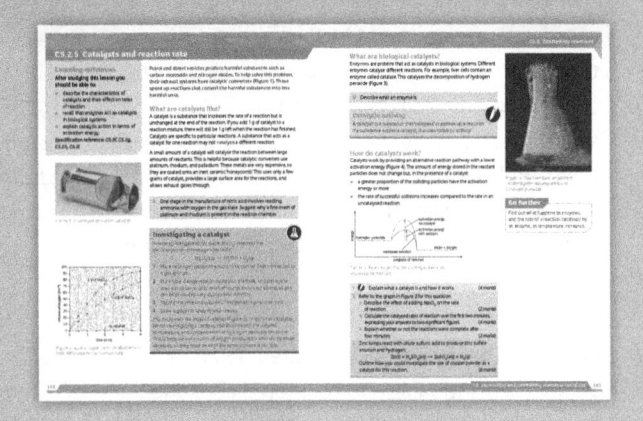

Target	Outcome	Checkpoint	
		Question	Activity
Aiming for GRADE 4	State that catalysts can be used to speed up chemical reactions.		Starter 1 and 2 Main 1 and 2 Plenary 1 and 2
	State that enzymes are biological catalysts.	B	Starter 1
	Record reaction times for reactions involving catalysts.		Main 1
Aiming for GRADE 6	Define the term catalyst and describe how catalysts work.	A, 1	Starter 2 Main 2 Plenary 1
	Explain how surface area affects the action of a catalyst.	A	Starter 2
	Process experimental data to demonstrate the effect of different catalysts on rate of reaction.		Main 1
Aiming for GRADE 8	Explain in detail how catalysts affect rate of reaction.	1, 3	Main 2 Plenary 1
	Explain using collision theory how a catalyst works.	1	Starter 2
	Use experimental data to calculate the effects of different catalysts on rate of reaction.	2	Main 1

Maths
In Main 1 students plot graphs and calculate the reaction rate in an enzyme-catalysed reaction (M4a, M4c).

Literacy
In Main 2 students write a specification for a catalyst.

Key words
catalyse, enzymes

kerboodle
A Kerboodle highlight for this lesson is **Literacy sheet: Catalysts**. Refer to the **Content map** on Kerboodle for a full list of resources and assessment.

The Practical Skills lesson for PAG *8 Measuring rates of reaction* could follow this lesson.

182

C5.2 Controlling reactions

Starter	Support/Extend	Resources
Speeding up reactions (5 minutes) Ask students if they have ever heard of biological washing powders. Ask them to suggest what makes them biological. They explain that they contain enzymes, and explain that enzymes are biological catalysts. Explain that a catalyst is a substance that speeds up a reaction without being used up. **Catalysts for thermal decomposition** (10 minutes) Introduce catalysts as a substance that speeds up a reaction without being used up. Then ask students to use their understanding from the previous lesson to explain why a powdered catalyst would be more effective than the same volume of catalyst as a solid. Ensure students understand that the difference is caused by surface area and the reactants being able to access more of the catalyst, rather than the powdered catalyst being "faster" than the solid catalyst.	**Extend:** Separate the catalyst from the chlorate salt to show that it is not used up.	

Main	Support/Extend	Resources
Investigating catalysts (35 minutes) Ask pairs of students to investigate the catalytic decomposition of $25\,cm^3$ of 10 vol hydrogen peroxide, with manganese(IV) oxide, potassium iodide, and catalase as three examples of a catalyst. Using a gas syringe, students collect the gas produced and record its total volume every 10 s for 2 minutes. (If gas syringes are not available, use a method similar to that shown in Starter 1, and record the time taken to produce a given height of foam.) Students plot a graph that they can then use to measure the rate of reaction. SAFETY: Hydrogen peroxide is an oxidising agent and an irritant. Manganese(IV) oxide is harmful. Iodide is harmful. Follow CLEAPSS advice for disposal procedures. Wear eye protection and wash hands after completing the practical. If food stuffs are used, dispose of appropriately and sterilise surfaces after use. **Catalyst specification** (5 minutes) Ask students to write a specification for a catalyst. This should include essential characteristics, such as increasing the rate of reaction, not being used up in the reaction, as well as desirable characteristics, such as being cheap and readily available.	**Extend:** Allow students to investigate the effect of other catalysts (e.g., potassium manganate(VII)) on this reaction, and plot the data on the same axes.	**Practical:** Investigating catalysis

Plenary	Support/Extend	Resources
Label (10 minutes) Give students an unlabelled reaction profile diagram, for a reaction with and without a catalyst, and ask them to annotate it for the catalytic decomposition of hydrogen peroxide using manganese(IV) oxide as the catalyst. **Changing conditions** (10 minutes) Give each student a mini-whiteboard. Ask students to consider the decomposition reaction of hydrogen peroxide, and state whether the rate of reaction will be faster, slower, or whether it is not possible to know, when conditions are changed as follows: 1 a catalyst is added 2 the temperature is increased 3 the concentration is decreased 4 the temperature is increased and the concentration is decreased 5 catalyst is added, temperature is decreased, and concentration is increased.	**Support** Provide students with the labels to add in the correct places.	**Interactive:** The effect of catalysts

Homework	Support/Extend	Resources
Design an A3 poster to summarise your learning about the effects of temperature, concentration, surface area, and catalysts on rate of reaction. Include examples of experiments and explanations using collision theory.		

Checkpoint
C5.2 Controlling reactions

Overview of C5.2 Controlling reactions

In this chapter students have studied how reaction rates are measured and controlled, including the effects of temperature, concentration, pressure, surface area, and catalysts on rates of reaction. They should be able to define the term rate of reaction, have carried out meaningful practical investigations, and interpreted results including graphs to find rates of reaction. They should be able to apply collision theory to explain the effects of different factors on rates of reaction, understanding, for example, that increasing the concentration or pressure leads to more frequent collisions.

Students should have monitored the rate of a reaction that produces a gaseous product using appropriate apparatus. In studying the effect of temperature, they should be able to explain the effect of changing temperature on rate of reaction, and use experimental data to find the rate of reaction at different temperatures. They should link this with work on activation energy in C3.2 *Energetics*. They should also understand that the rate of reaction increases with increasing concentration or pressure of the reactants, and explain these effects. They should be able to demonstrate and explain the effect of surface area on rate, including surface area to volume ratio.

Students have studied the effect of catalysts and should be able identify catalysts in reactions, compare different catalysts, and describe how they work, including the effect of surface area. They should recall that enzymes are biological catalysts.

MyMaths

You can find additional support for the maths skills covered in this chapter on **MyMaths**, including plotting graphs and calculating their gradients to determine rates of reaction.

PAGs

All students are expected to have carried out the PAG *8 Measuring rates of reaction*. A full lesson plan for each PAG is provided in the Practical skills chapter. PAG *8 Measuring rates of reaction* should be completed after lesson C5.2.5 *Catalysts and reaction rate*.

kerboodle

For this chapter, the following assessments are available on Kerboodle:
C5.2 Checkpoint quiz: Controlling reactions
C5.2 Progress quiz: Controlling reactions 1
C5.2 Progress quiz: Controlling reactions 2
C5.2 On your marks: Controlling reactions
C5.2 Exam-style questions and mark scheme: Controlling reactions

C5.2 Controlling reactions

Checkpoint follow-up lesson

A student's route through this lesson can be determined using the Checkpoint assessment. Percentage pass marks are supplied in the Checkpoint teacher notes.

For each successive route through it is assumed that the student can perform to their current route as well as previous routes. For example, students working at Aiming for 6 are assumed to be secure in Aiming for 4 knowledge and understanding and working towards achieving all the learning objectives for Aiming for 6.

	Aiming for 4	**Aiming for 6**	**Aiming for 8**
Learning outcomes	Describe the effect of changing temperature, concentration, surface area, and adding a catalyst to rate of reaction.	Use collision theory to explain the effect of changing temperature, concentration, surface area, adding a catalyst, and changing pressure on rate of reaction.	Justify a method for measuring rate of reaction.
	Describe a rate of reaction graph.	Use collision theory to explain the shape of a rate of reaction graph.	Interpret a rate of reaction graph including using mathematical processes.
Starter	**Particles (5 minutes)** Ask students to work in pairs to draw particle diagrams to represent high temperature and low temperature, high concentration and low concentration, high surface area and low surface area.		
	Magnesium and acid (5 minutes) Demonstrate the reaction between magnesium and hydrochloric acid by putting a small piece of magnesium ribbon and 50 cm^3 of hydrochloric acid in a conical flask (appropriate safety precautions should be taken, including wearing eye protection). Ask students for the word equation for the reaction. Write this on the board and then discuss how the reaction could be monitored (mass loss as hydrogen is lost to the atmosphere, collect the gas, or monitor pH). Ask – which would be the most useful dependent variable and why?		
Differentiated checkpoint activity	**Revision book (45 minutes)** Explain that students will be producing a section of a revision book to summarise the topic *Controlling reactions*. Students answer each question on the differentiated worksheets. They will need A4 paper, rulers, and coloured pencils. You may wish to allow students to use desktop publishing packages to present their work.		
	The Aiming for 4 sheet provides structured tasks to support students in revising and summarising the information to include in their revision book section. They may like to cut and paste the completed sections from the sheet, in which case they will need scissors and glue sticks.	The Aiming for 6 sheet provides questions to guide the content students include as they prepare their revision book section.	The Aiming for 8 sheet provides fewer prompt questions which cover more advanced content. Students design their work to be interesting and informative. They are provided with questions on the sheet which it should answer.
	Kerboodle resource: C5.2 Checkpoint follow-up: Aiming for 4, C5.2 Checkpoint follow-up: Aiming for 6, C5.2 Checkpoint follow-up: Aiming for 8		
Plenary	**Revision book review (5 minutes)** Ask students to lay out their revision book sections on benches around the room. Students should then choose another person's section to review. They should read the other person's section and decide on two strong points about the work, and one point that could be improved on.		
	Key learning (5 minutes) Ask student pairs to choose three key learning points from the chapter. Review these as a class. Address any misconceptions should they arise.		
Progression	Aiming for 4 students should identify the effect on rate of reaction of increasing or decreasing temperature, surface area, or concentration. They should also describe the effect of adding a catalyst. Students should begin to use collision theory to explain these observations.	Aiming for 6 students should be able to use collision theory to explain observations and make predictions. They should begin to calculate gradients on rate of reaction graphs and relate this to rate of reaction.	Aiming for 8 students should be able to justify which method is best for monitoring the rate of a particular chemical reaction. They should start using collision theory to support their justification.

C5.3 Equilibria
C5.3.1 Reversible reactions

Specification links:

5.3a Recall that some reactions may be reversed by altering the reaction conditions.

5.3b Recall that dynamic equilibrium occurs in a closed system when the rates of forward and reverse reactions are equal.

CM5.3i Use arithmetic computation and ratio when measuring rates of reaction.

CM5.3ii Draw and interpret appropriate graphs from data to determine rate of reaction.

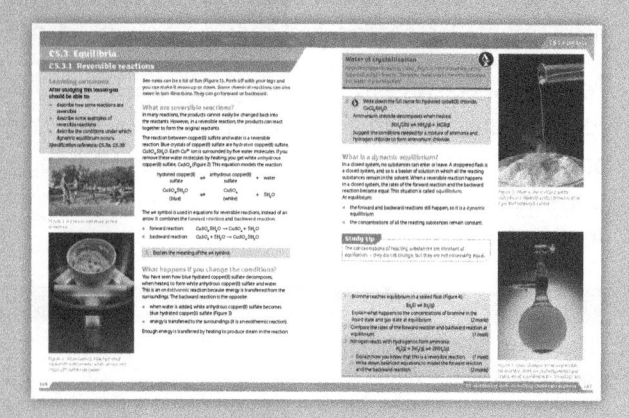

Target	Outcome	Checkpoint	
		Question	Activity
Aiming for GRADE 4	State that some reactions are reversible.	A	Starter 1
	State one example of a reversible reaction.	C, 1	Main 1
			Plenary 1
	Describe the concentrations of reacting substances as constant in a dynamic equilibrium.	1	Main 2
			Plenary 2
Aiming for GRADE 6	Explain the meaning of the ⇌ symbol.	A, 3	Starter 1
	Describe how some chemical reactions can be reversed by altering the reaction conditions.	C	Starter 2
			Main 1
			Plenary 1
	Explain why, in dynamic equilibrium reactions, the rates of the forward and backward reactions are equal.	2	Main 2
			Plenary 2
Aiming for GRADE 8	Write balanced equations for a reversible reaction to model the forward and backward reactions.	3	Main 1
			Plenary 1
	Suggest the conditions needed to reverse a given chemical reaction.	C	Starter 2
	Explain in detail the conditions under which dynamic equilibria occur.		Main 2
			Plenary 2
			Homework

Literacy
In Main 2 students explain a model for dynamic equilibrium, and critique the model.

Key words
hydrated, anhydrous, forward reaction, backward reaction, endothermic, equilibrium, dynamic

C5.3 Equilibria

Starter	Support/Extend	Resources
Interpret (5 minutes) Show students a balanced symbol equation for an equilibrium reaction. Ask students to suggest what the reversible arrow symbol means. Use questions and answers to ensure students understand that it signifies that the forward reaction happens at the same time as the backward reaction. **Colourful equilibrium** (10 minutes) Ask students to predict what would happen at each of the following stages: • 10 cm³ of hydrochloric acid is added to a beaker with a few drops of universal indicator solution (solution turns red/acidic) • 10 cm³ of sodium hydroxide is added to the solution (solution turns green/neutralised) • a further 2 cm³ of sodium hydroxide added to the solution (solution turns blue/alkali) • 4 cm³ of hydrochloric acid added to the solution (solution turns yellow/acidic) Point out to students that the indicator is undergoing an equilibrium reaction and changing colour.		**Interactive:** Interpret

Main	Support/Extend	Resources
Reversible reactions (25 minutes) Ask pairs of students to put half a spatula measure of hydrated copper(II) sulfate into an ignition tube, heat it, and note their observations. Students should then allow the tube to cool and, using a dropping pipette, add one drop of water and observe. Repeat. Ask students to explain why this is an equilibrium reaction, with the use of labelled equations that highlight the colour changes and energy changes. SAFETY: Copper sulfate is harmful. If the water is added to a hot boiling tube the glass could fracture due to thermal shock. Be aware of burns due to using the Bunsen burner to heat the boiling tube. Wear chemical splash-proof eye protection and wash hands after completing the practical. **Dynamic equilibrium model** (15 minutes) Give small groups of students a tray and polystyrene balls in two colours. Students should put 10 balls of each colour in the tray and 5 balls of each colour outside the tray. Ask students to work together to take balls out at the same rate as balls are being introduced to the tray. Ask students to explain how this can model a dynamic equilibrium, and to critique the model. How is the model like, and how is it not like, an equilibrium reaction?	**Extend:** Ask students to write balanced symbol equations with state symbols for the equilibrium. **Extend:** Ask students to develop their own dynamic equilibrium model using a sink and tap or an escalator.	**Practical:** Reversible reactions

Plenary	Support/Extend	Resources
Chemical test (5 minutes) Ask students to suggest what the reversible reaction of anhydrous copper(II) sulfate to hydrated copper(II) sulfate (shown in Figure 3) could be used for (test for water). **More models** (10 minutes) Ask students to use their evaluation of the dynamic equilibrium model from Main 2 to create a better model.	**Extend:** Demonstrate the use of cobalt(II) chloride. Ask students to write an equation to show this reversible reaction.	

Homework	Support/Extend	Resources
Explain why an equilibrium reaction is a chemical reaction and not a physical change. Illustrate your explanations with an example and a balanced symbol equation.		

kerboodle
A Kerboodle highlight for this lesson is **Literacy interactive: Reversible reactions**. Refer to the **Content map** on Kerboodle for a full list of resources and assessment.

HIGHER TIER
C5.3.2 Equilibrium position

Specification links:

5.3c Predict the effect of changing reaction conditions on equilibrium position and suggest appropriate conditions to produce as much of a particular product as possible.

WS1.2a Use scientific theories and explanations to develop hypotheses.

WS1.4c Use SI units and IUPAC chemical nomenclature unless inappropriate.

M1c Use ratios, fractions, and percentages.

CM5.3iv Use proportionality when comparing factors affecting rate of reaction (M1c).

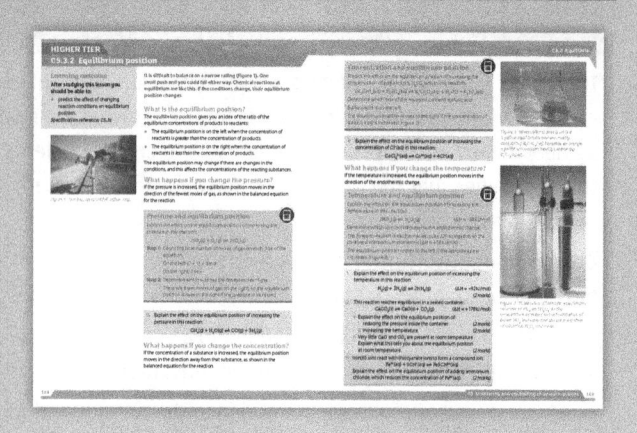

Target	Outcome	Checkpoint Question	Checkpoint Activity
Aiming for GRADE 6	Describe the effect of changing pressure on a given equilibrium system.		Starter 2 Main 1 and 2 Plenary 1 and 2
	Describe the effect of changing concentration on a given equilibrium system.		Starter 2
	Describe the effect of changing temperature on a given equilibrium system.		Starter 2 Main 1 and 2 Plenary 1 and 2 Homework
Aiming for GRADE 8	Explain fully the effect of changing pressure on a given equilibrium system.	A, 2	Starter 2 Main 1 and 2 Plenary 1 and 2
	Explain fully the effect of changing concentration on a given equilibrium system.	B, 3	Starter 2
	Explain fully the effect of changing temperature on a given equilibrium system.	1, 2	Starter 2 Main 1 and 2 Plenary 1 and 2 Homework

Maths
In Starter 1 students balance symbol equations. Throughout the lesson students use proportionality when comparing factors affecting the position of equilibrium (M1c).

Literacy
In Main 1 students write predictions about the position of equilibrium. In completing the Homework task, students write an explanation of the effect of changing temperature on a dynamic equilibrium.

Key words
equilibrium position

kerboodle
A Kerboodle highlight for this lesson is **Bump up your grade: Equilibrium**. Refer to the **Content map** on Kerboodle for a full list of resources and assessment.

C5.3 Equilibria

Starter	Support/Extend	Resources
Dynamic equilibrium (5 minutes) Students use the interactive to complete a paragraph to summarise reversible reactions and the energy changes involved. **Model equilibrium** (10 minutes) Explain that systems in dynamic equilibrium behave a bit like unruly children – they do the opposite of what you might expect. If the conditions of an equilibrium reaction are changed, the equilibrium position changes to counteract the effect of that change. Ask pairs of students to discuss and predict the effect on a dynamic equilibrium of: 1 heating (favours the endothermic reaction to reduce the temperature) 2 increasing the pressure (favours the side with fewer moles of gas to reduce the pressure) 3 cooling (favours the exothermic reaction to increase the temperature) 4 adding a catalyst (no effect on position of equilibrium but reaction is faster) 5 removing product (makes more product) 6 removing reactant (makes more reactant).	**Support:** Ask students to use the symbol equations in the Student Book to write word equations for the reactions.	**Interactive:** Dynamic equilibrium

Main	Support/Extend	Resources
Haber process (15 minutes) Introduce the Haber process. Ask students to write the balanced symbol equation for the production of ammonia, including state symbols. Explain that the forward reaction is exothermic and the reverse reaction is endothermic. Point out that the reactant side has a greater number of moles of gas than the product side (i.e., in the same sized container at the same temperature, the reactants alone would exert a higher pressure than the product alone). Ask students to predict the effect of changing the temperature or the pressure on the equilibrium position. **Dynamic equilibrium** (25 minutes) Demonstrate the effect of changing conditions on an equilibrium mixture of brown nitrogen(IV) oxide and colourless dinitrogen tetroxide held in a gas syringe. On compressing the syringe slightly, a colour change is seen as the position of equilibrium changes. Changing the temperature using a warm water bath or ice bath also causes a colour change. Encourage students to predict the effect of a proposed change, and then demonstrate it. There is no need to use the term 'Le Chatelier's principle' at this stage. Focus simply on the effect of changing conditions on the position of equilibrium.	**Extend:** Ask students to predict the effect of adding a catalyst to the system.	**Practical:** Dynamic equilibrium

Plenary	Support/Extend	Resources
Predict the yield (5 minutes) Ask students to consider the Haber process and suggest the effect on yield of the following changes: 1 increase in temperature (reduce yield) 2 decrease in temperature (increase) 3 increase in pressure (increase) 4 decrease in pressure (reduce) 5 adding a catalyst (no change). **Summarise** (10 minutes) Ask students to complete the following sentences: 1 In a dynamic equilibrium where the forward reaction is exothermic... 2 In a dynamic gaseous equilibrium where there are more moles of reactants than products... 3 In a dynamic equilibrium when a catalyst is added...	**Extend:** Ask students to consider the same changes in conditions for the potassium dichromate(VI) and sulfuric acid equilibrium.	

Homework	Support/Extend	Resources
Consider the Contact process as detailed in Student Book section *Pressure and equilibrium position* and in Student Book spread C6.1.4. Students should explain the effect of changing temperature on the reaction, given that the forward reaction is exothermic.		

HIGHER TIER
C5.3.3 Choosing reaction conditions

Specification links:

5.3c Predict the effect of changing reaction conditions on equilibrium position and suggest appropriate conditions to produce as much of a particular product as possible.

WS1.2a Use scientific theories and explanations to develop hypotheses.

WS1.2b Plan experiments or devise procedures to make observations, produce or characterise a substance, test hypotheses, check data, or explore phenomena.

WS1.2c Apply knowledge of a range of techniques, instruments, apparatus, and materials to select those appropriate to the experiment.

WS1.4c Use SI units and IUPAC chemical nomenclature unless inappropriate.

WS2a Carry out experiments.

WS2b Make and record observations and measurements using a range of apparatus and methods.

M1c Use ratios, fractions, and percentages.

CM5.3i Use arithmetic computation and ratio when measuring rates of reaction (M1a, M1c).

CM5.3iii Determine gradients of graphs as a measure of rate of change to determine rate (M4d, M4e).

CM5.3iv Use proportionality when comparing factors affecting rate of reaction (M1c).

Target	Outcome	Checkpoint	
		Question	Activity
Aiming for GRADE 6	Describe the factors that affect the equilibrium yield of a reaction.		Starter 2 Main Plenary 1 and 2 Homework
	Explain the optimum pressure for producing a high yield of a particular product in an equilibrium reaction.	2	Starter 2 Main Plenary 1 and 2 Homework
	Explain the optimum temperature for producing a high yield of a particular product in an equilibrium reaction.	2	Main Plenary 1 and 2 Homework
Aiming for GRADE 8	Explain why removing the product of a reversible reaction moves the equilibrium position to the right.	A	Main Plenary 1 and 2 Homework
	Justify the choice of a compromise pressure for a particular equilibrium reaction.	B, 2	Starter 2 Main Plenary 1 and 2 Homework
	Justify the choice of a compromise temperature for a particular equilibrium reaction.	1, 2	Main Plenary 1 and 2 Homework

Maths
In Main 1 and Plenary 2 students use proportionality when comparing factors affecting the position of equilibrium (M1c).

Literacy
In Main 1 students write a pitch to explain the compromise conditions for a given reaction, and in completing the Homework task students write a newspaper article about industrial reaction conditions.

Key words
equilibrium yield, Le Chatelier's principle

C5.3 Equilibria

Starter	Support/Extend	Resources
Atom economy revisited (5 minutes) Ask students to look at the balanced symbol equation for the reaction between carbon monoxide and hydrogen in Student Book section *How is methanol made?*. Ask them to state the atom economy for this reaction. **Predicting pressure** (10 minutes) Show students a balanced symbol equation with state symbols of a reaction where the rate of the forward reaction is decreased by pressure (i.e., where there are fewer gas molecules on the left hand side). Ask students to suggest what effect increasing the pressure will have on the reaction. They are likely to say "increase the rate". Explain that it will actually decrease the rate. See if any students can predict why.	**Extend:** Ask students to explain how they can see from the equation that it has 100% atom economy, without needing to calculate it.	

Main	Support/Extend	Resources
Methanol pitch (40 minutes) Ask students to work in small groups to create a 2-minute pitch to explain the compromise operating conditions of a methanol production plant. Students should comment on why low temperatures and low pressures would produce the greatest yield, but are not used. Students should justify the choice of conditions used. They then present their pitches. Whilst each pitch is being presented, students should write down one thing they thought was good about the pitch and one piece of constructive criticism.	**Extend:** Give each group a different industrial reversible reaction to make their pitch on (e.g., Contact process, ethanol production).	**Activity:** Methanol pitch

Plenary	Support/Extend	Resources
Yield up or down? (10 minutes) Interactive in which students investigate a familiar equilibrium system. Students predict how the yield of the forward reaction will be affected by a range of changes in conditions. **Pitch perfect** (5 minutes) After all students have presented their pitch, students vote for their favourite.	**Support:** Give students the science department's marking policy to refer to when they vote.	**Interactive:** Yield up or down?

Homework	Support/Extend	Resources
Write a newspaper article about how reaction conditions are chosen by industrial chemists. Include one reversible reaction as a case study.		

kerboodle
A Kerboodle highlight for this lesson is **Literacy sheet: Altering conditions.** Refer to the **Content map** on Kerboodle for a full list of resources and assessment.

Checkpoint
C5.3 Equilibria

Overview of C5.3 Equilibria

In this chapter students have studied reversible reactions and dynamic equilibria. They should be able to state examples of reversible reactions and represent these in equations. They should be able to describe how some reactions can be reversed by altering the reaction conditions, and recall that dynamic equilibrium occurs in a closed system when the rates of forward and reverse reactions are equal. They should understand that when a reversible reaction reaches equilibrium it does not stop – it continues, with opposing reactions occurring at the same rate. They should also be aware that when equilibrium is reached the concentrations of the reactants and products are not necessarily equal – in many equilibrium reactions the position of equilibrium lies well over to one side.

The majority of this topic is for higher-tier students, who should be able to predict and explain the effect of changing pressure, concentration, and temperature on a given equilibrium system. They should understand the effect of these factors on the equilibrium yield of a reaction, and explain the optimum pressure and temperature conditions for producing a high yield of a particular product, applying Le Chatelier's principle concerning concentration, temperature, and pressure. Higher-tier students should be able to explain why removing the product of a reversible reaction moves the equilibrium position to the right. They should be able to justify the choice of a compromise pressure and temperature for a particular equilibrium reaction. They should link this work with C3.2 *Energetics* where they learnt that thermal decompositions are always endothermic, and that endothermic reactions are favoured by heating. They should reinforce their studies of reaction profiles by applying these to equilibria reactions.

MyMaths

You can find additional support for the maths skills covered in this chapter on **MyMaths**, including plotting and interpreting graphs, and calculations using ratios and proportionality.

kerboodle

For this chapter, the following assessments are available on Kerboodle:
C5.3 Checkpoint quiz: Equilibria
C5.3 Progress quiz: Equilibria 1
C5.3 Progress quiz: Equilibria 2
C5.3 On your marks: Equilibria
C5.3 Exam-style questions and mark scheme: Equilibria

Checkpoint follow-up lesson

A student's route through this lesson can be determined using the Checkpoint assessment. Percentage pass marks are supplied in the Checkpoint teacher notes.

For each successive route through it is assumed that the student can perform to their current route as well as previous routes. For example, students working at Aiming for 6 are assumed to be secure in Aiming for 4 knowledge and understanding and working towards achieving all the learning objectives for Aiming for 6.

C5.3 Equilibria

	Aiming for 4	**Aiming for 6**	**Aiming for 8**
Learning outcomes	Calculate an average rate of reaction.	Calculate a rate of reaction at given times, using a graph of practical results.	Use Le Chatelier's principle to explain how the composition of an equilibrium mixture can be altered.
	Describe in simple terms how temperature and surface area affect the rate of a reaction.	Explain how collision theory can be used to explain the effect of temperature, surface area, pressure, and concentration on rate of reaction.	
Starter	**Post-it competition (5 minutes)** You will need Post-it notes and a board marked off into two areas. Ask for two volunteers to come to the front of the classroom. Explain that they will be competing to make as many pictures on Post-it notes as they can. They each have a minute to draw a flower and colour it on as many Post-it notes as possible, before sticking these on the board in their own marked area. Ask another student to time the minute and a fourth student to count the numbers of pictures produced. **Who won? (5 minutes)** Ask the class who won the competition, and how they could tell. Ask how this links to rates of reactions. Draw out that the pen and Post-it notes were similar to reactants, and the completed picture similar to products. (You can discuss here how models are useful but break down, e.g., the person drawing is not part of the model.) The number of pictures drawn represents the amount of product and the minute is the reaction time. Calculate each competitor's 'rate' and remind students that the average rate of reaction is calculated using the equation: average rate = (amount of reactant used or amount of product formed)/time.		
Differentiated checkpoint activity	**Rates and equilibria (40 minutes)** Aiming for 4 and Aiming for 6 students carry out some simple practical investigations using the differentiated worksheets. They will need support in performing these practicals. Aiming for 4 students will need: • task 1 – a stopwatch, some sugar, a teaspoon, a beaker of lukewarm water, and a beaker of hot water • task 2 – two test tubes containing dilute hydrochloric acid, a stopwatch, a magnesium strip, and the same mass of powdered magnesium (explain to students that the volumes of acid and the masses of magnesium are the same). The substances required should already be prepared for students (e.g. in small weighing boats or test tubes). Aiming for 6 students will need a beaker, a small strip of magnesium, dilute hydrochloric acid, a trough, and a measuring cylinder. They may need access to graph paper. Aiming for 8 students work independently to produce a poster about equilibria using the differentiated worksheet. These students will need A3 or A4 paper and coloured pencils.		
	Aiming for 4 students time: • how long it takes to dissolve a teaspoonful of sugar in lukewarm water compared with hot water • the reaction between a strip of magnesium metal and dilute hydrochloric acid compared with the same reaction using powdered magnesium. They then complete a series of questions and draw a cartoon strip. Students will need calculators.	Aiming for 6 students react a small strip of magnesium with dilute hydrochloric acid, and collect the hydrogen gas formed using an inverted measuring cylinder in a water bath. They use their results to plot a graph of volume of hydrogen gas against time. They use this graph to calculate the rate at given times. Students will need calculators. The sheet guides them through the process and provides a series of questions and tasks to consolidate their understanding, including drawing a cartoon strip and giving a written explanation for each factor.	The Aiming for 8 sheet encourages students to design their own poster on equilibria. They should choose a suitable reversible reaction, include full balanced equations and particle diagrams, and explain the effect of changing conditions on the positon of equilibrium.
	Kerboodle resource: C5.3 Checkpoint follow-up: Aiming for 4, C5.3 Checkpoint follow-up: Aiming for 6, C5.3 Checkpoint follow-up: Aiming for 8		
Plenary	**Monitoring reactions (10 minutes)** Ask student pairs to suggest how they could monitor the rate of a fuel burning in oxygen, such as a candle or ethanol in a spirit burner. Then one student describes why changing a factor such as temperature affects the rate (without naming the factor), for example, 'increasing this means that particles have more energy and whizz around faster, so more collisions take place.' The other student guesses the factor being described, and adds one piece of information to the description. Ask pairs to describe at least two factors in this way, swapping roles.		
Progression	Aiming for 4 students should show understanding that at hotter temperatures particles are moving faster and will collide more, and that a larger surface area means more particles are available on the surface to react.	Aiming for 6 students plot the results on a graph and use this to calculate the rate at given times. They should demonstrate an understanding of the effects of temperature, surface area, concentration, and pressure on rates of reaction.	Aiming for 8 students should demonstrate an understanding of Le Chatelier's principle and the effect of changing conditions on the positon of equilibrium.

C5 Monitoring and controlling chemical reactions

C5 Monitoring and controlling chemical reactions: Topic summary

C5.1 Monitoring chemical reactions
C5.2 Controlling reactions
C5.3 Equilibria

Spec ref	Statement	Book spreads
C5.1a	Explain how the concentration of a solution in mol/dm³ is related to the mass of the solute and the volume of the solution	C5.1.4
C5.1b	Describe the technique of titration	C5.1.5
C5.1c	Explain the relationship between the volume of a solution of known concentration of a substance and the volume or concentration of another substance that react completely together	C5.1.6
C5.1d	Describe the relationship between molar amounts of gases and their volumes and vice versa	C5.1.7
C5.1e	Calculate the volumes of gases involved in reactions using the molar gas volume at room temperature and pressure (assumed to be 24 dm³)	C5.1.7
C5.1f	Explain how the mass of a solute and the volume of the solution is related to the concentration of the solution	C5.1.4
C5.1g	Calculate the theoretical amount of a product from a given amount of reactant	C5.1.1
C5.1h	Calculate the percentage yield of a reaction product from the actual yield of a reaction	C5.1.2
C5.1i	Define the atom economy of a reaction	C5.1.2
C5.1j	Calculate the atom economy of a reaction to form a desired product from the balanced equation	C5.1.2
C5.1k	Explain why a particular reaction pathway is chosen to produce a specified product given appropriate data	C5.1.3
C5.2a	Suggest practical methods for determining the rate of a given reaction	C5.2.1
C5.2b	Interpret rate of reaction graphs	C5.2.1, C5.2.2, C5.2.3, C5.2.4
C5.2c	Describe the effect of changes in temperature, concentration, pressure, and surface area on rate of reaction	C5.2.2, C5.2.3, C5.2.4
C5.2d	Explain the effects on rates of reaction of changes in temperature, concentration, and pressure in terms of frequency and energy of collision between particles	C5.2.3
C5.2e	Explain the effects on rates of reaction of changes in the size of the pieces of a reacting solid in terms of surface area to volume ratio	C5.2.4
C5.2f	Describe the characteristics of catalysts and their effect on rates of reaction	C5.2.5
C5.2g	Identify catalysts in reactions	C5.2.5
C5.2h	Explain catalytic action in terms of activation energy	C5.2.5
C5.2i	Recall that enzymes act as catalysts in biological systems	C5.2.5
C5.3a	Recall that some reactions may be reversed by altering the reaction conditions	C5.3.1
C5.3b	Recall that dynamic equilibrium occurs in a closed system when the rates of forward and reverse reactions are equal	C5.3.1
C5.3c	Predict the effect of changing reaction conditions on equilibrium position and suggest appropriate conditions to produce as much of a particular product as possible	C5.3.2, C5.3.3

Maths

Spec ref	Statement	Book spread Main content	Maths chapter
CM5.1i	Calculations with numbers written in standard form when using the Avogadro constant	C5.1.4, C5.1.7	2
CM5.1ii	Provide answers to an appropriate number of significant figures	C5.1.6	5
CM5.1iii	Convert units where appropriate particularly from mass to moles	C5.1.4, C5.1.6, C5.1.7	11
CM5.1iv	Arithmetic computation, ratio, percentage, and multistep calculations permeates quantitative chemistry	C5.1.1, C5.1.2	3

CM5.1v	Arithmetic computation when calculating yields and atom economy	C5.1.1–3	3
CM5.1vi	Change the subject of a mathematical equation	C5.1.3	10
CM5.2i	Arithmetic computation, ratio when measuring rates of reaction		3
CM5.2ii	Drawing and interpreting appropriate graphs from data to determine rate of reaction	C5.2.1–5	13, 14
CM5.2iii	Determining gradients of graphs as a measure of rate of change to determine rate	C5.2.1–5	14
CM5.2iv	Proportionality when comparing factors affecting rate of reaction	C5.2.4	14
CM5.3i	Arithmetic computation, ratio when measuring rates of reaction	C5.3.1, C5.3.3	3
CM5.3ii	Drawing and interpreting appropriate graphs from data to determine rate of reaction	C5.3.1	13, 14
CM5.3iii	Determining gradients of graphs as a measure of rate of change to determine rate	C5.3.3	14
CM5.3iv	Proportionality when comparing factors affecting rate of reaction	C5.3.2, C5.3.3	14

Working scientifically

Spec ref	Statement	Main content	WS chapter
WS1.2a	Use scientific theories and explanations to develop hypotheses.	C5.1.2, C5.2.3, C5.3.3	WS3
WS1.2b	Plan experiments or devise procedures to make observations, produce or characterise a substance, test hypotheses, check data, or explore phenomena.	C5.1.2, C5.2.1, C5.3.3	WS3, WS4
WS1.2c	Apply knowledge of a range of techniques, instruments, apparatus, and materials to select those appropriate to the experiment.	C5.1.2, C5.2.1, C5.3.3	WS4
WS1.2d	Recognise when to apply knowledge of sampling techniques to ensure any samples collected are representative.	C5.1.2, C5.2.1	
WS1.3a	Present observations and other data using appropriate methods.	C5.2.1–5	WS6
WS1.3b	Translate data from one form to another.	C5.2.1–4	WS6
WS1.3c	Carrying out and representing mathematical and statistical analysis, to include arithmetic means, mode, and median.	C5.1.1–4, C5.1.6, C5.1.7, C5.2.1–4	WS5
WS1.3d	Represent distribution of results and make estimations of uncertainty.	C5.2.1–4	WS8
WS1.3e	Interpret observations and other data.	C5.2.1–4	WS7
WS1.3f	Present reasoned explanations.	C5.1.3, C5.2.2–4	WS7
WS1.3g	Evaluate data in terms of accuracy, precision, repeatability, and reproducibility.	C5.2.1–4	WS5, WS7
WS1.3h	Identify potential sources of random and systematic error.	C5.2.1–4	WS8
WS1.3i	Communicate the scientific rationale for investigations, methods used, findings, and reasoned conclusions.	C5.2.1–4	
WS1.4a	Use scientific vocabulary, terminology, and definitions.	C5.1.4, C5.1.6, C5.1.7, C5.2.5	WS2
WS1.4b	Recognise the importance of scientific quantities and understand how they are determined.	C5.1.6	
WS1.4c	Use SI units and IUPAC chemical nomenclature unless inappropriate.	C5.1.4, C5.1.6, C5.1.7, C5.2.2–4, C5.3.2, C5.3.3	
WS1.4d	Use prefixes and powers of ten for orders of magnitude.	C5.1.7	
WS1.4f	Use an appropriate number of significant figures in calculation.	C5.1.7	WS5
WS2a	Carry out experiments.	C5.1.2, C5.1.5, C5.2.1, C5.3.3	
WS2b	Make and record observations and measurements, using a range of apparatus and methods.	C5.1.2 C5.1.5 C5.2.1–4, C5.3.3	
WS2c	Present observations using appropriate methods.	C5.1.5	

C6 Global Challenges

C6.1 Improving processes and products
C6.1.1 Fertilisers — GCSE CHEMISTRY ONLY

Specification links:

6.1g Explain the importance of the Haber process in agricultural production.

WS1.4a Use scientific vocabulary, terminology, and definitions.

M1c Use ratios, fractions, and percentages.

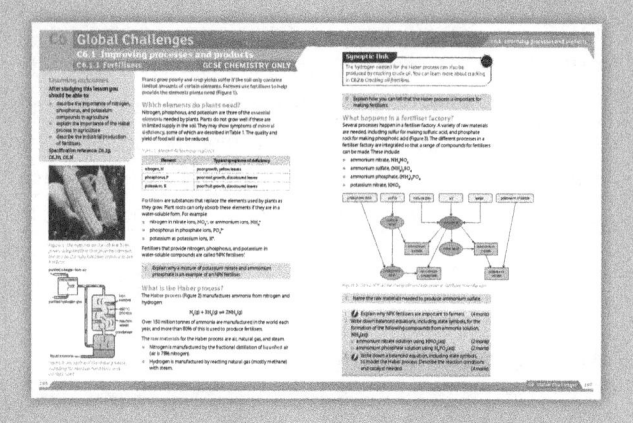

Target	Outcome	Checkpoint Question	Checkpoint Activity
Aiming for GRADE 4	State that fertilisers contain essential elements needed by plants and name the elements in NPK fertilisers.	A, 1	Starter 1
	State that ammonia is manufactured from hydrogen and nitrogen in the Haber process.		Starter 2, Main 1
	Recognise compounds that could be suitable for use as fertilisers.		Main 1 and 2, Plenary 1 and 2
Aiming for GRADE 6	Describe the typical symptoms of a deficiency of nitrogen, phosphorus, or potassium in plants.		Starter 1, Main 2
	Give the equation for the Haber process and describe the sources of its raw materials.	3	Starter 2, Main 1
	Describe the industrial production of fertilisers.	C	Starter 2, Main 1, Homework
Aiming for GRADE 8	Explain that plants can take up essential elements only in a water-soluble form, and give the formulae of suitable ions.	1	Starter 1
	Justify the importance of the Haber process in agriculture.	B	Plenary 1
	Explain in detail the industrial production of fertilisers and write equations for their formation.	2	Main 1

Maths
In Plenary 2 students calculate percentage composition (M1c).

Literacy
In Main 1 students write an informative advertisement for fertilisers. In Main 2 students make a flow chart to explain the details of the Haber process.

Key words
essential elements, mineral deficiency, fertilisers, Haber process, raw materials, liquefied

C6.1 Improving processes and products

Starter	Support/Extend	Resources
Plant nutrition (5 minutes) Ask students to explain why plants need the following three primary macronutrients: 1 nitrogen (to make amino acids and proteins) 2 phosphorus (to make DNA and RNA) 3 potassium (needed in the enzymes involved in respiration and photosynthesis). **Ammonia** (10 minutes) Show a video clip about the production of ammonia. Ask students to note the equation for the Haber process, the raw materials, the reactants, and the conditions for the reaction as they watch the video clip.	**Extend:** Ask students to find out about the secondary macronutrients and micronutrients needed by plants.	

Main	Support/Extend	Resources
Haber process flow chart (20 minutes) Ask students to use Figure 3 and the text in the Student Book to make a flow chart that explains where the raw materials for the Haber process are obtained, how they are turned into the reactants, what the conditions for the Haber process are, and why the unreacted gases are recycled. Students should include equations to illustrate any reactions, including the phase change of the ammonia that allows it to be tapped off.	**Extend:** Ask students to add to their flow chart to explain how ammonia is used to make fertiliser.	
Advertise fertilisers (20 minutes) Ask students to make an informative advert for fertilisers. Allow them to choose between an internet advert, a radio advert, a magazine advert, or a leaflet. Students should explain why fertilisers are important, which elements should be present, and the effect of a deficiency of each element on crops.	**Support:** Use desktop publishing software to make a pro forma advert for students to complete.	**Activity:** Advertise fertilisers

Plenary	Support/Extend	Resources
Agriculture (5 minutes) Ask students to write a short paragraph to explain why the Haber process is important to agriculture.		
Percentage composition (10 minutes) Ask students to calculate the percentage of nitrogen in different ammonium salts, such as ammonium nitrate, NH_4NO_3, and ammonium chloride, NH_4Cl.	**Extend:** Ask students to calculate the percentage of nitrogen in ammonium sulfate, $(NH_4)_2SO_4$.	**Interactive:** Percentage composition

Homework	Support/Extend	Resources
Outline the key stages in the production of the fertiliser ammonium nitrate.		

GCSE CHEMISTRY ONLY
C6.1.2 Making fertilisers

Specification links:

6.1h Compare the industrial production of fertilisers with laboratory syntheses of the same products.

WS1.2a Use scientific theories and explanations to develop hypotheses.

WS1.2b Plan experiments or devise procedures to make observations, produce or characterise a substance, test hypotheses, check data, or explore phenomena.

WS1.2c Apply knowledge of a range of techniques, instruments, apparatus, and materials to select those appropriate to the experiment.

WS1.2d Recognise when to apply knowledge of sampling techniques to ensure any samples collected are representative.

WS1.2e Evaluate methods and suggest possible improvements and further investigations.

WS2a Carry out experiments.

WS2b Make and record observations and measurements using a range of apparatus and methods.

M1c Use ratios, fractions, and percentages.

M2a Use an appropriate number of significant figures.

M2b Find arithmetic means.

Target	Outcome	Checkpoint Question	Checkpoint Activity
Aiming for GRADE 4	Describe some steps in the preparation of a fertiliser.		Starter 2, Main 1
	Use laboratory apparatus to prepare a neutral solution of ammonium sulfate.		Main 1
	State some differences between laboratory preparation and industrial production.		Main 2, Plenary 1 and 2
Aiming for GRADE 6	Describe how to prepare a compound found in fertilisers such as ammonium sulfate.		Main 1 and 2
	Use laboratory apparatus to prepare a compound found in fertilisers.		Main 1
	Describe the features of batch and continuous processes.		Main 2, Plenary 1 and 2
Aiming for GRADE 8	Explain in detail and with balanced equations how to prepare, in the school laboratory, pure dry samples of compounds found in fertilisers.	A, B, 2	Main 1 and 2
	Use laboratory apparatus competently to prepare, in the school laboratory, pure dry samples of compounds found in fertilisers.	1	Main 1 and 2
	Explain why batch processes are used for making small amounts of speciality chemicals and continuous processes are used for bulk chemicals.	3	Plenary 1

Maths
In Starter 1 (Extend) students balance symbol equations (M1c). In Main 1 they record readings to an appropriate number of decimal places and calculate the mean (M2a, M2b).

Literacy
In Main 1 students write an outline method for completing a titration. In Plenary 1 students justify the use of batch or continuous processes.

Key words
batch process, continuous processes

C6.1 Improving processes and products

Starter	Support/Extend	Resources
Name that fertiliser (5 minutes) Give students the names of pairs of acids and bases (e.g., ammonium hydroxide and nitric acid). Ask them to name the salt produced in a reaction between the two solutions that could be used as a fertiliser (ammonium nitrate). **Ammonia as a fertiliser** (5 minutes) Students use the interactive to complete a paragraph explaining why ammonia is not a very good fertiliser and needs to be converted to other chemicals.	**Extend:** Ask students to write balanced symbol equations for the neutralisation reactions.	**Interactive:** Ammonia as a fertiliser

Main	Support/Extend	Resources
Making ammonium sulfate fertiliser in the lab (30 minutes) Ask pairs of students to make ammonium sulfate fertiliser using a titration method: 1 Put dilute sulfuric acid in a burette and use a graduated pipette to accurately measure dilute ammonia solution into a small conical flask. 2 Add dilute sulfuric acid from the burette, 1 cm³ at a time, and swirl the conical flask until the solution is neutral (tested by dipping a glass rod into the solution and testing on blue litmus paper). 3 Note the titre and repeat until concordant results are obtained. 4 Put the resultant solution in an evaporating dish and heat it until about half of the water has evaporated off. 5 Leave the rest of the solution to evaporate slowly to leave crystals of ammonium sulfate. Ask students to write an outline of this method, generate a suitable results table to record their titres, and write an equation to model the neutralisation reaction. SAFETY: Ammonia and dilute sulfuric acid are corrosive. Wear eye protection and wash hands after the practical. Do not boil to dryness and keep the room well ventilated. Warn asthmatics not to breath in ammonia fumes. **Industrial process versus laboratory synthesis** (10 minutes) Tell students that they used a batch process to make ammonium sulfate fertiliser in Main 1, but that the industrial production of this fertiliser uses a continuous process, which runs all the time. Ask students to predict how the following factors differ in batch and continuous processes: 1 rate of production 2 cost of equipment 3 number of workers needed 4 ease of automating the process.	**Support:** Students could use a measuring cylinder to react 25 cm³ of ammonium hydroxide solution and 12.5 cm³ of sulfuric acid of the same concentration. Ask students to test the solution with litmus paper and use a dropping pipette to add more acid or alkali until neutralisation is complete.	**Practical:** Making ammonium sulfate fertiliser in the lab

Plenary	Support/Extend	Resources
Batch and continuous processes (5 minutes) Ask students to write a couple of sentences to justify why batch processes are used to make small amounts of speciality chemicals, while continuous processes are used for bulk chemicals. **Compare and contrast** (10 minutes) Read out statements based on Table 1 in the Student Book, which compares batch and continuous processes. Ask students to decide whether each statement relates to the industrial manufacture or laboratory preparation of fertilisers.		

Homework	Support/Extend	Resources
Explain why ammonia is not a very useful agricultural fertiliser.	**Support:** Ask students to list the properties of ammonia.	

kerboodle
A Kerboodle highlight for this lesson is **Extension: Fertilisers**. Refer to the **Content map** on Kerboodle for a full list of resources and assessment.

GCSE CHEMISTRY ONLY — HIGHER TIER
C6.1.3 The Haber process

Specification links:

6.1d Explain the trade-off between rate of production of a desired product and position of equilibrium in some industrially important processes.

6.1e Interpret graphs of reaction conditions versus rate.

WS1.3e Interpret observations and other data.

WS1.3f Present reasoned explanations.

CM6.1iii Determine gradients of graphs as a measure of rate of change to determine rate (M4d, M4e).

CM6.1iv Use proportionality when comparing factors affecting rate of reaction (M1c).

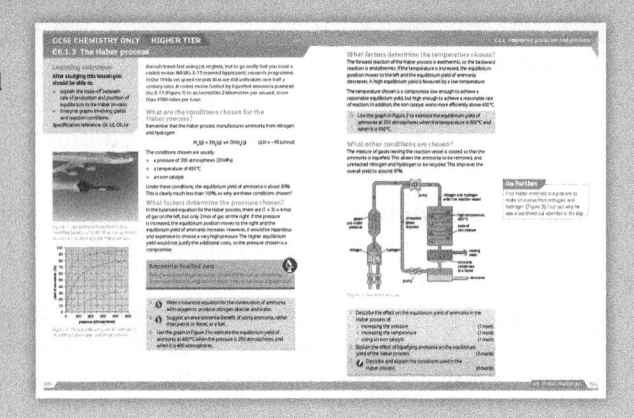

Target	Outcome	Checkpoint Question	Checkpoint Activity
Aiming for GRADE 6	Write the equation and describe the conditions chosen for the Haber process.	1, 3	Starter 1, Main 1
↓	Interpret yield–temperature graphs and deduce the yield of ammonia at different temperatures.	D, 1b	Main 1
↓	Interpret yield–pressure graphs and deduce the yield of ammonia at different pressures.	C, 1a	Main 1
Aiming for GRADE 8	Describe and explain in detail the conditions used in the Haber process.	A, B, 2, 3	Main 1 and 2, Plenary 1 and 2
↓	Use knowledge of rates and equilibria to justify the temperature used for ammonia production.		Starter 1, Main 1 and 2, Plenary 1
↓	Use knowledge of rates and equilibria to justify the pressure used for ammonia production.		Starter 1, Main 1 and 2, Plenary 1

Literacy

In Main 1 students create an animated presentation or poster about the Haber process. In completing the Homework task students summarise the Haber process in a text message.

C6.1 Improving processes and products

Starter	Support/Extend	Resources
Maximise yield (5 minutes) Display the balanced symbol equation for the Haber process. Ask students to justify the use of high pressure but low temperature conditions to maximise the yield. **The importance of ammonia** (10 minutes) Briefly introduce that the Haber process is used to turn nitrogen in the air into ammonia. Give a few examples of the uses of ammonia (e.g., as a fertiliser) and ask students to explain why the Haber process is important to the farming industry.	**Support:** Remind students that the greater the number of moles of gas, the higher the pressure.	

Main	Support/Extend	Resources
Haber process conditions (30 minutes) Ask students to create an animated presentation, or a poster, to show how the equilibrium yield of ammonia changes with temperature and pressure. The presentation or poster should include an equation for the reaction, the graph shown in Figure 2, as well as conclusions that are consistent with the data displayed in the graph. Students could also use what they have learnt about equilibrium reactions in previous lessons to explain their conclusions. **Peer assessment** (10 minutes) Students show their animated presentation or poster to another group. The other group points out three positive aspects of the presentation or poster, and gives two suggestions for improvement. Encourage students to look carefully at the justifications given for the choice of temperature used for ammonia production.		**Activity:** Haber process conditions

Plenary	Support/Extend	Resources
Explain (5 minutes) Ask students to explain the industrial benefit of the following stages of the Haber process: 1 Removal of ammonia (pushes equilibrium position to the right) 2 Cooling of the gases that leave the reactor (to liquefy ammonia and easily separate it from the unreacted gases) 3 Recycling of unreacted hydrogen and nitrogen (saves money and resources). **The Haber process** (5 minutes) Interactive activity in which students decide if statements about the Haber process are true or false and then complete a paragraph on the conditions of the Haber process.	**Support:** Provide students with the reasons to match to the correct stages.	**Interactive:** The Haber process

Homework	Support/Extend	Resources
Summarise the Haber process in a text message.		

kerboodle

A Kerboodle highlight for this lesson is **WebQuest: The Haber process**. Refer to the **Content map** on Kerboodle for a full list of resources and assessment.

GCSE CHEMISTRY ONLY — HIGHER TIER
C6.1.4 The Contact process

Specification links:

6.1d Explain the trade-off between rate of production of a desired product and position of equilibrium in some industrially important processes.

6.1e Interpret graphs of reaction conditions versus rate.

WS1.3f Present reasoned explanations.

M4e Draw and use the slope of a tangent to a curve as a measure of rate of change.

CM6.1iii Determine gradients of graphs as a measure of rate of change to determine rate (M4d, M4e).

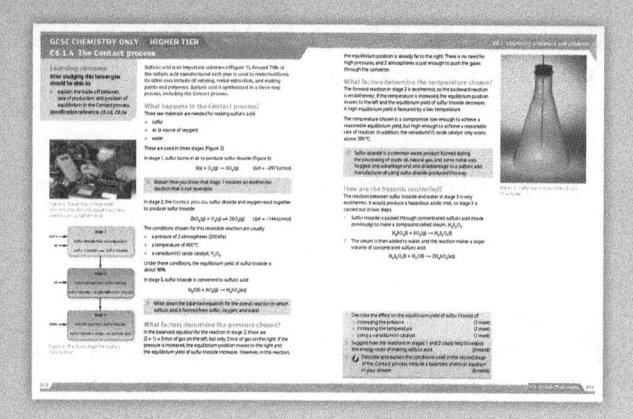

Target	Outcome	Checkpoint	
		Question	Activity
Aiming for GRADE 6	Write the equations and describe the conditions chosen for the Contact process.	A, B	Starter 1 and 2 Main 1 Plenary 1
	Describe the effect on equilibrium yield of increasing temperature and pressure.	1	Main 2
	Explain why some stages of the Contact process are hazardous.		Main 1 Homework
Aiming for GRADE 8	Describe and explain in detail the conditions used in the Contact process.	3	Main 1
	Use knowledge of rates and equilibria to justify the temperature and pressure used in the Contact process.	2	Main 1 Homework
	Explain in detail how the hazards in the manufacture of sulfuric acid are controlled.		Main 1 Homework

Maths
In Main 2 students interpret graphs of yield versus reaction conditions (M4e).

Literacy
In Plenary 1 students write brief summaries. In completing the Homework task students justify the use of oleum in the manufacture of sulfuric acid.

C6.1 Improving processes and products

Starter	Support/Extend	Resources
Maximise yield (5 minutes) Show the balanced symbol equation describing the dynamic equilibrium for the Contact process and the enthalpy change for the reaction. Ask students to suggest and justify the conditions needed to maximise the yield. **Combustion of sulfur** (10 minutes) Ask students to suggest what substance is made when sulfur burns in a Bunsen Burner flame. Students write a word equation and balanced symbol equation with state symbols.	**Support:** Label the equation to show the exothermic and endothermic reactions, and the side with more moles and fewer moles of reactants. **Support:** Demonstrate the reaction for students.	**Interactive:** Maximise yield

Main	Support/Extend	Resources
Sulfuric acid (30 minutes) Ask students to make a flow chart about how sulfuric acid is manufactured, including any hazards involved. Then ask students to make up questions about the Contact process, and swap these with a partner. The partner answers the questions, and returns their answers to the question writer for peer assessment. **Interpret a graph** (10 minutes) Provide students with a graph of yield of sulfur trioxide versus temperature. Ask students to describe and explain what the graph shows.	**Support:** Provide students with an outline flow chart with the key sections (temperature, pressure, catalyst, and safety) already labelled. **Extend:** Ask students to add to their flow chart details about how the hazards in the manufacture of sulfuric acid are controlled.	**Activity:** Sulfuric acid

Plenary	Support/Extend	Resources
Sticky note (5 minutes) Give each student a sticky note and ask them to summarise the Contact process and the compromise reaction conditions used. **Uses of sulfuric acid** (10 minutes) Demonstrate the use of sulfuric acid as a dehydrating agent. In a fume cupboard, half-fill a beaker with granulated sugar and add some concentrated sulfuric acid. As hydrogen and oxygen are removed from the sugar molecules, a carbon skeleton grows.	**Extend:** Ask students to write a balanced symbol equation for the reaction.	

Homework	Support/Extend	Resources
Justify why sulfur trioxide is reacted with oleum rather than water in the production of sulfuric acid.		

GCSE CHEMISTRY ONLY — HIGHER TIER
C6.1.5 Making ethanol

Specification links:

6.1f Explain how the commercially used conditions for an industrial process are related to the availability and cost of raw materials and energy supplies, control of equilibrium position, and rate.

WS1.1d Discuss ethical issues arising from developments in science.

M1c Use ratios, fractions, and percentages.

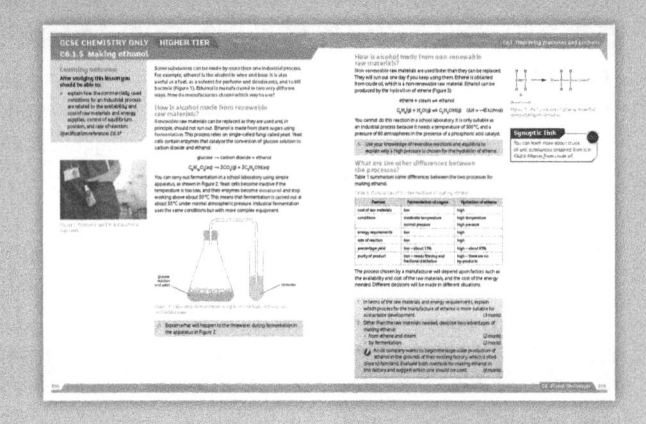

Target	Outcome	Checkpoint Question	Checkpoint Activity
Aiming for GRADE 6 ↓	Describe how to make ethanol from sugar in the school laboratory.		Main 1
	Describe steps in the production of ethanol from ethene and explain why the raw materials are non-renewable.		Main 2 Plenary 1 and 2
	Describe differences between the two methods of ethanol production.	1, 2	Main 2 Plenary 1 Homework
Aiming for GRADE 8 ↓	Explain in detail the production of ethanol from glucose, and explain why the raw materials are renewable.	A	Main 2
	Explain in detail the production of ethanol from ethane.	B	Main 2 Plenary 2
	Explain how the conditions for an industrial process are related to the availability and cost of raw materials and energy supplies, control of equilibrium position, and rate.	2, 3	Starter 1 Main 2 Plenary 1 Homework

Maths
In Main 2 (Extend) students calculate atom economy (M1c).

Literacy
In Plenary 1 students explain how ethanol can be made from renewable or finite resources. In completing the Homework task students write a justification for which is the better method for making ethanol as a fuel for cars.

Key words
renewable, fermentation, denatured, non-renewable, hydration

204

C6.1 Improving processes and products

Starter	Support/Extend	Resources
Burning money (5 minutes) Provide students with two hypothetical ways to produce a substance that is an important industrial chemical that can be sold for a high price: • The first reaction has a 90% yield for the useful product, but a toxic by-product that cannot be sold and is very difficult to dispose of is also produce. The reaction requires high pressure. • The second reaction has a 60% yield for the useful product, but the by-product can be sold though only for a small price. The reaction required high temperature. Ask students to choose which reaction they would use to produce the useful product. They should justify their choice. **Synoptic ethanol** (10 minutes) Show students the displayed formula of ethanol. Ask them to draw a dot-and-cross diagram, identify the type of bonding, and write the molecular formula for ethanol.	**Extend:** Ask students to write a balanced symbol equation for this reaction. **Extend:** Ask students to explain why ethanol has a lower melting point than water.	

Main	Support/Extend	Resources
Make ethanol (40 minutes) Set up an ice bath, a warm water bath (approximately 35 °C), and a hot water bath (approximately 60 °C) on each bench. Ask pairs of students to place 50 cm³ of yeast and sugar solution in each of four conical flasks. Ask students to put a balloon on the neck of each conical flask to collect qualitative data. Students place one flask in each water bath and leave one at ambient temperature. Allow at least 20 minutes for fermentation to occur, during which time students can tackle Main 2. Then ask students to observe the size of the balloons as an indicator of the rate of fermentation. While the reaction is occurring, ask students to predict the temperature at which most ethanol will be made. Students write a balanced symbol equation for the reaction. They could also outline an experiment to collect quantitative data. **Index cards** (15 minutes, during Main 1) Give each student an index card. On one side they should summarise making ethanol using fermentation, and on the reverse making ethanol using ethene. Then lead a discussion comparing the two processes, drawing out the points that the conditions for an industrial process are related to the availability and cost of raw materials and energy supplies, controlling the equilibrium position, and reaction rate.	**Support:** Use a blue balloon for the lowest temperature, green for ambient, yellow for warm, and red for hot. **Extend:** Ask students to explain why the balloon contracted at the coldest temperature. **Extend:** Ask students to calculate the atom economy for each method.	**Practical:** Make ethanol

Plenary	Support/Extend	Resources
Renewable or non-renewable? (5 minutes) Ask students to explain why ethanol made from fermentation is considered a renewable resource, but ethanol made from ethene is not. **Producing ethanol** (10 minutes) Provide students with statements that describe the process of fermentation to produce ethanol. Students put the statements in the correct order. They then do the same for the industrial process of producing ethanol.	**Support:** Use questions and answers to establish that ethene is made from crude oil, a finite resource, whereas sugar is made from crops.	**Interactive:** Producing ethanol

Homework	Support/Extend	Resources
Justify which is the better method for making ethanol as a fuel for cars, as it is used in Brazil and other countries.		

C6.1.6 Extracting metals

Specification links:

6.1a Explain, using the position of carbon in the reactivity series, the principles of industrial processes used to extract metals, including extraction of a non-ferrous metal.

WS1.4a Use scientific vocabulary, terminology, and definitions.

M1a Recognise and use expressions in decimal form.

M1c Use ratios, fractions, and percentages.

CM6.1i Use arithmetic computation and ratio when measuring rates of reaction (M1a, M1c).

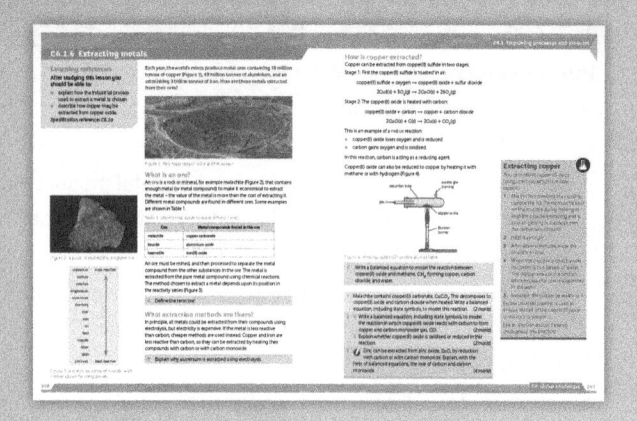

Target	Outcome	Checkpoint	
		Question	Activity
Aiming for GRADE 4 ↓	State a definition of the term ore.	A	Starter 1
	Describe some stages in the extraction of copper.		Main, Plenary 2
	Use laboratory apparatus to heat a sample of copper(II) oxide and charcoal.		Main
Aiming for GRADE 6 ↓	Outline the steps in extracting a metal from its ore.		Main, Plenary 1 and 2, Homework
	Describe how copper is extracted from copper(II) oxide.	2	Main, Plenary 2, Homework
	Prepare a sample of copper from copper(II) oxide.		Main, Plenary 2
Aiming for GRADE 8 ↓	Explain, using the position of carbon in the reactivity series, how the industrial process used to extract a metal is chosen.	B, 3	Plenary 1
	Explain the extraction of copper from different ores using chemical equations, and describe each part of the process as oxidation or reduction.	C, 1, 2	Homework
	Prepare a sample of copper from copper(II) oxide and explain why an excess of charcoal is used.		Main

Maths
In Main 1 (Extend) students calculate the yield of copper extracted from malachite (M1a, M1c).

Key words
ore, redox

206

C6.1 Improving processes and products

Starter	Support/Extend	Resources
Extracting metals (10 minutes) Use the Interactive activity to help students complete a paragraph introducing the concept that some metals have to be extracted from their ores and that carbon is sometimes used in the extraction process. **Ores** (5 minutes) Show students a selection of copper ores, for example, malachite, cuprite, chalcopyrite, and some native copper. Ask students to suggest the connection (all different forms that copper can be found in the Earth's crust).	**Support:** Give students only the copper samples and ask them to classify them as native metal, ore, mineral, and compound. **Extend:** Ask students to suggest the reason for using sodium carbonate. (The sodium carbonate does not take part in the reaction. It melts and provides an interface between the iron oxide and the carbon.)	**Interactive:** Extracting metals

Main	Support/Extend	Resources
Extracting copper (40 minutes) Remind students that copper exists naturally in ores such as malachite, which contains copper(II) carbonate mixed with other substances. Explain that they will extract copper from malachite in two stages (Main 1 and Main 2). Ask pairs of students to obtain copper(II) oxide from malachite: 1 Put 3 spatula measures of copper(II) carbonate into a boiling tube. 2 Using test-tube holders, hold the tube at a 45° angle in a blue Bunsen burner flame and heat it strongly. 3 When all of the powder has changed colour from green to black, remove the tube from the heat and allow it to cool in a boiling-tube rack. The black powder is copper(II) oxide. Ask students to briefly record how they obtained copper(II) oxide from copper(II) carbonate. Students then extract the copper from the copper(II) oxide: 1 Mix the cooled copper(II) oxide with an approximately equal volume of powdered charcoal. 2 Place the mixture in a metal bottle-top from which the plastic seal has been removed, and use tongs to hold the bottle-top in the hottest part of a Bunsen burner flame. 3 When the mixture glows red, remove it from the flame and observe the red-brown copper that has formed. Through discussion, establish that carbon can be placed above copper in the reactivity series, meaning that it has been able to reduce copper(II) oxide.	**Extend:** Ask students to measure the mass of malachite used in Main 1 and the mass of copper collected at the end of Main 2. Use these values to estimate the percentage copper content of the ore. **Extend:** Ask students to measure the mass of malachite used in Main 1 and the mass of copper collected at the end of Main 2. Use these values to estimate the percentage copper content of the ore.	**Practical:** Extracting copper

Plenary	Support/Extend	Resources
Reactivity series (5 minutes) Display a reactivity series with hydrogen and carbon listed. Ask students to annotate the list to show the native metals, those collected by smelting (extraction using carbon), and electrolysis. **Extraction of copper** (10 minutes) Demonstrate the reduction of copper(II) oxide using hydrogen, as shown in Figure 4 in the Student Book.	**Support:** Explain that some metals have to be reduced using hydrogen. Show these on the reactivity series.	

Homework	Support/Extend	Resources
Make a table to compare the extraction of copper from its ores by smelting, by displacement with a more reactive metal, and by reduction with hydrogen.	**Support:** Give each method and their advantages and disadvantages.	

kerboodle
A Kerboodle highlight for this lesson is **WebQuest: Find an extraction, ore else**. Refer to the **Content map** on Kerboodle for a full list of resources and assessment.

C6 Global Challenges

C6.1.7 Extracting iron

Specification links:

6.1a Explain, using the position of carbon in the reactivity series, the principles of industrial processes used to extract metals, [including extraction of a non-ferrous metal].

WS1.4a Use scientific vocabulary, terminology, and definitions.

M1c Use ratios, fractions, and percentages.

CM6.1i Use arithmetic computation and ratio when measuring rates of reaction (M1a, M1c).

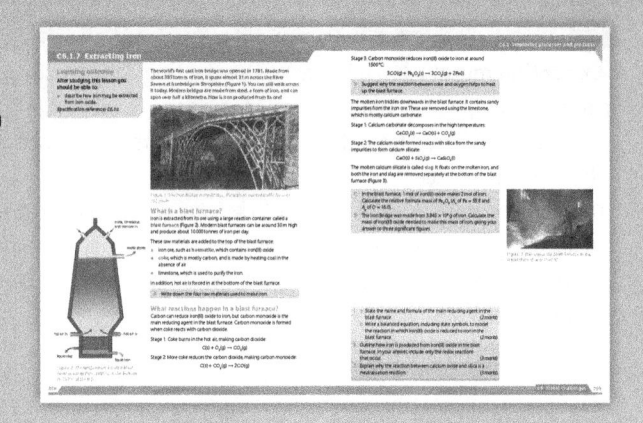

Target	Outcome	Checkpoint	
		Question	Activity
Aiming for GRADE 4 ↓	State that iron is produced from iron ore and coke.		Starter 1 and 2 Main 1 Homework
	State that iron ore is converted into iron at high temperature in the blast furnace.		Main 1 Homework
	State that the reaction that produces iron is a reduction reaction.		Main 2
Aiming for GRADE 6 ↓	Name all the raw materials used to make iron.	A	Starter 1 and 2 Main 1 Homework
	Describe the main processes that occur in the blast furnace to produce iron ore.		Starter 1 Main 1 and 2 Homework
	Write equations for the reactions that occur in the blast furnace in the production of iron ore.	1	Main 2 Homework
Aiming for GRADE 8 ↓	Explain why each of the raw materials used in iron production is needed.		Starter 1 and 2 Main 1 and 2 Homework
	Explain in detail how iron is extracted from iron ore.	B, 2	Main 1
	Distinguish the reactions that occur in the blast furnace as combustion, oxidation, redox, or neutralisation.	1, 2, 3	Main 2

Maths
In Main 1 and Main 2 students balance symbol equations (M1c).

Literacy
In Main 1 students write a script for a podcast.

Key words
blast furnace, haematite, coke, slag

C6.1 Improving processes and products

Starter	Support/Extend	Resources
Blast furnace (5 minutes) Use the interactive to introduce the blast furnace for extracting iron to students. Students label the different parts of the blast furnace. **Raw material or product?** (10 minutes) show students pictures of coke (or charcoal), haematite, limestone, slag, and pig iron. Ask students to classify them as either raw materials or products from the blast furnace.		**Interactive:** Blast furnace

Main	Support/Extend	Resources
Iron extraction podcast (30 minutes) Ask students to write a script for a three-minute podcast to explain how iron is extracted from iron ore in the blast furnace. Scripts should include an introduction, a main section with the explanation, and a summary of the key points in the extraction process. **Blast furnace equations** (10 minutes) Ask students to note down all the chemical reactions that occur in the blast furnace. Students should then classify each reaction as combustion, oxidation, redox, or neutralisation. Some reactions will have more than one classification.	**Support:** Give students key phrases to include in their podcast. **Extend:** Use recording software to allow students to record their podcast. The best examples could be uploaded to the school's website or VLE for use as a revision resource. **Support:** Give students the definitions for each type of chemical reaction. **Extend:** Ask students to explain how carbon can be both oxidised and reduced in the same chemical reaction.	**Activity:** Iron extraction podcast

Plenary	Support/Extend	Resources
Predict reactions (5 minutes) Explain that zinc can be extracted from zinc oxide in a blast furnace using zinc ore, limestone, and carbon as the raw materials. Ask students to predict the reactions that occur. Ask students to justify their prediction. **Make iron** (10 minutes) Explain that iron can be made using a displacement reaction. This method is used to weld railway tracks together. Remind students of the thermite reaction demonstrated in C3.1.5 and C3.3.1 (refer to these lessons for more details).	**Extend:** Ask students to compare and contrast the thermite reaction with the blast furnace as a means of making iron.	

Homework	Support/Extend	Resources
Label the key parts of the blast furnace and add equations to illustrate the reactions that are occurring.		

kerboodle

A Kerboodle highlight for this lesson is **Go further: Transitional elements and variable oxidation states**. Refer to the **Content map** on Kerboodle for a full list of resources and assessment.

C6.1.8 Extracting aluminium

Specification links:

6.1b Explain why and how electrolysis is used to extract some metals from their ores.

WS1.4 Use scientific vocabulary, quantities, units, symbols, and nomenclature.

M1c Use ratios, fractions, and percentages.

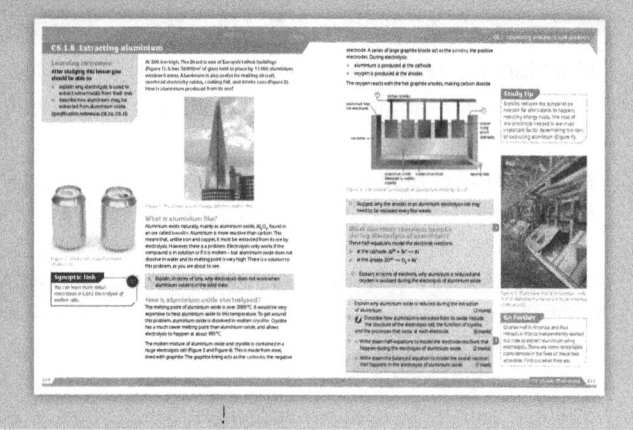

Target	Outcome	Checkpoint	
		Question	Activity
Aiming for GRADE 4 ↓	State that aluminium is extracted from aluminium oxide by electrolysis.		Main 1 and 2 Homework
	Describe some stages in the process of extracting aluminium from its ore.		Main 1 and 2
	State that the electrolysis of aluminium oxide produces aluminium and oxygen.		Main 1 and 2 Homework
Aiming for GRADE 6 ↓	State that the main ore of aluminium is bauxite, and explain why aluminium has to be extracted by electrolysis.		Starter 2 Main 1 and 2 Plenary 1 Homework
	Describe how aluminium is extracted from its oxide.		Main 1 and 2 Plenary 2 Homework
	Name the substances formed at each electrode in the electrolysis of aluminium oxide, and explain why the anode needs replacing frequently.	B	Main 1 and 2 Plenary 1 and 2 Homework
Aiming for GRADE 8 ↓	Explain why aluminium oxide is dissolved in cryolite before electrolysis.	A	Main 1 and 2
	Explain in detail each stage of the extraction of aluminium from its ore and write a balanced equation to model the overall reaction.	2, 3	Main 1 and 2
	Write equations for the processes that occur at each electrode and describe them as oxidation or reduction.	C, 1, 3	Main 1 and 2 Plenary 2 Homework

Maths
In Starter 2 (Extend) students write balanced symbol and half equations (M1c).

Literacy
In Main 2 students make a flow chart to show how aluminium is extracted from the Earth.

Key words
bauxite, cryolite

210

C6.1 Improving processes and products

Starter	Support/Extend	Resources
Uses of aluminium (5 minutes) Give small groups of students a tray of aluminium items (e.g., foil, drinks can, drinks bottle, saucepan). Ask students to suggest what the items have in common. **Aluminium reactivity** (10 minutes) Ask students to suggest where aluminium is in the reactivity series. They are likely to suggest that it is near the bottom, because it does not appear to react with the air, water, or other substances (e.g., in cooking). However, aluminium is a fairly reactive metal but is protected from reactions by an aluminium oxide coating on its surface. Using gloves and in a well-ventilated area, wipe a piece of cotton wool soaked with mercury(II) chloride over the surface of a piece of aluminium foil. This will remove the oxide layer and the aluminium will react highly exothermically with oxygen in the air.	**Extend:** Ask students to write a balanced symbol equation and half equations for this reaction. [H]	

Main	Support/Extend	Resources
Aluminium production (40 minutes) Provide an unlabelled diagram of the electrolytic cell for aluminium production (see Figure 3). Ask students to annotate the diagram to: 1 Describe the electrolysis of aluminium oxide in terms of ions moving. 2 Write an equation to summarise the electrolysis. 3 Explain why cryolite is added. 4 Explain why carbon electrodes need to be replaced frequently. Students then make a flow chart to describe how aluminium ore is mined from the Earth and how aluminium is extracted from it. Students should include equations for the electrolysis of aluminium.	**Support:** You may wish to show a video of the industrial electrolysis of aluminium. **Extend:** Ask students to write half equations for the reactions at the electrodes and classify them as oxidation or reduction. [H]	**Activity:** Aluminium production

Plenary	Support/Extend	Resources
Electrolysis extraction (5 minutes) Students use the interactive to complete a paragraph on electrolysis and how it is used to extract metals from their ores. **Dot-and-cross** (10 minutes) Ask students to draw dot-and-cross diagrams for the half equations in the electrolysis of aluminium oxide.	**Extend:** Ask students to draw the dot-and-cross diagrams to illustrate the balanced symbol equation for the electrolysis of aluminium oxide.	**Interactive:** Electrolysis extraction

Homework	Support/Extend	Resources
Draw a labelled particle diagram to explain how molten aluminium oxide undergoes electrolysis.		

kerboodle
A Kerboodle highlight for this lesson is **Homework: Improving processes and products**. Refer to the **Content map** on Kerboodle for a full list of resources and assessment.

HIGHER TIER
C6.1.9 Biological metal extraction

Specification links:

6.1c Evaluate alternative biological methods of metal extraction.

WS1.1a Understand how scientific methods and theories develop over time.

WS1.1e Explain everyday and technological applications of science.

WS2a Carry out experiments.

WS2b Make and record measurements using a range of apparatus and methods.

M2c Construct and interpret frequency tables and diagrams, bar charts, and histograms.

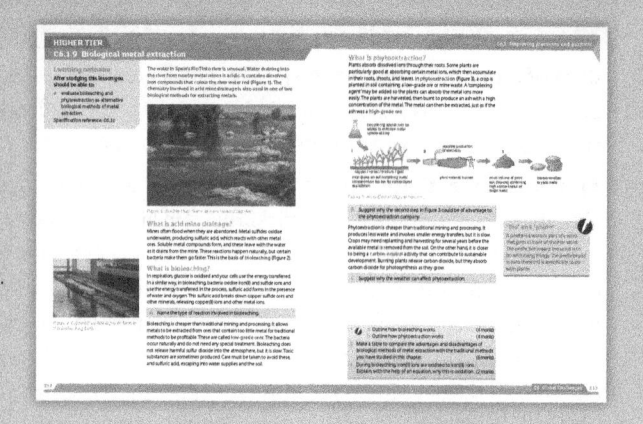

Target	Outcome	Checkpoint	
		Question	Activity
Aiming for GRADE 6	Describe the process of bioleaching.	1	Main 1, Plenary 1 and 2
	Describe the process of phytoextraction.	1	Main 2, Plenary 1 and 2
	Describe some advantages and disadvantages of bioleaching and phytoextraction.		Plenary 2, Homework
Aiming for GRADE 8	Explain the process of bioleaching in detail.	A, 3	Main 1, Plenary 1 and 2
	Explain the process of phytoextraction in detail.	B, C	Main 2, Plenary 1 and 2
	Compare bioleaching and phytoextraction with alternative methods of metal extraction and evaluate them.	2	Plenary 2, Homework

Maths
In Starter 2 students draw a pie chart (M2c).

Literacy
In Plenary 2 students compare and contrast different metal extraction methods.

Key words
bioleaching, low-grade ores, phytoextraction, high-grade ore, carbon-neutral, prefix

212

C6.1 Improving processes and products

Starter	Support/Extend	Resources
Uses of copper (5 minutes) Show students a selection of copper products (e.g., plumbing pipes, wire, and cooking pans). Ask students to suggest which properties of copper make it fit for each purpose. **Elements of the Earth** (10 minutes) Ask students to draw a pie chart to show the different elements in the Earth's crust (46% oxygen, 28% silicon, 8% aluminium, 5% iron, 4% calcium, 3% sodium, 2% magnesium, 2% potassium, and the rest is all other elements).	**Extend:** Ask students to suggest and justify which method of extraction should be used for each metal listed.	

Main	Support/Extend	Resources
Bioleaching and phytoextraction (20 minutes) Explain that many metal ores are oxides, mixed with other substances, in rock. Ask pairs of students to measure 25 cm³ of dilute sulfuric acid into a conical flask and add excess copper(II) oxide until the solution is blue. Students should then filter the mixture and extract the copper from the filtrate by electrolysis or the displacement reaction with iron. Then introduce students to the process of phytoextraction. Students should draw a flow chart to summarise the process then create a table to compare phytoextraction and bioleaching.	**Extend:** Ask students to write half equations for the reduction of the copper(II) ions.	**Practical:** Bioleaching and phytoextraction

Plenary	Support/Extend	Resources
Extracting metals (5 minutes) Students choose the correct words to complete a paragraph on the extraction of copper. they then sort statements according to whether they describe bioleaching or phytoextraction. **Compare and contrast** (10 minutes) Ask students to make a table about bioleaching and phytoextraction to compare the environmental, social, and economic consequences of these metal extraction methods.	**Extend:** Ask students to focus on copper extraction and add smelting and electrolysis to the table. Students should justify what they think is the best method of copper extraction.	**Interactive:** Extracting metals

Homework	Support/Extend	Resources
Rate metal extraction techniques (smelting, electrolysis, extraction with hydrogen, bioleaching, and phytoextraction) from most to least carbon-neutral, and justify your order.		

kerboodle
A Kerboodle highlight for this lesson is **WebQuest: Alternative methods of extracting metals**. Refer to the **Content map** on Kerboodle for a full list of resources and assessment.

GCSE CHEMISTRY ONLY
C6.1.10 Alloys

Specification links:

6.1m Describe the composition of some important alloys in relation to their properties and uses.

WS1.1b Use models to solve problems, make predictions, and to develop scientific explanations and understanding of familiar and unfamiliar facts.

WS2a Carry out experiments.

WS2b Make and record measurements using a range of apparatus and methods

M1c Use ratios, fractions, and percentages.

M3c Substitute numerical values into algebraic equations using appropriate units for physical quantities.

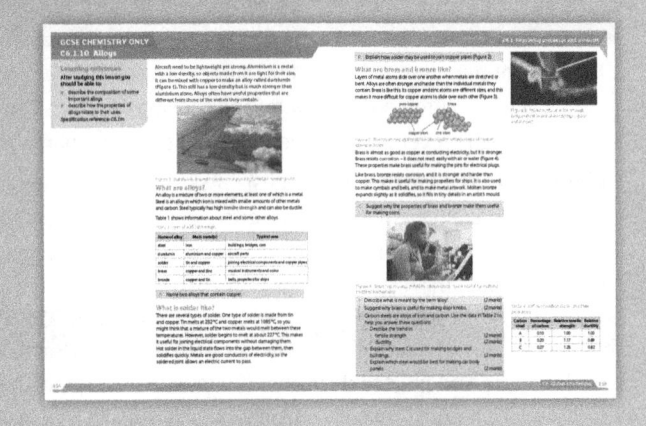

Target	Outcome	Checkpoint Question	Checkpoint Activity
Aiming for GRADE 4	State a definition of the term alloy.	1	Starter 1 and 2
	State that solder is used to join electrical components and copper pipes.		Main 2, Plenary 1
	Describe some uses of brass and bronze.		Plenary 1
Aiming for GRADE 6	Name some alloys, list the metals they contain, and outline their typical uses.	A	Starter 1, Plenary 1, Homework
	Describe the composition of solder and how its properties differ from those of its component metals.		Main 1, Main 2
	Describe the properties of brass and bronze and how these differ from those of their component metals.		Plenary 1
Aiming for GRADE 8	Use the properties of an alloy to evaluate its suitability for a particular use.	3	Main 2, Plenary 1
	Describe in detail the properties of solder and relate these to its use.	B	Main 2, Plenary 1
	Explain in detail the properties of brass and bronze and how these relate to their uses.	C, 2	Starter 2, Plenary 1

Maths
In Main 2 students calculate density (M3c). In completing the Homework (Extend) task students calculate the percentage of gold in different alloys (M1c).

Key words
tensile strength, corrosion

C6.1 Improving processes and products

Starter	Support/Extend	Resources
Alloys (5 minutes) Give a definition of an alloy, and name some, for example steel (mainly iron), duralumin (aluminium and copper), solder (tin and copper), brass (copper and zinc), and bronze (copper and tin). **Model alloys** (10 minutes) Give pairs of students 12 marbles or polystyrene balls, a tray, and sticky tack. Remind them of the particle model of a solid and ask them to make a model of a metal crystal. Then give students a smaller ball and ask them to add this to their structure. Ask for suggestions as to what they have made (an alloy) and how this added component may affect the metal's properties.	**Support:** Use questions and answers to establish the particle arrangement in a solid.	

Main	Support/Extend	Resources
Making solder (40 minutes) Pairs of students make solder: 1 Weigh out 1 g of lead into a crucible. 2 Using a blue Bunsen burner flame, heat strongly until the lead is molten, then add a spatula measure of carbon powder. 3 Add 1 g of tin and use a spatula to mix the substances thoroughly. 4 Remove from the heat and pour the metal onto a ceramic tile to cool. Ask students to state the composition of solder and draw a particle diagram to represent the structure. They then compare the properties of the solder made with the properties of tin and lead. 1 Assess hardness by trying to scratch the surface of each metal. 2 Use a top-pan balance and a Eureka can to measure the mass and volume of the metal samples in order to calculate their densities. 3 Compare melting points by heating small samples of each metal simultaneously on a crucible lid supported on a pipe-clay triangle. Students should design suitable results tables and draw conclusions from their results. Ask students to suggest the uses of solder based on its properties, compared with those of the pure metals.	**Extend:** Ask students to describe the bonding in solder. **Extend:** Allow students to use a secondary source to research the reported densities of tin, lead, and solder so that they can then comment on the accuracy of their results.	**Practical:** Making solder

Plenary	Support/Extend	Resources
Splat! (5 minutes) Ask student pairs to write the alloys listed in Table 1 on an A3 piece of paper in large text, spread out across the page. Then read out uses of the alloys as listed in the table. Students put their hand as quickly as possible on the name of the correct alloy. The first person in each pair to put their hand on the correct word gets a point. **Identifying alloys** (10 minutes) Interactive activity in which students match steel alloys with different compositions of carbon to their properties and uses.	**Support:** Prepare the A3 sheets in advance.	**Interactive:** Identifying alloys

Homework	Support/Extend	Resources
Look at the display of images of different gold jewellery, focusing on the hallmarks. Suggest what the hallmarks mean and why gold is often alloyed.	**Extend:** Calculate the percentage of pure gold in gold with different carat ratings.	

kerboodle

A Kerboodle highlight for this lesson is **Literacy interactive: Useful alloys**. Refer to the **Content map** on Kerboodle for a full list of resources and assessment.

GCSE CHEMISTRY ONLY

C6.1.11 Corrosion

Specification links:

6.1n Describe the process of corrosion and the conditions that cause corrosion.

WS2a Carry out experiments.

WS2b Make and record measurements using a range of apparatus and methods.

WS2c Present observations using appropriate methods.

WS2d Communicate the scientific rationale for investigations, methods used, findings, and reasoned conclusions.

M1c Use ratios, fractions, and percentages.

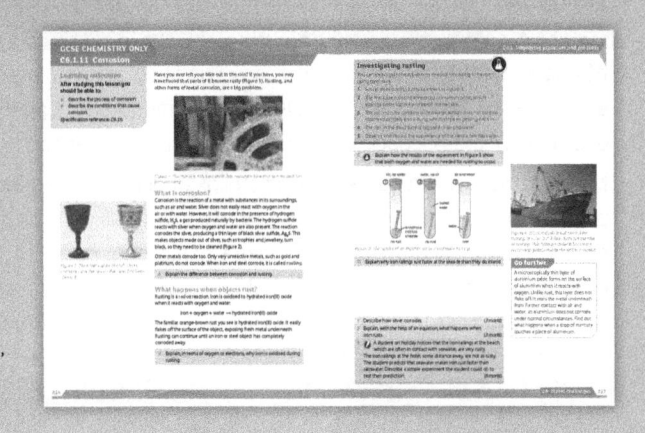

Target	Outcome	Checkpoint	
		Question	Activity
Aiming for GRADE 4	State that metals more reactive than platinum and gold corrode over time and need polishing to make them shiny again.		Starter 1 and 2 Main 2 Plenary 1
	State that rusting is the term used to describe the corrosion of iron and steel.	A	Starter 1 Main 1
	Investigate rusting experimentally and record some data.		Main 1
Aiming for GRADE 6	Define corrosion as the reaction of a metal with substances in its surroundings.		Starter 2 Main 2 Plenary 1
	Describe the process of rusting and use the equation to explain in terms of oxygen why iron is oxidised during rusting.	B, 2	Main 1 Homework
	Use experimental results to show that both oxygen and water are needed for rusting to occur.	C	Main 1
Aiming for GRADE 8	Using silver as an example, describe the process of corrosion in detail.	1	Main 2
	Describe in detail the process of rusting and explain in terms of electrons why iron is oxidised during rusting.	B	Main 1
	Explain using experimental data the factors that affect the rate at which rusting occurs.	A, D, 3	Main 1

Maths
In Main 1 and Plenary 1 students balance symbol equations (M1c).

Literacy
In completing the Homework task students design a poster to explain what rust is.

Key words
rusting, redox

216

C6.1 Improving processes and products

Starter	Support/Extend	Resources
What's gone wrong? (5 minutes) Display some images of rusted vehicles, buildings, and other structures. Ask students to suggest what has happened and why this is a problem. Elicit from students that rusting is the term used to describe the corrosion of iron and steel. **Corrosion demo** (10 minutes) Show students the Group 1 metals lithium, sodium, and potassium (as seen in C4.1.1, Main 1). Point out that they are stored under oil and encourage students to predict why this is so. Demonstrate cutting the metals. Draw students' attention to the freshly cut surface in each case and ask them to comment on the speed of corrosion.	**Extend:** Ask students to explain the rate of corrosion in terms of the electronic structure of the atoms.	

Main	Support/Extend	Resources
What causes iron to rust? (30 minutes) This practical should be begun a week in advance, for discussion in this lesson. Students should work in pairs. 1. Put an iron nail into each of three test-tubes in a test-tube rack. Label to tubes A–C. 2. Put half a spatula measure of calcium oxide in tube A and seal it with a bung. 3. Half-fill test-tube B with boiled water, add a small volume of oil to form a layer on top, and seal the test-tube with a bung. 4. Half-fill test-tube C with tap water and leave it open to the air. 5. Leave for 1 week and observe the nails. If possible, arrange for students to take a photograph of their experiment at the same time each day. Ask students to compare the images to draw conclusions consistent with their results. Encourage students to write a word equation for the reaction and explain why it is considered to be a redox reaction. Discuss the difficulty inherent in writing the balanced symbol equation for the reaction and encourage students to write a half equation focusing on the reaction of iron. **Corrosion** (10 minutes) Ask students to use the Student Book and secondary sources to find out about everyday examples of silver, brass, and copper corroding in air. Students should use an image search engine to find examples of corrosion and then annotate each image with an equation to explain the reaction that occurs.	**Extend:** Students could also investigate rusting using brine.	**Practical:** What causes iron to rust?

Plenary	Support/Extend	Resources
Corrosion equations (5 minutes) Ask students to complete part-written equations that model the corrosion of iron and silver. **Acidic corrosion** (10 minutes) Ask students to carry out a thought experiment to consider the effect of acidic conditions on the rate of corrosion for metals used in construction, and to write a couple of sentences to describe their ideas.	**Extend:** Ask students to explain why these are examples of redox reactions. **Support:** Demonstrate the reaction of iron and zinc in dilute sulfuric and nitric acids. **Extend:** Students could put foils of different metals into an acidic tank.	**Interactive:** Corrosion equations

Homework	Support/Extend	Resources
Design a poster to explain what rust is.		

kerboodle
A Kerboodle highlight for this lesson is **Working Scientifically: Investigating rusting**. Refer to the **Content map** on Kerboodle for a full list of resources and assessment.

GCSE CHEMISTRY ONLY
C6.1.12 Reducing corrosion

Specification links:

6.1o Explain how mitigation of corrosion is achieved by creating a physical barrier to oxygen and water and by sacrificial protection.

WS2a Carry out experiments.

WS2b Make and record measurements using a range of apparatus and methods.

WS2c Present observations using appropriate methods.

WS2d Communicate the scientific rationale for investigations, methods used, findings, and reasoned conclusions.

M1c Use ratios, fractions, and percentages.

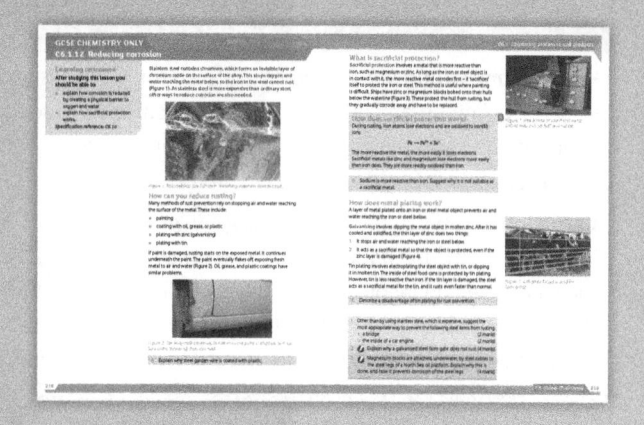

Target	Outcome	Checkpoint	
		Question	Activity
Aiming for GRADE 4 ↓	Describe methods of preventing corrosion.		Starter 1 and 2 Main 1 and 2 Plenary 1 and 2
	State that ships have sacrificial anodes that protect the hull from rusting.		Main 2
Aiming for GRADE 6 ↓	Explain how different methods of corrosion prevention work.	A	Main 2 Homework
	Explain how sacrificial protection works.	B, 3	Main 2
	Describe how galvanising and tin plating protect metals.	C, 2	Main 2
Aiming for GRADE 8 ↓	Suggest appropriate ways of preventing corrosion in different situations.	1	Plenary 2
	Explain with ionic equations how sacrificial protection works.		Main 2 Plenary 2
	Explain the difference in the rate of corrosion if zinc or tin plate is damaged.		Main 1

Maths
In Starter 1 (Extend) students write balanced equations and half equations (M1c).

Literacy
In Starter 2 students write sentences to define key words. In Main 2 students explain how each method of rust prevention works.

Key words
sacrificial protection, galvanising

C6.1 Improving processes and products

Starter	Support/Extend	Resources
Recall rusting (5 minutes) Ask students to recall a word equation for rusting. Then ask them to suggest how to prevent rusting (remove water and/or oxygen). **Define** (10 minutes) Give students the following terms: grease, oil, paint, galvanising, plating, oxidation, corrosion, rust. Students write a sentence defining each word then create a crossword. They then swap with a partner.	**Extend:** Ask students to write half equations for the corrosion of iron.	

Main	Support/Extend	Resources

Prevent iron rusting (40 minutes) Before the lesson, make a corrosion indicator by warming a solution of 5 g of gelatine in 100 cm^3 of water and then dissolving 0.2 g of potassium hexacyanoferrate(III) in the solution. In the lesson, ask pairs of students to carry out the following steps:
1 Clean six nails with cleaning solution and dry them with paper towels.
2 Put one nail into a test-tube to act as a control.
3 Put five steel nails, each treated in one of the following ways, into separate, labelled test-tubes:
  a wrap in cling film
  b paint with nail varnish and allow to dry
  c coat with grease
  d wrap in a piece of magnesium ribbon (allowing some of the nail to remain exposed)
  e wind a piece of copper wire around the nail (allowing some of the nail to remain exposed).
4 Add enough corrosion indicator to cover each nail.
5 Leave for 30 minutes, during which time students can draw a suitable results table to record their observations, and tackle Main 2.
After 30 minutes, ask students to observe the nails. Dark blue patches indicate the presence of rust. Ask students to explain how each method of rust prevention works, completing their explanations as homework if necessary.
Index cards (15 minutes, during Main 1) Give each student an index card. On one side they should summarise a method of corrosion prevention, along with some examples of items for which that method might be used, and on the reverse they should explain how the method prevents corrosion.
	Extend: Allow students to investigate galvanised nails and scratched galvanised nails.
	
	Extend: Write ionic equations **H** to explain how sacrificial protection works, using the Student Book for guidance.
		Practical: Prevent iron rusting

Plenary	Support/Extend	Resources
Classifying corrosion prevention (5 minutes) Ask students to classify each method of corrosion prevention as barrier, sacrificial, or both. **Rust prevention** (10 minutes) Display pictures of different uses of iron (e.g., cooking pans, cars, bicycles, bridges, buildings). Ask pairs of students to suggest which method of rust prevention would be best for each, and explain why.	**Support:** Discuss the different methods of rust prevention and their common uses as a class.	**Interactive:** Classifying corrosion prevention

Homework	Support/Extend	Resources
Carry out internet research to find out and explain why stainless steel does not corrode, but mild steel does.		

kerboodle
A Kerboodle highlight for this lesson is **Literacy sheet: Rusting**. Refer to the **Content map** on Kerboodle for a full list of resources and assessment.

GCSE CHEMISTRY ONLY
C6.1.13 Different materials

Specification links:

6.1p Compare quantitatively the physical properties of glass and clay ceramics, polymers, composites, and metals.

6.1q Explain how the properties of materials are related to their uses and select appropriate materials, given details of the usage required.

WS1.1e Explain everyday and technological applications of science.

WS1.3f Present reasoned explanations.

WS2a Carry out experiments.

WS2b Make and record measurements using a range of apparatus and methods.

WS2c Present observations using appropriate methods.

WS2d Communicate the scientific rationale for investigations, methods used, findings, and reasoned conclusions.

M2b Find arithmetic means.

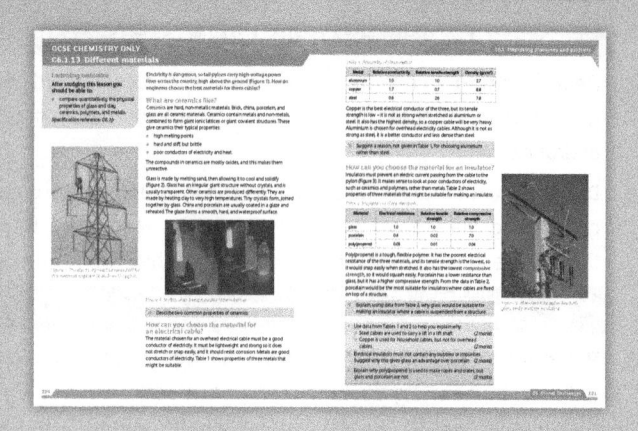

Target	Outcome	Checkpoint Question	Checkpoint Activity
Aiming for GRADE 4	Describe brick, china, porcelain, and glass as ceramics.		Starter 1, Main 1 and 2
	Use given information to compare the properties of different metals.		Main 1, Plenary 2
	Use given information to compare the properties of different insulators.		Main 1, Plenary 2
Aiming for GRADE 6	Describe the properties of a typical ceramic material.	A	Main 1, Plenary 1 and 2
	Given appropriate data, select a metal to use for a particular purpose	B	Main 2, Homework
	Given appropriate data, select an insulator to use for a particular purpose	C	Main 2, Homework
Aiming for GRADE 8	Relate the properties of different ceramic materials to their structures.	2	Plenary 1
	Justify choices of metals for different purposes.	1	Main 2, Plenary 2, Homework
	Justify choices of insulating materials for different purposes.	3	Main 2, Plenary 2, Homework

Maths
In Main 1 students calculate a mean from repeated readings (M2b).

Literacy
In Main 1 and Plenary 2 students generalise the properties of materials. In Plenary 1 (Extend) students critique each other's sentences in terms of scientific accuracy and grammatical correctness.

Key words
ceramics, compressive strength

220

C6.1 Improving processes and products

Starter	Support/Extend	Resources
Classify materials (5 minutes) Briefly introduce what ceramics, glass, and composite materials are. Then ask students to work in pairs to come up with two examples of each. **Tennis rackets** (10 minutes) Show students a solid wooden tennis racket, a laminated wood tennis racket, and a modern carbon-fibre tennis racket. Ask students to suggest tennis rackets have changed.	**Support:** Give students a list of examples and have them match to the correct material type. **Extend:** Prompt students to classify glass objects as a sub-class of ceramics.	**Interactive:** Classify materials

Main	Support/Extend	Resources
Properties of materials (30 minutes) Allow pairs of students to investigate the properties of some of the materials classified in Starter 1. Each pair should test one material. You may wish to conduct the flexibility tests as a demonstration (both for safety and to reduce waste). 1 To test flexibility: Clamp the material to be tested to the end of the desk, with the end of the material extending beyond the edge. Clamp a ruler to the end of the desk vertically, with the top of the ruler (0 cm) level with the free end of the material. Hang a 200 g mass on the free end of the material and measure the deflection of the free end after 30 seconds. This test is also used in C2.2.1, Main 1, so you may wish to exclude it here. 2 To test hardness: Put a ball bearing on top of the material to be tested and place a large tube vertically over the top of the ball bearing. Drop a 1 kg mass from the top of the tube onto the ball bearing and measure the diameter of the dent left in the material with a ruler. 3 To test toughness: Put the material to be tested in a vice. Suspend a hammer so that it will swing and hit the material after being lifted back. Lift the hammer to a measured height and let it swing to hit the material. Repeat five times for each material, measuring the angle of bend in the material each time. Calculate a mean angle for each material. Ask students to suggest general properties for each group of materials and consider how these relate to their uses. SAFETY: Be careful not to drop masses on feet. Do not test Pyrex or glass as they will shatter in some of the tests. Wear eye protection. **Label** (10 minutes) Provide a diagram of overhead power cables and a pylon. Ask students to label the metal, glass, ceramic, and polymers and explain which properties of each material make it suitable for the purpose.	**Support:** Provide the relevant properties for students to cut and stick onto their diagram.	**Practical:** Properties of materials

Plenary	Support/Extend	Resources
Finish the sentences (5 minutes) Ask students to complete the following sentences. Each sentence should either compare the properties of the given material with those of a different type of material, or relate the properties of the material to its structure. 1 A clay ceramic is... 3 A polymer is... 2 A glass is... 4 A metal is... **Generalise** (10 minutes) Ask students to generalise the properties of glass, clay, ceramics, polymers, and metals in the following orders: 1 good insulators to good conductors 3 high density to low density 2 high melting point to low melting point 4 weak to strong.	**Extend:** Ask three students to read out a sentence for others to comment on its scientific accuracy and grammatical correctness. **Extend:** Ask students to justify their ordering of the materials.	

Homework	Support/Extend	Resources
Choose a product at home, such as a Thermos flask, list the materials that it is made from, and explain why each material is chosen for this function.		

GCSE CHEMISTRY ONLY

C6.1.14 Composite materials

Specification links:

6.1p Compare quantitatively the physical properties of glass and clay ceramics, polymers, composites, and metals.

6.1q Explain how the properties of materials are related to their uses and select appropriate materials, given details of the usage required.

WS1.1e Explain everyday and technological applications of science.

WS1.3f Presenting reasoned explanations.

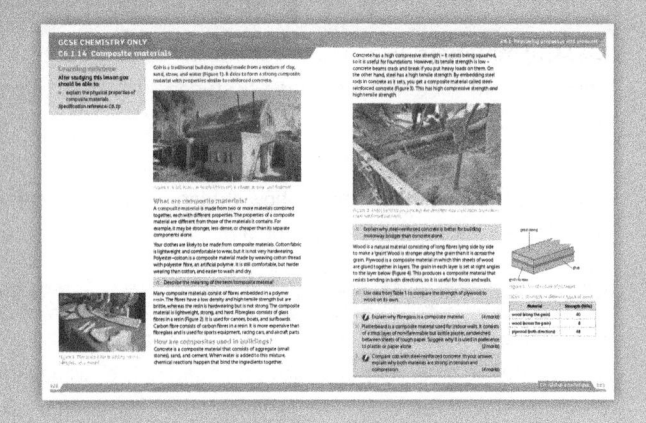

Target	Outcome	Checkpoint Question	Checkpoint Activity
Aiming for GRADE 4	State that composite materials are made from at least two different materials.		Starter 1 and 2 Main 2 Plenary 1 and 2
	Describe the structure of fibre-based composite materials and give some examples.	1	Starter 2 Main 2 Plenary 1 and 2
	Give examples of composite materials used in buildings and describe what they are used for.		Starter 2 Main 1 Plenary 1 and 2 Homework
Aiming for GRADE 6	Define the term composite material.	A	Starter 1 and 2 Main 2 Plenary 1 and 2 Homework
	Explain the physical properties of fibre-based composite materials and relate these to their uses.		Main 1 and 2 Plenary 1 Homework
	Explain the physical properties of composite materials used in buildings.	B, 3	Main 2
Aiming for GRADE 8	Explain the advantages of the properties of a composite material over those of the materials it contains, given an example.	2	Plenary 2
	Compare the physical properties of different fibre-based composite materials.		Main 1
	Compare quantitatively the physical properties of composite materials used in buildings.	C	Main 1 and 2

Literacy
In Main 2 students design a poster about composite materials used in buildings. In Plenary 2 students explain what a composite is, using an example.

Key words
composite material, resin

C6.1 Improving processes and products

Starter	Support/Extend	Resources
Model composites (5 minutes) Show students a picture of pink wafer biscuits. Ask them to suggest how these model plywood, which is a type of composite. **Compare and contrast** (10 minutes) Provide samples of wood, MDF, and plywood. Ask students to explain why wood is not a composite, but MDF and plywood are.	**Extend:** Ask students to list the advantages and disadvantages of each material. Students should then justify which material they would choose to make a coffee table.	

Main	Support/Extend	Resources
Investigate composites (20 minutes) Ask students to predict which would be stronger: a block of ice made from pure water, or a block of ice made from pure water with cotton wool in the mould. Students should use science to explain their prediction. Next, ask students to suggest how to test the strength of each block. Give student pairs samples of the ice and the ice composite. Students should mount the blocks between two bricks and record the maximum mass that can be supported before the ice breaks. Finally, ask students to explain how the materials they have just investigated are similar to composites used in building. **Composites in building** (20 minutes) Display a picture of reinforced concrete and remind students about the composites examined in Starter 2. Ask students to design a poster explaining, in terms of properties, how and why different composites are used in building.	**Extend:** Give students data about the physical properties of composite materials used in buildings, and ask them to use the data to compare the materials.	**Activity:** Investigate composites

Plenary	Support/Extend	Resources
Classify composites (5 minutes) Ask students to match the composite to what it is made from and its use (e.g., plywood – wood, glue – furniture). **Composite example** (10 minutes) Ask students to explain what a composite is, using an example. Students' explanations should include a labelled diagram to explain how the material qualifies as a composite, and should state at least one use of the material.	**Extend:** Ask students to explain which property has been modified in the composite.	**Interactive:** Classify composites

Homework	Support/Extend	Resources
Survey your home and list the composite materials you can identify. Explain what makes the materials composites.	**Extend:** Explain why each composite is fit for its use.	

kerboodle

A Kerboodle highlight for this lesson is **Podcast: Improving processes and products**. Refer to the **Content map** on Kerboodle for a full list of resources and assessment.

C6.1.15 Choosing materials

Specification links:

6.1i Describe the basic principles in carrying out a life-cycle assessment of a material or product.

6.1j Interpret data from a life-cycle assessment of a material or product.

6.1q Explain how the properties of materials are related to their uses and select appropriate materials, given details of the usage required.

WS1.1e Explain everyday and technological applications of science.

WS1.3f Present reasoned explanations.

M2b Find arithmetic means.

M4a Translate information between graphical and numeric form.

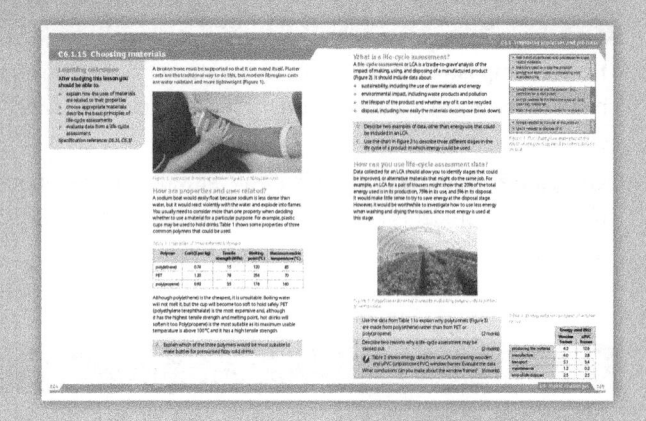

Target	Outcome	Checkpoint Question	Checkpoint Activity
Aiming for GRADE 4	State why one material would be more suitable than another for a particular purpose.		Starter 1 and 2 Main 1 and 2
	Explain what a life-cycle assessment (LCA) is.		Main 1 Plenary 1 Homework
	Describe the stages in the life cycle of a product, given data.	C	Main 1 Plenary 1 Homework
Aiming for GRADE 6	Choose the most appropriate material for a particular purpose, given data on a range of properties, and briefly explain this choice.	A	Starter 1 and 2 Main 1 Plenary 2
	Describe the basic principles of carrying out an LCA.	B, 2	Main 1 Plenary 1
	Interpret data from the LCA of a material or product.		Main 1 Plenary 2
Aiming for GRADE 8	Explain in detail the choice of an appropriate material for a particular purpose.	A, 1	Main 1 and 2 Plenary 2
	Describe in detail the process of carrying out an LCA.		Main 1 Plenary 1
	Evaluate data from an LCA and draw conclusions about the material or product.	3	Main 1

Maths
In Main 1 students estimate LCA figures. In Plenary 2 students display data as a tally chart and calculate the mean (M2b, M4a).

Literacy
In completing the Homework task students create a flow chart.

Key words
life-cycle assessment

C6.1 Improving processes and products

Starter	Support/Extend	Resources
Choose a material (5 minutes) Give students some examples of everyday items such as drinks bottles, plates, and cutlery. Ask students to identify the material(s) each product is made from, and to suggest why each material was chosen.	**Extend:** Provide students with water bottles made of glass, plastic, and metal. Ask students to justify the use of each material and evaluate which they think makes the best water bottle.	
Evaluate shopping bags (10 minutes) Give small groups of students a selection of different shopping bags (e.g., different sizes, long-life, reusable, paper, card, plastic, biodegradable plastic). Ask each group to choose the bag that is most suitable for carrying tinned food home from a shop, and to justify their decision. Repeat for different scenarios (wrapping new clothes, carrying muddy PE kit, taking a birthday present to a party). Using questions and answers, elicit a list of factors to consider when choosing a shopping bag (e.g., price, size, durability, aesthetics, environmental impact).		

Main	Support/Extend	Resources
Paper or plastic? (30 minutes) Explain what a life-cycle assessment (LCA) is. Then show students a plastic shopping bag and a paper shopping bag. Ask them to complete a simple LCA for each product. Students should focus on Figure 2 in the Student Book to help them consider the factors involved in an LCA. Students should generate a numerical value for each part of the LCA, and an overall value. Ask students to conclude which is the better bag.	**Support:** Prompt students to list the inputs and outputs for each bag in terms of raw materials, energy use, and environmental impacts, and then give each factor a subjective rating on a scale from 1 to 10. **Extend:** Ask students to explain why this method of LCA is a subjective measure.	**Activity:** Paper or plastic?
Cooking pans (10 minutes) Ask students to draw a labelled diagram of a cooking pan, and to annotate the materials that each part is made from.	**Support:** Show students a simple metal pan with a plastic handle and ask them to justify the use of metal and plastic. **Extend:** Show students a copper pan, a steel pan with PTFE coating and a plastic handle, a ceramic pan, and a plastic pan. Ask students to suggest how each pan is used, and how the materials enable the fulfilment of this function.	

Plenary	Support/Extend	Resources
Life-cycle assessment (5 minutes) Show students the parts of the product life cycle and ask them to order them.		**Interactive:** Life-cycle assessment
Vote (10 minutes) Collect data from the class in a tally chart to show the LCA values determined for each bag in Main 1. Ask students to calculate an average from the data and decide which bag the class think is best.	**Extend:** Ask students to consider the effect of the plastic bag charge, compared with the free distribution of plastic bags.	

Homework	Support/Extend	Resources
Design a flow chart to show how to calculate the LCA of a product.		

kerboodle

A Kerboodle highlight for this lesson is **WebQuest: Life-cycle assessment**. Refer to the **Content map** on Kerboodle for a full list of resources and assessment.

C6.1.16 Recycling materials

Specification links:

6.1k Describe a process in which a material or product is recycled for a different use, and explain why this is viable.

6.1l Evaluate factors that affect decisions on recycling.

WS1.1f Evaluate associated personal, social, economic, and environmental implications.

WS1.1g Make decisions based on the evaluation of evidence and arguments.

M1c Use ratios, fractions, and percentages.

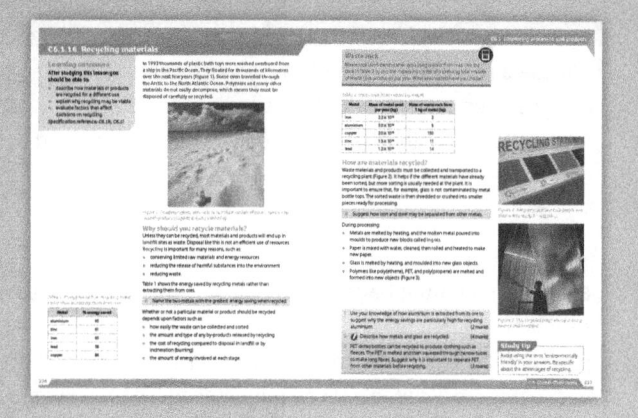

Target	Outcome	Checkpoint	
		Question	Activity
Aiming for GRADE 4 ↓	Describe some benefits of recycling materials.		Main 1 Plenary 1 and 2
	State one factor to consider before deciding whether or not to recycle a material.		Main 1
	Describe methods of sorting materials before they are recycled.	B	Main 2 Homework
Aiming for GRADE 6 ↓	Explain the benefits of recycling materials.		Main 1 and 2 Plenary 1 and 2
	Describe several factors to consider before deciding whether or not to recycle a material.		Main 1 Plenary 1
	Explain why it is important to sort materials before recycling and describe how some materials are sorted.	3	Main 2
Aiming for GRADE 8 ↓	Interpret data to evaluate the recycling of different materials.	A, 1	Starter 1 Main 1
	Process numeric data to demonstrate the relative benefit of recycling different materials.		Starter 1 Main 1
	Explain in detail how materials are recycled.	2	Main 2

Maths
In Main 1 students calculate the mass of waste rock produced from the use of aluminium per year, the percentage yield, and the energy saved in using recycled aluminium (M1c).

Literacy
In Plenary 2 students write a radio jingle.

Key words
landfill, recycling, ingots

226

C6.1 Improving processes and products

Starter	Support/Extend	Resources
Aluminium (10 minutes) Students complete the interactive where they complete a summary of how aluminium is obtained (mining of aluminium ore, purification, electrolysis). They then calculate the mass of waste rock produced per year from the use of aluminium.	**Extend:** Ask students to calculate the percentage yield of aluminium.	**Interactive:** Aluminum
Where does it come from? (5 minutes) Ask students to make a list of materials in everyday use in the UK. Then ask students to briefly state where these materials have come from (e.g., wood from trees, copper extracted from ores and purified, glass from sand or recycled).	**Extend:** Ask students to classify the materials as sustainable or non-renewable.	

Main	Support/Extend	Resources
Recycling metals (25 minutes) Ask students to consider the recycling of aluminium drinks cans. On an A5 sheet of blue paper, students should first write a simple LCA for aluminium drinks cans made from newly extracted aluminium. They should then use a red pen to list the disadvantages and a green pen to list the advantages of using newly extracted aluminium to make drinks cans. On an A5 sheet of light green paper, students should complete the same exercise for recycled aluminium cans. Encourage students to use Table 1 to calculate the energy saved by using recycled aluminium. Finally, ask students to use the drinks can example to suggest factors to consider when deciding whether or not to recycle a material. (Are the energy inputs for recycling lower? What is the quality of the recycled material?) Students should use all of their work to run a class debate on the motion 'Aluminium drinks cans should not be recycled'.	**Extend:** This could be developed into a class debate.	**Activity:** Recycling metals
Separating for recycling (15 minutes) Explain to students that, before a material can be recycled, it needs to be separated from the materials it is mixed with. Display three different mixtures: aluminium cans and steel/tin cans; containers made from different plastics (see their recycling symbols); glass jars with paper labels. Ask student pairs to work out how to separate each mixture, and to make a simple poster to display their findings. (Use magnets to separate the cans; use the recycling symbols, or density differences, to separate the plastics; soak in water to separate the paper and glass.)		

Plenary	Support/Extend	Resources
Review (5 minutes) Hold up each material from Main 2 in turn and ask for volunteers to share their thoughts.	**Extend:** Ask students to evaluate whether it would be best to reuse, recycle, or just dispose of the product in landfill after use.	
Radio jingle (10 minutes) Ask pairs of students to write a radio jingle to state the benefits of recycling and encourage people to recycle.	**Support:** You may wish to play examples of jingles such as those used on commercial radio stations in which advertisers sponsor a feature such as the weather.	

Homework	Support/Extend	Resources
Find out where you can recycle glass, paper, cardboard, metal, and chemical waste in your local area.		

kerboodle

A Kerboodle highlight for this lesson is **Homework: Improving processes and products**. Refer to the **Content map** on Kerboodle for a full list of resources and assessment.

Checkpoint

C6.1 Improving processes and products

Overview of C6.1 Improving processes and products

In this wide-ranging chapter, much of which is for students taking GCSE Chemistry rather than Combined Science, students have studied many chemical processes, starting with the manufacture of fertilisers. GCSE Chemistry students should recall that fertilisers contain essential elements needed by plants, and explain the importance of the Haber process in the industrial production of ammonia, using knowledge of rates and equilibria. They should be able to describe and compare batch and continuous processes.

Applying their work on the reactivity series in C4.1.6 *Reactivity of elements*, all students should be able to explain how the process used to extract a metal is chosen. They should be able to outline the extraction of copper from different ores, and use the terms oxidation and reduction. They should be able to describe the processes that occur in a blast furnace to extract iron. Students should be able to explain why and how electrolysis is used to extract more reactive metals such as aluminium from their ores. Higher-tier students have also studied biological metal extraction, including evaluation and comparison of the processes of bioleaching and phytoextraction.

In studying the applications of metals, GCSE Chemistry students should be able to define the term alloy and describe the composition of some important alloys in relation to their properties and uses. They should be able to define corrosion, discuss conditions that cause corrosion, and describe methods of preventing corrosion.

GCSE Chemistry students should be able to define the term composite, and to compare and give examples of the uses of various materials, including metals, ceramics, polymers, and fibre-based composites. In describing how appropriate materials are chosen for a purpose, all students should be able to describe how a life-cycle assessment is used and interpret data from such an assessment. They should be able to describe a process in which a material or product is recycled, and explain the benefits of this.

Extending their work on equilibrium conditions, higher-tier GCSE Chemistry students should be able to describe and explain the conditions used in industrially important processes such as the Contact process. They should understand how the conditions chosen in manufacturing processes are related to considerations of rate and equilibrium, as well as costs of raw materials and energy supplies, as applied to two methods of ethanol production.

MyMaths

You can find additional support for the maths skills covered in this chapter on **MyMaths**, including calculations involving ratios and percentages, recording to an appropriate number of decimal places, calculating means, and working with graphs and pie charts.

kerboodle

For this chapter, the following assessments are available on Kerboodle:
C6.1 Checkpoint quiz: Improving processes and products
C6.1 Progress quiz: Improving processes and products 1
C6.1 Progress quiz: Improving processes and products 2
C6.1 On your marks: Improving processes and products
C6.1 Exam-style questions and mark scheme: Improving processes and products

C6.1 Improving processes and products

Checkpoint follow-up lesson

A student's route through this lesson can be determined using the Checkpoint assessment. Percentage pass marks are supplied in the Checkpoint teacher notes.

For each successive route through it is assumed that the student can perform to their current route as well as previous routes. For example, students working at Aiming for 6 are assumed to be secure in Aiming for 4 knowledge and understanding and working towards achieving all the learning objectives for Aiming for 6.

	Aiming for 4	**Aiming for 6**	**Aiming for 8**
Learning outcomes	Use the reactivity series to give examples of metals that can be extracted by electrolysis, can be extracted by reduction with carbon, or are native.	Explain the metal extraction method used for metals listed in the reactivity series.	Evaluate modern and traditional methods of metal extraction.
	Describe the Haber process.	Compare how fertilisers are made in a laboratory compared with their manufacture in industry.	Justify compromises in reaction conditions and rates of industrial processes.
	Describe how a material can be recycled.	Explain the importance of recycling.	Evaluate the factors that affect recycling.
Starter	**Mnemonic (5 minutes)** Ask students in small groups to generate or recall a mnemonic to help them memorise the order of elements in the reactivity series. Then ask each group to share their mnemonics and, as a class, note down the best one from the list.		
	Samples (5 minutes) Give small groups of students sealed labelled samples of bauxite, haematite, carbon, aluminium oxide, cryolite, limestone, and slag. Ask them to classify the samples into two groups. Ask each student group to share their classifications. Through question and answer, guide the students to the classifications of the aluminium group (bauxite, carbon, aluminium oxide, and cryolite) and the iron group (haematite, carbon, limestone, and slag).		
Differentiated checkpoint activity	**Spider diagram (40 minutes)** Explain that students will be producing a set of revision notes to summarise the topic *Improving processes and products*. Students answer each question on the differentiated worksheets. They will need A4 lined paper, coloured pencils, and highlighter pens.		
	The Aiming for 4 sheet provides structured tasks to support students in revising and summarising the information to include in their revision notes.	The Aiming for 6 sheet provides questions to guide the content students include in their revision notes. It prompts them to use a highlighter to focus on the key points.	The Aiming for 8 sheet provides fewer prompt questions which cover more advanced content.
	Kerboodle resource: C6.1 Checkpoint follow-up: Aiming for 4, C6.1 Checkpoint follow-up: Aiming for 6, C6.1 Checkpoint follow-up: Aiming for 8		
Plenary	**Revision notes review (5 minutes)** Ask students to lay their notes out on benches around the room. Students choose another person's notes to review. They should look at the objectives of the lesson and make a comment about each objective, stating if the notes fully, partially, or did not cover the objective. Students should then conclude by writing a comment that gives one area for development, as well as something that has been completed excellently.		
	True or false? (5 minutes) Read statements about the Haber process and metal extraction. Students should put their thumbs up if they think it is true and thumbs down if they think it is false. Any misconceptions can then be addressed.		
Progression	Aiming for 4 students should recall the reactivity series and state which metals can be extracted by each method. They should develop this by explaining why each method is used. Students should be able to describe recycling, and this can be extended to consider the pros and cons of recycling. Students should be able to recall the stages of the Haber process and then build on this by contrasting how fertilisers are made in industry compared with in the laboratory.	Aiming for 6 students should be able to use the reactivity series to explain which method of metal extraction is used for each metal. They should build on this by outlining modern methods of metal extraction. Students should be able to explain the importance of recycling and this can be built upon to evaluate recycling. Students should be able to contrast the methods of making fertiliser in a laboratory and in industry, and should build on this to explain why reaction conditions are a compromise in industry.	Aiming for 8 students should be able to justify metal extraction methods that are used, including using new technologies. They should start to evaluate recycling in terms of environmental and economic factors. Students should be able to justify compromise conditions in industry. Encourage them to consider unfamiliar industrial systems such as the Contact process.

C6 Global Challenges

GCSE CHEMISTRY ONLY
C6.2 Organic chemistry
C6.2.1 Alkanes

Specification links:

6.2a Recognise functional groups and identify members of the same homologous series.

6.2b Name and draw the structural formulae, using fully displayed formulae, of the first four members of the straight-chain alkanes, [alkenes, alcohols, and carboxylic acids].

6.2c Predict the formulae and structures of products of reactions of the first four and other given members of the homologous series of alkanes, [alkenes, and alcohols].

WS1.4a Use scientific vocabulary, terminology, and definitions.

M4a Translate information between graphical and numeric form.

M4c Plot two variables from experimental or other data.

M5b Visualise and represent two-dimensional (2D) and three-dimensional (3D) forms, including 2D representations of 3D objects.

CM6.2i Represent three-dimensional (3D) shapes in two dimensions and vice versa when looking at chemical structures, [e.g. allotropes of carbon] (M5b).

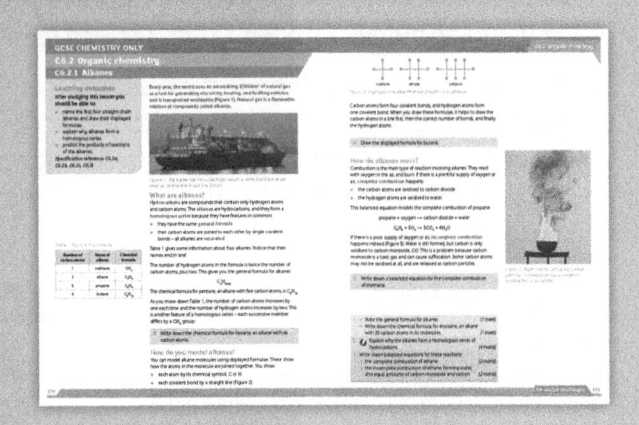

Target	Outcome	Checkpoint Question	Checkpoint Activity
Aiming for GRADE 4	State a definition of hydrocarbons as compounds that contain hydrogen and carbon atoms only.		Starter 1 Homework
	Name the first four straight-chain alkanes.		Main
	State that alkanes transfer energy to the surroundings when they burn and that they are commonly used as fuels.		Starter 2
Aiming for GRADE 6	Explain what members of the alkane homologous series have in common.	2	Main Plenary 1
	Write down the formulae of the first four straight-chain alkanes.		Main Plenary 1
	State the products of complete and incomplete combustion and describe the problems associated with the products of incomplete combustion.		Starter 2
Aiming for GRADE 8	Deduce the general formula of alkanes and use it to work out the formula of any alkane.	A, 1	Main Plenary 1
	Draw the displayed formula of any alkane, given the number of carbon atoms.	B	Plenary 2
	Use chemical equations to model the processes of complete and incomplete combustion.	C, 3	Starter 2

Maths
In Main 1 students generate and interpret 2D and 3D representations of molecules (M5b). In Main 2 students display data in charts, tables, and graphs (M4a, M4c).

Key words
hydrocarbons, alkanes, homologous series, general formula, saturated, complete combustion, incomplete combustion

C6.2 Organic chemistry

Starter	Support/Extend	Resources
Methane (5 minutes) Show students a ball-and-stick model of methane. Ask which elements it is made of. Ask students to list all the information they can about this compound. Point out that, since it is made up of the elements carbon and hydrogen only, it is a hydrocarbon. Ensure that students realise that there are a huge number of different hydrocarbons.	**Support:** Prompt students to list the molecular formula, molecular mass, and type of bonding. **Extend:** Ask students to predict the properties of the compound.	
Bunsen burner magic (10 minutes) Ask students to set up a Bunsen burner and turn it to a blue flame. Explain that this is burning methane to make just carbon dioxide and water – this is complete combustion. Ask students to write an equation for this. Repeat with the safety flame – this is incomplete combustion. Explain that this forms carbon monoxide, carbon, carbon dioxide, and water. Point out that, during both complete and incomplete combustion, energy is transferred to the surroundings.	**Support:** Allow students to write word equations. **Extend:** Encourage students to write balanced symbol equations with state symbols, and to explain why combustion is an example of an oxidation reaction.	

Main	Support/Extend	Resources
Alkanes (20 minutes) Give pairs of students a molecular model kit and explain which pieces represent carbon atoms, hydrogen atoms, and covalent bonds. Display the formulae of the first four alkanes and ask them to make molecular models of these. Tell students the names of these alkanes and ask them to design and complete a table with three columns: name, molecular formula, and displayed formula. Provide students with the melting point, boiling point, and density of the first four alkanes. Ask students to display this data in a suitable manner and describe any patterns in the data.	**Support:** Provide students with the information to write in the table. **Extend:** Ask students if they can generate the general formula for the homologous series from studying the models. **Extend:** Demonstrate the combustion of a selection of alkanes for students to note that short-chain alkanes light more easily and burn with a cleaner flame than longer-chain alkanes.	**Activity:** Alkanes

Plenary	Support/Extend	Resources
What's the formula? (5 minutes) Ask students to use the general formula of alkanes to determine the molecular formulae of several alkanes with a given number of carbon atoms.	**Extend:** Ask students to give the name of each alkane, as well as its molecular formula.	
Sort alkanes (10 minutes) Students use the interactive to match the name of the first four alkanes with the correct molecular formula and displayed formula.	**Extend:** Include organic compounds that do not fit any of the classifications.	**Interactive:** Sort alkanes

Homework	Support/Extend	Resources
From looking at the structural formula of butane, list all the information that you can about this compound.	**Support:** Focus on bonding, structure, where butane can be found, molecular formula, general formula, and family of chemicals. **Extend:** Draw the structures of other alkanes that have the same molecular formula but with a branched rather than a straight chain.	

kerboodle

A Kerboodle highlight for this lesson is **Bump up your grades: All about alkanes.** Refer to the **Content map** on Kerboodle for a full list of resources and assessment.

GCSE CHEMISTRY ONLY
C6.2.2 Alkenes

Specification links:

6.2a Recognise functional groups and identify members of the same homologous series.

6.2b Name and draw the structural formulae, using fully displayed formulae, of the first four members of the straight-chain [alkanes,] alkenes, [alcohols, and carboxylic acids].

6.2c Predict the formulae and structures of products of reactions of the first four and other given members of the homologous series of [alkanes,] alkenes, [and alcohols,].

WS1.4a Use scientific vocabulary, terminology, and definitions.

M1c Use ratios, fractions, and percentages.

M5b Visualise and represent two-dimensional (2D) and three-dimensional (3D) forms, including 2D representations of 3D objects.

CM6.2i Represent three-dimensional (3D) shapes in two dimensions and vice versa when looking at chemical structures, [e.g. allotropes of carbon] (M5b).

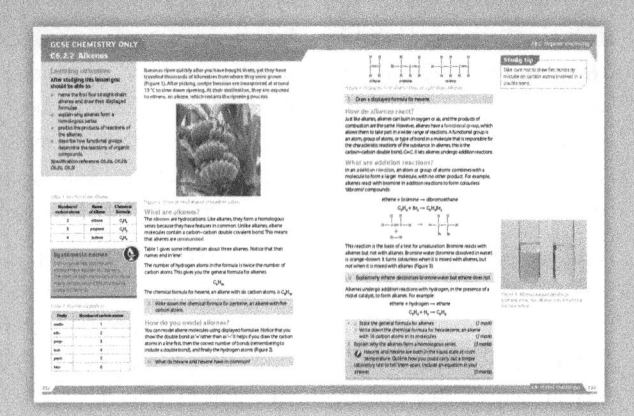

Target	Outcome	Checkpoint Question	Checkpoint Activity
Aiming for GRADE 4	Recognise the alkene functional group.		Starter 1 and 2 Main 2 Plenary 1
	Name the first four straight-chain alkenes.		Starter 1 and 2
	State that alkenes decolorise bromine water but alkanes do not.		Main Plenary 2
Aiming for GRADE 6	Explain what members of the alkene homologous series have in common.	2	Main
	Draw the displayed formulae of the first four straight-chain alkenes		Starter 2 Main
	Explain the term addition reaction and why alkenes decolorise bromine water but alkanes do not.	D	Main Homework
Aiming for GRADE 8	Deduce the general formula of alkenes and use it to work out the formula of any alkene.	A, 1	Starter 1
	Draw the displayed formula of any alkene, given the number of carbon atoms and the position of the double bond.	C	Plenary 1
	Explain with equations why alkenes decolorise bromine water but alkanes do not.	3	Main Plenary 2 Homework

Maths
In Plenary 2 (Extend) students write balanced symbol equations (M1c). In Starter 2 students represent molecules in 2D and 3D (M5b).

Literacy
In completing the Homework task students write a procedure to use bromine water as an indicator to test for unsaturation.

Key words
alkenes, unsaturated, systematic names, functional group, addition reaction

C6.2 Organic chemistry

Starter	Support/Extend	Resources
Identifying alkenes (5 minutes) Display the names and displayed formulae of the first four straight-chain alkenes and ask students to determine the molecular formula of each. **Molecular models** (10 minutes) Display the names and molecular formulae of the first four straight-chain alkenes. Ask students to use a molecular model kit to model these compounds and then draw the displayed formula of each.	**Extend:** Include all the isomers of butene and pentene. **Support:** Allow students to work in pairs and encourage them to start with the carbon chain and then add the hydrogen atoms. **Extend:** Ask if students can determine the general formula.	**Interactive:** Identifying alkenes

Main	Support/Extend	Resources
Reactions of alkenes (40 minutes) Set up three stations around the room. Students visit each station in pairs or groups of three. Ask students to complete the following reactions: 1 The bromine water test to show an addition reaction with hexene compared with hexane. 2 Polymerisation by the free-radical-initiated addition reaction of phenylethene (styrene) to make poly(phenylethene), commonly known as polystyrene. 3 Combustion in a spirit burner of hexene compared with hexane. Students should write a general and a specific equation for each of the reactions observed. SAFETY: Wear chemical splash proof eye protection and gloves. CLEAPSS Hazcards 015B; 045A & C; 071; 040A; 029; 071. (Keep away from naked flames.) Keep room well ventilated. Warn asthmatics.	**Extend:** The bromine water test can be used to compare the reactants and products of microscale cracking of paraffin.	**Practical:** Reactions of alkenes

Plenary	Support/Extend	Resources
Butene (10 minutes) Show students ball-and-stick models of but-1-ene and but-2-ene. Ask students to draw the displayed formula for each compound and note its molecular formula and the homologous series it belongs to. **Sort substances** (5 minutes) Give students hypothetical results a reaction with bromine water for four substances A, B, C, and D. Students use the results to identify the substances that are alkenes and the substances that are alkanes.	**Extend:** Ask students to list the similarities and differences between these compounds. **Extend:** Give molecular formula for A, B, C, and D. Students should use these to write balanced symbol equations for the reactions that occurred with bromine water.	

Homework	Support/Extend	Resources
Write a procedure for using bromine water as a test for an unsaturated hydrocarbon.	**Extend:** Predict the effect if iodine water were used instead of bromine water.	

kerboodle

A Kerboodle highlight for this lesson is **Calculation sheet: Drawing and naming organic compounds.** Refer to the **Content map** on Kerboodle for a full list of resources and assessment.

GCSE CHEMISTRY ONLY
C6.2.3 Alcohols

Specification links:

6.2a Recognise functional groups and identify members of the same homologous series.

6.2b Name and draw the structural formulae, using fully displayed formulae, of the first four members of the straight-chain [alkanes, alkenes,] alcohols, [and carboxylic acids].

6.2c Predict the formulae and structures of products of reactions of the first four and other given members of the homologous series of [alkanes, alkenes, and] alcohols.

WS1.4a Use scientific vocabulary, terminology, and definitions.

M1c Use ratios, fractions, and percentages.

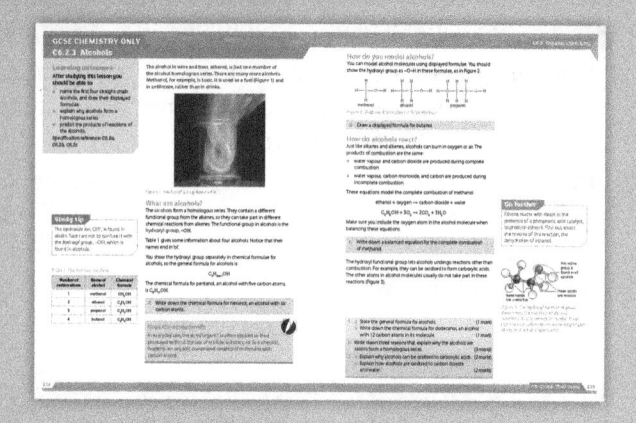

Target	Outcome	Checkpoint	
		Question	Activity
Aiming for GRADE 4 ↓	Recognise the alcohol functional group.		Starter 1, Plenary 1
	Name the first four straight-chain alcohols.		Starter 1
	State that alcohols burn in air and state the products of this reaction.		Starter 2, Main 1
Aiming for GRADE 6 ↓	Explain what members of the alcohol homologous series have in common.	2	Plenary 1
	Draw the displayed formulae of the first four straight-chain alcohols.	B	Homework
	Write word equations to model the oxidation reactions of alcohols.	C	Main 1 and 2, Plenary 2
Aiming for GRADE 8 ↓	Deduce the general formula of alcohols and use it to work out the formula of any alcohol.	A, 1	Plenary 1, Homework
	Draw the displayed formula of any alcohol, given the number of carbon atoms.		Homework
	Explain how alcohols can be oxidised to form carboxylic acids.	3	Main 2, Plenary 2

Maths
In Starter 2 and Main 2 (Extend) students write balanced equations (M1c).

Literacy
In Plenary 1 students write a bullet-point summary of the features of alcohols. In Plenary 2 students write an explanation of how wine turns to vinegar.

Key words
alcohols, hydroxyl group, organic compound

C6.2 Organic chemistry

Starter	Support/Extend	Resources
Match alcohols (5 minutes) Students use the interactive to match the name of the first four alcohols with the correct molecular formula and displayed formula. **Dehydration of ethanol** (10 minutes) Explain to students that alcohols can also be used as fuels, undergoing complete combustion to form carbon dioxide and water. Ask students to write a word equation and balanced symbol equation with state symbols for the combustion of alcohols.	**Extend:** Ask students to list the key features of members of the alcohol homologous series. **Support:** Students use methanol as their alcohol. **Extend:** Students use pentanol as their alcohol	**Interactive:** Match alcohols

Main	Support/Extend	Resources
Comparing the reactions of alcohols (20 minutes) Ask students to design a suitable table to record their observations. Then ask pairs of students to light three separate spirit burners, one filled with methanol, one with ethanol, and the third with propan-1-ol. Students consider how easily the alcohols ignite, and observe the cleanness of the flame. Then ask students to write equations for these reactions. SAFETY: Wear eye protection. CLEAPSS Hazcard 040A & B; 084A. Keep room well ventilated. **Properties of alcohols** (20 minutes) Carry out demonstration reactions to compare the properties of methanol, ethanol, and propan-1-ol. 1 Half-fill separate test-tubes with each alcohol. Add a few drops of universal indicator. Then add a cube of sodium with sides of length of approximately 2 mm to each test-tube and observe. 2 Place about 3 cm³ of acidified potassium dichromate(VI) in each of three clean dry boiling tubes using dropping pipettes. Then add about 1 cm³ of each alcohol to the tubes. Using a test-tube holder, hold the tubes just above the gas cone in a blue Bunsen burner flame until the mixtures are boiling. Explain that acidified potassium dichromate(VI) is an oxidising agent, and that the alcohols are oxidised to form carboxylic acids. Point out that other oxidation agents can be used instead of potassium dichromate(VI), including potassium manganate(VII), which is used in C6.2.4, Starter 2. Ask students to use the results to draw conclusions. SAFETY: Wear chemical splash-proof eye protection. CLEAPSS Hazcard 040A & B; 084A; 088; 078. Keep room well ventilated.	**Extend:** The iodoform reaction can be used to distinguish between methanol and ethanol. (Demonstration only: Hazcard 104.) **Extend:** Ask students to write a balanced symbol equation for the oxidation of the alcohols using [O] as a simplified representation of the oxidising agent.	**Practical:** Comparing the reactions of alcohols

Plenary	Support/Extend	Resources
Homologous series (5 minutes) Ask students to write a bullet-point list of the features of the homologous series of alcohols including the general formula. **Wine to vinegar** (10 minutes) Use universal indicator to measure the pH of freshly opened wine and wine that has been left open for a month (wine vinegar). Explain that vinegar contains an acid called ethanoic acid. Ask students to write an explanation of how wine becomes wine vinegar when the bottle is left open to the air.		

Homework	Support/Extend	Resources
Draw a table with three columns with the following column headings: name, molecular formula, displayed formula. Complete the table for the first 10 straight-chain alcohols.		

kerboodle

A Kerboodle highlight for this lesson is **Literacy skills: Uses of alcohols.** Refer to the **Content map** on Kerboodle for a full list of resources and assessment.

GCSE CHEMISTRY ONLY

C6.2.4 Carboxylic acids

Specification links:

6.2a Recognise functional groups and identify members of the same homologous series.

6.2b Name and draw the structural formulae, using fully displayed formulae, of the first four members of the straight-chain [alkanes, alkenes, alcohols, and] carboxylic acids.

WS1.4a Use scientific vocabulary, terminology, and definitions.

M1c Use ratios, fractions, and percentages.

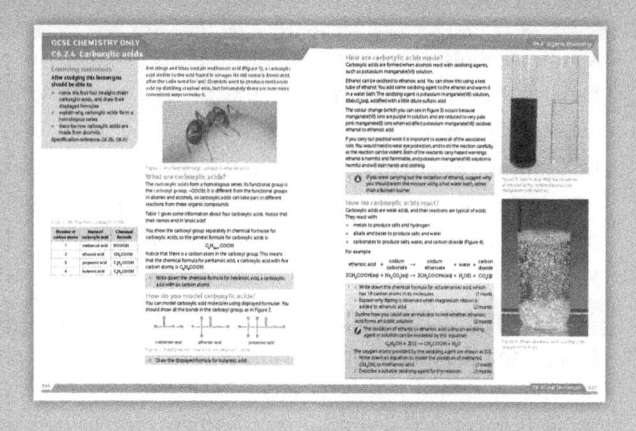

Target	Outcome	Checkpoint	
		Question	Activity
Aiming for GRADE 4 ↓	Recognise the carboxylic acid functional group.		Starter 1 Main 2 Homework
	Name the first four straight-chain carboxylic acids.		Starter 1 Main 2
	State that carboxylic acids are formed when alcohols are oxidised.	3	Starter 2 Plenary 2
Aiming for GRADE 6 ↓	Explain what members of the carboxylic acid homologous series have in common.		Main 2
	Draw the displayed formulae of the first four straight-chain carboxylic acids.	B	Main 2
	Describe with word equations the reactions of carboxylic acids.	1b, 2	Main 1 Plenary 1 Homework
Aiming for GRADE 8 ↓	Deduce the general formula of carboxylic acids and use it to work out the formula of any carboxylic acid.	A, 1a	Main 2
	Draw the displayed formula of any carboxylic acid, given the number of carbon atoms.		Main 2
	Describe in detail with equations the reactions of carboxylic acids.		Main 1 and 2

Maths
In Starter 1 students calculate the relative formula mass of the first four carboxylic acids (M1c).

Literacy
In Main 2 students make index cards about the carboxylic acid homologous series. In Plenary 1 students write a prediction about the properties of ethanoic acid, and explain their prediction.

Key words
carboxylic acid, carboxyl group

C6.2 Organic chemistry

Starter	Support/Extend	Resources
Carboxylic acid relative formula mass (5 minutes) Ask students to calculate the relative formula mass of each of the carboxylic acids shown in Table 1. **Oxidisation of ethanol** (10 minutes) Half-fill a test-tube with ethanol and add acidified potassium manganate(VII) solution. Put the test-tube in a warm water bath and return to the experiment at the end of the lesson. Explain that the acidified potassium manganate(VII) acts as an oxidising agent. SAFETY: Wear eye protection. CLEAPSS Hazcards 040A; 081. No naked flames.	**Extend:** Ask students to calculate the percentage of oxygen in these compounds. **Extend:** Acidified potassium dichromate(VI) may be used instead of acidified potassium manganate(VII).	

Main	Support/Extend	Resources
Properties of ethanoic acid (30 minutes) Give each pair of students three test-tubes in a rack and ask them to follow the steps below: 1 Ask them to half-fill each test-tube with ethanoic acid solution. They should add universal indicator to the first, half a spatula measure of potassium carbonate to the second, and one piece of magnesium ribbon to the third. Ask students to record any observations in a table. 2 Students should then half-fill a beaker with ethanoic acid solution. Ask students to submerge the ends of two graphite rods in this solution and, using connecting wires and crocodile clips, make a series circuit with a power supply and a lamp or ammeter/multimeter. Ensuring the carbon rods do not touch, students should then turn on the power supply and observe whether current flows. SAFETY: Wear eye protection. CLEAPSS Hazcards 038A; 032; 095A; 059A; 047A. Finally, ask students to write a conclusion that explains their observations. Encourage students to write equations to illustrate each reaction. **Index cards** (10 minutes) Give each student an index card. On one side they should summarise the key properties of the carboxylic acid homologous series, and on the reverse they should write the displayed formulae of the first four carboxylic acids.	**Support:** To help students compare and contrast the reactions of ethanoic acid with those of a strong acid, start by demonstrating the reactions using a strong acid such as dilute hydrochloric acid. **Extend:** Ask students to deduce the general formula of carboxylic acids, and to then use this to work out the formula of the carboxylic acid which has 10 carbon atoms.	**Practical:** Properties of ethanoic acid

Plenary	Support/Extend	Resources
Predict the reaction (5 minutes) Students match up the reactants and products of a series of word equations to describe the reactions between ethanoic acid and a metal, metal carbonate, and strong alkali. They then complete the balanced symbol equations with state symbols. **Oxidisation of ethanol: observations** (10 minutes) Return to the reaction from Starter 2 and ask students to note any observations. Students should then explain the observed colour change, and also explain why the reaction mixture was heated but not using a naked flame such as a Bunsen burner.	**Support:** Give students the general equations for the reactions between acids and metals, metal carbonates, and alkalis. **Extend:** Display the ionic equation for the reaction and ask students to interpret it.	**Interactive:** Predict the reaction

Homework	Support/Extend	Resources
Remember that carboxylic acids are weak acids (they ionise partially in solution). Predict the pH of propanoic acid, and predict whether or not it would conduct electricity. Explain your predictions.		

C6.2.5 Alkanes from crude oil

Specification links:

6.2j Describe the separation of crude oil by fractional distillation.

6.2k Explain the separation of crude oil by fractional distillation.

6.2l Describe the fractions as largely a mixture of compounds of formula C_nH_{2n+2}, which are members of the alkane homologous series.

6.2m Explain how modern life is crucially dependent upon hydrocarbons and recognise that crude oil is a finite resource.

6.2n Recall that crude oil is a main source of hydrocarbons and is a feedstock for the petrochemical industry.

WS1.1c Understand the power and limitations of science.

WS1.1f Evaluate associated personal, social, economic, and environmental implications.

WS1.1e Explain everyday and technological applications of science.

WS1.3f Present reasoned explanations.

WS1.4a Use scientific vocabulary, terminology, and definitions.

Target	Outcome	Checkpoint Question	Checkpoint Activity
Aiming for GRADE 4	Name some uses of crude oil and state that it is a fossil fuel.	1	Starter 2
	State that crude oil is a mixture of hydrocarbons from the homologous series of alkanes which can be separated into fractions by fractional distillation.		Main Plenary 1
	Name some fractions of crude oil.		Main Plenary 1
Aiming for GRADE 6	Explain how crude oil forms and why it is described as non-renewable.		Starter 2
	Explain how the properties of alkanes are related to the number of carbon atoms in the molecule and state the general formula for an alkane.	B, 2	Main Plenary 2
	Name the fractions of crude oil in order of increasing boiling point.	C	Main Plenary 1
Aiming for GRADE 8	Explain in detail why crude oil is a finite resource.	A	Starter 2
	Explain in detail the separation of crude oil by fractional distillation.	B, 2, 3	Main Plenary 1 Homework
	Justify the uses of different fractions obtained from crude oil.		Main

Literacy
Students write a flow chart to describe and explain the process of fractional distillation.

Key words
Crude oil, fossil fuel, finite resource, fraction alkane, hydrocarbon, homologous series, general formula, saturated

kerboodle
A Kerboodle highlight for this lesson is **Homework: Organic chemistry**. Refer to the **Content map** on Kerboodle for a full list of resources and assessment.

238

C6.2 Organic chemistry

Starter	Support/Extend	Resources
Crude oil and hydrocarbons (10 minutes) Interactive activity in which students put a series of statements that describe the formation of crude oil in the correct order. They then match the name, chemical formula, and structural formula for the first four alkanes. **Formation of crude oil** (10 minutes) Provide students with a list of statements about the formation of crude oil. Ask students to work in pairs to put them in the correct order. Come together as a class to discuss the correct order.	**Extend:** Use questions and answers to generate the list of stages on the board as a class.	**Interactive:** Crude oil and hydrocarbons

Main	Support/Extend	Resources
Distillation of crude oil (40 minutes) Display the formulae of methane, ethane, propane, and butane. Tell students that these four substances are hydrocarbons because they contain only hydrogen and carbon atoms. There are very many hydrocarbons and these four belong to a homologous series called alkanes. All alkanes have the same general formula (C_nH_{2n+2}) and their carbon atoms are joined to each other by a single covalent bond - they are saturated. Explain that crude oil is a mixture of hydrocarbons, mostly alkanes. Then demonstrate the fractional distillation of synthetic crude oil. 1 Soak mineral wool in synthetic crude oil and place it in a boiling tube with a side arm. 2 Insert a bored bung with a thermometer held with its bulb adjacent to the side arm. 3 Connect a delivery tube to the side arm, with its other end in a collecting tube in an ice bath. 4 Gently heat the boiling tube with a Bunsen burner, and notice when the temperature has stabilised (around 80 °C). 5 When the temperature rises again, quickly change the collecting tube for a new one. 6 Repeat four times, collecting five fractions and leaving a residue in the boiling tube. Each fraction can be collected over about 50 °C up to about 300 °C. The residue remains on the mineral wool, making the sixth. 7 Carefully pour each fraction onto mineral wool held on a watch glass, then ignite each fraction using a lighted taper. Whilst pouring the fractions, ask students to note their relative viscosities (fractions boiling at higher temperatures are more viscous). Ask students to link this property to the uses of each fraction, as shown in Figure 4. Then ask students to consider the relative ease with which the fractions catch fire, and to link this property to the uses of each fraction. SAFETY: Wear eye protection and complete in a well-ventilated room.	**Extend:** Whilst pouring the fractions, ask students to note their relative viscosities (fractions boiling at higher temperatures are more viscous). Ask students to link this property to the number of carbon atoms of the hydrocarbons in each fraction, as well the uses of each fraction, as shown in Figure 4. Then ask students to consider the relative ease with which the fractions catch fire, and to link this property to the uses of each fraction.	**Practical:** Distillation of crude oil

Plenary	Support/Extend	Resources
Summarising fractions (5 minutes) Ask students to create a table to summarise the different fractions from the distillation of crude oil and their properties. **Summarising alkanes** (10 minutes) Ask students to design and complete a table with three columns: name, molecular formula, and displayed formula and to complete the table with the first four alkanes.	**Extend:** Encourage students to add the uses for each fraction.	

Homework	Support/Extend	Resources
Draw labelled diagrams to explain why hydrocarbons with smaller molecules have a lower boiling point than hydrocarbons with larger molecules.	**Support:** See C2.3.2, which looks at intermolecular forces of attraction between molecules.	

C6.2.6 Cracking oil fractions

Specification links:

6.2m Explain how modern life is crucially dependent upon hydrocarbons and recognise that crude oil is a finite resource.

6.2o Describe the production of materials that are more useful by cracking.

WS1.1c Understand the power and limitations of science.

WS1.1f Evaluate associated personal, social, economic, and environmental implications.

WS1.1e Explain everyday and technological applications of science.

WS1.4a Use scientific vocabulary, terminology, and definitions.

M1c Use ratios, fractions, and percentages.

M2c Construct and interpret frequency tables and diagrams, bar charts, and histograms.

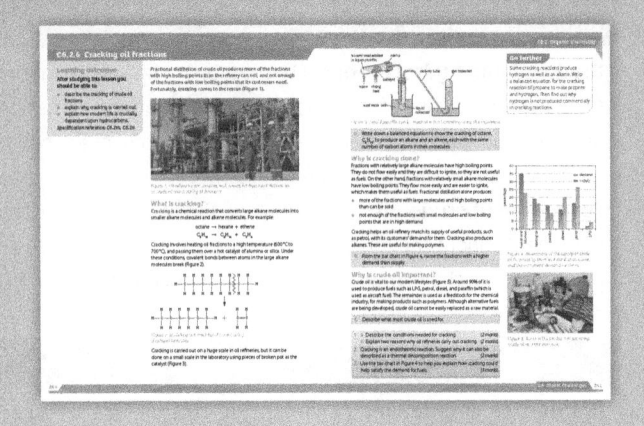

Target	Outcome	Checkpoint Question	Checkpoint Activity
Aiming for GRADE 4 ↓	State that during cracking large alkane molecules are broken down into smaller ones.		Starter 2
	State that cracking is carried out to convert hydrocarbons with long-chain molecules into more useful ones with shorter-chain molecules.		Starter 1 and 2
	Describe some uses of substances obtained from crude oil.	C	Homework
Aiming for GRADE 6 ↓	Describe the process of cracking and the conditions needed.	1	Main
	Explain why cracking is carried out.	1	Starter 1, Main
Aiming for GRADE 8 ↓	Explain, with balanced chemical equations, the process of cracking.	A, 2	Starter 2, Main, Plenary 2
	Explain in detail how cracking helps to satisfy the demand for specific fuels and other substances.	B, 3	Starter 1, Main, Homework

Maths
In Starter 2 students write balanced symbol equations (M1c). In Starter 1 and in completing the Homework task students interpret a bar chart (M2c).

Literacy
In Main students write a risk assessment.

Key words
cracking

kerboodle
A Kerboodle highlight for this lesson is **WebQuest: Cracking**. Refer to the **Content map** on Kerboodle for a full list of resources and assessment.

240

C6.2 Organic chemistry

Starter	Support/Extend	Resources
Supply and demand (5 minutes) Ask students to study Figure 4, which shows supply and demand for different crude oil fractions. Is there greater demand for fractions with bigger or smaller molecules? Which fractions are in greater supply? Tell students that oil-refining companies perform chemical reactions, called cracking, to help match the supply of useful products with customer demand. **Model cracking** (10 minutes) Ask pairs of students to use a molecular model kit to make an octane molecule. Then tell them that a process called cracking can be used to convert large alkane molecules into smaller alkane molecules and alkene molecules. Ask them to model this by breaking up their octane molecules to form hexane and ethene, and to write a balanced chemical equation for the reaction. Tell students that this reaction is an example of cracking.		

Main	Support/Extend	Resources
Cracking (40 minutes) Ask pairs of students to carry out cracking and collect the gases produced: 1 Place a mineral wool plug in the bottom of a boiling tube. Using a dropping pipette, add about 2 cm³ of liquid paraffin. 2 Clamp the tube near its mouth so that it is tilted slightly upwards from horizontal, and place a pile of catalyst in the centre of the tube. 3 Fit a delivery tube and set up the apparatus so that the end of the delivery tube fitted with a Bunsen valve is immersed in a trough half-filled with water. Fill two test-tubes with water and stand them inverted in the trough. 4 Strongly heat the catalyst for a few minutes, then move the flame to the mineral wool to vaporise some of the liquid paraffin. Focus on keeping the catalyst hot. Do not collect the first gas produced as this is air from the tube. 5 When there is a steady stream of bubbles, collect two test-tubes of gas and seal them with a bung under the water. 6 Use a lighted splint to test the first tube of gas. Then add a few drops of 0.01 mol/dm³ bromine water to the second test-tube and shake until decolorised. Perform these tests on the liquid paraffin and compare the results. Ask students to draw a labelled diagram of the experiment and add annotation to explain how the reaction occurs. Students should include brief notes explaining why cracking is done, and write a word equation to model the cracking of one of the substances in paraffin, octane, to form ethene and hexane. Finally, students should write a brief risk assessment for the experiment, aimed at the next GCSE class to carry out this experiment. SAFETY: Medicinal paraffin (liquid paraffin – a mixture of alkanes of chain length C20 and greater) is flammable and bromine water is harmful. Wear eye protection throughout and wash hands after completing the experiment. To prevent suck-back, do not stop heating until the delivery tube is removed from the water bath. If suck-back looks likely to happen, lift the whole apparatus so that the delivery tube is removed from the water bath. CLEAPSS Hazcards 015B; 045B.	**Support:** This practical requires a lot of dexterity. Suck-back is a safety concern. You may wish to demonstrate this experiment and give students pre-prepared tubes of an alkane and alkene to test with bromine water. **Extend:** Explain that the position in the molecule where the split occurs during cracking is not always predictable. The result is therefore a mixture of products, always a saturated molecule and an alkene. Ask students to write equations to illustrate all the possible cracking reactions for octane, and to suggest how the mixture of products could be separated (fractional distillation).	**Practical:** Cracking

Plenary	Support/Extend	Resources
Ethane and ethene (5 minutes) Interactive activity in which students sort statements according to whether they describe ethane, ethene, or both. **Explain** (10 minutes) Give groups of students a set of cards with a key word written on each, to include cracking, alkane, alkene, hydrocarbon, bromine water, saturated, unsaturated, supply, demand, and non-renewable. Ask students to select a card at random and show the rest of the group, but not look at it themselves. The rest of the group should describe the word and time how long it takes for the student holding the card to correctly guess the word. The person with the shortest guessing time is the winner of that round. Repeat for as long as time allows.		**Interactive:** Ethane and ethene

Homework	Support/Extend	Resources
Study Figure 4 in the Student Book and explain in detail what this shows.		

GCSE CHEMISTRY ONLY
C6.2.7 Addition polymers

Specification links:

6.2d Recall the basic principles of addition polymerisation by reference to the functional group in the monomer and the repeating units in the polymer.

M1c Use ratios, fractions, and percentages.

M5b Visualise and represent two-dimensional (2D) and three-dimensional (3D) forms, including 2D representations of 3D objects.

CM6.2i Represent three-dimensional (3D) shapes in two dimensions and vice versa when looking at chemical structures, [e.g. allotropes of carbon] (M5b).

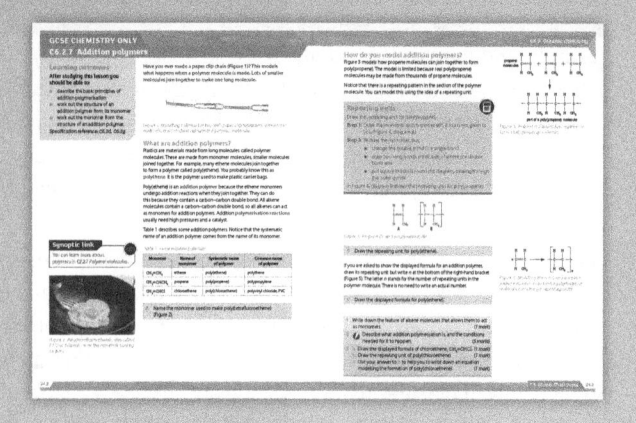

Target	Outcome	Checkpoint Question	Checkpoint Activity
Aiming for GRADE 4	State that substances whose names begin with the prefix 'poly' are polymers.		Main 2
	State the features of alkene molecules that allow them to act as monomers.	1	Starter 1, Main 1 and 2
	Recognise the polymer formed from a given monomer.		Main 2
Aiming for GRADE 6	Determine the systematic name of a polymer from its formula and vice versa.		Main 2
	Describe the formation of addition polymers.	1	Main 1, Plenary 1 and 2, Homework
	Draw the repeating unit of a polymer, given the formula of the polymer.	B	Main 2
Aiming for GRADE 8	Give the systematic and common names of polymers formed from a given monomer.		Main 2
	Explain in detail the conditions required for the formation of addition polymers.	2	Main 1
	Write an equation to model the formation of a polymer given the structure of the monomer or polymer.	C, 3	Main 1

Maths
In Starter 1, Main 1, and Plenary 1 students use 3D models and 2D formulae to represent polymers (M5b). In Starter 1 (Extend) students calculate relative formula mass (M1c).

Key words
addition polymer, polymerisation reactions

C6.2 Organic chemistry

Starter	Support/Extend	Resources
Formulae (5 minutes) Ask students to draw the displayed formulae of ethene, propene, and chloroethene.	**Support:** Refer students to Table 1. **Extend:** Ask students to calculate the relative formula masses of ethene, propene, and chloroethene.	
Dissolve polystyrene (10 minutes) Polystyrene can be dissolved in propanone. Provide students with packing foam and allow them to spray propanone onto the plastic and observe it dissolve. You could dissolve pieces of foam packaging in 100 cm³ of propanone in a beaker.	**Extend:** Show students the structure of polystyrene and ask them to suggest the name and structure of the monomer.	

Main	Support/Extend	Resources
Model addition polymerisation (25 minutes) Ask each student to use a molecular model kit to make a molecule of ethene. Then explain that under high pressure and in the presence of a catalyst, one bond from the C=C double bond breaks and a new bond forms, joining two monomers together. Ask pairs of students to model this, then join with others until the whole class has made one long molecule. Using questions and answers, establish the structures of the monomer (ethene) and polymer (poly[ethene]) and write an equation. Then repeat the process for poly(propene).	**Extend:** Ask students to discuss possible reasons for the conditions needed for addition polymerisation. They could also suggest their own way of modelling a polymer.	
Polymer table (15 minutes) Ask students to draw a table with five columns: monomer name, monomer structure, polymer name, polymer structure, polymer uses. Students should complete the table for poly(ethene) and poly(propene), using the Student Book for reference.	**Extend:** Ask students to include other addition polymers, such as polyvinyl chloride (PVC).	**Activity:** Polymer table

Plenary	Support/Extend	Resources
Necklace model (5 minutes) Display a necklace made of beads. Ask students to suggest how this can be used to model an addition polymer. (The necklace is the polymer and each bead is a monomer.)	**Extend:** Show a necklace made of more than one type of bead, and ask what this is modelling (an addition polymer made from more than one monomer, that is, a co-polymer).	
Poly(tetrafluoroethene) (10 minutes) Interactive activity in which students identify the structure of the monomer, the repeating unit of the polymer, and state the type of polymerisation used, when given a section of the structure of poly(tetrafluoroethene).	**Support:** Refer students to Figure 1.	**Interactive:** Poly(tetrafluoroethene)

Homework	Support/Extend	Resources
Draw a pictorial flow chart to explain how a generic alkene (RR'C=CR"R"') can form an addition polymer.		

kerboodle
A Kerboodle highlight for this lesson is **Maths skills: Draw addition polymers.** Refer to the **Content map** on Kerboodle for a full list of resources and assessment.

GCSE CHEMISTRY ONLY
C6.2.8 Biological polymers

Specification links:

6.2h Recall that DNA is a polymer made from four different monomers called nucleotides and that other important naturally occurring polymers are based on sugars and amino acids.

WS1.4a Use scientific vocabulary, terminology, and definitions.

M5b Visualise and represent two-dimensional (2D) and three-dimensional (3D) forms, including 2D representations of 3D objects.

CM6.2i Represent three-dimensional (3D) shapes in two dimensions and vice versa when looking at chemical structures, [e.g. allotropes of carbon] (M5b).

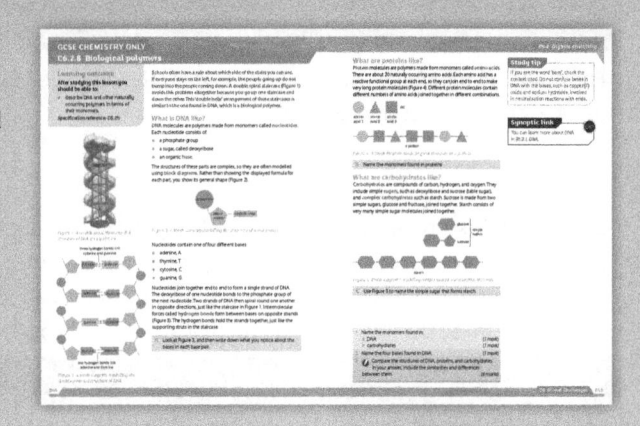

Target	Outcome	Checkpoint Question	Checkpoint Activity
Aiming for GRADE 4 ↓	State that DNA is a biological polymer with a double-helix structure.		Starter 1 and 2
	State that proteins are biological polymers made from amino acids.		Plenary 1 Homework
	State that carbohydrates are biological polymers made from sugars.		Plenary 1 and 2
Aiming for GRADE 6 ↓	Describe the monomer units used to make DNA.	A, 1a, 2	Starter 1 and 2 Main
	Describe the monomer units used to make proteins.	B	Plenary 1 Homework
	Describe the monomer units used to make carbohydrates.	C	Plenary 1 and 2
Aiming for GRADE 8 ↓	Describe in detail the structure and bonding in a DNA molecule.	3	Starter 1 and 2 Main
	Describe in detail the structure of a protein molecule.	3	Homework
	Describe in detail the structure of a carbohydrate molecule.	3	Plenary 1 and 2

Maths
In Starter 2 students make 3D models of DNA (M5b).

Literacy
In Main 1 students write a paragraph about the structure of DNA. In Plenary 2 students explain why bread eventually tastes sweet when it is chewed.

Key words
DNA, nucleotides, base, block diagrams, hydrogen bonds, protein, amino acids, carbohydrates, sugars, complex carbohydrates

C6.2 Organic chemistry

Starter	Support/Extend	Resources
DNA model (5 minutes) Show students a model of DNA and ask them to suggest what they will be studying in the lesson. Encourage students to share any information they already know about DNA. Ensure that students know that DNA has a double-helix structure. **Label DNA** (10 minutes) Ask students to use the student book to label a diagram of a DNA double helix with the key parts.	**Extend:** Ask students to describe each part of the diagram.	**Interactive:** Label DNA

Main	Support/Extend	Resources
Extracting DNA from a kiwi fruit (40 minutes) Ask groups of students to extract the DNA from a kiwi fruit. 1 Peel a kiwi fruit and blend it with a little sodium chloride and water until it is a viscous paste. 2 Sieve the paste and collect the liquid in a conical flask. 3 Add 2 tablespoons of washing-up liquid and swirl to mix, then leave for 10 minutes in a warm water bath. 4 Half-fill a test-tube with the mixture and add protease. 5 Tilt the test-tube to 45° and slowly pour in well-chilled ethanol so that a layer is formed on top of the mixture. 6 The white clumps that form are DNA, which can be collected using a glass rod and dried on a paper towel. Allow students to dry their DNA sample and use sticky tape to fix it into their notes. Then ask students to write a paragraph to explain what the sample is made from. SAFETY: Ethanol is highly flammable and harmful. Protease is harmful. Wear eye protection and wash hands after the practical. CLEAPSS Hazcard 040A; 033.		**Practical:** Extracting DNA from a kiwi fruit

Plenary	Support/Extend	Resources
Classifying polymers (5 minutes) Show students the structures of polypeptides, amino acids, monosaccharides, and polysaccharides. Ask students to classify them based on their structures. **Starch and sugar** (10 minutes) If science department policy allows, ask students to wash their hands thoroughly before giving them each a small piece of bread. Ask them to keep chewing the bread for about 3 minutes and then describe the taste (it becomes sweet as amylase in the saliva breaks the starch down into sugars). Ask students to use Figure 5 and their observation to explain what has happened.	**Support:** Give students the functional group(s) required for each classification.	**Interactive:** Classifying polymers

Homework	Support/Extend	Resources
Make a flick book to show the formation of a protein molecule. The flick book should consist of a series of images on thin card roughly 10 cm by 10 cm in size. Each image should be slightly different and should show how two glycine molecules join to make a dipeptide, and then show the reactions continuing to build up a protein molecule. Stack the images and staple them together at the top-left-hand corner. Flicking through the book should create an animation of the reaction.	**Extend:** You may have advanced computing skills and be able to make a computer animation.	

kerboodle

A Kerboodle highlight for this lesson is **Literacy sheet: Natural polymers.** Refer to the **Content map** on Kerboodle for a full list of resources and assessment.

GCSE CHEMISTRY ONLY HIGHER TIER
C6.2.9 Condensation polymers

Specification links:

6.2e Explain the basic principles of condensation polymerisation.

6.2f Describe practical techniques to make a polymer by condensation and addition.

WS1.1b Use models to solve problems, make predictions, and to develop scientific explanations and understanding of familiar and unfamiliar facts.

WS1.2a Use scientific theories and explanations to develop hypotheses.

WS1.2b Plan experiments or devise procedures to make observations, produce or characterise a substance, test hypotheses, check data, or explore phenomena.

WS1.2c Apply knowledge of a range of techniques, instruments, apparatus, and materials to select those appropriate to the experiment.

WS1.4a Use scientific vocabulary, terminology, and definitions.

WS2a Carry out experiments.

WS2b Make and record observations and measurements using a range of apparatus and methods.

CM6.2i Represent three-dimensional (3D) shapes in two dimensions and vice versa when looking at chemical structures, [e.g. allotropes of carbon] (M5b).

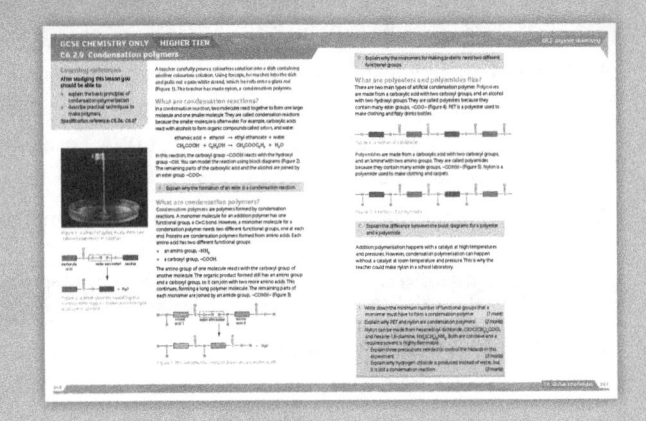

Target	Outcome	Checkpoint Question	Checkpoint Activity
Aiming for GRADE 6	Define the term condensation reaction and represent condensation reactions using block diagrams.		Main Plenary 1 Homework
↓	Describe the structure of monomer units used to make condensation polymers.	B, 1	Main Plenary 1 Homework
	Describe a practical technique that can be used to make a condensation polymer.		Main
Aiming for GRADE 8	Write balanced chemical equations to model condensation polymerisation reactions.	A	Main
↓	Describe in detail the formation of condensation polymers.	C, 2	Main Plenary 2 Homework
	Compare the conditions required for condensation and addition polymerisation.	3	Plenary 1

Literacy
In completing the Homework task students write a flow chart to explain how a condensation polymer is formed.

Key words
condensation reaction, esters, condensation polymers, polyesters, polyamides

246

C6.2 Organic chemistry

Starter	Support/Extend	Resources
Uses of artificial condensation polymers (5 minutes) Ask students to list uses of polyamides and polyesters. **Esters** (5 minutes) Students complete the Interactive to describe what esters are and how they are made. Then use the Interactive to introduce condensation polymerisation. Students sort statements according to whether they describe addition polymerisation or condensation polymerisation.	**Support:** Encourage students to refer to the Student Book. **Extend:** Give students a selection of polyamide and polyester products to classify.	**Interactive:** Esters

Main	Support/Extend	Resources
Making nylon (40 minutes) Ask students to suggest what would happen if a basic –NH$_2$ group reacted with a carboxylic acid. Then ask students to draw a block diagram to model diaminohexane and decanedioic acid. Demonstrate the nylon rope trick. Solution A is 0.4 mol/dm^3 1,6-diaminohexane and solution B is 0.15 mol/dm^3 decanedioyl dichloride solution dissolved in hexane. 1 Carefully add about 1 cm depth of solution A to a microbeaker. 2 Very gently pour a similar depth of solution B into the beaker (it will float and form a two-phase mixture). 3 Push forceps tips to the bottom of the beaker and draw them through the layers slowly. At the interface, a nylon rope will form and be pulled by the forceps. 4 Put the end of the nylon rope on a glass rod and rotate the glass rod to continue to draw the nylon. Explain that this is a condensation reaction, and ask students to write an equation or block diagram to describe the reaction observed. SAFETY: 1,6-diaminohexane (solution A) and decanedioyl dichloride (solution B) are corrosive and hexane (solution B) is highly flammable and harmful. Wear eye protection and nitrile gloves whilst completing the practical in a well-ventilated lab. Do not touch the nylon unless it has been washed well under cold running water. CLEAPSS Hazcards 003B; 041; 106; 045A & B; CLEAPSS Recipe Book 0062.	**Extend:** Encourage students to write a balanced symbol equation for this reaction, and to write a detailed description of the formation of the polymer. **Extend:** Encourage students to write a detailed description of the formation of an ester.	**Practical:** Making nylon

Plenary	Support/Extend	Resources
Compare and contrast (5 minutes) Ask students to draw a table to compare and contrast addition polymerisation and condensation polymerisation. The table should include examples of each type of polymer and the monomers it is made from. **Interpret formulae** (10 minutes) Ask students to look at Figure 3, which shows how peptides are formed. Students should write a similar equation for making a polyester and a polyamide, as shown in Figures 4 and 5.	**Support:** Provide the types of information that students should include, such as the reaction conditions and the number of different products formed.	

Homework	Support/Extend	Resources
Make a flow chart to explain how a condensation polymer is formed.		

kerboodle

A Kerboodle highlight for this lesson is **Animation: Polymerisation**. Refer to the **Content map** on Kerboodle for a full list of resources and assessment.

GCSE CHEMISTRY ONLY
C6.2.10 Producing electricity using chemistry

Specification links:

6.2p Recall that a chemical cell produces a potential difference until the reactants are used up.

6.2q Evaluate the advantages and disadvantages of hydrogen/oxygen and other fuel cells for given uses.

WS1.1g Make decisions based on the evaluation of evidence and arguments.

WS1.1i Recognise the importance of peer review of results and of communicating results to a range of audiences.

M1c Use ratios, fractions, and percentages.

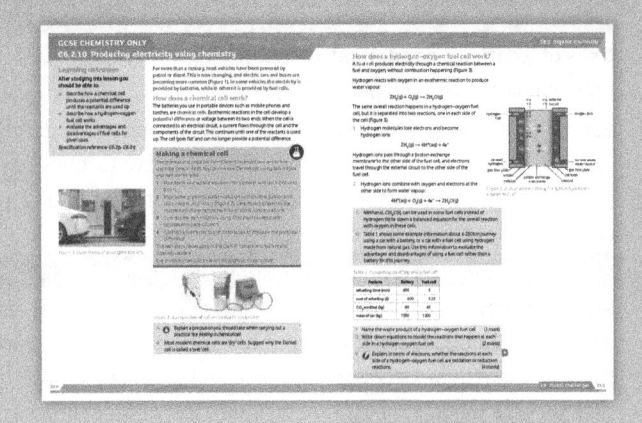

Target	Outcome	Checkpoint Question	Checkpoint Activity
Aiming for GRADE 4	State that a chemical cell produces a potential difference until the reactants are used up.		Main 1 Plenary 1
	Name the waste product of a hydrogen–oxygen fuel cell.	1	Main 2 Plenary 2
	Make a chemical cell.	A	Main 1
Aiming for GRADE 6	Explain how a chemical cell works.		Main 1
	Describe how a hydrogen–oxygen fuel cell works and write equations to model the reactions that occur.	2	Main 2 Homework
	Make a chemical cell, name the two electrodes, and record its maximum potential difference.		Main 1
Aiming for GRADE 8	Evaluate the advantages and disadvantages of chemical cells for given uses.	B, C, D	Plenary 2
	Explain in terms of electrons whether the reaction on each side of a hydrogen–oxygen fuel cell is an oxidation or reduction reaction.	3	Main 2
	Investigate the factors that affect the potential difference produced by a chemical cell.		Main 1

Maths
In Starter 1 students write balanced symbol equations (M1c).

Literacy
In completing the Homework task students draft a letter to an MP.

Key words
chemical cells, potential difference, fuel cell

C6.2 Organic chemistry

Starter	Support/Extend	Resources
Hydrogen/oxygen explosion (5 minutes) Ask students to predict what happens when a balloon filled with hydrogen is ignited with a splint. Encourage students to write a word and balanced symbol equation for the reaction. **Reactivity series recap** (10 minutes) Ask students to list the reactivity series, and to describe what it shows (the relative reactivity of metals). Then tell students that you can make use of the different reactivities of metals to make a chemical cell, as shown in Figure 2.	**Extend:** Ask students to suggest the sign of the enthalpy change, and to determine which species was oxidised and which was reduced. **Support:** Refer students to C6.1.6 to revise the reactivity series.	

Main	Support/Extend	Resources
Make a chemical cell (20 minutes) Allow pairs of students to make half-cells from a metal strip dipped in a dilute solution of a salt of the metal (e.g., magnesium in magnesium sulfate solution, copper in copper(II) sulfate solution). Students should choose two half-cells, and then connect them by draping a salt bridge between them made from a piece of filter paper soaked in saturated brine. They should then connect the metal strips to a voltmeter and measure the potential difference that each cell produces. Ask students to design a results table to record their data and then draw conclusions consistent with the results. SAFETY: Wear eye protection and consult CLEAPSS Hazcards. **Visual summary** (20 minutes) Show students Figure 3. Use questions and answers to build up the half equations at each electrode, and the overall equation. Ask students to discuss in small groups whether they think hydrogen fuel cells could soon replace other batteries in everyday use. Then ask students to design a visual summary that summarises the hydrogen fuel cell theory. Students should include the applications, drawbacks, and benefits of the hydrogen fuel cell. In this activity, ensure that students realise that a hydrogen–oxygen fuel cell produces just one waste product – water.	**Support:** Encourage students to look at the reactivity series to help them draw conclusions. **Extend:** Ask students to consider what happens when the reactants are used up (a potential difference is no longer produced). **Extend:** Ask students to identify oxidation and reduction reactions in fuel cells, and to explain their decisions using ideas about electron transfer.	**Practical:** Make a chemical cell

Plenary	Support/Extend	Resources
Fruity cell (5 minutes) Insert an iron nail and a piece of magnesium ribbon into a citrus fruit. Connect these to a voltmeter and ask students to explain the observation. **Fuel a car** (10 minutes) Students use the interactive to complete a paragraph summarising hydrogen fuel cells and their uses to fuel cars. They then sort statements according to whether they describe advantages or disadvantages of used hydrogen fuel cells in cars.	**Extend:** The cell may produce enough voltage to light an LED. **Support:** Demonstrate a small-scale 'squeaky pop' test and use questions and answers to elicit the pros and cons.	**Interactive:** Fuel a car

Homework	Support/Extend	Resources
Draft a letter to an MP about research into hydrogen-powered vehicles. Make a persuasive argument for extra funding being made available, stressing the problems that will arise if the present situation continues, and the problems that the research needs to solve.		

kerboodle
A Kerboodle highlight for this lesson is **WebQuest: Is hydrogen the perfect fuel?** Refer to the **Content map** on Kerboodle for a full list of resources and assessment.

C6 Global Challenges 249

Checkpoint
C6.2 Organic chemistry

Overview of C6.2 Organic chemistry

In this chapter students have studied organic chemistry, including the topic of functional groups and homologous series which is for GCSE Chemistry students only. Chemistry students should be able to name and draw formulae of the first four members of the straight-chain alkanes, alkenes, alcohols, and carboxylic acids. They should be able to describe the complete and incomplete combustion of the alkanes, and the addition reactions of alkenes. They should be able to recall the combustion reactions of alcohols as well as their oxidation to form carboxylic acids, and describe the reactions of carboxylic acids.

The topic of separating alkanes from crude oil is studied by all students, who should recall the process of fractional distillation to separate and explain the uses of different fractions of alkanes obtained from crude oil. They should understand that cracking is carried out to convert hydrocarbons with long-chain molecules into more useful ones with shorter-chain molecules, and be able to describe the process.

Polymerisation is another GCSE Chemistry topic, and students should be able to describe the formation of addition polymers from alkenes and draw the repeating unit given the formula of a polymer. In studying biological polymers they should be able to describe the monomers and structure of DNA, protein, and carbohydrate molecules. Higher-tier students should be able to explain the process of condensation polymerisation, including practical techniques.

Finally in this chapter, GCSE Chemistry students have studied fuel cells and should be able to describe how a hydrogen–oxygen fuel cell works, write equations to model the reactions that occur, and evaluate different types of fuel cell.

MyMaths

You can find additional support for the maths skills covered in this chapter on **MyMaths**, including using 2D and 3D representations of molecules, displaying data in charts, tables, and graphs, and calculations involving ratio and proportion.

kerboodle

For this chapter, the following assessments are available on Kerboodle:
C6.2 Checkpoint quiz: Organic chemistry
C6.2 Progress quiz: Organic chemistry 1
C6.2 Progress quiz: Organic chemistry 2
C6.2 On your marks: Organic chemistry
C6.2 Exam-style questions and mark scheme: Organic chemistry

Checkpoint follow-up lesson

A student's route through this lesson can be determined using the Checkpoint assessment. Percentage pass marks are supplied in the Checkpoint teacher notes.

For each successive route through it is assumed that the student can perform to their current route as well as previous routes. For example, students working at Aiming for 6 are assumed to be secure in Aiming for 4 knowledge and understanding and working towards achieving all the learning objectives for Aiming for 6.

C6.2 Organic chemistry

	Aiming for 4	Aiming for 6	Aiming for 8
Learning outcomes	Recognise and name compounds from the alkanes, alkenes, alcohols, and carboxylic acids homologous series.	Describe the first four straight-chain alkanes, alkenes, alcohols, and carboxylic acids.	Used balanced chemical equations to illustrate the combustion of organic compounds, the reaction of alkenes with bromine water, hydrogen, or polymerisation, and the oxidation of carboxylic acids.
	Describe what crude oil is and why fractional distillation is important.	Explain how fractional distillation separates crude oil.	Explain how modern life is crucially dependent upon hydrocarbons and recognise that crude oil is a finite resource.
	Recall the general properties of each homologous series.	Describe cracking and explain why it is useful.	Use examples to explain the difference between addition and condensation polymerisation.
Starter	**Sort that chemical (5 minutes)** Limited to the first four straight-chain alkanes, alkenes, alcohols, and carboxylic acids, give small groups of students a selection of cards with names of chemicals, structural formulae, molecular formulae, and molecular models. Students should group these by homologous series.		
	Molecular models (5 minutes) Give pairs of students a molecular model kit and ask them to make ethane, ethene, ethanol, and ethanoic acid. You may wish to provide the molecular formula of each compound to help them. Students could then compare the differences (functional group) and similarities (same number of carbon atoms) between the molecules.		
Differentiated checkpoint activity	**Flow chart (40 minutes)** Explain that students will be producing a flow chart to summarise the topic *Organic chemistry*. Students answer each question on the differentiated worksheets. They will need A3 paper, rulers, pencils, and coloured pencils.		
	The Aiming for 4 sheet provides structured tasks to support students in revising and summarising the information to include in their flow chart. Students should work in small groups.	The Aiming for 6 sheet provides questions to guide the content students include in their flow chart. Students should work in small groups. They will need access to the Student Book.	The Aiming for 8 sheet provides fewer prompt questions which cover more advanced content.
	Kerboodle resource: C6.2 Checkpoint follow-up: Aiming for 4, C6.2 Checkpoint follow-up: Aiming for 6, C6.2 Checkpoint follow-up: Aiming for 8		
Plenary	**Flow chart review (5 minutes)** Ask students to swap their flow chart with another student. Students should use the school marking policy to assess the work.		
	Bingo! (5 minutes) Students will need a piece of card and coloured pencils. Ask students to draw a 3 × 3 grid to form a Bingo card. They should choose four of the key words to write into their Bingo card, and colour in two of the cells. Collect the cards and re-distribute them randomly. Give the definitions of the key terms and if students think they have that term, they can cross it out. The first person to have all four words correctly crossed off could be given a prize.		
Progression	Aiming for 4 students should recall the key features of alkenes, alkanes, alcohols, and carboxylic acids and classify examples into these groups. They should aim to learn the general reactions of these substances and write word equations to illustrate these. Students should be able to describe the importance of crude oil and work towards explaining how fractional distillation separates it.	Aiming for 6 students should be able to draw the structural formula of the first four straight-chain alkanes, alkenes, alcohols, and carboxylic acids. They should be able to explain how fractional distillation separates crude oil and why cracking is useful. Students should work towards illustrating the combustion of organic compounds and the reaction of alkenes with bromine water, hydrogen, or polymerisation, and the oxidation of carboxylic acids with balanced symbol equations.	Encourage Aiming for 8 students to balance more complex symbol equations, and classify organic chemical reactions as addition, condensation, oxidation, reduction, and redox.

C6.3 Interpreting and interacting with Earth Systems
C6.3.1 Forming the atmosphere

Specification links:

6.3a Interpret evidence for how it is thought the atmosphere was originally formed.

6.3b Describe how it is thought an oxygen-rich atmosphere developed over time.

WS1.1a Understand how scientific methods and theories develop over time.

WS1.3e Interpret observations and other data.

M1c Use ratios, fractions, and percentages.

M2c Construct and interpret frequency tables and diagrams, bar charts, and histograms.

M4a Translate information between graphical and numeric form.

CM6.3i Extract and interpret information from charts, graphs, and tables (M2c, M4a).

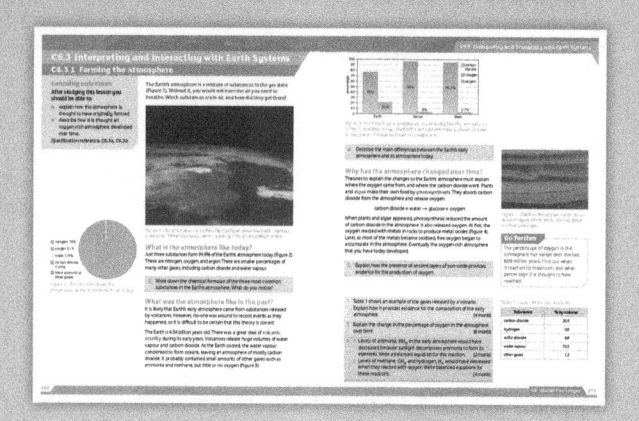

Target	Outcome	Checkpoint Question	Checkpoint Activity
Aiming for GRADE 4	Name the main gases in the atmosphere.		Starter 2, Plenary 2
	State that the early atmosphere was mostly carbon dioxide.		Main 1, Plenary 1
	State that photosynthesis may have caused the percentage of oxygen in the atmosphere to increase over time.		Starter 1, Main 2, Plenary 1
Aiming for GRADE 6	Describe the composition of the atmosphere.		Starter 2, Plenary 2
	Explain how the Earth's early atmosphere is thought to have formed.		Main 1, Plenary 1
	Explain how an oxygen-rich atmosphere may have developed over time.	B, 2	Starter 1, Main 2, Plenary 1
Aiming for GRADE 8	Describe in detail the composition of the atmosphere.	A	Starter 2, Plenary 2
	Interpret evidence about the formation of the early atmosphere.	1	Main 1, Homework
	Interpret evidence about changes in the atmosphere over time.	C, 3	Main 1, Homework

Maths
In Starter 1 (Extend) students write balanced symbol equations, and in Starter 2 (Extend) and Plenary 2 (Extend) students convert percentages to fractions (M1c). In Starter 2 and Plenary 2 students draw bar charts and pie charts (M2c, M4a).

Literacy
In Main 2 students write a prediction about the result of a gas test, and explain their prediction.

Key words
volcanic activity, algae, photosynthesis

C6.3 Interpreting and interacting with Earth Systems

Starter	Support/Extend	Resources
Photosynthesis and the atmosphere (5 minutes) Ask students to write an equation for photosynthesis and to explain the importance of this chemical reaction to life on Earth. **Display data: bar chart** (10 minutes) Ask students to make a bar chart to show the composition of dry air using data from Figure 2.	**Extend:** Encourage students to write the balanced symbol equation. **Extend:** Ask students to convert the percentages into fractions.	**Interactive:** Photosynthesis and the atmosphere

Main	Support/Extend	Resources
Flick book (25 minutes) Ask students to make a flick book to describe the key stages in the development of the Earth's atmosphere. The flick book should consist of a series of images on thin card roughly 10 cm by 10 cm in size. Each image should be slightly different and should show how the Earth's atmosphere developed. Students should stack the images and staple them together at the top-left-hand corner. Flicking through the book should create an animation of the development of the atmosphere. **Gases in the atmosphere** (15 minutes) Ask groups of students to set up apparatus to collect oxygen made by *Elodea*. 1 Put a sample of *Elodea* in a beaker, then add about 200 cm³ of water. 2 Trap the *Elodea* under an upturned funnel. 3 Fill a test-tube with water and then invert it over the stem of the funnel, ensuring that the lip of the test-tube is below the water level. This allows any gas to be collected by displacement. 4 Leave this apparatus on a sunny windowsill or set up a lamp to shine on it, then leave it next to a lamp overnight. 5 Carefully remove the test-tube from the beaker. Keeping the mouth under water, stopper the test-tube tightly with a bung before turning it over. Explain to students that they are going to test the gas in the tube with a glowing splint. Ask students to write a prediction about what they think the results of this gas test will be, and why, before carrying out the test. Point out that the experiment shows that plants produce oxygen gas in photosynthesis, and it is likely that this process caused the percentage of oxygen in the atmosphere to increase over time.	**Support:** Remind students of the gas tests in C4.2.1. **Extend:** Allow student groups to collect a second test-tube of gas from *Elodea* at the same time as they collect the first test-tube. Ask students to predict the results of testing the gas collected with limewater (SAFETY: wear eye protection, CLEAPSS Hazcard 018), undertake this test, and explain their result. Point out that respiration (in plants as well as in animals) produces carbon dioxide.	**Practical:** Gases in the atmosphere

Plenary	Support/Extend	Resources
List (5 minutes) Provide students with individual statements to put in the correct order, to explain the leading theory about how the current atmosphere was formed. **Display data: pie chart** (10 minutes) Ask students to draw two pie charts, showing the composition of the atmospheres on Venus and Mars, using data from Figure 3. Students should then compare their pie charts with Figure 2 in the Student Book, which shows the composition of the Earth's atmosphere.	**Extend:** Ask students to convert the percentages into fractions.	

Homework	Support/Extend	Resources
Create a timeline with sketches to explain the development of the Earth's atmosphere.	**Extend:** Use the internet to research where the evidence for this model comes from, and note this on the timeline.	

kerboodle

A Kerboodle highlight for this lesson is **WebQuest: The history of the atmosphere**. Refer to the **Content map** on Kerboodle for a full list of resources and assessment.

C6.3.2 Pollution and the atmosphere

Specification links:

6.3f Describe the major sources of carbon monoxide, sulfur dioxide, oxides of nitrogen, and particulates in the atmosphere and explain the problems caused by increased amounts of these substances.

WS1.4a Translate information between graphical and numeric form.

M1c Use ratios, fractions, and percentages.

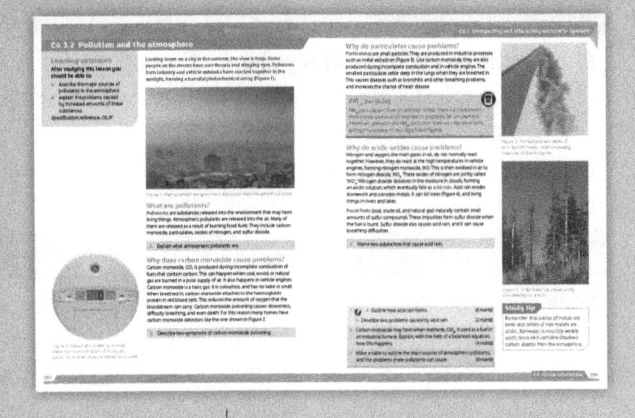

Target	Outcome	Checkpoint Question	Checkpoint Activity
Aiming for GRADE 4 ↓	State that carbon monoxide is a pollutant that may harm living things.	A	Plenary 1 and 2
	State that particulates are pollutants that may harm living things.	A	Starter Plenary 1 and 2
	State that nitrogen oxide and sulfur dioxide are pollutants that may harm living things.	C	Main Plenary 1 and 2
Aiming for GRADE 6 ↓	Describe how carbon monoxide is produced and explain the effect it has on the body.	B, 2, 3	Plenary 1 and 2
	Describe how particulates are produced and explain the effect they have on the body.	3	Starter 1 Plenary 1
	Describe how acidic oxides are produced and explain the effect they have on living organisms.	1a, 3	Main Plenary 1 and 2
Aiming for GRADE 8 ↓	Explain in detail the health problems caused by increased amounts of carbon monoxide in the atmosphere.	3	Plenary 1 and 2
	Explain in detail the health problems caused by increased amounts of particulates in the atmosphere.	3	Starter 1 Plenary 1 and 2
	Explain in detail the health problems caused by increased amounts of acidic oxides in the atmosphere.	1b, 3	Main Plenary 1 and 2

Maths
In Main 2 (Extend), Plenary 2 (Extend), and in completing the Homework task (Extend) students write balanced chemical equations (M1c).

Key words
pollutants, particulates, acid rain, fossil fuels

C6.3 Interpreting and interacting with Earth Systems

Starter	Support/Extend	Resources
Clouds in a bottle (10 minutes) Allow pairs of students to make a cloud in a bottle to demonstrate how particulates can increase cloud cover. 1 Place a small amount of water in an empty plastic drinks bottle. 2 Light a match and tap it out so that it is smouldering, and suck the smoke into the bottle. Replace the cap. 3 Squeeze the bottle and observe. This can be repeated several times. Discuss how particulates can be respiratory irritants.	**Extend:** Ask students to use what they have learnt about incomplete combustion to suggest what the particulates are made up of.	
Equations (5 minutes) Ask students to write combustion equations for the combustion of: • nitrogen to form nitrogen monoxide • nitrogen to form nitrogen dioxide • a hydrocarbon to form carbon dioxide and water • a hydrocarbon to from carbon, carbon monoxide, and water • sulfur to form sulfur dioxide.	**Support:** Write word equations. **Extend:** Write balanced symbol equations with state symbols.	

Main	Support/Extend	Resources
Acid rain (30 minutes) Ask students to draw a labelled diagram to illustrate how acid rain is formed, the effects of acid rain, how acid rain can be reduced, and how the effects of acid rain can be managed. Encourage students to colour-code their labels, using black to explain how acid rain is formed during industrial processes and the combustion of fuels in car engines, red for the negative effects of acid rain, green for how acid rain can be reduced, and yellow for how the negative effects of acid rain can be managed.	**Support:** Give students an outline diagram and the labels to colour code and then cut out and stick onto the diagram. **Extend:** Ensure that students include balanced symbol equations for the formation of acid rain.	**Activity:** Acid rain

Plenary	Support/Extend	Resources
Match (5 minutes) Provide students with a list of pollutants and a separate list of their effects. Students should match them up. The effects should include any health issues associated with the pollutants. **Atmospheric pollutants** (10 minutes) Students put statements in order to describe how acid rain is formed. they then complete a paragraph to describe the different health issues associated with pollutants.	**Extend:** Also provide a balanced symbol equation for the formation of each pollutant for students to match with the pollutants and their effects.	**Interactive:** Atmospheric pollutants

Homework	Support/Extend	Resources
Ask students to draw a labelled diagram to describe how acid rain is formed from industry pollution and car engines.	**Support:** Write word equations. **Extend:** Write balanced symbol equations with state symbols.	

kerboodle

A Kerboodle highlight for this lesson is **Literacy sheet: Atmospheric pollution**. Refer to the **Content map** on Kerboodle for a full list of resources and assessment.

C6.3.3 Climate change

Specification links:

6.3c Describe the greenhouse effect in terms of the interaction of radiation with matter within the atmosphere.

6.3d Evaluate the evidence for additional anthropogenic (human activity) causes of climate change and describe the uncertainties in the evidence base.

6.3e Describe the potential effects of increased levels of carbon dioxide and methane on the Earth's climate and how these effects may be mitigated.

WS1.1f Evaluate associated personal, social, economic, and environmental implications.

WS1.1h Evaluate risks both in practical science and the wider societal context.

CM6.3i Extract and interpret information from charts, graphs, and tables (M2c, M4a).

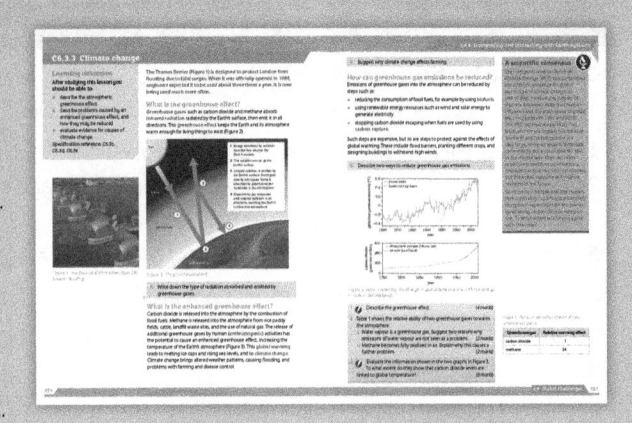

Target	Outcome	Checkpoint Question	Checkpoint Activity
Aiming for GRADE 4	State that the greenhouse effect keeps the Earth and its atmosphere warm enough for living things to exist.		Main 1 Plenary 1 and 2
	State that an increase in greenhouse gases is causing global warming.		Starter 2 Main 1 Plenary 1 and 2
	Describe the importance of reducing emissions of greenhouse gases.		Main 2 Homework
Aiming for GRADE 6	Describe the atmospheric greenhouse effect.	1	Main 1
	Explain the problems caused by an enhanced greenhouse effect.	B	Starter 1 Main 1 Homework
	Explain methods for reducing emissions of greenhouse gases.	C	Main 2 Homework
Aiming for GRADE 8	Explain the greenhouse effect in terms of the interaction of radiation with matter within the atmosphere.	A, 2	Main 1 Plenary 2
	Evaluate evidence for causes of climate change.	3	Starter 2 Main 1 Plenary 1 and 2
	Evaluate the effectiveness of methods for reducing greenhouse gas emissions.		Main 2 Plenary 2 Homework

Maths
In Main 2 students calculate their daily carbon footprint.

Literacy
In completing the Homework task students write a radio advert.

Key words
greenhouse gases, infrared radiation, greenhouse effect, anthropogenic, global warming, climate change, biofuels, carbon capture

C6.3 Interpreting and interacting with Earth Systems

Starter	Support/Extend	Resources
Polar ice (5 minutes) Show an image of the extent of the polar ice caps in 1800, 1900, 2000, and the present day. Ask students to speculate on what the images show. **Greenhouse gases** (10 minutes) Demonstrate an experiment to consider the effect of greenhouse gases. 1 Place 100 cm³ of water into each of two conical flasks. 2 Fill one flask with methane. 3 Seal each flask tightly with a bored bung holding a thermometer with its bulb in the water. 4 Put the flasks under a heat lamp. Ask students to predict what will happen to the temperature of each flask and suggest why they think this. Leave the experiment and return to it in Plenary 1.	**Support:** Use a data logger with a temperature probe and display the graph of the live data. **Extend:** Record the temperature every 5 minutes and ask students to plot a line graph of the results.	

Main	Support/Extend	Resources
The greenhouse effect (20 minutes) Give students an A4 sheet of paper and ask them to fold it in half. Students should entitle one half of the page 'Greenhouse effect (natural)' and the second 'Enhanced greenhouse effect (resulting from human activity)'. Ask students to draw a labelled diagram to explain each phenomenon. **Calculate your daily carbon footprint** (20 minutes) Ask students to make a list of all the daily activities that may contribute to their carbon footprint. There are a number of online calculators that can be used for this. Once they have calculated their carbon footprint, ask students to list three ways in which they could reduce their carbon footprint, and outline the steps they could take to achieve this.	**Extend:** Show students a black body radiation curve of the Earth and indicate which regions of the electromagnetic spectrum are absorbed by different gases in the atmosphere.	**Activity:** The greenhouse effect

Plenary	Support/Extend	Resources
More greenhouse gases (5 minutes) Return to the demonstration begun in Starter 2. Students should note that the temperature of the water in both flasks has risen, but the temperature of the water in the methane-filled flask has risen more than that in the air-filled flask. **The greenhouse effect** (10 minutes) Provide students with a list of statements about the greenhouse effect and the steps that can be taken to reduce greenhouse emissions. Students sort the statements according to whether they are true or false. They then label a diagram of the greenhouse effect to highlight the key points.	**Extend:** Students correct the false statements.	**Interactive:** The greenhouse effect

Homework	Support/Extend	Resources
Write a short radio jingle (no more than 1 minute) about the enhanced greenhouse effect, its impact on the Earth, and how people could change their lives to reduce the effect.		

kerboodle
A Kerboodle highlight for this lesson is **Working Scientifically: Evidence for global warming**. Refer to the **Content map** on Kerboodle for a full list of resources and assessment.

C6.3.4 Water for drinking

Specification links:

6.3g Describe the principal methods for increasing the availability of potable water in terms of the separation techniques used.

M2c Construct and interpret frequency tables and diagrams, bar charts, and histograms.

M4a Translate information between graphical and numeric form.

CM6.3i Extract and interpret information from charts, graphs, and tables (M2c, M4a).

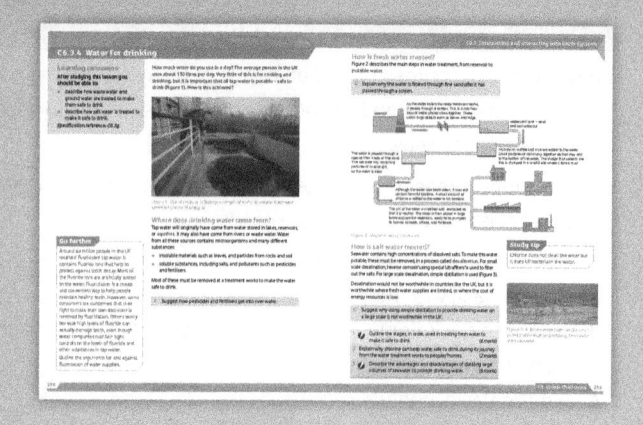

Target	Outcome	Checkpoint	
		Question	Activity
Aiming for GRADE 4 ↓	Describe where drinking water comes from.		Starter 1 and 2, Main, Homework
	State that water has to be treated before it is safe to drink.		Main, Plenary 1
	State that seawater can be made safe to drink using desalination to remove dissolved salts.		Main
Aiming for GRADE 6 ↓	Name the substances that are present in rivers and waste water.		Main
	Describe how ground water and waste water are treated in order to make them safe to drink.	B, 1, 2	Main, Plenary 1, Homework
	Describe how salt water is treated to make it safe to drink.		Main, Homework
Aiming for GRADE 8 ↓	Explain the sources of the substances present in rivers and waste water.	A	Main
	Evaluate the arguments for and against the fluoridation of drinking water.		Homework
	Evaluate the advantages and disadvantages of distilling large volumes of seawater to provide drinking water.	C, 3	Main, Homework

Maths
In Starter 2 students draw a pie chart and in Plenary 2 (Extend) students make a tally chart (M2c, M4a). In Plenary 2 students estimate how much water is used per person.

Literacy
In Plenary 1 students write a tweet about how water is treated.

Key words
aquifers, potable water, desalination

C6.3 Interpreting and interacting with Earth Systems

Starter	Support/Extend	Resources
Drinking water (5 minutes) Ask students to work in small groups to list all the possible sources of water for drinking. **Pie chart** (10 minutes) Ask students to draw a pie chart to show the percentages of fresh water and seawater on Earth (97% oceans and seas, 3% freshwater). Then ask students to consider how drinking water could be made from the available water.	**Support:** Display images of boreholes, wells, reservoirs, springs, and glaciers. **Extend:** Ask students to suggest where fresh water occurs on Earth, (e.g., lakes, rivers, glaciers).	

Main	Support/Extend	Resources
Analysis and purification of water samples (40 minutes) Ask students to write an outline method of how to use distillation to make pure water from salt water. Then allow pairs of students to set up a simple distillation apparatus to distil salt water. 1 Half-fill a large flask with salt water and add a few anti-bumping granules. 2 Connect up a condenser and a beaker to collect the distillate. Include a thermometer to measure the temperature of the vapour entering the condenser during the distillation. 3 Use a Bunsen burner to boil the salt water. (SAFETY: Wear eye protection.) Once students have collected the distillate, they should test the purity of the sample by measuring the boiling point (a pure sample will boil at 100 °C) and the pH.	**Extend:** Ask students to suggest how they could determine if there were other than sodium chloride in the original sample.	**Practical:** Analysis and purification of water samples

Plenary	Support/Extend	Resources
Water purification methods (5 minutes) Interactive activity in which students label a diagram of a simple distillation set-up. **Calculate your daily water use** (10 minutes) Ask students to use a water calculator (available on the Internet) to calculate how much water they each use on average each day.	**Extend:** Ask students to make a tally chart to display the class data.	**Interactive:** Water purification methods

Homework	Support/Extend	Resources
Design and complete a table to explain how the following water treatment processes work: distillation, desalination, filtering, sterilising. For each process, students should determine whether the resulting water is pure and potable or just potable.	**Support:** Provide a writing frame for students to complete. **Extend:** Ask students to tackle the task in Student Book section *Go further*, to outline the arguments for and against fluoridation of water supplies.	

kerboodle

A Kerboodle highlight for this lesson is **Literacy interactive: Water safe to drink**. Refer to the **Content map** on Kerboodle for a full list of resources and assessment.

Checkpoint

C6.3 Interpreting and interacting with Earth systems

Overview of C6.3 Interpreting and interacting with Earth systems

In this chapter students have studied the Earth's atmosphere. They should be able to describe its composition, and how it formed, including how an oxygen-rich atmosphere may have developed over time. They should be able to describe pollution in the atmosphere, including sources of carbon monoxide, particulates, sulfur dioxide, and oxides of nitrogen, and explain the problems caused by these pollutants to human health and to other living things.

In studying climate change, students should be able to describe the greenhouse effect, stating that it keeps the Earth and its atmosphere warm enough for living things to exist. They should be able to explain the problems caused by an enhanced greenhouse effect in terms of global warming and evidence for this, and recall ways of reducing emissions of greenhouse gases.

Students have studied drinking water, and should be able to describe how water is treated in order to make it safe to drink, including the desalination of seawater. They should be able to evaluate the arguments for and against the fluoridation of drinking water, and also describe how waste water is treated.

MyMaths

You can find additional support for the maths skills covered in this chapter on **MyMaths**, including plotting and interpreting graphs, and calculations using ratios and proportionality.

kerboodle

For this chapter, the following assessments are available on Kerboodle:
C6.3 Checkpoint quiz: Interpreting and interacting with Earth systems
C6.3 Progress quiz: Interpreting and interacting with Earth systems 1
C6.3 Progress quiz: Interpreting and interacting with Earth systems 2
C6.3 On your marks: Interpreting and interacting with Earth systems
C6.3 Exam-style questions and mark scheme: Interpreting and interacting with Earth systems

C6.3 Interpreting and interacting with Earth systems

Checkpoint follow-up lesson

A student's route through this lesson can be determined using the Checkpoint assessment. Percentage pass marks are supplied in the Checkpoint teacher notes.

For each successive route through it is assumed that the student can perform to their current route as well as previous routes. For example, students working at Aiming for 6 are assumed to be secure in Aiming for 4 knowledge and understanding and working towards achieving all the learning objectives for Aiming for 6.

	Aiming for 4	Aiming for 6	Aiming for 8
Learning outcomes	Describe how crude oil formed and describe why it is a finite resource.	Describe the difference between alkanes and alkenes and how they can be distinguished.	Describe in detail how fractional distillation and cracking are carried out on an industrial scale.
	Name and draw the first four alkanes.	Describe how fractional distillation takes place.	
	Describe how alkanes can be distinguished from alkenes.	Describe how cracking takes place and why it is an important industrial process.	
Starter	**Products from crude oil (5 minutes)** Ask students to come up with a list of products or substances that they use in everyday life that originate from crude oil.		
	Using fuels (10 minutes) Reiterate that crude oil provides us with numerous substances, including fuels. Carry out a practical of burning a fuel in a spirit burner, and passing the gases formed through limewater and an inverted U-tube containing calcium carbonate. Discuss that when hydrocarbon fuels burn they produce water and carbon dioxide, unless they do not have enough oxygen to react with and they will produce carbon monoxide.		
Differentiated checkpoint activity	Explain to students that they will be using the differentiated Checkpoint follow-up sheets and that this will involve them completing a series of tasks to revise the key material from the chapter.		
	Aiming for Grade 4 students will complete three tasks. First they order statements to describe how crude oil was formed. They then complete a table to summarise the name, formula, and structure of the first four alkanes. Finally they test substances to see whether they are alkanes or alkenes. They will need to be provided with the apparatus and chemicals required to test an alkene and an alkane with bromine water (or be shown a demonstration of this). It is up to you to carry out a full risk assessment before this practical and to decide on the suitability of this activity for your students.		
	Aiming for Grade 6 students will create a leaflet to summarise alkanes, alkenes, fractional distillation, and cracking.		
	Aiming for Grade 8 students create a leaflet on the processing of crude oil. Students should use the Internet or other resources to carry out research to include in their leaflets.		
	Kerboodle resource: C6.3 Checkpoint follow up: Aiming for 4, C6.3 Checkpoint follow up: Aiming for 6, C6.3 Checkpoint follow up: Aiming for 8		
Plenary	**Reviewing leaflets (5 minutes)** Ask students to lay their leaflets around the room. Students should then choose another person's leaflet to review. They should read the other person's leaflet and decide on two strong points about the leaflet and one point that could be improved on. Aiming for Grade 4 students should peer-assess each other's completed sheets, or mark their sheets against the correct answers if more appropriate for the ability level.		
	Key points (5 minutes) Ask students to decide as a pair three key learning points from the chapter. Review these as a class. Address any misconceptions should they arise.		
Progression	The Aiming for 4 checkpoint follow-up sheet is highly structured and provides students with detailed instructions and extra support for each task.	The Aiming for 6 checkpoint follow-up sheet provides a series of questions that students should aim to answer with their leaflet. For extra support, students could work in pairs.	The Aiming for 8 Checkpoint follow-up sheet provides brief guidance on what the leaflet should cover and students should be looking to work independently.

C6 Global Challenges 261

C6 Global challenges: Topic summary

C6.1 Improving processes and products
C6.2 Organic chemistry
C6.3 Interpreting and interacting with Earth Systems

Spec ref	Book spreads
C6.1a	C6.1.6, C6.1.7
C6.1b	C6.1.8
C6.1c	C6.1.9
C6.1d	C6.1.3, C6.1.3, C6.1.3 H S
C6.1e	C6.1.3, C6.1.3 H S
C6.1f	C6.1.5 H S
C6.1g	C6.1.1 S
C6.1h	C6.1.2 S
C6.1i	C6.1.15
C6.1j	C6.1.15
C6.1k	C6.1.16
C6.1l	C6.1.16
C6.1m	C6.1.10 S
C6.1n	C6.1.11 S
C6.1o	C6.1.12 S
C6.1p	C6.1.13, C6.1.14 S
C6.1q	C6.1.13, C6.1.14, C6.1.15 S
C6.2a	C6.2.1, C6.2.2, C6.2.3, C6.2.4 S
C6.2b	C6.2.1, C6.2.2, C6.2.3, C6.2.4 S

Spec ref	Book spreads
C6.2c	C6.2.1, C6.2.2, C6.2.3, C6.2.4 S
C6.2d	C6.2.7 S
C6.2e	C6.2.9 H S
C6.2f	C6.2.9 H S
C6.2g	S
C6.2h	C6.2.8 S
C6.2i	S
C6.2j	C6.2.5
C6.2k	C6.2.5
C6.2l	C6.2.5
C6.2m	C6.2.5, C6.2.6
C6.2n	C6.2.5, C6.2.6
C6.2o	
C6.2p	C6.2.10 S
C6.2q	C6.2.10 S
C6.3a	C6.3.1
C6.3b	C6.3.1
C6.3c	C6.3.3
C6.3d	C6.3.3
C6.3e	C6.3.3
C6.3f	C6.3.2
C6.3g	C6.3.4
C6.3h	S
C6.3i	S

Maths

Specification		Book spread	
Spec ref	Statement	Main content	Maths chapter
CM6.1i	Arithmetic computation, ratio when measuring rates of reaction	C6.1.6, C6.1.7	3
CM6.1ii	Drawing and interpreting appropriate graphs from data to determine rate of reaction		13, 14
CM6.1iii	Determining gradients of graphs as a measure of rate of change to determine rate	C6.1.3, C6.1.4	14 S
CM6.1iv	Proportionality when comparing factors affecting rate of reaction	C6.1.3	14 S
CM6.2i	Represent three-dimensional shapes in two dimensions and vice versa when looking at chemical structures, e.g. allotropes of carbon	C6.2.1, C6.2.2, C6.2.7, C6.2.8, C6.2.9	16 S
CM6.3i	Extract and interpret information from charts, graphs and tables	C6.3.1, C6.3.3, C6.3.4	6
CM6.3ii	Use orders of magnitude to evaluate the significance of data		8

Working Scientifically

Specification		Book spread	
Spec ref	Statement	Main content	WS chapter
WS1.1a	Understand how scientific methods and theories develop over time, to include new technology allowing new evidence to be collected and changing explanations as new evidence is found.	C6.1.9, C6.3.1	WS2
WS1.1b	Use models to solve problems, make predictions and to develop scientific explanations and understanding of familiar and unfamiliar facts.	C6.1.10, C6.2.9	WS2
WS1.1c	Understand the power and limitations of science.	C6.2.5, C6.2.6	WS1
WS1.1d	Discuss ethical issues arising from developments in science.	C6.1.5	WS1
WS1.1e	Explain everyday and technological applications of science.	C6.1.9, C6.1.13, C6.1.14, C6.1.15, C6.2.5, C6.2.6	WS1
WS1.1f	Evaluate associated personal, social, economic and environmental implications.	C6.1.16, C6.2.5, C6.3.3, C6.2.6	WS1
WS1.1g	Make decisions based on the evaluation of evidence and arguments.	C6.1.16, C6.2.10	WS1
WS1.1h	Evaluate risks both in practical science and in the wider societal context.	C6.3.3	WS1, WS4
WS1.1i	Recognise the importance of peer review of results and of communicating results to a range of audiences.	C6.2.10	WS2
WS1.2a	Use scientific theories and explanations to develop hypotheses.	C6.1.2, C6.2.9	WS3
WS1.2b	Plan experiments or devise procedures to make observations, produce or characterise a substance, test hypotheses, check data, or explore phenomena.	C6.1.2, C6.2.9	WS3, WS4
WS1.2c	Apply knowledge of a range of techniques, instruments, apparatus, and materials to select those appropriate to the experiment.	C6.1.2, C6.2.9	WS4
WS1.2d	Recognise when to apply knowledge of sampling techniques to ensure any samples collected are representative.	C6.1.2	
WS1.2e	Evaluate methods and suggest possible improvements and further investigations.	C6.1.2	
WS1.3e	Interpret observations and other data.	C6.1.3, C6.3.1	WS7
WS1.3f	Present reasoned explanations.	C6.1.3, C6.1.4, C6.1.13, C6.1.14, C6.1.15, C6.2.5	WS7
WS1.4a	Use scientific vocabulary, terminology, and definitions.	C6.1.1, C6.1.6, C6.1.7, C6.1.8, C6.2.1, C6.2.2, C6.2.3, C6.2.4, C6.2.6, C6.2.8, C6.2.9, C6.3.2	WS2
WS2a	Carry out experiments.	C6.1.9, C6.1.2, C6.1.10, C6.1.11, C6.1.12, C6.1.13, C6.2.9	
WS2b	Make and record observations and measurements, using a range of apparatus and methods.	C6.1.9, C6.1.10, C6.1.11, C6.1.12, C6.1.13, C6.1.2	
WS2c	Present observations using appropriate methods.	C6.1.11, C6.1.12, C6.1.13	
WS2d	Communicate the scientific rationale for investigations, methods used, findings, and reasoned conclusions.	C6.1.11, C6.1.12, C6.1.13	

C6 Global Challenges

C7 Practical skills
Practical activity groups
C1 Reactivity trend

Specification links:

PAG C1 Demonstrate safe use and careful handling of gases, liquids, and solids, including careful mixing of reagents under controlled conditions, using appropriate apparatus to explore chemical changes and/or products.

WS2a Carry out experiments.

WS2b Make and record observations and measurements using a range of apparatus and methods.

WS2c Present observations using appropriate methods.

WS2d Communicate the scientific rationale for investigations, methods used, findings, and reasoned conclusions.

M1c Use ratios, fractions, and percentages.

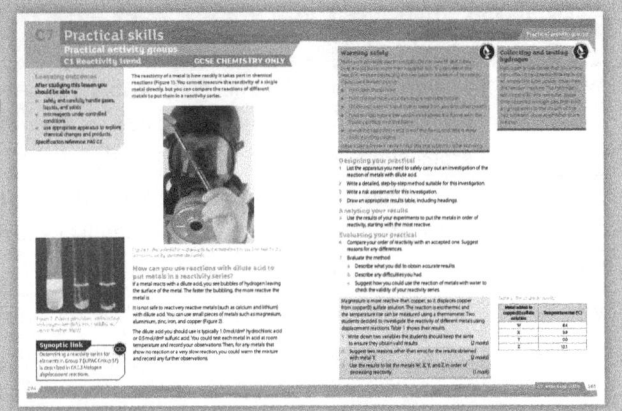

Target	Outcome	Checkpoint Question	Checkpoint Activity
Aiming for GRADE 4	Safely perform reactions between some metals and an acid.		Main
	Describe the products of the reaction between a metal and an acid as solid, liquid, or gas.		Starter 1 Starter 2 Main
	Describe some observations when reacting a metal with an acid.		Starter 1 Main
Aiming for GRADE 6	Perform reactions between a range of metals and an acid as directed.		Main
	Collect and test the products of the reaction between a metal and an acid.		Starter 1 Main
	Describe accurately observations when reacting metals with an acid, and place metals in an order of reactivity.	3	Main
Aiming for GRADE 8	Select metals to safely react with an acid, warming if necessary.		Main
	Collect, test, and identify the products of the reaction between a metal and an acid.		Starter 1 Starter 2 Main
	Describe accurately observations when reacting metals with an acid, and place metals in the correct order of reactivity.	3	Starter 1 Main

Maths

In Starter 1 (Extend) students use ratio to carry out calculations involving moles (M1c). In Plenary 1 (Extend) students suggest how to calculate rate of reaction.

Literacy

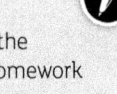

In the Main activity students write a detailed plan for the investigation of reactivity trends. In completing the Homework task students write a 'how-to' guide about handling gases, liquids, and solids safely.

Practical activity groups

Starter	Support/Extend	Resources
Make and test hydrogen (10 minutes) show students a picture of the experimental set-up for a test tube half-filled with hydrochloric acid and a piece of magnesium, with an inverted boiling tube of the top of a test tube. Ask students to predict what gas is being collected in the boiling tube (hydrogen) and what test they can carry out to confirm the identity of the gas (squeaky pop test).	**Extend:** Ask students to explain why the hydrogen does not escape from the open boiling tube as long as its mouth is facing downwards.	
Complete equations (5 minutes) Ask students to write a general word equation for the reaction of an acid with a metal. Students should then adapt this for the reaction of the metal with hydrochloric acid and with sulfuric acid.	**Extend:** Ask students to use mole calculations to show that $1\,mol/dm^3$ of hydrochloric acid will produce the same concentration of H^+ ions as $0.5\,mol/dm^3$ sulfuric acid.	

Main	Support/Extend	Resources
Reactivity trend (40 minutes) Carry out practical activity C1 *Reactivity trend* in the Student Book. First ask students to write a plan to investigate how different metals react with dilute acid. Students should identify the independent variable (different metals), the dependent variable (observations), and the control variables (type, volume, and concentration of acid). Students' plans should take the form of a step-by-step method, including safety information and a risk assessment. Once students' plans have been checked, ask them to carry out the practical, recording their results in an appropriate table. In a first lesson students could undertake planning and risk assessment and carry out the practical activity, A second lesson could be used for students to write a final report of the practical activity, including analysis and evaluation of results.	**Support:** Give students a writing frame that defines the key variable terms and suggests an outline method.	**Practical:** PAG C1 Reactivity trend

Plenary	Support/Extend	Resources
Qualitative to quantitative (10 minutes) Explain that students' observations from the Main activity, such as observing the reaction mixture bubbling, and hearing a squeaky pop, are qualitative. Ask them to suggest how quantitative data could be collected.	**Support:** Display examples of equipment, such as gas syringes or a balance, that could be used to measure the amount of gas produced. **Extend:** Ask students to suggest how the rate of reaction could be calculated for each reaction.	
Accuracy (5 minutes) Remind students that accuracy means how close to the truth results and/or conclusions are. Use questions and answers to determine where the 'truth' can be found (e.g., a textbook, a trusted website, a teacher). Then show students the reactivity series (see Student Book C4.1.6, Figure 2) and ask them to comment on the accuracy of their results.		

Homework	Support/Extend	Resources
Ask students to write a 'how-to' guide about handling gases, liquids, and solids safely.	**Support:** Ask students to write a guide for the specific substances they have used that day (e.g., hydrogen gas, hydrochloric acid solution, and calcium).	

C2 Electrolysis

Specification links:

PAG C2 Use appropriate apparatus and techniques to draw, set up, and use electrochemical cells for separation and production of elements and compounds.

PAG C2 Use appropriate qualitative reagents and techniques to analyse and identify unknown samples or products, including gas tests.

WS2a Carry out experiments.

WS2b Make and record observations and measurements using a range of apparatus and methods.

WS2c Present observations using appropriate methods.

WS2d Communicate the scientific rationale for investigations, methods used, findings, and reasoned conclusions.

M1c Use ratios, fractions, and percentages

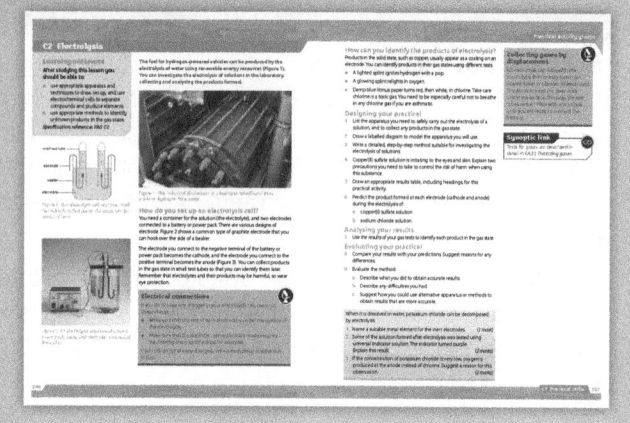

Target	Outcome	Checkpoint Question	Checkpoint Activity
Aiming for GRADE 4 ↓	Set up a simple electrolysis cell.		Main
	Identify the product at each electrode as a solid, a liquid, or a gas.		Starter 1 / Main
	Identify some of the products of electrolysis.	2	Starter 1 / Main / Plenary 1
Aiming for GRADE 6 ↓	Use a full range of apparatus to set up a suitable cell to collect the products of electrolysis.		Main
	Collect the products of electrolysis for testing.		Starter 1 / Main
	Use appropriate methods to identify the products of electrolysis.	2	Starter 1 / Main / Plenary 2
Aiming for GRADE 8 ↓	Use a full range of apparatus to set up an electrolysis cell and independently solve any problems with the functioning of the cell.	1	Starter 2 / Main / Plenary 2
	Independently collect all the products of electrolysis for testing.		Main
	Use appropriate methods to identify all the products produced at the anode and cathode of an electrolysis cell.	2, 3	Main / Plenary 2

Maths
In completing the Homework task students calculate percentage yield (M1c).

Literacy
In the Main activity students write a detailed plan for undertaking electrolysis.

266

Practical activity groups

Starter	Support/Extend	Resources
Hoffman voltameter (10 minutes) Demonstrate the Hoffman voltameter to electrolyse acidified water (SAFETY: wear eye protection). Tap off the gases and allow pairs of students to test them. You can use the same apparatus to electrolyse brine, and then test the chlorine gas that is produced. **Spot the mistake** (5 minutes) Show students a variety of electrolysis set-ups, each with a different problem (e.g., a solid electrolyte, electrodes touching each other, power supply not connected). Ask students to evaluate each set-up and suggest how the equipment could be modified so that it could be used for electrolysis.	**Extend:** Ask students to write the half equation for the process that occurs at each electrode.	

Main	Support/Extend	Resources
Electrolysis (40 minutes) Carry out practical activity C2 *Electrolysis* in the Student Book. First ask students to write a plan to investigate the electrolysis of copper(II) sulfate solution and of brine, and to collect and test the products. Students' plans should take the form of a step-by-step method, including safety information, along with a labelled diagram of an electrolytic cell and a risk assessment. Once students' plans have been checked, ask them to carry out the practical, recording their results in an appropriate table. SAFETY: Wear eye protection, Keep lab well ventilated. Warn asthmatics not to breathe in fumes. In a first lesson students could undertake planning and risk assessment and carry out the practical activity. A second lesson could be used for students to write a final report of the practical activity, including analysis and evaluation of results.	**Support:** Give students the statements for the method and ask them to order them. **Extend:** Task students with outlining how they can collect the products and determine which gases are produced.	**Practical:** PAG C2 Electrolysis

Plenary	Support/Extend	Resources
Petri dish electrolysis (10 minutes) Ask students to explain why, when a mixture of potassium chloride solution and universal indicator are connected to two carbon electrodes the universal indicator changes colour. Ask students to predict what the colour change will be. **Collection by displacement** (5 minutes) State that chlorine dissolves in water. Ask students to explain why displacement is not a suitable method for collecting this gas.	**Extend:** Ask students to write equations to model the processes that are taking place.	

Homework	Support/Extend	Resources
Ask students to suggest how they could modify the method in the electrolysis practical activity to calculate the percentage yield of the products.		

C3 Separation techniques

Specification links:

PAG C3 Safely use a range of equipment to purify and/or separate chemical mixtures, including distillation.

WS2a Carry out experiments.

WS2b Make and record observations and measurements using a range of apparatus and methods.

WS2c Present observations using appropriate methods.

WS2d Communicate the scientific rationale for investigations, methods used, findings, and reasoned conclusions.

M3c Substitute numerical values into algebraic equations using appropriate units for physical quantities.

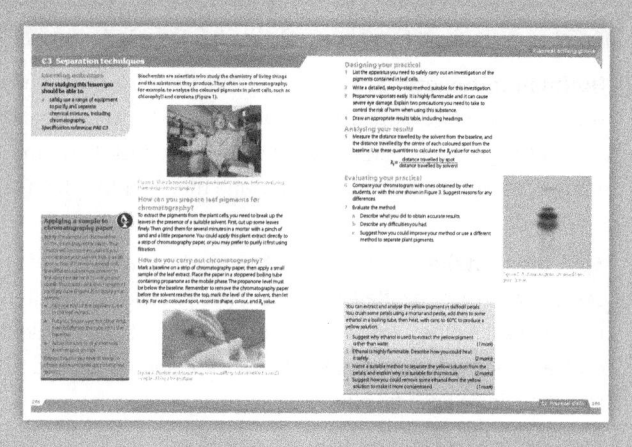

Target	Outcome	Checkpoint	
		Question	Activity
Aiming for GRADE 4 ↓	Apply given pigments or dyes to chromatography paper.		Main
	Carry out chromatography to separate the components of a pigment or dye.		Main
	Recognise the number of substances in a pigment or dye from the number of spots in the chromatography trace.		Main / Plenary 1
Aiming for GRADE 6 ↓	Follow instructions to prepare samples for chromatography and apply them to chromatography paper.		Main
	Use a chromatography tank with accuracy and precision to separate the components of a pigment or dye.		Main
	Accurately measure the distance travelled by each spot from the baseline.		Starter 2 / Main
Aiming for GRADE 8 ↓	Independently prepare samples for chromatography and use a capillary tube to apply them to chromatography paper.		Main
	Choose a suitable solvent and independently set up a chromatography tank to separate the components of a pigment or dye.		Main / Plenary 2
	Calculate the retention factor (R_f value) for each spot on a chromatogram.		Starter 2 / Main

Maths
In Starter 2 and in the Main activity, students calculate R_f values (M3c).

Literacy
In the Main activity students write a detailed method for extracting and separating the pigments in a leaf cell.

Practical activity groups

Starter	Support/Extend	Resources
Paper chromatography (10 minutes) Ask students to write a flow chart to describe how to carry out paper chromatography. **R_f factors** (5 minutes) Show students a sketch of a chromatogram with labels to the baseline, the distances from the baseline to the centres of separated spots, and the distance from the baseline to the solvent front. Ask students to use the formula shown in C2.1.6 *Calculating an R_f value* to calculate the retention factor for each substance.	**Extend:** Ask students to evaluate paper chromatography as a means of identifying substances.	

Main	Support/Extend	Resources
Separation techniques (40 minutes) Carry out practical activity C3 *Separation techniques* in the Student Book. First ask students to use the outline method provided in the Student Book to write a detailed method for extracting and separating the pigments in a leaf cell, including safety information. Once students' plans have been checked, ask them to carry out the practical. (SAFETY: Take care if using flammable materials.) Once the solvent front has passed the last separated spot, the chromatogram can be removed from the solvent tank. Students should mark the level of the solvent front using a pencil. The chromatogram can then be allowed to dry in the air. Once dry, students should measure the distance travelled by the solvent front and by each pigment spot. Ask students to record this data in a table and use it to calculate the R_f for each pigment. In a first lesson students could undertake planning and risk assessment, carry out the practical activity, and leave the chromatogram to dry. A second lesson could be used for students to write a final report of the practical activity, including analysis and evaluation of results.	**Support:** Provide students with the extracted pigments from plant cells.	**Practical:** PAG C3 Separation techniques

Plenary	Support/Extend	Resources
Explain (10 minutes) Explain that different substances are attracted to the solvent and to the paper to different degrees. Ask students to use this idea to explain how chromatography separates different pigments in leaf cells. **Choose a solvent** (5 minutes) Ask students to suggest how to choose a solvent to separate the pigments in nail polish.	**Support:** Provide an explanation as separate sentences for students to order. **Extend:** Encourage students to relate their explanation to the chromatogram that they have produced.	

Homework	Support/Extend	Resources
Ask students to explain how to make their paper chromatography results reliable (repeat the experiment until they get similar results, or another group gets similar results) and how they can check accuracy (look up R_f values from a trusted source).		

C7 Practical skills 269

C4 Distillation

Specification links:

PAG C4 Safely use a range of equipment to purify and/or separate chemical mixtures, including distillation.

PAG C4 Safely use appropriate heating devices and techniques, including use of a Bunsen burner and a water bath or electric heater.

PAG C4 Use appropriate apparatus to make and record a range of measurements accurately, including the measurement of temperature.

WS2a Carry out experiments.

WS2b Make and record observations and measurements using a range of apparatus and methods.

WS2c Present observations using appropriate methods.

WS2d Communicate the scientific rationale for investigations, methods used, findings, and reasoned conclusions.

M1c Use ratios, fractions, and percentages.

M3c Substitute numerical values into algebraic equations using appropriate units for physical quantities.

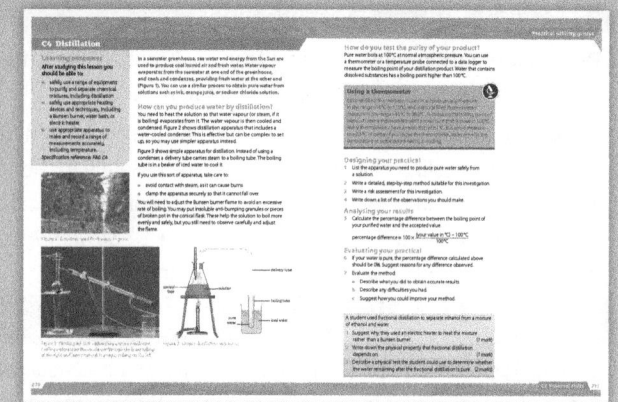

Target	Outcome	Checkpoint	
		Question	Activity
Aiming for GRADE 4 ↓	Safely light and use a Bunsen burner for heating.		Main
	Recognise distillation apparatus and state that it is used to separate mixtures.		Main
	Use a thermometer to record temperature.		Starter 1, Main
Aiming for GRADE 6 ↓	Use a Bunsen burner, water bath, or electric heater safely as directed.	1	Main
	Set up and use distillation apparatus as directed to separate a mixture.		Main
	Measure temperature accurately to ± 1 °C.		Starter 1, Main
Aiming for GRADE 8 ↓	Use a Bunsen burner, water bath, or electric heater safely, and independently decide when it is appropriate to use each.	1	Main
	Independently set up and use distillation apparatus to separate a mixture.		Main
	Measure temperature accurately to ± 0.5 °C and use this to evaluate the purity of a product.		Starter 2, Main, Plenary 2

Maths
In Plenary 2 students calculate percentage difference (M1c, M3c).

Literacy
In the Main activity students write a detailed plan to distil water and test the purity of the distillate.

270

Practical activity groups

Starter	Support/Extend	Resources
Types of thermometer (10 minutes) Show students different types of thermometer (e.g., clinical thermometer, mercury-filled thermometer, spirit-filled thermometer, infrared thermometer, temperature probe with data logger). Compare the use of each thermometer to measure the temperature, discussing the sensitivity, range, and accuracy of each. **Pure water** (5 minutes) Provide small groups of students with labelled samples of mineral water, distilled water, de-ionised water, tap water, and rainwater. Ask students to arrange the samples in order of purity. Then explain that only the distilled water is pure, as this is the only one that contains only water molecules.	**Extend:** Describe different scenarios and ask students to choose an appropriate thermometer to use. Students should suggest why their chosen thermometer is a good choice.	

Main	Support/Extend	Resources
Practical activity: Distillation (40 minutes) Carry out practical activity C4 *Distillation* in the Student Book. First ask students to write a plan to distil water and test the purity of the distillate. Students' plans should take the form of a step-by-step method, including a labelled diagram of a simple distillation set-up and safety information. Students should then write a second plan, to test the purity of the distillate. Once students' plans have been checked, ask them to carry out the practical, recording any key observations. (SAFETY: Wear eye protection.) In a first lesson students could undertake planning and risk assessment and carry out the practical activity. A second lesson could be used for students to write a final report of the practical activity, including analysis and evaluation of results.	**Support:** Provide statements describing the method and ask students to use these to annotate their diagram. **Extend:** Ask students to write an alternative method to check the purity of the distillate using the freezing point.	**Practical:** PAG C4 Distillation

Plenary	Support/Extend	Resources
Fractional distillation (10 minutes) Ask students to state the similarities and differences between simple distillation and fractional distillation. **Calculate percentage difference** (5 minutes) Ask students to use the formula in the Student Book to calculate the percentage difference between the boiling point observed in the Main activity and the actual boiling point for water. Students should comment on the accuracy of their results.	**Support:** Demonstrate the fractional distillation of an ethanol-water mixture. **Extend:** Ask students to write equations with state symbols to show the physical changes occurring.	

Homework	Support/Extend	Resources
Ask students to suggest how the simple distillation apparatus in Student Book C2.1.5 Figure 2 could be modified to increase the yield of the distillate.		

C5 Identification of species

Specification links:

PAG C5 Use appropriate qualitative reagents and techniques to analyse and identify unknown samples or products, including flame tests and precipitation reactions.

PAG C5 Safely use appropriate heating devices and techniques, including use of a Bunsen burner.

WS2a Carry out experiments.

WS2b Make and record observations and measurements using a range of apparatus and methods.

WS2c Present observations using appropriate methods.

WS2d Communicate the scientific rationale for investigations, methods used, findings, and reasoned conclusions.

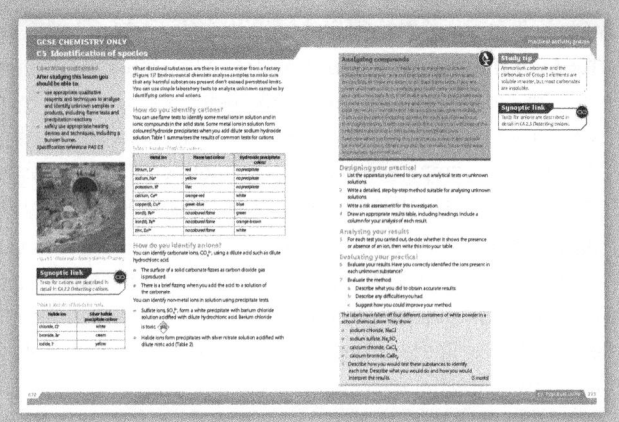

Target	Outcome	Checkpoint	
		Question	Activity
Aiming for GRADE 4 ↓	Perform flame tests and record the results.		Main
	Add sodium hydroxide solution to a solution containing a metal ion and record observations.		Main
	Use tests to identify some unknown anions.	1	Starter 1, Main
Aiming for GRADE 6 ↓	Perform flame tests and identify a wide range of metal ions.		Starter 2, Main
	Use sodium hydroxide solution to identify a wide range of metal ions in solution.		Main
	Follow instructions and perform tests to identify some unknown anions.		Starter 1, Main
Aiming for GRADE 8 ↓	Independently use the correct procedure to perform a flame test and use the results to identify a wide range of metal ions.		Main
	Independently use sodium hydroxide to identify a wide range of metal ions in solution.		Main
	Perform tests independently and with precision and accuracy to identify unknown anions.		Main, Plenary 2

Literacy

In the Main activity students write a detailed plan for the identification of species.

Practical activity groups

Starter	Support/Extend	Resources
Identify the halide (10 minutes) Tell students to imagine they have a sample of each sodium halide, silver nitrate solution, and dilute nitrate solution. Ask students to write a brief description of how they could identify the halide in the sodium halide solutions. **Guess the metal ion** (5 minutes) In a fume cupboard, carefully spray a mixture of ethanol and a metal salt solution into a blue Bunsen burner flame from a pump-operated spray bottle. Ask students to identify the metal from the colour of the resultant fireball.	**Support:** Prompt students to use Table 2 in the Student Book.	

Main	Support/Extend	Resources
Practical activity: Identification of species (40 minutes) Carry out practical activity C5 *Identification of species* in the Student Book. Ask students to write a plan to test first for the cation and then for the anion in an unknown solution. Encourage students to plan their method using a logical process. Students' plans should take the form of a step-by-step method, including safety information. Once students' plans have been checked, ask them to carry out the practical, recording their results in an appropriate table. Students should then use these results to identify the substance. (SAFETY: Wear eye protection.) In a first lesson students could undertake planning and risk assessment, and carry out the practical activity. A second lesson could be used for students to write a final report of the practical activity, including analysis and evaluation of results.	**Support:** Explain that as there is only one solute, once they have a positive result for an ion, no further testing needs to be done. **Extend:** Ask students to design a flow chart to show their method.	**Practical:** PAG C5 Identification of species

Plenary	Support/Extend	Resources
Predict (10 minutes) Ask students to predict the results of flame tests, precipitation tests, or the addition of dilute acid for the following solutions: 1 potassium chloride 2 iron(III) sulfate 3 copper(II) carbonate. **Red flames** (5 minutes) Lithium ions and calcium ions both produce red flames in a flame test. Ask students to outline an additional test to determine which of these ions is present in a solid sample.	**Support:** Focus students on Table 1 in the Student Book to make their predictions. **Extend:** Ask students to write equations to show the reactions occurring.	

Homework	Support/Extend	Resources
Ask students to write a procedure for the identification of ammonium ions.		

C6 Titration

Specification links:

PAG C6 Use appropriate apparatus and techniques for conducting and monitoring chemical reactions, including appropriate reagents and/or techniques for the measurement of pH in different situations.

PAG C6 Use appropriate qualitative reagents and techniques to analyse and identify unknown samples or products, including the determination of concentrations of strong acids and strong alkalis.

PAG C6 Use appropriate apparatus to make and record a range of measurements accurately, including volumes of liquids.

WS2a Carry out experiments.

WS2b Make and record observations and measurements using a range of apparatus and methods.

WS2c Present observations using appropriate methods.

WS2d Communicate the scientific rationale for investigations, methods used, findings, and reasoned conclusions.

M1c Use ratios, fractions, and percentages.

M2a Use an appropriate number of significant figures.

M2b Find arithmetic means.

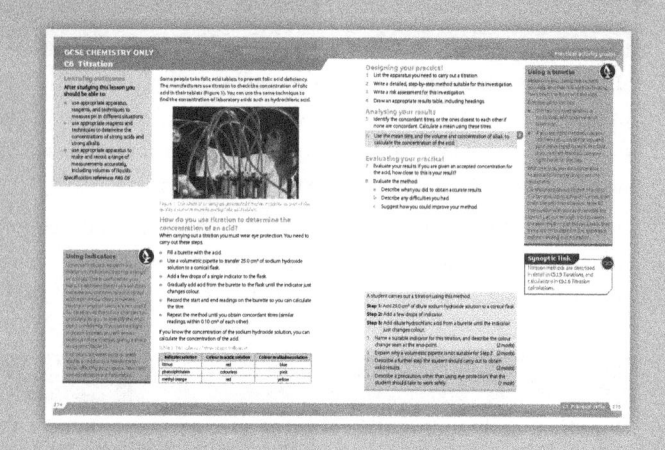

Target	Outcome	Checkpoint	
		Question	Activity
Aiming for GRADE 4 ↓	Make some progress in carrying out an acid–alkali titration.		Main
	Record some data when carrying out an acid–alkali titration.		Starter 1, Main
	Describe some steps taken in an acid–alkali titration to ensure that the results are accurate.	2, 3	Starter 2, Main
Aiming for GRADE 6 ↓	Perform an acid–alkali titration and obtain a titre value.		Main
	Record initial and final burette readings and calculate a titre value.		Main
	Make some progress in titration calculations.		Plenary 1
Aiming for GRADE 8 ↓	Perform an acid–alkali titration to obtain concordant titre values.		Main
	Record initial and final burette readings to two decimal places and select suitable titres to calculate a precise mean titre.		Starter 1, Main
	Use titration data to calculate the concentration of an unknown acid or alkali and fully evaluate the experimental procedure.		Plenary 1, Plenary 2

Maths
In the Main activity students record readings to an appropriate number of decimal places and calculate the mean (M2a, M2b). In Plenary 1 students calculate the concentration of an acid (M1c).

Literacy
In the Main activity students write a detailed plan for titration.

Practical activity groups

Starter	Support/Extend	Resources
Results table (10 minutes) Ask students to draw a results table for a titration, to record a rough result and results for up to four runs. **Acid or base?** (5 minutes) Show students the stock bottles of a concentrated acid (clean neck) and a concentrated alkali (white solid deposits on the neck). Then ask students to suggest why the acid and not the alkali should be put in a burette (deposits from the alkali could clog up the tap).	**Extend:** Ask students to explain how concordant results improve reliability (reproducibility).	

Main	Support/Extend	Resources
Practical activity: Titration (40 minutes) Carry out practical activity C6 *Titration* in the Student Book. First ask students to use the outline plan provided in the Student Book to write a detailed plan to titrate a strong acid such as hydrochloric acid of unknown concentration against 25 cm^3 of 0.1 mol/dm^3 sodium hydroxide solution. Students' plans should take the form of a step-by-step method, including safety information. Once students' plans have been checked, ask them to carry out the practical, recording their results in an appropriate table. (SAFETY: Wear eye protection. CLEAPSS Hazcard 047A; 091.) In a first lesson students could undertake planning and risk assessment and carry out the practical activity. A second lesson could be used for students to write a final report of the practical activity, including analysis and evaluation of results.	**Support:** Give students statements with missing information for them to fill in, such as the reagents, volumes, and names of equipment. **Extend:** Encourage students to stop titrating when they have two concordant results only.	**Practical:** PAG C6 Titration

Plenary	Support/Extend	Resources
Calculate acid concentration (10 minutes) Students should use their mean titre, the concentration and volume of the sodium hydroxide solution, and the balanced symbol equation to calculate the concentration of the acid titrated in the Main activity. **Which indicator?** (5 minutes) Display a titration curve for a weak acid and a strong base. On it, mark the position where methyl orange and phenolphthalein change colour. Ask students to explain which of these two indicators is suitable for the titration depicted in the titration curve.	**Support:** Provide students with the calculation steps with blanks for them to fill in with the readings from their experiment. **Extend:** Ask students to write an ionic equation for the reaction.	

Homework	Support/Extend	Resources
Ask students to make a list of procedural problems that could lead to an incorrect volume being recorded from a burette (e.g., an air bubble in the tap, leaving the funnel in the top, parallax error when reading the scale).		

C7 Production of salts

Specification links:

PAG C7 Safely use a range of equipment to purify and/or separate chemical mixtures including evaporation, filtration and crystallisation

PAG C7 Use of appropriate apparatus to make and record a range of measurements accurately, including mass and volume of liquids

PAG C7 Use and handle gases, liquids, and solids safely and carefully, including careful mixing of reagents under controlled conditions, using appropriate apparatus to explore chemical changes and/or products.

WS2a Carry out experiments.

WS2b Make and record observations and measurements using a range of apparatus and methods.

WS2c Present observations using appropriate methods.

WS2d Communicate the scientific rationale for investigations, methods used, findings, and reasoned conclusions.

M1c Use ratios, fractions, and percentages.

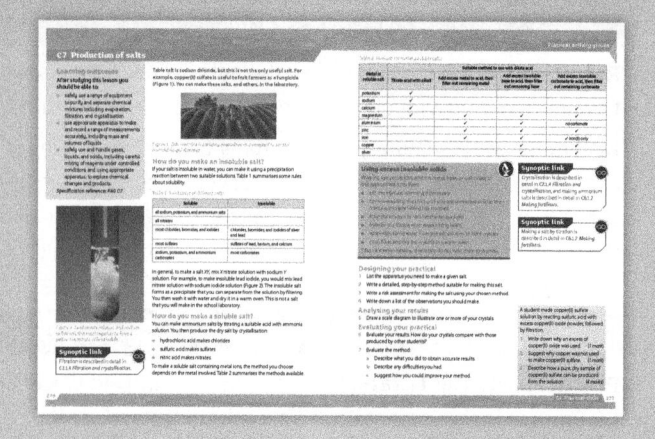

Target	Outcome	Checkpoint Question	Checkpoint Activity
Aiming for GRADE 4	Carry out a reaction to produce an insoluble salt.		Starter 1 Main
	Carry out a reaction to produce a soluble salt.		Main
	Describe measures taken to obtain accurate results.	1, 2, 3	Main
Aiming for GRADE 6	Follow instructions to prepare a sample of an insoluble salt.		Starter 1
	Follow instructions to prepare a sample of a soluble salt.		Main
	Describe measures taken to obtain accurate results and suggest improvements to the method.	1, 2, 3	Main Plenary 1
Aiming for GRADE 8	Independently prepare a pure sample of an insoluble salt.		Main
	Independently prepare a pure sample of a soluble salt.		Main
	Fully evaluate the method used to prepare a salt.		Starter 1 Main Plenary 1

Maths
In the Main activity (Extend) students calculate percentage yield (M1c).

Literacy
In the Main activity students write a detailed plan for the production of a salt. In completing the Homework task students design a flow chart.

Practical activity groups

Starter	Support/Extend	Resources
Make an insoluble salt (10 minutes) Ask students to write an equation for the precipitation reaction between sodium iodide solution and lead nitrate solution. Encourage students to outline how they would collect a dry sample of the salt. **Sort** (5 minutes) Read out examples of salts and ask students to say whether they are soluble in water or are insoluble in water.	**Extend:** Ask students to write an ionic equation for the reaction. **Support:** Refer students to Table 1 in the Student Book.	

Main	Support/Extend	Resources
Practical activity: Production of salts (40 minutes) Carry out practical activity C7 *Production of salts* in the Student Book. First ask students to use the outline plan provided in the Student Book to write a detailed plan to make salts by reacting a metal, an alkali, and a metal carbonate with hydrochloric acid. Students' plans should take the form of a step-by-step method, including safety information. Once students' plans have been checked, ask them to carry out the practical to prepare and collect samples of salts. SAFETY: As lead salts are toxic, chemical splash-proof eye protection should be worn. CLEAPSS Hazcard 057A. In a first lesson students could undertake planning and risk assessment and carry out the practical activity. A second lesson could be used for students to write a final report of the practical activity, including analysis and evaluation of results.	**Support:** Provide calcium, calcium carbonate, and calcium hydroxide for students to react with hydrochloric acid, so that they use the same metal each time. **Extend:** Ask students to use mole calculations to determine the percentage yield of each experiment.	**Practical:** PAG C7 Production of salts

Plenary	Support/Extend	Resources
Justify the method (10 minutes) Ask pairs of students to place a piece of calcium carbonate in a test-tube half-filled with dilute sulfuric acid, repeat with dilute hydrochloric acid of the same concentration and volume, and compare the reactions. Students to explain the observation made (calcium sulfate is insoluble and forms a layer on the calcium carbonate, preventing it from completing the reaction with sulfuric acid). Ask students to suggest a more suitable method to make calcium sulfate. CLEAPSS Hazcards 047A; 098A. **Equations** (5 minutes) Ask students to write equations for all the reactions that they have studied. Foundation candidates should write only word equations; most candidates should write balanced symbol equations; and the most able could write ionic equations.	**Support:** Provide students with the word equations for the two reactions, annotated to show which substances are soluble and which are insoluble. **Extend:** Ask students to write an ionic equation for the reaction.	

Homework	Support/Extend	Resources
Ask students to design a flow chart to explain how to make all the different dry salts detailed in Table 1 in the Student Book.		

C7 Practical skills

C8 Measuring rates of reaction

Specification links:

PAG C8 Use appropriate apparatus to make and record a range of measurements accurately, including mass, time, and volumes of liquids and gases.

PAG C8 Make and record appropriate observations during chemical reactions, including the measurement of rates of reaction by a variety of methods such as production of gas and colour change.

WS2a Carry out experiments.

WS2b Make and record observations and measurements using a range of apparatus and methods.

WS2c Present observations using appropriate methods.

WS2d Communicate the scientific rationale for investigations, methods used, findings, and reasoned conclusions.

M4a Translate information between graphical and numeric form.

M4b Understand that $y = mx + c$ represents a linear relationship.

M4c Plot two variables from experimental or other data.

M4d Determine the slope and intercept of a linear graph.

M4e Draw and use the slope of a tangent to a curve as a measure of rate of change.

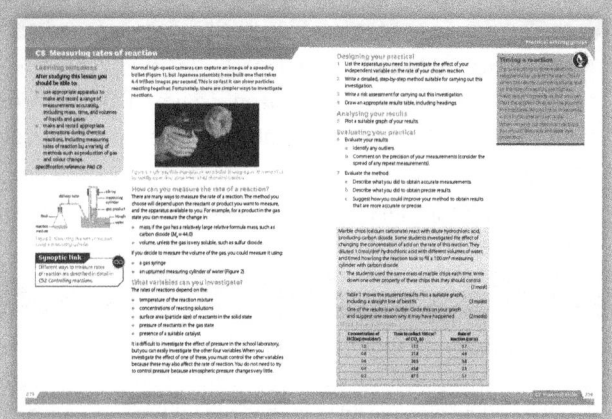

Target	Outcome	Checkpoint	
		Question	Activity
Aiming for GRADE 4 ↓	Describe at least one method of measuring the rate of a reaction.		Main Plenary 1
	Make some steps in carrying out experiments to measure reaction rates.		Starter 2 Main
	Describe the outcome of a rate experiment in simple terms.		Main Plenary 1
Aiming for GRADE 6 ↓	Describe methods that can be used to measure the rate of a reaction.		Main Plenary 1
	Carry out experiments to investigate how different variables affect reaction rate.	1	Starter 2 Main
	Plot a suitable graph and describe how the reaction rate has been affected by the variable under investigation.	2	Main Homework
Aiming for GRADE 8 ↓	Describe in detail methods that can be used to measure the rate of a reaction.		Main Plenary 1
	Design experiments to investigate in detail how different variables affect reaction rate.	1	Starter 2 Main Plenary 1
	Plot results to produce a graph of rate versus the variable under investigation, and fully justify conclusions.	2, 3	Main Homework

Maths
In completing the Homework task students plot and interpret a graph to find the rate of reaction (M4a, M4b, M4c, M4d, M4e).

Literacy
In the Main activity students write a detailed plan for measuring rate of reaction.

278

Practical activity groups

Starter	Support/Extend	Resources
Slow-mo whoosh (10 minutes) Explain that it is easier to measure the rate of some reactions than others. Ask students to create a list of key features a reaction needs to make recording the rate easy, for example, needs to be enough to measure but not too slow, needs to have a property that changes and can be measured (colour, pH, etc).		
Choose the set-up (5 minutes) Give students descriptions of different reactions, including what the state of the reactants and products and any other key properties (i.e., precipitate formed, colour change, or change in pH, etc). Ask students to suggest a method that could be used to measure the rate of reaction.	**Extend:** Only give students word equations and balanced symbol equations for the reactions.	

Main	Support/Extend	Resources
Practical activity: Measuring rates of reaction (40 minutes) Carry out practical activity C8 *Measuring rates of reaction* in the Student Book. First ask students to write a plan to react magnesium ribbon pieces with different concentrations of hydrochloric acid, and to measure the rate of reaction by monitoring the volume of gas produced every 10 seconds for a few minutes, or by calculating the mass change. Students' plans should take the form of a step-by-step method, including safety information, focusing on variables and measuring equipment. Once students' plans have been checked, ask them to carry out the practical, recording their results in an appropriate table. (SAFETY: Wear eye protection. CLEAPSS Hazcards 059A; 047A; 048.) In a first lesson students could undertake planning and risk assessment and carry out the practical activity. A second lesson could be used for students to write a final report of the practical activity, including analysis and evaluation of results.	**Support:** Ask students to draw a labelled diagram of their planned apparatus, annotating it with information about the reaction and how it will be monitored. **Extend:** Ask students to investigate more than one variable from the list in the Student Book.	**Practical:** PAG C8 Measuring rates of reaction

Plenary	Support/Extend	Resources
Outline a method (10 minutes) Students should suggest an outline method to monitor how the rate of reaction between magnesium and dilute hydrochloric acid changes when the surface area of the magnesium is varied.	**Support:** Show students magnesium as ribbon, turnings, and powder.	
Dilute and strong (5 minutes) Show students concentrated orange squash, and then dilute it. Show students a bottle of vinegar and a bottle of sulfuric acid. Ask students to point to the strong acid and the weak acid, and to a dilute solution and a concentrated solution. Tackle any misconceptions.	**Extend:** Ask students to write ionic equations for the strong acid and weak acid.	

Homework	Support/Extend	Resources
Ask students to sketch a graph to determine the rate of reaction for calcium carbonate reacting with hydrochloric acid. Students should annotate their graphs to show how to calculate the rate of reaction using tangents to the curve.		

Answers

C1.1 The particle model

C1.1.1 In-text questions
A Atoms, ions, molecules
B The distance between the particles (they are close in the liquid state but far apart in the gas state)
C Particles in the gas state have space to move into.

C1.1.1 Using maths: Drawing 3D objects
A 2D diagram is easy to draw but only shows one layer of particles. An isometric diagram shows more layers of particles and gives a sense of depth, but is difficult to draw and some particles are hidden.

C1.1.1 Spread questions
1 Particles in a gas can move in all directions. *(2 marks)*
2 Particles in a liquid can move around each other. *(2 marks)*
3 The space between the particles increases (the particles stays the same size). *(2 marks)*

C1.1.2 In-text questions
A Freezing juice – reverse by warming the ice (water in its solid state) until it melts. Mixing sand with water – reverse using a funnel and filter paper. Dissolving sugar in water – reverse by evaporating the water.
B Any two reasonable answers, for example burning wood and burning magnesium.
C The C and H particles (atoms) in methane, and the O particles (atoms) in oxygen, must separate from one another.

C1.1.2 Literacy – Chemical: noun or adjective?
All substances are chemicals. The shampoo itself must be a mixture of chemicals.

C1.1.2 Go further: Making cupcakes
Mixing the cake ingredients and icing ingredients together are both physical changes, since no new substances are made. Cooking the cake ingredients is a chemical change, since new substances are made. Baking powder contains sodium bicarbonate and one or more acid salts. The sodium bicarbonate, acid salts, and water will react together in the cake mixture to produce carbon dioxide, which lightens and softens the mixture.

C1.1.2 Spread questions
1 Three chemical changes, e.g. cooking an egg, steel nail going rusty, making a salt and water from an acid and an alkali, methane burning. *(6 marks)*
Three physical changes, e.g. melting an ice cube, mixing sand with water, boiling water.
2 In a chemical change new substances are made, but not in a physical change. Many physical changes are easy to reverse but many chemical changes are not. *(2 marks)*
3 In a chemical change, the particles break up and then join together in different ways, such as when methane reacts with oxygen to form carbon dioxide and water. In a physical change, the particles stay the same but their arrangement and movement may change, such as when water freezes to form ice. *(6 marks)*

C1.1.3 In-text questions
A $1.27 \times 10^7 \div 1 \times 10^9 = 1.27 \times 10^{-2} = 0.0127$ m
B 330 mm
   Need a large area for the drawing.
C $55 \times 6 = 330$ mm (this will only fit on a sheet of A4 paper from corner to corner).
D Electrostatic forces of attraction

C1.1.3 Using maths: The space between atoms
$$\frac{(5.1 \times 10^{-9}\,\text{m})}{(6.0 \times 10^{-10}\,\text{m})} = 8.5$$

C1.1.3 Spread questions
1 No forces shown. Particles in the gas are too close together. *(3 marks)*
2 The distances are only a little more in the liquid. The forces are only a little weaker in the liquid. *(2 marks)*
3 The water particles are not packed close together in ice; they are further apart in the solid than the liquid. Solid state, because the particles are in fixed positions. *(3 marks)*

C1.2 Atomic structure

C1.2.1 In-text questions
A The 2 in O_2 shows that an oxygen molecule contains two oxygen atoms. Carbon dioxide molecules also contain one carbon atom, so their formula is CO_2.
B The nucleus would be too small to see.
C The nucleus contains protons and neutrons, which have a much higher mass than electrons.

C1.2.1 Using maths – How big are atoms, molecules, and bonds?
Diameter of oxygen atom = $2 \times 0.073 = 0.146$ nm
Oxygen–oxygen bond length = 0.121 nm
The atoms are bigger than the distance between their centres. The atoms must be squashed together.

C1.2.1 Spread questions
1 An atom has a positively charged nucleus consisting of protons and neutrons, surrounded by negatively charged electrons. *(6 marks)*
2 $+1.60 \times 10^{-19}$ C *(1 mark)*
3 $\frac{(1.673 \times 10^{-27}\,\text{kg})}{(9.109 \times 10^{-31}\,\text{kg})} = 1837$ times greater (to four significant figures)
So the relative mass for an electron is 0.000 544 5 to four significant figures. Table 1 gives values to one significant figure, so this agrees with the table as it is 0.0005 to one significant figure. *(4 marks)*

C1.2.2 In-text questions
A 6 protons, 6 electrons
B 12 neutrons
C <not 4.>
   $^{1}_{1}$H has 1 proton, 0 neutrons, and 1 electron.
   $^{2}_{1}$H has 1 proton, 1 neutron, and 1 electron.
   $^{3}_{1}$H has 1 proton, 2 neutrons, and 1 electron.

C1.2.2 Using maths: Calculating the number of neutrons
$23 - 11 = 12$ neutrons

C1.2.2 Spread questions
1 Atomic number is the number of protons in the nucleus of an atom. Mass number is the total number of protons and neutrons in the nucleus of an atom. Isotopes of an element are atoms with the same numbers of protons and electrons, but different numbers of neutrons (or same atomic number but different mass number). Ions are charged particles formed when atoms lose or gain electrons. *(6 marks)*
2 $^{16}_{8}$O has 8 protons, 8 neutrons, and 8 electrons.
   $^{18}_{8}$O has 8 protons, 10 neutrons, and 8 electrons.

Answers

$^{56}_{26}$Fe has 26 protons, 30 neutrons, and 26 electrons.
$^{56}_{26}$Fe^{2+} has 26 protons, 30 neutrons, and 24 electrons. *(12 marks)*

3   Although their mass numbers are the same, their atomic numbers are different, so they must be different elements.
X has 18 protons, 22 neutrons, and 18 electrons.
Y has 20 protons, 20 neutrons, and 20 electrons. *(2 marks)*

C1.2.3 In-text questions

A   Atoms of an element are identical in that they contain the same numbers of protons and electrons, but they can be different because isotopes with different numbers of neutrons exist. The atoms of different elements contain different numbers of protons and electrons, but they can be similar in that they may contain the same number of neutrons.
B   Protons and neutrons had not been discovered then.
C   The blindfolded player will move through the field without hitting anything, but they will bump into the picnic basket every so often.
D   Bohr used mathematical models but the other scientists carried out experiments.

C1.2.3 Working scientifically: Developing theories

The plum-pudding model was rejected. An atomic model containing a nucleus was proposed. Niels Bohr was then able to work out that electrons must occupy energy levels or shells.

C1.2.3 Go further: Protons and neutrons

Proton: 1917, Ernest Rutherford
Neutron: 1932, James Chadwick (he had previously worked with Rutherford).

C1.2.3 Spread questions

1   It was difficult to obtain evidence that atoms existed because they could not do the experiments needed then. *(1 mark)*
2   Helium is $\frac{4}{2}$He, so an alpha particle contains two protons and two neutrons. *(2 marks)*
3   They knew the alpha particles and electrons have opposite charges and that the electrons do not have enough mass to push alpha particles away. If electrons are negatively charged, the nucleus must be positively charged. *(4 marks)*

C2.1 Purity and separating mixtures

C2.1.1 In-text questions

A   Helium is 4 and titanium is 48. The mass of three helium atoms equals the mass of a carbon atom, so if the A_r of carbon is 12, the A_r of helium must be 12 ÷ 3 = 4. The mass of one titanium atom equals the mass of four carbon atoms, so if the A_r of carbon is 12, the A_r of titanium must be 4 × 12 = 48.
B   Methane molecules each contain one carbon atom and four hydrogen atoms.
C   N = 2, H = 8, S = 1, O = 4
D M_r of H$_2$O = 18, M_r of CH$_4$ = 16, M_r of Al$_2$(SO$_4$)$_3$ = 342

C2.1.1 Using maths: Brackets in chemical formulae

2 N atoms, 8 H atoms, 1 S atom, 4 O atoms

C2.1.1 Spread questions

1   A_r of N = 14, *(1 mark)*
    A_r of Cl = 35.5, *(1 mark)*
    A_r of Na = 23 *(1 mark)*
2   M_r of O$_2$ = 32, *(1 mark)*
    M_r of CO$_2$ = 44, *(1 mark)*
    M_r of NH$_3$ = 17, *(1 mark)*
    M_r of NaCl = 58.5 *(1 mark)*
3   M_r of Al(OH)$_3$ = 78, *(1 mark)*
    M_r of (NH$_4$)$_2$CO$_3$ = 96 *(1 mark)*

C2.1.2 In-text questions

A   PbO$_2$
B   C$_2$H$_4$O
C   In order left to right: 36.5 / 40.0 / 58.5 / 18.0
D   M stands for molecular. It could be misleading because not all substances exist as molecules

C2.1.2 Spread questions

1   S *(1 mark)*, CH$_2$ *(1 mark)*, CH$_2$O *(1 mark)*
2   M_r of CuO = 79.5, *(1 mark)*
    M_r of HNO$_3$ = 63, *(1 mark)*
    M_r of H$_2$O = 18 *(1 mark)*
3   M_r of copper nitrate = 79.5 + (2 × 63) − 18 *(1 mark)*
    = 187.5 *(1 mark)*

C2.1.3 In-text questions

A   A scientist would say that it is impure because it is a mixture of substances.
B   Answer should include: mixture looks better, tastes better, is easier to swallow.
C   The melting point of the ring gold is different from the melting point of pure gold, and it melts over a range of temperatures. Pure gold melts at one temperature which can be measured accurately.

C2.1.3 Practical activity: Determining melting point

Answer should include: slow heating allows the temperature of the whole sample to increase, mixing ensures that the sample is all at the same temperature.

C2.1.3 Spread questions

1   The water still contains other substances *(1 mark)*
    not just water. *(1 mark)*
2   Sea water contains a lot of dissolved salt *(1 mark)*
    and is more impure than fresh water. *(1 mark)*
3   The steels are not pure iron *(1 mark)*
    because their melting points are different to pure iron. *(1 mark)*
    Adding carbon reduces the melting point of iron *(1 mark)*
    because the melting points of the steel are all lower than iron. *(1 mark)*
    The more carbon is added, the greater the difference in melting point. *(1 mark)*
    Example given, e.g. 0.2% carbon gives 1466 °C but 1.6% carbon gives 1352 °C. *(1 mark)*

C2.1.4 In-text questions

A   Solvent: water Solute: copper sulfate
B   Copper oxide must be insoluble if it is black and you get a black residue. Copper sulfate is soluble, so its particles are small enough to pass through the filter paper.
C   The solubility of the solute or crystals decreases as the temperature goes down.

C2.1.4 Spread questions

1   Filtration removes insoluble impurities such as sand. *(1 mark)*
    The salts are dissolved *(1 mark)*
    so their particles are small enough to pass through the filter paper with the water. *(1 mark)*
2   Answer should include the points for one mark each, to 6 marks maximum:
    add copper oxide to sulfuric acid
    filter mixture
    to remove any unreacted copper oxide
    heat the filtrate
    to remove water
    stop heating (when it becomes saturated) so that crystals form
    filter the crystals
    dry the crystals with an oven or paper.

281

3   Answer should include these points for one mark each, to 4 marks maximum:
add the mixture to ethanol
until all the sugar is dissolved
filter the mixture
to remove the undissolved sodium chloride
evaporate the water (to produce sugar).

C2.1.5 In-text questions
A   100 °C because that is the boiling point of water.
B   Ethanol is flammable (it is used as a fuel), so it could catch fire with a flame.
C   Ethanol has the lower boiling point so its vapours reach the top of the fractionating column without condensing. Water has the higher boiling point so it condenses on the cooler part of the fractionating column.

C2.1.5 Spread questions
1   Boiling point *(1 mark)*
2   The water leaves the ink but the pigment does not *(1 mark)*
    the pigment gets more concentrated *(1 mark)*
    so the colour of the ink gets darker.
3   When the ethanol has left the mixture, the temperature of the fractionating column increases *(1 mark)*
    until water vapour is able to reach the top without condensing. *(1 mark)*

C2.1.6 In-text questions
A   to prevent the solvent dissolving the sample out of the paper
B $R_f = \frac{3}{12} = 0.25$

C2.1.6 Spread questions
1   a C2 is in the drink *(1 mark)*
       because it has the same R_f as one of the spots in the drink. *(1 mark)*
    b The drink contains one more substance *(1 mark)*
       which is not one of the three permitted colours. *(1 mark)*
    c R_f for C1 = 0.42, *(1 mark)*
       R_f for C3 = 0.90 *(1 mark)*
2   Three similarities for one mark each, to three marks maximum:
    both involve a mobile phase and a stationary phase
    the stationary phase is silica or alumina
    both separate the components in mixtures
    the separation in both depends on the distribution between the phases.
    Three differences for one mark each, to three marks maximum:

Feature	Thin-layer chromatography	Gas chromatography
mobile phase	solvent	carrier gas
chromatogram shows	R_f values	travel times
temperature	room temperature	high (in an oven)
analysis	just separates components	also measures amounts
detection	visual	a detector

3   Helium is unreactive or inert, *(1 mark)*
    but oxygen would react with the sample. *(1 mark)*

C2.1.7 In-text questions
A   The brown colouring has produced three different coloured spots (blue, red, and yellow).
B   Each peak represents a different substance, and there is more than one peak in the chromatogram.
C   Copper sulfate is soluble in water but glass is insoluble, so the copper sulfate dissolves but the glass does not. During filtration, the glass stays behind as a residue. The water can be removed by evaporation during crystallisation of the filtrate to leave copper sulfate crystals.
D   The mixture swept up from the floor may have contained other substances that are soluble in water (and so would form part of the filtrate).

C2.1.7 Working scientifically: Information from a gas chromatogram
The chromatograms contain more than one peak, so the wax must have contained more than one substance.

C2.1.7 Spread questions
1   Fractional distillation, *(1 mark)*
    because this method relies on substances in the liquid state having different boiling points. *(1 mark)*
2   Each colour itself might contain two more different substances with the same R_f value *(1 mark)*
    and colour. *(1 mark)*
    The scientist could use gas chromatography to check; *(1 mark)*
    if the colour produces more than one peak it is impure. *(1 mark)*
3   Mix the leaves with propanone to dissolve the pigments. *(1 mark)*
    Filter to remove any pieces of leaf. *(1 mark)*
    Use paper chromatography / thin layer chromatography, *(1 mark)*
    with propanone as the mobile phase. *(1 mark)*

C2.2 Bonding

C2.2.1 In-text questions
A   Mercury is the only metal that is liquid at room temperature, and bromine is the only non-metal that is liquid at room temperature.
B   Carbon is a non-metal, so it should be dull not shiny, and be an electrical insulator not a conductor.
C   Magnesium oxide is alkaline and in the solid state. Sulfur dioxide is acidic and in the gas state.

C2.2.1 Spread questions
1   Suitable table, with one mark for each property to six marks maximum, e.g.

	Ions formed	Reaction with each other	Oxides
Metal elements	Positive by losing electrons	None – they mix to form alloys	Solutions are alkaline
Non-metal elements	Negative by gaining electrons	Produce compounds that consist of molecules	Solutions are acidic

2   Answer should include:
    connect battery, lamp, and sample *(1 mark)*
    in series *(1 mark)*
    the lamp should light if the sample is a metal (or graphite) *(1 mark)*
    but not if it is a non-metal. *(1 mark)*
3   Air is an electrical insulator, *(1 mark)*
    so the elements it contains are likely to be non-metals. *(1 mark)*
4   Answer should include:
    dissolve the oxide in water *(1 mark)*
    test the solution with universal indicator / suitable *named* indicator *(1 mark)*
    it would turn blue or purple / correct colour change if the element was a metal *(1 mark)*
    it would turn orange or red / correct colour change if the element was a non-metal. *(1 mark)*

Answers

C2.2.2 In-text questions
A 2, 8, 8, 18
B O 2.6 and Mg 2.8.2
C Potassium is in Group 1 and Period 4, and its atomic number is 19.

C2.2.2 Spread questions
1. A period is a row in the periodic table *(1 mark)*
   a group is a column in the periodic table. *(1 mark)*
2. 5 electrons *(1 mark)*
3. **a** X is in Period 3 *(1 mark)*
   because the electronic structure has three numbers in it. *(1 mark)*
   X is in Group 0 *(1 mark)*
   because its outer shell is full / it contains the maximum number of electrons. *(1 mark)*
   The atomic number of X is 18 *(1 mark)*
   because (2 + 8 + 8) = 18 *(1 mark)*
   b Argon *(1 mark)*
   (because argon has an atomic number of 18)
4. N 2.5, *(1 mark)*
   Al 2.8.3, *(1 mark)*
   Cl 2.8.7 *(1 mark)*

C2.2.3 In-text questions
A An aluminium atom loses its three outer electrons. A nitrogen atom gains three electrons to complete its outer shell.
B Mg^{2+} 2.8 and O^{2-} 2.8
C Electron diagram for Mg: three circles with 2, 8 and 2 dots or crosses
Electron diagram for Mg^{2+}: two circles with 2 and 8 dots or crosses; bracketed with 2+ at top right

C2.2.3 Spread questions
1. Electron diagram for O: two circles *(1 mark)*
   with 2 and 6 dots or crosses *(1 mark)*
   Electron diagram for O^{2-}: two circles with 2 and 8 dots or crosses *(1 mark)*
   bracketed with 2− at top right *(1 mark)*
2. The lithium ion has the same nucleus as the lithium atom *(1 mark)*
   and this is different to the helium nucleus. *(1 mark)*
3. **a** H: one circle with one dot or cross; *(1 mark)*
   H^-: one circle with two dots or crosses *(1 mark)*
   b The H^+ has no electrons, *(1 mark)*
   it is just a hydrogen nucleus (a proton for ^1H). *(1 mark)*
   c Hydrogen forms positive ions like metals do *(1 mark)*
   and negative ions like non-metals do. *(1 mark)*

C2.2.4 In-text questions
A The outer electrons of two sodium atoms transfer to the outer shell of an oxygen atom, forming Na^+ ions and O^{2-} ions.
B Strong electrostatic force of attraction between oppositely charged ions.
C Diagram showing alternate positive circle and negative circle. Positive circles labelled sodium and negative circles labelled chlorine.
D Space-filling models show ions close together but do not show the bonds. Ball-and-stick models do not show ions close together.

C2.2.4 Using maths: Models of giant ionic lattices
Answer should include:
Ball-and-stick model shows detail inside the structure but space-filling model does not
Ball-and-stick model shows ionic bonds but space-filling model does not
Space-filling model shows ions touching but ball-and-stick model does not
Space-filling model shows relative sizes of ions but ball-and-stick model does not.

C2.2.4 Spread questions
1. Electron diagram for Mg^{2+}:
   - two circles with 2 and 8 dots *(1 mark)*
   - bracketed with 2− at top right *(1 mark)*
   Electron diagram for O^{2-}:
   - two circles with 2 and 8 crosses *(1 mark)*
   - bracketed with 2− at top right *(1 mark)*
2. The two outer electrons *(1 mark)*
   of a magnesium atom transfer to the outer shells *(1 mark)*
   of two chlorine atoms *(1 mark)*
   forming Mg^{2+} ions and Cl^- ions. *(1 mark)*
3. Potassium bromide contains potassium ions and bromide ions *(1 mark)*
   attracted to each other by ionic bonds *(1 mark)*
   and arranged in a giant ionic lattice. *(1 mark)*

C2.2.5 In-text questions
A Its molecules each consist of two hydrogen atoms joined by a covalent bond.
B There are two shared pairs of electrons between the carbon and oxygen atoms.
C A covalent bond is an electrostatic force of attraction between the nucleus of each bonded atom and the shared electrons.
D Space-filling model: gives a rough indication of the size of atoms. Does not show the bonds.
Ball-and-stick model: Shows 3D shape of molecule. Size of atoms and bonds not correct and suggests bonds are fixed in place.
Displayed formula: Simply shows the atoms and bonds in a molecule. Doesn't show 3D shape or size of atoms and bonds.

C2.2.5 Working scientifically: Models of simple molecules
Answer should include:
The space-filling model and displayed formula show the element symbols but the ball-and-stick model does not
The ball-and-stick model and displayed formula show the covalent bonds but the space-filling model does not
The space-filling model shows the relative sizes of the atoms but the other two do not
All three give you an idea of the shape of a water molecule
None of them show the electrons involved in bonding.

C2.2.5 Spread questions
1. A shared <u>pair</u> of electrons *(1 mark)*
2. **a** Correct number of bonding (shared) electrons *(1 mark)*
   Correct number of non-bonding (not shared) electrons *(1 mark)*
   b Answer should include:
   Only the dot-and-cross diagram shows the electrons involved in bonding *(1 mark)*
   Only the dot-and-cross diagram shows that there are electrons not involved in bonding *(1 mark)*
   The dot-and-cross diagram does not show the relative sizes of the atoms (but the space-filling model does) *(1 mark)*
3. Correct number of bonding electrons *(1 mark)*
   Correct number of non-bonding electrons *(1 mark)*
4. Covalent bonds between <u>atoms</u> *(1 mark)*
   intermolecular forces between <u>molecules</u> *(1 mark)*
   which are weaker than covalent bonds *(1 mark)*

C2.2.6 In-text questions
A It has a regular arrangement that repeats many times.
B This is the empirical formula for graphite, used because graphite has a giant structure.

C There are very many atoms in the structure.
D The number of silicon and oxygen atoms in silicon dioxide depends on the amount of silicon dioxide you have. SiO_2 is the simplest ratio of silicon to oxygen atoms. The formula does not indicate the total number of atoms in a sample of silicon dioxide and does not show that it has a giant covalent structure.

C2.2.6 Using maths: Empirical formulae of giant covalent structures
Answer should include: the formula is SiO_2 because on average silicon and oxygen atoms are in the ratio 1 : 2. Not all the atoms are shown, for example, the fourth oxygen atom is missing from the top silicon atom. If you count the atoms, there are 15 Si atoms but only 22 O atoms (there should be 30).

C2.2.6 Go further: Large molecules that are not giant
Answer should include: there are 60 carbon atoms. The molecule is not a giant covalent structure because its pattern does not repeat very many times. Therefore its molecular formula is used not its empirical formula.

C2.2.6 Spread questions
1. Very many non-metal atoms (1 mark)
   joined by covalent bonds (1 mark)
   to form a large repeating regular pattern. (1 mark)
2. A nanotube is made from very many atoms (1 mark)
   not just a few; it has a lattice structure or pattern that repeats many times. (1 mark)
3. Two similarities for one mark each:
   both have regular patterns that repeat
   atoms are joined by covalent bonds
   in both structures one atom is bonded to four others.
   Difference: diamond is made of one element but silica is made from two elements / it is a compound. (1 mark)

C2.2.7 In-text questions
A Many propene molecules join together end to end.
B The straight lines represent covalent bonds (because the atoms are all non-metal atoms).
C There are very many atoms in the structure.

C2.2.7 Go further: Thermosoftening and thermosetting polymers
Thermosoftening polymers include: poly(ethene), used for carrier bags; poly(propene), used for crates and ropes; and poly(chloroethene) or PVC, used for drain pipes and electricity cable insulations. Thermosetting polymers include: urea formaldehyde, used for electrical fittings; and melamine formaldehyde, used for worktops and tableware.

C2.2.7 Spread questions
1. Two natural polymers for one mark each, e.g.
   - proteins (or named example such as keratin)
   - complex carbohydrates (or named example such as starch)
   - DNA.
   Two artificial polymers for one mark each, e.g.
   - poly(ethene)
   - poly(propene)
   - nylon.
2. Between atoms: covalent bonds, (1 mark)
   between polymer molecules: weak intermolecular forces (1 mark)
   and (in thermosetting polymers) covalent bonds (1 mark)
3. Advantages:
   - simple to draw (1 mark)
   - gives an idea of the polymer molecules being long (1 mark)
   - shows that molecules are linked in thermosetting polymers. (1 mark)
   Limitations:
   - no atoms are shown (1 mark)
   - intermolecular forces are not shown (1 mark)
   - lines are used to represent both the polymer molecules and the covalent bonds between molecules. (1 mark)

C2.2.8 In-text questions
A They are packed together in a regular way forming a giant metallic lattice. Mercury is a metal, and this is the arrangement of atoms in a metal in the solid state.
B Metallic bonds are strong electrostatic forces of attraction between delocalised electrons and positively charged metal ions.
C The electrons are not moving. Also, they are too large compared to the ions and you cannot see their charge.
D **Figure 4** Advantages: shoes electrons as a diffuse 'sea' of negative charge, rather than fixed points; Disadvantages: does not give indication to how many electrons have been donated from the metal atoms.
   Figure 5 Advantages: shows how many electrons have been donated by the metal atoms; Disadvantages: Shows electrons in fixed positions.

C2.2.8 Using maths: Models of metals
Answer should include: in both diagrams, the ions are not touching and the electrons are too large for the size of the ions. The isometric diagram gives an idea of the 3D structure, but is difficult to draw and the electrons are shown as a cloud of negative charge not as particles. The elevation view is easy to draw and shows electrons as particles, but you cannot see their charge or particles in layers behind

C2.2.8 Spread questions
1. Positively charged metal ions (1 mark)
   packed together to form a giant lattice (1 mark)
   and surrounded by a 'sea' of delocalised electrons. (1 mark)
   There are strong (1 mark)
   electrostatic forces of attraction (1 mark)
   between the positively charged metal ions and the negative charged delocalised electrons. (1 mark)
2. Both bonds involve strong electrostatic attractions between oppositely charged particles. (1 mark)
   These are oppositely charged ions in ionic bonds, (1 mark)
   and positively charged metal ions and negatively charged electrons in metallic bonds. (1 mark)
3. Answer should include:
   - each atom only has one outer electron (like Group 1) (1 mark)
   - each metal ion has one positive charge (like ions produced by Group 1 metals) (1 mark)
   - the student might show two outer electrons in each atom (1 mark)
   - a 2+ charge in each ion (1 mark)
   - twice the number of electrons in the 'sea' of delocalised electrons. (1 mark)

C2.2.9 In-text questions
A Mendeleev's predicted elements might not exist. He had to make an exception to his order of elements for tellurium and iodine.
B The discoveries showed that Mendeleev's table could be used to make predictions which could be tested, and found true.
C Tellurium has a lower atomic number than iodine (52 versus 53), the modern Periodic Table is arranged in order of increasing atomic number.

C2.2.9 Spread questions
1. Mendeleev arranged the elements in order of increasing atomic weight, (1 mark)
   tellurium has a higher atomic mass than iodine (128 versus 127). (1 mark)

Answers

2   Electronic structure of the atom was not known then, *(1 mark)* atomic number as the number of protons in the nucleus was not known until after Mendeleev had died. *(1 mark)*
3   It is important in science to publish your work, *(1 mark)* the first person to do this usually gets the credit for a discovery. *(1 mark)*

C2.2.10 In-text questions
A   It would not matter that Mendeleev had not predicted the existence of helium and argon if they were not elements.
B   Mendeleev's Periodic Table was able to accommodate a whole new group of elements, even though it had not been predicted. This gave support to his table.
C   They all have a full outer shell.

C2.2.10 Spread questions
1   Their outer shells contain six electrons / their electronic structures end in 6. *(1 mark)*
2   a 1 mark for each correct electronic structure: 2.2, 2.8.2, and 2.8.8.2.
    b They have two electrons in their outer shells so they are in Group 2. *(1 mark)*
       This means that they are metals. *(1 mark)*
       Oxygen is a non-metal. *(1 mark)*
       Metals react with non-metals to form ionic compounds. *(1 mark)*
3   Answer should include:
    Mendeleev made some accurate predictions. *(1 mark)*
    Mendeleev failed to predict the Group 0 elements. *(1 mark)*
    Mendeleev's table could fit in the new group. *(1 mark)*
    The position of the new group followed his order *(1 mark)*
    of increasing atomic weight or relative atomic mass (seen by the top numbers in the section of the Periodic Table). *(1 mark)*

C2.3 Properties of materials

C2.3.1 In-text questions
A   Diamond and graphite have very many strong covalent bonds that must be broken.
B   Each carbon atom in graphite is only covalently bonded to three other carbon atoms, leaving one unbonded electron which becomes delocalised. Each carbon atom in diamond is covalently bonded to four other carbon atoms, so has no unbonded electrons.
C   Each carbon atom has three covalent bonds, so graphene and nanotubes should have delocalised electrons.

C2.3.1 Spread questions
1   The carbon atoms in nanotubes are joined together by strong *(1 mark)*
    covalent bonds. *(1 mark)*
2   a Each carbon atom has three covalent bonds *(1 mark)* so there are unbonded electrons that become delocalised. *(1 mark)*
    b Buckyballs are balls not tubes *(1 mark)* so there is nowhere for the delocalised electrons to move to. *(1 mark)*
3   Answers could include the following for one mark each, to a maximum of six marks:
    Both have high melting points *(1 mark)*
    because they have very many strong *(1 mark)*
    covalent bonds. *(1 mark)*
    Diamond is hard but graphite is slippery *(1 mark)*
    because graphite has layers *(1 mark)*
    attracted by weak forces *(1 mark)*
    but all the carbon atoms in diamond are joined by covalent bonds. *(1 mark)*

Graphite conducts electricity but diamond does not *(1 mark)*
graphite has delocalised electrons but diamond does not *(1 mark)*
carbon atoms in graphite are covalently bonded to three other atoms but in diamond they are covalently bonded to four other atoms. *(1 mark)*

C2.3.2 In-text questions
A   Some bonds are broken when water melts but all the remaining bonds are broken when it boils.
B   25 °C: solid; 30 °C: liquid; 700 °C: gas
C   Weak intermolecular forces because ice cream melts at a low temperature (room temperature).
D   Carbon dioxide is made of simply molecules that, when solid, are held together by weak intermolecular forces. The molecules easily separate at room temperature so carbon dioxide goes from solid to vapour.

C2.3.2 Working scientifically: Sublimation
Carbon dioxide exists as simple molecules with weak intermolecular forces. The molecules easily separate from one another.

C2.3.2 Go further: Freeze-drying
Food is cooled so that the water in it freezes. The air pressure around it is reduced. The food is warmed just enough for the water to sublime, leaving as water vapour and producing dried food.

C2.3.2 Spread questions
1   −183 °C: solid; *(1 mark)*
    −162 °C: liquid *(1 mark)*
2   Weak intermolecular forces break, rather than strong covalent bonds. *(2 marks)*
3   Air is in the gas state at room temperature *(1 mark)* so the bonds between its particles must be very weak. *(1 mark)*
4   Answer should include the following points for one mark each, to six marks maximum:
    iron, sodium chloride, and silica have strong bonds / oxygen has weak bonds *(1 mark)*
    iron has metallic bonds *(1 mark)*
    forces of attraction between metal ions and delocalised electrons *(1 mark)*
    sodium has ionic bonds *(1 mark)*
    forces of attraction between oppositely charged ions *(1 mark)*
    silica has covalent bonds *(1 mark)*
    oxygen has weak intermolecular forces / forces between molecules. *(1 mark)*

C2.3.3 In-text questions
A   Diamond has a giant covalent structure. Many covalent bonds break at once when a force is applied.
B   The polymer molecules must not be in a lattice or regularly arranged (they are randomly arranged or tangled), and they have weak intermolecular forces between them.
C   Graphite has delocalised electrons.

C2.3.3 Go further: Metalloids
The metalloids are boron, silicon, germanium, arsenic, antimony, and tellurium; selenium, polonium, and astatine are also sometimes included in the list. They are found next to the zig-zag line separating metals from non-metals.

C2.3.3 Spread questions
1   Sodium chloride has a giant covalent structure. When a large force is applied, the strong ionic bonds break. *(2 marks)*
2   No, they do not conduct electricity [*no marks for this statement, but zero for question if answer is yes*].
    There are no delocalised electrons *(1 mark)*
    because they are with the atoms as outer electrons. *(1 mark)*

3   Answer should include the relevant properties and the reasons for them, e.g.
    For copper, to a maximum of three marks:
    conducts electricity (1 mark)
    because it has delocalised electrons (1 mark)
    flexible / malleable / ductile (1 mark)
    because its layers of ions can slide over each other. (1 mark)
    For the polymer, to a maximum of three marks:
    does not conduct electricity (1 mark)
    because it has no charged particles / delocalised electrons (1 mark)
    flexible (1 mark)
    because its polymer molecules are attracted by weak intermolecular forces. (1 mark)

C2.3.4 In-text questions
A   Nanoparticles are 1 nm to 100 nm in diameter; buckminsterfullerene is in this range but methane is not.
B $\frac{100\,000\,nm}{31\,nm} = 3225.8 = 3230$, to three significant figures
C   Ratio is 0.6 /nm.
D   0.6/nm

C2.3.4 Spread questions
1   Their surface area to volume ratio (1 mark)
    is much greater than the same substance in bulk/ (1 mark)
    their surface area is very large (1 mark)
    compared to the same mass of material in bulk. (1 mark)
    [Maximum 2 marks]
2   Sensible advantage for 1 mark, e.g. bacteria in sock are killed, sock will not get smelly (1 mark)
    Bacteria in the environment may be killed (1 mark)
    if the nanoparticles are washed out / escape / do not get broken down. (1 mark)
3   Answer should include:
    nanoparticulate titanium dioxide is transparent (1 mark)
    so it is invisible on the skin (1 mark)
    bulk titanium dioxide is white / visible on the skin (1 mark)
    both forms absorb ultraviolet light (1 mark)
    people may prefer their sunscreen to be invisible (1 mark)
    possible risk of harm to health from nanoparticulate sunscreen / identified hazard. (1 mark)

C3.1 Introducing chemical reactions

C3.1.1 In-text questions
A   Na, Mg, Al, Fe, Cu
B O_2, Br_2, N_2, Ar, H_2
C C_5H_{12}

C3.1.1 Go further: Allotropes of phosphorus
White phosphorus exists as P_4 molecules but red phosphorus has a chain-like structure. Red phosphorus ignites at about 300 °C, but white phosphorus ignites at just 30 °C.

C3.1.1 Spread questions
1   Bromine in the liquid state exists as diatomic molecules (1 mark)
    not single atoms (or giant molecules). (1 mark)
2   I_2, (1 mark)
    Ne, (1 mark)
    P, (1 mark)
    Pb, (1 mark)
    Zn (1 mark)
3   a   CO, (1 mark)
        SO_2, (1 mark)
        SO_3 (1 mark)
    b C_2H_6, (1 mark)
        C_3H_8, (1 mark)
        C_4H_{10} (1 mark)

C3.1.2 In-text questions
A   They tell you the charge on the ion, 2+ for iron(II) and 3+ for iron(III).
B $FeCl_2$ and Fe_2O_3
C   A unit of ammonium carbonate contains two ammonium ions and one carbonate ion.

C3.1.2 Spread questions
1   a F^-, (1 mark)
        Cs^+, (1 mark)
        Sr^{2+} (1 mark)
    b   HF, (1 mark)
        CsBr, (1 mark)
        SrO (1 mark)
2   NH_4OH, (1 mark)
    $Al(NO_3)_3$, (1 mark)
    $Fe_2(SO_4)_3$ (1 mark)
3   Hydrogen ions, H^+, (1 mark)
    nitrate ions, NO_3^-, (1 mark)
    sulfate ions, SO_4^{2-} (1 mark)
4   Answer should include six of the following for one mark each to a maximum of six marks. It tells you that the substance:
    is an ionic compound (1 mark)
    contains two (1 mark)
    ammonium ions (1 mark)
    for every one (1 mark)
    carbonate ion (1 mark)
    contains four different elements / named elements (1 mark)
    contains 14 atoms (in a unit) (1 mark)
    is neutral overall. (1 mark)

C3.1.3 In-text questions
A   No atoms are created or destroyed in the reaction. The same particles are there at the start and the end, so the mass stays the same.
B   Smoke and products in the gas state escape from the log as it burns, so the ashes contain fewer particles or atoms than the log it came from.
C $4.40 - 1.20 = 3.20\,g$

C3.1.3 Spread questions
1   No atoms are created or destroyed in chemical reactions (1 mark)
    so the total mass stays the same. (1 mark)
2   a   Carbon dioxide escapes from the reaction mixture (1 mark)
        because the system is non-enclosed. (1 mark)
    b $1.03 - 0.66\,(1) = 0.37\,g$ (1 mark)
3   Oxygen atoms from the air (1 mark)
    combine with copper atoms (1 mark)
    which adds to the original mass of copper. (1 mark)

C3.1.4 In-text questions
A   One sulfur atom reacts with one oxygen molecule to produce one sulfur dioxide molecule.
B   There are equal numbers of atoms of each element on both sides (one titanium atom, four chlorine atoms, and two magnesium atoms).
C   Water, because NaOH(aq) means sodium hydroxide dissolved in water.

C3.1.4 Spread questions
1   The law of conservation of mass states that no atoms are created or destroyed in chemical reactions (1 mark)
    so the total mass stays the same; (1 mark)
    there are equal numbers of atoms of each element (1 mark)
    on both sides of the equation. (1 mark)
2   a $2Mg + O_2 \rightarrow 2MgO$ (1 mark)
    b $2Fe + 3Cl_2 \rightarrow 2FeCl_3$ (1 mark)

Answers

    c $Ca + 2H_2O \rightarrow Ca(OH)_2 + H_2$ *(1 mark)*
    d $C_2H_5OH + 3O_2 \rightarrow 2CO_2 + 3H_2O$ *(1 mark)*
3 Two similarities for one mark each to two marks maximum:
- All show reactants
- All show products
- All show reactants becoming products

Three differences for one mark each to three marks maximum:
- Only word equations give the names
- Only balanced equations give the formulae / how the atoms are rearranged
- Only balanced equations show the relative amounts of substance involved
- State symbols are the only way to tell the physical state of each substance

Sensible concluding statement for one mark, e.g. balanced equation with state symbols provides most information / balanced equations do not require knowledge of the names / word equations provide limited information / require knowledge of chemical names.

C3.1.5 In-text questions [H]
A $Mg \rightarrow Mg^{2+} + 2e^-$, $O_2 + 4e^- \rightarrow 2O^{2-}$
B $Ba^{2+}(aq) + SO_4^{2-}(aq) \rightarrow BaSO_4(s)$
C Na^+ and Cl^-.

C3.1.5 Spread questions [H]
1 A half equation shows the change that happens to one reactant in a reaction. *(1 mark)*
An ionic equation shows how oppositely charged ions *(1 mark)* form an ionic compound. *(1 mark)*
2 $Ca \rightarrow Ca^{2+} + 2e^-$ *(1 mark)*
$Br_2 + 2e^- \rightarrow 2Br^-$ *(1 mark)*
3 a $Pb(NO_3)_2(aq) + 2NaI(aq) \rightarrow PbI_2(s) + 2NaNO_3(aq)$
1 mark for correct formulae, 1 mark for correct balancing, 1 mark for correct state symbols
    b $Pb^{2+}(aq) + 2I^-(aq) \rightarrow PbI_2(s)$
1 mark for correct formulae, 1 mark for correct balancing, 1 mark for correct state symbols

C3.1.6 In-text questions [H]
A $2 \times 2 = 4$ mol
B $2.54 \times 6.02 \times 10^{23} = 1.53 \times 10^{24}$ atoms
C The molar mass of carbon is 12 g/mol, so 1 mol has a mass of 12 g which is the reading on the balance.

C3.1.6 Go further: Base units [H]
The seventh is the candela, cd, the base unit for luminous intensity, notice that it is cd not Cd (the chemical symbol for cadmium).

C3.1.6 Spread questions [H]
1 The mole is the amount of any substance that contains the same number of entities *(1 mark)*
as there are atoms in 12 g *(1 mark)*
of carbon-12 / ^{12}C atoms. *(1 mark)*
2 The Avogadro constant is the number of entities in 1 mol. *(1 mark)*
    a $12.0 \times 6.02 \times 10^{23} = 7.22 \times 10^{24}$ atoms *(2 marks)*
    b $1.0 \times 3 \times 6.02 \times 10^{23} = 1.81 \times 10^{24}$ atoms *(2 marks)*
    c $0.5 \times 45 \times 6.02 \times 10^{23} = 1.35 \times 10^{25}$ atoms *(2 marks)*

3 Aluminium: 27 g/mol, *(1 mark)* [H]
water: 18 g/mol, *(1 mark)*
copper: 63.5 g/mol, *(1 mark)*
table sugar: 342 g/mol, *(1 mark)*
sodium chloride: 58.5 g/mol *(1 mark)*

C3.1.7 In-text questions [H]
A molar mass = $\dfrac{\text{mass}}{\text{amount}}$
B amount of NH_3 in 6.8 g = $6.8 \div 17 = 0.4$ mol
amount of H_2 needed = $(0.4 \div 2) \times 3 = 0.6$ mol
mass of H_2 needed = $2 \times 0.6 = 1.2$ g
C amount of Mg = $4.8 \div 24 = 0.2$ mol
amount of MgO = $8.0 \div 40 = 0.2$ mol
ratio of Mg : MgO = 0.2 : 0.2 = 1 : 1
equation must be: $2Mg + O_2 \rightarrow 2MgO$ (or $Mg + \frac{1}{2}O_2 \rightarrow MgO$)

C3.1.7 Spread questions
1 molar masses: CaO = 56 g/mol; $CaCO_3$ = 100 g/mol *(1 mark)*
amount of CaO = $(28 \times 10^6) \div 56 = 5 \times 10^5$ mol *(1 mark)*
amount of $CaCO_3 = 5 \times 10^5$ mol *(1 mark)*
mass of $CaCO_3$ = 100 g/mol × 5×10^5 mol = 5×10^7 g (or 50 tonnes) *(1 mark)*
2 molar masses: C = 12 g/mol; CO_2 = 44 g/mol; H_2 = 2 g/mol *(1 mark)*
amount of C = $1.8 \div 12 = 0.15$ mol *(1 mark)*
amount of $CO_2 = 6.6 \div 44 = 0.15$ mol *(1 mark)*
amount of $H_2 = 0.6 \div 2 = 0.3$ mol *(1 mark)*
ratio of C : CO_2 : H_2 = 0.15 : 0.15 : 0.3 = 1 : 1 : 2 *(1 mark)*
equation must be: $C + 2H_2O \rightarrow CO_2 + 2H_2$ *(1 mark)*
3 a amount of $H_2 = 1.0 \div 2 = 0.5$ mol *(1 mark)*
amount of $O_2 = 4.0 \div 32 = 0.125$ mol *(1 mark)*
amount of $H_2O = 4.5 \div 18 = 0.25$ mol *(1 mark)*
    b Hydrogen must be in excess / oxygen must be limiting *(1 mark)*
because only 0.25 mol of hydrogen is needed (to make 0.25 mol of H_2O, and 0.5 mol is present) *(1 mark)*
$(0.25 \div 2) = 0.125$ mol of oxygen is needed *(1 mark)*
(and this is the amount present).

C3.2 Energetics

C3.2.1 In-text questions
A Measure the temperature change in the surroundings. An increase means an exothermic reaction.
B One example of an exothermic reaction, e.g. combustion, neutralisation, explosions. One example of an endothermic reaction, e.g. reaction between citric acid and sodium hydrogencarbonate, photosynthesis.
C The polystyrene is a thermal insulator and reduces the transfer of energy by heating.

C3.2.1 Go further: More about endothermic reactions
Answers should include: aluminium is produced by the electrolysis of aluminium oxide. This is expensive because a lot of electricity is needed.

C3.2.1 Spread questions
1 The lid reduces energy transfers by heating *(1 mark)* to and from the surroundings. *(1 mark)*
2 The temperature may go up because of the heating *(1 mark)* so you might think the reaction is exothermic when it is not. *(1 mark)*

3 a Exothermic reaction: Experiment 2 because the temperature goes up *(1 mark)*
  Endothermic reaction: Experiment 1 because the temperature goes down. *(1 mark)*
 b No reaction *(1 mark)*
  (because the temperature stayed the same).
 c Answer to include these points:
- Room temperature was 20.8 °C. *(1 mark)*
- In Experiment 1, energy is transferred from the surroundings by heating. *(1 mark)*
- In Experiment 2, energy is transferred to the surroundings by heating *(1 mark)*
- until the reaction mixtures reached room temperature. *(1 mark)*

C3.2.2 In-text questions
A Energy is transferred to the surroundings when bonds are made. Energy is transferred from the surroundings to break bonds.
B Bonds broken: Energy transferred from the surroundings to the bond.
 Bonds made: Energy transferred from the bond to the surroundings.
C The heating supplies the activation energy needed to start the reaction.

C3.2.2 Using maths: Energy change
2346 − 2253 = 93 kJ (or 2253 − 2346 = −93 kJ)

C3.2.2 Spread questions
1 The amount of energy transferred to break bonds is less *(1 mark)*
 than the energy transferred when new bonds form *(1 mark)*
 so the energy change is negative. *(1 mark)*
 (and overall energy is transferred to the surroundings).
2 Activation energy is the minimum *(1 mark)*
 amount of energy needed for a reaction to start. *(1 mark)*
3 Each energy profile diagram should include:
 correct axes and shape of line *(1 mark)*
 all formulae correct *(1 mark)*
 activation energy correctly identified and labelled *(1 mark)*
 net energy transfer correctly identified and labelled. *(1 mark)*
 a Sketch shows reactants ($CH_4 + 2O_2$) above products ($CO_2 + 2H_2O$). Peak to reactants line labelled "activation energy". Reactants line to products line labelled "energy transferred". *(4 marks)*
 b Sketch shows reactants ($CaCO_3$) below products ($CaO + CO_2$). Peak to products line labelled "activation energy". Reactants line to products line labelled "energy transferred". *(4 marks)*

C3.2.3 In-text questions [H]
A Bond energies of double and triple bonds are higher than those of single bonds.
B 2 × 347 = 694 kJ/mol
C It is a relatively strong covalent bond.

C3.2.3 Working scientifically: Mean bond energies [H]
The C–H bond in methane is stronger than average (435 compared to 413), so the C–H bond in some other substances must be weaker.

C3.2.3 Spread questions [H]
1 The reaction is endothermic. *(1 mark)*
2 a i (4 × 464 kJ/mol) = 1856 kJ/mol *(1 mark)*
  ii (2 × 436 kJ/mol) + (1 × 498 kJ/mol) = 1370 kJ/mol *(1 mark)*
 b Net energy transfer = 1856 − 1370 = +486 kJ/mol *(1 mark)*
 c The reaction is endothermic *(1 mark)*
  because the energy change is positive. *(1 mark)*
3 Energy transferred to break bonds = (1 × 945) + (3 × 436)
  = 2253 kJ/mol *(1 mark)*
 Energy transferred when bonds made = (6 × 391) = 2346 kJ/mol *(1 mark)*
 Energy change = 2253 − 2346 = −93 kJ/mol *(1 mark)*
 The reaction is exothermic *(1 mark)*
 because the energy change is negative. *(1 mark)*

C3.3 Types of chemical reaction

C3.3.1 In-text questions
A Magnesium is oxidised to magnesium oxide while copper oxide is reduced to copper. Oxygen is transferred in the reaction.
B Magnesium atoms are oxidised to magnesium ions when they lose electrons: $Mg \rightarrow Mg^{2+} + 2e^-$
 Copper(II) ions are reduced to copper atoms when they gain electrons: $Cu^{2+} + 2e^- \rightarrow Cu$

C3.3.1 Spread questions
1 a $Zn + CuO \rightarrow ZnO + Cu$ *(1 mark)*
 b Zinc gains oxygen *(1 mark)*
  and is oxidised to zinc oxide *(1 mark)*
  while copper oxide loses oxygen *(1 mark)*
  and is reduced to copper. *(1 mark)*
 c Zinc is the reducing agent *(1 mark)*
  because it reduces copper oxide / gains oxygen / removes oxygen from copper oxide. *(1 mark)*
2 $Zn \rightarrow Zn^{2+} + 2e^-$ *(1 mark)*
 $Cu^{2+} + 2e^- \rightarrow Cu$ *(1 mark)*
3 a $Fe \rightarrow Fe^{3+} + 3e^-$ [1 mark for correct formulae, 1 mark for balancing]
  $Cl_2 + 2e^- \rightarrow 2Cl^-$ [1 mark for correct formulae, 1 mark for balancing]
 b Iron atoms lose electrons *(1 mark)*
  and are oxidised *(1 mark)*
  to iron(III) ions *(1 mark)*
  while chlorine atoms gain electrons *(1 mark)*
  and are reduced *(1 mark)*
  to chloride ions. *(1 mark)*
 c Iron is the reducing agent / chlorine is the oxidising agent *(1 mark)*
  because iron reduces chlorine atoms to chloride ions / loses electrons / transfers electrons to chlorine atoms *(1 mark)*
  and chlorine oxidises iron to iron(III) ions / gains electrons / accepts electrons from iron atoms. *(1 mark)*

C3.3.2 In-text questions
A Acidic: hydrogen ions, H^+; alkaline: hydroxide ions, OH^-
B It is weakly alkaline because its pH is more than 7 but closer to 7 than 14.
C It is neutral because universal indicator is green at pH 7 and this means neutral.

C3.3.2 Go further: Single indicators
Methyl orange is red below pH 3.1, yellow above pH 4.4, and orange between these two values.

Answers

C3.3.2 Spread questions
1. **a** It produces hydrogen ions, H⁺(aq) *(1 mark)*
   and these make solutions acidic. *(1 mark)*
   b It produces hydroxide ions, OH⁻(aq) *(1 mark)*
   and these make solutions alkaline. *(1 mark)*
2. Alkalis are bases that are soluble in water so all alkalis are bases *(1 mark)*
   but not all bases are soluble in water. *(1 mark)*
3. Answers should include the following:
   - Indicators are easy to use / pH meters are more difficult to use. *(1 mark)*
   - pH meters give accurate results / indicators give estimates. *(1 mark)*
   - pH meters give readings precise to one or two decimal places / indicators are usually precise to a whole number or to one decimal place. *(1 mark)*
   - universal indicator gives the relative amount of acidity or alkalinity / litmus only gives whether it is acidic, neutral, or alkaline. *(1 mark)*

C3.3.3 In-text questions
A Ammonium chloride
B Sodium nitrate, NaOH + HNO$_3$ → NaNO$_3$ + H$_2$O
C The reaction mixture contains Na⁺ ions and PO$_4^{3-}$ ions. These make Na$_3$PO$_4$ (and H⁺ and OH⁻ ions make water).

C3.3.3 Spread questions
1. Potassium sulfate *(1 mark)*
2. Acid reacting with alkali or a base *(1 mark)*
   to form a salt plus water *(1 mark)*
   H⁺(aq) + OH⁻(aq) → H$_2$O(l) / hydrogen ions react with hydroxide ions to form water *(1 mark)*
3. **a** Calcium nitrate *(1 mark)*
   b CaO(s) + 2HNO$_3$(aq) → Ca(NO$_3$)$_2$(aq) + H$_2$O(l)
   Correct formulae *(1 mark)*
   balanced *(1 mark)*
   correct state symbols *(1 mark)*

C3.3.4 In-text questions
A Sodium chloride, Na$_2$CO$_3$(aq) + 2HCl(aq) → 2NaCl(aq) + H$_2$O(l) + CO$_2$(g)
B Calcium chloride
C Sodium sulfate, 2Na(s) + H$_2$SO$_4$(aq) → Na$_2$SO$_4$(aq) + H$_2$(g)

C3.3.4 Go further: Aqua regia
It contains concentrated nitric acid and concentrated hydrochloric acid. 'Aqua regia' means 'royal water'.

C3.3.4 Spread questions
1. Ammonium chloride *(1 mark)*
2. **a** Magnesium chloride *(1 mark)*
   b MgCO$_3$(s) + 2HCl(aq) → MgCl$_2$(aq) + H$_2$O(l) + CO$_2$(g)
   Correct formulae *(1 mark)*
   balanced *(1 mark)*
   correct state symbols *(1 mark)*
3. Answer should include the following to a maximum of six marks:
   Observations: aluminium disappears / gets smaller *(1 mark)*
   bubbles produced *(1 mark)*
   Explanation: aluminium sulfate is soluble *(1 mark)*
   bubbles are hydrogen gas *(1 mark)*
   Equation: 2Al(s) + 3H$_2$SO$_4$(aq) → Al$_2$(SO$_4$)$_3$(aq) + 3H$_2$(g)
   Correct formulae *(1 mark)*
   balanced *(1 mark)*
   correct state symbols *(1 mark)*

C3.3.5 In-text questions [H]
A CH$_3$CH$_2$COOH(aq) ⇌ CH$_3$CH$_2$COO⁻(aq) + H⁺(aq)
B HCl(aq) → H⁺(aq) + Cl⁻(aq)
C They may have the same hydrogen ion concentration, and this is linked to pH.

C3.3.5 Spread questions [H]
1. Dilute ethanoic acid has a lower ratio of acid to volume of solution than concentrated ethanoic acid *(1 mark)*
   so it is has a lower hydrogen ion concentration *(1 mark)*
   and a higher pH. *(1 mark)*
2. Hydrochloric acid is fully ionised in solution *(1 mark)*
   but propanoic acid is only partially ionised. *(1 mark)*
3. The concentration reduces by two factors of 10 / 10² *(1 mark)*
   so its pH must increase *(1 mark)*
   by 2. *(1 mark)*

C3.4 Electrolysis

C3.4.1 In-text questions
A Combination of 'cat' from cathode and 'ion'; and 'an' from 'anode' and 'ion'.
B Lead and bromine are harmful.
C Sodium at cathode and chlorine at anode.

C3.4.1 Spread questions
1. Both contain ions *(1 mark)*
   but only molten potassium hydroxide conducts electricity *(1 mark)*
   because its ions can move *(1 mark)*
   a Potassium at the cathode *(1 mark)*
   iodine at the anode *(1 mark)*
   because potassium ions are positively charged and iodide ions are negatively charged *(1 mark)*
   b Calcium at the cathode *(1 mark)*
   chlorine at the anode *(1 mark)*
   because calcium ions are positively charged and chloride ions are negatively charged *(1 mark)*
2. Aluminium at the cathode *(1 mark)*
   Al³⁺ + 3e⁻ → Al *(1 mark)*
   This is reduction / gain of electrons *(1 mark)*
   Oxygen at the anode *(1 mark)*
   2O²⁻ → O$_2$ + 4e⁻ *(1 mark)*
   This is oxidation / loss of electrons *(1 mark)*

C3.4.2 In-text questions
A Platinum is expensive.
B Water is H$_2$O, two hydrogen atoms to one oxygen atom, so twice as much hydrogen is produced.
C Hydrogen at cathode and chlorine at anode.

C3.4.2 Spread questions
1. (Brown) copper metal forming on the cathode *(1 mark)*
   bubbles of oxygen forming on the anode *(1 mark)*
2. **a** Na⁺ and H⁺ (1) Cl⁻ and OH⁻ *(1 mark)*
   b Hydrogen at the cathode *(1 mark)*
   chlorine at the anode *(1 mark)*
3. Answer should include:
   - Electrons travel through wires when there is an electric current *(1 mark)*
   - Ions form when atoms or groups of atoms gain or lose electrons *(1 mark)*
   - Two substances are produced during electrolysis *(1 mark)*
   - One substance at the anode / one substance at the cathode *(1 mark)*
   - Electrolysis only works when ions are free to move *(1 mark)*

- Ions cannot move from place to place in the solid state / can only move from place to place in the liquid state and when dissolved *(1 mark)*

Go further
$4H^+(aq) + 4e^- + 4OH^-(aq) \rightarrow 2H_2(g) + 2H_2O(l) + O_2(g) + 4e^-$
Make water from the hydrogen ions and hydroxide ions, and cancel out electrons:
$4H_2O(l) \rightarrow 2H_2(g) + 2H_2O(l) + O_2(g)$
Cancel out two water molecules on each side:
$2H_2O(l) \rightarrow 2H_2(g) + O_2(g)$

C3.4.3 In-text questions
A Cathode, the tap; anode, chromium; electrolyte, chromium nitrate (or other named soluble chromium salt).
B Anode: $Cr \rightarrow Cr^{3+} + 3e^-$. Cathode: $Cr^{3+} + 3e^- \rightarrow Cr$.
C Anode: $Cu \rightarrow Cu^{2+} + 2e^-$. Cathode: $Cu^{2+} + 2e^- \rightarrow Cr$.

C3.4.3 Spread questions
1 Metal ions are positive *(1 mark)*
   and the cathode is negative *(1 mark)*
2 Make the steel the cathode *(1 mark)*
   make a piece of tin the anode *(1 mark)*
   use an electrolyte of tin nitrate (or named soluble tin salt) *(1 mark)*
   connect to a direct current supply *(1 mark)*
3 a The electrolyte does not contain their ions / only contains copper(II) ions (as the metal ions) *(1 mark)*
     their ions cannot be attracted to the cathode *(1 mark)*
   b Silver and gold are valuable metals *(1 mark)*
     so they can purified and sold *(1 mark)*

Go further
Sulfuric acid. It increases the conductivity of the electrolyte.

C4.1 Predicting chemical reactions

C4.1.1 In-text questions
A Li, Na, K will float, Rb and Cs will sink.
B Answer in the range 35 °C to 45 °C (accepted value is 39 °C).
C Their atoms lose electrons.

C4.1.1 Using maths: Density
Lithium, sodium, and potassium should float because their densities are less than the density of water. Rubidium and caesium should sink because their densities are more than the density of water.

C4.1.1 Spread questions
1 Blue / purple *(1 mark)*
   because potassium hydroxide solution is alkaline. *(1 mark)*
2 a $2Cs(s) + 2H_2O(l) \rightarrow 2CsOH(aq) + H_2(g)$
     Correct formulae *(1 mark)*
     correctly balanced *(1 mark)*
     correct state symbols *(1 mark)*
   b Rubidium atoms lose their *outer* electron less easily than caesium atoms *(1 mark)*
     but more easily than potassium atoms, *(1 mark)*
     and the more easily the electrons are lost, the more reactive the metal. *(1 mark)*
3 Answer should including the following points for one mark each, to six marks maximum:
   - it should have typical properties of metals / stated typical properties, e.g. electrical conductor, shiny when freshly cut
   - solid state or liquid state at room temperature (*depends on melting point given*)
   - melting point in the range 20 °C to 25 °C because melting point decreases down the group
   - it should sink in water
   - density in the range 2.5 g/cm³ to 3.0 g/cm³
   - it should react explosively with water because reactivity increases down the group
   - $2Fr(s) + 2H_2O(l) \rightarrow 2FrOH(aq) + H_2(g)$
   - francium hydroxide should be (strongly) alkaline.

C4.1.2 In-text questions
A Answer in the range −200 °C to −240 °C [accepted value is −220 °C]
B $2Fe(s) + 3Cl_2(g) \rightarrow 2FeCl_3(s)$
C Their atoms gain electrons.

C4.1.2 Spread questions
1 Answer in the range 320 °C to 350 °C [accepted value is 337 °C] *(1 mark)*
   boiling points increase down the group / change by about 100–120 °C each time *(1 mark)*
2 a A violent / very vigorous / explosive reaction *(1 mark)*
     because caesium is the (second) most reactive Group 1 metal and fluorine is the most reactive halogen *(1 mark)*
     flame / white product *(1 mark)*
   b $2Cs(s) + F_2(g) \rightarrow 2CsF(s)$
     Correct formulae *(1 mark)*
     correctly balanced *(1 mark)*
     correct state symbols *(1 mark)*
   c Chlorine atoms gain electrons to their <u>outer</u> shell less easily than fluorine atoms *(1 mark)*
     more easily than bromine atoms *(1 mark)*
     and the more easily electrons are gained, the more reactive the halogen. *(1 mark)*
3 Answer should include the following points for one mark each, to four marks maximum:
   - solid state at room temperature
   - shiny because metals are shiny / iodine crystals are shiny
   - it should react very slowly with metals because reactivity decreases down the group
   - $2Na(s) + At_2(s) \rightarrow 2NaAt$ / equation for other metal

C4.1.3 In-text questions
A Bromine is more reactive than iodine.
B (Brown) iodine solution is produced.
C potassium chloride and iodine water
   potassium bromide and chlorine water
   potassium bromide and iodine water
   potassium iodide and chlorine water
   potassium iodide and bromine water
   Table with one column for each potassium solution and one row for each halogen water.
D potassium chloride takes part in two reactions, potassium bromide takes part in one reaction, potassium iodide takes part in no reactions
E $Cl_2 + 2I^- \rightarrow 2Cl^- + I_2$

C4.1.3 Practical activity: Halogen displacement reactions
You would need to test:
Potassium chloride with chlorine solution and iodine solution.
Potassium bromide with chlorine solution, bromine solution, and iodine solution.
Potassium iodide with chlorine solution, bromine solution, and iodine solution.
Chlorine would take part in two reactions, bromine would take part in one reaction, and iodine would not take part in any reactions at all.

C4.1.3 Go further: Extracting bromine
Seawater is evaporated to concentrate it, chlorine is bubbled through to displace bromine. The bromine is removed in air, dried with sulfuric acid, and cooled and condensed.

Answers

C4.1.3 Spread questions
1. chlorine + lithium iodide → lithium chloride + iodine (*1 mark*)
2. It should displace astatine (*1 mark*)
   because iodine is more reactive than astatine. (*1 mark*)
3. a Fluorine is more reactive than chlorine. (*1 mark*)
   b $F_2(g) + 2NaCl(aq) → 2NaF(aq) + Cl_2(aq)$
   Correct formulae (*1 mark*)
   correctly balanced (*1 mark*)
   correct state symbols (allow (g) for chlorine) (*1 mark*)
   c $F_2 + 2Cl^- → 2F^- + Cl_2$
   Correct formulae (*1 mark*)
   correctly balanced (*1 mark*)
   Fluorine gains electrons and is reduced, (*1 mark*)
   chloride ions lose electrons and are oxidised. (*1 mark*)

C4.1.4 In-text questions
A He 2, Ne 2.8, Ar 2.8.8
B Answer in the range −140 °C to −160 °C [accepted value is −152 °C].
C Answer in the range 3.30 kg/m³ to 3.60 kg/m³ [accepted value is 3.43 kg/m³].

C4.1.4 Spread questions
1. They have complete / full outer shells (*1 mark*)
   so no tendency to lose, gain, or share electrons. (*1 mark*)
2. Helium and neon are less dense than air / the others are more dense than air, (*1 mark*)
   the mass of the balloon must be less than the mass of air it replaces for it to rise. (*1 mark*)
3. Answers should include the following for one mark each to a maximum of six marks:
   - solid / liquid state at room temperature
   - shiny because metals are shiny
   - conducts electricity because metals conduct
   - malleable not brittle when solid
   - these are properties typical of a metal
   - (much) higher density than the other Group 0 elements
   - because its atoms will be close together
   - unreactive / might react to make some compounds
   - because its outer shell is full.

C4.1.5 In-text questions
A Steel is stronger and harder than sodium. Sodium reacts vigorously with water but iron / steel rusts very slowly.
B Sodium is a Group 1 element which forms white or colourless compounds, but the other solutions contain transition metal ions, which are usually coloured.
C Iron(II) sulfate is green and iron(III) chloride is orange.

C4.1.5 Go further: Vanadium ions
Vanadium is named after Vanadis, the goddess of beauty in Scandinavian mythology. Ions include:
- VO_3^- and VO_2^+, yellow
  VO^{2+}, blue
  V^{3+}, green
  V^{2+}, violet

C4.1.5 Spread questions
1. Group 1 ions are colourless / transition metal ions are coloured, (*1 mark*)
   Group 1 ions always have a 1+ charge / transition metal ions can have difference charges. (*1 mark*)
2. a A catalyst is a substance that increases the rate of a reaction (*1 mark*)
   without being used up. (*1 mark*)
   b V^{5+} (*1 mark*)

3. c The compound is an ionic compound (*1 mark*)
   with strong ionic bonds (*1 mark*)
   it is a transition metal compound (and these are coloured). (*1 mark*)
4. They are unreactive (*1 mark*)
   so they will not take part in the electrolysis reactions, (*1 mark*)
   they are good conductors of electricity, (*1 mark*)
   they have high melting points so they are in the solid state / do not melt easily. (*1 mark*)

C4.1.6 In-text questions
A Iron is more reactive, so iron can displace copper but copper cannot displace iron.
B Francium and fluorine

C4.1.6 Practical activity: Rate of bubbling
It would be unsafe. The water or acid would bubble when it boiled, so you would not be able to tell if the bubbles were due to a reaction.

C4.1.6 Practical activity: Displacement reactions
The pairs that would react would be:
Copper(II) sulfate solution with zinc and copper.
Zinc sulfate solution with magnesium, zinc, and copper.
Magnesium sulfate solution with magnesium, zinc, and copper.
Magnesium would take part in two reactions, zinc would take part in one reaction, and copper would not take part in any reactions.

C4.1.6 Spread questions
1. Group 1: potassium and sodium (*1 mark*)
   Group 2: calcium and magnesium (*1 mark*)
   Group 3: aluminium (*1 mark*)
   Transition metals: zinc, iron, copper, silver, gold, platinum (*1 mark*)
   (*zinc is not strictly a transition metal but is treated as one at GCSE level*)
   Trend: going down the reactivity series, Group 1, then Group 2, then Group 3, then transition metals (*1 mark*)
2. Sodium and potassium both react with water (*1 mark*)
   so you cannot see if they displace each other from solutions of their compounds. (*1 mark*)
3. Answer should include the following for one mark each, to six marks maximum:
   - Add to water. (*1 mark*)
   - Compare the rate of bubbling with other known metals. (*1 mark*)
   - If safe in water, add to dilute hydrochloric acid. (*1 mark*)
   - Compare the rate of bubbling with other known metals. (*1 mark*)
   - Add a piece of the metal to solutions of metal compounds. (*1 mark*)
   - See which, if any, of the other metals it displaces / gets coated in. (*1 mark*)

C4.2 Identifying the products of chemical reactions

C4.2.1 In-text questions
A $Ca(OH)_2(aq) + CO_2(g) → CaCO_3(s) + H_2O(l)$
B So that chlorine dissolves int he water to form a solution that can interact with the litmus paper.
C $4H_2 + O_2 → 2H_2O$

291

C4.2.1 Spread questions
1. Chlorine: dampen a piece of litmus paper and hold over substance. If it is chlorine, litmus paper turns red the white. *(2 marks)*
Oxygen: put a glowing splint near container of gas. If it is oxygen the splint will relight. *(2 marks)*
2. Collect a sample of the gas from Lake Nyos. Place a lighted splint near the mouth of the container. If the sample is hydrogen it will ignite with a squeaky pop. If the sample is carbon dioxide the splint will go out. *(4 marks)*
3. a $H_2O(l) + CO_2(g) \rightarrow H_2CO_3(aq)$
   b precipitate can dissociate into ions and dissolve in water

C4.2.2 In-text questions
A cheaper, disposable so you don't need to clean, made of wood not metal
B React with sodium hydroxide. Iron(II) would give a green precipitate and iron(III) would give an orange-brown precipitate.

C4.2.2 Spread questions
1. flame test to give orange-red flame *(2 marks)*
react with Group 1 hydroxide to produce blue precipitate *(2 marks)*
2. Reactivity decreases down the group, so lithium would not displace sodium from sodium hydroxide and so you would not get a result. Would produce white precipitates not coloured precipitates. Lithium, sodium, and potassium are all in Group 1 so could give false positive results. *(3 marks)*
3. Carry out a flame test. Calcium chloride would produce an orange-red flame.
React with an excess of sodium hydroxide. The white calcium hydroxide precipitate will not dissolve, but the white zinc hydroxide precipitate will. *(6 marks)*

C4.2.3 In-text questions
A $BaCl_2(aq) + Na_2SO_4(aq) \rightarrow BaSO_4(s) + 2NaCl(aq)$
B $MgCO_3(s) + 2HCl(aq) \rightarrow CO_2(g) + H_2O(l) + MgCl_2(aq)$
C $AgNO_3(aq) + NaCl(aq) \rightarrow AgCl(s) + NaNO_3(aq)$

C4.2.3 Spread questions
1. a Carry out in a fume cupboard. Wear gloves and eye protection. *(2 marks)*
   b Barium sulfate is not soluble so will pass through the body. *(2 marks)*
2. a Add a few drops of dilute hydrochloric acid, collect the gas and pass through limewater. If limewater turns cloudy, the original solution had carbonate ions. *(2 marks)*
   b Acid reacts with any other ions in the solution. *(2 marks)*
3. Take a sample of each solution. Add a few drops of nitric acid then a few drops of silver nitrate. Solution that forms yellow precipitate is sodium iodide. *(2 marks)*
Of the remaining two solutions, take another sample and add a few drops of hydrochloric acid. Collect any gas given off and pass through limewater. The solution that produces a gas that causes limewater to go cloudy (carbon dioxide) is potassium carbonate. *(2 marks)*
Take a sample of the remaining solution. add a few drops of hydrochloric acid and then barium chloride solution. A white precipitate should form to confirm the solution was potassium sulfate. *(2 marks)*

C4.2.4 In-text questions
A Sensitive (can detect small traces of substance), accurate, and quick.
B You can use the area under the peak to work out the amount of alcohol in the blood sample.

C $(12 \times 4) + (1 \times 10) = 58$

C4.2.4 Spread questions
1. Any two from:
Can analyse small quantities of substance and identify small amounts of substance within a sample.
Instrumental techniques are very accurate.
Can analyse a sample quickly and can run all the time. *(2 marks)*
2. Gas chromatography separates the substances and mass spectrometry easily identifies them. *(2 marks)*
3. 3358: O—H; 2974: C—H; 1274: C—O; 880: C—C *(4 marks)*

C5.1 Monitoring chemical reactions

C5.1.1 In-text questions
A Maximum mass it is possible to make from a given mass of reactants.
B $\dfrac{4.8g}{(1 \times 16)} \times (2 \times 18) = 10.8g$
C $\dfrac{10.8g}{(2 \times 27)} \times (2 \times 408) = 163.2g$

C5.1.1 Spread questions
1. a 44 *(1 mark)*
   b $\dfrac{6g}{(1 \times 12)} \times (1 \times 44)$ *(1 mark)*
   = 22 g *(1 mark)*
2. M_r of $CuCO_3$ = 123.5 and M_r of CuO = 79.5 *(1 mark)*
$\dfrac{24.7g}{(1 \times 123.5)} \times (1 \times 79.5)$ *(1 mark)*
= 15.9 g *(1 mark)*
3. a $2Al(s) + 6HCl(aq) \rightarrow 2AlCl_3(aq) + 3H_2(g)$
Correctly balanced *(1 mark)*
correct state symbols *(1 mark)*
   b amount of Al = 1.35 g / 27 g/mol *(1 mark)*
= 0.05 mol *(1 mark)*
   c amount of H_2 = (0.05 / 2) × 3 = 0.075 mol *(1 mark)*
   d molar mass of H_2 = 2 g/mol *(1 mark)*
yield of H_2 = 0.075 mol × 2 g/mol = 0.15 g *(1 mark)*
Alternative working, without moles:
$\dfrac{1.35g}{(2 \times 27)} \times (3 \times 2)$ *(1 mark)*
= 0.15 g *(1 mark)*

C5.1.2 In-text questions
A 2.97 g ÷ 3.24 g × 100 = 91.7%
B The filtrate is blue and there is a blue tinge on the filter paper.
C 4 ÷ 48 × 100 = 8.3%

C5.1.2 Spread questions
1. 12.7 kg ÷ 16.3 kg × 100 *(1 mark)*
= 77.9% *(1 mark)*
2. 4 ÷ 36 × 100 *(1 mark)*
= 11.1% *(1 mark)*
3. Answer should include the following for one mark each to a maximum of six marks:
Similarities:
All have atom economies less than 100%.
All produce one other product.
Differences:
The other product is different.
The reactants are different.
Conclusion (process identified with reason), e.g.
Methane and steam is best because it has highest atom economy.
Methane and steam not so good because it produces carbon monoxide / toxic gas.

Carbon and steam not so good because it produces carbon dioxide / greenhouse gas.
Electrolysis of water second best atom economy but oxygen is the other product / useful product / not toxic.

C5.1.3 In-text questions

A If the raw materials are expensive, it may be better to choose a reaction pathway that uses cheaper raw materials.
B Chlorine is toxic and hydrogen chloride is acidic.

C5.1.3 Spread questions

1. Total M_r of desired products = 111 + 44 = 155 *(1 mark)*
   Total M_r of all products = 111 + 18 + 44 = 173 *(1 mark)*
   Atom economy = (155 / 173) × 100 = 89.6% (to three significant figures) *(1 mark)*
2. Three from the following, for one mark each to a maximum of three marks:
   - yield of the product
   - atom economy of the reaction
   - usefulness or otherwise of by-products
   - rate of the reaction
   - equilibrium position
   - cost of raw materials.
3. **a** Hydration of ethene appears to be more desirable because it:
   - has a higher atom economy *(1 mark)*
   - has a higher yield *(1 mark)*
   - has a higher rate of reaction. *(1 mark)*
   Must not just quote the figures – it must be a comparison
   b i A substance formed in a reaction in addition to the desired product. *(1 mark)*
   ii It may make fermentation more desirable because:
   - it will improve the atom economy *(1 mark)*
   - the atom economy will become 100% *(1 mark)*
   - it will reduce the overall costs of the process. *(1 mark)*

C5.1.4 In-text questions

A There are 1000 cm³ in 1 dm³, so 25 cm³ = (25 cm³ ÷ 1000) = 0.025 dm³
B Volume = (150 cm³ ÷ 1000) = 0.15 dm³
Concentration = (0.75 g ÷ 0.15 dm³) = 5.0 g/dm³
C Volume = (50 cm³ ÷ 1000) = 0.05 dm³
Amount of NaCl = (0.45 g ÷ 58.5 g/mol) = 7.692 × 10⁻³ mol
Concentration = (7.692 × 10⁻² mol) ÷ 0.05 dm³ = 0.154 mol/dm³

C5.1.4 Go further: mg/dl

There are 1000 mg in 1 g, and 10 dl in 1 dm³.
1 mg/dl = 0.01 g/dm³ (so you divide by 100).

C5.1.4 Spread questions

1. Volume = (500 cm³ ÷ 1000) = 0.5 dm³ *(1 mark)*
   Concentration = (36.5 g ÷ 0.5 dm³) = 73 g/dm³ *(1 mark)*
2. **a** amount in mol = concentration in mol/dm³ × volume in dm³ *(1 mark)*
   b volume in dm³ = amount in mol ÷ concentration in mol/dm³ *(1 mark)*

3. **a** amount = 0.5 mol/dm³ × 2 dm³ *(1 mark)*
   = 1 mol *(1 mark)*
   b volume = 0.5 mol ÷ 2 mol/dm³ *(1 mark)*
   = 0.25 dm³ *(1 mark)*
   c amount = 0.125 mol/dm³ × 0.500 dm³ = 0.0625 mol *(1 mark)*
   molar mass of KI = (39 + 127) = 166 g/mol *(1 mark)*
   mass of KI = 0.0625 mol × 166 g/mol = 10.4 g *(1 mark)*

C5.1.5 In-text questions

A A burette
B molar mass of NaOH = 23 + 16 + 1 = 40 g/mol
amount of NaOH = 1.00 g ÷ 40 g/mol = 0.025 mol
volume = 250 cm³ ÷ 1000 = 0.250 dm³
concentration = 0.025 mol ÷ 0.250 dm³ = 0.100 mol/dm³
C A volumetric pipette is more accurate.
D Repeat the titration until you get at least two concordant titres.
E Work out the difference to calculate the volume of acid.

C5.1.5 Spread questions

1. To find the concentration of an acid or an alkali *(1 mark)*
2. Swirl the flask, *(1 mark)*
   add acid drop by drop near the end-point *(1 mark)*
3. **a** (48.90 cm³ − 24.35 cm³) *(1 mark)*
   = 24.55 cm³ *(1 mark)*
   b 24.40 cm³ and 24.35 cm³ *(1 mark)*
   c (24.40 cm³ + 24.35 cm³) ÷ 2 *(1 mark)*
   = 24.38 cm³ *(1 mark)*

C5.1.6 In-text questions

A amount in mol = concentration in mol/dm³ × volume in dm³
B 0.085 mol/dm³
C 0.25 mol/dm³

C5.1.6 Spread questions

1. Volumes: 0.025 dm³ NaOH and 0.02625 dm³ HCl *(1 mark)*
   Amount of NaOH = 0.200 mol/dm³ × 0.025 dm³ = 0.005 mol *(1 mark)*
   Amount of HCl = 0.005 mol *(1 mark)*
   Concentration of HCl = 0.005 mol / 0.02625 dm³ *(1 mark)*
   = 0.190 mol/dm³ *(1 mark)*
2. Volumes: 0.025 dm³ NaOH and 0.0164 dm³ H_2SO_4 *(1 mark)*
   Amount of NaOH = 0.25 mol/dm³ × 0.025 dm³ = 0.00625 mol *(1 mark)*
   Amount of H_2SO_4 = (0.00625 mol ÷ 2) = 0.003125 mol *(1 mark)*
   Concentration of H_2SO_4 = 0.003125 mol / 0.0164 dm³ *(1 mark)*
   = 0.191 mol/dm³ *(1 mark)*
3. **a** Volume of NaOH = 0.02775 dm³ *(1 mark)*
   Amount of NaOH = 0.01 mol/dm³ × 0.02775 dm³
   = 2.775 × 10⁻⁴ mol *(1 mark)*
   b Amount of acid = (2.775 × 10⁻⁴ mol ÷ 3) *(1 mark)*
   = 9.25 × 10⁻⁵ mol *(1 mark)*
   c Concentration of acid = (9.25 × 10⁻⁵ mol) ÷ 0.025 dm³ *(1 mark)*
   = 3.7 × 10⁻³ mol/dm³ *(1 mark)*

C5.1.7 In-text questions
A 24 dm³
B 0.5 dm³

C5.1.7 Go further: Standard temperature and pressure
100 000 Pa and 273 K (0 °C)

C5.1.7 Spread questions
1 a volume = 0.25 mol × 24 dm³/mol = 6 dm³ (*1 mark*)
   b volume = 1.125 mol × 24 dm³/mol = 27 dm³ (*1 mark*)
2 a amount = 2880 dm³ ÷ 24 dm³/mol = 12 mol (*1 mark*)
   b molar mass of H_2 = 2 g/mol (*1 mark*)
      mass = 12 mol × 2 g/mol = 24 g (*1 mark*)
3 a molar mass of H_2O = 18 g/mol (*1 mark*)
      amount = 1 g ÷ 18 g/mol = 0.0556 mol (*1 mark*)
   b 2 mol of H_2O produces 1 mol of O_2
      0.0556 mol of H_2O produces 0.0278 mol of O_2 (*1 mark*)
      volume = 0.0278 mol × 24 dm³/mol = 0.667 dm³ (*1 mark*)
   c total volume = 3 × 0.667 dm³ (*1 mark*)
      2.00 dm³ (*1 mark*)

C5.2 Controlling reactions

C5.2.1 In-text questions
A A high rate because (amount of product) / (time taken) will be a large value
B $\frac{32}{80}$ = 0.40 cm³/s
C Mean rate = (21 cm³ − 0 cm³) / (30 s − 0 s)
   = 21 cm³/30 s = 0.7 cm³/s

C5.2.1 Spread questions
1 A measure of how quickly reactants are used or products are formed in a reaction (*1 mark*)
   rate = (amount of reactant used) / (time taken) or
   rate = (amount of product formed) / (time taken) (*1 mark*)
2 a rate = $\frac{60 \text{cm}^3}{150 \text{s}}$ (*2 marks*)
      = 0.4 cm³/s (*1 mark*)
   b The reaction has finished at 150 s (*1 mark*)
      because no more hydrogen was produced after that / the graph is horizontal. (*1 mark*)
3 Answer should include six of the following points for one mark each:
   • put dilute hydrochloric acid in a flask
   • connect a gas syringe
   • add calcium carbonate and stopper the flask
   • record the time and volume at intervals
   • draw a graph of volume against time
   • the rate is equal to the gradient
   • calculate the gradient at different times.

C5.2.2 In-text questions
A When particles collide with enough energy for a reaction to happen
B 0.038 / s
C 38.5 / s

C5.2.2 Spread questions
1 1/time (*1 mark*)
   because the rate at 40 °C is 0.004/s (*1 mark*)
2 The rate of reaction decreases (*1 mark*)
   because the particles move more slowly and collide less often (*1 mark*)

and a lower proportion of particles have the activation energy (or more) (*1 mark*)
3 a 0.046 /s (allow 0.044–0.048) (*1 mark*)
   b The particles move more quickly and collide more often (*1 mark*)
      a greater proportion of particles have the activation energy (or more) (*1 mark*)
      so the rate of successful collisions increases (*1 mark*)
      doubles (*1 mark*)
   c The student would have to cool the mixture below room temperature to get below 20 °C, (*1 mark*)
      above 80 °C the reaction would be dangerously fast / the mixture would be too hot to handle safely (*1 mark*)

C5.2.3 In-text questions
A The concentration of hydrochloric acid is decreased. The rate of collisions decreases, so the rate of successful collisions decreases.
B The reaction time is also affected by the temperature of the reaction mixture, so this must be kept the same to make it a fair test.

C5.2.3 Using maths: Limiting reactants
Ratio of volumes = 80/40 = 2
Ratio of masses = 0.08/0.04 = 2
The two ratios are the same, so magnesium (not hydrochloric acid) must be the limiting reactant.

C5.2.3 Spread questions
1 The rate of reaction decreases (*1 mark*)
   because the rate of collisions decreases, (*1 mark*)
   so the rate of successful collisions decreases. (*1 mark*)
2 The rate of reaction increases (*1 mark*)
   because the reactant particles become more crowded, (*1 mark*)
   so the rate of collisions / successful collision decreases. (*1 mark*)
3 a 0.0485 /s (*1 mark*)
      [0.048–0.049]
   b Rate is 0.013 /s at 1.0 mol/dm³ but 0.059 /s at 2.0 mol/dm³, (*1 mark*)
      rate increases (*1 mark*)
      number of successful collisions must have increased (*1 mark*)
      4.5 times (*1 mark*)

C5.2.4 In-text questions
A The iron bar will have a small surface area to volume ratio but the filings will have a large surface area to volume ratio. This means they will react quickly but the bar will not.
B Easier to compare repeat results.
C Some hydrochloric acid would be lost and this would affect the recorded mass.
D The reaction time is also affected by the temperature and concentration of the hydrochloric acid, so these must be kept the same to make it a fair test.

C5.2.4 Practical activity: Investigating the effect of particle size
The loss in mass is also affected by the mass of calcium carbonate, so it must be kept the same to make it a fair test.
Without the cotton wool plug, acid would be lost and the loss in mass would be greater than expected. It would make the measured rate of reaction appear to be greater than it really is.

Answers

C5.2.4 Spread questions
1   a   Powder: 6 min *(1 mark)*
        Lump: 8.5 min *(1 mark)*
    b   Powder rate = 0.90 g / 6 min *(1 mark)*
        = 0.15 g/min *(1 mark)*
        Lump rate = 0.90 g / 8.5 min *(1 mark)*
        = 0.11 g/min *(1 mark)*
    c   The powder reacted faster / had a greater rate of reaction. *(1 mark)*
        The powder has a larger surface area to volume ratio *(1 mark)*
        More particles are available for collisions. *(1 mark)*
        Greater chance of collisions / rate of successful collisions *(1 mark)*
        Accept the reverse argument for the lumps.
2   Custard powder is explosive *(1 mark)*
    because its particles are very small *(1 mark)*
    so have a large surface area *(1 mark)*
3   a   molar mass of CO_2 = 12 + (2 × 16) = 44 g/mol *(1 mark)*
        amount of CO_2 = 0.90 g / 44 g/mol = 0.0205 mol *(1 mark)*
        volume = 0.0205 mol × 24 000 g = 490 cm³ *(1 mark)*
    b   The volume of gas is too large / a very large gas syringe would be needed. *(1 mark)*

C5.2.5 In-text questions
A   Platinum and rhodium are catalysts for the reaction. The fine mesh provides a large surface area for the reaction to happen on, and it allows the mixture of ammonia and oxygen through.
B   An enzyme is a protein that acts as a catalyst in biological systems.

C5.2.5 Go further: Enzymes and temperature
The shape of the active site changes and the enzyme becomes denatured. The rate of reaction increases with temperature until about 40 °C, when the enzyme becomes denatured and the rate of reaction decreases.

C5.2.5 Spread questions
1   A catalyst is a substance that increases the rate of a reaction *(1 mark)*
    without being used up in the reaction. *(1 mark)*
    It provides an alternative pathway with a lower activation energy, *(1 mark)*
    so a greater proportion of colliding particles have the activation energy (or more) *(1 mark)*
2   a   It increases the rate of reaction, *(1 mark)*
        adding a lot more does not increase the rate by much more. *(1 mark)*
    b   rate with 0.2 g = 49 cm³ / 2 min *(1 mark)*
        = 25 cm³/min *(1 mark)*
        rate with 2 g = 73 cm³ / 2 min *(1 mark)*
        = 37 cm³/min *(1 mark)*
    c   They were not complete, *(1 mark)*
        because the lines were not horizontal. *(1 mark)*
3   Answer includes the following points for one mark each to six marks maximum:
    - put a measured volume of dilute sulfuric acid into a flask
    - add some lumps of zinc to the acid
    - connect a gas syringe and start a stop clock
    - record the volume of gas at intervals
    - repeat but also add copper powder
    - draw graphs of volume of gas against time
    - more hydrogen / rate of hydrogen production should be greater with copper
    - repeat with different masses of copper powder.

C5.3 Equilibria

C5.3.1 In-text questions
A   The reaction is reversible.
B   Keep it cool / cool it down.

C5.3.1 Working scientifically: Water of crystallisation
Cobalt(II) chloride-6-water

C5.3.1 Spread questions
1   The concentrations become constant, *(1 mark)*
    because the rates of the forward reaction and backward reaction are equal. *(1 mark)*
2   They are equal *(1 mark)*
3   a   The equation has the reversible symbol / ⇌ *(1 mark)*
    b $N_2(g) + 3H_2(g) \rightarrow 2NH_3(g)$ (forward reaction) *(1 mark)*
        $2NH_3(g) \rightarrow N_2(g) + 3H_2(g)$ (backward reaction) *(1 mark)*

C5.3.2 In-text questions [H]
A   There are fewer moles of gas on the left (2 versus 4) so the equilibrium position moves to the left if the pressure is increased.
B Cl^- ions are on the right so the equilibrium position moves to the left if the concentration of Cl^- ions is increased.

C5.3.2 Spread questions [H]
1   The forward reaction is exothermic so the backward reaction is endothermic, *(1 mark)*
    increasing the temperature moves the equilibrium position to the left / in the direction of the backward reaction. *(1 mark)*
2   a   i   There are fewer molecules of gas on the left, *(1 mark)*
            so reducing the pressure moves the equilibrium position to the right. *(1 mark)*
3   ii The forward reaction is endothermic, *(1 mark)*
            so increasing the temperature moves the equilibrium position to the right. *(1 mark)*
    b   The equilibrium position must lie to the left, *(1 mark)*
        because CaO and CO_2 are on the right. *(1 mark)*
4   The equilibrium position will move to the left, *(1 mark)*
    because reducing the concentration of a substance moves the position in the direction of that substance (and Fe^{3+} ions are on the left). *(1 mark)*

C5.3.3 In-text questions [H]
A   By Le Chatelier's principle the equilibrium position moves to oppose the change and produce more methanol / the rate of the backward reaction decreases / the equilibrium position moves in the direction of the substance with the decreased concentration.
B   At high pressure the equilibrium position lies to the right but very high pressures are expensive / hazardous so this pressure is a compromise.

C5.3.3 Go further: Le Chatelier's principle [H]
He tried to make ammonia by heating nitrogen and hydrogen to 600 °C in the presence of an iron catalyst. There was some air in the apparatus by accident, which caused an explosion. Even so, Le Chatelier was convinced he had made ammonia so he patented the process (ahead of Fritz Haber, who actually got it to work).

C5.3.3 Spread questions
1   The forward reaction is exothermic so the backward reaction is endothermic, *(1 mark)*
    at low temperature the equilibrium position lies to the left, *(1 mark)*
    but the reaction rate would be low *(1 mark)*
    (so this temperature is a compromise).
2   a i There are fewer molecules of gas on the right, *(1 mark)*
           so increasing the pressure moves the equilibrium position to the right. *(1 mark)*
3   ii The forward reaction is exothermic, *(1 mark)*
           so increasing the temperature moves the equilibrium position to the left. *(1 mark)*
    b High pressures are expensive / hazardous / need expensive equipment, *(1 mark)*
       at low temperatures the equilibrium position lies to the left *(1 mark)*
       but the rate of reaction would too low. *(1 mark)*
4   Catalysts increase the rate of reaction, *(1 mark)*
    producing a higher yield in a given time / reduce time taken to reach equilibrium. *(1 mark)*

C6.1 Improving processes and products

C6.1.1 In-text questions
A   Potassium nitrate contains K and N, ammonium phosphate contains N and P.
B   A lot of ammonia is made and most of it is used for fertilisers.
C   Sulfur, natural gas, air, water

C6.1.1 Spread questions
1   They provide nitrogen, phosphorus, and potassium *(1 mark)*
    in a water-soluble form *(1 mark)*
    needed by plants for healthy growth / to grow well, *(1 mark)*
    produce good quality food / high yield. *(1 mark)*
2   a $NH_3(aq) + HNO_3(aq) \rightarrow NH_4NO_3(aq)$ [1 for equation, 1 for state symbols]
    b $3NH_3(aq) + H_3PO_4(aq) \rightarrow (NH_4)_3PO_4(aq)$ [1 for equation, 1 for state symbols]
3   $N_2(g) + 3H_2(g) \rightleftharpoons 2NH_3(g)$ *(1 mark)*
    450 °C *(1 mark)*
    200 atm *(1 mark)*
    iron catalyst *(1 mark)*

C6.1.2 In-text questions
A   Potassium sulfate is soluble so it passes through the filter paper, dissolved in water.
B $2KOH(aq) + H_2SO_4(aq) \rightarrow K_2SO_4(aq) + 2H_2O(l)$
C $2NH_3(aq) + H_2SO_4(aq) \rightarrow (NH_4)_2SO_4(aq)$

C6.1.2 Spread questions
1   a Two from the following for one mark each to two marks maximum:
       - Acids / alkalis are irritant / corrosive.
       - Ammonia solution gives off an irritating sharp smell.
       - Hot solutions / naked flames are produced if heating with a Bunsen burner.
    b One mark for each control measure, one mark for the reason for doing it. The two control measures must match the hazards, e.g.
       - wear gloves / eye protection *(1 mark)*
         to avoid contact with skin / eyes. *(1 mark)*
       - work in a ventilated area / in a fume cupboard *(1 mark)*
         to avoid breathing in ammonia. *(1 mark)*
       - use tongs / tie hair back *(1 mark)*
         to avoid contact with hot objects / naked flames. *(1 mark)*
2   Two sensible reasons for one mark each to two marks maximum, e.g.
    - factory uses machinery
    - factory needs to make acids / ammonia from raw materials
    - factory needs to purify raw materials or product
    - factory produces larger amounts.
    Accept reverse arguments for laboratory preparation.
3   Batch processes: two reasons for one mark each to two marks maximum, e.g.
    - low rate of production
    - large number of workers needed / higher wage costs
    - more frequently shut down
    - difficult to automate the processes.
    Continuous processes: two reasons for one mark each to two marks maximum, e.g.
    - high rate of production
    - smaller number of workers needed / lower wage costs
    - infrequently shut down
    - easier to automate the processes.

C6.1.3 In-text questions
A   200 atmospheres: 40%, 400 atmospheres: 55%
B   300 °C: 67%, 400 °C: 19%

C6.1.3 Go further: Fritz Haber
He developed chemical warfare in World War 1, including the use of chlorine. He carried out his tests even after his wife committed suicide because of his work. The Allies regarded him as a war criminal. He invented Zyklon B, a toxic gas which the Nazis later used to murder people in concentration camps.

C6.1.3 Spread questions
1   a increases *(1 mark)*
    b decreases *(1 mark)*
    c no change *(1 mark)*
2   The concentration of ammonia in the gas state in the mixture is reduced *(1 mark)*
    so the position of equilibrium will move to the right *(1 mark)*
    increasing the equilibrium yield. *(1 mark)*
3   The answer should include the following points for one mark each to a maximum of six marks:
    - 200 atmospheres pressure
    - high pressure favours a high equilibrium yield
    - a very high pressure is expensive / hazardous
    - 450 °C temperature
    - low temperature favours a high equilibrium yield
    - rate of reaction is too low at low temperatures
    - idea of compromise pressure / temperature
    - iron catalyst (to increase rate of reaction)

C6.1.4 In-text questions
A ΔH is negative and the reversible symbol $\rightleftharpoons$ is not used.
B $2S(s) + 3O_2(g) + 2H_2O(l) \rightarrow 2H_2SO_4(aq)$
C V_2O_5

Answers

C6.1.4 Spread questions
1. a increases *(1 mark)*
   b decreases *(1 mark)*
   c no change *(1 mark)*
2. The reactions in both stages are exothermic *(1 mark)* transferring energy by heating *(1 mark)* which can be used to increase the temperature of the reactants in Stage 2. *(1 mark)*
3. $2SO_2(g) + O_2(g) \rightleftharpoons 2SO_3(g)$ *(1 mark)*
   The answer should also include the following points for one mark each to a maximum of five marks:
   - 2 atmospheres pressure
   - high pressure favours a high equilibrium yield
   - equilibrium positions already on the right
   - 450 °C temperature
   - low temperature favours a high equilibrium yield
   - rate of reaction is too low at low temperatures
   - idea of high pressure not needed / compromise temperature
   - vanadium(V) oxide catalyst (to increase rate of reaction).

C6.1.5 In-text questions
A It will go milky / cloudy white because of the carbon dioxide produced.
B There are fewer moles of gas on the right-hand side of the equation, so as the pressure increases the position of equilibrium moves to the right, increasing the equilibrium yield of ethanol.

C6.1.5 Spread questions
1. Fermentation, because plant sugars are renewable / crude oil is non-renewable, *(1 mark)* fermentation has lower energy requirements *(1 mark)* so less fuel needed. *(1 mark)*
2. a Two from the following for one mark each:
   - faster process
   - purer product
   - higher percentage yield
   - atom economy is 100% / no by-product.
   b Two from the following for one mark each:
   - uses less energy
   - can be carried out with simpler equipment
   - suitable if no oil is available / lots of farmland is available
   - produces carbon dioxide which could be sold, e.g. for fire extinguishers / fizzy drinks.
3. The answer should compare the two processes and recommend one of them. For example, including the following points for one mark each to a maximum of six marks:
   - farmland nearby for growing crops / oil company has ready supply of oil (or ethene)
   - raw materials cheaper for fermentation
   - lower energy costs for fermentation
   - fermentation better for sustainable development
   - higher rate of reaction for hydration of ethene
   - higher yield for hydration of ethene
   - purer product from hydration of ethene
   - higher atom economy for hydration of ethene.
   Accept opposite arguments for each process.

C6.1.6 In-text questions
A A rock or mineral that contains enough metal to make it worthwhile extracting
B Aluminium is more reactive than carbon.
C $4CuO + CH_4 \rightarrow 4Cu + CO_2 + 2H_2O$

C6.1.6 Spread questions
1. $CuCO_3(s) \rightarrow CuO(s) + CO_2$ [1 mark for equation, 1 mark for state symbols]
2. a $CuO(s) + C(s) \rightarrow Cu(s) + CO(g)$ [1 mark for equation, 1 mark for state symbols]
   b Copper(II) oxide is reduced *(1 mark)* because it loses oxygen (to form copper). *(1 mark)*
3. $ZnO + C \rightarrow Zn + CO$ / $2ZnO + C \rightarrow 2Zn + CO_2$ *(1 mark)*
   $ZnO + CO \rightarrow Zn + CO_2$ *(1 mark)*
   Carbon and carbon monoxide are reducing agents. *(1 mark)*
   They remove oxygen / accept oxygen / gain oxide from zinc oxide. *(1 mark)*

C6.1.7 In-text questions
A Iron ore (haematite), coke, limestone, air
B The coke is burning / the reaction is exothermic, so energy is transferred to the surroundings by heating.

C6.1.7 Spread questions
1. a Carbon monoxide, *(1 mark)*
      CO *(1 mark)*
   b $Fe_2O_3(s) + 3CO \rightarrow 2Fe(l) + 3CO_2(g)$ [1 mark for correct symbols, 1 mark for balancing]
2. Carbon is oxidised to carbon dioxide when it reacts with oxygen. *(1 mark)*
   Carbon dioxide is reduced to carbon monoxide when it reacts with carbon. *(1 mark)*
   Iron(III) oxide is reduced to iron when it reacts with carbon monoxide. *(1 mark)*
3. Calcium oxide is alkaline / a base *(1 mark)*
   silica is acidic, *(1 mark)*
   because metal oxides are bases and non-metal oxides are acids / a base reacts with an acid (to make a salt). *(1 mark)*

C6.1.8 In-text questions
A The ions can only vibrate about fixed positions / cannot move from place to place.
B They will burn away as the oxygen reacts with them.
C Aluminium is reduced because aluminium ions gain electrons. Oxygen is oxidised because oxide ions lose electrons.

C6.1.8 Go further: The Hall–Héroult process
Both were born in 1863 and both died in 1914. Hall's life was just 8 days longer than Héroult's. Both discovered the process in 1886 and patented it.

C6.1.8 Spread questions
1. Aluminium oxide loses oxygen / aluminium ions gain electrons. *(2 marks)*
2. Answer should include the following points for one mark each to six marks maximum:
   - graphite cathode and anodes
   - aluminium oxide dissolved in
   - molten cryolite
   - to reduce temperature
   - electric current passed through
   - aluminium forms at cathode / equation given
   - oxygen forms at anode / equation given
   - anodes react with oxygen / burn / produce carbon dioxide.

3 **a** $Al^{3+} + 3e^- \rightarrow Al$ *(1 mark)*
   $2O^{2-} \rightarrow O_2 + 4e^-$ *(1 mark)*
   b $2Al_2O_3 \rightarrow 4Al + 3O_2$ *(1 mark)*

C6.1.9 In-text questions
A Oxidation / redox
B The electricity could be used in the process / sold to increase the profits.
C The growth of the plants depends on the weather.

C6.1.9 Spread questions
1 **a** Bacteria *(1 mark)*
   oxidise iron(II) ions and sulfide ions *(1 mark)*
   producing sulfuric acid *(1 mark)*
   which breaks down copper sulfide minerals / releases copper(II) ions / releases soluble metal ions. *(1 mark)*
   b Plants *(1 mark)*
   absorb metal (ions) through their roots *(1 mark)*
   the plants are harvested and burnt *(1 mark)*
   the ash contains a high(er) concentration of metal *(1 mark)*

2 Suitable table, three advantages and three disadvantages for one mark each to six marks. Allow only one mark for two opposites. For example:

	Biological	Traditional
Advantages	Uses less energy	Fast
	Cheap	Large scale
	Less pollution / waste	Takes little time to make a profit
	Low-grade ores may be used	
	Close to being carbon-neutral	
Disadvantages	Slow	Uses more energy
	Takes a long time to make a profit	Expensive
	Small scale	More pollution / waste
	May release toxic substances / sulfuric acid	High-grade ores needed
		May release sulfur dioxide
		Not carbon-neutral

3 $Fe^{2+} \rightarrow Fe^{3+} + e^-$ *(1 mark)*
   iron(II) ions lose electrons. *(1 mark)*

C6.1.10 In-text questions
A Two from: duralumin, brass, bronze
B Heated to melt it. Molten solder runs into gap between pipes, then cools and solidifies.
C Resists corrosion, so coins stay shiny. Strong and hard, so they don't bend or get worn away easily.

C6.1.10 Spread questions
1 A mixture of two or more elements *(1 mark)*
   at least one of which is a metal *(1 mark)*
2 Strong and hard, so it doesn't bend or get worn away easily *(1 mark)*
   resists corrosion, so it stays shiny *(1 mark)*
3 **a** **i** As the percentage of carbon increases, the tensile strength increases. *(1 mark)*
   ii As the percentage of carbon increases, the ductility decreases. *(1 mark)*
   b Steel C has a high tensile strength so it resists stretching *(1 mark)*
   and a low ductility so it does not bend easily. *(1 mark)*
   c Steel A because it has a high ductility *(1 mark)*
   so it is bent into shape easily *(1 mark)*
   or,
   Steel B because it can be bent into shape more easily than Steel C *(1 mark)*
   but is stronger than Steel A. *(1 mark)*

C6.1.11 In-text questions
A Corrosion is the general term for the reaction of a metal with substances in its surroundings, but rusting only applies to iron and steel corrosion.
B Iron gains oxygen / loses electrons (to form iron(III) ions, Fe^{3+})
C Only the nail exposed to air and water rusted. The ones exposed to air only, or to water only, did not rust.
D Iron railings at the seaside are exposed to higher concentrations of dissolved salt (from seawater) than those inland.

C6.1.11 Go further: Aluminium
Mercury combines with aluminium to form a mercury–aluminium amalgam. This destroys the protective aluminium oxide layer, so the aluminium corrodes. Mercury is not usually allowed aboard aircraft in case it spills and touches aluminium aircraft parts.

C6.1.11 Spread questions
1 Silver reacts with hydrogen sulfide *(1 mark)*
   in the presence of oxygen and water *(1 mark)*
   to produce black silver sulfide. *(1 mark)*
2 Iron reacts with air/oxygen and water *(1 mark)*
   to form hydrated iron(III) oxide *(1 mark)*
   iron + oxygen + water $\rightarrow$ hydrated iron(III) oxide *(1 mark)*
3 Answer should include the following for one mark each to a maximum of six marks:
   - Set up tubes containing an iron or steel nail
   - One nail in rainwater / freshwater and one nail in seawater / salt solution
   - Set up a control tube with a nail and no water
   - Use the same volume of water / same size or mass of nail
   - Leave the tubes for the same time
   - Measure amount of rusting, e.g. by observation, change in mass of nail
   - Repeat the experiment.

C6.1.12 In-text questions
A It keeps the air and water away from the steel, and stops the steel rusting.
B Sodium is too reactive / it will react vigorously with air and water.
C The steel will rust faster than normal if the tin layer is damaged.

C6.1.12 Spread questions
1. a Use paint *(1 mark)*
   because this is cheap / attractive. *(1 mark)*
   b Use oil *(1 mark)*
   because this will also lubricate the engine parts. *(1 mark)*
2. The gate is plated with zinc *(1 mark)*
   which stops air and water reaching the steel *(1 mark)*
   the zinc also acts as a sacrificial metal / corrodes in preference to the steel *(1 mark)*
   this works even if the zinc is damaged. *(1 mark)*
3. This is sacrificial protection *(1 mark)*
   to stop the steel legs rusting. *(1 mark)*
   Magnesium is more reactive than iron *(1 mark)* so it corrodes in preference to the steel / loses electron more easily. *(1 mark)*

C6.1.13 In-text questions
A Two from: high melting points / hard and stiff / brittle / poor conductors of electricity and heat / unreactive.
B Aluminium will not rust but steel will.
C Glass has a high tensile strength.

C6.1.13 Spread questions
1. a Two from the following for one mark each:
   - steel has a high tensile strength
   - it will not snap easily from the weight of the lift
   - steel rusts but it will be protected by oil or grease in the machinery.
   b Two from the following for one mark each:
   - household cables are shorter / thinner than overhead cables
     the extra weight of the copper is not important
     the better conductivity of copper is important.
2. Glass is transparent (but porcelain is not) *(1 mark)*
   so the bubbles or impurities will be easier to see. *(1 mark)*
3. Glass and porcelain are stronger than poly(propene) *(1 mark)*
   but they are brittle, *(1 mark)*
   whereas poly(propene) is tough and flexible. *(1 mark)*

C6.1.14 In-text questions
A A material made from two or more different materials, with properties different from the materials it contains.
B Concrete will crack and break under a heavy load, but steel-reinforced concrete is stronger in tension and compression and will hold a greater load.
C Plywood is stronger than wood alone / stronger in both directions / 20% stronger than wood along the grain / six times stronger than wood across the grain.

C6.1.14 Spread questions
1. Fibreglass contains two different materials *(1 mark)*
   with different properties, *(1 mark)*
   glass fibre and a resin, *(1 mark)*
   its properties are different from its individual components. *(1 mark)*
2. Two of the following for one mark each to two marks:
   - plaster alone is brittle so easily damaged / broken
   - paper alone is tough but not rigid
   - plasterboard should be strong / hard / non-flammable.
3. Cob contains straw which is strong in tension *(1 mark)*
   reinforced concrete contains steel which is strong in tension, *(1 mark)*
   cob contains clay / sand which is strong in compression *(1 mark)*
   reinforced concrete contains concrete which is strong in compression. *(1 mark)*

C6.1.15 In-text questions
A PET because it has the highest tensile strength (and its low maximum usable temperature does not matter for this use).
B Two from: sustainability / raw material use / environmental impact / waste products / pollution/ lifespan / how easily recycled/ disposal / how easily materials decompose.
C Energy used in processing and manufacturing, energy in use or maintenance, disposal.

C6.1.15 Spread questions
1. It is cheapest *(1 mark)*
   and melting point / usable temperature does not matter. *(1 mark)*
2. Identify stages for improvement *(1 mark)*
   identify alternative materials. *(1 mark)*
3. Answer should include six of the following for one mark each to six marks maximum:
   production of uPVC needs three times more much energy
   greatest amount of energy in uPVC is for production of the material
   uPVC needs less energy in manufacture
   wooden frames need more energy to transport them / 1.5 times more energy
   greatest amount of energy in wooden frames is for transport
   wooden frames need six times more energy to maintain them
   both use the same amount of energy at disposal
   wooden frames need 17.0 MJ in total and uPVC frames need 21.5 MJ in total
   uPVC frames need more energy overall.

C6.1.16 In-text questions
A Aluminium and copper
B Iron and steel are magnetic, so a powerful magnet could be used to separate them from other non-magnetic metals.

C6.1.16 Using maths: Waste rock
zinc $\quad 1.3 \times 10^{10} \times 11 = 1.43 \times 10^{11}$ kg
aluminium $\quad 5.0 \times 10^{10} \times 3 = 1.5 \times 10^{11}$ kg
lead $\quad 1.2 \times 10^{10} \times 14 = 1.68 \times 10^{11}$ kg
copper $\quad 2.0 \times 10^{10} \times 150 = 3.0 \times 10^{12}$ kg
iron $\quad 2.2 \times 10^{12} \times 2 = 4.4 \times 10^{12}$ kg

Assumed that all the metal used each year comes from ores (which it does not due to recycling).

C6.1.16 Spread questions
1. Aluminium is extracted from its ore using electricity *(1 mark)*
   rather than by reduction with carbon monoxide / carbon. *(1 mark)*
2. They are sorted *(1 mark)*
   and crushed *(1 mark)*
   then melted *(1 mark)*
   and moulded into ingots / new objects. *(1 mark)*
3. Other materials will contaminate the PET, *(1 mark)*
   get stuck in the narrow tubes, *(1 mark)*
   harm the properties of the fibres. *(1 mark)*

C6.2 Organic chemistry

C6.2.1 In-text questions
A C_6H_{14}
B Correct displayed formula of butane
C $CH_4 + 2O_2 \rightarrow CO_2 + 2H_2O$

C6.2.1 Spread questions
1. a C_nH_{2n+2} *(1 mark)*
   b $C_{20}H_{42}$ *(1 mark)*
2. They are hydrocarbons because they contain hydrogen and carbon *(1 mark)*
   only. *(1 mark)*

3   They form a homologous series because they have the same general formula *(1 mark)* and are all saturated. *(1 mark)*
4   a $C_2H_6 + 3½O_2 \rightarrow 2CO_2 + 3H_2O$ / $2C_2H_6 + 7O_2 \rightarrow 4CO_2 + 6H_2O$
        1 mark for correct substances, 1 mark for balancing
    b $C_2H_6 + 2O_2 \rightarrow CO + C + 3H_2O$
        1 mark for correct substances, 1 mark for balancing

C6.2.2 In-text questions
A C_5H_{10}
B   Correct displayed formula of hexene
C   Ethene has a carbon–carbon double bond / is unsaturated, so it reacts with bromine to form a colourless (dibromo) compound. Ethane does not have a double bond so it cannot do this.

C6.2.2 Working scientifically: Systematic names
Their molecules both contain six carbon atoms (and they are both hydrocarbons).

C6.2.2 Spread questions
1   a C_nH_{2n} *(1 mark)*
    b $C_{16}H_{32}$ *(1 mark)*
2   They have the same general formula. *(1 mark)*
    They are all unsaturated / have the same functional group / C=C bond. *(1 mark)*
    They have similar chemical reactions. *(1 mark)*
3   Put some hexane in a test tube and hexene in another test tube. *(1 mark)*
    Add orange-brown *(1 mark)*
    bromine water (and shake). *(1 mark)*
    Hexene decolorises bromine water but hexane does not. *(1 mark)*
    $C_6H_{12} + Br_2 \rightarrow C_6H_{12}Br_2$ *(1 mark)*

C6.2.3 In-text questions
A $C_6H_{13}OH$
B   Correct displayed formula of butanol
C $CH_3OH + 1½O_2 \rightarrow CO_2 + 2H_2O$ or $2CH_3OH + 3O_2 \rightarrow 2CO_2 + 4H_2O$

C6.2.3 Spread questions
1   a $C_nH_{2n+1}OH$ *(1 mark)*
    b $C_{12}H_{25}OH$ *(1 mark)*
2   Three from the following for one mark each to three marks total:
    • they have the same general formula
    • they have the same functional group / hydroxyl group / –OH group
    • they have similar chemical reactions
    • each successive member differs by a CH_2 group.
3   a   Alcohol molecules contain the hydroxyl group / –OH group. *(1 mark)*
        This allows them to be oxidised to carboxylic acids. *(1 mark)*
    b   The carbon atoms can be oxidised to carbon dioxide (by combustion). *(1 mark)*
        The hydrogen atoms can be oxidised to water (by combustion). *(1 mark)*

C6.2.4 In-text questions
A $C_5H_{11}COOH$
B   Correct displayed formula of butanoic acid.
C   Ethanol is flammable so it could set on fire with a flame from a Bunsen burner.

C6.2.4 Spread questions
1   a $C_{17}H_{35}COOH$ *(1 mark)*
    b   Magnesium reacts with ethanoic acid *(1 mark)*
        to produce hydrogen. *(1 mark)*
2   Add universal indicator *(1 mark)*
    it should turn orange or yellow. *(1 mark)*
    [not red as it is a weak acid]
3   a $CH_3OH + 2[O] \rightarrow HCOOH + H_2O$ *(1 mark)*
    b   Potassium manganate(VII) *(1 mark)*
        acidified *(1 mark)*
        with sulfuric acid *(1 mark)*

C6.2.5 In-text questions
A   Crude oil is made extremely slowly / takes a long time to form / takes millions of years to form.
B   They have different boiling points.
C   Petrol, paraffin, diesel, heating oil, fuel oil

C6.2.5 Go further: Using fractions

Fraction	Typical use(s)
LPG	heating, bottled camping gas
petrol	fuel for cars
paraffin	fuel for aircraft
diesel	fuel for cars, lorries, buses
heating oil	heating
fuel oil	fuel for ships and power stations
bitumen	roads, waterproofing roofs

C6.2.5 Spread questions
1   Fuel *(1 mark)*
    feedstock for the chemical industry *(1 mark)*
2   Oil is heated / boiled *(1 mark)*
    vapours rise through the column *(1 mark)*
    cool and condense *(1 mark)*
    at different heights. *(1 mark)*
3   The larger / longer the molecules the stronger the intermolecular forces *(1 mark)*
    and the higher the boiling points. *(1 mark)*

C6.2.6 In-text questions
A $C_8H_{18} \rightarrow C_4H_{10} + C_4H_8$
B   LPG, petrol, diesel
C   Fuels

C6.2.6 Spread questions
1   a   High temperature / 600 °C to 700 °C *(1 mark)*
        (alumina or silica) <u>catalyst</u> *(1 mark)*
    b   Helps to match the supply of fractions with the demand for them *(1 mark)*
        produces alkenes to use for making polymers *(1 mark)*
2   Heating is needed *(1 mark)*
    a single reactant breaks down to form two products. *(1 mark)*
3   The supply of fuel oil, heating oil, and paraffin is greater than the demand for it *(1 mark)*
    but the demand for LPG, petrol, and diesel is greater than the supply, *(1 mark)*
    cracking will convert the fractions in oversupply into those in undersupply. *(1 mark)*

Answers

C6.2.7 In-text questions
A Tetrafluoroethene
B Repeating unit for poly(ethene)
C Displayed formula for poly(ethene)

C6.2.7 Spread questions
1. The carbon–carbon double bond (*1 mark*)
2. Many small monomer molecules (*1 mark*)
   join together (*1 mark*)
   to make a long polymer molecule (*1 mark*)
   under high pressure (*1 mark*)
   and with a catalyst. (*1 mark*)
3. a Displayed formula of chloroethene (*1 mark*)
   b Repeating unit of poly(chloroethene) (*1 mark*)
   c Displayed formulae to model the formation of poly(chloroethene) (*1 mark*)

C6.2.8 In-text questions
A C and G always go together, and A and T always go together
B Amino acids
C Glucose

C6.2.8 Spread questions
1. a nucleotides (*1 mark*)
   b (simple) sugars (*1 mark*)
2. Adenine, thymine, cytosine, guanine (*1 mark*)
3. Answer should include the following for one mark each to six marks maximum:
   - they are polymers
   - they contain monomers
   - DNA is made from nucleotides
   - proteins are made from amino acids
   - complex carbohydrates are made from (simple) sugars
   - DNA contains four different monomers / nucleotides
   - proteins contain about 20 different monomers / amino acids
   - sucrose contains two different simple sugars / glucose and fructose.

C6.2.9 In-text questions [H]
A Two molecules react together to form one larger molecule and one smaller molecule.
B The two groups must react with each other, and the growing polymer must still have one of these groups at each end.
C The monomers in the polyester are joined by –COO– groups, and the monomers in the polyamide are joined by –CONH– groups.

C6.2.9 Spread questions [H]
1. Two (*1 mark*)
2. They are formed from monomers (*1 mark*)
   which react together in condensation reactions. (*1 mark*)
3. a Three sensible precautions with reasons for one mark each, e.g.
   - wear gloves to avoid skin contact with the substances
   - avoid naked flames to stop the flammable solvent igniting
   - wear eye protection to avoid contact with the eyes
   - work in a fume cupboard to avoid inhaling harmful vapours.
   b Hexanedioyl chloride has an –OCl group rather than the –OH group (*1 mark*)
   found in a carboxylic acid (*1 mark*)
   a small molecule is produced (as well as the polymer). (*1 mark*)

C6.2.10 In-text questions
A Wear eye protection to avoid substances splashing in eyes / wear gloves or use forceps to avoid skin contact.
B It uses solutions / liquids in containers.
C $2CH_3OH + 3O_2 \rightarrow 2CO_2 + 4H_2O$
D Advantages: quicker refuelling time, less carbon dioxide emitted, car weighs less
Disadvantage: more expensive to refuel
Neutral point: neither release carbon dioxide during the journey

C6.2.10 Spread questions
1. Water (vapour) (*1 mark*)
2. $2H_2(g) \rightarrow 4H^+(aq) + 4e^-$ / $H_2(g) \rightarrow 2H^+(aq) + 2e^-$ (*1 mark*)
   $4H^+(aq) + O_2(g) + 4e^- \rightarrow 2H_2O(g)$ (*1 mark*)
3. The reaction at the hydrogen side / fuel side / anode is oxidation (*1 mark*)
   because hydrogen loses electrons. (*1 mark*)
   The reaction at the oxygen side / cathode is reduction (*1 mark*)
   because hydrogen ions gain electrons. (*1 mark*)

C6.3 Interpreting and interacting with Earth Systems

C6.3.1 In-text questions
A N_2, O_2, Ar. They are all elements.
B The early atmosphere had more carbon dioxide, and less nitrogen and oxygen.
C It shows that oxygen must have been produced for the metal to react with.

C6.3.1 Go further: A very oxygen-rich atmosphere
280 million years ago, 35%.

C6.3.1 Spread questions
1. There was a lot of volcanic activity on the early Earth (*1 mark*)
   volcanic gases are mostly carbon dioxide (*1 mark*)
   and water vapour, (*1 mark*)
   so these are likely to have been present in the early atmosphere. (*1 mark*)
2. Photosynthesis (*1 mark*)
   from plants and algae (*1 mark*)
   released oxygen into the atmosphere. (*1 mark*)
   This reacted with metals, (*1 mark*)
   but when these were oxidised (*1 mark*)
   free oxygen formed. (*1 mark*)
3. a $2NH_3 \rightarrow N_2 + 3H_2$
   1 mark for correct substances, 1 mark for balancing
   b $CH_4 + 2O_2 \rightarrow CO_2 + 2H_2O$
   1 mark for correct substances, 1 mark for balancing
   $2H_2 + O_2 \rightarrow 2H_2O$
   1 mark for correct substances, 1 mark for balancing

C6.3.2 In-text questions
A Harmful substances released into the air
B Two from: drowsiness, difficulty breathing, death
C Nitrogen dioxide / NO_2 *and* sulfur dioxide / SO_2

C6.3.2 Using maths: PM$_{10}$ particles
1×10^{-5} m

C6.3.2 Spread questions
1. a Sulfur (*1 mark*)
   in fuel forms sulfur dioxide. (*1 mark*)
   Nitrogen and oxygen react (*1 mark*)
   at high temperatures (in engines) (*1 mark*)
   to produce NO_x / oxides of nitrogen / NO_2. (*1 mark*)

301

These dissolve in the clouds to produce an acidic
solution. *(1 mark)*
    b Two from the following for one mark each:
- erodes stonework
- corrodes metals
- kills trees
- kills living things in river / lakes.

2 Incomplete combustion happens *(1 mark)*
because of a poor supply of air / oxygen *(1 mark)*
$CH_4 + O_2 \rightarrow CO + 2H_2O$
1 mark for correct substances, 1 mark for balancing

3 Suitable table, one mark for each correct box to a maximum of 8, e.g.

Pollutant	Source	Problem
Carbon monoxide	incomplete combustion, vehicle engines	toxic gas / symptoms of poisoning
Particulates	incomplete combustion, vehicle engines, metal extraction	bronchitis, increased chance of heart disease
Oxides of nitrogen	vehicle engines	acid rain / stated effect of acid rain
Sulfur dioxide	burning fossil fuels	acid rain / stated effect of acid rain / breathing difficulties

C6.3.3 In-text questions
A Infrared radiation
B Sensible suggestions, such as change in temperature means different crops must be planted, animals may not cope with the higher temperatures, droughts and flood cause problems with crops, warmer weather may bring more insect pests.
C Reduce consumption of fossil fuels, use renewable energy resources, carbon capture

C6.3.3 Working scientifically: A scientific consensus
There is no 'right' answer to this question – it is intended to provoke thought and discussion. Answer should include agree or disagree, with reasons. For example, agree because we are allowing carbon dioxide levels to rise when the link between carbon dioxide levels and global warming is known, without fully understanding the results of this. Disagree because there may be other factors involved in global warming, or global warming itself is not proved.

C6.3.3 Spread questions
1 Infrared radiation is emitted by the Earth's surface *(1 mark)*
absorbed by greenhouse gas molecules *(1 mark)*
which emit infrared radiation in all directions *(1 mark)*
warming the Earth and its atmosphere. *(1 mark)*
2 a Most water vapour is produced naturally *(1 mark)*
excess water leaves the atmosphere as rain. *(1 mark)*
    b This produces carbon dioxide (and water vapour) *(1 mark)*
which also have a warming effect. *(1 mark)*
3 Conclusion for one mark, backed up by five of the following points for one mark each:
- mean temperature generally increases over time
- carbon dioxide levels generally increase over time
- example(s) of change with timescale given
- comment that annual mean temperatures vary about the 5-year mean
- there have been periods / stated dates when mean temperature has fallen

- the method used to obtain carbon dioxide levels changed
- the timescale for the graphs is not identical (1880–2010, and 1750–2010)
- similar trends but no causal link shown.

C6.3.4 In-text questions
A They are washed into the river from fields when it rains.
B The screen removes large objects such as leaves and twigs that would block the sand filter.
C The UK has a lot of fresh water / energy supplies are expensive in the UK.

C6.3.4 Go further: Fluoridation
For: protects against tooth decay, cheap, convenient, levels of fluoride are tightly controlled.
Against: takes away the right to choose, high levels cause damage to teeth.

C6.3.4 Spread questions
1 Stages in correct order, e.g.
- screened or sieved to remove large objects *(1 mark)*
- settlement for remove sand and soil *(1 mark)*
- aluminium sulfate and lime added to clump particles together *(1 mark)*
- filtration through a bed of sand *(1 mark)*
- chlorine added to kill bacteria *(1 mark)*
- pH checked and corrected. *(1 mark)*

2 Chlorine kills bacteria *(1 mark)*
which may be harmful to health. *(1 mark)*
3 **Advantages:** uses sea water (which is abundant on the coast) *(1 mark)*
useful where there is little fresh water *(1 mark)*
useful where energy resources are cheap *(1 mark)*
heating kills bacteria. *(1 mark)*
Disadvantages: uses a lot of energy *(1 mark)*
expensive. *(1 mark)*

C7 Practical skills

PAG C1 Reactivity trend
Designing your practical
1 The apparatus list should include:
- test tubes
- test tube rack
- test tube holder
- dropping pipette
- Bunsen burner (or beaker and kettle to heat water)
- wooden splints
- dilute acid, for example, 1.0 mol/dm³ hydrochloric acid or ethanoic acid, or 0.5 mol/dm³ sulfuric acid
- metals to test, turnings, foil, or ribbon.

2 The method should include:
- adding a small volume of acid to test tubes
- adding a known amount of each metal to the acid
- recording observations, including results of tests for hydrogen
- a description of how to heat the mixture and repeat the observations.

3 Suitable precautions include wearing eye protection, pointing test-tubes away from people, not overfilling test-tubes or overheating the acid, adequate ventilation in case of harmful products (e.g., hydrogen sulfide from impurities in iron filings, if used).

4 Here is an example of a suitable results table to record expected observations.

Answers

Metal	Observations in cold acid	Observations in warm acid

Analysing your results
5   Correct interpretation of results, for example metals listed in the correct order using the student's results.

Evaluating your practical
6   A comparison should be made between the student's reactivity series and an accepted series, for example the ones shown in the Student Book. Reasons should be suggested for any differences, for example only a limited range of reaction types was used.
7   a   Precautions for accurate results, for example the same mass or amount of metal and acid each time, allowing sufficient time to collect hydrogen, ensuring that bubbling continues after heating is stopped.
    b   Difficulties, if any, are described, for example problems collecting sufficient hydrogen to test.
    c   The answer could include repeating the experiment using water instead of acid, using the observations from all four situations (cold and warm acid or water) to produce a reactivity series, and noting that hydrogen is also produced when metals react with water.

Spread questions
1   Two of the following for 1 mark each: amount or mass of metal, volume of solution, concentration of solution, same starting temperature, same observation time, recording maximum temperature rise.
2   No reaction because metal Y was copper   *(1 mark)*
    or metal Y was a less reactive metal than copper.   *(1 mark)*
3   Z, W, X, Y.   *(1 mark)*

PAG C2 Electrolysis of solutions
Designing your practical
1   The apparatus list should include:
    - a battery / power pack
    - leads with crocodile clips
    - two electrodes (inert, such as carbon / graphite)
    - test tubes / ignition tubes to collect gases
    - electrolytes to test, for example, sodium chloride solution, copper(II) sulfate solution.
2   A suitable labelled diagram, drawn with the aid of a ruler. PAG C2 Figure 2 in the Student Book gives an example.
3   The method should include:
    - how to set up the electrolysis cell
    - electrical connections needed
    - how to set up the test tubes to collect products in the gas state
    - an outline of what to do and observe once the battery is connected
    - an outline of gas tests for hydrogen, oxygen, and chlorine.
4   Two suitable precautions, for example, using eye protection, gloves, and forceps.
5   Here is an example of a suitable results table to record expected observations.

Electrolyte	Observations at cathode	Observations at anode
copper(II) sulfate solution		
sodium chloride solution		

A table for gas tests may be included too.
6   Here are the correct predictions.

Electrolyte	Product at cathode	Product at anode
copper(II) sulfate solution	copper	oxygen
sodium chloride solution	hydrogen	chlorine

Analysing your results
6   Correct interpretation of results, for example:
    - a lighted splint ignites the gas with a pop – hydrogen
    - a glowing splint relights – oxygen
    - damp blue litmus paper turns red, then white – chlorine.

Evaluating your practical
7   Predictions for the product at each electrode are compared with the results obtained. Reasons for differences are given, for example, insufficient product to obtain a reliable test result.
8   a   Precautions for accurate results, for example, each electrode is correctly identified, sufficient product is collected for testing.
    b   Difficulties, if any, are described, for example, problems collecting sufficient product, difficulties completing the circuit.
9   c   Alternative apparatus might be a power pack if battery used, larger electrodes. Alternative method might be using Hofmann apparatus.

Spread questions
1   Inert metal named, for example, platinum / gold / copper.   *(1 mark)*
2   The solution was alkaline   *(1 mark)*
    because potassium hydroxide formed / hydroxide ions (and potassium ions) were left in solution   *(1 mark)*
    Hydroxide / OH⁻ ions   *(1 mark)*
    are discharged instead of chloride / Cl⁻

PAG C3 Separation techniques
Designing your practical
1   The apparatus list should include:
    - plant leaves
    - sand
    - propanone
    - a mortar and pestle
    - a boiling tube with bung or a beaker with lid
    - chromatography paper
    - a capillary tube
    - a pencil and ruler.
2   The method should include:
    - cutting up leaves
    - grinding leaves with sand and propanone in a mortar
    - applying the extract to the baseline on the chromatography paper
    - developing the chromatogram
    - a description of how to determine R_f values.
3   Two suitable precautions, for example, using eye protection and gloves, no flames, adequate ventilation.
4   Here is an example of a suitable results table to record the expected observations.

Spot number	Spot colour and shape	Distance travelled by spot (mm)	R_f value

303

The student should also record the distance travelled by the solvent.

Analysing your results

5 The distances travelled by the solvent and the spots are recorded to the nearest millimetre, and R_f values are calculated correctly.

Evaluating your practical

6 A comparison is made between the student's chromatogram and other students' results and Figure 3. Reasons are suggested for any differences, for example, a different solvent may be used in Figure 3, the solvent may have travelled a different distance (longer distances give better separation), the exact centre of each spot may be determined differently.

7 a Precautions for accurate results, for example, a small concentrated spot is made on the baseline, a long length of chromatography paper is used, distances are measured to ±1 mm.
 b Difficulties, if any, are described, for example, obtaining a small concentrated spot, different spots merging, deciding the exact centre of each spot.
 c Improving the method might include using longer chromatography paper to achieve a better separation, investigating using different solvents, for example, ethanol, or a mixture of solvents. Different methods could include two-dimensional paper chromatography, thin-layer chromatography, or other named chromatography methods.

Spread questions

1 The pigment is soluble in ethanol but not in water. *(1 mark)*
2 Heat it using a hot water bath *(1 mark)*
 with water heated in a kettle / without a naked flame. *(1 mark)*
3 Filtration *(1 mark)*
 because the petals are insoluble. *(1 mark)*
4 Use (fractional) distillation / evaporation. *(1 mark)*

PAG C4 Distillation

Designing your practical

1 The apparatus list should include:
 - a flask
 - a Bunsen burner with tripod, gauze, and a heat-resistant mat, or electrical heater
 - condensing apparatus, for example, a bung and delivery tube with a boiling tube and beaker of iced water, or a condenser with beaker
 - anti-bumping granules or broken pot
 - a solution to distil
 - a thermometer
 - a test tube rack.

2 The method should include:
 - heating the solution in the flask until it boils
 - cooling and condensing the steam
 - measuring the boiling point of the distillate.

3 At least two risks specific to this practical activity should be identified. For example:

Hazard	Risk	Control
hot surfaces	skin burns	avoid contact with hot surfaces
hot liquid escaping during heating	skin burns, damage to eyes	use anti-bumping granules

4 Suitable observations include the appearance of the solution before and after distillation, the appearance of the distillate, the boiling point of the distillate.

Analysing your results

5 The percentage difference is calculated. For example, a measured boiling point of 101 °C has a percentage difference of +1%.

Evaluating your practical

6 Reasons for any differences from 0%, for example, the water is not pure, the thermometer is not correctly calibrated, the resolution of the thermometer is too low.

7 a Precautions for accurate results, for example, avoiding solution splashing over through the delivery tube, boiling gently, sufficient cooling, using an accurate thermometer.
 b Difficulties, if any, for example, problems setting up the apparatus or heating.
 c Improvements to the distillation and determination of boiling point, for example, use a condenser if one was not used, use a calibrated thermometer.

Spread questions

1 Ethanol is flammable, so the electric heater is safer than a Bunsen burner. *(1 mark)*
2 Boiling point. *(1 mark)*
3 Boil the water and measure the temperature while boiling, *(1 mark)*
 which should be 100 °C. *(1 mark)*

PAG C5 Identification of species

Designing your practical

1 The apparatus list should include:
 - test tubes
 - a test tube rack
 - dropping pipettes
 - flame test loops
 - a Bunsen burner with gauze and a heat-resistant mat
 - reagents needed for each test:
   o dilute sodium hydroxide solution (for cation tests)
   o dilute hydrochloric acid (for carbonate ion tests)
   o barium chloride solution and dilute hydrochloric acid (for sulfate ion tests)
   o silver nitrate solution and dilute nitric acid (for halide ion tests).

2 The method should include descriptions of how to safely and accurately carry out:
 - flame tests
 - hydroxide precipitate tests
 - tests for carbonate ions, sulfate ions, and halide ions.

3 At least two risks specific to this practical activity should be identified. For example:

Hazard	Risk	Control
naked flame	skin burns	tie back hair; tuck in ties
barium chloride solution is toxic	poisoning	wear gloves

4 Here is an example of a suitable results table.

Unknown compound	Test carried out	Result of test	What the test shows

Answers

Analysing your results
5. Correct interpretation of results, for example, cations and anions correctly identified in unknown substances, and compounds named if required.

Evaluating your practical
6. Analyses are compared with the identity of each substance. Reasons are suggested for any differences, for example, there was insufficient sample to gain clear results, contamination between samples and test solutions.
7. a Precautions for accurate results, for example, avoiding contamination, repeating if results are unclear.
   b Difficulties, if any, for example, problems determining the colour of the precipitate in halide ion tests, or problems determining flame test colours.
   c Improvements to the method, for example, make concentrated solutions to test, carry out a single test on each substance in turn to reduce the chance of contamination.

Spread questions
1. The answer should include the following points.
   - Dissolve each powder in water. *(1 mark)*
   - Add dilute hydrochloric acid, then barium chloride solution – the sample that forms a white precipitate is sodium sulfate. *(1 mark)*
   - Add dilute sodium hydroxide solution to the remaining three samples – the one that does not form a precipitate is sodium chloride. *(1 mark)*
   - Add dilute nitric acid, then silver nitrate solution to the remaining two samples. The one that forms a white precipitate is calcium chloride *(1 mark)* – the one that forms a cream precipitate is calcium bromide. *(1 mark)*

PAG C6 Titration

Designing your practical
1. The apparatus list should include:
   - a burette stand or a stand, boss, and clamp
   - a burette
   - a plastic funnel
   - a volumetric pipette
   - beakers
   - a conical flask
   - a white tile
   - a named indicator
   - a named acid and alkali.
2. The method should include descriptions of:
   - how to set up the burette
   - how to carry out a titration
   - expected observations at the end-point.
3. At least two risks specific to carrying out a titration should be identified. For example:

Hazard	Risk	Control
naked flame	hair or clothes setting on fire	tie back hair; tuck in ties
dilute acids and alkalis are harmful	damage to eyes and skin	wear eye protection and gloves

4. Here is an example of a suitable results table.

	Run 1	Run 2	Run 3	Run 4
Final burette reading (cm^3)				
Initial burette reading (cm^3)				
Titre (cm^3)				
Tick if concordant				

Analysing your results [H]
5. Concordant titres (within 0.10 cm^3 of each other) are identified, and the mean titre calculated.
6. The concentration of acid is correctly calculated.

Evaluating your practical
7. The closeness of titres is discussed, and reasons suggested for any variation, for example, missing the end-point, incorrect use of the volumetric pipette. The closeness of the experimental concentration to the accepted concentration is discussed.
8. a Precautions for accurate results, for example, making sure the burette is vertical, correct use of the volumetric pipette, adding acid dropwise near the end-point.
   b Difficulties, if any, for example, problems using the volumetric pipette or burette, determining the end-point, reading the burette.
   c Improvements to the method (which will depend upon comments made in part b), for example, using white paper or black and white paper behind the burette, adding acid dropwise near the end-point.

Spread questions
1. Named single indicator *(1 mark)* with the appropriate colour change, *(1 mark)* for example, phenolphthalein, pink to colourless; litmus, blue to red; methyl orange, yellow to red.
2. It delivers a fixed volume / 25 cm^3 rather than allowing you to read a titre. *(1 mark)*
3. Repeat the titration *(1 mark)* until concordant results are obtained. *(1 mark)*
4. Suitable safety precaution (not eye protection) for 1 mark, for example, fill the burette below eye level, use a funnel when filling it, wear gloves.

PAG C7 Production of salts

Designing your practical
1. The apparatus list will depend upon the salt being made, but all should include:
   - a filter funnel
   - filter paper
   - an evaporating basin
   - apparatus to dry the crystals (warm oven, filter paper or tissue paper, access to windowsill).

   Apparatus for making an insoluble salt will also include:
   - beakers
   - a stirring rod
   - suitable named reagents.

   Apparatus for making a soluble salt by titration will also include:
   - a burette stand, or stand, boss, and clamp
   - a burette
   - a plastic funnel
   - a volumetric pipette

305

- beakers
- a conical flask
- a white tile
- suitable named reagents, including a named single indicator solution.

Apparatus for making a soluble salt using excess insoluble solid will also include:
- beakers
- a stirring rod
- a Bunsen burner (optional)
- suitable named reagents.

2 The method should include descriptions of how to:
- produce the insoluble salt or salt solution
- purify and dry the salt.

3 At least two risks specific to producing the chosen salt should be identified. For example:

Hazard	Risk	Control
naked flame	hair or clothes setting on fire	tie back hair; tuck in ties
dilute acids and alkalis are harmful	damage to eyes and skin	wear eye protection and gloves

4 Suitable observations should include the appearance of the reagents before the reaction, what happens during the reaction, and any changes during purification and crystallisation.

Analysing your results
5 Diagram (or photo) of crystals made.

Evaluating your practical
6 The appearance of the final product is discussed, and comparisons made with other students' crystals.
7 a Precautions for accurate results, for example, ensuring reaction is complete, filtration to remove unreacted reagents, careful crystallisation.
   b Difficulties, for example, slow filtering, splashing during evaporation, poorly shaped crystals.
   c Improvements to the method (which will depend on comments made in part b), for example, reduce the amounts of reagents used, heat more gently.

Spread questions
1 The excess ensures the reaction is complete / all the sulfuric acid has reacted. *(1 mark)*
2 Copper is too unreactive / does not react with sulfuric acid. *(1 mark)*
3 Heat to evaporate some of the water, *(1 mark)*
   cool to form crystals, *(1 mark)*
   filter / decant / pour off the liquid, *(1 mark)*
   dry the crystals using an oven / paper. *(1 mark)*
4 The reaction would produce sodium sulfate (and water), *(1 mark)*
   but it would be too dangerous to do / sodium is too reactive to use safely / the reaction would be violent. *(1 mark)*

PAG C8 Measuring rates of reaction

Designing your practical
1 The apparatus list will depend on the reaction being investigated and the variable chosen, but should include:
- apparatus for carrying out the reaction, for example, suitable containers
- measuring apparatus, for example, for volumes, masses, and times
- the reagents required.

2 The method should include descriptions of how to:
- carry out the reaction
- measure the required quantities
- measure the rate of reaction
- vary the independent variable
- keep control variables constant.

3 At least two risks specific to the chosen method of measuring the rate of reaction should be identified. For example:

Hazard	Risk	Control
fine powders	may react vigorously and spray reactants out of the container	mix reactants cautiously
inverted measuring cylinder (used to measure gas volumes) releases water during the reaction	water could overflow from the container	use a container with a volume sufficient to contain the water displaced during the reaction

4 The results table will vary depending on the investigation, but should include columns for independent and dependent variables.

Analysing your results
5 A suitable graph of rate of reaction against the independent variable chosen.

Evaluating your practical
6 a Outliers, if any, are identified on the graph and in writing.
   b Comment is made on the spread of measurements where repeats have been made.
7 a Precautions for accurate results, for example, starting and stopping the stop clock at the correct times, use of appropriate measuring apparatus for volumes and masses.
   b Precautions for precise results, for example, repeats, a sensible range in the independent variable.
   c Improvements to the method, for example, alternative apparatus or method to measure the rate of reaction, carrying out repeats if these were not done.

Spread questions
1 Surface area or size. *(1 mark)*
2 The graph should have these features:
- Vertical axis is rate of reaction, horizontal axis is concentration, scales chosen so that plotted points occupy >50% of the axis area. *(1 mark)*
- Points are plotted within a gridline of the correct position. *(1 mark)*
- A straight line is drawn (need not go through the origin). *(1 mark)*

3 (0.6, 3.8) circled. *(1 mark)*

One mark for any of the following reasons: concentration of acid was too high, temperature was higher than for the others, stop clock was stopped too soon, stop clock was started late, measuring cylinder was not completely full of water at the start. *(1 mark)*

OXFORD
UNIVERSITY PRESS

Great Clarendon Street, Oxford, OX2 6DP, United Kingdom

Oxford University Press is a department of the University of Oxford.
It furthers the University's objective of excellence in research,
scholarship, and education by publishing worldwide. Oxford is a
registered trade mark of Oxford University Press in the UK and in
certain other countries

© Oxford University Press 2016

The moral rights of the authors have been asserted

First published in 2016

All rights reserved. No part of this publication may be reproduced,
stored in a retrieval system, or transmitted, in any form or by any
means, without the prior permission in writing of Oxford University
Press, or as expressly permitted by law, by licence or under terms agreed
with the appropriate reprographics rights organization. Enquiries
concerning reproduction outside the scope of the above should be sent
to the Rights Department, Oxford University Press,
at the address above.

You must not circulate this work in any other form and you must
impose this same condition on any acquirer

British Library Cataloguing in Publication Data
Data available

978 0 19 835988 3

10 9 8 7 6 5 4 3 2 1

Paper used in the production of this book is a natural, recyclable
product made from wood grown in sustainable forests.
The manufacturing process conforms to the environmental regulations
of the country of origin.

Printed in Great Britain

COVER: EYE OF SCIENCE/SCIENCE PHOTO LIBRARY